D1508353

ACCOUNTING HANDBOOK FOR NONACCOUNTANTS

Second Edition

ACCOUNTING HANDBOOK FOR NONACCOUNTANTS

Second Edition

CLARENCE B. NICKERSON

Professor of Business Administration Emeritus
Harvard University Graduate School of
Business Administration

CBI Publishing Company, Inc.
51 Sleeper Street
Boston, Massachusetts 02210

Library of Congress Cataloging in Publication Data

Nickerson, Clarence B   1906—
    Accounting handbook for nonaccountants.

    Includes bibliographical references and index.
    1. Accounting.   I. Title.
HF5635.N63   1979   657   79-1368
ISBN 0-8436-0765-3

To L. T. N.

CONTENTS

FOREWORD

The enormous growth of trade and travel in the past quarter century has convincingly demonstrated to Americans that all the world does not speak English. In response, men and women all over the country spend time boning up on Swahili or wrestling with Russian declensions.

But the person who would not think of leaving for Paris without a French phrasebook is perfectly confident of being able to sight-read corporate income statements or balance sheets and understand exactly what they are saying. This illusion has cost overconfident investors a great deal of money. It has been equally damaging to corporations, which have fallen steadily in public esteem in recent years. If the typical American today suspects that management speaks with forked tongue, it is at least partly due to having read false meanings into the accounting reports of U.S. business.

Accounting is a language both figuratively and literally. It is a set of recognized symbols, arranged according to established rules and principles in such a way that they convey meaning. It has its own vocabulary and syntax. And like any language, it has certain ambiguities. Anyone who wants to read accounting statements must study both its basic concepts and its eccentricities.

In this revised second edition of *Accounting Handbook for Nonaccountants*, Professor Nickerson again offers nonaccountants a basic course in the language of accountancy, as currently spoken by those fluent in the tongue. Like any good language teacher, he starts his students reading immediately and reading something of significance, not just Dick and Jane stuff. The income statement of the General Electric Company, which the reader encounters early in the book, is what a multibillion-dollar corporation tells its stockholders about its performance in a turbulent year for the U.S. economy. In the pages that follow, the readers are introduced one by one to the accounting problems that had to be argued out to produce such an income statement and its companions, the balance sheet and the cash flow estimates.

This is not a book that could be titled *Accounting Made Easy*. I am glad that it is not. Accounting, as distinct from bookkeeping, is not an easy subject. It is a rigorous discipline that deals with complex problems, many of which have never been solved in the sense that the problems of Euclidean geometry have been solved. Any student of philosophy will tell you that value theory is one of the stickiest subjects in his field. And any student of economics will say that forecasting is at the same time the weakest area of his performance and the ultimate test of his theories. An accounting statement is both an evaluation and a forecast.

Some years years ago, the American Institute of Certified Public Accountants set up a committee headed by the late Robert Trueblood, of Touche, Ross & Co. The committee defined the fundamental objective of financial statements as "to provide users with information for predicting, comparing, and evaluating enterprise earning power," with earning power defined as the ability to generate cash.

The more you study that statement, the more you will find in it. It defines the duties of the accountant in terms of the use that is made of accounting statements. In doing so, it puts his obligation to the user of the statement ahead of his obligation to the maker of the statement (the company management). And by rating prediction on a par with evaluation and comparison, it deprives the accountant of the convenient explanation that he is simply reporting what happened and is in no way responsible for the conclusions someone may draw from what he reports.

The Trueblood report is perhaps somewhat ahead of accounting as it is practiced today. But it indicates without any question the way accounting is developing.

The financial statements of U.S. corporations are the most accurate and informative in the world. The rules enforced by the Securities & Exchange Commission, the AICPA, and the various stock exchanges, epecially the New York Stock Exchange, ensure that. There is no comparison between the statements of U.S. companies and the cryptic, uninformative reports that are made to the stockholders in other nations.

Nevertheless, both the auditors and the companies that employ them are under fire today because financial statements too often have failed to tell the public all that it should know. The problem has been complicated, of course, by the violent inflation that has distorted the relation between the dollar figures and the assets or liabilities they represent; but that is only part of the trouble. The hard fact is that the "generally accepted accounting principles" so dear to the accounting profession have not kept up with the sophisticated problems presented by modern business.

The profession is well aware of this, and so is the SEC. Accounting is going to change profoundly in the years ahead. It is going to come to grips with reporting and estimating problems it is now evading. Although many experts will disagree with me, I think it is going to change in the direction of acknowledging more responsibility to the external users of financial statements — the investors, stockholders, and creditors — and less to the management of the company making the reports. If I am right, the public is going to be deluged with information that formerly was reserved for management's eyes only, information about profit lines and profit margins, contingent liabilities and leasing deals, sales forecasts, and pension fund liabilities.

If the public does not take the trouble to study accounting, all this new information will be bewildering rather than helpful. For the plain truth is that a majority of the public understands only a fraction of the material that already is available to it. Professor Nickerson is known as the author of accounting books for accountants, and he is also known for his ability to teach this language to a broader audience — those who speak no accounting and those who think they are at home in the language of Shakespeare when they have never really progressed beyond an eighth-grade reader.

To paraphrase the accountant's certificate: I have examined the statements prepared by Professor Nickerson and find them in accordance with generally accepted accounting principles, fairly and fully presenting the state of the discipline at this time. Furthermore, I think the country would be a great deal better off if everyone entertaining an opinion about corporate performance studied this book before voicing it.

John L. Cobbs
Editor, *Business Week*

PREFACE TO THE SECOND EDITION

In recent years it has become evident that a significant number of nonfinancial executives and managers at all levels in business are interested in knowing something more, or different, about accounting than either broad generalizations or narrow mechanics of bookkeeping. While nonfinancial managers need not be experts in accounting, they will often require a sufficient facility with this language both to be able to understand the accounting data received and to communicate with others in accounting terms, particularly with accountants who supply vital information. Indeed, since accounting data is used for management purposes internally, and since much of the accounting data reported externally is reported by management, as well as on management, proper accounting and financial reporting are responsibilities of businessmen in general, not just of internal and external accountants.

It was with the needs of such nonfinancial managers in mind that this book was written originally, and with such individuals in mind that this book has been revised to include up-to-date information. At the time the first edition of this book was published, the Financial Accounting Standards Board had just been established. Early in its deliberations, the FASB adopted the accounting principles which had been settled upon and pronounced in the opinions of the Accounting Principles Board. Thus these published opinions, along with many of the accounting research and terminology bulletins of the American Institute of Certified Public Accountants, continue to be in force as authoritative statements of accepted principles and practices and are referred to, as such, in this second edition.

In addition to information from statements published by the FASB, this edition also includes new information in the financial accounting area from other sources. Among the subjects discussed are financial statements issued both at year-end and during the year, depletion accounting, and in view of continued inflation, inventory valuation at market above cost, and replacement cost data on inventories, property, plant, and equipment required by the SEC. New material in the management accounting area includes a discussion of the budgeting process, with attention paid to zero-base budgeting, as well as to other advances in budget formulation.

As in the first edition, employing the word "handbook" in the book title is intended to suggest its usefulness as a reference source on individual subjects. The index at the back of the book has been designed to assist such use. Beyond this purpose, the arrangement of Chapters 1 through 20 provides an orderly course of study for the reader who wishes to undertake a more comprehensive program in improving his ability to analyze and understand financial statements. Topics are arranged essentially in the same order as items appearing in typical income statements, funds flow statements, and balance sheets.

Similarly, Chapters 21 through 23 enable the study of cost accounting and control in logical progression, while Chapters 24 through 27 concentrate on cost-price-volume relationships and the selection of relevant costs for various purposes, including pricing and the selection and replacement of fixed assets. Finally, Chapters 28 through 31 deal with various means of setting goals and measuring performance, such as budgeting, formal long-range planning, and percentage return on investment.

As well as providing information on accounting and financial matters, this book also is designed to assist, encourage, and develop the reader's thinking about these subjects. Accounting techniques, conventions, and principles — with reasons for their adoption — are discussed at length. So too are alternatives that are available, have been discarded, or might be adopted in the future. Emphasis is also placed, however, on the many areas where judgment is called for in arriving at solutions and where pat answers are not available or should not be given. Solutions here are highly dependent on the facts of the given situation and on their interpretation. The solutions also may depend on subjective views and on personal values regarding customary practices. Historical background is included in the text at various points for the benefit of the reader who wishes to develop a deeper understanding.

The reader will find that this book differs from a number of other accounting books for nonaccountants, particularly in its approach through the income and funds flow statements rather than through the balance sheet; in its de-emphasis on the mechanics of bookkeeping while stressing the importance of transaction analysis; and in its treatment at greater depth of critical accounting areas, such as depreciation, inventory valuation, cost accounting, and budgeting. Yet in common with many accounting textbooks and handbooks, explanations of the reasoning underlying accounting practice form the great bulk of the discussions of accounting theory. Such discussions frequently are written off as being "theoretical" and are automatically assumed to be impractical. But *Accounting Handbook for Nonaccountants* proceeds with the conviction that in order to *really* understand an accounting practice, one must understand the reasoning behind it.

Clarence B. Nickerson

ACKNOWLEDGMENTS

Materials from Opinions of the Accounting Principles Board and from Accounting Research and Terminology Bulletins, Final Edition, copyright 1953, 1959, 1962, 1964, 1965, 1966, 1967, 1968, 1969, 1970, 1971 by the American Institute of Certified Public Accountants, Inc., are reprinted at various points in the book as authoritative views on the accounting principles or procedures under discussion.

Certain parts of the sections on cost accounting and control have been adapted by permission from the text of my casebook *Managerial Cost Accounting and Analysis* published in 1962 by the McGraw-Hill Book Company, Inc., New York.

Tables in Appendix 2, to be used in connection with Chapter 27, Fixed Asset Selection and Replacement, have been adapted by permission from *Tables for the Analysis of Capital Expenditures*, by Jerome Bracken and Charles Christenson, published by the Harvard Business School and copyright © 1961 by the President and Fellows of Harvard College.

Permission to reprint material from annual reports has been granted by the General Electric Company, Koppers Company, Inc., and Litton Industries, Inc.

Material from the Financial Accounting Standards Board is reprinted with permission. Copyright © by Financial Accounting Standards Board, High Ridge Park, Stamford, Connecticut 06905, U.S.A. Copies of the complete documents from which excerpts have been taken are available from the FASB. Where appendices are not reprinted here, it should be noted that such appendices are an integral part of any FASB document.

ACCOUNTING HANDBOOK FOR NONACCOUNTANTS

Second Edition

CHAPTER 1

Elements of Financial Reporting

The purpose of this chapter is to assist the nonfinancial manager in understanding more clearly the basic concepts and conflicts underlying financial reporting in the United States. Such knowledge is essential for proper understanding and interpretation of financial statements.

While it is commonly recognized that financial statements are prepared in accordance with "generally accepted accounting principles," there is far less understanding as to what the term "accounting principles" really means and as to how such principles become generally accepted. The present chapter offers background and definitions in this area and traces some key influences on the development of financial reporting.

Background and Definitions

The roots of accounting practices and principles lie deep in business history. Over centuries of business activity, a considerable degree of uniformity in accounting practice has evolved as ideas have been generated, tested, and carried forward or discarded depending on their usefulness and practicality. Each generation of managers, not accountants alone, has contributed to this development and to the formulation of what have become known as "generally accepted accounting principles."

The importance of these principles and the degree of uniformity engendered by their general acceptance should not be minimized. Yet the question is often raised, reasonably enough: If there is widespread agreement in principle among accountants, why is there so much diversity in practice? Confusion on this point is due partly to how the words "accounting principles" relate to detailed rules of conduct and partly to the failure to appreciate that business complexities can generate the need for legitimate variations of an accepted general rule of conduct. This does not mean that all differences in practice are correct or that efforts aimed at narrowing such differences are not important. Rather, it means that in the complicated world of business there can be variations in practice without departure from principle.

What Is an Accounting Principle?

The dictionary definition that comes nearest to describing what most accountants mean by the word "principle" is: "A general law or rule adopted or professed as a guide to action; a settled ground or basis of conduct or practice. . . ."

A principle of any type develops slowly, gaining general acceptance only after years of experience, and this has been true of accounting principles. As noted in an earlier day by the American Institute of Certified Public Accountants: "Initially, accounting postulates are derived from experience and reason; after postulates so derived have proved useful, they become accepted as principles of accounting. When this acceptance is sufficiently widespread, they become a part of the 'generally accepted accounting principles' which constitute for accountants the canons of their art."

Also, "Care should be taken to make it clear that, as applied to accounting practice, the word 'principle' does not connote a rule from which there can be no deviation. An accounting principle is not a principle in the sense that it admits of no conflict with other principles. In many cases the question is which of several partially relevant principles has determining applicability."[1]

In addition, individual cases often warrant different accounting treatment in order to record and present facts in the most rational, meaningful, truthful, and economic manner. Still another reason for variations is that within the boundaries of a general principle, and even under the same circumstances, there are often several different but acceptable ways to reasonably account for a financial event.

At a later date the Accounting Principles Board (APB) of the American Institute of Certified Public Accountants defined the term "generally accepted accounting principles" as follows: "Generally ac-

---

[1] Accounting Terminology Bulletin No. 1 (New York: American Institute of Certified Public Accountants, 1953), paragraphs 17 and 18.

cepted accounting principles incorporate the consensus at a particular time as to which economic resources and obligations should be recorded as assets and liabilities by financial accounting, which changes in assets and liabilities should be recorded, when these changes should be recorded, how the assets and liabilities and changes in them should be measured, what information should be disclosed and how it should be disclosed and which financial statements should be prepared.

"*Generally accepted accounting principles* therefore is a technical term in financial accounting. Generally accepted accounting principles encompass the conventions, rules, and procedures necessary to define accepted accounting practice at a particular time. The standard of 'generally accepted accounting principles' includes not only broad guidelines of general application, but also detailed practices and procedures.

"Generally accepted accounting principles are conventional — that is, they become generally accepted by agreement (often tacit agreement) rather than by formal derivation from a set of postulates or basic concepts. The principles have developed on the basis of experience, reason, custom, usage, and, to a significant extent, practical necessity."[2]

Development of Accounting Practice and Financial Reporting

Since the stock market crash of 1929 and the depression of the 1930s, there has been accelerating action toward narrowing variations in accounting practice; putting into writing and gaining the general acceptance of accounting principles, rules, and regulations; and in general improving the quality of financial reporting. Many individuals have influenced these developments through speeches, articles, and books. Government bodies, business organizations (including individual companies), and professional societies have made substantial and effective contributions to the process. Without rating one contribution above another, here are some comments on a few of these influential forces.

The stock exchanges. Through listing requirements and making recommendations by letter and pamphlet to member companies, the stock exchanges—particularly, the New York Stock Exchange—have been a much more constructive and effective influence on the improvement of financial reporting than is perhaps generally recognized.

---

[2] Accounting Principles Board Statement No. 4 (New York: American Institute of Certified Public Accountants, 1971), paragraphs 137, 138 and 139.

The Securities and Exchange Commission (SEC).   This organization has broad authority over prospectuses issued to obtain capital by the sale of securities to the public and over annual reports required to be filed with the commission by publicly held companies.

The commission has not attempted to develop extensive rules and regulations for accounting practice. In general, it has sought to do two things: 1. obtain from companies the type of information and degree of disclosure it believed was intended by the securities laws under which its authority was established; and 2. assure itself that the information supplied was accounted for in comformance with generally accepted accounting principles, consistently applied. Any rules, regulations, and opinions issued by the commission were considered necessary to meet these objectives.

In recent years the SEC has assumed a more active role in establishing accounting rules, and has expanded its disclosure requirements for financial reporting in prospectuses, in proxy statements to stockholders, and in the various reports that must be filed with the commission.

The information and disclosure requirements of the SEC have improved the quality of financial reporting by furthering its integrity. And they have directly and indirectly improved its completeness, since, for many companies, information that must be filed with the commission has exceeded what these companies had customarily furnished to stockholders. As a matter of fairness to their stockholders, such companies have been moved to supply them with essentially the same amount of information furnished to the commission, since such information is for the most part a matter of public record and therefore available to competitors and others who might take the trouble to search for it.

In many companies, it is the practice to note in their annual reports that a copy of Form 10-K (the principal financial report filed with the SEC) will be sent to any stockholder on request. It is my understanding, however, that only a small percentage of stockholders have taken up this offer.

A few companies have placed a copy of Form 10-K in their annual reports as their major presentation of financial statements.

The Accounting Principles Board (APB).   For a number of years, the Accounting Principles Board of the American Institute of Certified Public Accountants, through painstaking study of specific problems (during which the views of all interested parties were sought), developed a series of opinions on the accounting treatment that should be followed in meeting these problems. Although not always greeted with universal acclaim, these opinions became "generally accepted accounting principles" as issued.

It was an institute rule that "departures from Board Opinions must be disclosed in footnotes to the financial statements or in independent auditors' reports when the effect of the departure on the financial statements is material."

Although the rule applied technically to members of the American Institute of Certified Public Accountants only, other outside auditors as well as company internal accountants were strongly influenced by it. Thus, while absolute compliance with board opinions was not required, a high degree of compliance was obtained as a practical matter since no company financial officer or independent auditor would take lightly having to disclose and defend a departure from a board opinion.

After some years, however, strong resistance developed to the opinions presented, or about to be presented, by the board, on a number of highly controversial issues. The resistance was not silenced by the board's logic, reasoning, or powers of persuasion. Some of its published opinions would not have been effective without the backing of the SEC and, on occasion, the SEC did not see fit to provide such backing. The board finally succumbed to a combination of resistance and lack of necessary support from companies and professional organizations, as well as from the SEC.

The Financial Accounting Standards Board (FASB). In 1973, the Financial Accounting Standards Board of seven full-time, salaried members was established. This nongovernmental board is financed by contributions from businesses as well as from accounting firms. It replaced the Accounting Principles Board, which had consisted of eighteen members, all of whom were members of the American Institute of Certified Public Accountants serving on a part-time basis with no financial compensation.

Early in its deliberations, the FASB adopted the accounting principles which had been settled upon and pronounced in the opinions of the APB. Thus these published opinions, along with many of the accounting research and terminology bulletins of the American Institute of Certified Public Accountants, continue to be in force as authoritative statements of accepted principles and practices.

The SEC noted in its Accounting Series Release No. 150 (1973) that the pronouncements of the FASB are to be considered to constitute substantial authoritative support for accounting and reporting procedures and practices used in preparing financial statements to be filed with the commission. Thus it gave an initial blessing to the board and, in general, has supported its work since that time.

The statement is sometimes made that the FASB now establishes generally accepted accounting principles in this country. This is true in a literal sense, but seems to imply a dictatorial function and does not give credit to the manner and spirit in which the board actually operates.

The board is well aware that, in a democracy at least, no seven individuals could count on establishing an accounting principle that would be generally accepted without first sounding out a great many of those who would be affected by the proposal and finding strong support for it.

Exceptions to this generalization could occur in cases where they simply place their stamp of approval on a principle that was already widely practiced, or simply outlaw what was commonly recognized as the relatively undesirable practice of a small minority.

In keeping with this viewpoint, the FASB, as a significant part of its procedure in drawing up its formal statements, seeks comments, opinions, and suggestions on its problems and proposals from a large number of individuals and groups most interested and concerned.

Moreover, as a practical matter, companies must account for financial events as they take place, whether or not there exist FASB pronouncements on how these events should be recorded and reported. When some new type of financial event occurs, therefore, a significant body of practice is established long before the FASB has had time to publish a statement on it.

Much of the work of the staff operating under the FASB is to study existing practices in connection with specific problems on which pronouncements are to be made, and to present summaries of these studies to the board.

It is evident from the steps just described that the FASB does not attempt to establish generally accepted accounting principles all by itself. One can assume that in studying existing practices and in seeking views on its problems and proposals from so many sources, and in such volume, it aims to use this assistance in molding pronouncements that will be generally acceptable.

That it seeks this assistance does not minimize the importance of the FASB in spearheading a narrowing of differences on accounting practice and in applying pressure for the solidification of views on what should constitute generally accepted accounting principles. But it is not the responsibility of the FASB alone to establish accounting principles, and a tacit recognition exists that in the long run the real authority of FASB pronouncements rests in their general acceptability.

Other influences on financial reporting. Through research, committee work, and publications, various professional associations have contributed substantially over the years to the development of accounting theory and practice. These have included the American Institute of Certified Public Accountants, already mentioned, the American Accounting Association, the National Association of Accountants, and the Financial Executives Institute, as well as a variety of organizations of bankers, credit men, financial analysts, and others.

The financial press, generally speaking, has been a constructive force. And even when its criticisms of financial reporting have been unduly harsh, it has served to publicize important issues.

With particular reference to uniformity in accounting practice, many industrial associations have developed uniform systems of accounting, which, although not adopted universally or in every aspect by the memberships, have narrowed the differences in practice among companies within each industry.

In the public utility, transportation, banking, and insurance industries, mandatory uniform systems of accounting and/or reporting have been established by state and federal commissions. Unfortunately, the emphasis on regulation, and particularly on rate-regulation, has made these systems less appropriate for other purposes. Also, the commissions have tended to freeze such systems and have not allowed them to develop in line with the evolution of generally accepted accounting principles.

Pressures for Uniformity

Despite the progress made in recording generally accepted accounting principles and practices, and in narrowing the range of variations in practice, many financial analysts and others have been impatient with the rate and degree of progress. This impatience, and some dissatisfaction with both the concept and output of the Accounting Principles Board, led to the replacement of that board by the Financial Accounting Standards Board. Many proposals for other changes have also been made.

While there has been general agreement on the desirability of narrowing the acceptable range of variations in practice, there have been, and still are, marked differences of opinion as to the degree of uniformity that should be sought and the manner and speed with which it should be achieved.

As might be expected, financial analysts and members of the banking fraternity in general have been highly vocal in favoring the development of greater uniformity in financial reporting. Economists and government officials concerned with gathering business statistics to forecast, judge, or control various aspects of the nation's economy have expressed a similar view.

Academicians concerned with accounting matters have written extensively in this area. They have tended to stress the need for developing uniformity in accounting on an intellectual basis rather than relying heavily on the slower process of selection through experience.

Financial and accounting executives in business, backed by other members of top management, have, in general, been sympathetic to the narrowing of variations through an evolutionary process based on experience. They have tended to resist regimented uniformity and to believe that reporting a company's financial condition and operations is management's responsibility, best met by allowing a reasonable degree of freedom in accounting practice within the boundaries of broad, generally accepted accounting principles and conventions.

Public accountants have been actively concerned with the development of greater uniformity in accounting practice for years. But their views tend to be divided among those suggested for financial analysts, academicians, and financial and accounting executives in business. Major differences in beliefs lie in the degree of uniformity or freedom of choice that should be sought in accounting practice, and the degree of pressure that should be applied to achieve it, particularly the extent to which it should be brought about by regimentation as opposed to voluntary acceptance.

Conflicts of Opinion in Establishing Accounting Principles

These divergent views on achieving uniformity in accounting practice have been major factors underlying conflicts in establishing what should henceforth be considered acceptable accounting and reporting procedures.

Also, although accountants, whether public or private, are commonly thought of as being reserved and unemotional, this is far from the truth when it comes to expressing their preferences in accounting practice. Here they are aggressive, articulate, and highly vocal. These human factors are at least a partial explanation of why it takes some time for an accounting practice to become a generally accepted accounting principle, and to get such a principle down in writing.

Reporting by Management or on Management?

Much of the conflict in the matter of regimented uniformity, as opposed to considerable freedom of choice in accounting practice, stems from differences in viewpoint as to the intent underlying the reporting process. Simply stated, one viewpoint stresses reporting *by* management and the other reporting *on* management. Both viewpoints accept the obvious function of financial reports as statements of a company's financial condition and results.

Financial reports as management communications. If one holds strongly to the view of financial reporting as a means of management communication to stockholders and others, then management should logically have both the freedom and the responsibility to account for and report on financial matters in ways that will properly reflect the financial condition of the company and the results of its operations.

Satisfactory communication, however, involves the use of language that is understood by both receiver and sender. Thus the sender must record and report financial data according to rules and practices that are generally understood and accepted. He must also call specific attention to any material departures from such rules and practices.

This view of financial statements as management communications understandably favors required adherence to only relatively broad principles and conventions. The more detailed any prescribed rules and practices become, particularly as the range of allowable practices is narrowed within a given area, the less freedom of action is left for management to decide what it considers to be the most desirable appropriate practice in the given case.

The belief here is that highly regimented uniformity in practice results in an oversimplification of financial statements, implying a degree of comparability between the published statements of different companies that actually exists in appearance only. In some cases, such regimentation inevitably forces management to furnish statements which they do not believe are proper representations of financial condition and results.

Financial reports as means of measuring management performance. If one holds strongly to the view of financial reports as means of measuring management performance, then management should logically have little or no freedom in determining what and how financial information is recorded and reported. This conclusion is based partly on the grounds that an examinee should not be allowed to determine the nature of his examination and partly on the belief that because of a possible management conflict of interest here such restriction is necessary to insure objectivity and truthfulness in financial reporting.

There are some, unfortunately, who combine this view with one favoring the regimentation of accounting practices in great detail, including enforced drastic reduction of the allowable range of practices within a given area. The combination of these views minimizes the degree of trust that should be placed in management's willingness and ability to properly account for its stewardship and places undue reliance on regimentation as the means for achieving proper accounting and financial reporting.

Reporting Both by and on Management

The fact is, of course, that financial reporting involves reporting both by management and on management. This is generally recognized, though many people differ greatly in the emphasis they place on one of these aspects versus the other. This difference in viewpoint has in many cases been a significant obstacle in arriving at an agreement to adopt or eliminate some accounting practice.

Management Implications

Too often reporting decisions have been left exclusively to financial executives and accounting firms. It should be remembered that the annual report is a report *by* management as well as *on* management. Therefore, it behooves managers to enter into decisions regarding what and how to report, since these are basically "management" decisions.

Nonfinancial executives should join with financial executives in discussions of draft proposals of statements to be made by the Financial Accounting Standards Board, and should make their views known to the board. While they may not always be happy with the board's conclusions, they should bear in mind that the alternative to the voluntary development of accounting principles through such a board is complete government regulation. It should also be recognized that to be effective a board like this needs moral support far more than financial support.

The top managements of companies should assist in the development of greater uniformity in accounting practices by the voluntary elimination of those that a prudent businessman would recognize as less supportable from the viewpoint of public interest than other available practices. Included in the term "public interest" is the ability to compare the financial aspects of one company with those of another.

They should continue to seek improvements in their financial reporting with the aim of making it more informative and useful, particularly to stockholders and prospective stockholders.

They should make known in annual reports to stockholders and elsewhere their interest in the matters listed above. Expression of these views might help to overcome the woeful lack of public realization of the extent to which improvements in financial reporting in the United States have come about voluntarily from within companies, rather than from requirements forced upon them.

The difference between voluntary financial reporting and regimented financial reporting can be seen most dramatically by comparing the highly informative financial reports of American companies with reports published abroad in countries where methods of accounting and financial reporting are prescribed in great detail. The least that can be concluded from such a comparison is that financial reporting by government edict provides no guarantee as to the quality of the information supplied. Beyond this, it appears that government regimentation of financial accounting invites resistance and leads to only minimal reporting. It seems evident that high quality in financial reporting is in fact dependent on the sympathetic interest and cooperation of company management.

Underlying the financial statements reported to stockholders and others externally is a variety of accounting statements and reports for internal use presenting in detail the financial results of activities at each level of management. These statements and reports are designed to help managers guide, measure, and judge — in financial terms — the operations under their supervision.

The first responsibility of a manager with respect to such statements and reports is, of course, to educate himself to understand them. His next responsibility is to make effective use of them, including discussing them intelligently with those who report to him and those to whom he reports. A final responsibility is to work jointly with accountants toward improving the accuracy, propriety, and usefulness of the accounting information with which he is furnished.

CHAPTER 2

The Income Statement: Policy and Practice

The typical company annual report to stockholders starts with a presentation of the financial highlights of the year. Two items always presented, generally at the top of the list, are sales and net earnings. These and other types of figures highlighted are illustrated in Exhibit 1, an example from the 1977 annual report of the General Electric Company.

Additional items highlighted are the operating results in terms of revenues and net earnings for each of seven industry segments served by the company. Also, the operating results in terms of revenues and net earnings are given for each of three major geographic segments of the company's business.

Emphasis on income items. Note that most of the figures in the example represent *action* that has taken place, largely involving or reflecting revenues and expenses. Only the figures for borrowings, share owners' equity, and total capital invested have any reference to the *standing* of the business as of the close of the years covered. The figures are presented as key indicators of how well the company has fared financially; what it has done with its earnings in terms of dividend distribution and retention in the business; and where it seems to be heading as evidenced by figures for the previous year, which are shown beside those for the year being reported.

The particular items highlighted, commonly found in the annual reports of other companies as well, are indicative of the greater emphasis investors place on the *income statement*, which shows revenues and expenses in some detail, as compared with the *balance sheet* which lists a company's assets, liabilities, and stockholders' equity. Relatively few balance sheet items are highlighted at the outset of annual reports, although significant changes in these items are commonly discussed in the accompanying narrative. The narrative, of course, also discusses

EXHIBIT 1
General Electric Financial Highlights

	(In millions; per share amounts in dollars)		Percent increase
	1977	1976	
	For the year		
Sales of products and services to customers	$17,519	$15,698	12%
Other income	390	274	42
Total revenues	17,909	15,972	12
Net earnings applicable to common stock	1,088	931	17
	At year end		
Short- and long-term borrowings	$ 2,056	$ 1,933	6%
Shareholders' equity	5,943	5,253	13
Total capital invested	8,131	7,305	11
	Measurements		
Net earnings per common share	$ 4.79	$ 4.12	16%
Dividends declared per General Electric common share	2.10	1.70	24
Operating margin as a percentage of sales	9.7%	9.7%	
Earnings as a percentage of sales	6.2	5.9	
Percent earned on average share owners' equity	19.4	18.9	
Percent earned on average total capital invested	15.8	15.1	
Borrowings as a percentage of total capital invested	25.3	26.5	

many important matters in nonfinancial terms, such as new products introduced during the year, changes in management, and the company's share in the various markets served.

Importance of expression in monetary units. The first figure in the foregoing example, that for sales, is a key indicator of the company's volume of activity for the year as well as its gross revenue. While it is possible in some companies to express sales in physical terms, such as weight in pounds or tons, the great majority of companies have no such physical common denominator. Thus the monetary unit, in our case the dollar, provides not only the means for expressing sales in financial terms, but also the only common denominator for combining dissimilar products sold to show the volume of sales activity for the company as a whole. For internal management reports it also permits combining sales of various products by useful categories, such as sales by individual salesman, customer, and district.

Similarly, the monetary unit as a common denominator permits the combining of dissimilar activities into meaningful summaries and the reporting of them by product lines, cost centers, departments, divisions, and the company as a whole. Finally, monetary expression makes it possible to summarize a company's properties, liabilities, and owners' equity, as well as changes in them, in balance sheets, funds flow statements, and other reports.

Emphasis on net earnings. While, as noted earlier, the sales figure is important as both an indicator of volume of activity and a statement of gross revenue, a company's net earnings figure is of paramount interest to share owners and prospective share owners. This interest is so well known that interest in the "bottom line" has become a common expression for an interest in final results in all sorts of activities.

This interest is anticipated in the present example, which highlights net earnings in five different ways: 1. total dollars; 2. net earnings per share of common stock; 3. percentage of sales; 4. percent earned on average share owners' equity; and 5. percent earned on total capital invested.

These ratios and others will be discussed in Chapter 4, "The Income Statement: Ratio Analysis." The point here is the emphasis placed on net earnings in a representative annual report, such as that of the General Electric Company.

Importance of comparative data. The General Electric Company has provided figures for the previous year for purposes of comparison, since figures of the type presented are not particularly meaningful for one year alone. This has been a practice of GE and other companies for many years and is a requirement for financial statements submitted to the Securities and Exchange Commission. Moreover, like other companies, GE presents a ten-year comparative summary of these and other financial data in another section of its annual report.

While past performance does not necessarily provide desirable or valid standards for the future, figures from the past do provide a perspective for judging current performance and noting trends that affect the company's financial condition and prospects. The least that can be said for the comparison of current performance with past performance is that it serves to signal areas that merit investigation.

In addition to studying the comparative data and developing other comparisons from a company's published financial statements, one should check actual reported performance against forecasts made earlier by company officers or professional financial analysts. Apart from satisfying one's curiosity as to how matters turned out relative to these forecasts, it should be possible to determine over time the degree of reliability that might reasonably be placed on such estimates.

Comparing performance with budget.   In a majority of companies, there is a formal process of budgeting by which plans and goals are put into writing, in financial terms. The budget, by time periods, should provide a more valid basis of comparison as performance takes place than records of the past (such comparisons will be noted later). Yet, unless one is directly involved in the operations of a particular business, its budget is not available for current performance comparisons. And even when the budget is available as a basis for comparison, businessmen also compare current results against records of the past as an additional check on performance.

Consistency in accounting practice.   Comparisons with the past can be misleading if data have not been accounted for and reported consistently. In recognition of this danger, consistency in accounting practice has long been accepted as a major accounting convention. Indeed, an auditor is expected to include in his report on a company's financial statements his opinion as to whether the financial results are stated "in conformity with generally accepted accounting principles applied on a basis consistent with that of the preceding year." If consistency has not been maintained, the auditor is expected to call specific attention to any material changes in practice that have taken place.

Consistency is obviously a virtue in terms of assuring data that may be compared rationally from period to period. There is, however, no virtue in being consistently wrong or in avoiding the adoption of better practices in favor of maintaining mediocrity. Essentially, the convention of consistency supports the application of good practices and their replacement only by significantly better practices. It properly aims to discourage shifts in practice from period to period that arise from carelessness, capriciousness, or ulterior motives.

Comparisons with other companies.   Investors and others judge the financial results and condition of a company by making comparisons with the same types of data for other companies, particularly other companies within the same industry. Comparisons are made by studying published financial statements and data collected by trade associations, credit and investment organizations, and other bodies.

Just as consistency in accounting treatment is desirable for valid comparisons of financial data from year to year within a company, so too is uniformity of accounting treatment, *within reason*, desirable for valid comparisons between companies. The words, "within reason" are used here to emphasize that uniformity in practice does not necessarily in itself lead to the most valid, correct, or desirable statements of financial results or condition for any given company at any given time. Moreover, blind adherence to uniformity in accounting practice can deceive by providing an appearance of comparability in situations which are not truly comparable.

Difficulties in Understanding Financial Statements

Based on a knowledge of simple arithmetic, a reader of the financial highlights in an annual report can readily understand that "revenue" less "expense" equals "net income." Such simplification applied to an income statement, however, can provide only a superficial understanding of events and may well encourage undue confidence in the reader who neither really knows the meaning of "revenue" or "expense" as used in the statement, nor has any appreciation of the complications, estimates, or reasoning involved in deriving figures for these items.

This lack of true understanding has been furthered by the common practice of furnishing only simplified financial statements in annual reports to stockholders. Fortunately, most companies will furnish more detailed information on request, often a copy of the company's Form 10-K report to the SEC. Thus the reader who wants more detailed information on a company can get it and not be limited strictly to information geared to the least sophisticated stockholder. Since few stockholders request such information, however, the average stockholder is likely to be left with a false impression as to the depth of his understanding of his company's financial statements.

The real difficulties in understanding financial statements lie both in the inherent complexities of the operations which these statements reflect and in the need on the part of the reader for understanding the conventions, principles, and practices by which financial data are recorded, allocated, and reported. The degree of possible understanding in any given situation is also dependent, of course, on the quantity and quality of the information provided.

Problems in understanding financial statements are compounded by the fact that so much of the language used in such statements consists of everyday words used in a technical sense. Furthermore, the use of numbers inevitably gives these statements an appearance of exactness which is deceiving, considering the amount of judgment, opinion, and convention underlying the amounts reported.

Forms of Income Statements

The financial statements of revenues, expenses, and the difference between the two for given time periods are commonly presented in one of two basic forms: the *single-step* or the *multiple-step*. The elements of the single-step form of income statement for manufacturing and merchandising business may be illustrated as shown in Exhibit 2.

Single-step statements are so called because there are no intermediate steps showing profit or income figures in arriving at net income. In this particular example, a single step is taken in arriving at a figure for net income, which is independent of whatever extraordinary items of income and expense might have been experienced during that period. The example is therefore really one of taking two steps in arriving at final net income.

The elements of a multiple-step form of income statement for the same types of business may be illustrated as shown in Exhibit 3.

EXHIBIT 2
Single-Step Form of Income Statement

	Year Ended December 31	
	1977	1976
Sales, less returns and allowances	$89,731,224	$81,427,649
Other income	743,012	677,111
Total revenues	90,474,236	82,104,760
Costs and expenses		
Cost of goods sold	68,447,490	60,251,113
Selling, general and administrative expenses	15,096,582	13,934,940
Other expense	766,831	737,417
State and federal income taxes	3,005,624	3,760,089
Total costs and expenses	87,316,527	78,683,559
Net income before extraordinary items of income or expense	3,157,709	3,421,201
Add or (deduct) extraordinary items of income or expense (net of related income tax $367,807)	(385,862)	—
Net income	$ 2,771,847	$ 3,421,201
Earnings per share of common stock:		
Earnings before extraordinary item	$1.34	$1.44
Extraordinary item	.16	—
Net earnings	$1.18	$1.44

EXHIBIT 3
Multiple-Step Form of Income Statement

	Year Ended December 31	
	1977	1976
Sales, less returns and allowances	$89,731,224	$81,427,649
Less—cost of goods sold	68,447,490	60,251,113
Gross margin	21,283,734	21,176,536
Less—Selling, general and administrative expenses	15,096,582	13,934,940
Net operating income	6,187,152	7,241,596
Add or (deduct) other income and expense	(23,819)	(60,306)
Net income before income tax	6,163,333	7,181,290
Less—State and federal income taxes	3,005,624	3,760,089
Net income before extraordinary items of income or expense	3,157,709	3,421,201
Add or (deduct) extraordinary items of income or expense (net of related income tax $367,807)	(385,862)	—
Net income	$ 2,771,847	$ 3,421,201
Earnings per share of common stock:		
Earnings before extraordinary item	$1.34	$1.44
Extraordinary item	.16	—
Net earnings	$1.18	$1.44

Those who use the single-step form do so partly because of its simplicity and partly because they believe that the multiple-step form can mislead stockholders and others into placing undue importance on figures for the revenue left after deducting only certain types of expenses. In this connection, they consider it improper to apply the word income (or profit) to any figure short of the revenue left after deducting all of the expenses that should logically be applied against gross revenue.

Those who favor the multiple-step form believe that there is something to be gained from showing the gross margin realized above the purchase cost, or manufacturing cost, of goods sold. They also believe it is useful to show the net income from operations prior to taking into account other items of income and expense, including income taxes.

More importantly, the segmentation of cost and revenue figures and the provision of subtotals are aids in locating major areas of loss or gain when comparing current figures with previous periods or with budgeted figures. In particular, segmentation helps to separate changes in trading gains and losses (i.e., changes in sales revenue and the cost of goods sold, and their effect on profit) from the effect on profit of changes in operating expenses.

Time Periods for Income Statements

It has been customary for many years to prepare income statements on an annual basis. For the majority of companies, the calendar year has been the annual period selected. For some of the remainder, the anniversary date of the beginning of the company has marked the start of a new fiscal year. For others, the annual period covered has been the "natural business year," such as the end of a season, whether that be the end of a crop year or the Christmas season. At such a time, there is a lull in business, inventories are at a low point, and it is a natural time to "take stock" and see how the company fared for the twelve months just ended. For many diversified companies, however, the seasonal pattern differs among divisions so that there is no natural business year for the company as a whole for purposes of financial reporting.

In addition to the annual income statement, it has become customary, and indeed is an SEC reporting requirement, for companies to provide quarterly information on key figures such as sales, operating profit, net income, and earnings per share. Complete income statements are prepared monthly for internal management use. The annual income statement is not only the most important of these financial reports, but for most companies, it is the only income statement based on figures audited by a public accountant and therefore the only one on which he states his opinion.

The Accounting Principles Board, in its Opinion No. 28, described the type of information that should appear in interim statements, including information on changes in accounting principles and practices adopted by the company reporting.[1]

The Financial Accounting Standards Board in its Statement of Financial Accounting Standards No. 3 presented an amendment to APB No. 28. The gist of this amendment was that if an accounting change is made in other than the first interim period of an enterprise's fiscal year, the cumulative effect of the change on retained earnings at the beginning of that year shall be included in the determination of net income of the first interim period of the year of change (by restatement of that period's financial information).[2]

---

[1] Accounting Principles Board Opinion 28, "Interim Financial Reporting," AICPA New York, May 1973.

[2] Statement of Financial Accounting Standards No. 3, "Reporting Accounting Changes in Interim Financial Statements," FASB, Stamford, Conn., Dec. 1974.

Accounting Problems. . .

Most of the difficult problems in accounting policy and practice, as distinguished from operational problems such as those connected with the design and operation of a computer-based information system, stem from the custom of reporting periodically on the condition of a business and on its revenues, expenses, and net income for given periods of time.

Ancient moneylenders, among the earliest bookkeepers, were largely concerned with records of amounts owed by debtors to them and owed by them to creditors (depositors) who had left money with them for safekeeping. Then, as now, one could be well aware of what he owed, as well as what he was owed. The only accounting problem was one of accuracy in recordkeeping, unless one includes the problem of determining when an account should be written off as uncollectible. The problem of "casting-up" accounts, i.e., adding up accounts and determining balances periodically, was not difficult.

Even for early traders and merchants, whose activities and properties were much more extensive than those of the moneylenders, accounting problems were relatively simple. Bookkeeping was a matter of recording, day by day, completed financial transactions between the enterprise and other parties. Essentially, it involved recording monetary amounts for what came into a business and what left it, with appropriate journal explanations and classification by accounts in a ledger or ledgers.

Profit or loss for the business as a whole was determined on a formal basis only at the end of a company's life, as, for example, when a joint venture was concluded or a partnership was dissolved, and the net gain or loss to be divided among the participants or partners was computed, and the books of account were closed.

. . . Related to Time Periods

It was when businessmen began to want a periodic reckoning of how their businesses stood, and a measure of profit or loss for periods shorter than the life of an enterprise, that problems in accounting policy and practice really began. This demand for periodic measurement accompanied, and was stimulated by, recognition of the concept of a business enterprise as a going concern of unlimited life.

Problems in the periodic measurement of financial condition and results of operations occur because the purchase (or acquisition by other means) of labor, services, goods, and other properties including legal claims is not matched neatly by the sale, exhaustion, or disposal of these same items (or of properties or services created by them) within the same time period for which "an accounting" must be made. The latter is a month, a quarter, a year, or any other period short of the entire life of the given enterprise.

To state this another way, financial transactions involving *costs* are not matched neatly in the same accounting period by financial transactions involving *revenues*. Under these conditions, there are problems in determining what can reasonably be considered as a company's revenues for a given period and the costs to be charged appropriately against them.

Similarly, there are problems in determining appropriate monetary amounts for a company's assets on hand at the end of a period, and for its liabilities and the net worth of its owners at that time. Periodic measurement thus forces the exercise of judgment and experience in making estimates, allocations, and valuations, and a combination of judgment, convention, and rules in arriving at the most appropriate accounting treatment under the given circumstances for each type of item to be recorded and reported.

Representative problems in this area are illustrated by the following questions:

> What costs incurred during a period should a manufacturing business identify with inventories remaining on hand at the close of that period?
>
> What costs should be identified with goods sold during that period?
>
> What costs should be charged as operating costs of the period not directly identified with either inventories or goods sold?
>
> How should the amount of depreciation on plant and equipment for a given period be determined?
>
> Should depreciation on manufacturing facilities be charged to goods produced by them or simply be "written off" as period costs?
>
> If goods produced are to be charged for depreciation of the facilities used to produce them, on what basis should the charges be made?
>
> How should the amount of revenue be determined each month when goods sold are paid for on an installment basis over several months?
>
> Should research and development costs on a project be charged off as expenses each month as incurred or be carried forward to be charged against revenues on that project when, as, and if received?

We shall be examining these and similar problems later. For the moment, let us simply acknowledge that a number of methods for dealing with such problems have become generally accepted, including a variety of alternative practices. Those practices which have gained widest acceptance have done so gradually over the years. Their acceptability has been established by voluntary growth in use, not by edict, vote, or to any appreciable extent by persuasive writings.

Fortunately, superior practices have tended to increase in use, and inferior practices to pass from circulation, although not as rapidly or extensively as some people might have wished. To be sure, many practices have been affected by rulings and opinions of governmental, legal, and professional bodies but the roots of these decisions have rested in the test of experience. In most instances, the rulings and opinions handed down have simply stated which practices currently in use are to be considered as the only acceptable practices in the future.

. . .Within Generally Accepted Principles

Even where an accounting principle has become generally accepted, practice usually requires the exercise of judgment in specific cases. For example, generally accepted accounting principles require that the cost of a machine be allocated to accounting periods over its expected useful life in a systematic and rational manner.

This clearly involves judgment both in estimating the probable useful life of the machine and in selecting the method by which its cost will be allocated over that life in a systematic manner. Indeed, there are also likely to be problems of judgment in determining what the machine actually cost. And there are bound to be such problems if the machine was built in a company's own shops instead of being purchased from an outside source.

Judgment will always be necessary in making a variety of estimates, allocations, and valuations in connection with accounting problems of the type under discussion. Also, short of complete political or professional dictatorship, judgment will always be necessary, and desirable up to some point, in selecting appropriate accounting methods or practices for handling such problems.

. . . of Valuation

An early method of measuring profit or loss for an accounting period was to compare how a company stood financially at the end of a given period with its financial condition at the beginning of that period.

Expressed in terms of the major classifications of items in a balance sheet, assets minus liabilities as of the end of the period would be compared with a similar figure for the beginning of that period. The difference, adjusted for any capital entering the business and any capital or earnings withdrawn from the business during the period, would measure the profit or loss for that period.

The same earnings figure can be computed as the difference between owners' equity (including retained earnings) at the beginning and end of the given time period, adjusted as just quoted.

Both of these ways of measuring profit or loss may be illustrated by figures adapted from the General Electric Company's Statement of Financial Position in its annual report for 1977, as shown in Exhibit 4.

EXHIBIT 4
Income Determination by Deduction

A. By comparison of assets less liabilities

Excess of assets over liabilities (in millions)		
Total assets December 31, 1977	$13,696.8	
Total liabilities December 31, 1977	7,622.5	$6,074.3
Total assets December 31, 1976	$12,049.7	
Total liabilities December 31, 1976	6,677.8	5,371.9
Net increase in 1977		$ 702.4
Add back dividends declared in 1977		476.9
		$1,179.3
Adjust for changes in capital		
New shares issued	$ 2.6	
Amounts received for stock in excess of par value	50.1	
Decrease in treasury stock	26.0	
Increase in minority interest	12.4	91.1
Net earnings applicable to common stock 1977		$1,088.2

B. By comparison of share owners' equity including retained earnings

Share owners' equity December 31, 1977	$ 5,942.9	
Minority interest December 31, 1977	131.4	$6,074.3
Share owners' equity December 31, 1976	$ 5,252.9	
Minority interest December 31, 1976	119.0	5,371.9
Net increase in 1977		702.4
Add back dividends declared in 1977		476.9
		$1,179.3
Adjust for changes in capital as in A above		91.1
Net earnings applicable to common stock 1977		$1,088.2

When a company's profit or loss for a period is calculated as the difference between its financial position at the beginning and at the end of that period, as reflected in its balance sheets, the amount calculated is obviously dependent on the values placed on the items making up the positions at those two periods of time. Accounting difficulties in this connection are discussed as problems of valuation.

Thus, selecting one basis of valuation rather than another for any given item is a problem of deciding which basis is most appropriate under the given circumstances. Different bases will, of course, cause differences in the computed worth of a business at either end of an accounting period, as well as corresponding differences in the profit or loss computed for that period.

The words "value," "valuation," and "worth" are used here in a technical sense. While valuation in arriving at worth does involve establishing a monetary amount for a given property or legal claim, as of a given time, that amount 1. is affected by accounting conventions, practices, and rules; 2. probably involves the exercise of judgment in making estimates, allocations, and computations; and 3. is more likely to be based on historical cost than on market value.

. . . of Matching Costs and Revenues

The profit or loss figure derived by deduction from balance-sheet data is, of course, the same as that arrived at in a company's income statement, as shown by the General Electric Company's figures in Exhibit 5. The latter, however, provides important information on the company's costs and revenues, which is not revealed when the net profit or loss figure alone is found by deduction from balance-sheet data.

In arriving at net income through the subtraction of costs from revenues, it is evident that if problems should arise in the process they would be in determining what should be recognized as constituting revenues and expenses of the accounting period. These are commonly spoken of as problems in the "proper matching of costs and revenues by accounting periods."

Since the balance sheet and income statement dovetail so nicely when it comes to the figure for net profit or loss, and since this figure can be affected both by balance sheet valuations and also by determinations as to what constitutes the costs and revenues of a period, we can realize that these approaches from different directions must somehow be reconciled, one with the other, in order to come out to the same net profit or loss.

We shall be examining valuation problems and problems in the proper matching of costs and revenues, together with relationships be-

EXHIBIT 5
Statement of Earnings
General Electric Company and Consolidated Affiliates

For the years ended December 31 (In millions)	1977	1976
Sales of products and services to customers	$17,518.6	$15,697.3
Operating costs:		
Employee compensation, including benefits	6,555.5	5,849.9
Materials, supplies, services, and other costs	8,753.9	7,726.0
Depreciation, depletion, and amortization	522.1	486.2
Taxes, except those on income	239.0	258.8
Increase in inventories during the year	(249.9)	(151.5)
	15,820.6	14,169.4
Operating margin	1,698.0	1,527.9
Other income	390.3	274.3
Interest and other financial charges	(199.5)	(174.7)
Earnings before income taxes and minority interest	1,888.8	1,627.5
Provision for income taxes	(773.1)	(668.6)
Minority interest in earnings of consolidated affiliates	27.5	28.3
Net earnings applicable to common stock	$ 1,088.2	$ 930.6
Earnings per common share (in dollars)	$ 4.79	$ 4.12

tween the two, in depth. For the moment, let us note that acquisitions of goods, services, and properties are entered in the accounts at their cost. At the close of an accounting period, it is necessary, under current accounting practice, to determine to what extent these costs should be charged as expenses of the current period of carried forward in the accounts to be charged as expenses in later periods. This is a combined problem of balance-sheet valuation and period-cost determination.

For some items, the problem can be approached from either of these two ways to arrive at the same end result, as we shall note later when discussing the valuation of inventories on a cost basis.

In other instances, however, the valuation approach is the dominant concern and period-cost determination is subordinated to it. Thus if, on the grounds of conservatism in asset valuation, a company decides to value its inventories at market values which are below the recorded costs of these goods, the loss resulting from this lower valuation will have to be accounted for as a period cost.

In still other cases, period cost or revenue considerations are dominant and valuation subordinated. Thus, if the market value of inventories is above their costs, the gain in valuation will not be taken, under the principle that revenue should not be recognized until a sale takes place. This matter of inventory valuation will be considered further in the chapter to follow, as we examine the elements of an income statement in more detail.

"Current Value" Accounting

For many years the income statement, and the proper matching of costs and revenues therein, has been of greater interest to investors and prospective investors, as well as to company managements, than the balance sheet and the valuation of assets within it.

In recent times, however, increases in the rate of inflation have raised questions about the justification of continuing to carry assets at their historical costs when such costs are markedly lower than would be the estimated costs to replace them. These questions have raised interest on the part of some, and concern, if not fear, on the part of others, in what has become known as "current value" accounting.

This term has come into use for lack of a better one. It does not result in providing financial statements which represent a company's value in the sense of earning power, nor what it might fetch in either an outright sale or by gradual liquidation. It does provide for the valuation of assets at figures that are more current than the historical costs as entered in the accounts at the time they were acquired.

Since current value accounting is not a currently accepted practice, its possible benefits, or detriments, as either a substitute for historical-cost accounting, or as supplementary information, are matters of conjecture and opinion. We shall be discussing various aspects of current value accounting in later chapters, particularly in Chapter 19 on accounting for property, plant and equipment, where revaluation would have major consequences.

We have noted in the present chapter that one way of computing a company's profit or loss for an accounting period is by first comparing assets minus liabilities at the end of a period with a similar figure for the beginning of that period. The difference is then adjusted for any capital entering the business and any capital or earnings withdrawn from the business during the period, to measure the profit or loss for that period.

It can be appreciated that if assets were to be revalued in substantial amounts at the close of an accounting period, this could have a profound effect on the profit or loss computed by the method described in the previous paragraph. As we shall note later, however, part of the revaluation would presumably be matched by an adjustment to stated capital, so that only part of the revaluation would affect the computed profit or loss. Whatever the effect might be, it would correspondingly affect the profit or loss as reported in the income statement. Thus the balance sheet would move forward as the dominant financial statement and the income statement would become subordinated to it.

Since current value accounting is not a currently accepted practice, these matters may appear to be of only academic interest. Strong pressures are developing, however, for moving in the direction of current value accounting. The possible effects of such accounting, whether favorable or unfavorable, should then be matters of interest and concern to those who publish financial statements as well as to those who receive them.

CHAPTER 3

The Income Statement: Revenues and Expenses

In the preceding chapter, we noted the common practice of furnishing only simplified financial statements in annual reports to stockholders based on the assumption that the average stockholder is unsophisticated in matters of accounting and finance.

Another contemporary concept is that of the stockholder as an investor who is periodically trying to decide whether he will continue to hold his stock in a company, sell it, or buy more. He is considered to have a cold, analytical viewpoint, with no sentiment or loyalty to the company attached to it.

This is, of course, the investment approach of large stockholders, such as mutual funds and institutions. It is an understandable viewpoint for smaller stockholders as well. Except in closely held companies, the average stockholder has nothing to do with managing the company in which he has invested and very little, if anything, to do with changing its management. Apart from speaking up at a stockholders' meeting, writing letters to the president, and consuming or not consuming the company's products, he can express his support or lack of support of the company, its management, and its policies only by holding, increasing, or unloading his investment in it.

There is no doubt that many managements feel the pressure of this analytical viewpoint, whether from stockholders, prospective stockholders, or the writings of financial analysts. This pressure can be useful to the extent that it prevents management complacency and stimulates good management performance, along with adequate and accurate financial reporting. It can be harmful, however, if it leads management to become overly concerned with a company's current position and short-run performance, to the detriment of its long-run best interests and those of its more steady stockholders.

This concept of the analytical stockholder assumes that he is most interested in short-run performance and if not satisfied with the current performance or near-term prospects of his present holdings, he will switch his investments to other companies where the performance and prospects appear to be better.

In order to hold the favor of such stockholders and to woo new stockholders of the same type, some managements will not only adopt operating policies aimed at short-run gains, but on occasion will also change their accounting practice to less conservative alternative practices in order to improve the short-run appearance of performance.

For example, even some of our most respected companies have for this reason shifted to less conservative practice in inventory valuation (specifically, LIFO to FIFO); in accounting for depreciation (accelerated to straight-line); and in accounting for investment tax credits (deferral to "flow-through").

The explanation generally given for such changes is that they have been made to bring the company's practices in line with those of other companies in the same industry. Such a statement is not the whole truth, nor does it necessarily justify such changes in accounting practice. It may simply indicate that the desire or pressure for uniformity can lead a company, and indeed an industry, in the wrong direction.

This preoccupation with reporting favorably on a company's current position and performance is in marked contrast to the ultraconservatism in accounting policy and financial reporting of an earlier day. For example, compare this viewpoint with the following statement in the annual report of the National Lead Company for 1894 by William P. Thompson, then president of that company.

"The policy of this company remains precisely as it has been since its inauguration, and is very simple. First, the unqualified protection of the property in all its departments and in its business, and second, to make fair and reasonable profits, and distribute same among its shareholders whenever deemed wise and prudent to do so."

Although we should not return to the degree of management paternalism of those days which led to gross understatement of assets, and the creation of "hidden reserves" unknown to the average stockholder, the quality of financial reporting of many companies today could benefit from the adoption of more conservative policies than they are now exercising.

Revenue Recognition . . .

Having in mind the interest of the analytical investor in a company's current position, some theorists have pressed enthusiastically for the valuation of all assets at current values as of the end of each accounting period. In Chapter 19 we shall examine price-level adjustments for changes in the purchasing power of money and consider problems in the revaluation of fixed assets in terms of market values and replacement costs as well as other possible adjustments for the effects of inflation. However, for the moment, we shall consider only the periodic revaluation of inventories in terms of their current values.

It has long been a common practice to write inventories down to their market values at the close of an accounting period if such values are less than the inventories cost. This is both a matter of conservatism with respect to balance-sheet presentation and a belief that such a drop in value should be accounted for as a loss during the period in which it takes place rather than carried forward to the period during which the materials or goods involved are sold.

Consistent valuation at market would require, however, that inventories be written up to market when market is above cost. This would not only mean writing up inventories to reflect gains from holding materials and goods as prices rose, but in manufacturing businesses it would also include writing up a profit element for inventories of finished goods. The question then is: Should any of these gains be accounted for as earned income?

Many theorists, who are enthusiastic about the consistent valuation of inventories at market, are mainly interested in having assets stated at current values. They propose that gains from inventory write-ups be accounted for as holding gains not to be brought into earned income until the goods involved are sold. Some, however, would like to see these gains brought into earned income for the period during which the rise in market value reflected in the inventory write-ups has taken place.

Regardless of how the gain might be accounted for, even the most opportunistic of businessmen have voiced no enthusiasm for writing up inventories to reflect market values above costs, except in a few special cases such as in the mining of gold. Underlying their lack of enthusiasm is their experience that it is relatively easy to buy, make, or hold an item but that it can be very difficult to sell it. Moreover, the higher market value for an inventoried item today may well drop tomorrow for reasons completely beyond the control of the company stocking it.

Therefore, businessmen consider it best not to count as a gain an apparent rise in the market value of materials and goods on hand. Also, in a manufacturing business, although it is pleasant to think that value has been created through the production of an item, the only certainty is that costs have been incurred. Whether or not the product proves to have any value, and if so, how much, is dependent on finding a prospective buyer, coming to terms on price, and completing the sale through delivery.

For the practical reasons indicated, it has long been an accepted rule among businessmen not to value inventories above their costs and, therefore, not to recognize revenue on materials or goods until they have been sold. Another way the rule is stated is that revenue should not be anticipated, i.e., it should not be recognized until realized through a sale.

In recent years, the SEC has required larger companies to include as supplementary information in their Form 10-K reports the estimated replacement costs of inventories, the cost of goods sold, property, plant, and equipment, and depreciation expense. The aim has been to try to determine the usefulness to investors of such information, and the difficulties and expense to companies in getting it.

The possible benefits and reservations with respect to this type of information will be discussed more fully in Chapter 19. For the moment let us note simply that both the SEC and the companies involved are warning that there are limitations to the usefulness of the information being supplied. In particular they are stressing that this replacement cost data should not be used to indicate the effect of inflation upon a company's net income, i.e., should not be used to restate its reported net income.

In the case of inventories, this means that if their replacement cost is higher than the historical cost at which they are being shown in the balance sheet, this can be regarded as an interesting aspect of a company's current working-capital position, but the difference between the two should not be considered as having as yet been earned.

... of Sales

To a salesman, a sale takes place when he gets an order from a customer, and his sales manager is likely to be sympathetic to this view. Happy though this event may be to both of them, however, the hard-headed accountant will not enter it as a sale in the records. It will be recorded appropriately by the accountant or someone else as a statistical record of an order received. The accountant realizes that information on the receipt and backlog of orders is important to managers and should be reported to them, but he believes such information should be reported as orders received and on hand, not as realized revenue.

When goods have been shipped, in the sense of having at least been placed in the hands of a common carrier, the accountant will accept the fact that delivery has been made and, accordingly, will then record the event as a sale.

Thus, for the majority of companies, the word "sales" in an income statement means goods shipped during the given accounting period. The monetary amount indicated for these sales is the amount thereby recognized as the revenue realized on these shipments. The purchasers of these goods, if commercial customers, will record in their accounts as purchases the monetary amounts of these shipments as billed to them when shipment is made. Thus one man's revenue is another man's cost.

Sales may be extended to cover "fees" for services performed as well as other items of income such as commissions, rents, and royalties. More exact information is given in the income statement, however, if these specific titles are used rather than the general term "sales."

For sales involving the shipment of goods, there is normally a passing of legal title, which is evidence that a sale has in fact taken place. In other types of business transactions, however, revenue recognition is not dependent on the passing of legal title. If a company performs some type of service, for example, which was requested by the one served, there is no transfer of property and hence nothing on which to pass title. Even so, assuming that everything about the transaction is in order, the company that has performed the service is entitled to bill its customer and to recognize revenue.

... of Performance

There are many situations involving long-term contracts in which revenue will be recognized as work progresses even though title to whatever is produced will not pass until the contract is completed.

In the construction of a ship, for example, revenue will be recognized each accounting period in accordance with work performed during that period as measured either by percentage of completion or by completion of identifiable portions of the work. As a precaution, something less than the full proportion of revenue will be recognized at such times (or a reserve will be established from revenue) to make good whatever parts of the work may fail to come up to expectations, or to provide for possible higher costs than planned later in the contract.

Commonly, interim recognitions of revenue on long-term contracts are matched in timing with billing arrangements agreed to by the customer or client. To illustrate, the following schedule of payments is common on contracts for the construction of houses in at least one section of the country, and contractors there time their recognition of revenue to the same schedule:

10% when foundation is completed.
20% when house is boarded in and roof shingled.

20% when rough wiring, plumbing, and heating have been
   installed, inspected, and passed by local authorities.
20% when plastered, including skim coat.
20% when completed and ready for occupancy.
10% forty-three days after completion.

The important point in the foregoing is that revenue recognition is
tied to performance for another party. The party recognizing the revenue
has delivered something, performed some service, or taken some action
for which he is entitled to payment, eventually if not immediately. The
party on the other side of the transaction normally will recognize at the
same time that he has purchased or incurred as a cost whatever it was
that the party recognizing the revenue has supplied. Under this view, it
is not enough to have received an order, to have been paid for something
in advance, or to have made something for stock; revenue is recognized
only after performance for another party has taken place.

There are some, however, who do not share that view. They hold
that the important point is assurance of income. Thus, if the income on
an order is assured, it is appropriate to recognize revenue at the time the
order is received.

For example, it used to be common practice among flour millers, at
the end of an accounting period, to value at market: grain on hand, grain
ordered, sales orders for flour on hand, and future contracts outstanding
for the purchase or sale of grain. The net effect of all this was that profit
was taken on flour sales at the time orders were received. The argument
of those who did this was that their operations were fully hedged, trade
custom dictated the honoring of contracts, and these factors taken
together assured income on whatever orders were received.

In more recent years, major flour millers have swung to the general
practice in other industries of not recognizing income from sales until
the delivery or performance of whatever was ordered has taken place.

... of Income Tax

Those who are enthusiastic about recording inventory gains, and accounting for profit as goods are manufactured or as orders are received,
do not usually carry their enthusiasm to the point of suggesting that
such gains or profits be reported as taxable income. Similarly, those who
record in their accounts, and state in reports to stockholders, income on
long-term contracts as work progresses, commonly defer reporting income on such contracts for tax purposes until their completion.

Those selling goods on an installment payment basis will commonly record in their accounts, and state in reports to stockholders,
sales revenue as of the time such goods are delivered to customers.

However, they will defer reporting for tax purposes the income on these sales until after the costs of the goods sold have been recovered by installments received.

Timing differences in recognizing revenues or gains and expenses or losses, as between a company's own financial accounting and its reporting for income tax purposes, are of sufficient importance to be discussed more fully later. At the moment, let us simply note that there are such differences. Where options are available which permit these differences, the natural tendency is for a company to be more conservative in computing net income for tax purposes than in its own accounting.

This should not be taken to imply that there is anything sharp or immoral in the practice. The government does not expect a company to report for any given period any more revenue, or any less expense, than required or allowed for in the law.

Moreover, management is responsible for controlling a company's tax expense to the best of its ability, just as it is responsible for controlling any other expense. It must take care, however, that steps resulting in short-run tax savings are also in the company's long-run best interests.

... of Trade Discounts

In many industries, catalog or list prices serve as basing points for pricing purposes. The real price charged any given class of buyer is determined by the application of a discount, or chain of discounts, to these catalog or list prices. No knowledgeable buyer pays the "full" price.

Under these conditions, sales reported for financial accounting purposes represent revenue net of trade discounts. However, for purposes of internal measurement and control, sales are commonly reported by customer classes, as well as in total; one type of classification being by amount of trade discount.

In some companies, classified sales are first shown at "full selling price" and the amount of discount taken is then subtracted in arriving at the real sales figure. The purpose here is to assist in the comparative analysis of sales to different classes of customers by relating all sales to common base prices.

... of Cash Discounts

The question whether cash discounts are a financial expense, a selling expense, or a reduction in sales revenue has been debated for many years. Arguments can be advanced in support of each of these concepts. Consider:

Treating the discount as a *financial expense* assumes that it is granted in order to receive payment earlier as it is a matter of either matching what competitors are doing or of offering something competitors are not offering.

Treating the discount as a *reduction in sales revenue* may likewise be an assumption of competitive reduction in price. Then, again, it may be a more complicated assumption that prices are set high enough to allow for this discount. Therefore, it is appropriate to subtract the cash discount in arriving at the real sales figure, which is net sales.

The basic assumption here is that since the granting and taking of cash discounts are common practices in the given trade the net effect is that industry-wide prices are forced upward to provide for them. The thought also is that since prompt payment is the normal expectation, the buyer who cannot meet this expectation pays a higher price by the loss of the discount.

... of Returns and Allowances

The sales value of goods returned is another of the items subtracted from sales in arriving at net sales. The only accounting problem here is that goods returned in the current accounting period may have been sold in the previous period. Therefore, to treat them as a reduction from current sales is an incorrect matching of costs and revenues.

However, unless the returns are unusually heavy in any one period, there is no serious distortion of results. The figures for sales returns will simply lag somewhat behind the sales figures. This is an example where costs and revenues are not likely to be matched exactly for any single accounting period, but the resulting distortions are not likely to be material and will balance out over time.

Trade discounts, discussed earlier, are treated by some companies as allowances in the income statement. Where this is the practice, the discount percentages involved are not likely to be high. Other items accounted for under this title are adjustments for billing errors and after-the-fact adjustments of selling prices for one reason or another. The latter situation may be one where the quality of goods is not up to the customer's expectations but he is willing to keep them if such an allowance is granted.

Cost of Goods Sold ...

This title, which is sometimes listed in an income statement as "cost of sales," covers the cost of the goods themselves that are shipped. It does not cover the expenses of selling and shipping these goods, or ordinarily any storing, office, or general administrative expenses involved in company operations.

When revenue consists of items such as fees, rents, and royalties, or where commissions are the only source of revenue even though goods or tangible properties are involved in the transactions, there is no category similar to cost of goods sold in the income statement. The revenue is shown under an appropriate title, and operating costs are then listed and subtracted in arriving at net operating income.

. . . for Goods Not Inventoried

When goods not carried in inventory by the supplier are sold, the supplier has no problem in determining his cost of goods sold. For example, when a wholesaler receives an order from a retailer for goods, which are to be shipped directly to the retailer from the manufacturer, the wholesaler has no difficulty in determining the cost of the goods sold in the transaction. He will bill the retailer at the selling price for the goods, and the cost of goods sold will be determined by the invoice sent to him by the manufacturer.

There could be a problem of delay in the preparation of financial statements, however, if a shipment was made at the very end of the month and the seller had to wait a few days to receive the invoice from the factory covering the cost of the goods. If it was urgent to push through the preparation of financial statements, the cost of such goods could doubtless be estimated with great accuracy since the wholesaler would surely want to know, before accepting an order from a retailer, what the goods were going to cost him.

. . . When Inventories Are Involved

In merchandising and manufacturing businesses where inventories are maintained, the cost of goods sold is established in one of several ways: directly, or by deflating sales figures, or by a process of deduction.

Determining cost directly. If detailed inventory records are maintained in both quantity and money, the cost of goods sold can be established directly as sales take place. This can be done from summaries of entries in these records for withdrawals from stock, although this may be a cumbersome approach to the problem.

Another direct method is to establish the cost of goods sold by costing each line of a copy of each sales invoice, using data from a stock list of unit costs or file of standard unit costs. For large manufactured goods, the cost records kept on them during production provide their total cost at time of shipment.

In some retail establishments, each item available for sale will have a two-part tag attached to it. One part shows the sales price and the other the cost of the item in code. At the time of sale, the cost tags are sent to the accounting department where they are decoded and summarized to find the cost of goods sold.

Whatever the mechanics may be, the steps described indicate that in many companies it is practicable to establish the cost of goods sold by a direct approach.

Deflating sales figures.   A shortcut in establishing the cost of goods sold directly for monthly financial statement purposes is to maintain classifications of sales by product groups having the same percentage of mark-up (gross margin) and to deflate the sales in each group by the appropriate percentage.

For example, if the sales of a product group having a known gross margin of 40% are $200,000 for the period, the cost of goods sold would be established as 60% of this, or $120,000.

In some establishments, such as some garages, the problem is further simplified by providing for a uniform margin on all goods sold through taking a loss or gain on goods at the time of purchase. Thus, if the advertised selling price on an accessory was $10.00, its cost to the garage $6.50, and the garage wanted to meet its uniform margin of 40% at time of sale, it would account for a loss of $0.50 per unit at the time of purchase. Thereafter, it would account for a cost of $6.00 on each of the units sold.

Establishing cost by deduction.   Where it is not possible or practicable to establish the cost of goods sold directly, or to establish it by deflating sales figures, it is necessary to determine it by deduction.

An inventory record or account has four elements: 1. what was on hand at the beginning of the period; 2. what came in during the period; 3. what went out during the period; and 4. what was left at the end of the period. The total of the last two items is equal to the total of the first two items, as illustrated in the following figures:

On hand at the beginning	$1,515,983	Went out	$6,736,490
Came in	6,515,858	On hand at the end	1,295,351
	$8,031,841		$8,031,841

If any three of these figures are known, it is possible to find the fourth by deduction. Thus, if all except the ending inventory is known here, it can be found by subtracting $6,736,490 (what went out) from $8,031,841 (the sum of the beginning inventory plus what came into the account).

In every case, the amount on hand at the beginning of the period would either be zero or a known amount that had been established at the close of the previous period. Under a proper accounting system, whatever came in would be recorded.

Thus, at the close of the period, what came in can be added to what was on hand at the beginning of the period to establish the total amount to be accounted for. If what went out is known, as would be the case when the cost of goods sold for the period is established directly, a figure for the closing inventory can be established by deduction.

The term "a figure for the closing inventory can be established" is used here, rather than "the closing inventory can be established," in recognition of the fact that an inventory figure found by deduction in this way may not be absolutely correct because of thefts, clerical errors, mistakes made in issuing goods or materials, and failure to account properly for spoilage. Therefore, it is necessary to make a physical inspection and count the stock on hand periodically in order to make corrections in inventory records and concomitant adjustments in the cost of goods sold. This is particularly important with respect to year-end financial statements.

However, the ability to establish the cost of goods sold directly, and the closing inventory by deduction, is still of great value, since monthly financial statements can be prepared without having to stop operations to make a physical inspection and count the stock on hand. If considered desirable, an allowance can be made each month, based on experience, setting up a reserve to take care of estimated corrections that will have to be made at the next physical inventory time.

The effect of inventory adjustments may also be spread by inspecting and counting a few items each day, particularly when they have reached a low reorder point, and correcting the accounts accordingly.

Using the inventory record figures from the previous illustration, a schedule of the cost of goods sold for the given period would appear as shown in the following table (the assumption for the moment is that we are dealing with a merchandising business, thus additions to inventory arise from purchases):

Inventory January 1, 1977	$1,515,983
Purchases	6,515,858
	$8,031,841
Inventory December 31, 1977	1,295,351
Cost of goods sold	$6,736,490

This information would appear in a company's internal reporting, either as a separate schedule or as a section of the income statement immediately after the net-sales figure. In the interest of simplicity of presentation, a schedule of this type would not usually be included in a published statement. .

For internal financial statements, the schedule of cost of goods sold is commonly presented in this way. This is normal even when the cost of goods sold has, in fact, been established directly and the ending inventory found by deduction, i.e., the schedule under these conditions makes it appear that the cost of goods sold has been found by deduction when it has in fact been established directly.

Schedule of Cost of Goods Sold

In a manufacturing business, there are three major inventory classifications to be considered: raw material; work in process; and finished goods. For internal use, it is considered desirable to present the monetary amount and activity (flow of costs) with respect to each of these inventories. The schedule of cost of goods sold in a manufacturing business is thus more involved than in a merchandising business. The manufacturer has to undertake both purchasing and manufacturing in order to have his goods for sale, whereas the merchant has only to engage in the purchasing process.

A simplified form of this schedule is shown in Exhibit 6. The figures in this exhibit for inventories in total and cost of goods sold are the same as those we saw earlier in the tables for the assumed merchandising business. The point of using them again here is to stress the similarity of the deductive process even though the input figures differ in nature.

Inventory Valuation and Cost of Goods Sold

There are a variety of problems common to both the valuation of inventories and the determination of the cost of goods sold. These are so important that a later chapter on inventory valuation will discuss them in detail. A few comments at this point, however, may be helpful to a better understanding of the income statement.

First-in, first-out basis. As a matter of good housekeeping, as well as to minimize spoilage, it is common practice for companies stocking anything to use or sell the oldest units first, the next oldest next, and so on. In line with the practice just stated, many companies in determining the cost of goods sold make the assumption that the oldest lots

EXHIBIT 6
Schedule of Cost of Goods Sold

For the Year Ending December 31, 1977

Inventories January 1, 1977			
Raw material	$ 333,927		
Work in process		$ 194,748	
Finished goods			$ 987,308
Add: raw material purchases	1,385,824		
Total	$1,719,751		
Less: raw material inventory			
12/31/77	298,090		
Raw material used	$1,421,661		
Add: manufacturing costs			
direct labor	1,267,207		
factory overhead expenses	3,862,827		
Total material and manufacturing			
costs		6,551,695	
Total		$6,746,443	
Less: work in process inventory			
12/31/77		203,247	
Cost of goods completed			6,543,196
Total			$7,530,504
Less: finished goods inventory			
12/31/77			794,014
Cost of goods sold			$6,736,490

have been used first, whether or not this is actually the case physically. The closing inventories are costed as representing the most recent acquisitions.

This method of pricing, or costing, is known as the *first-in, first-out* method of inventory valuation (FIFO). Although called a method of inventory valuation, the words actually apply to the costing of the units leaving the inventory account. The inventory remaining is costed by reference to cost data covering the latest units to enter the account, up to the quantity on hand.

Average cost. In other companies, it is believed that short-run fluctuations in the cost of items inventoried cause undesirable fluctuations in the cost of goods sold, and in computed profits, when inventory valuation is on a FIFO basis. To minimize the effect of such fluctuations, they compute average costs for both the cost of goods sold and closing inventories.

Depending upon the cost accounting system in use, the average cost of each type of item stocked is computed either by simply averaging the beginning inventory and all units entering for the period, or by arriving at a new average unit cost with each incoming lot, i.e., adding the cost of incoming units to the cost of units on hand and dividing the total by the total units involved.

Last-in, first-out basis.   Quite a number of companies, for reasons discussed later in Chapter 17 dealing with inventory valuation, make the assumption that goods sold have come from the most recent acquisitions or production. The closing inventories are costed as representing the beginning inventories, plus or minus whatever increments or decrements have taken place between the beginning and end of the period.

This method of pricing or costing, known as the *last-in, first-out* method of inventory valuation (LIFO), results essentially in matching the replacement cost of goods sold, rather than their actual historical cost, against sales revenue.

Standard cost.   In Chapter 22 on standard costing, we shall note how standard costs of products are developed and used. For the moment, let us consider simply that standard costs are expected costs under given conditions. In a manufacturing plant, standard costing can provide the expected cost of material, labor, and factory overhead on each type of product. One of the uses of such standard costs is to establish the cost of goods sold for a period by multiplying the quantity of each type of product sold by its standard cost.

Variances between the actual and standard material, labor, and factory overhead expenses are computed each period on all work performed. These are treated completely as losses or gains for the period, or they are apportioned between closing inventories and the cost of goods sold to arrive at an approximation of actual costs for each.

Where inventories are maintained at standard cost, and all variances between actual and standard costs are treated as losses or gains for the period, some companies show them as separate items in the income statement. Others show them as adjustments to the cost of goods sold.

Under the latter practice, the adjusted cost of goods sold figure is obviously a hybrid. The reason for this is that the adjusted cost is composed of the standard cost of the goods shipped during the period which had been in the beginning inventory at standard cost; the actual cost of goods both worked upon and shipped during the period; and the variances between the actual cost and standard cost of goods worked upon during the period but remaining in inventory at standard cost at the end of the period.

Inventory Costs vs. Period Costs

Among the important problems to be discussed in the chapter on inventory valuation is the question: What costs incurred during a period should be identified with goods remaining on hand at the close of the period and thus be carried forward to the new period, and what costs should be charged off as expenses of the period?

As an example in this area, we have just noted that under a standard cost system some companies will carry inventories forward from one period to another at their standard costs. Thus they treat all variances between actual cost and standard cost as losses or gains for the period during which they arose, regardless of when goods with which they might be identified are sold.

Differences of opinion in this area are sharpest with respect to items of factory overhead, particularly those manufacturing costs which are not affected by short-run changes in the volume of production. Some accountants believe that all such costs should be charged off as expenses of the period and that inventories should be charged with direct costs only.

This aspect of what is known loosely as "direct costing" is a matter on which there is considerable difference of opinion and we shall be examining it later. For the moment, let us note that "the exclusion of all overheads from inventory costs does not constitute an accepted accounting procedure."[1]

Although the statement just quoted allows great latitude as to what items of overhead, and how much of each, shall be included in the valuation of inventories, it is clear that the use of direct costs alone is not accepted by certified public accountants as an allowable practice for external financial reporting purposes. Moreover, since published financial statements are supposed to reflect financial data as recorded in a company's accounts, the matter is not simply one of external financial reporting but one that must be carried out in the company's accounting records.

By having met this requirement, however, a company can keep its accounts in as much detail as it wishes, depending only on how much it is willing to spend on accounting. It can therefore account for direct

---

[1]Accounting Research Bulletin 43, *Restatement and Revision of Accounting Research Bulletins* (New York: American Institute of Certified Public Accountants, Inc., 1953), Chapter 4, Statement 3.

costs and nondirect overhead costs separately and report only direct costs internally if it sees fit to do so.

Since general acceptance allows considerable leeway in determining the types and amounts of overhead costs to be treated as inventory costs, there are naturally wide differences in practice in this area. The allowance of freedom in practice here, however, is in recognition of differences in situations and cost accounting complexities. It is not a license for looseness, capriciousness, or manipulation. Management is expected to use judgment in the adoption of cost accounting procedures considered appropriate for the given situation, and the company's public accountant is expected to pass upon the appropriateness of the procedures selected, in the same light.

Consistency in practice.   The public accountant is particularly careful to check that his client has been consistent in his valuation procedures from period to period, or, if not, that any material change has been noted in the company's financial reporting. Consistency in practice is important.

For example, if inventories at the close of a period are valued on a different basis than the one applied to the beginning inventories, that will cause a difference in the cost of goods sold and computed profit for the period. Consistency does not refer to maintaining the same prices or costs but means only that the same valuation and cost accounting procedures will be used, particularly, the same methods of cost allocation.

In most companies, the general character of inventories changes relatively slowly, although they are subject to turnover and fluctuations in quantities, prices, and costs. Thus there are no valid reasons for frequent shifts in methods of cost accounting and inventory valuation.

This does not mean, however, that changes should never take place. Obviously, a poor practice should not be maintained just for the sake of consistency. Progress requires that changes be made as better methods are developed.

The merits of consistency in practice can be overrated if carried to the point of believing that it makes little difference what practices are followed as long as they are followed consistently. One may be led to believe, for instance, that no matter how inventories are valued, as long as they are valued consistently on the same basis, the cumulative profit will come out to the same figure over a number of years.

Even if this be true, however, the critical problem is not simply one of being sure that profit will average out over time to the same figure. Rather, the critical problem is that of the psychological effect of a company's financial statements on those who have an interest in that company and who may thereby be moved to take some action that they would not have taken had the financial statements shown different figures.

For example, present stockholders might be moved to sell, hold, or buy stock in the company; prospective stockholders to buy or not buy its stock; creditors to grant or not grant credit; company executives to be optimistic or pessimistic, thus affecting their company decisions; and company employees to be hopeful or not hopeful, relative to wage and salary increases and bonuses.

The stress on consistency in practice is to ensure comparability of financial statements from period to period by avoiding the changes in reported financial results that would arise from the lack of such consistency. Consistency in practice, however, cannot avoid the short-run fluctuations in reported financial results arising from other causes.

For example, it cannot avoid the effects on cost of goods sold, and on computed profit, of changes from period to period in the quantity and types of inventory, and of changes in material prices and operating costs. The extent of the monetary effect of these changes is highly dependent on a company's cost accounting and inventory valuation practices quite apart from the question of the consistent application of these practices.

To illustrate, a company could a. consistently charge inventories with little more than their direct costs, or b. consistently charge inventories with their direct costs plus relatively heavy amounts of overhead costs. When changes took place in the physical size of the inventory between the beginning and end of a period, the effect on the cost of goods sold and on computed profit for that period would differ considerably, depending upon whether it had adopted practice a. or practice b.

In most manufacturing companies, where goods are manufactured for stock rather than on the basis of individual customers' orders, the fluctuations in sales (shipments) from period to period tend to be more marked than fluctuations in production. This is because production can be leveled out to a degree, in order to keep men and facilities employed and to produce most economically, whereas sales are dependent on customers' demands which are more subject to seasonal and other fluctuations.

In these businesses, therefore, the rate of production is relatively stable, while sales fluctuate from period to period. Thus the reconciliation between these two different rates of activity is taken care of by additions to, or reductions from, inventories of finished goods.

Under these conditions, the more modest the charges of factory overhead costs per inventory unit the greater the fluctuations in the computed profit from period to period. This is because the majority of factory overhead costs will be charged off each period, and profit enjoyed in any one period will depend highly on the sales volume achieved in that period.

In contrast to this, where goods inventoried are charged for a significant amount of factory overhead costs and production volume is relatively steady, the absorption and release of these costs by inventory fluctuations are stabilizing factors, which reduce the size of the fluctuations in computed profit from period to period.

Thus, in this latter situation, computed operating results per period are influenced by both production volume and sales volume. Conversely, when inventories are charged with little more than their direct costs the only volume influence on computed profit is that of sales.

Inventory Valuation at Lower of Cost or Market

Except under LIFO, it is common practice to price inventories at the close of an accounting period at the lower of their cost or market value. Although this practice is supported by certified public accountants, it obviously does not meet their tenet of consistency in practice, the merits of which we have just reviewed.

Valuation at lower of cost or market is, however, justified on the grounds of conservatism in balance-sheet presentation and recognition of losses during the period in which they take place. When inventories are presented in financial statements at cost under this practice, they are stated conservatively, that is, in the sense of being stated below their market value, no matter what types of cost and how many dollars of each have been included in the valuation.

For example, if finished goods are stated at a cost which includes a full complement of factory overhead, this cost must still be below the market value of these goods, under the practice of valuation at the lower of cost or market. Otherwise, they would not be stated at their cost but at their market value instead.

Market value for raw material inventories commonly means their valuation at replacement cost, that is, what it would cost to replace the inventory on the date of the valuation at prices then in effect for purchases from the regular sources of supply in lot sizes commonly purchased.

The valuation of work-in-process inventories at market also commonly involves the use of replacement cost. The cost elements are the same as the given company has used when valuing the same inventory on a cost basis. Thus, for example, if freight-in was included as a cost element in valuing the inventory at cost it would also be included in valuing the same inventory at its replacement cost.

Another approach in establishing a market value for work in process is that of working backward from the current selling price of finished goods. The estimated selling and administrative expenses, and the estimated remaining conversion costs, are subtracted from this price to arrive at what is considered to be a market valuation. This approach is appropriate when there has been a decided drop in the selling price of the type of goods to which the work in process is committed and no change has taken place in their replacement cost.

Since considerable clerical work is involved in each of these approaches, the reader can appreciate that many companies forego these valuation refinements and simply report such inventories at either their actual or standard cost.

The same concepts of market valuation in terms of replacement cost, or of working backward from the current selling price of finished goods as just described for inventories of work in process, are found in the valuation of finished goods inventories at market.

Valuation at Replacement Cost Above Historical Cost

Earlier in this chapter we noted the process of establishing the period cost of goods sold by deduction. Figures were used to illustrate the results of the process as follows:

Inventory, January 1, 1977	$1,515,983
Purchases	6,515,858
	$8,031,841
Inventory, December 31, 1977	1,295,351
Cost of Goods Sold	$6,736,490

We can visualize here that if the ending inventory was reduced to a market value (replacement cost) which was below its historical cost, the cost of goods sold found by deduction would be increased by exactly the difference in the two valuations. In this way the inventory loss would be charged to the current period in line with the discussion in the preceding paragraphs.

Similarly, if the ending inventory was valued at a market value (replacement cost) above its historical cost, the cost of goods sold would be correspondingly reduced, and the net income before taxes for the period increased, in the same amount. As we have noted, however, this is not an accepted accounting practice. And, as we have also noted, the SEC in asking companies to furnish supplementary information in Form 10-K on the replacement costs of their inventories cautioned investors against using this information as adjustments to reported net income.

Gross Margin

Once the cost of goods sold has been established, either by a direct process, or by deduction after having established closing inventory valuations, this cost is subtracted from net sales to arrive at a figure for the gross margin (gross profit) in a multiple-step form of income statement. This figure is the amount of revenue over and above that necessary to cover the purchasing cost or manufacturing cost of the goods sold. It represents all the revenue available to cover selling and administrative expenses and to provide an operating profit, if any, for the period.

The inclusion of the gross margin figure is considered by those who favor the multiple-step form of income statement to provide a useful checking point on operating results. If the figure is out of line, as measured against past results, or a budget, they consider it desirable to analyze variances at this point by causes before moving on to the selling and administrative expenses.

Selling Expenses

It should be noted that selling expenses listed in an income statement appear after the figure for gross margin. They are not included in inventory valuations. In other words, they are accounted for as period costs and not as inventory costs.

Practice varies among companies with respect to the specific types of cost that are included under the title of "selling expenses." In published financial statements, the title covers a wide range of costs brought together into one figure to simplify statement presentation.

For internal management use, selling expenses are listed in considerable detail by type of expense and by organizational areas of responsibility such as the advertising department, order handling department, and each district sales office.

In general terms, selling expenses consist of two major types: order getting and order handling. Order-getting expenses are those such as advertising, salesmen's salaries and commissions, and sales office costs. Order-handling expenses are those such as costs of order editing and filling, warehousing, and shipping.

The majority of expenses included under the title of selling expenses in an income statement do not necessarily bear any direct relationship to the sales figure in that statement. And the shorter the period covered by the statement the less likely it is for there to be any relationship between these figures.

This is particularly true of order-getting expenses, partly because the realization of sales is dependent on a number of factors in addition to efforts expended to achieve them, and partly because the figure for sales in an income statement represents the sales value of shipments.

The term "a proper matching of costs and revenues" does not necessarily mean in this instance an exact matching of sales revenues and the selling expenses that helped to generate them. It means only that sales revenues, which have been recognized as properly belonging to a given period, are joined in statement presentation by expenses, which are identified as being properly chargeable to that period.

Some years ago, it was suggested that order-getting costs should be identified with orders gotten and be carried forward in the accounts to the period during which the goods involved were shipped. At that point in time, they would be charged off as expenses in order to have a proper matching of costs and revenues.

This suggestion was not, however, taken up by practitioners, presumably on the grounds of conservatism. Thus it continues to be common practice to treat such costs as expenses during the period in which they are incurred, although now and then an exception to this practice is made.

For example, when a large expenditure for advertising takes place near the end of a period, or a new catalog is printed at that time, the expenditure is often carried forward in the accounts as a deferred charge to be expensed in the next period or periods, as seems appropriate.

General and Administrative Expenses

These expenses are considered to be operating expenses to be deducted in an income statement in arriving at operating income. They are not identified with goods purchased or produced, or with selling operations. Therefore, they are accounted for as period costs, not inventory costs.

From a budgeting and control viewpoint, these are managed costs, and in the short run many are fixed costs. They are regulated over time by management decisions and do not necessarily bear any direct relationship to production or sales volume in the short run.

As presented in an income statement, they fit within the term "a proper matching of costs and revenues" only in the sense that they are considered to be proper charges to the period in which they take place.

Income from Operations

In many companies, it is considered desirable to arrive at a figure for income from operations before taking into account income from other sources, as well as nonoperating expenses. *Operations* simply means the regular major activities of the business. The presentation of a figure for income from operations provides a useful checking point for comparisons with past performance, with the performance of other companies, and with a budget when presented internally for management use.

Other income and other expense.   There can be a number of sources of income or causes of expense, which are either apart from regular operations or so unusual as to best be treated separately in order to maintain the integrity of the figure for operating income.

For example, losses or gains on the disposal of plant and equipment are typically accounted for as "other expense" or "other income." Similarly, "interest income" and "interest expense" are included in this section of the income statement.

Although it can be argued that a company borrows money or extends credit as a necessary and regular part of its operations, interest is commonly treated as a nonoperating matter. The exception to this, of course, are those institutions where interest represents a major item of income or expense or both.

Provision for Income Taxes

The word "estimated" is often used in place of "provision for" in the title for this item in the income statement. In any event, provision for state and federal income taxes is an estimate in the sense that it is based on assumptions as to revenue and expense and on calculations that may or may not prove to be acceptable to the taxing authorities. It is also a provision in the sense that it is the amount provided for the purpose indicated, even though not paid in full as of the close of the period covered by the statement.

A question that has been debated at length is whether this figure, as shown in the income statement presented to stockholders, should represent the estimated tax on the pretax income reported to them or the estimated tax on the taxable income as reported for the same period on income tax returns. We shall discuss this matter later, particularly in Chapter 16 "Problems in the Timing of Revenues and Expenses," and in Chapter 19 "Accounting for Property, Plant, and Equipment."

In Summary

The income statement, although appearing to be a simple document, is in actuality a greatly condensed financial summary of a series of highly complex activities and events. In particular, the income statement for a manufacturing business is not an easy matching of costs and revenues in arriving at a figure of net income for the period.

On the one hand, sales in such a statement represent happy events of fruition when goods which have involved so much research and development, production, sales, and administrative effort finally pass through the shipping room door on the way to the customer. The cost of goods sold section of the income statement, or a separate schedule for the same data, reflects the activities of purchasing, receiving and storing materials, issuing them into production, and converting them to finished products by the application of labor, under supervision, and the use of production and service facilities. In short, selling expenses represent all of the activities of promoting and soliciting business and of handling and filling orders.

On the other hand, general and administrative expenses cover a wide range of activities not directly connected with production and sales, including long-range planning, the results of which will not be reflected in financial statements for months or years to come.

An income statement thus presents on one page a digest in financial terms of a wide range of complicated events, even in a small company. Although it may have its shortcomings, it is still a remarkable document to reflect so much activity, so effectively, in such little space.

CHAPTER 4

The Income Statement: Ratio Analysis

Ratios in themselves control nothing, nor do they provide explanations of what has happened. Thus there is danger that they may serve as inadequate, unwise, or faulty goals and measures of performance. Ratio analysis does however provide the means for spotting situations that appear to be out of line. When noted, these are the areas that merit investigation by those running the business or at least bear watching by stockholders and outside analysts. Its usefulness for these purposes should not be obscured by concern for its limitations.

P. M. Stanton Company Example

To illustrate the use of ratio analysis in measuring a company's performance from items in its income statements, we shall examine the 1977 income statement for the P. M. Stanton Company (Exhibit 7).[1]

P. M. Stanton used a brief multiple-step form of income statement, which company management considered to be adequate information for stockholders (and which is fully adequate for our present discussion). For internal use, the company prepared detailed income statements by divisions and for the company as a whole, as well as a statement of sales by product lines and by major markets served. Since figures standing by themselves mean but little, the company, in line with SEC reporting requirements, provided figures for the previous year as a basis against which to measure the results of the year just

---

[1]The P. M. Stanton Company is a fictitious company created for illustrative purposes here and in other sections of the book. The figures used have been adapted in large part from those of an actual company to insure their practicality.

ended. For comparative purposes, it also provided a ten-year schedule of financial highlights.

For internal comparative purposes, figures for the current and previous year were provided in detail as well as budgeted figures for the year just ended. Actual and budgeted figures in summary form were also provided for the ten-year period.

It was noted in Chapter 2 that the typical company annual report starts with a presentation of the financial highlights of the year, showing summaries of revenues and expenses and emphasizing net income in total dollars and per common share. Thus by the time the analyst arrives at the formal income statement in the annual report, he already knows the major features of the financial story for the year and how the story ended. He can, therefore, proceed to examine the income statement from top to bottom in a more leisurely fashion. This we shall now do with respect to the income statement of the P. M. Stanton Company.

Sales Comparisons

We can see in this case that sales were considerably better (by $1,169,000) in 1977 than in 1976. Moreover, had the company's ten-year summary been included here with Exhibit 7, the reader could have seen that this was an unusually large increase relative to earlier years and that the trend of sales had been upward over the past nine years.

The sales figure is the most important measure of a company's activity in terms of revenue, and a figure that should be of interest to all who are concerned about a given enterprise. Granted that "the bottom line" (net income) is a matter of top importance, it should be remembered that revenue is a major determinant of net income. A dollar that ends up as net income must first have come into the company as revenue.

Not too many years ago, it was not common practice for companies to publish sales figures for fear that such information in the hands of competitors could be harmful. In recent years, the trend has been toward furnishing sales data by major divisions of a business, as well as for the business as a whole.

As we noted earlier, since 1974 annual reports to stockholders of companies filing with the SEC must include line-of-business information. Also, in accord with the Statement of Financial Accounting Standards No. 14 of the FASB (December 1976) sales figures for the major segments of a business enterprise must be separately disclosed.

EXHIBIT 7

P. M. Stanton Company's 1977 Income Statement

	For the Years Ended	
	Dec. 31, 1977	Dec. 31, 1976
Net sales	$9,990,486	$8,821,121
Cost of goods sold	6,736,490	6,360,782
Gross margin	$3,253,996	$2,460,339
Selling expense	1,482,635	1,365,342
General and administrative expenses	595,605	538,517
Total selling, general and administrative expenses	2,078,240	1,903,859
Income from operations	1,175,756	556,480
Other income and other expense: Bond interest, 1977 bond redemption expenses (Note A) less other income ($13,444 and $29,228), net	66,523	26,522
Income before provision for taxes	1,109,233	529,958
Provision for federal income tax	487,864	219,744
Provision for state income tax	65,545	33,499
Net income	$ 555,824	$ 276,715
Net income per common share (Both years shown are based on 295,371 shares outstanding on December 31, 1977)	$ 1.88	$ 0.94

Note A. On October 15, 1977 the company retired the outstanding First Mortgage 6% Bonds by payment of $800,000 principal and $26,075 premium.

The idea of publishing sales data by product lines, however, other than by major divisions, and also of publishing profitability data by product lines, has met resistance. This is not only for competitive reasons but because of the difficulties and the arbitrary decisions involved in making allocations of revenues and joint costs among divisions and among product lines within divisions.

On the one hand, it is difficult enough, even under internally agreed-upon ground rules, to make cost and revenue allocations that are satisfactory for purposes of internal management and control, and it is often fruitless for these purposes to even attempt to allocate some types of cost.

On the other hand, it is much more difficult to make cost and revenue allocations that will enable one to state publicly, with any degree of assurance and without a host of qualifications, what the profit is on any given product line for any given period of time.

Internally, the management of P. M. Stanton Company would have been well aware of what was happening to sales month by month compared with sales for the same period and year-to-date of the previous year and compared also with budgeted figures for the current year. For analytical and control purposes, sales would be broken down in various ways such as by division, product line, sales district, individual salesman, and type of customer. Results in these categories would, where practicable, be compared in total dollars with past results and budgeted figures. Also, differences between these figures would be broken down to specific differences in volume, selling price, and product mix.

Cost of Goods Sold and Gross Margin Comparisons

With an increase in sales one would naturally expect an increase in the total cost of the goods sold, as indeed was the case in P. M. Stanton where this cost increased by $376,000 in 1977 compared with 1976. Since there was a margin between the selling price and the cost of goods sold this cost increase was well below the increase in net sales; by $793,000:

Increase in net sales	$1,169,000
Increase in cost of goods sold	376,000
Increase because of margin	$ 793,000

This difference of $793,000 can, of course, also be seen by comparing the gross margin of 1977 with that of 1976 in Exhibit 7.

Percentage Comparisons

As we have noted, the amounts of change when expressed in dollars for sales, cost of goods sold, and gross margin are significant in P. M. Stanton's case, and this can be seen just by looking at them relative to the figures for the same categories in the income statement for 1976 in Exhibit 7. Their significance may also be measured, however, by the use of percentages.

For example, sales in 1977 were 13.3% above sales in 1976. This is a healthy looking percentage increase in itself, and it looks even better when viewed against a background of general business conditions for that year. Also, although the evidence has not been included here, this percentage increase was a high figure for that year in the industry in which the company was located and a higher rate of growth than P. M. Stanton had enjoyed in any of the previous nine years.

While sales increased by 13.3%, the cost of goods sold increased by only 5.9%. This difference, when reflected in gross margin, had a leverage effect strong enough to increase the margin by 32.8%.

We cannot tell from Exhibit 7 the causes of this difference in rate of increase between sales and the cost of goods sold, although internally the company could probably identify most, if not all, of them. The following are illustrative of possible causes:

1. In addition to an increase in the volume of units sold, the difference in gross margin could have been that higher prices were received without a corresponding increase in costs, or that a better product mix was realized in the sense that a higher proportion of the sales were of units having higher profit margins than the previous year. (Both of these possible causes had in fact been experienced but were not the full explanation of the better gross margin.)
2. The cost of goods sold was, in fact, lower per product unit than the previous year, perhaps because material costs were lower, or cheaper substitutes were found; new methods, or machines, or new designs helped to cut costs; labor and machine utilization was more efficient; machines continued to be used after having been fully depreciated; or higher volume of operations resulted in spreading fixed costs over more units, thereby lowering unit costs. (This had been, in fact, a major cause of the lower cost of goods sold per unit.)
3. The higher volume of sales drew down inventory that had been built up in previous years and had been carried in the accounts at a low valuation per unit. If this *was* one of the causes, it probably could not be expected to continue for long in the future since there was a limit to the extent to which the company could reduce its inventories and still remain in business. Moreover, continued expansion of sales would require the support of larger inventories than had been maintained in the past. (It can be seen in Exhibit 6 (Chapter 3) that the inventory of finished goods had been reduced during the year by $193,294. These goods had, in fact, been carried in the accounts at very conservative figures for their factory overhead cost content.)

Selling and G & A Expense Comparisons

With increased sales and production activity, it was natural for selling and general and administrative expenses in the P. M. Stanton Company to increase in 1977 compared to 1976.

Selling expense. In P. M. Stanton's case, this item included rather heavy costs for outward freight and trucking as well as costs of the company's finished goods storing and shipping departments, along with the usual selling expenses such as sales department salaries and commissions, sales department space and operating costs, and advertising. This expense increased by $117,000 for 1977, or 8.5% above 1976.

While this increase was greater than the percentage increase in the cost of goods sold, it was still well below the percentage increase in sales. The latter, as noted previously, was affected by higher prices on some items, by a higher percentage of higher-margin goods, and by increased volume.

Still, it seems evident that P. M. Stanton's selling expenses were not directly variable with changes in sales volume and, therefore, that some of them were fixed or semivariable in nature. A study over several accounting periods should, of course; reveal the general pattern of relationship between selling expenses and sales, but this is a matter beyond our concern at the moment.

As a final note on selling expenses in this case, there was a lag between the incurrence and payment of some expenses which could cause a slight distortion of costs for any one period. For example, it was a common practice in this company to push shipments strenuously during the third period in each quarter, and particularly during the last period of the year, in order to be able to report higher figures for sales and net income.

Sales commissions on shipments, however, were not paid until the period following shipment. Thus commissions, as a percentage of sales, were lower than normal in the last period of the quarter and year and higher than normal in the first period of the quarter and year. Although these effects tended to balance out by quarters and for the year as a whole, they would not do so completely with a marked upward or downward trend in sales, as took place in 1977.

General and administrative expenses. These increased by $57,000 for 1977, or 10.6% above 1976. Actually, this increase was higher than should have been expected on the basis of the company's experience in recent years. Many of these expenses were relatively fixed in nature, although bonuses were based on the profitability of operations, and some costs moved upward by steps, as when general wage and salary increases for office employees were instituted. Now and then, an unusually high expense was experienced, as when a new computerized information system was installed.

A number of the office costs did, however, tend to move upward or downward with shifts in the volume of sales and production activity. Some of these were really discretionary in nature, and their correlation with sales or production activity was largely a matter of spending psychology; spending tended to increase during periods of "good" business and to decrease as sales receded.

Income from Operations Comparisons

The net financial effect of the increase in sales, cost of goods sold, and selling and G & A expenses in 1977 for P. M. Stanton was an increase in the income from operations of $619,000 for 1977, or 111.3% above 1976.

The figure for income from operations is an important measure of performance, and in this instance a pleasant result for the year. To be sure, other expenses, other income, and income taxes remain to be accounted for before arriving at net income. But the responsibility for and control of these items is not the same as for operating revenues and expenses.

The increase of 111.3% in operating income from a sales increase of 13.3% and much lower percentage increases in costs and expenses is a dramatic result. Nonetheless, since leverage can work either way, it would be well to reflect soberly on what the effect on income from operations would have been had the shift in sales, costs, and expenses been in the reverse direction.

With respect to the remaining items in the P. M. Stanton income statement, it can be seen that net other expenses and income taxes for 1977 were somewhat more than double their amounts for 1976, leaving net income showing an increase of $279,000 and a total slightly better than double that for the previous year.

Percentage of Net Sales

Another form of ratio analysis which can be applied to items in the income statement is illustrated in Exhibit 8. The analysis of costs, expenses, and income as percentages of net sales is particularly useful in comparing the income statements of a given company from year to year, and for comparing actual results with budgeted percentages. Because of differences in situations, and in accounting practices, comparisons of this type between companies, and with common or average figures for a given trade or industry, are somewhat less useful.

Moreover, even if the situations and practices were alike, a difference in the percentage for a given item between one company and another would not necessarily mean that one was correct and the other not. Neither might be what it could, or should, be. Nonetheless, these

EXHIBIT 8
P. M. Stanton Company's Percentages of Net Sales

	For the Years Ended	
	Dec. 31, 1977	Dec. 31, 1976
Net sales	100.0%	100.0%
Cost of goods sold	67.4	72.1
Gross margin	32.6%	27.9%
Selling expense	14.8	15.5
General and administrative expenses	6.0	6.1
Total selling, general and administrative expenses	20.8%	21.6%
Income from operations	11.8%	6.3%
Other income and other expense	.7	.3
Income before provision for taxes	11.1%	6.0%
Provision for federal income tax	4.9	2.5
Provision for state income tax	.7	.4
Net income	5.5%	3.1%

comparisons are useful by calling attention to differences between companies and thereby marking areas which at least bear watching.

Now and then one hears a businessman say that the common percentages gathered by his trade association are of no use to him, since his situation is different. The point is, of course, that he should compare his percentages with those of his trade association. Where there are differences, he should, of course, investigate to be sure that they are indeed caused by his situation and not by inefficiency or some other condition that should be changed.

Ratios of the type presented in Exhibit 8 should be viewed with some caution since, being expressed as percentages of net sales, they are affected by changes in the dollars of net sales, as well as by changes in the dollar amounts of items being measured against them.

For an example, let us consider a simple change in selling price which would not only affect net sales but also the ratios of cost to it. Let us assume that an item selling for $1.00 per unit, with a manufacturing cost of $0.77 per unit, is increased in selling price to $1.10 with no change in its cost:

	Previously		With Change in Selling Price	
Selling price	$1.00	100%	$1.10	100%
Cost	.77	77	.77	70
Gross margin	$ .23	23%	$ .33	30%

If one looked at the percentage figures alone, one could be led to believe that a reduction in cost had taken place with a resulting increase in gross margin. While this was true in terms of percentage relationships to net sales, the facts were that the selling price had increased while the cost had remained unchanged.

For internal use, many companies combine the ratio analysis illustrated in Exhibit 8 with their internal detailed income statement (an expansion of Exhibit 7). Thus one looking at the combined statement can at least note the extent of the change in net sales between the periods illustrated and make some mental allowance for it, even though the effect of the change on the ratio is not spelled out.

Gross Margin Ratio

This ratio, which appears in the third item in Exhibit 8, is considered by many businessmen to be very important. Some merchants, for example, hold that unless it is possible to realize a certain percentage of gross margin determined by them as being necessary, it will not be possible to cover operating costs and reach a desired net income. Accordingly, they price their merchandise so as to realize this margin above their cost of these goods.

Others hold that preoccupation with percentage of gross margin is not wise and that a desired net income should be reached by concentration on the reduction and control of operating costs and pricing aimed at achieving high sales volume.

There is, of course, something to be said for each of these two approaches. Sales volume is certainly a matter of importance; there is small comfort in having a high percentage of gross margin if the volume in dollars of gross margin is inadequate to cover reasonable operating costs and provide a reasonable amount of net income.

On the other hand, high sales volume may provide social benefits, such as employment, but no joy to the owners of the business if the percentage of gross margin realized is inadequate to provide the number of dollars necessary to cover reasonable operating costs and leave a reasonable amount of net income.

No matter which of these approaches is taken, it can be seen that it is the total dollars of gross margin realized, rather than either percentage of gross margin or sales volume alone, that is of paramount importance. It is clear also that the attainment of reasonable operating costs is a highly important factor in reaching a desired net income.

Income from Operations Percentage

Earlier, we noted that the dollar figure for income from operations is regarded as an important measure of performance. So too is the percentage relationship of this figure to net sales, which was 11.8% in 1977 for the P. M. Stanton Company. In addition, many analysts are interested in observing the operating expense ratio. This is the ratio of total operating expenses, including the cost of goods sold, to net sales. For P. M. Stanton, this was 88.2% in 1977, which, when subtracted from net sales at 100%, left the figure of 11.8% as the ratio for income from operations.

Net Income to Net Sales Percentage

A key matter of interest to stockholders and others concerned with a company's welfare is its net income. Evidence of this interest was noted at the outset of Chapter 2, where in a listing of financial items highlighted by the General Electric Company in its annual report for 1977, it was found that net income was stressed, including net income as a percentage of net sales by major product categories.

Since this ratio expresses the relationship between the final figure and the beginning figure in the income statement, it is influenced by all of the items of revenue and expense appearing before it in that statement. Thus it is affected by changes in the price, product mix, and volume of the net sales base against which it is measured. In addition, it is affected by changes in the cost of goods sold and expenses subtracted from the net sales figure and by other income added to it.

Net income is a matter of such interest that it is also analyzed in ways other than as a percentage of net sales; which we shall now discuss.

Computation of Earnings per Share . . .

Stockholders and prospective stockholders are particularly interested in earnings per share of common stock. This figure is not directly useful in comparisons of one company with another, since the common stocks of the two are not likely to be comparable and therefore do not represent a common base of measurement.

However, it is a useful index of financial accomplishment in comparisons of results by periods for the same company. Observation of the

trend of these figures may be helpful in forecasting the probable profitability of the company in the near future.

The figure for earnings per share also provides a stockholder with a
ready means of computing one form of return on his investment by
relating it to the average price per share he paid for his holdings. Similarly, prospective stockholders can relate the earnings per share figure
to the current market value per share for the given stock as a measure
of the rate of return on the stock at its current price.

In fact, many hold that the latter computation of return on investment should also be made by the present stockholder in the belief
that whatever price he paid for his stock is water over the dam and its
current value should be regarded as the amount of his investment in it.
Nonetheless, many stockholders who are holding their stocks as long-
run investments maintain the homely view that what they paid for the
stock is what they have invested in it, as well as the base against which
they wish to measure return on investment.

The Accounting Principles Board (APB) considered the subject of
earnings per share to be of such importance that Part II of Opinion No.
9, *Reporting the Results of Operations*, and all of Opinion No. 15,
Earnings Per Share, were devoted to it.

... under Simple Capital Structures

Where a corporation's capital structure is simple — that is, where it
consists of common stock only, or of common stock and an insignificant amount of convertible securities, stock options, warrants, or other
rights that would, if converted, dilute the earnings per common share
— the computation and presentation of earnings per share is also simple.

The amount of net income for the period applicable to the common stock is divided by the weighted average number of shares of
common stock outstanding during the period. In determining the
number of shares outstanding, reacquired shares (including treasury
stock) are excluded.

When the number of shares outstanding is increased as a result of a
stock dividend or stock split, or decreased as a result of a reverse split,
the number of shares used in computing earnings per share should be
adjusted correspondingly for the entire period and for all periods presented for comparison.[2]

---

[2]See APB Opinion No. 9, *Reporting the Results of Operations* (December 1966),
paragraphs 36–39.

... Applicable to Common Stock

In many cases, not all of the net income reported for the period is applicable to common stock. This is the case in some consolidated statements of income, where allowance must be made for the minority interest in the net income of affiliated companies not fully owned. The General Electric Company, for example, showed the following data with respect to consolidated net income, minority interest in net income, and earnings per share in its annual report for 1977:

For the years ended December 31 (in millions)	1977	1976
Earnings before income taxes and minority interest	$1,888.8	$1,627.5
Provision for income taxes	(773.1)	(668.6)
Minority interest in earnings of consolidated affiliates	(27.5)	(28.3)
Net earnings applicable to common stock	$1,088.2	$ 930.6
Earnings per common share (in dollars)	$ 4.79	$ 4.12

In a ten-year summary in that same GE annual report, the company showed among other data that the average number of shares outstanding (in thousands) was 227,154 in 1977 and 225,791 in 1976. Thus earnings per common share had been computed as follows:

	1977	1976
Net earnings applicable to common stock (millions) ÷ Shares outstanding (thousands)	$\dfrac{\$1,088.2}{227,154} = \$4.79$	$\dfrac{\$930.6}{225,791} = \$4.12$

Another example of an item to be deducted from net income in arriving at earnings applicable to common stock is that of dividends on other classes of stock. The Philadelphia Electric Company and Subsidiary Companies, for example, showed the following data at the end of their annual report for 1977:

	For the Year Ended December 31	
	1977	1976
	(Thousands of Dollars)	
Net income	$173,439	$164,618
Preferred stock dividends	40,705	39,022
Earnings applicable to common stock	$132,734	$125,596
Shares of common stock-average (thousands)	70,844	65,606
Earnings per average share (dollars)	$1.87	$1.91

... Before and After Extraordinary Income or Expense

Net income reported for a given accounting period should reflect all items affecting profit or loss, which are recorded in the accounts during that period. The exceptions are a few rare items identified as prior period adjustments to be reflected in the statement of retained earnings as adjustments of the opening balance of retained earnings.

Items of income or expense judged to be significantly unusual in the sense that they are not typical of the ordinary activities of the enterprise, or not expected to recur frequently, should nonetheless be included in the final net income reported in the income statement. These are listed separately, net of the related income tax, as illustrated in Exhibit 2 and Exhibit 3 (Chapter 2).

Explanation of these items should be given in the income statement or in a note attached to it. Extraordinary items should be presented in this way in order to allow comparisons of operating results from period to period before as well as after taking them into account. They should be included in the income statement in arriving at final net income to avoid being overlooked. That is, if they are not included in the income statement, but instead are treated as adjustments of retained earnings, the danger is that such items may not then be taken into account by those attempting to judge the performance of a company over the years, since they may look only at the results reflected in its income statements.

Where a company has experienced and reported extraordinary items of income or expense, it is expected to show earnings per share both before and after taking such items into account.[3] Data from the Mobil Oil Corporation annual report for 1970 is a typical presentation of an extraordinary item of loss in the final section of a consolidated income statement and presentation of earnings per share of common stock both before and after such an item.

... Under Complex Capital Structures

There are a variety of complications in determining the appropriate number of shares for computing earnings per share under complex capital structures. Suggestions for handling these are presented in APB Opinion No. 15, *Earnings Per Share*, to which reference has already been made. For our purposes here, we shall deal only with basic considerations and a few of the major complications. The reader who does not care to become this much involved in the subject may prefer to

---

[3]See APB Opinion No. 9, paragraph 32, and Opinion No. 15, paragraph 13.

EXHIBIT 9
Mobil Oil Earnings

	Mobil Oil Corporation Year Ended December 31	
	1970	1969
Income before extraordinary item	$482,707,000	$456,498,000
Extraordinary item Write-off related to sale of fertilizer assets and withdrawal from retail fertilizer business in the United States, less applicable income tax reduction of $21,200,000	—	(21,983,000)
Net income	$482,707,000	$434,515,000
Per share Income before extraordinary item	$4.77	$4.50
Extraordinary item	—	(.22)
Net income	$4.77	$4.28

bypass this section and move on to the discussion of P. M. Stanton's earnings per share and other measures of net income.

Complex capital structures are those where, in addition to common stock, a company has a. outstanding other types of stock or types of debt convertible into common stock; b. other types of stock sharing in a company's earning potential even though not convertible to common stock; c. stock options, warrants, and purchase contracts; or d. an obligation to issue common stock upon the satisfaction of certain specified conditions.

The basic problem is the extent to which, if at all, these possibilities, which might lead to increases in the number of shares of common stock outstanding, should be included in determining the number of shares to be used in computing the earnings per share at any given time.

The basic answer is that each such case, on an individual basis, should be included in the computation, that is, provided there would have been a reduction (dilution) of earnings per share had the common stock contingent upon it been issued at the outset of the period for which earnings per share are being computed (or at the time of issuance of the convertible security, option, or other document if issued within that period).

Thus there would be no need to include items that would *not* have diluted earnings had issuances of common stock taken place at the times indicated. And, on the grounds of conservatism, items *should not* be included which would result in either increasing the earnings per share or reducing the loss per share for the given period.

Common stock equivalents. There are some types of securities (within the classifications of convertible debt and convertible preferred stock) whose principal attractiveness lies in their convertibility to common stock. These convertible securities afford the opportunity to share in a company's current and potential growth in earnings, while providing a modest return through interest or dividends. The APB considers that if such securities meet certain tests, they should be treated as common stock equivalents in determining the number of shares to be used in computing earnings per share.[4]

However, even though convertible securities are considered to be common stock equivalents, they should not be brought into the computation of earnings per share unless their inclusion would have a dilutive effect. They would have a dilutive effect if the portion of earnings for the period that would have been applicable to them (had they been converted to common stock at the start of the period) is greater than the amount of dividends or interest (net of tax effect) actually paid out or owed on them for the period.

In explanation of this point, when convertible securities are brought into the computation of earnings per share, the number of shares of common stock to which they would be entitled on conversion is included in the total number of shares to be used in the computation. These securities are computed as though they had, in fact, been converted at the outset of the period. This step taken alone would, of course, dilute the earnings per share, since the total earnings applicable to common stock would simply be divided by a larger number of shares.

However, since this computation assumes that these securities were converted at the outset of the period, it must also assume that neither the dividends nor interest (net of tax effect) actually paid or owed on them for the period would have been paid or owed. Therefore, the computation must assume that the amount of net earnings applicable to common stock would have been increased accordingly.

---

[4]Part of paragraph 33, APB Opinion No. 15, *Earnings Per Share:* "The Board believes that convertible securities should be considered common stock equivalents if the cash yield to the holder at times of issuance is significantly below what would be a comparable rate for a similar security of the issuer without the conversion option. Recognizing that it may frequently be difficult or impossible to ascertain such comparable rates, and in the interest of simplicity and objectivity, the Board has concluded that a convertible security should be considered as a common stock equivalent at the time of issuance if, based on its market price, it has a cash yield of less than 66⅔% of the then current bank prime interest rate." Part of paragraph 28: "The Board has concluded that determination of whether a convertible security is a common stock equivalent should be made only at the time of issuance and should not be changed thereafter so long as the security remains outstanding."

Whether the inclusion of the convertible securities as common stock equivalents will dilute or increase earnings per share in the computation is then dependent upon whether the amount that is in effect put back into net earnings applicable to common stock is less or greater than the portion of these earnings thereafter applicable to the convertible securities as common stock equivalents.

In the computation, if these common stock equivalents had contributed less to the common pool of net earnings than they could claim thereafter, their inclusion would have a dilutive effect on the computed earnings per share. If they had contributed more, the effect of their inclusion would be to increase the earnings per share.

As noted earlier, if the latter were the situation, these convertible securities would not be brought into the computation unless their inclusion would have a dilutive effect. Also, as a practical matter, they would not then be common stock equivalents, since their current value would lie in the return they were receiving as preferred stock or debt and not in their convertibility. In fact, if such a condition continued, it is probable that they would never be converted.

Other types of securities. In addition to convertible debt and convertible preferred stock, there are other types of securities which are or may be considered as common stock equivalents. These include stock options and warrants; stock purchase contracts; some types of securities which participate in earnings, or earnings potential, but are not convertible to common stock; and shares of common stock to be issued in the future merely with the passing of time. Of these, the most common are stock options and warrants, and we shall comment briefly on their inclusion in the computation of earnings per share.

As with convertible debt and convertible preferred stock, stock options and warrants are brought into the computation only when this would have a dilutive effect. Dilution would only take place in a period in which the average market price of the common stock obtainable by the exercise of the options or warrants was greater than their exercise price. Dilution would take place essentially because those who, in the computation, were assumed to have exercised their options or warrants would have put less into the company per share than the average market value for the period of the shares they purchased.

In the opinion of the APB, the amount of dilution reflected in earnings per share should be computed by application of the "treasury stock" method. Thus: "Under this method, earnings per share data are computed as if the options and warrants were exercised at the beginning of the period (or at time of issuance, if later) and as if the funds obtained thereby were used to purchase common stock at the average price during the period.[5]

The APB offers this illustration of treasury stock computation:

> For example, if a corporation has 10,000 warrants outstanding, exercisable at $54 and the average market price of the common stock during the reporting period is $60, the $540,000 which would be realized from exercise of the warrants would be an amount sufficient to acquire 9,000 shares; thus 1,000 shares would be added to the outstanding common shares in computing primary earnings per share for the period.[6]

In other words, it would be as though those who were assumed in the computation to have exercised their warrants had purchased 9,000 shares of stock already outstanding and had received in addition 1,000 shares which cost them nothing. Although these 1,000 shares would not have represented any additional capital entering the business, they would have been entitled to a proportionate share in the net earnings applicable to common stock. The 1,000 shares would therefore be added to the average number of shares of common stock actually outstanding during the period in computing the earnings per common share for the period.

Primary earnings and fully diluted earnings.   If a corporation's capital structure is complex, it is not adequate for it to show a single presentation of earnings per share under a title such as "Earnings Per Share of Common Stock."

If the capital structure consists only of common stock and common stock equivalents, the following type of presentation used at the conclusion of the income statement in the annual report of the Utah-Idaho Sugar Company for 1971 is appropriate.

Where there are outstanding convertible securities, stock options, warrants, and other types of securities which do not fall within the definition of common stock equivalents, but which, if assumed to have been converted or exercised at the start of the period (or time of issuance if later) would individually reduce the earnings per share of common stock for the period, there should be a dual presentation of earnings per share on the face of the income statement.

---

[5]APB Opinion No. 15, *Earnings Per Share*, paragraph 36.
[6]Footnote to paragraph 36.

EXHIBIT 10
Utah Idaho Sugar Company

	Year Ended February 28	
	1971	*1970*
Earnings per share of common stock and common stock equivalent (Note F):		
Earnings before extraordinary item	$1.34	$1.44
Extraordinary item	.16	—
Net earnings	$1.18	$1.44

Note F: Earnings per share were computed using the average number of shares of common stock and common stock equivalents outstanding during each year. Dilutive outstanding stock options were included as common stock equivalents.

The number of Utah-Idaho Sugar shares used in arriving at the earnings per share were established as:

	1971	*1970*
Average shares issued	2,373,000	2,373,000
Average shares in treasury	(15,336)	(2,327)
Dilutive stock options, based on the treasury stock method using average market prices	424	
Total shares	2,358,088	2,370,673

Earnings	*1971*	*1970*
Earnings before extraordinary item	$3,157,709	$3,421,201
Extraordinary item: Provision for loss on closing West Jordan, Utah, plant, less $367,807 income taxes	385,862	
Net earnings	$2,771,847	$3,421,201

The first of these presentations is referred to in APB Opinion No. 15 as "primary earnings per share." This income statement item involves the computation of earnings per share based on the weighted average number of common shares outstanding during the period, plus the number of common shares represented by the common stock equivalents.

The second presentation is referred to in APB Opinion No. 15 as "fully diluted earnings per share." This item involves the number of common shares and earnings computed in the first presentation, plus the number of common shares and adjustments of net income that must be brought into the computation in order to give current recognition to the potential dilutive effect of all contingent issuances of common stock.

An interesting example of the dual presentation of earnings per share appeared in the 1970 annual report of Monsanto Company at the conclusion of its income statement. Consider:

	1970	1969
Earnings a common share (dollars):		
Primary:		
Before extraordinary items	$2.17	$3.08
Including extraordinary items	1.83	3.28
Fully diluted:		
Before extraordinary items	2.17	3.03
Including extraordinary items	1.83	3.21

Monsanto offered this explanation of its dual presentation of earnings per share:

> The primary earnings a share of common stock are based on the weighted average number of common shares outstanding in each year plus the number of shares issuable upon the conversion of the convertible loan stock of Monsanto Textiles Limited and the exercise of outstanding stock options. Net income used in this computation is after deduction of dividends on the $2.75 Preferred Stock but before deduction of interest (less tax) on the convertible loan stock of Monsanto Textiles Limited.
>
> The fully diluted earnings a share are based on the number of shares used in the determination of primary earnings, plus the number of common shares issuable upon conversion of the $2.75 Preferred Stock and upon conversion of the debentures of Monsanto International Finance Company. Net income used in this computation is before deduction of dividends on the $2.75 Preferred Stock and before deduction of interest (less tax) on the convertible loan stock of Monsanto Textiles Limited and on the debentures of Monsanto International Finance Company.[7]

Exhibit 11 is a further explanation of how the Monsanto Chemical Company and subsidiaries computed earnings per share for the years 1969 and 1970.

P. M. Stanton's Earnings Per Share

Let us return to our analysis of the performance of the P. M. Stanton Company. With respect to net income, we have previously noted the

---

[7]Monsanto Company 1970 Annual Report, p. 17 note.

EXHIBIT 11

Monsanto Chemical Company and Subsidiaries, Computation of Earnings a Common Share
(In thousands of dollars except earnings a share)

Years Ended December 31

	1970 Primary	1970 Fully diluted	1969 Primary	1969 Fully diluted
Earnings before extraordinary items:				
Income	$ 77,873	$ 77,873	$ 109,366	$ 109,366
Deduct: Preferred dividends	6,363		6,333	
Remainder	71,510	77,873	103,033	109,366
Add: Interest (less tax) on:				
Convertible loan stock—Monsanto Textiles, Ltd.	745	745	416	416
Debentures—Monsanto International Finance, Co.		572		531
Total	745	1,317	416	947
Adjusted income	$ 72,255	$ 79,190	$ 103,449	$ 110,313
Earnings a share based on total shares indicated below	$ 2.17	$ 2.19(1)	$ 3.08	$ 3.03
Including extraordinary items				
Adjusted income as above	$ 72,255	$ 79,190	$ 103,449	$ 110,313
Extraordinary charges (credits)	11,343	11,343	(6,741)	(6,741)
Adjusted net income	$ 60,912	$ 67,847	$ 110,190	$ 117,054
Earnings a share based on total shares indicated below	$ 1.83	$ 1.88(1)	$ 3.28	$ 3.21
Shares for earnings computation (2):				
Weighted average shares outstanding	32,813,504	32,813,504	33,085,158	33,085,158
Add: Shares issuable upon conversion of Loan stock—Monsanto Textiles Limited	471,272	471,272	471,272	471,272
Debentures—Monsanto International Finance Co.		280,898		280,898
$2.75 preferred stock		2,591,579		2,579,147
Total	33,284,776	36,157,253	33,556,430	36,416,475

Notes:
1. Fully diluted earnings per share for 1970, because of the anti-dilution provision of Opinion No. 15 of the Accounting Principles Board are reported in the Company's income statement in amounts similar to those of primary earnings a share.
2. The exercise of outstanding stock options would have no dilutive effect on a share.

EXHIBIT 12
P. M. Stanton Company's Comparative Balance Sheets

	Dec. 31, 1977	*Dec. 31, 1976*
Assets		
Current assets:		
Cash	$ 929,375	$ 930,250
Accounts receivable	1,067,737	765,162
Inventories at cost on the last-in, first		
out basis	1,295,351	1,515,983
Prepaid assets	81,514	51,178
Total current assets	$3,373,977	$3,262,573
Property, plant and equipment at cost less		
allowances for depreciation of $945,569		
and $760,720	1,362,970	1,278,479
Investment in subsidiaries at cost	43,132	34,401
Deferred development expenses	80,069	116,878
	$4,860,148	$4,692,331
Liabilities		
Current liabilities:		
Bond sinking fund installment	$ —	$ 100,000
Accounts payable (trade)	332,200	153,220
Provision for pensions	163,500	177,300
Provision for federal income tax	417,300	226,675
Other accrued liabilities	246,800	224,974
Total current liabilities	$1,159,800	$ 882,169
Provision for deferred income tax	98,301	103,418
First Mortgage 6% Bonds due 1984 (Note A)	—	800,000
Capital		
Common stock of $1 par value, 350,000 shares		
authorized, 295,371 and 268,022 shares		
issued and outstanding (Notes B and C)	295,371	268,022
Paid-in surplus (Note C)	2,398,339	2,152,198
Retained earnings, per accompanying statement	908,337	486,524
	$4,860,148	$4,692,331

Note A. On October 15, 1977, the Company retired the outstanding First Mortgage 6% Bonds by payment of $800,000 principal and $26,075 premium.

Note B. At December 31, 1977, options to purchase 1,447 shares at $10 per share (not less than 95% of the market price at the time of granting) were outstanding and exercisable. Options terminate in 1980 or when the employee leaves the Company. During the year, options for 14,104 shares were exercised and options for 1,092 shares lapsed.

Note C. During 1977, paid-in surplus was increased by $126,936 excess of option price over par value of 14,104 shares issued upon exercise of options and $119,205 excess of market value over par value of 13,245 shares issued as a stock dividend. There were no changes in paid-in surplus during 1976.

EXHIBIT 12
(continued)

| | For the Years Ended | |
Statement of Retained Earnings	Dec. 31, 1977	Dec. 31, 1976
Retained earnings at beginning of period	$ 486,524	$ 209,809
Net income for the period	555,824	276,715
	$1,042,348	$ 486,524
Common stock dividend—5% (13,245 shares and $1,561 cash for fractional shares)	134,011	—
Retained earnings at end of period	$ 908,337	$ 486,524

total net income figures in Exhibit 7 and net income as a percentage of sales in Exhibit 8. Since we have just been discussing earnings per share, we might now note the earnings per share figures for P. M. Stanton at the bottom of Exhibit 7 where the figures for both years shown are based on 295,371 shares of common stock outstanding at the end of 1977.

Comparative balance sheets for the company, and notes applicable to them, are included here as Exhibit 12 to provide information on the stockholders' equity (ownership) and other data against which net income might be measured.

Notes B and C in Exhibit 12 indicate that during 1977 options for 14,104 shares of common stock were exercised and 13,245 shares issued as a stock dividend. Since these were included in the number of shares outstanding at the close of 1977, the use of the year-end figure in computing earnings per share for 1977 treated them as though they had been outstanding since the start of that year. The use of the same 1977 year-end figure in computing earnings per share for 1976 in Exhibit 7 put these figures on a more comparable basis with 1977 than would otherwise have been the case.

Earnings Related to Stockholders' Equity

Another measure of stockholders' earnings is the percentage relationship of these earnings to stockholders' equity. In the case of P. M. Stanton, all of the net income for the company was applicable to either common stock or common stock equivalents, since there were no other securities such as preferred stock outstanding.

Stockholders' equity, often called net worth, in P. M. Stanton consisted of outstanding common stock carried at a modest par value of $1 per share, plus paid-in surplus arising from the sale of this stock, or issurance of stock dividends (see Note C, Exhibit 12), plus retained earnings.

The percentage relationship of the net income to stockholders' equity would be computed as follows:

$$\frac{\text{Net income}}{\text{Stockholders' equity}} = \text{Percentage return on stockholders' equity}$$

Note that this is a measure of the return on the combination of what stockholders have put into the business and of retained earnings. It is not a measure of return on the current market value of the stock. In fact, the stockholders' equity reflected in the balance sheet, sometimes called the book value, may be far different at any given time than the market value of the stock it represents.

The net income to be used in the computation here for P. M. Stanton is, of course, the net income for 1977 of $555,824, as shown in Exhibit 7. However, the question is: Should the figure used for stockholders' equity be that at the beginning of the period, at the end of the period, or some type of average? The result in this particular case is quite different depending upon which of these figures is used, as follows:

Percentage Return on Stockholders' Equity

Based on equity at beginning of period	Based on equity at end of period	Based on average equity
$\dfrac{\$\ 555{,}824}{\$2{,}906{,}744} = 19.1\%$	$\dfrac{\$\ 555{,}824}{\$3{,}602{,}047} = 15.4\%$	$\dfrac{\$\ 555{,}824}{\$3{,}254{,}395} = 17.1\%$

The average figure used here is simply the average of the beginning and ending figures, since this is the only type of average that can be computed from P. M. Stanton's published data.

The base selected could depend on what had been used in the past, since one use of such a ratio is to compare it with similar ratios of the past in order to judge the trend of earnings relative to stockholders' equity. However, there is no reason why ratios for the past could not be recomputed on a different base if this seemed desirable.

Some analysts use the figure for equity at the beginning of the period on the grounds that this was the amount of stockholders' capital and retained earnings available to management at the outset of the period against which they believe the results of that period should be judged.

Thus, if losses had been suffered, they should not be measured against a base which had been lowered by them. If the equity had risen during the period as a result of earnings net of dividends paid, or by inputs of additional capital, there was always a practical question as to how quickly the company could make effective use of such additional funds to generate additional earnings.

From this viewpoint, it would therefore be best to omit them from the investment base in the short run in computing the percentage return on stockholders' equity.

Those who favor the use of average equity as the base do so, of course, because they believe that this was the average amount of stockholders' equity available to management for use in creating earnings during the period. Therefore, the earnings performance of the period should be measured against it.

Those who favor use of the figure for equity at the end of the period do so because they are more concerned about what is likely to happen in the near future relative to return on stockholders' equity than they are in judging the performance of the period just passed.

Percentage return on stockholders' investment. The return on stockholders' equity just discussed is a measure of the return on the recorded stockholders' capital put into the business, plus retained earnings. Although this is one measure of return on the stockholders' investment, an individual stockholder might be more interested in measuring earnings against the amount he had actually paid for his investment. To do this, he would simply measure the earnings per common share for the period against the average price he paid for his stock.

Thus, if a stockholder in P. M. Stanton had paid an average of $10 per share for his stock, the earnings for 1977 of $1.88 per share would represent a return on his investment of 18.8% (although not available to him except through dividends voted by the company's board of directors).

This stockholder might also be interested in the current percentage yield on his investment as expressed by the relationship of the dividends he had received for the year to the price he had paid for his stock. If, for example, he had received a cash dividend of $1 per share, the percentage yield on the $10 average price he had paid for his stock would be 10%.

In the present case, however, instead of a cash dividend, he would have received a stock dividend of 5%. Thus, if he held 100 shares at the time he received the dividend, his dividend of five shares would represent a return on his investment of 5% in terms of numbers of shares. In his investment records, however, he would record the five shares at no value (cost) to him.

If and when he sold these shares later, he would have the option of considering that they had cost him nothing. Thus whatever he received for them would be entirely income, or he could use the dividend to reduce the average cost of the shares held (bringing the average cost down from $10 to $9.52 per share), and any gain or loss per share on shares sold would be the difference between this adjusted cost and the price received per share.

It so happened that the market value of P. M. Stanton's stock on the date the stock dividend was declared was $10 per share, and the dollar amount of the dividend subtracted from retained earnings was therefore $134,011 (13,245 shares × $10 per share and $1,561 cash for fractional shares, as shown in Exhibit 12).

Thus the five shares received by the stockholder in our example would have had a market value of $50 and, in this sense, would have represented a 5% yield to him on his investment of $1,000. Had he paid $12.50 per share for his 100 shares, his dividend of five shares would have represented a yield of 4% to him in terms of their market value of $50 relative to his investment of $1,250.

Percentage relationship of earnings to market value of common stock. A measure of the demand for a company's common stock, as well as an indicator of the return an investor might get if he purchased it, is to be found by relating earnings per share on an annual basis to the current market value of the stock. Thus, if P. M. Stanton's common stock was selling for $12 per share, the rate of return based on earnings of $1.88 per share in 1977 would be 15.7%.

Similarly the percentage yield may be determined by relating the dividends on an annual basis to the current market value of the stock. Thus, if P. M. Stanton's common stock was selling for $12 per share and the annual dividend was $0.50 per share in cash, or in market value of stock, the yield would be 4.2%.

Price earnings ratio for common stock. Another measure of the current demand for a company's stock, as well as an indicator of the return that might be expected from making an investment in it, is in the price/earnings ratio. This is found by dividing the market price for the given stock by earnings per share on an annual basis. In the case of P. M. Stanton's common stock, this would show a ratio of 6.3 to 1, assuming a market price of $12 divided by $1.88 per share. In other words, the stock was selling for 6.3 times its earnings on an annual basis.

This measure, as well as the percentage relationship of earnings to the market value of common stock, is also useful in comparing one company with another, since ratios and percentages are more comparable than total earnings or earnings per share. The price/earnings ratio provides a market rating for the given stock that enables it to be compared, market-wise at least, not only with other companies in the same industry, but also with other companies in other industries.

A higher ratio or a lower percentage in the case of the percentage relationship of earnings to the market value of the stock, however, is not simply a current preferential market rating, but also an indicator that the market is counting on greater growth and larger earnings in the future than it expects from stocks currently showing a lower ratio or higher percentage of return.

Return on investment in assets. Still another measure of performance is that of the percentage relationship of earnings to assets, i.e., the return on investment in assets. The computation of this ratio may at first appear to be a simple matter but there are a number of basic questions to be met in connection with it. Consider:

Should the assets against which earnings are to be measured be total assets net of the allowance for depreciation? Total assets with property, plant, and equipment at cost without subtracting allowances for depreciation? Total assets less current liabilities? Total assets less current liabilities except for loans on which interest is being paid? Or total assets less intangible assets such as goodwill and deferred expenses?

Should the figures for whatever are taken as representing assets in the computation be the total of these assets at the start of the period, at the end of the period, or some type of average for the period?

Should the earnings figure used be that for operating income before other income and other expenses, including income taxes? Operating income less related income taxes but before other income and other expenses and their tax effects? Net income from all sources after taxes but before extraordinary items of income or expenses? Or net income?

In Chapter 31, we shall examine such questions in dealing at greater depth with the subject of return on investment as both a goal and measure of performance. In the meantime, one common form of this computation is to relate net income for the period to the total as-

sets, net of depreciation, as of the end of the period. In the case of
P. M. Stanton, the computation for 1977 would be as follows:

Net income for 1977

Total assets December 31, 1977

$$\frac{\$\ 555{,}824}{\$4{,}860{,}148} = 11.4\%$$

A more involved approach to this same result divides the return on
investment into two major aspects: the volume of sales for the period
relative to assets employed; and the matching of costs and revenues for
the period. This approach may be illustrated as follows:

$$\frac{\text{Net income} \quad \$\ 555{,}824}{\text{Sales} \qquad \$9{,}990{,}486} \times \frac{\text{Sales} \qquad \$9{,}990{,}486}{\text{Total assets} \ \$4{,}860{,}148} = \begin{array}{l}\text{Return on assets} \\ 11.4\% \text{ (rounded)}\end{array}$$

Net income as % of sales × Turnover of assets   = Return on assets
       5.5%   2.06   11.4% (rounded)

The point in taking this longer approach is that if the percentage
return on the investment in assets turns out to be different than expected or desired, it can be determined quickly whether the major
cause was in the relationship of costs and revenues or in the effectiveness with which assets were utilized for the period. It thus identifies
the major area in which further inquiry should be made.

Another common form of computing return on investment is to
relate net income to total gross assets; i.e., with fixed assets at cost
without subtracting the allowance for depreciation as follows:

Net income

Total gross assets

$$\frac{\$\ 555{,}824}{\$5{,}805{,}717} = 9.6\%$$

A final form of computing return on investment is to relate the net
income plus depreciation (known as "cash flow," and to be discussed
in the next chapter) to total gross assets, as follows:

Cash flow

Total gross assets

$$\frac{\$\ 807{,}079}{\$5{,}805{,}717} = 13.9\%$$

An uncommon, and more involved, form of computing return on
investment also relates cash flow to gross assets but recognizes in the
case of depreciable assets the need to account for the recovery of the
investment itself as well as whatever rate of return there may be on it.
This method is illustrated in detail in Chapter 31 and utilizes the
discounted cash flow method of computing return on investment described in Chapter 27.

Without attempting to present a detailed explanation at this point, let us note simply that in the case of P. M. Stanton this method would have shown a return of 10.66% compared to the return of 13.9% under the preceding method. While the nondepreciable assets, amounting to 59% of the total gross assets, would show a return of 13.9%, the depreciable assets, amounting to 41% of the total gross assets, would show a return of only 6% under the discounted cash flow method. The weighted average would thus be 10.66%.

Interest Coverage

A ratio of particular interest to bondholders is the number of times interest charges or requirements have been earned for the period. For this purpose, net income before taxes (since interest is deductible for tax purposes) and before interest is divided by the interest involved.

In the case of P. M. Stanton, interest on the bonds outstanding in 1976 was covered a little more than ten times by net income before interest and taxes as follows:

Income from operations	$556,480
Other income	29,228
Income before interest and taxes	$585,708
Bond interest less other income	$ 26,522
Other income	29,228
Bond interest	$ 55,750
Income before taxes and interest	$585,708
Bond interest	$ 55,750

$$\frac{\$585,708}{\$55,750} = 10.5 \text{ times}$$

Note: Data taken from Exhibit 7.

Dividend Coverage on Preferred Stocks

Preferred stockholders have a similar interest to bondholders in the number of times earnings are in excess of the dividends to which they are entitled. As stockholders, they are entitled to share only in income after taxes, even on a preferred basis, i.e., unlike interest, dividends on preferred stock are not tax deductible. Thus net income after taxes is divided by the preferred stock dividends payable in total for the period to determine the number of times the dividends were earned.

Cash Flow Analysis

An interesting development in recent years in financial reporting has been the growing awareness of investors, analysts, and business executives of the importance of funds flow analysis. Such an analysis serves to summarize the significant financial actions that have taken place in companies in which they have an interest and to identify major changes in the financial condition of those companies. The analysis summarizes financial actions and effects in all areas of a business, as reflected in all of its accounts, not simply in the actions and effects of revenues and expenses as dealt with in an income statement.

In line with this awareness, it has become common practice for publicly held companies to provide funds flow statements to stockholders in their annual reports, in addition to the usual income statements and balance sheets. Since 1971, at the recommendation of the Accounting Principles Board, the common title used for this statement has been "Statement of Changes in Financial Position." Other titles had previously been applied to these statements, such as "Source and Application of Funds," "Funds Flow Statement," and "Changes in Working Capital." In an earlier day they had occasionally been referred to as "Where-Got, Where-Gone" statements.[1] Here, however, we shall use "Funds Flow Statement" most frequently since it has the virtue at least of being brief.

For internal management use, many companies also prepare similar statements as projections of funds flow for future periods and include

---

[1]This descriptive title was introduced by William Morse Cole in *The Fundamentals of Accounting* (Boston: Houghton Mifflin, 1921).

them with the preparation of projected balance sheets and income statements in their formal planning (budgeting) process.

Being relatively new in terms of the long history of accounting practice, the form of this statement has not reached the degree of uniformity found in the design of balance sheets and income statements. Thus the statement varies in form, and sometimes in title, from company to company. But these are matters of minor importance, provided that the reader understands the substance of what is being presented.

Cash Flow vs. Funds Flow

In recent years, the term *cash flow* has come into common use in the financial press and in company financial reports. Whereas, as we have noted, a number of different titles for the same subject are found in the case of funds flow, the situation is even more confusing in the case of cash flow where the same title is used for a number of different subjects, including what others call funds flow.

Funds flow is a more important concept than cash flow, if for no other reason than that it encompasses a broader area which includes cash flow, as we shall later note, more specifically. Nevertheless, cash flow is an important matter in itself, and we shall examine it in this chapter before moving on to a consideration of funds flow in Chapter 6. We shall concern ourselves here with two of the three uses of the term cash flow, as follows:

1. As a term used commonly by financial analysts and defined by them as net income (after taxes) plus depreciation.
2. As referring to what has happened, or is expected to happen, to a company's cash account, i.e., the flow in and out of that account.

Cash Flow as a Term Used by Financial Analysts

In the financial press, it is common for analysts to speak of a company's cash flow as being net income (after taxes) plus depreciation for the given period. Sometimes, the same figure is stated as being income after taxes and before depreciation; and, again, as revenues less cash expenses for the period. The computation of the same cash flow figure in these three different ways is illustrated in the following table:

Net income	$555,824	Net sales	$9,990,486
Plus: depreciation	251,255	Less: cash expenses	9,183,407
Cash flow	$807,079	Cash flow	$ 807,079

	Per Income Statement	Cash Flow
Income before depreciation and taxes	$1,360,488	$1,360,488
Estimated depreciation	251,255	
Taxable income	$1,109,233	
Estimated taxes	553,409	553,409
Net income	$ 555,824	
Income after taxes and before depreciation (cash flow)		$ 807,079

A figure for cash flow is often presented as supplementary information in published financial reports, and it is sometimes described there as representing the company's internally generated funds or *cash throw-off*. In addition to depreciation, the amortization of deferred charges and other major noncash expenses are usually included in computing total cash flow in such reports.

Depreciation as an Element in Cash Flow

Common sense tells us that cash cannot be generated simply by making bookkeeping entries for depreciation expense, or by making entries for any other types of noncash expense. The financial analyst is well aware of this. Thus when he says that cash flow is net income plus depreciation, he means only that this is how he computes it. Starting with net income, he adds back depreciation to arrive at the figure for income after taxes and before depreciation. This is, of course, a more accurate description of cash flow than is its definition as net income plus depreciation.

We noted in the preceding table that cash flow can also be described as the net of revenues and cash expenses. Under this definition, it is clear that the amount of cash flow is not directly affected by any accounting charge for depreciation. Depreciation and other noncash expenses are subtracted from this figure to arrive at net income, if any. In a purely mechanical sense, therefore, depreciation and other noncash expenses can be added back to net income to arrive at the cash flow figure; and this is what the financial analyst does.

Indirect effects of changes in depreciation. While the amount of depreciation charged has no direct bearing on cash flow, a change in it may affect the flow indirectly. For example, an increase in depreciation expense may influence a company to raise its selling price, which is bound to have some effect on sales volume and the cash flow from sales.

Even if prices are not increased, if depreciation is increased in a company having taxable income, the amount of such income will thereby be decreased and the resulting tax decrease will reduce the required outward flow of cash for tax payments. It is, however, only a consolation and not a real joy when one's income tax is decreased and cash flow thereby improved, solely as a result of an increase in some other type of expense.

Except for these indirect effects, a change in the amount of depreciation expense will have no effect on cash flow. This should be kept in mind since now and then, after a company's depreciation expense has increased, someone will state that this need not be a matter of concern in view of the fact that the company's cash flow will rise by the same amount.

To be sure, if one defines cash flow as net income plus depreciation, it is true that there will be an increase in the depreciation component of cash flow. However, there will be exactly the same amount of decrease in the net income component of cash flow, leaving, therefore, no net change in the cash flow figure.

Importance of Cash Flow

Cash flow is important because it represents cash generated from operations which obviously helps to meet a company's needs for cash and thereby reduces, and in some cases eliminates, the need for additional short- or long-term loans, or additional capital for expansion.

Cash flow comes from customers. Instead of thinking of cash flow as net income plus depreciation, it is really preferable to think of it as a single net flow figure coming essentially from customers after allowing for cash expenses including income taxes. This single figure, then, is all there is to provide whatever reimbursement the company is to get for depreciation and other noncash expenses and net income, if any.

If the company's income statement shows a net loss, it is fruitless for one to hold that depreciation and other noncash expenses did provide cash flow to their full amounts which was subsequently lost to the extent of the loss for the period. The fact is that revenues from customers less cash expenses did not provide enough cash flow to reimburse the company fully for depreciation and other noncash expenses, let alone leave anything for profit.

The segmentation of cash flow into depreciation and net income sources becomes particularly meaningless when the amount of the loss in a period exceeds the amount of depreciation plus noncash expenses, as it has in some companies in times past. Under these conditions, cash expenses exceed revenues and there is no cash flow either for, or provided by, depreciation or net income.

There is a point, however, in thinking of cash flow by segments of net income, depreciation, and other major noncash expenses in that these figures can thereby be traced to and identified in the income statement. If the income statement shows a separate figure for cash flow, either as net sales less cash expenses or as income after taxes and before depreciation, the segmentation of cash flow into net income, depreciation, and other major noncash expenses is not necessary in identifying it in the income statement.

There is also some point in segmenting cash flow if one wishes to relate inward cash flow with uses of funds, for example, if one wishes to see whether more or less than the funds recovered from customers as reimbursement for depreciation has been invested in plant, machinery, and equipment during a given period.

Cash flow for reimbursement of depreciation.   It is clearly important to recover from customers the capital invested in buildings and equipment over the economic life of these assets. One hopes, therefore, that the cash flow for each accounting period is at least adequate to cover the depreciation that has taken place on these facilities. The recovery of capital invested is the major point; whether or not the capital recovered will be reinvested in the same types of facilities is a separate problem.

Similarly, where such facilities were financed originally through long-term debt, the recovery of capital invested, through customer reimbursement for depreciation, provides a means for retiring the debt. If the life of the facilities and the life of the debt are the same, and if the cash flow is at least enough to cover depreciation, the investment will have been recovered and the debt retired over this life, unless management has spent the money for something else as it was recovered. The latter point suggests why it is important to have a sinking fund requirement connected with a bond, as a means by which money is allotted to achieve a gradual reduction of bond indebtedness.

Cash flow from net income. That portion of cash flow which financial analysts attribute to net income is certainly of great importance in meeting whatever cash dividend policy a company has established, or may establish, on both common and preferred stock. What net income is left after allowing for cash dividends provides the means for expansion and/or replacement of facilities at costs higher than those recovered through customer reimbursement for depreciation.

To the extent that cash flow attributed to net income has not been committed to such uses or to the payment of dividends, it provides support for future dividends, interest payments on debt, and debt retirement. An adequate cushion of uncommitted funds thus generated is particularly important for these purposes when a company faces periods of net operating losses.

Danger in Overemphasis on Cash Flow

Important as cash flow is, there can be harmful effects from overstating its significance. For example, if a stockholder is led to believe that cash flow is superior to net income, either as something better to be had or as a better measure of management performance, this is unfortunate. Since net income is a part of cash flow, it may appear that cash flow is the more important of the two figures.

However, net income is a residual figure after all expenses, including noncash costs, have been covered. Therefore, unless net income is adequate the cash flow is bound to be inadequate. Thus net income is the key figure to serve as both a goal and a measure of management performance.

That part of cash flow not related to net income, although important, is simply a recovery of capital invested. If net income is negative, whatever cash flow there is represents only the conversion of assets, including deferred charges, into cash. It is thus a process of liquidation and not advancement.

It is, of course, important for management to protect the stockholders' capital through the recovery from customers of the cost of goods or services sold to them, including depreciation that has taken place on plant, machinery, and equipment used. But this is what the stockholders have the right to expect in the ordinary course of events. Managers should not count on receiving kudos for simply managing a circular process of investing and recovering investment, any more than they should expect commendation for the fact that a year's loss will provide a tax saving in a subsequent year of profit.

Danger in presenting cash flow on a per-share basis.   The danger of misleading the stockholder on the importance of cash flow is magnified when a company shows cash flow on a per-share basis as well as in total dollars in its financial reports.

The presentation of net income on a per-share basis may be helpful to the stockholder because he can then relate this figure to the average price he paid for his stock, as one measure of return on investment from his viewpoint. He can also relate it to the current market value per share of stock, as a measure of the current rating the market gives to the stock, either in terms of the current return on the investment at that price or the number of times the earnings per share the current market value per share represents. He can also relate net income per share to dividends paid per share to see quickly what portion of current earnings has been paid out in dividends and what portion retained in the business.

But how is the stockholder expected to interpret cash flow per share? It is bound to be higher than net income per share because it includes whatever reimbursement there may be for depreciation and other major noncash items as well as net income, if any. Surely, this is likely to encourage the unsophisticated stockholder to think that cash flow per share is better than net income per share, as something to be had or as a measure of management performance.

There is also the probability that he will try to relate this figure to the price he paid for his stock, as a measure of return on his investment. Does he know that a substantial portion, indeed perhaps all, of the cash flow per share on his stock for a given period simply represents turnover of his own capital in the business? Does he think that this is his share of cash in the business that might have been paid out to him in the same way that net income in the form of cash per share might have been paid out to him if not used for something else?

The answer to these questions, of course, is that the average stockholder does not really understand what is meant by cash flow per share. It is therefore unfortunate that such a figure ever appears in a company annual report. Perhaps it does the stockholder no serious harm. But it certainly does him no good, and it can mislead him, particularly if discussed in the financial report or by some financial analyst, as a palliative when earnings per share are nonexistent or inadequate.

Cash Flows Out as Well as In

While the cash flow figure standing by itself in a financial report highlights the inward flow of cash from net profit and reimbursement of depreciation and other major noncash expenses, it provides no warning that much, if not all, of what came in has already been expended. It tells where some money came from but not where it went. Thus the cash flow figure can lead the unsophisticated to believe that it is somewhere around the company and available for use in the future.

The cash flow figure alone will not help the stockholder to realize that in a going concern the bulk of the cash flow must be used to keep the company going, including paying off debt, and that the cash flow is not likely to be adequate to meet the investment needs of its goals for growth. The old Yankee custom of plowing back into the business each year an amount equal to depreciation plus one half of the net profit is too slow a growth pace for many modern companies even though, under this policy, investment and reinvestment absorb a large portion of the cash flow.

If the stockholder does some analyzing himself, and particularly if the company has provided him with a funds flow statement, he should be able to note the extent to which a. net income has, or has not, met the dividend requirements for the period; b. reimbursement for depreciation has been plowed back into buildings, machinery, and equipment; or c. reimbursement for depreciation has been used to retire debt by means of which those properties had been acquired. He should also be able to spot other major flows of funds in terms of their sources and applications and to reach some conclusions on the financial movements evidenced in the period under study.

Accrual Accounting vs. Cash Accounting

The definition of cash flow, as we have been examining it, implies that all revenues for the period have represented inward flows of cash, and that all costs and expenses charged against income for the period in arriving at the figure for cash flow have represented outward flows of cash, except for depreciation and other major noncash expenses. In the great majority of cases, however, neither the revenues nor the expenses implied as involving cash are wholly cash transactions. In this respect, the term cash flow and the various definitions commonly applied to it can be misleading.

The reader should remember that a figure presented as the cash flow for a period is not likely to be literally true to its title. Those who use the term cash flow assume that in a figure for it those elements which are not actually cash are the equivalent of cash for all practical purposes. Thus it is assumed that revenues included in arriving at the cash-flow figure for which payments have not yet been made will be paid within a short period.

Individuals commonly account for their revenues and expenses on a cash basis, and some companies do likewise. However, for all or part of their activities, the great majority of companies account for them on what is called the *accrual basis* in the presentation of their financial statements and tax returns. Accounting on an accrual basis means essentially that revenue is accounted for in the period during which it is considered to have been earned, whether or not the payment has been received in cash. Similarly, expenses are accounted for in the period in which they are considered to have been incurred, whether or not payment in cash is made for them in that same period.

Revenues: cash vs. accrual basis.   Earlier in this book, we noted that almost universally revenue is recognized only as a result of performance. Neither the mere receipt of an order nor of a payment in advance constitute revenue. We noted further that in the case of goods, or physical items of one type or another, the date of delivery is the typical time at which revenue is recognized. Delivery is effected when the goods sold are taken by the customer, delivered to him directly by the seller, or placed in the hands of a common carrier.

Services are earned as performed but revenue is recognized typically at time of billing the customer, which may be immediately following the completion of the service rendered or at some customary time such as the end of the month. On long-term contracts, by custom, or by specific agreement, customers are billed and revenue is recognized monthly or at definite stages or percentages of completion.

The major interest with respect to revenue determination in Chapter 3 was in the discussion of when revenue might reasonably be recognized and income anticipation be avoided. Now, in connection with our discussion of cash flow, the question is the extent to which revenue reported in an income statement is actually in the form of cash receipts or may be assumed to represent an inward flow of cash for all practical purposes.

In many retail stores, restaurants, and other types of business dealing directly with final consumers, a substantial percentage of sales are on a cash basis. Thus to this extent sales revenue and the inward cash flow for a given accounting period are synonymous.

Similarly, there are some transactions between businesses where trade custom involves simultaneous delivery and payment for goods or services.

Finally, there are many situations in which revenue is not recognized in the accounts until payment has been received, even though the customer, client, or patient may have been billed for goods delivered or services performed. Here, the businesses or individuals involved, such as doctors, lawyers, and management consultants, account for revenue on a cash basis, rather than on an accrual basis.

Throughout industry in general, however, the great bulk of sales volume is on a credit basis, and sales revenue is recorded when goods have been delivered or services performed. Thus the great majority of companies account for revenue on an accrual basis, rather than on a cash basis. As of the end of an accounting period, therefore, a substantial portion of the sales reported in income statements has not been realized in cash.

If it so happened that at the end of a given accounting period the amount owed a company by customers in total was exactly the same as the amount owed at the beginning of that period, the result would be that the cash received from customers for the period would be exactly equal to the sales of that period, even though payment was in part for sales actually made in a previous period.

In other words, if a customer has bought something on account during a period, but owes the same amount at the end of the period as he did at the beginning of that period, his purchases and cash payments during the period must have been equal in dollar amount.

Under these circumstances, the assumption made by the financial analyst that sales revenue represents an inward flow of cash is correct as far as the amount of cash is concerned but not strictly true with respect to the stated source.

However, since the amount owed by customers in total at the end of a period will never be the same as that owed at the beginning of the period, except by the oddest of circumstances, the sales reported for a period under the accrual method of accounting will never be exactly the same as the amount of cash received from customers during that period.

When the financial analyst assumes that sales revenue does represent an inward cash flow for all practical purposes, he is making one of two other assumptions: that changes in the amount owed by customers in total between the beginning and end of the period are not large enough to be significant; or that changes in these accounts are equivalent to cash changes since it is expected that the average customer's account will be paid in a reasonably short period of time.

As we shall note in Chapter 6, the funds flow concept includes the analysis of changes in the amount of accounts receivable between the beginning and end of the accounting period. In this respect, as well as in others, funds flow gives a more complete and accurate analysis of financial events than cash flow.

Expenses: cash vs. accrual basis. Just as there are companies that account for revenue on a cash basis, so too are there companies that account for expenses on a cash basis. There are, however, fewer of the latter since many companies that account for revenue on a cash basis will account for expenses on an accrual basis in order to have what they regard as a proper matching of costs and revenues.

For example, a restaurant might record most, if not all, of its income on a cash basis but account for its food and labor costs on an accrual basis each period in order to charge these operating costs against the operating revenues to which they applied. Moreover, restaurants and many other businesses which account for revenues on a cash basis must at least account for the use of owned buildings, machinery, and equipment on an accrual basis through periodic charges for depreciation which are noncash expenses.

In merchandising and manufacturing businesses where inventories must be maintained in order to remain in business, time elapses inevitably between the purchase of goods and materials, the incurrence of labor and other costs, and the sale of goods purchased or produced. The longer it takes to find a buyer for a given item, or the longer the manufacturing process, the longer the elapsed time will be.

Thus, in cases where inventories are maintained, some portion of the goods sold in any given period will have been carried forward from the previous period in the inventory as of the close of that period. To the extent that these inventoried goods sold had been paid for in the previous period, they would not represent an outward cash flow in the computed cost of goods sold for the given period.

In many cases where inventories are involved, some of the costs incurred in purchasing or producing some of the goods which are sold along toward the end of a given period will not have been paid for by the end of that period. To this extent, therefore, the computed cost of goods sold for the given period would not represent an outward flow of cash.

Looking beyond the cost of goods sold, other expenses which affect net income, and which would therefore be assumed to represent outward flows of cash under the financial analyst's definition of cash flow, are selling and administrative expenses and income taxes. Since time again elapses between the incurrence of most selling and administrative expenses and their payment in cash, and since income taxes are paid in arrears, the figures for these items as presented in most published income statements do not entirely represent outward flows of cash for the given period.

If it so happened that balances in inventory accounts and in current liability accounts were the same at the end of a period as they were at the beginning of that period, then all cash expenditures in connection with these accounts would in effect have flowed through them to become costs for the period. These cash expenditures, plus any expenses paid for directly in cash, would equal the total of cost of goods sold, selling and administrative expenses, and taxes, except for depreciation and other major noncash expenses.

For example, if a merchant's inventories were the same in dollar amount at the beginning and end of a given period, his cost of goods sold would be the same as his cost of goods purchased, as though the inventories had remained untouched. If it happened also that his debts relative to merchandise purchases were the same at the end of the period as they were at the beginning of that period, his cash payments to suppliers would be equal in dollar amount to his purchases and in turn equal to his cost of goods sold. In this sense, the cost of goods sold would represent an outward flow of cash.

The fact is, of course, that in an active business the inventories and liabilities connected with them, and the liabilities related to expenses, are never exactly the same at the end of a period as at the beginning of that period. In not making specific allowances for changes in inventories or liabilities in computing cash flow, the financial analyst has to again make one of two assumptions: that these changes from period to period are not large enough to make any significant difference; or that since these changes have either involved cash, or will involve cash in the near future, it is all right to include them as matters of cash flow connected with net income.

As we shall discuss in detail in the next chapter, funds flow analysis, as distinct from cash flow analysis, recognizes net income as a source of funds, defined in a broad sense and not restricted to cash. It also provides an analysis of changes in inventories and liabilities as either sources or applications of funds. In these respects, as well as in others, funds flow presents a more complete and correct analysis of financial events than does cash flow.

Cash Flow in Terms of the Cash Account

Sometimes, the discussion of cash flow refers to events which actually increase or decrease cash in a company's cash account. This is in contrast to the financial analyst's concept of cash flow, which, as we noted, is not in fact directly related to what happens to the cash account.

Cash, as a figure standing in the cash account, represents money on hand, or on bank deposit subject to demand, i.e., in a checking account subject to immediate withdrawal. Bank deposits which are subject to restrictions on withdrawal are accounted for as investments and not as cash.

To a company's financial vice-president and treasurer, the amounts and timing of inward and outward flows of cash are obviously matters of great importance. Depending upon individual company circumstances, they can also be matters of concern to other members of top management and to creditors, particularly commercial bankers to whom the company owes money.

The cash budget is a major control tool for planning, and for checking the inward and outward flows of cash, on a daily basis if necessary or at less frequent intervals. An example of the cash budget is to be found in Chapter 28.

Inward cash flow in the cash account.   With respect to inward cash flow, the cash account is increased when payments are received from customers regardless of when the goods or services for which they are paying were sold to them. Moreover, unlike what we have been calling the financial analyst's cash flow figure, the inward flow to the cash account includes such items as advanced payments and deposits from customers, monies received from the sale of properties or items other than goods and services, receipt of short- or long-term loans, additional capital from old or new stockholders, and on occasion gifts, grants, and refunds.

Outward cash flow in the cash account.   With respect to outward cash flow, the cash account is decreased for various items, many of which are the opposites of the inward flows just mentioned. Regardless of when costs and expenses are recognized and appear in the income statement, the cash account is affected only as payment is made for the goods, materials, or services purchased or expenses incurred. Moreover, again unlike the analyst's cash flow figure, the outward flow from the cash account includes such items as payments for rent in advance; purchases

EXHIBIT 13
Major Elements of Cash Flow in Terms of the Cash Account

Cash

Receipts	Disbursements
Capital from stockholders	Payments to trade and other creditors
Payments from customers	Payments for wages and salaries
Payments on sales of assets other than goods	Payments on accrued taxes and other accruals
Loans from creditors	Payments for expenditures and expenses paid immediately in cash
Interest on investments	Loans and advances made
Dividends on investments, including dividends from subsidiaries	Investments made
Advances, rebates, & refunds received	Interest paid
Grants, gifts, & subsidies received	Donations
	Rebates, refunds & allowances paid
	Payments on warranties and other losses
	Dividend payments
	Reduction of loans
	Retirements of capital

of plant, property, and equipment; payments of short- or long-term loans; retirement of capital; and payments of dividends.

Exhibit 13 illustrates the major sources and applications of cash with respect to the cash account.

All in all, it can be seen that cash flow as defined by the financial analyst and as it affects the cash account is quite different. Each is an important financial matter which should be given consideration but discussed separately, and the one should not be confused with the other.

In Summary

The term cash flow is used in a variety of senses, ranging from what has happened or is expected to happen in the cash account alone to the flow of funds, as we shall be examining it next in Chapter 6 with reference to a funds flow statement. Among financial analysts, it is defined as net income after taxes plus depreciation or by longer definitions which include other major noncash expenses in addition to depreciation.

Analyses of cash flow as just defined are useful in judging a company's financial strength relative to such matters as its ability to maintain or increase a given dividend rate, to replace or expand facilities, and to meet requirements for interest payments and debt retirement. Such analyses reveal funds generated from operations as distinct from funds obtained from additional capital invested in the business, from increased short- or long-term debt, or from the liquidation of assets.

A figure for cash flow is therefore not a complete picture of the funds entering a business during a given period. Moreover, cash flow by itself gives no indication as to what has happened to the funds received, and it may lead the unsophisticated stockholder to believe that they are around the company somewhere available for distribution. A greater danger, however, is that such a stockholder may be led to believe either that the cash flow figure is a better measure of his company's performance than net income or that the cash flow figure is more of a consolation than it should be if there is no net income.

These comments are not intended to imply that cash flow analysis is necessarily misleading. They are, however, intended to indicate that since cash flow analysis (as distinct from funds flow analysis) provides a useful but limited view of financial results, it should be interpreted with caution.

CHAPTER 6

Funds Flow Analysis

We shall concern ourselves in this chapter with a discussion of funds flow. This is a more important concept than cash flow since it encompasses a broad area which includes cash flow. Thus the analysis of funds flow provides a more complete and useful analysis of financial events.

At times, cash flow has been used carelessly, as an interchangeable word substituted for the term funds flow, or in conjunction with "statement" as the title of one form of funds flow statement. As we shall discuss, however, the two are not synonymous.

A summary of the flow of funds for an accounting period is now presented by companies in a *Statement of Changes in Financial Position*. These statements used to be called statements of source and application of funds. For brevity we shall refer to them here most commonly as funds flow statements.

Conceptual Framework of Funds Flow

A diagram such as that shown in Exhibit 14 is helpful to many nonfinancial managers in gaining a better understanding of the flow of funds into and out of a business, as well as within it. Unfortunately, it is often spoken of as a cash flow diagram, which is incorrect, since far more than the flow of cash is pictured in it.

More specifically, the diagram differs from the net-income-plus-depreciation cash flow concept of the financial analyst as well as being far more than a description of activity in the cash account. On the latter point, a brief study of Exhibit 14 reveals that only the boxes

EXHIBIT 14
Conceptual Framework of Funds Flow

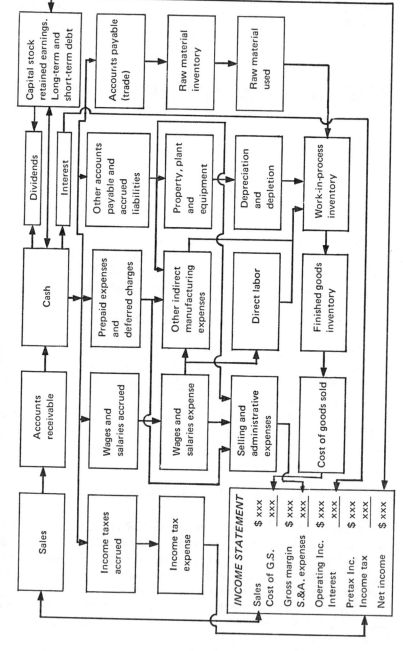

adjoining the box designated as "Cash" are literally involved in either the receipt or disbursement of cash.

In many noncash transactions it may well be that transfer has taken place of something that might be considered the equivalent of cash. But it is best to treat this as a matter of funds flow, rather than cash flow, in my opinion. If there is to be confusion here, it is better to have the reader of financial statements be confused about the term funds flow, and seek help to understand it, than to have him think he understands what has incorrectly been labeled a cash flow.

Cash vs. Funds

Many companies prepare statements of cash receipts and disbursements for internal management use and also various forms of statements which concentrate on changes in working capital. But here, we shall be concerned with broader statements of source and application of funds that are appropriate for use with other financial statements in reports to stockholders and others, as well as useful for management purposes. In such statements, the word "funds" has a broader meaning than that of "cash," and the flow of funds includes noncash, as well as cash, flows.

An example of noncash funds flow is to be seen in Exhibit 15 depicting inventory and cost flows in manufacturing. These same flows can be traced in Exhibit 14. Note that these are flows of resources expressed in monetary terms, but they are not cash flows.

Funds Defined

Funds have been defined commonly as "purchasing power," "spending power," and as "all financial resources arising from transactions with parties external to the business enterprise."[1]

The last part of the third definition is superfluous and indeed may be harmful if one believes that it implies only transactions with parties external to the business enterprise are important with respect to funds

---

[1]See APB Opinion No. 3, *The Statement of Source and Application of Funds*, paragraph 2; APB Opinion No. 19, *Reporting Changes in Financial Position*, paragraph 6; and Perry Mason, *"Cash Flow Analysis and the Funds Statements,"* Accounting Research Study No. 2 (American Institute of Certified Public Accountants, 1961), p. 54.

EXHIBIT 15

Inventory and Cost Flows in Manufacturing

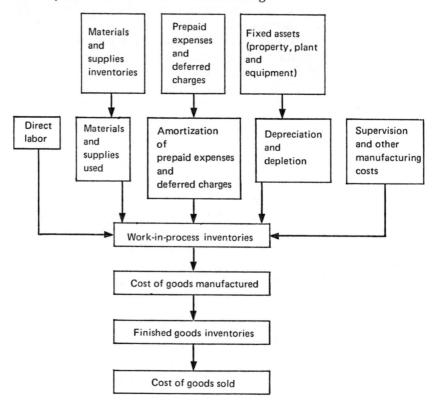

flow. Internal flows of funds are highly important financial events and, indeed, may be far more important than external flows in any given accounting period.

Business enterprises, being man-made entities, have no resources at the outset. Therefore, they can get initial resources only by transactions with external parties, including investments of capital by stockholders or other types of owners. Beyond this, although resources flow within an enterprise changing in form and accounting title as they do (e.g., when raw material moves into production and is then accounted for as work in process), they cannot be increased in total dollar amount except through profits arising from sales; from other revenues such as interest, rentals, and royalties; or from loans or further injections of capital — all of which involve transactions with parties external to the business enterprise.

To be sure, resources are in fact created within enterprises, and some resources gain in value or rise in replacement cost with the passing of time. But whatever gains are created or arise in these ways are not accounted for under American accounting practice until realized through sales to parties external to the business enterprise.

The emphasis on transactions with external parties can be harmful if it leads one to ignore the internal flow of funds or to treat them in summary as simply an incidental item or as a mere balancing factor in a funds flow statement. In any given accounting period, some aspect of a company's internal flow of funds may be a matter of far more importance and concern than the flow of funds relative to any single category of transactions with external parties in that period.

For example, the accumulation of an undesirably large inventory of finished goods can be a critical matter of more importance than many types of transactions with outsiders. Again, the reduction of cash and inventories to dangerously low levels in order to help finance purchases of machinery and equipment is a more important financial event to observe than the fact that these purchases involved transactions with parties external to the business enterprise.

It should also be recognized that every transaction with an outsider has an internal effect which is the more important part of the transaction as far as the company is concerned.

The word *funds* is so commonly associated with investments or with money put aside for carrying out some object as to cause some confusion when used in terms of a funds flow statement. Fortunately, the concept appears not too difficult to grasp even though difficult to define. Purchasing power comes close to defining it. In more homely terms, funds are the wherewithal by which things can be bought or done. I prefer the concept of "all financial resources," without reference to transactions with external parties, in keeping with the following statement by the Accounting Principles Board:

> The concept of "funds" underlying the preparation of a statement of source and application of funds should be consistent with the purpose of the statement. In the case of statements prepared for presentation in annual reports, a concept broader than that of working capital should be used which can be characterized or defined as "all financial resources," so that the statement will include the financial aspects of all significant transactions (e.g., "nonfund" transactions such as the acquisition of property through the issue of securities).[2]

---

[2] APB Opinion No. 3, *The Statement of Source and Application of Funds*, paragraph 9.

EXHIBIT 16

P. M. Stanton's Statement of Changes in Financial Position

	For the Years Ended	
	Dec. 31, 1977	Dec. 31, 1976
Source of funds:		
From operations:		
Net income	$ 555,824	$276,715
Depreciation	200,980	156,008
Amortization of deferred charges	50,275	65,685
Total	$ 807,079	$498,408
Common stock options exercised	141,040	—
Decrease in working capital	166,227	—
Miscellaneous	13,435	11,994
	$1,127,781	$510,402
Funds applied:		
Purchase of plant, machinery and equipment, less disposals	$ 285,471	$276,252
Redemption of long-term debt	800,000	100,000
Deferred development expense	26,901	37,925
Increase in working capital	—	67,405
Miscellaneous	15,409	28,820
	$1,127,781	$510,402

Funds Flow Statement

A common form of funds flow statement is illustrated in Exhibit 16. In the actual statement from which this exhibit was drawn, there were footnote explanations with reference to the common stock options exercised ($141,040) and the redemption of long-term debt ($800,000), but these explanations are not necessary for our present discussion. Also, although figures for the previous year were presented in the statement for comparative purposes in accordance with general practice, we shall refer only to the figures for 1977.

The reader will note that the flow of funds from operations, amounting to $807,079, is the same item we examined in Chapter 5 as an illustration of the financial analyst's concept of cash flow. More importantly, the reader will note that the funds flow statement goes well beyond this and shows not only the inward flow of funds from other sources in addition to those from operations but also, in net terms, where all of these funds have gone. It is, therefore, a complete summary of financial events for an accounting period and not simply a picture of funds generated through operations.

Dual Nature of Financial Events

A highly important point to note relative to the funds flow statement is that the total of funds applied is exactly equal to the total of funds in terms of sources. This is perfectly natural since, in an analysis of funds flow, one is observing the same funds from two points of view: 1. where they came from; and 2. where they went. A financial flow, like a river, has both a source and a destination.

In commonplace terms, one is looking at the same coin from two different sides. Since the same funds are involved, their identification in terms of applications must of course balance in total their identification in terms of sources. This dual nature of financial events, which can be observed clearly in the funds flow statement, is the essential basis for the practice of what is known as double-entry bookkeeping. Furthermore, although some skeptics may regard the fact that a balance sheet balances as simply a man-made contrivance through double-entry bookkeeping, the balancing is actually a reflection of the dual nature of financial events.

In any case, an understanding of the natural balancing of sources and applications of funds, as shown in a funds flow statement, can be helpful to an understanding of the logic underlying double-entry bookkeeping and the balance sheet. And this is one of the reasons why we are discussing funds flow before taking up the latter subjects in this book.

Changes in Working Capital

Another form of funds flow statement is illustrated in Exhibit 17. Here, the information from Exhibit 16 has been restated to emphasize the change that has taken place in working capital.

Working capital is the amount of capital invested in resources subject to relatively rapid turnover (current assets) such as cash, accounts receivable, and inventories less the amounts provided by short-term creditors (current liabilities) such as accounts payable, notes payable, and certain other accounts such as income taxes payable and expenses accrued. Stated in another way, working capital represents the portion of the owners' combined capital and retained earnings tied up in the current assets of a business.

In both Exhibit 16 and Exhibit 17, the change in working capital is shown as a single figure rather than as changes in the numerous ac-

EXHIBIT 17
P. M. Stanton's Statement of Sources and Uses of Working Capital

	For the Year Ended December 31, 1977
Sources of working capital	
From operations:	
Net income	$ 555,824
Depreciation	200,980
Amortization of deferred charges	50,275
Total	$ 807,079
Common stock options exercised	141,040
Miscellaneous	13,435
	$ 961,554
Uses of working capital	
Purchase of plant, machinery and equipment, less disposals	$ 285,471
Redemption of long term debt	800,000
Deferred development expense	26,901
Miscellaneous	15,409
	$1,127,781
Net decrease in working capital	($ 166,227)

counts from which a figure for working capital is derived. This is largely a matter of statement simplification or concentration on major financial events, although it does mean that important flows in working capital have been reduced to a single residual figure.

Exhibit 17 illustrates a common form of funds flow statement used by many of the leading companies in this country and presented by them under the title *Statement of Changes in Financial Position*. The arguments for this form are that it highlights the change in working capital, concentrates on major financial events, and avoids the use of the confusing word "funds."

The major objection to the form is that it appears to be stressing whatever net change has taken place in the amount of working capital during the period, which often is the least significant financial event to have taken place. In any case, the net change in working capital does not merit being highlighted in comparison with other major financial events. Incidentally, this emphasis on working capital is not in keeping with the title *Statement of Changes in Financial Position* under which the summary of funds flow for the period is presented.

If the purpose in highlighting working capital is to call attention to the fact that all of the funds dealt with in the statement flow in and out of the working capital category, this type of presentation does indicate that the analysis is broader than that of cash flow. Unfortunately, it stresses the function of the storage tank rather than the importance of the sources and applications of the flow.

Moreover, if changes in working capital are to be highlighted, it should be more appropriate to examine changes in the accounts from which the figure for working capital is derived rather than simply to observe the flow of funds in and out of that category.

In Exhibit 18, detail is presented on the changes between the beginning and the end of 1977 in the various accounts which resulted in the net decrease of $166,227 in working capital as presented in Exhibit 16 and Exhibit 17. The reader will note that during this period there were significant changes in accounts receivable, inventories, accounts payable, and in the provision for federal income tax, each of which was as important in amount as all but two of the items highlighted in Exhibit 16 and Exhibit 17.

Thus, as shown in Exhibit 18, the increase in accounts receivable, along with the decrease in the liability for sinking fund, represented important applications of funds. Similarly, the decrease in inventories, increase in accounts payable, and increase in the provision for federal income tax represented important sources of funds.

EXHIBIT 18

P. M. Stanton's Analysis of Changes in Working Capital

	For the Year Ended December 31, 1977	
Increases in working capital		
Increase in accounts receivable	$302,575	
Increase in prepaid assets	30,336	
Decrease in liability for sinking fund	100,000	
Decrease in provision for pensions	13,800	$446,711
Decreases in working capital		
Decrease in cash	875	
Decrease in inventories	220,632	
Increase in accounts payable	178,980	
Increase in provision for federal income tax	190,625	
Increase in other liabilities	21,826	612,938
Net decrease in working capital		($166,227)

Simplicity in financial statements is popularly held to be a virtue. But, there are times, as in the present case, when more complete information can be helpful to a better understanding of the situation. The use of the type of funds flow statement illustrated in Exhibit 16, supplemented by an analysis of working capital changes as illustrated in Exhibit 18, combines simplicity of presentation with reasonably complete information on funds flow. This combination is preferable to the form of statement presented in Exhibit 17.

Combining Working Capital Changes with Other Funds Flow

In Exhibit 19, another form of funds flow statement is illustrated. It represents a common form in cases where the company believes that changes in the individual accounts affecting working capital are important enough to be shown in detail along with other items of funds flow. A similar form of statement would result from combining the information presented in Exhibit 16 with that in Exhibit 18.

The net change in cash, or in cash and temporary investments in this case, is not commonly shown as a residual figure. Instead, it is listed with other items, and the total of funds from sources then balances the total of funds applied. This practice is much to be preferred. To show the change as a residual figure implies that the funds did in fact flow in and out of the cash, and temporary cash investment accounts, leaving, in the present case, a net decrease in these accounts for the period.

Unfortunately, this implication leads some to call this form of the funds flow statement a cash flow statement. Such a title not only causes confusion in the financial analyst's use of the term cash flow, but it also is an incorrect and misleading designation of the true nature of the statement. It should be evident that not all of the figures in either Exhibit 16 or Exhibit 18 represent actual flows of cash. Therefore, combining these data would not create a statement of cash flows. The result would still be a funds flow statement but in greater detail.

Funds Flow Statement Highlighting Cash

Changes in working capital can be brought together with other items of funds flow into a statement emphasizing the cash aspect of funds flow. Such a statement is illustrated in exhibit 20.

A statement prepared in this form can be useful for educational purposes when discussing cash flow and funds flow, while containing more detail than most companies would consider desirable for use in their annual report to stockholders. Moreover, while what happens in the cash account is of great interest and importance to the treasurer of

EXHIBIT 19
Consolidated Statement of Source and Application of Funds

Source of funds	
Operations:	
Net earnings	$ 4,692,327
Add charges not requiring cash expenditures:	
Depreciation, depletion and amortization	2,603,870
Amortization of deferred charges	323,829
Deferred Federal income taxes	270,000
	7,890,026
Increase in accounts payable	3,107,899
Increase in accrued liabilities and federal	
income taxes payable	413,200
Issuance of debentures	—
Other long-term debt	17,065,664
Issuance of common stock	63,327
Other—net	513,787
	29,053,903
Application of funds	
Increase in prepaid expenses	320,632
Increase in accounts receivable	3,521,385
Increase in inventories	3,242,514
Decrease in short-term notes payable	113,427
Unconsolidated foreign investments	
Net earnings, less amortization of excess costs	2,252,473
Other	1,058,312
Property, plant and equipment additions (net)	11,471,203
Increase in deferred charges	1,105,814
Retirement of long-term debt	5,675,534
Expenses to effect mergers	191,670
Increase in long-term notes receivable	270,863
	29,223,827
Increase (decrease) in cash and temporary	
cash investments	$ (169,924)

a company, it is only one of a number of important items of funds flow with which stockholders, and others including the treasurer, should be concerned.

Thus, while it is interesting to note the flow of cash into a business from customers and other sources for the period, and the outward flow of cash through expenditures — leaving in our example a net change of only $875 in the cash balance — preoccupation with these particular flows as they affect the cash account can detract attention from other effects of important financial events. The latter, in the

EXHIBIT 20
P. M. Stanton's Funds Statement Emphasizing Cash

Net sales			$9,990,486
Less increase in accounts receivable			302,575
Cash collected from customers			$9,687,911
Cost of goods sold		$6,736,490	
Selling, general and administrative expenses		2,078,240	
Total operating expenses		$8,814,730	
Less items not involving cash expenditures:			
Depreciation	$200,980		
Amortization of deferred charges	50,275		
Decrease in inventories	220,632		
Increase in accounts payable-trade	178,980		
Increase in accrued liabilities	21,826	672,693	
		$8,142,037	
Add: items involving cash expenditures			
Decrease in provision for pensions	$ 13,800		
Increase in prepaid assets	30,336		
Increase in deferred development expense	26,901	71,037	
Cash expenditures for operations			8,213,074
Cash generated from operations (before income taxes)			$1,474,837
Less: Bond interest and bond redemption expense, less other income			66,523
Cash internally generated (before income taxes)			$1,408,314
Less: Estimated state and federal income tax		$ 553,409	
Less: Increase in provision for federal income tax		190,625	
Income tax payments in cash			362,784
After tax cash internally generated			$1,045,530
Add: Cash from other sources:			
Common stock options exercised		$ 141,040	
Miscellaneous		13,435	154,475
			$1,200,005
Deduct other cash expenditures:			
Purchase of property, plant and equipment		$ 285,471	
Payment of bond sinking fund installment		100,000	
Redemption of long term debt		800,000	
Miscellaneous		15,409	$1,200,880
Net increase or (decrease) in cash			$ (875)

present case, include significant changes in working capital items; the investment in new property, plant, and equipment; and the retirement of long-term debt.

In other words, it is not so important to be able to uncover a company's flow of cash in a literal sense as it is to be able to grasp the major changes, broadly interpreted, that have taken place during a period in its financial condition. For this purpose, funds flow as presented in Exhibit 16, supplemented by Exhibit 18, is to be preferred over the statement illustrated in Exhibit 20.

Funds Flow Statement for a New Enterprise

A discussion of the first funds flow statement for a new enterprise may be helpful to a better understanding of the meaning of the word funds, the nature of the funds flow statement, and the dual nature of financial events.

In forming a new company, or in undertaking a new project or expansion in an existing company, it is both natural and usual to estimate in advance what investments and what expenditures will be required and where the funds are to come from to meet these financial requirements. This is good practice, whether or not a formal statement of expected source and application of funds is prepared in this connection.

This does not mean that planned sources and planned applications must necessarily be in balance. It is possible to start an undertaking without knowing clearly where all of the funds are to come from to meet planned uses, although this is more courageous than wise.

While sources and applications of funds may not always be in balance in the planning stage, this is not the case with funds involved in actual financial events. As we noted earlier, a flow of funds has to balance as to source and application, since these words simply refer to two views of the same funds: where they came from and where they went.

In any actual undertaking, it is possible to use only such funds as become available. Something must be done with funds as they become available even if their temporary use, in the case of funds in the form of cash, is simply to build up cash on hand or in a bank. Thus in any action involving a flow of funds the dual aspects of source and application are inherently in balance.

As we shall note later, these dual aspects of financial transactions are recorded under a formal system of double-entry bookkeeping. And it is, of course, from the accounting records that financial statements are developed, including the statement of changes in financial position.

Initial Sources of Funds

Let us assume that in starting a new manufacturing company we plan to finance this business at the outset largely through the sale of common stock to ourselves and to other members of the community and through a long-term loan from an insurance company based on a mortgage on the manufacturing plant we shall buy.

We plan to supplement these sources of funds through seasonal bank loans to assist in financing inventories and customers' accounts and through credit to be granted to the company by the suppliers of raw material and other items purchased, since payment for such items will not have to be made until from ten to thirty days or more after their purchase, depending upon the terms of each purchase.

Business as a separate entity.   One of the basic accounting concepts is that of the business enterprise as an entity separate and distinct from its owners. As such, it is perhaps even more accountable to the owners than to others also having a legitimate interest in the enterprise and therefore a proper right to obtain information concerning it.

A business corporation established under state laws is legally such a separate entity. Enterprises not incorporated are not separate legal entities, although their owners are required to make separate accountings for them for taxation and other purposes. Accounting convention calls for treating a business enterprise as a separate accounting entity. And, in any event, prudence should lead owners to make such an accounting separation and not mix a business with personal property and affairs.

With a business as a separate entity in mind, the additions or reductions of capital by investors — whether stockholders or other types of owners — and the payment of dividends or profits to them, represent transactions with parties external to the business enterprise. Thus the initial capital to start our manufacturing business, which we shall assume comes from the purchase of common stock in the business by ourselves and others for cash, is brought about by transactions with parties external to the enterprise.

In terms of source and application of funds with respect to these transactions, the new stockholders represent the source of the funds received, while the immediate, albeit temporary, use or application of these funds is simply to increase cash on hand. With respect to bookkeeping, the cash account would be increased with each payment received and each such entry would be matched by an entry in a common stock or capital account. Thus each transaction would be recorded in terms of both source and application of the funds involved.

Legal claims or rights as funds.   Let us assume that one of the founders of our new company holds patent rights to one of the products we plan to manufacture and is willing to receive shares of stock in exchange for these rights. When this is effected, he will have contributed funds to the business in the sense of a financial resource in the form of patent rights representing intangible property of financial value.

The provision of funds in this case will be recognized by the company through recording the shares of stock issued in the exchange (under the account title "Common Stock" or "Capital"), presumably at the same amount per share as paid by stockholders who bought their shares for cash. The use of funds will be recognized by recording the patent rights as one of the properties of the business at the same valuation recorded for the stock involved.

In a case such as this, it is the responsibility of the company's directors to determine the "fair value" of the property to be acquired and the number of shares of stock to be issued in exchange for it. This is, then, a matter of judgment on both sides of the transaction, since it requires those involved to judge not only the fair value of the property to be acquired but also the fair value of the stock to be issued in exchange for it.

The latter problem is not difficult in cases where a reasonable number of shares are currently being sold for cash. It can be difficult, however, in situations where there have been no recent cash sales of stock in a company that proposes to acquire some type of property by issuing stock in exchange for it.

Services as funds.   As another example of noncash source and use of funds, let us assume that one or more individuals will receive shares of stock in our company in lieu of salary, commissions or fees, or reimbursement of expenses incurred personally in connection with the organization of the company.

Here, the amount involved will be recorded by the company, on the one hand, as organization expense (a use of funds) and, on the other hand, as stock issued (a source of funds). Assuming that a proper valuation of the services rendered has been made, the net effect in terms of sources and uses of funds will be the same as though stock had been sold for cash and the cash then used to pay for the services rendered.

Credit as a source of funds. In the two examples given, we noted a concept of funds that is broader than that of cash or working capital. Another example is that of credit, a highly important segment of funds. Each supplier who grants credit provides funds to the purchaser under this concept.

The amount and source of the funds provided is recognized by the purchasing company through recording its indebtedness to the supplier in its accounting records at the time of purchase. The use (application) of these funds is recorded at the same time as an increase in the items on hand (expressed in monetary terms) for whatever items were purchased.

At this stage of procurement, no cash has been involved, although there has been both a provision and use of funds in a funds-flow sense. Carrying the point further, at the time such debts are paid the reduction of debt is an application of funds and the source of these funds is a reduction in cash.

Thus, from the purchasing company's viewpoint, the receipt of credit is an inward flow of funds and the payment of debt an outward flow of funds. Whether the flow is inward or outward, however, each flow has the two aspects of where it came from and where it went.

Debt as a source of funds. One of the ways of obtaining funds is, of course, by getting a loan, which is an inward flow of cash in a layman's sense. In terms of source and application of funds, the company receiving the loan recognizes its source through recording indebtedness to the lender for the amount involved. The use (application) of these funds is recorded at the same time as an increase in the company's cash account.

This is a situation in which, as far as the borrower is concerned, the funds involved are in the form of cash when received. However, if, as is likely to be the case, the lender is a bank, the granting of the loan involves simply a bookkeeping entry in the bank's accounting records and thus the funds loaned are in actuality in the form of credit. In this case, the definition of funds as "purchasing power" or "spending power" is most appropriate.

Initial Statement of Changes in Financial Position

Returning to the formation of our company, let us assume that the planned inital steps have been taken and that the following statement summarizes the source and application (use) of funds to date prior to the actual manufacture and sale of our products:

Application of Funds		Source of Funds	
Cash	$345,000	Accounts payable	$ 50,000
Raw material	50,000	Mortgage note	350,000
Plant and equipment	475,000	Common stock	500,000
Patents	20,000		
Organization expense	10,000		
	$900,000		$900,000

The reader will note that this statement is a summary of the flow of funds over a period of time. It shows where the funds came from to get this business started and how they have been used to date. It is, however, a description of only the net source or application of funds for the period in each category. It does not provide detail on the increases and decreases which took place within each category during the period in arriving at the net figure. Such detail would of course be available in the company's records if required for some reason.

The purpose of the statement of changes in financial position, however, is to highlight significant financial changes which have taken place during the given period. Thus, presentation of the net change in each category for the period as a whole is more appropriate than detail on the fluctuations in each category within the period.

Balance Sheet Comparison

In chapters soon to come, we shall examine the balance sheet in considerable detail. For the moment, we shall assume that the reader has examined published balance sheets from time to time, understands their format and purpose in general, and as a minimum knows that the *balance sheet* is a formal statement of the financial position of a business as of a given date showing:

1. The assets of a business expressed in monetary terms.
2. The liabilities outstanding against these assets.
3. The ownership of the business described in terms such as capital and retained earnings, or owners' equity.

Tying this to our discussion of funds flow, the assets as listed in a balance sheet show where the resources (funds) of the business are located as of the given date, by categories and monetary amounts. The asset side of the balance sheet is thus a static picture of the current use or application of funds.

Similarly, the liability and ownership categories listed by amounts on the other side of the same balance sheet present a static picture of the sources of these funds.

We have noted that from the beginning of an undertaking there will inevitably be a matching of funds provided and funds used. It follows that, if both the sources and applications of funds have been properly recorded to reflect this fundamental balance in the flow of funds, the total (or net) recorded financial resources on hand at any given time will be matched by balancing records of the origins of these resources. Thus a balance sheet, drawn from these records, balances.

This is not to say that each financial resource now on hand and reported in the balance sheet can easily be traced to its exact source. Once a dollar is in the till, for example, it is impossible to tell exactly where it came from. Some major items can be related, however, such as raw material inventory with accounts payable, and plant and equipment with mortgage notes. But identification in detail is not so important as the broad picture of financial resources and the major sources or means by which they were generated.

As the statement of changes in financial position for our company now stands, it is not only such a statement but also a balance sheet in simple form. The list of items under Application of Funds is a list of assets totaling $900,000 in monetary terms. The items under Source of Funds are liabilities of $50,000 and $350,000; and ownership is expressed as common stock of $500,000. Thus the total of these three items is $900,000, which balances with the total for the assets. These two statements will, however, be comparable only for the first accounting period of the company's existence.

Our manufacturing company had no resources to begin with. This being so, a balance sheet prepared at the close of the *first* accounting period will contain the same elements as the statement of changes in financial position for that period, since both statements will be reflecting the same net results of the flow of funds for this initial period.

After the first accounting period, however, the two statements will be quite different for our company. The statement of changes in financial position will reflect the net funds flow in terms of uses and sources for a given accounting period only. Essentially, it will highlight the funds flow by which the financial position of the company as shown in the balance sheet at the outset of that period has changed to the financial position shown in the balance sheet as of the close of that period. The latter will show the then-current applications and sources of funds reflecting the net result of funds flow since the origin of the company. This point will be clarified in the more detailed analysis of the balance sheet in Chapters 8–14, and in the steps involved in constructing funds flow statements that are presented in Chapter 15.

In Summary

The statement of changes in financial position (funds flow statement) provides a picture of financial action, showing in summary the flow of funds that has taken place over a given period of time within the business and between the business and parties external to it, i.e., showing by various categories where funds have come from during that period and where they have gone, and the amounts involved.

In such a statement, the sources and applications of funds are to be found under the following major classifications:

Applications of Funds	Sources of Funds
Net increases in assets	Net decreases in assets
Net decreases in liabilities	Net increases in liabilities
Net losses	From operations:
Dividends	Net income
Retirements of capital	Depreciation and amortization
	Increases in capital
	Gifts, grants, and subsidies

In contrast, the balance sheet is a static picture of financial position and not a picture of financial action.

It is a tabulation in monetary terms of the resources of a given entity, as of a given date, matched by a tabulation of the origins of those resources. It balances because the figures in it are drawn from accounting records in which financial events have been entered in conformity with the dual nature of the flow of funds involved, i.e., in terms of where they came from and where they went.

An important ability to be acquired by the nonaccountant who wishes to better understand and make more effective use of accounting is to visualize the flow of funds involved in any given financial event. In this way he will understand how the accounts are affected by such an event, and, in turn, know its effect on the financial statements drawn from the accounts.

For example, in the present chapter we noted the flow of funds connected with each financial event involved in the formation of a small manufacturing company. Further, we noted the effects of these

events on the company's accounts and, in the net, on its initial statement of changes in financial position and initial balance sheet.

The analysis of financial events in terms of funds flow, and their
effects on the accounts, is known commonly as transaction analysis.
We shall discuss this subject in more detail in the next chapter before
moving on to further consideration of the balance sheet.

CHAPTER 7

Analysis of Financial Transactions

There are differences of opinion as to how much of the bookkeeping process the nonfinancial manager should know as an aid to a better understanding of financial statements and reports and to a more effective use of accounting data in dealing with business problems.

Many people hold that a working knowledge of the process is not only helpful for the reasons just mentioned, but also that it promotes better understanding and communication between nonfinancial managers and accountants, which can lead to the development and use of the most appropriate accounting data for any given purpose.

In direct contrast, there are those who believe that all aspects of bookkeeping should be left to the bookkeepers. They are of the opinion that it is not necessary for nonfinancial managers to understand techniques in this area in order to understand and make effective use of accounting data.

Some people go beyond this and believe also that matters of accounting policy should be left to the experts, or professionals, and therefore not be of any concern to those who are not. Moreover, they believe that if there is something that the nonfinancial manager does not understand about a financial statement or report, or about some accounting data, he should turn to the expert for interpretation and advice. In their view, he should not attempt to have more than a rudimentary knowledge of accounting himself.

It can readily be agreed that one does not necessarily have to understand a process, particularly a more or less mechanical one, in order to use the output or results of that process. It is not necessary, for example, to understand how an internal combustion engine works in order to enjoy an automobile ride.

Nor is it necessary to understand stenography in order to understand the output of a stenographer. Shorthand and typewriting, although important, are simply the means by which what has been dictated is reproduced in useful form. The person giving the dictation, who is also the primary user of the stenographic output, can employ someone able to undertake these mechanics. The former does not need to understand or have any personal expertise in them himself, even when deciding that it is desirable to get a new typewriter, or a new secretary, or both.

So, too, with the mechanics of bookkeeping. There are no compelling reasons for most nonfinancial managers to learn about the bookkeeping process with respect to handling journals and ledgers, or making entries on cards or tapes, or programing for a computer. Nor is it really necessary for them to understand the mechanical processes of periodically drawing off account balances and adjusting and closing the books of account.

These duties and responsibilities may quite properly be left to the bookkeepers and operators of office machines, including computers. Of course, they should have proper supervision, internal check, and auditing to ensure correct accounting and to thwart embezzlement. The processing of data within the accounting system, like stenography, is important to those who are responsible for carrying out such an activity. But it is not a matter of great concern to others.

How Financial Events Affect the Accounts

Without debating the matter further, let us grant that it is more important for the nonfinancial manager to understand what information is provided by a specific type of account as reported in a financial statement, and the policy or practice determining it, than to be concerned about the mechanics of how information gets into an account or leaves it.

To really understand the information that comes out of a bookkeeping system, however, one should understand the information that goes into it. Such understanding is aided by the ability to visualize the flow of funds involved in any given financial event, and its effect on the accounts. In turn, the ability to visualize how given financial events affect the accounts enables one to understand more clearly the nature of data drawn from them. This is a matter of substance affecting the usefulness of accounting to nonfinancial managers and not simply a matter of bookkeeping mechanics.

Beyond this, the ability to express, both orally and in writing, how a given financial event has affected or would affect the accounts enables one to state succinctly the financial implications of that event. This ability is thus a distinct aid to communication on financial matters.

If the nonfinancial manager will extend his study and understanding of accounting to the point of being able to visualize and express how any given financial event is likely to affect the accounts, he will be better able to understand financial statements and use accounting data more effectively. Moreover, he will be better able to discuss with others the financial implications of events that have taken place or are proposed.

It is the development of these abilities in financial analysis and communication that is important and not the knowledge of how to keep a set of books.

Financial Transactions

Financial events which are, or might be, recorded in the accounts are known as *financial* or *accounting transactions.*

The word "financial" is used to indicate that the transaction has financial effects, or is measurable in monetary terms, although this does not necessarily mean that cash is actually involved in any given transaction.

The word "accounting" is sometimes used instead of financial and simply indicates that the event is one in which an entry in the accounts is involved.

The word "transaction" covers any event, operation, or action to be accounted for in monetary terms and is not limited to its more common meaning of a deal or trade between two parties.

Pro forma journal entries.   The results of the analysis of a financial transaction are commonly expressed in the form of journal entries that would be made to record it under a simple bookkeeping system. In such a system, each transaction is first recorded in chronological order in a book called a journal. A journal entry states for a given transaction the titles of the accounts affected and the monetary amount involved for each account.

While it is true that determining the appropriate journal entry for a financial transaction is the first step in the bookkeeping process, this is not our concern at the moment. We are concerned here with the analysis of financial transactions for purposes other than bookkeeping.

The expressing of the effect of any given financial transaction on the accounts in journal entry form is simply an orderly and efficient way of stating it in a manner that is widely understood. In fact, the use of pro forma journal entries to illustrate the effect of financial transactions, either proposed or that have taken place, is one of the ways in which accounting serves as "the language of business."

Dual nature of financial transactions.   In our discussion of funds flow and of the balance sheet, we noted the dual nature of each financial event. So, too, the analysis of a financial transaction, and expressing the effect of that transaction in journal entry form, must take its dual nature into account in determining what accounts are affected by it and in what amounts.

For any given transaction, the nonfinancial manager may perhaps be interested in its effect on only one of the accounts involved. However, the ability to visualize the two or more accounts affected, and the amount connected with each, enables one to have a better understanding of the financial implications of that transaction.

Moreover, it prevents overlooking some aspect of the transaction that could turn out to be of considerable importance in addition to the aspect that was thought to be of major interest.

The Nature of Accounts

Before further discussion of the analysis of financial transactions in journal entry form, it would be well to discuss the basic nature of the accounts in which the effects of these transactions are reflected.

Record keeping has changed considerably in recent years through the application of mechanical, electrical, and electronic data processing. Regardless of the means by which records are kept, however, or the forms in which they are kept, it is still practice, as it has been for centuries, to maintain both a chronological record of financial transactions and a classified record of the same events. Various types of subsidiary or supplementary records are also maintained but these are not of importance to us at the moment.

We have already noted that in a simple bookkeeping system a chronological record of financial transactions is maintained in a journal. The classified record of financial transactions in such a system is kept in a book called a ledger, which has a separate section for each of the accounts under which financial transactions are classified.

Traditionally, a transaction is first entered in the journal and then entered in (posted to) the ledger. Today, for convenience and time-saving, the entries are often made simultaneously, even in relatively simple bookkeeping systems.

As suggested, accounts may be kept in various forms. For example, they may be kept in bound books, on sheets, tapes or cards, or stored in an electronic data processing system to be printed out when desired. For discussion purposes, however, it is common practice to illustrate the accounts as though they were in the form of a large "T" as shown in the following illustration. Thus one side of the account is used for recording additions, the other for subtractions, and we shall follow this practice in our discussion here.

A "T" Account

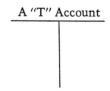

Although an account could be kept in a single column, as on the tape of a simple adding machine, in an active account having both additions and subtractions it would be necessary, or at least desirable, to strike a new balance with each entry, which would be time-consuming. Moreover, entries recorded in a single column only would be awkward when one wished to know how much had entered or left the account in total for a given period.

For some accounts, such as those for individual inventory items, or for individual customers, it may well be desirable to know the account balance at all times. Even where this is the case, however, it is usually considered desirable to record additions to, and subtractions from, the account in separate columns.

Some ancient bookkeeper, in a day when there was not so much concern about striking a new balance with every transaction entering an account, started the practice of entering all additions on one side of an account and all subtractions on the other. At such times as a balance was desired, both sides could be added, and one subtracted from the other.

This design of an account enabled a quick visual inspection of its activity. It also provided a simple means of summarizing what had come into an account and what had left it for any given period. And, for an account that showed much activity, it saved the bookkeeper a considerable number of calculations, which was important at a time when it was not possible to add, subtract, or strike a new balance automatically.

This basic design of an account remains in use today. And, for many accounts, a balance is struck only at the end of an accounting period in connection with the preparation of financial statements.

Debit and Credit

There is confusion about the words *debit* and *credit* that is difficult to overcome, as when the nonfinancial manager discovers that something he has thought to be to his credit turns out to be a debit.

The problem will be eased considerably for the reader who is willing to give up attempts to fit his common understanding of these words into his understanding of accounting practice. Instead, all he needs to understand is that in accounting practice debit simply means the left-hand side of an account and credit the right-hand side of an account.

In accounting practice, the abbreviation for debit is dr. and for credit, cr. Thus the "T" form illustration looks like this:

Any Account	
Debit or Dr. simply means the left-hand side of an account	Credit or Cr. simply means the right-hand side of an account

The Balance Sheet Equation

It will be helpful to an understanding of the nature of accounts, and to developing skill in the analysis of financial transactions, if the reader will first establish firmly in his mind the balance sheet equation in the form of: Assets = Liabilities + Owners' Equity.

It is particularly important to remember that assets are on the left-hand side of the equation, while liabilities and accounts for owners' equity are on the right. The reader will recall that owners' equity consists of capital and retained earnings. Reserves of various types are also really part of owners' equity until required for the.purposes for which they were created.

Balance sheet account balances.   Having in mind that the assets are on the left-hand side of the balance sheet equation, it will be helpful to remember further that by custom, under double-entry bookkeeping, balances of asset accounts are — with rare exceptions — to be found on the left-hand side of those accounts.

Another way of expressing this is that asset accounts have debit balances, as shown:

Any Asset Account	
Debit	Credit
Balance (asset accounts have debit balances)	

Again, having in mind that liabilities and accounts for owners' equity are on the right-hand side of the balance sheet equation, it will be helpful to remember further that the balances in these accounts are — with rare exceptions — to be found on the right-hand side of the "T" form, as shown in (A) and (B).

Another way of expressing this is that liability accounts, and accounts for owners' equity, have credit balances, as illustrated in (A) and (B).

(A) Any Liability Account		(B) Any Owners' Equity Account	
Debit	Credit	Debit	Credit
	Balance (Liability accounts have credit balances)		Balance (Owners' equity accounts have credit balances)

Knowing the balance sheet equation, we can visualize in the three foregoing "T" accounts that as of the date of a balance sheet the total of the debit balances in the asset accounts will be equal to the total of the credit balances in the liability and owners' equity accounts. Stated in another way, the total of the debits will equal the total of the credits.

Increases in balance sheet accounts.   Since it is common practice, as just described, to carry the balances of asset accounts on the left-hand side of the "T" form, it can be appreciated that custom would logically dictate that additions to them should also be entered on the left-hand side, which will of course add to their balances. Thus an addition to an asset account is commonly described as being a debit to that account. To illustrate:

Any Asset Account	
Debit	Credit
1. Balance at start of period	
2. Increases	

Similarly, since it is the custom to carry the balances of liability and owners' equity accounts on the right-hand side of those accounts, it is logical to enter also on the right-hand side additions to these accounts, which will of course add to their balances. Thus additions to liability or owners' equity accounts are commonly described as being credits to these accounts, as shown in "T" form (A) and (B):

(A) Any Liability Account		(B) Any Owners' Equity Account	
Debit	Credit	Debit	Credit
	1. Balance at start of period		1. Balance at start of period
	2. Increases		2. Increases

Decreases in balance sheet accounts.   If by custom there are to be two sides of an account — one for additions and one for subtractions — and one particular side of a type of account has been selected as the side in which additions are to be entered, then by deduction as well as by custom the other side of that account is slated for subtractions.

Thus a decrease in an asset is entered on the right-hand side of the given asset account and is commonly described as being a credit to that account, as shown in the following "T" form (A).

In contrast, decreases in liability and owners' equity accounts are entered on the left-hand side of the given accounts and are commonly described as being debits to those accounts, as in (B) and (C) respectively.

(A) Any Asset Account	
Debit	Credit
1. Balance at start of period	1. Decreases
2. Increases	

(B) Any Liability Account	
Debit	Credit
1. Decreases	1. Balance at start of period
	2. Increases

(C) Any Owners' Equity Account	
Debit	Credit
1. Decreases	1. Balance at start of period
	2. Increases

Balance sheet accounts are "real" accounts. The balance sheet accounts we have been discussing — namely asset, liability, and ownership accounts — are sometimes spoken of as "real" accounts. They are real in the sense that they cover all of the resources of the entity that can appropriately be stated in monetary terms, together with all of the claims to them.

Thus any financial activity, or activity having financial effects, will be reflected directly or indirectly in these accounts.

Expense and Revenue Accounts

There are two other types of accounts commonly in use — namely, expense accounts and revenue accounts. These are sometimes spoken of as "nominal" accounts, i.e., as accounts in name only, in contrast to the "real" accounts for assets, liabilities, and owners' equity.

Expense and revenue accounts are actually subdivisions of owners' equity. Regardless of how the accounts are handled, it is obvious that as each expense is incurred the owners of a business are that much poorer and with the receipt of each item of revenue they are that much better off.

However, if all accounting entries for expenses were debits to the owners' equity account "Retained Earnings," and all items of revenues were treated as credits to that account, the account would be a hodgepodge. There would be no clear record in the ledger as to what kinds of expenses had been incurred, and for how much, during any given period, nor would there be a clear record of the various types and amounts of revenue.

Accordingly, an appropriate number of expense and revenue accounts are carried in the ledger in order to accumulate this important information on a classified basis. At the close of an accounting period, generally at the close of each year rather than monthly, the balances in expense and revenue accounts are transferred by a series of steps to the owners' equity account "Retained Earnings."

The net effect of these steps is that the "Retained Earnings" account is increased or decreased by the net income or loss for the period, while the expense and income accounts have no balances left in them.

Thus at the beginning and end of the year, the only accounts in the ledger having balances are the "real" accounts for assets, liabilities, and ownership. These are reflected in the company's balance sheet as of those times.

During the year, expenses and revenue items are recorded in appropriate accounts which are "closed out" to "Retained Earnings" at the end of the year, leaving no balances in them. Information from these accounts is reflected in the company's income statement.

For purposes of monthly statements, information on balance sheet accounts and on income statement accounts can be drawn from the ledger without a formal "closing of the books of account." In some companies, however, the closing process takes place each month instead of at year-end only.

Expenses are debits.   Expense accounts have two sides, in common with the other accounts we have discussed, with the left side being for debit entries and the right for credit entries.

If charged directly to an owners' equity account, expenses would be debited to it as reductions in that account. In keeping with this concept, expenses as incurred are recorded on the debit side of expense accounts.

Although it may be somewhat misleading to say that expenses are debits, since other accounts are debited for things other than expenses, still if one keeps this concept in mind it is easy to visualize how expenses involved in any given financial transaction will affect the accounts and, in turn, affect the company's financial statements.

The credit side of expense accounts is used to record deductions from these accounts. Deductions are entered in an expense account to correct errors made on the debit side and to transfer amounts to other accounts, including the transfer made to close out the account at the end of an accounting period. Here is how this looks in "T" form:

Any Expense Account

Debit	Credit
An expense is entered on the debit side of an expense account when incurred.	Credit entries are made in an expense account to correct errors made on the debit side and to transfer amounts to other accounts, including the amount at the end of an accounting period to close the account.

Revenue items are credits.   Revenue accounts also have the usual two sides, the left side being for debit entries and the right side for credit entries, as for all accounts.

If allowed to affect an owners' equity account directly, revenue items would be credited to that account since they would represent additions to it. In keeping with this concept, revenue items — when recognized as such in accounting terms — are recorded on the credit side of revenue accounts. When this is kept in mind, it is easy to visualize how revenue involved in any given financial transaction will affect the accounts and, in turn, affect the company's financial statements.

As might be expected, the debit side of a revenue account is used to record reductions from recorded revenues, either to correct errors made on the credit side or to transfer amounts to other accounts. The latter includes the transfer made to close out the account at the end of an accounting period. Thus:

Any Revenue Account

Debit	Credit
Debit entries are made in a revenue account to correct errors made on the credit side and to transfer amounts to other accounts, including the amount to close the account at the end of an accounting period.	Revenues are entered on the credit side of revenue accounts when given accounting recognition (i.e., when recognized as having been earned).

Summary on the Nature of Accounts

We have noted that there are five types of accounts: asset, liability, owners' equity, expense, and income accounts.

The first three of these are known as balance-sheet accounts since their balances appear in condensed form in a company's balance sheet at the close of an accounting period. They are also known as "real" accounts since they account for all of the resources of a business and all of the claims to them. Moreover, they reflect directly or indirectly the results of all of the financial transactions in which the company engages.

The last two of the five types of accounts are known as income-statement accounts since they are reflected in condensed form in a company's income statement. They are also known as "nominal" accounts since they are actually reflected directly in the owners' equity account, commonly titled "Retained Earnings." Therefore, these are considered to be accounts in name only, or subdivisions of a real account, and not real accounts in themselves.

The accounts with which we are concerned have two sides, the left-hand side being known as the debit side and the right-hand side as the credit side. Entries in the accounts with respect to these two sides may be summarized as follows:

Debits	Credits
1. Balances of asset accounts.	1. Balances of liability and owners' equity accounts.
2. Additions to assets.	2. Additions to liabilities and to owners' equity accounts.
3. Expenses.	3. Revenues.
4. Deductions from liability and owners' equity accounts.	4. Deductions from asset accounts.
5. Corrections to and transfers of amounts from revenue accounts.	5. Corrections to and transfers of amounts from expense accounts.

Dual Aspect of Accounts and Transactions

In connection with our discussions of funds flow and the balance sheet, we noted the dual nature of financial transactions in terms of the natural balance between the sources and applications of funds. Essentially, each financial transaction involves funds in a broad sense. Their dual nature is simply a matter of identifying both where they came from and where they went.

Following up on this concept with accounts having two sides and the debit and credit mechanism provides a sensible and useful type of record keeping. It also provides the means for expressing the results of, or expected from, a financial event in simple terms that can be understood by anyone who has at least a rudimentary knowledge of the system.

Let us now see how typical financial transactions might be expressed (analyzed) in double-entry accounting.

Journal Entry Form

The results of the analysis of a financial transaction are commonly expressed in the form of journal entries that would be made to record it under a simple bookkeeping system. In fact, when one is asked to analyze a financial transaction, it is usually expected that the answer will be presented in journal entry form.

The journal entry states in uniform order the accounts affected and the monetary amount involved for each account. By custom, the debit entries involved are listed first, followed by the balancing credit entries (credit entries are indented to distinguish them from debit entries).

Similarly, the monetary amounts for debits are entered in one column, while the amounts for credits are entered in a second column to the right of the debit column.

Journal entries illustrated. Near the close of Chapter 6, the flow of funds in the initial steps of the formation of a company was illustrated and a statement was presented summarizing the source and application of these funds. We shall now use this same situation to illustrate the analysis of financial transactions in journal entry form.

The initial funds for the business were provided by the sale of common stock. So far as actual bookkeeping is concerned each sale of stock would have to be recorded separately.

However, this is not our interest at present. Here, we are concerned only with being able to visualize how typical financial transactions affect a company's accounts, since financial statements are based on data drawn from the accounts and such data are also used for a variety of other purposes.

For our immediate purpose, then, we are interested only in how the entire sales of common stock for cash amounting to $470,000 would affect the accounts. Therefore, we can analyze the total amount as though it were from only one transaction. Incidentally, there would doubtless be some expenses connected with the sale of stock but we shall ignore them in order to simplify our discussion.

It is easy to see that for one side of this transaction the asset "Cash" is increased. We know from our foregoing discussion that assets have left-hand (debit) balances and that to increase an asset account one makes a debit entry in it. Our debit entry to illustrate this transaction is thus: Dr: Cash $470,000.

The other side of the transaction in this case involves an increase in owners' equity under the account title "Common Stock." Again, we know from our foregoing discussion that owners' equity accounts have right-hand (credit) balances and that to increase such an account one makes a credit entry in it. Our credit entry to illustrate this side of the transaction is thus: Cr: Common Stock $470,000.

Bringing these two items together, the journal entry expression of the transaction is as follows:

Dr: Cash $470,000
   Cr: Common Stock $470,000

In an actual journal, if an explanation were considered necessary, it would be written in following the debit and credit entries. If a lengthy explanation were required, it would be entered in a voucher file elsewhere and only the file number would be included in the explanation section of the journal.

It can be seen that the dual aspect of a financial transaction is clearly indicated in the journal entry form of expression. In this instance, funds are pictured as entering the cash account and their source is indicated as the sale of common stock. Since the same funds are involved, the analysis of where they go is naturally balanced in monetary terms by the analysis of where they come from.

Another way of looking at this transaction is that the company's resources in the form of cash would increase by $470,000 and there would be a corresponding increase in the claims of stockholders.

Sale of Common Stock for Other Than Cash

In our example in Chapter 6, we assumed that one of the founders of our new company was to receive stock in exchange for the patent rights to one of the products we plan to manufacture. The "fair value" of the patent rights was assumed to be $20,000.

Similarly, some of the founders of the company were to receive shares of stock in lieu of salaries, commissions, or fees, or for expenses they had incurred personally in connection with the organization of the company.

Although a separate journal entry could be prepared to illustrate each of these financial transactions, they could also be combined in illustration as follows:

Dr: Patents	$20,000	
Organization Expense	10,000	
Cr: Common Stock		$30,000

In fact, the sale of the stock for the three different types of payment could be combined in one illustration. The reasoning here is that for analytical purposes we are interested only in the total effect on the accounts and not in the bookkeeping for individual sales, or types of sale, of stock.

Dr: Cash	$470,000	
Patents	20,000	
Organization Expense	10,000	
Cr: Common Stock		$500,000

A point to notice here is that the dual nature of financial transactions does not necessarily mean that each debit entry is matched by a credit entry for the same amount. Rather, it means only that the sum of the debit entries for any given transaction will equal the sum of the credit entries for that transaction.

In the analysis just noted, the assumed debit to "Organization Expense" can be considered appropriate under the concept of expenses as debits and indirect reductions in owners' equity.

The debit might, however, be justified by considering the organization expense account as a type of asset in the sense that a company organized is worth more than a company not yet organized. Being organized is thus a resource (asset), the cost of which is organization expense.

Under common practice, the two concepts are in a sense combined. Organization expense, at the time incurred, is regarded as a deferred charge and is carried along and listed under that classification on the asset side of the balance sheet until such time as there is revenue against which to amortize it.

Purchases of Goods or Materials on Account

One of the most common financial transactions in business is the purchase on account of goods, materials, and parts which are later to be sold or used in manufacturing goods for sale.

Although it is the practice in many companies to record purchases in one or more accounts separately for statistical purposes, and to leave the main inventory accounts untouched between the beginning and end of an accounting period, each purchase does in fact add to the goods, materials, or parts on hand and thus adds to the assets of a business.

In keeping with this fact, we shall visualize purchases of goods, materials, or parts as being debited to one or more inventory accounts since, as we have noted, additions to assets are entered as debits to asset accounts.

If a purchase is paid for immediately in cash, a credit to the cash account is the balancing factor in the transaction. If a purchase is on account, however, as is true of most commercial purchases, the balancing credit is an increase in the liability account titled "Accounts Payable."

Thus the purchase of $50,000 worth of raw materials on account would be visualized in terms of transaction analysis as follows:

```
Dr: Raw Material           $50,000
     Cr: Accounts Payable              $50,000
```

Borrowing Money

Arrangements were made in connection with our new company to borrow money to help finance the purchase of a plant, using a mortgage on the plant as collateral. It is likely that the receipt of the loan, the signing of a mortgage note for it, the payment for the plant, and the passing of title on it would all take place in the same office almost simultaneously. Nonetheless, it is more orderly for discussion purposes here to visualize the proceedings in steps.

Thus the loan of $350,000 taken by itself would be an increase in an asset matched by an increase in a liability. In terms of transaction analysis, it would be visualized as follows:

Dr: Cash	$350,000	
Cr: Mortgage Note Payable		$350,000

Purchase of Plant and Equipment

Although machinery and equipment purchased probably would not be paid for immediately, and might indeed be paid for in installments, we shall assume for our purposes that the items of plant, machinery, and equipment were purchased for cash. These transactions would thus involve the exchange of one asset for another and would be visualized in debit and credit form in total as follows:

Dr: Plant and Equipment	$475,000	
Cr: Cash		$475,000

With this illustration of the purchase of plant and equipment, we have completed the financial transaction analysis in the formation of our company. We shall not continue with this particular example. Instead, we shall briefly examine the financial transaction analysis of common types of transactions for any manufacturing corporation once in operation.

Production of Goods in Accounting Terms

Costs involved in the production of goods are accounted for typically under three classifications: type of expense; area of responsibility; and product.

At the moment, we are concerned only with the effect of typical financial transactions on a company's major accounts, which in turn affect its financial statements. For this purpose, we are concerned with a. accounting for costs by type of expense and by products (to the extent of identifying costs in summary form with inventories); b. the cost of materials used; and c. the cost of goods manufactured.

Accounting for Raw Material Used

We have already noted the analysis of a transaction involving the purchase of raw material. The transfer of raw material into "Work-in-Process" may be visualized in accounting terms as a flow or transfer from one asset to another:

Dr: Work-in-Process
    Cr: Raw Material

A somewhat more complete record of the transfer is visualized with the following entry:

Dr: Raw Material Used
    Cr: Raw Material

Such an assumed entry allows for accumulating the material used during an accounting period in an expense account by itself.

At the close of the period, the total in the account, along with amounts from other expense accounts for production costs, is visualized as being transferred to the inventory account for work in process.

Direct Labor Costs

In many companies, wages are recorded only as paid, with a corresponding credit to "Cash," except at the close of the period when it is necessary to recognize wages that have been earned but not yet paid.

A somewhat more orderly process is to first recognize the expense that has taken place, together with the liability connected with it, and then later to record the elimination of this liability by the payment of cash. The analysis of such transactions is visualized as follows:

1. Dr: Wages Expense (or Direct Labor)
    Cr: Wages Accrued

2. Dr: Wages Accrued
    Cr: Cash

At the close of the period, the accumulated wages expense (or direct labor) would be transferred to "Work-in-Process," as just suggested for raw material used.

Indirect Manufacturing Expenses Other Than Depreciation

Very minor items of indirect manufacturing expenses are paid in cash, but most involve credits to some type of liability account at the time they are incurred.

Wages and salaries, supervision, and other types of indirect labor debited to appropriate expense accounts are balanced by credits to wages and salaries accrued, as in the case of direct labor.

An expense such as electricity is likely to be credited to a liability account titled "Accounts Payable–Other" to distinguish it from accounts payable for materials and components. Supplies as purchased are also likely to be credited to "Accounts Payable–Other" and debited to an inventory account before being issued for use in production.

A few expenses such as rent are paid in advance and balanced by credits to cash. With the passing of time, the expense is recognized as having taken place for a given item and a debit is made to an expense account. This is then balanced by a credit to the appropriate prepaid expense account.

Expenses for repairs and maintenance undertaken by an outside contractor are balanced by credits to "Accounts Payable–Other." If undertaken by an inside crew, some rather complicated cost accounting is involved with which we need not concern ourselves at the moment.

Indirect manufacturing expenses are identified first by type of expense, in order to have a record in the ledger of their amount for each given time period, and transferred at the close of the period to "Work-in-Process," as in the cases of raw material and direct labor costs.

These comments on indirect manufacturing expenses have been concerned with steps taken in actually recording these expenses. The same steps are however visualized in the analysis of financial transactions involving indirect manufacturing expenses. Much more will be discussed about indirect manufacturing expenses in later chapters dealing with costs and cost accounting.

Accounting for Depreciation

The depreciation of manufacturing plant, machinery, and equipment may be visualized as the conversion of these fixed assets into manufactured products. From a manufacturing viewpoint, these facilities were purchased for the production of goods. In time they will be worn out or obsolete, and in recognition of this their cost should be borne by the products produced by, with, or in them over their useful lives.

Depreciation, being an expense, is easily visualized as a debit under the concept noted earlier that expenses are debits. The credit to this expense account at the close of the period in order to transfer it to "Work-in-Process" can also be easily visualized as the conversion of fixed assets into manufactured products.

The credit side of the transaction at the time depreciation is debited is, however, a little more difficult to comprehend. Whether depreciation is looked upon as an expense or a conversion of fixed assets, it would seem logical that the "Plant, Machinery, and Equipment" account should be reduced by the amount of depreciation which has taken place, and that it should therefore be credited.

However, as we shall discuss in Chapter 10, it is a generally accepted practice in the United States to carry fixed assets in the accounts at their historical cost and to credit an account commonly titled "Accumulated Depreciation" for the contra entries to "Depreciation Expense." Thus the historical cost of the fixed assets, supportable by documentary evidence, is kept separate from the accumulated depreciation on these assets which has been established by the exercise of policy and judgment.

Another point about depreciation expense is that it does not arise to be accounted for as do most expenses. Therefore, depreciation expense requires special attention.

Business activities such as the purchase and sale of goods, the earning of salaries and wages, and the flow of goods through a plant involve actions by people which signal that an accounting must be made, and clerical precedures are established for doing so.

But depreciation and expenses such as those involving the amortization of prepaid expenses and deferred charges take place silently, which means that someone has to look out for them accordingly. The entries that we have visualized as accounting for such expenses are actually entered in the accounting records as "adjusting entries" at the close of the period after all of the action, or people-related, entries have been made.

Cost of Goods Completed

This transaction analysis is determined either by detailed cost accounting records or by establishing the ending physical inventory of work in process, placing a cost valuation on it, and subtracting this amount from the sum of the beginning inventory and the material, labor, and other costs charged to "Work-in-Process" for the period.

Whatever method is used to determine this figure, or whatever accounting steps are involved in connection with the computation, the amount computed can then be visualized as being debited to "Finished Goods" and credited to "Work-in-Process." Thus the cost of goods completed during an accounting period represents the transfer of goods from one asset (inventory) account to another.

Cost of Goods Sold

As with the cost of goods completed, the cost of goods sold during an accounting period can be established by detailed cost accounting records or by a process of deduction.

Whatever the approach, the figure once determined can be visualized as an expense to be charged with other expenses against the revenues for the period in arriving at the period's net income. In terms of debit and credit, the transaction can be visualized initially as a debit to "Cost of Goods Sold" and a credit to "Finished Goods." It can then be visualized that the cost of goods sold would later be closed out along with other expense and revenue accounts, directly or indirectly, to "Retained Earnings."

Sales Transactions

With each sale, there is an increase in a company's accounts receivable or cash, and with this increase in assets the company and indirectly its owners are that much better off. In order to have a record of revenues in the ledger, however, no ownership account is credited for sales as they take place. Instead, credits are entered in one or more sales accounts depending upon what classifications of sales are desired.

The totals of sales accounts are closed out at the end of the period in arriving at the net profit or loss to be entered in the ownership account "Retained Earnings." A sale is expressed in journal entry form as follows:

Dr: Accounts Receivable (or Cash)
    Cr: Sales

There should really be no difficulty in either visualizing how a sale should be accounted for or in accounting for a sale that has taken place. The problem in accounting for sales lies in determining when, in fact, a sale has taken place, as we noted in Chapter 3.

Selling, Administrative, and Other Expenses

Transaction analysis with respect to sales and the cost of goods sold covers factors determining a company's gross margin for any given period. There remain selling, administrative, and other expenses to be deducted, and possibly some nonoperating income to be added, in arriving at net income before taxes. Finally, income taxes must be taken into account in arriving at the net income for the period.

Given the description of a transaction involving any type of expense, and the amount of expense involved, there should really be no difficulty in visualizing how it should be accounted for, or in actually accounting for it by type of expense other than perhaps some question of its exact classification. The main problems of accounting for expenses, however, are not those of identifying costs by type of expense.

Rather, the problems are those of cost allocation such as: How much of a given amount of cost of a given type should be charged to the current accounting period and how much deferred to later periods? Also, how should a given cost be allocated among departments or cost centers? And, again, on what basis should a given cost for a given period of time be charged to the goods produced during that period?

Problems of cost allocation will be discussed in later chapters. For the present, then, let us be content to be able to express in journal entry form how a given type of expense would probably affect a company's accounts and in turn its financial statements.

Payments from Debtors and to Creditors

Payments by customers for amounts owed by them on account can easily be visualized as the exchange of one asset for another. "Cash" is debited as the asset increased, while the "Accounts Receivable" account is credited as the asset decreased.

In payments to creditors, in which cash is flowing out rather than in, there is a reduction (debit) in the liability "Accounts Payable" and a reduction (credit) in the asset "Cash."

Accounting for Bad Debts

The estimated loss on bad debts relative to the sales made during a period is charged as an expense to the period in which the sales take place. At the same time, an allowance is created against which such accounts as prove later to be uncollectible are written off.

The charging of the expense and creation of the allowance can be visualized as follows:

Dr: Estimated Loss on Bad Debts
    Cr: Allowance for Bad Debts

The writing off of accounts deemed to be uncollectible can be visualized as follows:

Dr: Allowance for Bad Debts
    Cr: Accounts Receivable

Accounting for the Disposal of Fixed Assets

When a fixed asset subject to depreciation is sold, or otherwise disposed of, its cost is removed from the "Fixed Asset" account. The "Cash" account is increased for the amount, if any, received on disposal. The depreciation accumulated on it is charged to "Accumulated Depreciation" account. And a loss or gain on the disposal is recorded.

As an illustration, let us assume that a machine costing $20,000 has been depreciated on a straight-line basis under an estimated useful life of ten years but at the end of eight years is sold for $5,000. The disposal would be analyzed in accounting terms as follows:

Dr: Cash $ 5,000
    Accumulated Depreciation   16,000
        Cr: Property, Plant, and Equipment $20,000
        Gain on Disposal of Fixed Assets   1,000

Declaration and Payment of Dividends

Let us close our discussion of transaction analysis on a happy note by analyzing the declaration and payment of a dividend.

At the time the directors of a corporation vote in favor of (declare) a dividend, it becomes a legal obligation of that corporation. In accounting terms, the declaration can be analyzed as follows for whatever amount is involved:

Dr: Retained Earnings
    Cr: Dividends Payable

Upon payment of the dividend, the liability is of course eliminated and cash is reduced by the amount involved:

Dr: Dividends Payable
    Cr: Cash

In Summary

There are differences of opinion as to how much the nonfinancial manager might increase his understanding of financial statements, and his ability to make effective use of accounting data, by gaining a thorough knowledge of accounting techniques and particularly of bookkeeping.

In the discussion, I have stated the opinion that it is not necessary for the nonfinancial manager to concern himself with the clerical aspects of bookkeeping. These have been expressed as the "mechanics" that involve the "opening" of a "set of books," the journalizing of actual transactions, the "posting" of journal entries to general and subsidiary ledgers, and the "adjusting" and "closing" of the "books of account." My intent has not been to belittle the importance of these activities, but only to state my belief that there are no compelling reasons for most nonfinancial managers to learn about them.

However, I believe that it is important for the nonfinancial manager who wishes to be able to interpret financial statements reasonably well, and to make the most effective use of accounting data furnished to him, to understand the major policy aspects of accounting which are based on principles, concepts, and conventions that have been evolved over centuries of practical experience. Likewise, I believe it is important for him to understand the critical areas in which accounting decisions are highly dependent on judgment, opinion, and plain common sense.

Accounting policy and practice are, however, carried out by the manner in which financial events are recorded in the accounts and are reflected in the financial statements drawn from the accounts. It seems to me, therefore, that a full understanding of an accounting policy or practice includes an understanding as to how accounts are affected by it.

Accordingly, I urged that the nonfinancial manager extend his study and understanding of accounting to the point of being able to visualize and express how any given financial event is likely to affect

the accounts. Thus he will not only be better able to understand financial statements and use accounting data more effectively, but he will
also be better able to discuss with others the financial implications of
events that have taken place or are proposed.

For the benefit of the reader whose curiosity may have been
aroused relative to the mechanics of bookkeeping, or who, indeed, may
wish to keep his own books of account, Appendix 1, "The Accounting
Cycle," is presented at the end of this book.

CHAPTER 8

The Balance Sheet: Current Assets and Current Liabilities

For some years now, companies have been urged to substitute the title "Statement of Financial Position" for the financial statement commonly known as the "Balance Sheet." Custom is difficult to overcome, however, and the title "Balance Sheet" is still in common use. We shall use this old title here, if for no better reason than because it is briefer.

In our discussion of the funds flow statement, the balance sheet was described as a tabulation in monetary terms of the resources of a given entity, as of a given date, matched by a tabulation of the origins of these resources. The point of tying the balance sheet to funds flow was to note that a balance sheet balances as the natural result of accounting for the two aspects of a company's flow of funds — namely, where they came from and where they went.

A balance sheet is often defined simply as a statement of the assets, liabilities, and owners' equity of an entity, as of a given date. Often, too, it is described as a statement of the assets of an entity and the claims against them, including the claims of its owners, as of a given date. Such definitions are usually accompanied by definitions of assets, liabilities, and owners' equity.

It is common practice to illustrate the nature of a balance sheet by use of an equation, such as Assets = Liabilities + Owners' Equity, or Assets − Liabilities = Owners' Equity.

In an earlier day, the committee on terminology of the American Institute of Certified Public Accountants objected to definitions which suggested that the balance sheet is prepared by simply tabulating assets and claims against them. The committee held that historically the balance sheet is a summary of balances developed in books of account kept by double-entry methods, whereas a mere tabulation of assets and claims against them may be prepared without any such system of record keeping. Thus the committee considered that "balance sheet" is a technical term related to an accounting system and defined this financial statement as: "A tabular statement or summary of balances (debit and credit) carried forward after an actual or constructive closing of books of account kept according to principles of accounting."[1]

While this definition is technically correct, it notes only the mechanics by which the statement is prepared and gives no indication of the roots on which it is based or the significance of what it portrays. Moreover, it paints a rather dull picture of a bookkeeping process and discourages any thought of perhaps visualizing in the balance sheet the resources of a dynamic and colorful enterprise, and how these resources came about. It is perhaps wise, however, not to attempt to see too much romance in financial statements, and it may be even wiser to discount whatever romance is seen.

In any event, it must be admitted that this definition does caution that the balance sheet is simply a summary of balances of financial events recorded in accordance with accounting conventions. And one can deduce from this that such a statement is not necessarily an indicator of either current values or future prospects.

On the foregoing point, the Institute of Chartered Accountants in England and Wales has stated: "The primary purpose of the annual accounts of a business is to present information to the proprietors, showing how their funds have been utilized and the profits derived from such use. It has long been accepted in accounting practice that a balance sheet prepared for this purpose is an historical record and not a statement of current worth."[2]

Records of Historical Cost

As resources are brought into an enterprise, they are recorded at what is commonly described as their historical cost. Again quoting from the statement by the Institute of Chartered Accountants in England and Wales: "An important feature of the historical cost basis of preparing annual accounts is that it reduces to a minimum the extent to which

---

[1]Accounting Terminology Bulletin No. 1 (New York: American Institute of Certified Public Accountants, 1968), paragraph 21.

[2]Recommendations on Accounting Principles, N15-1 and 2 (London: The Institute of Chartered Accountants in England and Wales, 1961).

the accounts can be affected by the personal opinions of those responsible for them."[3]

Thus what is recorded and reported to stockholders are the results of financial transactions which, at least with respect to resources acquired, can be supported by documentary evidence and verified by audit. Accounting on an historical cost basis does not, however, avoid the need for the exercise of judgment and opinion in many areas.

For example, although judgment or opinion may not be called for in establishing the cost of a machine that has been purchased, determining the probable economic life of such a machine, and the amount of the historical cost properly chargeable to each accounting period as depreciation expense, is quite another matter.

The Going Concern Assumption

One of the reasons for maintaining records on an historical cost basis lies in the assumption of a "going concern" of unlimited life. This assumes that resources will continue to be used for the purposes for which they were acquired, and liabilities will not have to be met before their maturity. Under these conditions, it is considered neither necessary nor desirable for a balance sheet to be a statement of current worth or liquidation value.

It is, however, common practice to depart from the historical cost basis on the grounds of conservatism, when this seems appropriate.

For example, in many companies, inventories are written down to their market value when that value, as of the date of the balance sheet, is below the cost of these goods or materials.

On the same grounds, and because of the problems of uncertainty, probable lack of objectivity, and possible manipulation connected with upward revision of "values," it is not an accepted practice in this country to write up inventories, or any other resources, to amounts which are above their cost. This is unacceptable practice whether these higher amounts might be current market values, historical costs adjusted for price-level changes, or appraisals by company officers or others.

There is, however, growing agitation for restating financial statements to reflect general price-level changes, as supplementary information to statements based on historical costs. This matter, as well as

---

[3] *Ibid.*

restatements to reflect upward changes in market value, will be discussed in Chapter 19 in connection with accounting for property, plant, and equipment.

Balance Sheet Examples

The comparative balance sheets presented in Exhibit 21 for the P. M. Stanton Company are typical of published balance sheets in format and account classifications. In the annual report from which these statements were taken, the assets were listed on a left-hand page, with the liabilities and capital listed on the opposite right-hand page.

By contrast, in Great Britain it is customary to list assets on the right side, while liabilities and capital items are listed on the left. There is no more significance to this difference, however, than the fact that our British friends drive their cars on the left side of the road while we drive ours on the right.

Similarly, it will be noticed that current assets and current liabilities are the first items shown in their respective sides of the balance sheet. And the order of presentation on both sides is from the most to the least current items.

In contrast, it is customary to list the least current items first in public utility balance sheets in the United States since property, plant and equipment, and the sources from which they were financed, are the most important items presented. This public utility balance sheet format is also the common balance sheet arrangement for all types of companies in Great Britain.

Here again, the difference in format between countries, or between companies, is not important. But it is important for ease of analysis that for the same company the items be presented from period to period consistently by appropriate groupings and logical order of liquidity.

Definition of Assets

The committee on terminology used the bookkeeping identification of the term "asset" as it did in defining the term "balance sheet." The committee stated:

> The word *asset* is not synonymous with or limited to property but includes also that part of any cost or expense incurred which is properly carried forward upon a closing of books at a given date. Consistently with the definition of *balance sheet* previously

EXHIBIT 21
P. M. Stanton's Comparative Balance Sheets

	Dec. 31, 1977	Dec. 31, 1976
Assets		
Current assets:		
Cash	$ 929,375	$ 930,250
Accounts receivable	1,067,737	765,162
Inventories at cost on the last-in, first-out basis	1,295,351	1,515,983
Prepaid assets	81,514	51,178
Total current assets	$3,373,977	$3,262,573
Property, plant, and equipment at cost less allowances for depreciation of $945,569 and $760,720	1,362,970	1,278,479
Investment in subsidiaries at cost	43,132	34,401
Deferred development expenses	80,069	116,878
	$4,860,148	$4,692,331
Liabilities		
Current liabilities:		
Bond sinking fund installment	$ —	$ 100,000
Accounts payable (trade)	332,200	153,220
Provision for pensions	163,500	177,300
Provision for federal income tax	417,300	226,675
Other accrued liabilities	246,800	224,974
Total current liabilities	$1,159,800	$ 882,169
Provision for deferred income tax	98,301	103,418
First Mortgage 6% Bonds due 1984 (note A)	—	800,000
Capital		
Common stock of $1 par value, 350,000 shares authorized, 295,371 and 268,022 shares issued and outstanding (notes B and C)	295,371	268,022
Paid-in surplus (note C)	2,398,339	2,152,198
Retained earnings, per accompanying statement	908,337	486,524
	$4,860,148	$4,692,331

Note A. On October 15, 1977, the Company retired the outstanding First Mortgage 6% Bonds by payment of $800,000 principal and $26,075 premium.

Note B. At December 31, 1977, options to purchase 1,447 shares at $10 per share (not less than 95% of the market price at the time of granting) were outstanding and exercisable. Options terminate in 1980 or when the employee leaves the Company. During the year, options for 14,104 shares were exercised and options for 1,092 shares lapsed.

Note C. During 1977, paid-in surplus was increased by $126,936 excess of option price over par value of 14,104 shares issued upon exercise of options and $119,205 excess of market value over par value of 13,245 shares issued as a stock dividend. There were no changes in paid-in surplus during 1976.

suggested, the term asset, as used in balance sheets, may be defined as follows:

Something represented by a debit balance that is or would be properly carried forward upon a closing of books of account according to the rules or principles of accounting (provided such debit balance is not in effect a negative balance applicable to a liability), on the basis that it represents either a property right or value acquired, or an expenditure made which has created a property right or is properly applicable to the future. Thus plant, accounts receivable, inventory, and a deferred charge are all assets in balance-sheet classification.[4]

This definition at least warns the reader that the word asset as used in a balance sheet has a technical meaning that is somewhat different from, or goes beyond, his probable concept of an asset as simply a quality or thing that is good for one to have.

This does not mean, however, that the reader must necessarily learn the bookkeeping process in order to have a reasonable understanding of the term asset as used in balance sheets. For many people it may be easier to understand and discuss what an asset is by noting examples of assets, and their characteristics, rather than by attempting to define the term.

Also, going back to our discussion of source and application of funds, the reader will recall that assets can be viewed as uses or applications of funds or as representing where the funds of the enterprise are lodged as of the date of the balance sheet.

Under the latter concept, for example, it is not unusual for the proprietor of a business to say, "My money is all tied up in . . ." and then proceed to name items such as accounts receivable, inventories, and plant and equipment, and the dollar amounts of each on hand. Even items such as prepaid expenses and deferred charges can be identified as uses of his funds for the benefit of the future.

Current Assets

The reader will note that some of the assets listed in Exhibit 21 are grouped under the title "Current Assets." These are items in which the flow of funds is one of continuous circulation or turnover in the short run. They consist of cash on hand and in banks subject to withdrawal

---

[4]Accounting Terminology Bulletin No. 1 (New York: American Institute of Certified Public Accountants, Inc., 1968), paragraph 26.

for current use and other assets which are expected to be realized in cash, or sold, converted, or consumed within one year.

In some other companies, such as those in which an aging process is involved, the conversion period for some items, e.g., inventories, is longer than one year, yet they will nonetheless be listed as current assets. Here, the view is that an item is a current asset if conversion will take place during the normal operating cycle of the given type of business.

In an earlier day, a major determinant as to whether an item was or was not a current asset was the estimated speed with which it could be liquidated in the event that the company got into financial difficulty. In more recent years, under the assumption that most balance sheets are prepared for "going concerns," the normal turnover period for a given type of item in the given industry is the major determinant of the currency of an asset, rather than a set one year time limit for conversion.

In many quarters, nonetheless, a period of conversion beyond one year is considered to be an exception to the general rule.

Assets current only up to a limited amount.   There are cases where some of the units of a given type of item may properly be shown as current assets while the remainder should not. For example, it is often sound policy to continue to produce a given item, e.g., sulphur, because of the extremely heavy start-up costs once the plant is shut down, even though inventories are already in excess of short-run sales forecasts.

Under these circumstances, only such quantity as is expected to be sold within the coming year or normal operating cycle should be listed as a current asset. Where this continued production policy is followed, it is, of course, the expectation that the quantity treated as noncurrent inventory will in time be reduced by sale, or by being shifted to the current-asset category, as the volume of demand for the item rises.

Another example along the same lines is that of cash or temporary investments where some portion is being held for the purchase of property, plant, or equipment in the near future, or for the retirement of long-term debt. Here, intent is the guide as to whether or not the given item is a current asset.

The point, again, is that current assets are assets which turn over with regularity in the normal short-run operating cycle of a business. Regardless of title, if the asset is not being used or is not available for this purpose, it is not a current asset.

The inclusion as current assets of items which do not meet this test would result in a grouping of nonhomogeneous items that would be an obstacle in interpreting a given balance sheet and would destroy its comparability with balance sheets of other companies and with earlier balance sheets of the same company.

Current Liabilities

On the other side of the balance sheet, short-term debts are grouped under the title of current liabilities. As might be expected from the definition of current assets, current liabilities are those debts existing as of the balance-sheet date which will fall due for payment within one year or within the normal operating cycle of the given type of business. Note that this is not an estimate of the total expenditures, or outward cash flow, for the coming period. It is simply a statement of short-term indebtedness, as of the balance-sheet date, arising from financial transactions that have already taken place.

There is usually no problem in identifying whether a given debt is, or is not, a current liability. One is generally well aware of one's debts and of when they fall due.

A minor problem arises when, for example, a heavy amount of long-term debt falls due within the coming year but is to be paid off by funds obtained from substituted long-term indebtedness. The existing long-term indebtedness to be refunded would not under these conditions be shown in the balance sheet as a current liability. There are two reasons for this. One, because long-term indebtedness is not an item related to the continual circulation of funds in the ordinary activities of the company. Two, because the intent here is simply to substitute one long-term debt for another, even though cash will flow in and out of the company in this connection sometime within a year.

The Financial Accounting Standards Board dealt with this matter in its Statement of Financial Accounting Standards No. 6, May 1975, "Classification of Short-Term Obligations Expected to Be Refinanced."

The board held that a short-term obligation should not be classified as a current liability if the given enterprise intends to refinance the obligation on a long-term basis. However, this intent must be supported by the ability to consummate the refinancing demonstrated either by:

1. Issuance of a long-term obligation, or equity securities, after the balance-sheet date but before the balance sheet itself is issued, or
2. A financing agreement entered into before the balance sheet is issued that clearly indicates that the enterprise can refinance the obligation on a long-term basis.

As with current assets, the inclusion in current liabilities of unusual items not connected with the continual circulation of funds in the ordinary activities of the company would make it more difficult to interpret the balance sheet and destroy the comparability of that financial statement.

Working Capital and Net Working Capital

We have noted that both current assets and current liabilities are shown in a balance sheet as current items because of their characteristic of short-run rotation or turnover and because they are identified with the short-run activities of the given business. On the one hand, in terms of source and application of funds as rotation takes place, increases in current assets are applications of funds while decreases are sources of funds. On the other hand, increases in current liabilities are sources of funds while decreases are applications of funds.

The balance sheet does not show the flowing of the funds just noted. Instead, it shows by major categories where the funds (financial resources) of the business are located as of the given date and the amount in each category; and also, where these funds came from, by major categories of sources, and the amount in each category.

Those funds which are subject to short-run rotation or turnover are shown in the balance sheet as current assets. Temporary sources of funds usually also subject to short-run rotation or turnover are shown as current liabilities.

Generally speaking, a considerable portion of the current assets of a business are provided by incurring current liabilities. Similarly, it is through the orderly liquidation of current assets that current liabilities are met when due. Thus each is dependent on the other.

Normally, for most companies, there is a happy meshing of rotating current assets and rotating current liabilities. In merchandising, for example, a company purchases goods, thereby increasing inventories and increasing accounts payable. Customers buy goods, thereby increasing the company's accounts receivable and reducing its inventories. Customers pay their debts, thereby increasing the company's cash and reducing its accounts receivable. The cash is then used to reduce accounts payable, and so on in a rhythmic pattern.

Hopefully in the process, the amounts received from customers, resulting from the prices charged and volume sold, will be sufficiently higher than the cost of the goods involved to provide an adequate gross margin to cover operating expenses and to leave a reasonable amount for income taxes and return to the owners of the business.

If for some reason the rotation of the current assets becomes out of phase with the required rotation of the current liabilities, there can be difficulty in meeting current debts as they mature. Thus prudent management requires that there be a comfortable margin of current assets above current liabilities, the rough rule of thumb being the maintenance of a 2 to 1 ratio.

Stated in another way, no more than one half of the investment in current assets should be financed by short-term debt. On a going-concern basis such a margin enables a smooth financing of current operations, including meeting current debts as they mature. It also provides desirable protection to short-term creditors in the event the company involved gets into serious financial difficulty and is forced into liquidation, thereby ceasing to be a going concern.

The amount of funds involved in the margin between current assets and current liabilities is known as *working capital* or *net working capital*. Those who use the term net working capital with reference to this margin apply the term working capital to the funds invested in current assets. The latter concept is in keeping with the common practice, when speaking about the working capital needs of a business, of referring to the total funds required for cash, accounts receivable, inventories, and other current assets. It is not simply the difference between current assets and current liabilities.

Those who use the term working capital with reference to the margin between current assets and current liabilities have in mind that this is the amount of a company's capital being used to finance day-by-day operations while the remainder is tied up in other assets such as plant and equipment.

Although it is not a matter of great importance, we shall for present discussion purposes use the term net working capital with reference to the difference between current assets and current liabilities since this figure is after all a net figure and since working capital means something different than this to many people.

Source of Net Working Capital

Although it is reasonably obvious and logical that current liabilities represent in total the source of the funds for a substantial portion of the current assets of a business, the balance sheet does not indicate specifically the source of the remainder, or net working capital.

Perhaps identification of this source is not important. If one believes that long-term debt, owners' capital, and retained earnings together provide a common pool or source of funds in which the ratio of debt and owners' equity presumably will be controlled relative to the risks of the particular business, it is therefore a matter of indifference as to exactly which part of the pool provided what use of funds.

If one wishes to connect sources and applications more closely, however, it is logical that long-term debt should be related to long-term investments such as those in property, plant, and equipment, and not to investments in current assets. One could argue that net working capital, although subject to turnover, is really a long-term investment which might well be financed by long-term debt. However, a counter argument could be that, in contrast to investments in property, plant, and equipment acquired through such debt, investments in working capital are not subject to depreciation and therefore to reimbursement by customers for depreciation, by means of which the debt might gradually be liquidated.

Thus, the investment in net working capital, although subject to fluctuations, is not simply a long-term investment. By and large, it is a permanent investment which should therefore be financed by owners' capital or retained earnings and not by any form of debt.

Of even greater importance, if net working capital is considered to be a margin of protection for short-term creditors in the event that a company gets into financial difficulty, it is hardly appropriate for it to be provided by borrowing from long-term creditors. In general, then, one could say that owners' capital and retained earnings should be the sources of net working capital.

Difficulties relative to net working capital.   Financial difficulties in the area of net working capital can arise with any major shifts in the volume or nature of operations. Accounts receivable and inventories are particularly subject to shifts in amount, character, and rate of turnover. Expansion and shifts to new products and new markets increase the investment in these two items and, temporarily at least, slow down their rotation rate.

In the meantime, increased indebtedness falls due with the same degree of regularity as previously. Some creditors may not be as enthusiastic as the company about expansion or shifts in the nature of its operations, and it may be difficult to get additional short-term loans or credit. In the meantime also, if profits drop the current liability for income taxes will not rotate to the previous extent and taxes on past profits will have to be paid without being replaced by the same amount of tax liability.

If shifts in the nature of operations or drops in volume are drastic enough to cause losses, there will be a drain on cash to cover expenses and no inward cash flow from profits. Under these conditions, however, loss carrybacks with respect to income taxes can provide some relief.

With shifts of the type just illustrated, the burden of adjustment falls heavily on a company and may, or may not, be cushioned by assistance from creditors. The problem can be particularly acute if agreements with bondholders, commercial banks, or other creditors require that the margin between current assets and current liabilities shall not be allowed to drop below a stated figure.

The fear of shifts that will slow down the conversion of current assets, require additional investments in such assets, or drain cash in order to cover expenses not reimbursed by revenues explains why many companies often appear to be carrying larger than necessary cash balances or temporary investments in government bonds and thus currently are not making the most effective use of their net working capital.

Current Assets: Cash

As a figure standing in the cash account, cash represents money on hand or on bank deposit subject to demand, i.e., in a checking account subject to immediate withdrawal. Bank deposits subject to restrictions on withdrawal are accounted for as investments and not as cash.

Minor problems arise in accounting for cash, such as the question as to when the amount of a check outstanding for some time might properly be added back to the cash account on the grounds that it appears unlikely to ever be cashed. Problems also are found in handling the small amounts of petty cash kept on hand in an office for such matters as travel advances and minor expenses. But such problems are not our concern here.

Temporary Investments

The intent with respect to temporary investments, e.g., government bonds, should determine whether they should be listed as current assets or shown among other assets in a balance sheet.

To be listed as current assets, investments should be readily convertible to cash for use in financing other current assets or in reducing current liabilities. Thus temporary investments that are to be converted to cash, and the cash used for longer-run purposes, should not be listed among current assets. To do so would distort the company's net working capital position.

Investments in the capital stock of subsidiaries, representing long-term investments, should not be listed as temporary investments, even though the stock might be readily marketable. It is the intent with respect to an investment, as well as its marketability, that should determine where it should be placed in the balance sheet.

Since convertibility is a major point with respect to temporary investments, they should be shown at no higher figure than their market value on the date of the balance sheet. Some analysts hold that such investments should always be shown at their market value on that date. But the common practice is to show them at the lower of their cost or market valuation on the grounds of conservatism.

In some companies, it is the practice to carry temporary investments at cost, unless their market value has dropped well below what might be considered as a temporary fluctuation. Although it is not accepted practice to write-up temporary investments, when their market value is significantly above their cost it is desirable to state this value as a footnote to the balance sheet. The reasoning here is that this is a matter of fact which could be of importance to some readers of the balance sheet.

Notes and Accounts Receivable

Generally speaking, the notes and accounts receivable shown in a published balance sheet represent amounts owed to the company by its customers, arising from sales of goods or services to them. These are known as *trade receivables*. Other types of receivables in significant amounts are shown separately as *accounts receivable, other,* or by separate specific classifications, in keeping with the accounting convention of making full disclosure of material facts.

Under a rule adopted in 1934 by the membership of the American Institute of Certified Public Accountants: "Notes or accounts receivable due from officers, employees, or affiliated companies must be shown separately and not included under a general heading such as notes receivable or accounts receivable."[5]

Under certain conditions, receivables connected with government contracts should be identified separately.[6]

---

[5]See Accounting Research Bulletin No. 43, Chapter 1, Section A, paragraph 5.

[6]*Ibid.*, Chapter 11, particularly Section A, paragraphs 5 and 6, and discussion in paragraphs 21 and 22.

On the grounds of providing more accurate information, notes receivable should be shown separately from accounts receivable when they are a significant portion of the receivables. The reason for this is that particularly in the case of notes connected with installment sales, the collection period is usually longer than for accounts receivable.

Notes receivable are the debts of customers or borrowers acknowledged by them in signed written statements (promissory notes) and in which they have agreed to pay certain sums of money under stated conditions.

Accounts receivable, sometimes referred to as debts on open account, are debts of customers or others to the given company in which no promissory notes are involved. Companies are careful, however, to file documentary evidence of the transactions by which these debts arise. The evidence may be in the form of purchase orders or sales slips signed by the customer, shipping documents and/or receipts for goods delivered or services provided, and copies of invoices by which the amounts involved were charged.

When notes receivable and accounts receivable are shown separately in a balance sheet, it is a matter of indifference as to which is listed first. Neither should be shown as a current asset to the extent that they are not likely to be collected within the year or within the company's normal operating cycle.

One might argue that notes receivable should be shown first as being more potentially liquid since they can be discounted (have money advanced on) readily at a bank if cash is needed. Nonetheless, since the accounts receivable are likely to be collected from customers in a shorter period on the average than the notes receivable, they are more liquid in terms of the normal operating cycle.

Also, accounts receivable should certainly be regarded as being more liquid than such notes receivable as have been obtained from customers who could not pay for their purchases on open account when payment was due.

There is a tendency to believe that having a note receivable from a customer is somehow better than having an account receivable from him. This may be true as far as the same customer is concerned. But surely, one would prefer to have an account receivable from an honest customer, capable and willing to meet his indebtedness on time, than to hold the note of a customer who is always delinquent in meeting his payments.

Receivables pledged for loans. The extent to which receivables have been pledged (hypothecated) as security for loans should be stated in explanatory notes accompanying the balance sheet itself. Such notes are considered to be an integral part of the balance sheet and a statement to this effect generally appears in a published balance sheet.

It is often said that the average stockholder pays no attention to such notes. Nonetheless, they should be included in a financial report as a matter of full disclosure of material facts and for the benefit of those who are concerned enough to read them.

Allowance for Bad Debts

Since, theoretically at least, creditors rely on the convertibility of accounts receivable when granting credit to a company, it is important that such receivables be shown in the balance sheet at their conversion value. Also, on the grounds of both conservatism and a proper matching of costs and revenues, an estimate of probable loss from bad debts should be charged against the sales of each period instead of waiting until individual accounts prove to be uncollectible to account for such losses.

These steps are accomplished by the use of an expense account for the estimated loss on bad debts coupled with an allowance for bad debts account, which is increased each period to the extent considered necessary and reduced as individual accounts are found to be uncollectible and are "written off" against it. Accounts receivable not deemed uncollectible are carried forward from period to period in the accounting records for their full amount of indebtedness.

The balance in the allowance for bad debts account at the end of a period is carried forward to the next period. The difference between it and the accounts receivable balance carried forward at the same time is the company's estimated conversion value of accounts receivable on that date.

To provide more complete information, the accounts receivable should be shown in the balance sheet at their gross amount and the allowance for bad debts shown as a visible subtraction from this figure. This is particularly important in situations where bad debt losses are a significant factor in the profitability of operations.

The gross accounts receivable figure is a fact, supportable by documentary evidence, whereas the amount of allowance for bad debts is a matter of judgment. Unless the two are shown separately, it is not possible to measure over time the quality of the judgment exercised.

Some companies go beyond this and present as supplementary information an analysis of accounts receivable according to age and the amount of allowance for debts related to each classification. Many companies, however, apparently in the interest of simplification of balance-sheet presentation, show only a net figure for accounts receivable and give no indication of the amount of their allowance for bad debts.

Estimating bad debt losses. There are two common methods by which companies arrive at the estimated bad debt losses to be reported in their financial statements. One involves a percentage of sales; the other, percentages of accounts receivable.

Under the first method, each period is charged for an estimated loss on bad debts, and a corresponding figure is entered in the allowance for bad debts account. The latter is computed by applying a percentage to the sales figure for the period, the percentage being based on experience. Where a company has not been in business long enough to have had much experience with bad debts, it must simply guess as to a reasonable percentage or rely on a figure supplied by some source such as its banker, public accountant, or trade association as representing a reasonable percentage for the given trade at that time.

Under the second method, accounts are totaled by groups, according to age as of the balance-sheet date, such as those on the books for one month or less, those that are one to two months old, and so on. In arriving at the amount of allowance for bad debts, a very small percentage is applied to the youngest group, a higher percentage to the next group, and so on, until at some point such as the group for one year the percentage used for that group and each group thereafter is 100%. The percentage used for each group is based on judgment, backed by experience, of the bad debt probability of that group.

After these group computations are made, they are added together to determine the total amount that should be in the allowance for bad debts account as of the given date. This amount is then compared with the amount actually in the account and an adjustment made. The purpose of all this is to bring the account to the desired amount and, at the same time, to charge operations for the amount of the adjustment as the estimated bad debt loss for the period.

In some companies, the first method (percentage of sales) is used in computing the estimated bad debt loss and in setting up the allowance for bad debts for monthly financial statements; the second method (percentages of accounts receivable) is used at the end of each six months or year. This assures that reports for the latter periods will reflect more accurately the current collection experience, as established by the size of each age group then on hand, than would be the case if they reflected simply the application of the long-run loss-percentage experience to the sales for the period.

Physical Inventories

The term *inventory* applies to 1. goods on hand available for sale which were produced or acquired for this purpose; 2. goods being produced for the purpose of sale; and 3. raw materials, manufactured parts, and supplies intended to be used in the regular course of operations for the production of goods or furnishing of services for sale.

At the close of a fiscal year, and more frequently if practicable, it is common practice for companies to take a physical count of all items of inventory. In many companies, a portion of the inventory is counted each month, including all items which reach a predetermined low or reorder point. In addition, it is common practice to maintain continuous inventory records (cards, tapes, or disks) which provide for each type of item inventoried the balance on hand at all times, the receipts, and the issues. Such records are adjusted when shown to be out of line with a physical count.

Inventory classifications. For internal information and control purposes, companies find it useful to maintain inventory in a number of account classifications such as by major items, by location, and by product line. These are supported in detail by the records noted in the previous paragraph and by cost accounting records for goods in the course of production.

For external reporting purposes, however, inventories are presented in only one or a few classifications. In Exhibit 21, for example, inventories are shown as only one figure, although for internal use the P. M. Stanton Company had accounts for raw material, goods in process, and finished goods by various divisions and for the company as a whole. It also had some 27 product-line classifications for finished goods and a variety of accounts for raw materials. Underlying these major accounts in the company's ledgers were thousands of perpetual inventory records by individual items stored within its computerized information system.

Although it was not necessary for the company to furnish its stockholders with the detail used for internal purposes, it could have been helpful had the inventories been broken down by the three main components: raw material, goods in process, and finished goods. For example, inventories were reduced by some $220,000 during 1977, a year in which sales increased by nearly $1,200,000. Further knowledge with respect to the decrease in inventory could be useful information relative to prospects for the coming year.

It would be one thing, for instance, if the reduction had been largely in finished goods built up from surplus production in previous years and if inventories of raw material and goods in process were large enough, or were being built up, to support an expected continuation of high demand.

It would be quite another matter if, in order to meet sales demands in 1977, inventories across the board had been drained and no provision had been made to expand production to bring them back up to satisfactory levels or to meet an expected continuation of high demand.

Valuation of inventories at cost.   Earlier in this chapter, we noted that resources as acquired by a company are entered in its accounts at historical cost. On the assumption that the company will continue to exist for an indefinite period and that its resources will therefore be used for the purposes for which they were acquired, it is normally appropriate to continue to carry them in the accounts at historical cost and to present them in the balance sheets on this basis. On these grounds, many companies account for inventories, and present them in balance sheets, consistently from period to period at cost.

They believe valuation at cost is also appropriate with respect to the effect of inventory valuation on the income reported in an income statement, by enabling them to properly match costs and revenues with goods or services sold. Inventories valued at cost are carried forward at that value to the accounting period during which they are sold and, in this way, their cost is matched against the revenue received for them.

However, as we also noted earlier and shall examine later, on the grounds of conservatism with respect to both balance-sheet presentation and income determination, many companies depart from their normal practice of carrying and reporting inventories at cost, by writing them down to their market value when that value as of the date of the balance sheet is below their cost.

Alternative assumptions for the flow of materials.   In the valuation of inventories at cost, a company must decide the order in which it is to be assumed for costing purposes that materials move through the plant in a manufacturing business and the order in which goods are sold in both manufacturing and merchandising establishments. In particular, a company must decide whether to:

1. Identify materials and goods by specific lots related to specific invoices or cost records.
2. Assume that purchases or goods produced of the same type and grade have been mixed in storage and drawn on as a mixture.

3. Assume that materials or goods have been withdrawn from storage in the order in which they were purchased or produced (first-in, first-out), and therefore that the inventory remaining consists of materials or goods most recently purchased or produced.

4. Assume that the materials or goods withdrawn from storage represent the most recent acquisitions (last-in, first-out), and therefore that the inventory remaining has come from previous acquisitions.

It is not necessary under assumptions 2, 3, or 4 that the materials or goods shall actually move in the order assumed. These are costing concepts and not monetary identifications of physical movement. Normally, as a matter of good housekeeping, and avoidance of possible deterioration, the oldest units on hand of any given item will be used first regardless of cost accounting procedure.

Under the four alternative assumptions with respect to the flow of materials and goods, the valuation of inventories at cost would be as follows:

Under 1, materials or goods on hand would be identified with the specific invoices or cost sheets applicable to them.

Under 2, materials or goods on hand would be valued at their weighted average cost.

Under 3, materials or goods on hand would be identified with the most recent invoices or cost records for the quantities involved.

Under 4, to the extent that quantities on hand could in effect be assumed to have remained on hand since the time this method was adopted, the costs as of the time of adoption would apply. Increments to this quantity over the years would be priced at cost as of the time of acquisition. Decrements would be assumed to have come from the most recent increments.

In the United States, as far as income taxes and generally accepted accounting principles are concerned, a business enterprise is free to adopt any of the foregoing assumptions to all or any part of its inventory. The assumption adopted wth respect to each part of the inventory should be stated in the balance sheet or in the explanatory notes connected with that financial statement. In Exhibit 21, for example, the P. M. Stanton Company stated in its balance sheet that inventories were ". . . at cost on the last-in, first-out basis."

Consistency in practice is highly desirable for the sake of comparability of reported data. Therefore, changes in these assumptions from year to year should be avoided. If, however, a time comes when it appears highly desirable to change an assumption, as a change to be maintained and not simply as a change for the current period, it should be made and accompanied by a footnote to the balance sheet calling attention to the change and the reasons for it.

Types of cost to be taken into account.   The valuation of inventories at cost involves many problems of cost allocation and of cost identification with specific goods. In particular, such valuation involves judgment in determining in the light of individual circumstances the most suitable accounting treatment of a wide variety of costs. For maximum usefulness, each enterprise should be free to develop the details of its cost accounting to meet the needs of its management. At the same time, it should be expected to report its costs in broad categories in line with general accounting conventions and customs and procedures common to the given trade or industry.

The clearest inventory costs to be identified are those which appear on invoices for materials, goods, and supplies purchased, including adjustments for returns, allowances, and discounts.

To the extent practicable, other costs associated with the acquisition of materials, goods, and supplies, e.g., inward freight and delivery costs, should be charged to items purchased and included as part of the valuation of inventories at cost.

Some costs of this type, however, cannot be identified with materials or goods except by time-consuming and expensive clerical effort. Therefore, as a practical matter, these costs should be charged as expenses of the accounting period in which they are incurred and not included in the valuation of inventories at cost.

In a trading or merchandising enterprise, the valuation of inventories at cost should include only the costs that are directly connected with the goods acquired such as all costs on purchase invoices and transportation costs. Those costs involved in purchasing, receiving, and storing the goods, as well as selling and administrative expenses, should be charged as expenses of the accounting period in which they are incurred.

From a balance-sheet viewpoint, the costs not directly connected with goods acquired add nothing to their value or to the amount that might be recovered on them in a forced liquidation. Moreover, in the short run, most of those costs are not affected by fluctuations in the size of inventories, being more closely related to periods and the passing of time than with goods. They are therefore more properly treated as period costs than as costs which should be borne, in part at least, by inventories.

In a manufacturing business, the cost of raw materials, purchased parts, and supplies on hand at the close of a period involves only acquisition costs as noted for trading and merchandising enterprises.

The cost of materials in inventories of work in process and finished goods is established from cost accounting records and is dependent on the assumption adopted with respect to the flow of materials as described in the previous section.

In addition to the material element, the cost of work in process and finished goods includes direct labor and burden (manufacturing overhead). The latter covers items such as factory supervision, indirect labor, insurance, depreciation on plant, machinery and equipment, repairs, and maintenance. The application of labor and manufacturing overhead costs to products is dependent on the methods of wage payment for the specific enterprise, the nature of its production process, and the system of cost accounting in use. Judgment is required in determining the adequacy of the procedures of such a system in each situation.

Judgment is also involved in deciding the extent to which costs such as those arising from unusual operating conditions, excessive spoilage, or idle plant should be charged to the period and not included in the cost valuation of work in process and finished goods inventories.

As in the case of trading or merchandising companies, the selling and administrative expenses of a manufacturing enterprise should be excluded from inventory costs except for such portion of administrative expenses as may be identified with production activities.

Valuation of inventories at market.   When materials or goods have deteriorated, or have become damaged or obsolete, their valuation at cost is no longer appropriate. This assumes that the price they would bring on disposal is less than their cost, since the purpose for which they were purchased or made will not be carried out as intended. They should therefore be priced at their market value on the date of the balance sheet. Market value pricing is important for two reasons. One, for the sake of balance sheet conservatism. The other, so that the loss involved can be charged to the period in which the deterioration, damage, or obsolescence has taken place and not deferred to the period having the task of disposal.

We have already noted that on the grounds of conservative balance-sheet presentation and income determination many companies will write down their inventories of materials or goods which have not deteriorated or become damaged or obsolete to market when their market value is lower than their cost. Thus their inventories are valued at the lower of cost or market.

We should add that if consistent valuation at cost is the practice, the market value, when significantly lower than cost, should be stated as a footnote to the balance sheet in keeping with the convention of making full disclosure of important facts.

While there are a few situations, e.g., gold mining, where inventories are carried at market values above costs, the overwhelming majority of business enterprises do not follow such a practice. To do so could result in the anticipation of income which may never, in fact, be realized.

Here again, the main concept is one of a going concern engaged in the orderly conduct of its operations and not that of a concern about to go out of business. Income, under this concept, arises from a financial transaction with a party external to the business, commonly a sale, and not from simply holding or making for stock some materials or goods.

It is true that in some companies, in addition to those engaged in such activities as gold mining, parts of the inventory are carried at their market values because of a joint-cost situation in which it is difficult to allocate costs on a rational basis. Generally speaking, however, this is, in fact, a cost-allocation process under which some of the items produced jointly are given market values which are subtracted from the joint costs and the balance is charged to one or more products remaining. Thus, in total, no more than cost is involved.

Of course, if products that were given market values remain on hand while those charged with the residual costs are sold, there could be an anticipation of profit. Certainly, there would be one if it were found later that the items retained at market values could only be sold at a loss.

Prepaid Expenses

In the normal course of operations, payments are made in advance for a number of expenses which are to benefit, or at least are chargeable to, later accounting periods. The prepayment of rent, insurance premiums, and interest are such items, and they are accounted for as prepaid expenses at the time of payment.

When the proper time comes thereafter, charges are made to operations for items that had been prepaid, and the prepaid expense account is reduced accordingly. As of the balance-sheet date, the amount standing in the account is listed in the balance sheet as a current asset. In Exhibit 21, such an item was listed by P. M. Stanton under the title "Prepaid assets."

Prepaid expenses are an asset in the sense that they save the enterprise from having to spend the money involved at a later date. Granted that if the enterprise were forced into liquidation the payments made and accounted for as prepaid expenses might not be fully recovered. But, here again, most balance sheets are prepared on a going-concern basis. Thus the assumption is that the enterprise will be in regular operation during the periods in the future for which the expenses have been prepaid.

Current Liabilities: Examples

We have noted that current liabilities are those debts existing as of the balance-sheet date which fall due for payment within one year, or within the normal operating cycle of the given type of business. We noted further that current liabilities are major sources of the funds invested in current assets, and that, in turn, the liquidation of current assets enables the payment of current liabilities as they fall due.

These relationships indicated the importance of maintaining an adequate ratio of current assets to current liabilities to assure that the rotation of funds invested in current assets will be sufficiently timely and adequate in amount to meet current liabilities as they fall due. To achieve this, it is necessary that adequate net working capital be provided by stockholders' capital or retained earnings.

Examples of current liabilities are to be found in the balance sheets of the P. M. Stanton Company as presented in Exhibit 21.

It will be noted that P. M. Stanton's current liabilities in 1976 included the planned payment of a bond sinking fund installment of $100,000. This represented, essentially, a portion of the company's long-term debt which would become payable within six months to one year, in accordance with the indenture of the First Mortgage Bonds then outstanding. This was properly recognized as a current liability since it was not to be replaced by any other form of long-term debt and would have to be met within the company's normal operating cycle from the liquidation of current assets.

In line with common practice, accounts payable to the trade were kept separate by P. M. Stanton from other types of accounts payable.

The "trade" in this instance meant those who supplied the company with raw materials, manufactured parts, and supplies. In a merchandising business, it would represent those who had supplied the goods the company had for sale, or had sold. This separation from other types of accounts payable is of some importance to trade creditors and others who might become trade creditors, in seeing to what extent the company's inventories have been financed by this means and how promptly, on the average, it is paying off these debts.

In many companies, current liabilities would include notes payable, representing seasonal indebtedness to commercial banks and others for loans to help finance inventories and accounts receivable.

There are many other types of payables such as accrued wages, Social Security taxes payable, and employee income taxes withheld, which in P. M. Stanton's case were lumped in the balance sheet under the title "Other Accrued Liabilities," although, of course, in the company's records a separate account was kept for each type of liability.

The provision for pensions represented amounts computed in accordance with the company's pension plan, based on wages and salaries earned, which within the current time period would be paid into a pension fund administered outside of the company.

The provision for federal income taxes arises from the company's estimates of the amount of taxes it owes based on its computed earnings as recorded in its accounts and reported in its income statements. Although the provision for federal income taxes does provide funds, in the sense that "tax money" not payable immediately is available for use, the amount is subject to marked fluctuations. Thus it is unreliable as a steady source of funds in situations where operations, or the demand for a company's products or services, are subject to rapid and substantial shifts.

At the close of World War II, for example, many companies that had been producing goods for the armed forces found themselves with serious working capital problems. Their government contracts were cancelled, and there were long delays in getting reimbursement for funds already expended on them. Heavy investments had to be made to build up inventories of non-war products without any sales revenue to assist in the process. In the meantime the liability for income taxes fell due for payment while, temporarily, no taxable income was available which would provide either an offsetting tax liability or a cash flow with which to make payment.

CHAPTER 9

The Balance Sheet: Long-Term Investments

Many companies make long-term investments in other companies for the purpose of earning revenue, directly or indirectly, whether or not such investments give them control of the operations of the companies in which they have invested. Generally, such investments involve the purchase of common stock. However, they may also be in the form of purchases of preferred stock or bonds, or of advances or loans, and even of investments in property, plant, or equipment which are not related to the principal business of the company.

To simplify our discussion, we shall deal only with long-term investments in the form of common stock in companies that are expected to continue in operation as separate legal entities. In a later chapter, we shall examine business combinations in which the assets and liabilities of two or more companies are merged. But, at the moment, we are dealing with long-term investments, which will be accounted for as such and appear in the balance sheet under this title or perhaps as investments in subsidiaries.

Long-term investments are commonly listed in the investor's balance sheet as a single item between current assets and fixed assets. In the balance sheet of a British company, these investments are usually listed as one of the fixed assets.

Recording Common Stock Investments

Early in the preceding chapter, we noted that resources brought into a business are recorded at historical cost, and this is the practice with long-term investments. Thus when common stocks are purchased as long-term investments, they are entered in the accounts at their cost, including brokerage.

If the stocks acquired are paid for in cash, there is no problem in establishing what they cost. Difficult problems may be faced in establishing this amount, however, if payment is in the form of shares of the investor's common stock or other securities or in the form of other types of property.

Here, it is necessary to establish the cost by deciding, on the basis of available data, which is the fairest figure among: 1. the fair value of the stock acquired; 2. the fair value of the net assets underlying the stock acquired; or 3. the fair value of the stock or other property given in exchange for the stock acquired.

In essence, it is necessary under these conditions to establish the cost of the investment by determining, as being most appropriate, either the value of what was received or the value of what was given.

The Cost Method

Holdings of common stock in companies in which the investor has no significant influence over operating and financial policies are usually carried continually in the accounts of the investor at their original cost. The exception is where continued losses of the investee, or other evidence, indicate that there has been a permanent drop in the value of the holdings. In this case, judgment calls for writing down the investment accordingly.

Other than such possible write-downs, the investment account is not affected by whatever profit or loss might be experienced each period by the investee. The investor accounts for income on the investment only upon the receipt of dividends on the stock held. Any such dividends received by the investor in excess of its share of the earnings of the investee following the date of the investment are accounted for as a reduction in the investment. The reason is that since they have not been earned by the investor, they represent a return of part of the investment rather than a return on it.

The procedure of accounting for long-term investments at historical cost is known, naturally enough, as the cost method.

The Equity Method

In certain cases, the investor does have significant direct or indirect influence over the affairs of the investee. A particular example of this situation is where the company is identified as being a subsidiary of the controlling or parent company. In this circumstance, it is not adequate accounting simply to carry the investment in the investor's records at historical cost and to record income on the investment only as dividends are received.

To do so is to account for this important part of a business on a cash basis, while all other major aspects are being accounted for on the accrual basis. The investment amount shown each period in the investor's balance sheet at historical cost does not reflect changes that have taken place in the resources underlying the investment, except where losses have stimulated a write-down of the investment.

Moreover, recording income on the investment only as dividends are received does not reflect in the investor's income statement the underlying expenses and revenues as they take place. And it departs from the usual goal of having that statement present a proper matching of costs and revenues each accounting period.

On the grounds just stated, the Accounting Principles Board concluded that investments in common stock of unconsolidated foreign and domestic subsidiaries should be accounted for by the equity method in consolidated financial statements, assuming that the holdings treated as investments have been properly excluded from consolidation.[1] We shall examine consolidation briefly in a moment. But, at present, we are focusing only on holdings which are appropriately accounted for as investments.

The Accounting Principles Board also concluded:

> ... that parent companies should account for investments in the common stock of subsidiaries by the equity method in parent-company financial statements prepared for issuance to stockholders as the financial statements of the primary reporting entity.[2]
> ... that the equity method best enables investors in corporate joint ventures to reflect the underlying nature of their investment in those ventures.[3]
> ... that the equity method of accounting for an investment in common stock should also be followed by an investor whose investment in voting stock gives it the ability to exercise significant influence over operating and financial policies of an investee even though the investor holds 50% or less of the voting stock.[4]

---

[1]APB Opinion No. 18, *The Equity Method of Accounting for Investments in Common Stock* (New York: Accounting Principles Board, American Institute of Certified Public Accountants, March 1971), paragraph 14.

[2]*Ibid.*, paragraph 14.

[3]*Ibid.*, paragraph 16.

[4]*Ibid.*, paragraph 17.

Determining whether or not an investor has a significant influence over the operating and financial policies of the investee in deciding what method of accounting to apply to an investment is said to be a matter of judgment. But, surely, this should be no great problem for one who knows the details of the given situation and is operating in good faith.

If there is any question, it would be best to assume that the degree of influence is significant, since this view calls for the presentation in financial statements of more timely information on the investment than would otherwise be the case.

It is generally recognized that an investor can, in one way or another, exercise a significant influence over the operating and financial policies of an investee even though holding less than a majority of the investee's outstanding common stock. It is also generally recognized that the degree of influence exercised is not necessarily measured by the percentage of stock held.

The Accounting Principles Board accepted these views, but also noted:

> In order to achieve a reasonable degree of uniformity in application, the Board concludes that an investment (direct or indirect) of 20% or more of the voting stock of an investee should lead to a presumption that in the absence of evidence to the contrary an investor has the ability to exercise significant influence over an investee. Conversely, an investment of less than 20% of the voting stock of the investee should lead to a presumption that an investor does not have the ability to exercise significant influence unless such ability can be demonstrated.[5]

The equity method defined.   Under this method of accounting for long-term investments in common stock, the investment is first entered in the investor's accounts at its cost to the investor, including brokerage, in the same way as noted earlier for long-term investments that are carried continually at historical cost, i.e., the cost method.

Thereafter, however, accounting under the equity method is quite different. The major difference is that the investment account, or a subdivision of it, is either increased each period for the investor's share of the investee's realized net income, or decreased for its share of a loss.

At the same time, the amount of this income or loss is recorded in the investor's income accounts and later is shown as a separate item in

---

[5] *Ibid.*, paragraph 17.

its income statement. In arriving at the amount of the net income, or loss, intercompany gains or losses are eliminated, as in preparing consolidated statements which we shall turn to shortly.

In contrast, the reader will recall that under the cost method income on the investment is recognized only as dividends are received on the stock held. Under the equity method, income or loss on the investment is accounted for as described in the previous paragraph, while dividends received on the stock are simply accounted for as reductions in the investment.

Thus, under the equity method, the balance in the investment account, and its subdivisions if any, at the close of an accounting period represents the ownership claim (equity) on that date of the investor in the investee. In other words, the balance in the investment account represents the unamortized cost of the investment plus the investor's claim for its share of earnings realized and retained by the investee since the date of the investment. In addition, it includes any unpaid balance of advances or loans made by the investor to the investee.

The amount of this equity is equal to the amount of net assets underlying the investment, as would be presented in a consolidated balance sheet if the assets and liabilities of the investee had been consolidated with those of the investor. The equity is likely to be larger than the amount of net assets underlying the investment of the investee alone.

If losses were experienced by the investee after the date of the acquisition, the investment balance would of course have been reduced by the investor's share of them. If losses were extreme, the stage might eventually be reached where the investor's portion of them would have entirely eaten up the amount of its original investment.

However, the investor would not be likely to wait for such a stage. And sometime before this could happen the investment itself would have been abandoned, let alone the equity method of accounting for it.

The major point to understand about the equity method is that the investor's share of the earnings or losses of the investee are accounted for as income or loss by the investor each period as they take place. Under the cost method, income on the investment is recognized by the investor only as dividends are received, and losses are recognized only when it is judged that they are likely to be permanent and a write-down of the investment is therefore in order.

For the benefit of the reader who wishes to study the equity method of accounting for investments at somewhat greater depth, we shall now examine some additional points with respect to it.

Excess Investment Cost

Under the equity method, the cost of an investment in common stock, as entered in the records of the investor at the time of acquisition, is likely to be greater than the values at which the *net assets* underlying it are being carried in the accounts of the investee on that date. For our purposes, we shall use the term *excess investment cost* for this higher amount.

A higher amount is likely to have been paid either because the replacement cost, or because the market value, of the property, plant, and equipment underlying the stock acquired was higher than the historical cost at which these items had been recorded in the accounts of the investee at the time of their purchase. Thus the cause of some of the excess investment cost is likely to be inflation or a rise in market value or both.

Also, along with having paid a higher amount because of the cost or market increase in the tangible assets underlying the investment, the investor is likely to have paid something to cover the underlying intangible asset known as goodwill, an asset which would not have been recorded in the accounts of the investee.

That part of the excess investment cost applicable to underlying *tangible assets,* which are subject to loss of useful life through depreciation, will lose its value as time passes. Such losses will not, however, be accounted for as expenses or losses in the investee's accounts, since the excess would not have been recorded in them. The earnings computed each period by the investee will not therefore take any depreciation of this excess into account.

When the investor records each period its share of the investee's earnings, it must make an adjustment for the estimated amount of depreciation on its excess investment cost, since as time passes this excess will be lost through the depreciation of the tangible assets underlying it. The adjustment affects both the investment account and the account for income on the investment.

An illustrative example.   Let us assume that a company (the investor) has paid $20,000,000 for stock in a company (the investee) over which it has sufficient control as to be required to account for its investment under the equity method. Let us assume further for simplification that all of the assets underlying this investment are tangible assets subject to depreciation, and that at the time of the investment their book value at historical cost in the records of the investee was $18,000,000. The investment which would have been recorded by the investor at $20,000,000 thus contained an excess investment cost of $2,000,000.

If the average life of the underlying assets was expected to be 20 years, the investee would charge off $900,000 each year for depreciation on this $18,000,000 portion of its assets, assuming straight-line depreciation. If its operations were at least breaking even, it would recover this $900,000 each year from customers and reinvest it in the business. The investor must go beyond this, however, and recognize in its accounting the additional depreciation of $100,000 each year on the $2,000,000 of excess investment cost.

To further our example, let us assume that for the first year after the investment was made the investor's share of the earnings recorded in the books of the investee was $3,000,000, after allowing for all costs including $900,000 of depreciation. The investor would then recognize these earnings in its books:

Investment in Company X (Investor's claim on investee's retained earnings since the date of the investment)	$3,000,000	
Income on investments (The portion of the investee's earnings reported by the investor as income)		$3,000,000

The investor would next, however, make an adjusting entry to recognize the depreciation that had taken place on the excess investment cost as follows:

Income on investments (The portion of the investee's earnings reported by the investor as income)	$100,000	
Investment in Company X (A credit to the original investment)		$100,000

By use of the words in parentheses above, I wish to distinguish within the investment account the original investment from the investor's claim on retained earnings since the date of the investment; also, to make a distinction between the amount of the investor's computed earnings the investor can claim from the investee and the amount it would report as income.

In our example, the balance in the investment account would contain two elements: the investor's claim on earnings of the subsidiary since the date of the investment and not yet received as dividends; and the amount of the original investment less the amount of excess investment cost that had been written off as depreciation.

After 20 years in the present case, the "excess" would have been written off. And the investment, other than the amount claimed for retained earnings, would be at $18,000,000, thus matching the book value of the assets underlying it at the time the investment was made.

If both the original investment and claims to earnings after the investment date were recorded in a single investment account, that account would have had the following entries:

Original investment	$20,000,000
Add: Investor's claim on earnings as	
recorded by investee	3,000,000
	$23,000,000
Less: Amortization of excess investment cost	100,000
Balance in investment account	$22,900,000

The $22,900,000 figure would be reported in the investor's balance sheet as the amount of the investment as of the end of the period. If dividends had been received from the investee during the period, they would have been subtracted before arriving at the balance to be reported.

The $22,900,000 figure could be interpreted as representing $20,000,000 of original investment plus a $2,900,000 claim on earnings retained by the investee. This view could be supported on the grounds that the latter figure is the amount which the investee has reported as income on this investment, and also that it is desirable to maintain the original investment cost of $20,000,000 in the account.

However, since the reported income of $2,900,000 was brought down from $3,000,000 as a result of writing off the excess investment cost by $100,000, it is more logical to consider that the remaining amount of the original investment is now $19,900,000. Moreover, the legal claim of the investor on the retained earnings of the investee is, in fact, $3,000,000. Thus the $22,900,000 would more logically be regarded as representing $19,900,000 of remaining original investment cost plus a legal claim for $3,000,000 of the investee's retained earnings.

This view is further supported by noting that if the investee were to pay dividends equal to the amount of its retained earnings the investor would receive $3,000,000, not $2,900,000. Of this, $2,900,000 would be the receipt in cash for what it had already reported as income on the investment, while $100,000 would be the recovery in cash for what it had already recognized as a reduction in the figure for its original investment.

Amortization of excess paid for goodwill. To the extent that the excess investment cost cannot be related to specific tangible or intangi-

amount represented by them in the investments figure appearing in the parent company balance sheet.

Similarly, the consolidated income statement would include the revenues and expenses of the subsidiaries consolidated, in place of the parent company's share of the net income of such subsidiaries that would appear as a single figure in the parent company's income statement. As a minor point, provision must also be made in the consolidated income statement for any minority stockholders' share of the net income or loss of the subsidiaries consolidated.

Thus, although the details of balance-sheet presentation differ between the parent company's treatment of investments in subsidiaries on the equity basis and the substitution under consolidation of the subsidiaries' assets and liabilities underlying those investments, the total (or net) amount involved is the same.

Similarly, the parent company's share of the net income (or loss) of subsidiaries is the same amount in the parent company income statement under the equity method as in the consolidated income statement, although the presentation is different.

Need for uniformity. If the financial statements of two completely independent companies that have had no dealings of any kind between them were to be combined, the only problems in the consolidation would be those caused by whatever lack of homogeneity there might be in the nature of the items to be combined, in the account classifications applied to those items, and in the methods of accounting for them.

Problems of these types can also be met in the preparation of consolidated financial statements for a parent and its subsidiaries. To avoid them, it is necessary for the consolidating companies to maintain uniformity to the extent practicable in accounting policy and practice, including uniform accounts for major types of assets, liabilities, revenues, and expenses.

As long as these needs are met, each operating unit can then proceed to account for its financial activities and position in such ways, and in as much detail, as it believes necessary or desirable for internal management purposes.

Adjustment for intercompany relationships. A parent company and its subsidiaries are obviously not completely independent companies. Accordingly, the preparation of consolidated financial statements for a parent and its subsidiaries also involves problems connected with the ownership of one by the other.

When the financial statements of a parent company and its subsidiaries are in effect combined to form consolidated financial statements, adjustments must be made with respect to ownership equities, intercompany transactions, and the assets, liabilities, and net worth affected by such transactions. These adjustments are made only on the worksheets used in consolidating the data and not in the actual accounts of either the parent company or its subsidiaries.

Without going into all the details of consolidation, the process may be most easily visualized by starting with a picture in mind of a parent company balance sheet in which the investment in subsidiaries is listed among the assets as a separate single figure. To simplify the discussion, we shall assume that the subsidiaries included in this figure are all to be consolidated in the financial statements of parent and subsidiaries, and that all have been accounted for in the parent company records under the equity method.

Thus, as described earlier under the equity method, at the close of each accounting period the Investment in Subsidiaries account in the parent company, as reported in its balance sheet, represents the unamortized cost of the investments, plus the parent company share of the undistributed earnings of the subsidiaries since the investments were made and any outstanding advances or loans made by the parent company to the subsidiaries. (Any outstanding advances or loans made by the subsidiaries to the parent company would of course be deducted.)

Adjustment of the investment in subsidiaries. The major difference between the consolidated balance sheet and the balance sheet of the parent company is that in the former the subsidiaries' assets and liabilities are substituted for the investment in the subsidiaries' figure of the parent company's balance sheet. Where the parent company does not own 100% of the common stock of its subsidiaries, the total of the subsidiaries' assets and liabilities are nonetheless brought into the consolidated balance sheet.

The reason for this consolidation is that the parent company is attempting to show the combined resources and liabilities of parent and subsidiaries as a single accounting entity; the ownership interest of the minority stockholders is shown in the balance sheet as the balancing factor.

Earlier, in discussing accounting for investments in the common stock of subsidiaries by the equity method, we noted that the cost of such investments is likely to be greater than the value at which the parent company's share of the underlying net assets are being carried in the accounts of the investee on the date of the investment.

Similarly, in consolidation, the net amount of the subsidiaries' assets and liabilities brought into a consolidated balance sheet is likely to be less than the investment cost in the parent company's balance sheet for which they are being substituted. (To avoid having to keep making allowances for the minority interest, we shall assume in our discussion that the subsidiaries are 100% owned by the parent.)

This difference, which we defined as an excess cost when discussing the equity method, is identified to the extent practicable with specific tangible and intangible assets of the subsidiaries for which the excess cost is assumed to have been paid, again in the same manner as under the equity method. Whatever amount of excess cost cannot be so identified is assumed to have been paid for goodwill.

In consolidation, the amounts of the excess cost identified with specific tangible and intangible assets of the subsidiaries are commonly added to them in bringing them into the consolidated balance sheet. The balance of the excess cost not so identified is brought into the consolidated balance sheet under the title of goodwill.

In some companies, however, the total of the excess cost is simply brought into the consolidated balance sheet under a title such as that used by the Eastman Kodak Company — namely, "unamortized excess cost of investments in consolidated subsidiaries over net assets acquired."[7]

By bringing the excess cost into the consolidated balance sheet, along with the assets and liabilities of the subsidiaries as carried in their accounts, the items in that balance sheet are equal in the net to the investment cost of subsidiaries in the parent company's balance sheet for which they are being substituted.

The excess cost in consolidation is subject to amortization or depreciation on the same terms as the assets with which it is identified, as under the equity method, and goodwill must be amortized over a reasonable period but not in excess of 40 years.

Adjustment for intercompany transactions. Since the consolidated financial statements are intended to present the combined companies as a single accounting entity, it is necessary to make adjustments for

---

[7]Eastman Kodak Company, 1977 Annual Report, p. 28.

intercompany sales and purchases, intercompany indebtedness, intercompany profit on goods still in inventory, and so forth.

Intercompany sales and purchase transactions are eliminated, for example, so that sales will not be counted twice in the consolidated income statement, once inside and again to outsiders, and also so that profit will not be anticipated, i.e., so that profit will not be shown on sales made within the family but only on sales to outsiders. The need for such adjustments is expressed by the American Institute of Certified Public Accountants as follows:

> In the preparation of consolidated statements, intercompany balances and transactions should be eliminated. This includes intercompany open account balances, security holdings, sales and purchases, interest, dividends, etc. As consolidated statements are based on the assumption that they represent the financial position and operating results of a single business enterprise, such statements should not include gain or loss on transactions among the companies in the group. Accordingly, any intercompany profit or loss on assets remaining within the group should be eliminated; the concept usually applied for this purpose is gross profit or loss. However, in a regulated industry where a parent or a subsidiary manufactures or constructs facilities for other companies in the consolidated group, the foregoing is not intended to require the elimination of intercompany profits to the extent that they are ordinarily capitalized in accordance with the established practice of the industry.[8]

The major point of the previous sentence is that in the case of a regulated company, e.g., a public utility, the rates the company is allowed to charge for its services are based in large part on what is considered to be a reasonable return on the assets employed, the majority of which consists of facilities. The investment in the manufacturing divisions of the company would obviously not be allowed to be included in the investment base used in determining rates to be allowed the utility divisions.

Unless a profit were allowed in the sale of facilities by manufacturing divisions to the utility divisions, the company would never be able to realize a profit from producing them since, not having been charged for such a profit, the utility divisions would not be able to recover it in the rate structure as either reimbursement for depreciation or return on the investment.

---

[8]Accounting Research Bulletin Number 51, *Consolidated Financial Statements*, August 1959, paragraph 6.

Apart from control over the quality, cost, and delivery of facilities, there would be no point in manufacturing for internal use, since no profit or return on investment could be realized from it. Moreover, the company would be giving up whatever return it might be making by having the investment in manufacturing property, plant, and equipment invested elsewhere instead.

The following statement from the 1977 Annual Report of the American Telephone and Telegraph Company illustrates the application of adjustment for intercompany transactions:

> Most of the telephone equipment, apparatus and materials used by the companies consolidated has been manufactured or procured for them by Western Electric Company, Incorporated, the principal subsidiary not consolidated. Contracts with the telephone companies provide that Western's prices to them shall be as low as to its most favored customers for like materials and services under comparable conditions. Items purchased from Western by the telephone companies are entered in their accounts at cost to them, which includes the return realized by Western on its investment devoted to this business.

Although the sentence referred to earlier in ARB Number 51 deals only with regulated companies, it should also be applicable to transactions between other affiliated companies involving materials, plant, and equipment purchased for use rather than as goods or components for resale.

Nonconsolidated Controlled Companies

In some companies, one or more of the subsidiaries will not be treated on a consolidated basis. Instead, they will simply be listed as investments in both the consolidated and parent company balance sheets and accounted for on the equity basis described earlier. The reason for such treatment of a subsidiary (thereby excluding its assets, liabilities, revenues, and expenses from consolidation with those of the parent company and consolidated subsidiaries) is because it is engaged in a markedly different type of business than the parent company.

For example, AT&T has a number of nonconsolidated subsidiaries. The largest among them is Western Electric Company, which manufactures telephone equipment, apparatus, and materials. The Bell System is a consolidation of telephone operations. Thus Western Electric is treated as an investment and not consolidated even though its products are used by the telephone industry.

In recent years, the trend toward diversification through the acquisition of a controlling number of shares of companies in a wide variety of industries has further complicated the problem of determining which subsidiaries should be presented in financial statements on a consolidated basis. Particularly in what have become known as conglomerates, there may be no dominant industry among the varied holdings to serve as the primary basis on which to decide whether a given subsidiary should be included in or excluded from consolidation.

One can argue that in such companies consolidation can result only in a hodgepodge of numbers without any real meaning, and therefore consolidation should be avoided and investments simply presented in financial statements as such.

The counter to this, however, is that the presentation of consolidated data under major account classifications should be at least somewhat more informative about the financial affairs of the company than would be the case if all holdings were accounted for simply as investments. Moreover, consolidation, by providing more detail, provides more checking points against which to measure from period to period the trends of a company's financial affairs.

Reporting by Segments of a Business

Along with the increase in conglomerates created by acquisitions and mergers in recent years, there has been a marked trend toward diversification of products and services within companies through research and development and expansion into new areas, by means other than through buying the common stock or property of an existing company.

The whole movement toward diversification led many financial analysts to complain that the financial statements of diversified companies defied analysis because they combined unrelated elements. Accordingly, these analysts urged that such companies present supplemental information on the financial condition and results of the major segments of their business.

Many companies complied voluntarily with this demand, particularly where their segments were in quite different types of industries and physically separated. Formal requirements for financial reporting for segments of a business enterprise were established by the Financial

Accounting Standards Board as of December 1976, in its Statement of Financial Accounting Standards No. 14. These requirements are supported by the SEC through requiring companies to report this information in their Form 10-K annual report to the commission.

The two most important figures to be reported by industry segments are those for sales, and the operating profit or loss. Sales to unaffiliated customers and sales or transfers to other industry segments of the enterprise must be separately disclosed. It is recognized that the operating profit or loss reported by a segment may represent the contribution of that segment to profit or loss and not net profit or loss. For example, it may not have had deductions from it for items such as corporate expenses, income taxes, and interest.

Where unconsolidated subsidiaries are being accounted for under the equity method described earlier in this chapter, the reporting enterprises' equity in their net income must also be reported by industry segments, as well as the enterprises' equity in the net assets of these subsidiaries.

Other items to be reported by industry segments are, in brief, as follows:

1. The aggregate amount of identifiable assets (i.e., identifiable by industry segment).
2. The aggregate amount of depreciation, depletion, and amortization expense.
3. The amount of capital expenditures for the period (i.e., additions to property, plant, and equipment).
4. Information on foreign operations covering revenue (sales), operating profit or loss, and identifiable assets.
   a. Where revenue from sales to unaffiliated customers is 10 percent or more of consolidated total assets as reported in the enterprise's income statement.
   b. Where identifiable assets of the enterprise's foreign operations are 10 percent or more of consolidated total assets as reported in the enterprise's balance sheet.
5. Information about major customers so that if 10 percent or more of the revenue of an enterprise is derived from sales to any single customer, that fact and the amount of revenue from each such customer shall be disclosed.

The exhibit from the 1977 annual report of Koppers Company, Inc. is a good example of the presentation of information on operations by industry segments required by Statement No. 14 of the FASB and by Form 10-K of the SEC. Intersegment sales were not disclosed in this table because of immateriality.

The Koppers Company, Inc. annual report also included six pages describing the nature of operations in each industry segment, as well as tables showing the growth in sales and operating income over a ten-year period by industry segments. A table of sales and descriptions by major end markets was also presented which included discussion of major developments during 1977 and developments expected beyond 1977. Incidentally, Koppers' annual report incorporated all material required in Form 10-K filed with the SEC and was a comprehensive and outstanding presentation of information on the company's operations and financial situation.

The tables and explanations from the 1977 annual report of the General Electric Company are in keeping with the FASB Statement No. 14 requirements for reporting industry segment and geographic segment information. It is interesting to note that GE reports not only segment operating profit but net earnings by segments as well. In computing net earnings, general corporate expenses and interest and other financial charges are allocated to the industry segments. The methods of allocating these costs are described in notes following the tables in the annual report and are included in this chapter.

Translation of Foreign Currency Financial Statements and Foreign Currency Transactions

Many American companies have subsidiaries or long-term investments in foreign countries whose financial statements are incorporated in their own financial statements by consolidation, combination, or the equity method of accounting. In this process, the financial statements from foreign countries must be translated for measurement and expression in dollars. Also, adjustments are often required to convert the figures to accepted American accounting practice.

Many additional companies engage in foreign currency transactions that must be converted to dollar terms.

In recognition of the accounting problems that arise in connection with these foreign activities the Financial Accounting Standards Board developed its Statement No. 8, Accounting for the Translation of Foreign Currency Transactions and Foreign Currency Financial Statements (October 1975). Treatment in detail is to be found in this statement. We shall deal only with some of its major points here.

EXHIBIT 22

Koppers Company, Inc.
Operations by Industry Segment

Year ended December 31, 1977

($ Thousands)	Organic Materials	Forest Products	Metal Products	Road Materials	Environ- mental Elements	Engineering and Construction	Other	Consolidated
Sales	$427,778	$296,265	$194,668	$174,101	$70,757	$189,793	$2,327	$1,355,689
Operating profit before general corporate overhead	$ 47,191	$ 24,162	$ 12,931	$ 18,873	$ 3,462	$ 19,990	$ 840	$ 127,449
Other income	103	1,325	540	1,915	128	153	2,912	7,076
Equity in earnings of affiliates	1,735	286	18	193	—	—	—	2,232
Operating income	$ 49,029	$ 25,773	$ 13,489	$ 20,981	$ 3,590	$ 20,143	$3,752	136,757
General corporate overhead								13,272
Interest expense								10,485
Income before income taxes								$ 113,000
Identifiable assets as of Dec. 31, 1977	$278,027	$164,082	$123,507	$140,114	$37,344	$ 71,481	$ —	$ 814,555
General corporate assets (principally cash)								37,345
Total assets								$ 851,900
Depreciation and depletion	$ 13,871	$ 10,429	$ 4,479	$ 10,247	$ 810	$ 430	$ 415	$ 40,681
Capital investments	$ 46,375	$ 16,810	$ 7,699	$ 27,769	$ 896	$ 873	$4,100	$ 104,522

EXHIBIT 23

General Electric Company Industry Segment Information

(In millions)

Revenues

For the years ended December 31

	Total revenues	
	1977	1976
Consumer products and services	$ 4,148.1	$ 3,452.6
Industrial products and components	3,698.1	3,269.8
Power systems	3,217.6	2,998.4
Technical systems and materials	4,144.6	3,688.6
Utah International Inc.	965.1	1,002.9
Foreign multi-industry operations	2,562.1	2,333.6
Net earnings of GE Credit Corp.	67.2	57.1
General corporate items and eliminations	(893.9)	(831.4)
Total	$17,908.9	$15,971.6

Segment operating profit

For the years ended December 31

	1977	1976
Consumer products and services	$ 482.8	$ 397.1
Industrial products and components	366.7	302.4
Power systems	162.7	154.4
Technical systems and materials	473.7	399.3
Utah International Inc.	389.2	359.7
Foreign multi-industry operations	210.8	201.0
Net earnings of GE Credit Corp.	67.2	57.1
Total segment operating profit	2,153.1	1,871.0
General corporate items and eliminations	(64.8)	(68.8)
Interest and other financial charges	(199.5)	(174.7)
Total	$ 1,888.8	$ 1,627.5

Assets

At December 31

	1977	1976
Consumer products and services	$ 1,791.9	$ 1,643.7
Industrial products and components	1,925.1	1,726.9
Power systems	2,152.8	2,153.8
Technical systems and materials	2,128.3	1,896.0
Utah International Inc.	1,386.0	1,235.5
Foreign multi-industry operations	1,849.0	1,654.3
Investment in GE Credit Corp.	600.0	548.5
General corporate items and eliminations	1,863.7	1,191.0
Total	$13,696.8	$12,049.7

	Intersegment sales		External sales and other income	
	1977	1976	1977	1976
	$ 181.9	$ 157.8	$ 3,966.2	$ 3,294.8
	431.5	395.8	3,266.6	2,874.0
	153.9	151.6	3,063.7	2,846.8
	148.0	118.1	3,996.6	3,570.5
	—	—	965.1	1,002.9
	49.4	41.0	2,512.7	2,292.6
	—	—	67.2	57.1
	(964.7)	(864.3)	70.8	32.9
	$ —	$ —	$17,908.9	$15,971.6

Net earnings
For the years ended December 31

1977	1976
$ 255.9	$ 203.5
191.1	160.4
75.5	61.4
247.5	201.3
196.2	181.3
70.6	74.7
67.2	57.1
(15.8)	(9.1)
—	—
$1,088.2	$ 930.6

Property, plant and equipment
For the years ended December 31

	Additions		Depreciation, depletion & amortization	
	1977	1976	1977	1976
	$ 127.0	$ 86.3	$ 101.0	$ 95.5
	147.7	115.0	83.8	77.3
	81.6	72.0	73.2	79.6
	203.8	176.5	126.3	110.2
	131.6	213.6	66.9	67.5
	115.9	69.6	52.7	41.0
	—	—	—	—
	14.9	7.4	18.2	15.1
	$ 822.5	$ 740.4	$ 522.1	$ 486.2

Consumer products and services consists of major appliances (which also includes appliance service), air conditioning equipment, lighting products, housewares and audio products and services, television receivers and broadcasting and cablevision services.

Industrial products and components includes components (appliance controls, small motors and electronic components); industrial capital equipment (construction, automation, and transportation); maintenance, inspection, repair and rebuilding of electric and mechanical apparatus; and a network of supply houses offering products of General Electric and other manufacturers.

Power systems includes steam turbine-generators, gas turbines, nuclear power reactors and nuclear fuel assemblies, transformers, switchgear, meters, and installation and maintenance engineering services.

Technical systems and materials consists of jet engines for aircraft, industrial and marine applications; electronic and other high-technology products and services primarily for space applications and national defense; materials (engineering plastics, silicones, industrial cutting materials, laminated and insulating materials, and batteries); medical and communications equipment; and time sharing, computing, and remote data processing.

Utah International Inc. is engaged in mining coking coal (principally in Australia), uranium, steam coal, iron, and copper. In addition, Utah engages in oil and natural gas production, ocean shipping (primarily in support of mining operations) and land acquisition and development.

EXHIBIT 23 (continued)
Geographic Segment Information
(In millions)

Revenues | For the years ended December 31 | |

| | Total revenues | |
Revenues	1977	1976
United States	$14,560.4	$12,878.9
Far East including Australia	1,056.2	1,040.0
Other areas of the world	2,916.7	2,564.6
Elimination of intracompany transactions	(624.4)	(511.9)
Total	$17,908.9	$15,971.6

Included in United States revenues were export sales to unaffiliated customers of $2,101.2 million in 1977 and $1,914.5 million in 1976. Of such sales, $1,216.9 million in 1977 ($1,179.7 million in 1976) were to customers in Europe, Africa

Net earnings	For the years ended December 31	
	1977	1976
United States	$ 846.3	$ 633.2
Far East including Australia	161.6	194.5
Other areas of the world	83.5	103.5
Elimination of intracompany transactions	(3.2)	(0.6)
Total	$ 1,088.2	$ 930.6

Revenues, net earnings, and assets associated with foreign operations are shown in the tabulation above. At December 31, 1977, foreign operation liabilities, minority interest in equity and GE interest in equity were $1,798.7 million, $131.3 million

Foreign multi-industry operations consist principally of foreign affiliates who manufacture products primarily for sale in their respective home markets.

General Electric Credit Corporation, a wholly-owned nonconsolidated finance affiliate, engages primarily in consumer, commercial and industrial financing, principally in the United States. Products of companies other than General Electric constitute a major portion of products financed by GECC.

In general, it is the Company's policy to price internal sales as nearly as practicable to equivalent commercial selling prices.

In computing net earnings, general corporate expenses and interest and other financial charges have been allocated to the industry segments. General corporate expenses are allocated principally on the basis of cost of operations, with certain exceptions and reductions which recognize the varying degrees to which affiliated companies maintain their own corporate structures. Interest and other financial charges are allocated to parent company components based principally on cash flow, and affiliated companies generally service their own debt. In addition, provision for income taxes ($773.1 million in 1977, $668.6 million in 1976) is allocated based on the total corporate effective tax rate, except for the Credit Corporation and Utah whose income taxes are calculated separately. Minority interest ($27.5 million in 1977, $28.3 million in 1976) is allocated to operating components having responsibility for investments in consolidated affiliates.

Intersegment sales		External sales and other income	
1977	1976	1977	1976
$ 340.3	$ 274.5	$14,220.1	$12,604.4
204.0	132.3	852.2	907.7
80.1	105.1	2,836.6	2,459.5
(624.4)	(511.9)	–	–
$ –	$ –	$17,908.9	$15,971.6

and the Middle East; and $574.2 million in 1977 ($371.9 million in 1976) were to customers in the Far East and Australia.

Assets	At December 31
1977	1976
$10,491.5	$ 9,262.6
871.2	792.7
2,414.8	2,069.0
(80.7)	(74.6)
$13,696.8	$12,049.7

and $1356.0 million, respectively. On a comparable basis at December 31, 1976, foreign operation liabilities, minority interest in equity and GE interest in equity were $1,520.1 million, $118.9 million and $1,222.7 million, respectively.

The objective of translation is presented in paragraph 6 of the statement as follows:

> 6. For the purpose of preparing an enterprise's financial statements, the objective of translation is to measure and express (a) in dollars and (b) in conformity with U.S. generally accepted accounting principles the assets, liabilities, revenue, or expenses that are measured or denominated in foreign currency. Remeasuring in dollars the assets, liabilities, revenue, or expenses should not affect either the measurement bases for assets and liabilities or the timing of revenue and expense recognition otherwise required by generally accepted accounting principles. That is, translation should change the unit or measure without changing accounting principles.

With respect to foreign currency transactions:

> 7. The objective of translation requires that the following shall apply to all foreign currency transactions of an enterprise other than forward exchange contracts.
>   a. At the transaction date, each asset, liability, revenue, or expense arising from the transaction shall be translated into (that is, measured in) dollars by use of the exchange rate in effect at that date, and shall be recorded at that dollar amount.
>   b. At each balance sheet date, recorded dollar balances representing cash and amounts owed by or to the enterprise that are denominated in foreign currency shall be adjusted to reflect the current rate.
>   c. At each balance sheet date, assets carried at market whose current market price is stated in a foreign currency shall be adjusted to the equivalent dollar market price at the balance sheet date (that is, the foreign currency market price at the balance sheet date multiplied by the current rate).

The foreign financial statements that are to be included by consolidation, combination, or the equity method in an enterprise's financial statements must first be prepared or converted so as to conform with U.S. generally accepted accounting principles. The foreign currency figures are then translated into dollars in accordance with the requirements set by Statement No. 8.

A digest of major requirements is as follows:

Assets and liabilities carried in the foreign accounts at prices in past exchanges (past prices) shall be translated at historical exchange rates.

EXHIBIT 24

Litton Industries, Inc. and Subsidiary Companies
Notes to Financial Statements

For the Years Ended July 31, 1977 and July 31, 1976

NOTE A: SUMMARY OF SIGNIFICANT ACCOUNTING POLICIES

Translation of Non-U.S. Currencies

Earnings from operations and currency adjustments presented in the Consolidated Statement of Earnings in accordance with the provisions of Statement of Financial Accounting Standards No. 8 are as follows:

	Total		Per Share	
	1977	1976	1977	1976
	(thousands of dollars)			
Operations (after tax)	$62,225	$45,522	$1.58	$1.11
Currency adjustments (after tax)	(6,319)	(17,634)	(.18)	(.49)
	$55,906	$27,888	$1.40	$ .62

Assets and liabilities of operations located outside the United States have been translated to U.S. dollars at year-end market rates, except that inventories, property, plant and equipment, cost of businesses purchased over corresponding net assets, and other minor accounts have been translated at rates prevailing when acquired.

Income and expense items have been translated at average rates during the year, except that those income and expense accounts that relate to assets and liabilities translated at historical rates have been translated to U.S. dollars on the same basis as the related assets and liabilities.

All currency gains and losses are included in the determination of net earnings for the period in which rates change.

Assets and liabilities carried in the foreign accounts at prices in current purchase or sale exchanges (current prices) or future exchanges (future prices) shall be translated at the current exchange rate.

Revenue and expense transactions shall be translated at the average exchange rate for the period covered by the income statement. However, revenue and expenses that relate to assets and liabilities translated at historical rates (such as depreciation expense) shall be translated at the historical rates used to translate the related assets or liabilities.

The note from the 1977 annual report of Litton Industries, Inc. illustrates the type of explanation given in such a report on the translation of non-U.S. currencies.

CHAPTER 10

The Balance Sheet: Property, Plant, and Equipment

Because of their permanent nature, in the sense of being kept on hand for a number of years and not being subject to the rapid turnover associated with current assets, items of property, plant, and equipment are commonly spoken of as *fixed assets.* In contrast to properties such as materials and goods, fixed assets are purchased for use in connection with producing or earning revenue and not for sale in the ordinary course of business. Thus they are recorded in the accounts and presented in the balance sheet in terms of the intent with which they were acquired and not simply according to their physical characteristics.

Land and buildings acquired for speculation by a realtor, for example, would not fit into the definition of fixed assets even though physically fixed in nature and subsequently held for a long time waiting for a buyer. Neither, of course, would such property be treated as a current asset. Instead, it would be accounted for as a noncurrent investment.

As a practical matter, minor items of property purchased for use and not for resale, e.g., small tools, are generally not accounted for as fixed assets. In some companies, they are treated as expenses at the time of purchase, while in others they are accounted for as supplies.

Accounting for property, plant, and equipment is such a critical factor in determining the amount of net income each period in many companies that a later chapter will be entirely devoted to it. At present, our discussion will center on major points, with particular reference to balance-sheet presentation.

Fixed-Asset Valuation at Historical Cost

In the United States, it is common practice to record property, plant, and equipment at cost at time of acquisition and to carry these items in appropriate accounts at such costs until they are sold or become worn out or obsolete and discarded.

The costs of fixed assets subject to wear, obsolescence, or inadequacy are amortized over their estimated useful lives by periodic charges to operations for depreciation and depletion. The fixed-asset accounts themselves are not reduced as a result of such charges; instead, an offsetting account with a title such as "Accumulated Depreciation and Depletion" is built up. At the close of each period, the amount of the balance in this account is shown in the balance sheet as a visible deduction from the total of the fixed assets to which it applies.

Thus the reader is informed as to the historical cost of the fixed assets, the amount to date written off on them through charges for depreciation and depletion, and—by deduction—the amount of their historical cost remaining to be amortized over their estimated remaining useful lives. In this way, the verifiable facts of historical costs are kept separate from the judgmental amounts of accumulated depreciation and depletion.

The amount of change in these two types of accounts from period to period and the ratio of one to the other, as well as the difference between the two, provide indications of the company's policies with respect to depreciation and depletion, fixed-asset replacement, and expansion and the average age of fixed assets on hand, as measured by the amount of depreciation and depletion taken and the amount remaining to be taken.

Problems in Establishing Cost

It might at first appear that there should be no problems in arriving at the cost of any given item of property, plant, or equipment. A given cost would be assumed to be part of the cost of an item if it would not have been incurred had the item not been acquired.

This test can easily be applied, for example, to some of the costs involved in the purchase of a machine. Here, the price is stated on the invoice covering the purchase, while freight and delivery costs are readily ascertainable from shipping documents.

But what is the true price of the machine if the transaction involves the trading-in of an old machine, the allowance on which is far in excess of the amount that could reasonably have been received had the old machine been sold to some other user or as scrap for cash?

Again, if an engineer has been brought in to install the machine and get it running smoothly, should his costs of transportation, hotel room, and meals, as well as his fee properly be considered as part of the cost of the machine to be amortized over its useful life?

Also, if the floor where the machine is to be located has to be strengthened because of the weight of the machine, is this a part of the cost of the machine, of the building, or just a maintenance expense?

Finally, should the heavy spoilage of products before the machine is running properly be considered as part of its cost?

Where a company produces a machine for its own use, there are additional problems in determining cost, such as in deciding what indirect manufacturing and overhead costs should be charged to it. Again, should research, development, and experimental costs involved in bringing out the first model of a machine be charged to it, prorated between it and later machines, or written off as an operating expense not chargeable to any machines?

Problems of the various types suggested in the foregoing paragraphs will be discussed later in Chapter 19, "Accounting for Property, Plant, and Equipment." In the meantime, we shall simply recognize that establishing the historical cost of fixed assets can involve complications. It should also be stated that income tax considerations tend to be a deciding factor when dealing with borderline costs where reasons can be developed either for expensing or for capitalizing any given item.

While it might be permissible to expense an item for tax purposes and to capitalize it for other financial reporting purposes, the general practice is to account for it in the same way for all purposes. This is partly a matter of accounting simplification and partly because it is more difficult to support the expensing of an item of cost for tax purposes if the company has considered it appropriate to capitalize it instead of expensing it for other purposes.

Problems in Accounting for Depreciation

The Committee on Terminology of the American Institute of Accountants (later, the American Institute of Certified Public Accountants) described depreciation accounting succinctly and most appropriately in the following terms: "Depreciation accounting is a system of accounting which aims to distribute the cost or other basic value of tangible capital assets, less salvage (if any), over the estimated useful life of the unit (which may be a group of assets) in a systematic and rational manner. It is a process of allocation, not of valuation."[1]

Problems arise in determining the probable useful life of the depreciable tangible asset, its probable salvage value, and the most

---

[1] Accounting Terminology Bulletin No. 1, *Review and Résumé* (American Institute of Certified Public Accountants, August 1953).

appropriate system of allocating its cost, or other value at which it entered the accounts, over its estimated useful life.

Attempting to estimate the probable salvage value of a long-lived depreciable asset is an academic exercise best avoided. The chances are that the costs of removal and disposal will more than offset whatever salvage value is realized.

In many cases, however, salvage, or trade-in value, is an important factor to be taken into consideration in determining the amount of cost to be amortized over the number of years a company expects to use a given fixed asset. The major airlines, for example, realized substantial amounts on the disposal of their DC-3s to smaller airlines, as they were replaced by newer and larger models.

Problems in Estimating Useful Life

The economic life of a tangible capital asset is dependent largely on the factors of physical wear and tear, obsolescence, and inadequacy. Estimating useful life can be very difficult and generally involves judgment, experience, and — wisely or not — some subjective reasoning.

The Internal Revenue Service has a pamphlet, *Depreciation Guidelines and Rules*, which states service lives for broad classes of depreciable assets considered by the IRS to be appropriate in establishing depreciation charges to be deducted in arriving at taxable income.[2] These guidelines have been particularly helpful in reducing disputes between taxpayers and the government. But since they are only guidelines for broad classifications of depreciable assets, they do not relieve management of the responsibility for exercising judgment in determining the probable useful lives of individual items.

Moreover, the guidelines, or any other estimated years of useful life based on experience may not be correct. Indeed, they may be very misleading, with respect to new types of depreciable assets or assets used in connection with new products or new markets.

When jet airplanes were first purchased, for example, experience with propeller-driven planes did not serve as a particularly useful guide in deciding on the probable economic life of the jets.

In addition to the factors of physical life and obsolescence, the decision to discontinue the use of a given depreciable asset may be dependent on both objective and subjective views of safety and, in some cases, esthetic considerations if not whims. The useful life of a ship, for example, comes to an abrupt end if government inspectors declare it unseaworthy; at least, until it is reconditioned.

---

[2]Washington, D.C., United States Treasury Department.

Again, some executives will decide to discontinue the use of a piece of equipment or other property when its appearance becomes unattractive even though it is still serviceable. Others, who are not so moved by the beauty of their surroundings or so concerned about the public image of the company as affected by the appearance of its physical facilities, will continue the use of such an item as long as it meets purely physical or economic requirements.

Similarly, in corporate life as in family life, there is some tendency to keep up with the Joneses. And this has a bearing on decisions as to when an item should be replaced by a better and usually more expensive one.

The factor of obsolescence is the most difficult element to forecast in estimating the useful life of a depreciable asset, since it is not necessarily subject to a repetitive or rhythmic pattern. Obsolescence may be that of the facilities to make, house, or display a product or service; or the product or service itself; or more likely a combination of the two with the one being more dominant than the other at any given time.

The factor of inadequacy is somewhat akin to obsolescence and may bring an asset to the end of its useful life as far as a given company is concerned. Thus a facility may in time be found inadequate to meet a growing demand for a given product or service and have to be replaced.

A power plant in a rapidly growing area, for example, may not be obsolete in the sense that if another plant its size were to be built it would be markedly different. But it may well be approaching inadequacy where it is located and thus have to be replaced.

Depreciation: Straight-Line and Accelerated

In addition to determining the historical cost for a depreciable asset, it is necessary to select the method by which the net cost or other value shall be systematically allocated over the asset's estimated useful life.

The major methods in use result in charging an equal amount of depreciation each period of useful life (straight-line) or in charging the heaviest amount in the first period and a declining amount each period thereafter (accelerated).

Under the straight-line method, a fixed percentage is applied to the asset's cost, or other carrying value, net of its estimated salvage value, if any. For example, if the given asset has an estimated life of five years, the depreciation rate is 20% per year.

Under one accelerated method, known as the double-declining balance, a fixed percentage (double that of the percentage which would be used under straight-line) is applied each period to the declining balance as it stood at the beginning of that period.

Thus if the given asset has an estimated life of five years the depreciation rate is 40% applied to the declining balance. If the asset cost $10,000, the depreciation taken on it the first year under this method would amount to $4,000. (Under the double-declining balance method, it is customary to apply the percentage to the cost or other carrying value of the asset without allowance for any estimated salvage value.) In the second year, the depreciation would be $2,400 ($6,000 × 40%); in the third year $1,440; and in the fourth year $864. This would leave $1,296 as the balance at the beginning of the year five representing the remaining cost to be written off.

If there is not expected to be any salvage value, the company is likely to switch to the straight-line method toward the end of an asset's life in order both to have more equal charges in the later years of life and to fully depreciate the asset; that is, a fixed percentage applied to a declining balance would never fully depreciate the asset, hence the change to straight-line depreciation in order to do so.

Under the other accelerated method, known as the sum-of-the-years-digits, a percentage which declines each period is applied to the asset's cost, or other carrying value, net of its estimated salvage value if any. The rate of depreciation each year is found by dividing the number of years remaining by the sum of the year's digits. Thus if the given asset has an estimated life of five years the depreciation rates for these years would be computed as follows:

Years		Depreciation Rates	
1	Year 1.	$\dfrac{5}{15}$	$= 33\frac{1}{3}\%$
2	2.	$\dfrac{4}{15}$	$= 26\frac{2}{3}$
3	3.	$\dfrac{3}{15}$	$= 20$
4	4.	$\dfrac{2}{15}$	$= 13\frac{1}{3}$
5	5.	$\dfrac{1}{15}$	$= 6\frac{2}{3}$
Sum-of-years-digits	15		100.0%

Assuming that the cost of the given asset net of its salvage value is $15,000:

Depreciation Year 1 33⅓% × $15,000 = $5,000 or $\frac{5}{15}$ × $15,000 = $5,000

2 26⅔% × $15,000 = $4,000 or $\frac{4}{15}$ × $15,000 = $4,000

3   20% × $15,000 = $3,000 or $\frac{3}{15}$ × $15,000 = $3,000

4 13⅓% × $15,000 = $2,000 or $\frac{2}{15}$ × $15,000 = $2,000

5   6⅔% × $15,000 = $1,000 or $\frac{1}{15}$ × $15,000 = $1,000

$15,000 $15,000

The calculation might also be made as follows:

$\frac{\text{Net cost \$15,000}}{\text{Sum-of-years-digits 15}}$ = $1,000 per digit

Year 1   5 digits × $1,000 = $ 5,000
2   4 digits × $1,000 = $ 4,000
3   3 digits × $1,000 = $ 3,000
4   2 digits × $1,000 = $ 2,000
5   1 digit × $1,000 = $ 1,000
$15,000

Other Methods of Depreciation

In some situations, it is possible to establish depreciation rates on a unit of production basis. Such a method attempts to combine a uniform depreciation charge per unit of product from a product costing viewpoint, with depreciation based on use from a depreciation on facilities viewpoint. For the latter purpose, the depreciation charge is thus allied with physical wear, and probably with sales activity, but may well not take obsolescence into account.

In many industries, for example, the rate of obsolescence increases in depression periods because machine-tool builders are under pressure to bring out new and better models in order to make any sales at all. On balance, although the unit of production method may appear to be attractive, it has only limited application and may not provide adequately for the factor of obsolescence.

There are some theoretical arguments supporting the use of a method of depreciation under which depreciation charges start at a low figure the first year and rise each year thereafter at an increasing rate (the annuity or sinking-fund method) but few, if any, companies use such a method.

Accelerated Depreciation for Tax Purposes

Although some companies report depreciation expense in their published financial statements on the same basis as reported for income tax purposes, there is no requirement that they do so. Accordingly, many companies report depreciation on an accelerated basis for income tax purposes and on a straight-line basis for all other purposes. In this way, the higher depreciation taken in the early years of the life of a depreciable asset under accelerated depreciation reduces for those years the amount of taxable income on which taxes are to be paid. In order for this practice to be of any value, there must of course be some taxable income which would thereby be reduced and income taxes temporarily saved.

In the later years of the life of the depreciable asset, the charges for depreciation expense under accelerated depreciation are lower than they would be under straight-line depreciation. Therefore, the taxable income and income taxes are higher. The total amount of depreciation that can be taken as a deductible expense for tax purposes is of course the same regardless of the method of depreciation—that is, 100% of the cost of the depreciable asset less its salvage value at the end of its useful life.

The point in deducting heavier depreciation for income tax purposes in the earlier years of the useful life of a depreciable asset is so that the company involved may temporarily have the use of money which otherwise would have gone to the government in payment of taxes at an earlier date. In terms of present value, a dollar saved in taxes now is greater than the value of a dollar that would otherwise be saved later.

Assuming that income before depreciation and income taxes is at least adequate to cover all costs including depreciation on an accelerated basis, the tax differential between the use of accelerated depreciation and the use of straight-line depreciation in any given year is equal to the difference in the depreciation expense between the two methods multiplied by the company's income tax rate for that year.

TABLE 1

Year	Accelerated depreciation	Straight-line depreciation	Difference in accelerated	Tax rate	Differential tax saving or expense	Accumulated tax saving at period end
	(a)	(b)	(c) c = a − b	(d)	(e) (e = c × d)	(f)
1	$ 5,000	$ 3,000	+ $2,000	48%	+ $960	$ 960
2	$ 4,000	$ 3,000	+ $1,000	48%	+ $480	$1,440
3	$ 3,000	$ 3,000	-0-	48%	-0-	$1,440
4	$ 2,000	$ 3,000	− $1,000	48%	− $480	960
5	$ 1,000	$ 3,000	− $2,000	48%	− $960	-0-
Total	$15,000	$15,000	-0-	48%	-0-	-0-

Let us take the example of a machine whose cost, net of its salvage value, is $15,000 and whose estimated life is five years. And let us assume that the total net income of the company is such as to place it in the 48% tax bracket. In this case, the tax differential each year with respect to this machine between the use of the sum-of-the-years-digits method and straight-line depreciation would be as shown in Table 1.

Although, as indicated by Table 1, the accumulated tax saving is reduced in the later years of the useful life of a depreciable asset and is eliminated completely by the end of that life, a company using accelerated depreciation for tax purposes would always have the use of a significant amount of interest-free "tax money." The reason for this is that the company would continually be replacing worn-out or obsolete depreciable assets with new ones and it would probably also be adding new facilities for expansion purposes.

These temporary tax savings and the income that can be realized on their use are of considerable assistance in financing the addition and replacement of depreciable assets. Moreover, the ability to charge heavier depreciation for tax purposes in the early years of their useful lives helps to reduce the risk involved in such investments.

Of course, the stimulation to make these investments, and thereby to stimulate the national economy, is considered to be a justification for allowing the use of accelerated depreciation for tax purposes. This is so even in cases where straight-line depreciation would seem to represent a more rational amortization of historical cost.

Interestingly, in almost every other major country in the world, the depreciation percentages allowed for income tax purposes in the early years of a depreciable asset's life are markedly higher than in the United States.

Deferred income taxes related to depreciation. If a company reports depreciation on an accelerated basis for income tax purposes and on a straight-line basis in its published financial statements, it is expected to show as its estimated income tax expense in the published statements the amount for which it would have been liable had it reported depreciation on a straight-line basis for tax purposes.

Thus the estimated tax should be an amount allocated to the accounting period for published statement purposes and not the amount of income tax to be actually paid for that period. The difference between these amounts is carried to a deferred income tax account. In the early years of life of a depreciable asset, the differences in these two amounts would be additions to the deferred income tax account and in the later years of life deductions from that account.

Assuming that a company following this practice is continually replacing depreciable assets as they wear out or become obsolete, and is likely to be adding facilities for expansion, there will always be a balance in this account to represent the amount and stated source of funds provided by the use of accelerated depreciation for federal income tax purposes. The balance in the deferred income tax account at the close of a period is shown as an item standing by itself on the liabilities side of the balance sheet.

An example may be helpful to an understanding of the accounting for deferred income taxes. Let us take the case of the same machine used earlier and assume that we can identify the income realized from the use of this machine as being $5,000 per year before deducting depreciation and income tax.

On the one hand, if the company reported depreciation for income tax purposes on the *sum-of-the-years-digits* basis, the results would be as shown in Table 2.

On the other hand, if the company reported depreciation for income tax purposes on the *straight-line* basis, the results would be as shown in Table 3.

The most significant difference between the figures in the two preceding tables is, of course, in the matter of *cash flow*, as Table 4 shows.

Thus, by using accelerated depreciation for income tax purposes, the company would have the use of funds which it would otherwise have had to pay earlier to the government. The total cash flow is, of course, the same under both methods, being reimbursement for the capital lost through depreciation of $15,000 and total net income of $5,200.

Granted that, unless a large increase in the income tax rate is expected in the near future, it should be advantageous for a company to

TABLE 2

Year	Income before depreciation & income tax	Accelerated depreciation	Income before tax	Income tax at 48%	Net income after tax	Cash flow
	(a)	(b)	(c) c = a - b	(d)	(e) e = c - d	(f) f = a - d, f = b + e
1	$ 5,000	$ 5,000	$ -0-	$ -0-	$ -0-	$ 5,000
2	5,000	4,000	1,000	480	520	4,520
3	5,000	3,000	2,000	960	1,040	4,040
4	5,000	2,000	3,000	1,440	1,560	3,560
5	5,000	1,000	4,000	1,920	2,080	3,080
Total	$25,000	$15,000	$10,000	$4,800	$5,200	$20,200

TABLE 3

	Income before depreciation & income tax	Straight-line depreciation	Income before tax	Income tax at 48%	Net income after tax	Cash flow
	(a)	(b)	(c) c = a - b	(d)	(e) e = c - d	(f) f = a - d, f = b + e
Each year	$ 5,000 X 5	$ 3,000 X 5	$ 2,000 X 5	$ 960 X 5	$1,040 X 5	$ 4,040 X 5
Total	$25,000	$15,000	$10,000	$4,800	$5,200	$20,200

use accelerated depreciation for tax purposes, the question might well then be raised as to why it might not also be desirable to use the same basis of depreciation for all other reporting purposes.

Some companies do in fact use accelerated depreciation for all reporting purposes on the grounds that 1. it is simpler to do so; 2. facilities require more maintenance as they get older and, therefore, higher maintenance costs in later years tend to balance off higher depreciation charges taken in the early years of useful life; and 3. owing to uncertainty as to the probable years of useful life, particularly with respect to obsolescence of products as well as of facilities, it is wise to take heavier depreciation in the early years of a depreciable asset.

TABLE 4

Year	Cash flow under accelerated depreciation for income tax purposes	Cash flow under straight-line depreciation for income tax purposes	Difference in favor of or against accelerated depreciation	Cumulative difference in favor of accelerated depreciation
	(Col. f) (a)	(Col. f) (b)	(c)	(End of year) (d)
1	$ 5,000	$ 4,040	+ $960	$ 960
2	4,520	4,040	+ 480	1,440
3	4,040	4,040	-0-	1,440
4	3,560	4,040	- 480	960
5	3,080	4,040	-· 960	-0-
Total	$20,200	$20,200	-0-	-0-

Most companies, however, which show depreciation on an accelerated basis for tax purposes, report depreciation to their stockholders and others on a straight-line basis. In part, this procedure is supported simply by the belief that the straight-line method represents the most equitable allocation of the cost of depreciable assets over their years of useful life. This also seems particularly appropriate where selling prices are strongly influenced by costs.

Another reason lies in the belief that the use of straight-line depreciation helps to level out stated profit from period to period. Accelerated depreciation causes distortions in stated profit, unless there is great regularity from period to period in expenditures for replacement and expansion of facilities.

A further reason for using straight-line depreciation for financial reporting to stockholders and others, particularly in a new company, is to avoid the depressing effects on stated profits that would result from the use of accelerated depreciation in the early years of life of depreciable assets acquired.

The pressure on management to use straight-line depreciation for reporting purposes other than for taxation is very strong. This is particularly so when competitors in the same industry are using this basis and when the management in question feels the need to have its company regarded favorably in financial circles in order for it to obtain funds at a competitive cost for future expansion.

As stated earlier, if a company reports depreciation on an accelerated basis for income tax purposes and on a straight-line basis in its published financial reports, under generally accepted accounting principles it is expected to show as its estimated income tax expense in the published statements the amount for which it would have been liable

TABLE 5

Year	Income before depreciation & income tax (a)	Depreciation (b)	Income before tax (c) c = a - b	Estimated tax (d)	Net income after tax (e) e = c - d	Tax actually payable (f)	Tax deferred (g) g = d - f	Cash flow (h) h = a - f h = b + e + g
1	$ 5,000	$ 3,000	$ 2,000	$ 960	$1,040	$ -0-	+ $960	$ 5,000
2	5,000	3,000	2,000	960	1,040	480	+ 480	4,520
3	5,000	3,000	2,000	960	1,040	960	-0-	4,040
4	5,000	3,000	2,000	960	1,040	1,440	- 480	3,560
5	5,000	3,000	2,000	960	1,040	1,920	- 960	3,080
	$25,000	$15,000	$10,000	$4,800	$5,200	$4,800	-0-	$20,200

had it reported depreciation on a straight-line basis for tax purposes. The difference between the estimated amount and the amount actually to be paid for that period is carried to a *deferred income tax account*. The manner in which this would be accounted for is illustrated in Table 5.

The point is that, although the use of accelerated depreciation on this depreciable asset for deferred income tax purposes has benefited temporarily the company's cash flow, there has been no net tax saving on this asset over its useful life. If the company has benefited from this procedure, the benefit has come only from the temporary use of "tax money" with no expense for interest.

Although there would be no net tax saving in our example, and eventually the early tax savings would be offset by higher tax payments in the later years of the life of the asset, it should be acknowledged that all companies of any size are continually replacing their depreciable assets and are probably adding to the total from time to time in order to expand their operations.

Under these conditions, there would always be a favorable balance of deferred income taxes and thus funds provided from this source for use by the company at no interest cost.

No income tax allocation. Not everyone has been happy with the generally accepted accounting practice, as illustrated in our deferred income tax account example, of depreciation taken on an accelerated basis for income tax purposes and reported to stockholders and others on a straight-line basis.

More specifically, some people believe that the income tax expense shown in reports to stockholders should be the same as that computed in income tax returns as far as accelerated depreciation is concerned. Thus there will be no income tax allocation in this connection and, therefore, no deferred tax account.

Whatever income tax gain or loss there might be in any given period between the use of accelerated depreciation for income tax purposes and the use of straight-line depreciation would *flow-through* to net income. This procedure is illustrated in Table 6.

Column (e) in this flow-through table is the net income after tax, with depreciation on a straight-line basis adjusted by the tax gain or loss each period arising from the use of accelerated depreciation. Thus the tax gain or loss from using accelerated depreciation for tax purposes can be seen to flow through to net income as shown in Table 7.

With respect to reported results in the early years of the life of a machine, the procedure illustrated in Tables 6 and 7 places a company

TABLE 6

Year	Income before depreciation and income tax	Depreciation	Income before tax	Income tax payable	Net income after tax	Cash flow
	(a)	(b)	(c) c = a - b	(d)	(e) e = c - d	(f) f = a - d f = b + e
1	$ 5,000	$ 3,000	$ 2,000	$ -0-	$2,000	$ 5,000
2	5,000	3,000	2,000	480	1,520	4,520
3	5,000	3,000	2,000	960	1,040	4,040
4	5,000	3,000	2,000	1,440	560	3,560
5	5,000	3,000	2,000	1,920	80	3,080
Total	$25,000	$15,000	$10,000	$4,800	$5,200	$20,200

TABLE 7

Year	Net income after tax straight-line depreciation	Tax gain or loss using accelerated depreciation	Net income after tax adjusted for gain or loss per period from use of accelerated depreciation
	(Col. e) (a)	(Col. e or Col. c) (b)	(Col. e) (a) ± (b)
1	$1,040	+ $960	$2,000
2	1,040	+ 480	1,520
3	1,040	-0-	1,040
4	1,040	- 480	560
5	1,040	- 960	80
Total	$5,200	-0-	$5,200

in the best light in both the worlds of depreciation and income taxation. This is because it allows the presentation of depreciation on a straight-line basis, which is lower in those years than it would be on an accelerated basis. At the same time, it permits the company to show its income tax expense on an accelerated basis, which is lower in those years than it would be if it were computed with depreciation on a straight-line basis.

One of the reasons why the procedure is not a generally accepted accounting practice is that it is not uniformly consistent. For all practical purposes, it places the accounting for income tax expense on a cash basis, whereas other expenses are accounted for on an accrual or allocated basis.

Regulatory commissions and flow-through.   The Interstate Commerce Commission, Federal Power Commission, and some of the state regulatory commissions require companies coming under their jurisdiction to use the flow-through method when depreciation is taken on an accelerated basis for tax purposes and reported to them on a straight-line basis.

Such companies must also report to their stockholders and others on the flow-through basis. But they are allowed, if they wish to do so, to also report by stated adjustments to the flow-through figures or otherwise what the results would be when computed under generally accepted accounting principles.

Without debating the point here at length, the major contention of those regulatory commissions requiring flow-through is that in public utility and transportation companies replacements of facilities are being made continuously. Moreover, since such companies are continually growing, the tax deferred, if tax allocation were to be practiced, would always show a balance which would grow with the years and never be drawn down. It is held that such a practice would provide a company continually with the use of funds which do not rightfully belong to it.

The aim of the regulatory commissions which require flow-through is therefore to force the companies affected to increase their stated net income by the amount of tax savings enjoyed in the early years of the life of facilities through the use of accelerated depreciation for tax purposes. If the net income so computed provides a rate of return on the company's assets in excess of that considered allowable for rate-making purposes, the given commission will require an adjustment in the rates charged by the company to its customers.

The income tax benefits from the use of accelerated depreciation may therefore not simply flow-through for the benefit of stockholders, but also flow-through and beyond them for the benefit of the company's customers.

Supposedly, if in later years the use of accelerated depreciation had an unfavorable effect on net income after taxes because of a drop in expenditures for the replacement of facilities, or a reduction rather than expansion of facilities, an increase in the rates charged to customers would be allowed if the company's return on investment was inadequate by the established rate-making standards.

The drop in expenditures for facilities would, however, be the result of depression conditions for either or both the specific industry and industry in general and hardly the time that increases in rates could politically or practically be put into effect. It would not have been any consolation to the dying electric street-railway companies, for example, to have been told that they could increase rates to recover funds which had been denied them in earlier years.

The fact is that the "tax money" involved, whether viewed as a temporary, long-time, or perpetual income tax saving, should really not be regarded as the property of either the stockholder or the customer. It represents funds left with, and thereby made available to, the business as a separate entity through a specific income tax provision, which was intended to stimulate the economy by encouraging investment in new facilities for replacement and expansion and reducing the risk involved in doing so.

Surely, the intent of the provision is defeated if the result is simply to flow funds immediately into the pockets of stockholders or to save some of the flow of funds out of the pockets of customers.

If a company's purchase of a given facility has been wise, the benefits will come in due time from the lower costs or from the additional quantity or quality of goods or services as a result of its use. In addition, the expenditure may provide esthetic, safety, or ecological benefits.

Accounting for Depletion

Through mining, pumping, or some other process, units of a natural resource such as oil are removed for use or sale from the area in which they were formed or developed by nature. When the resource area becomes exhausted, in the sense that no more units can be removed from it and sold economically, it will of course no longer be of any value as a natural resource.

Thus, whatever capital has been invested in it will no longer be recoverable, except for what might be salvaged in the way of usable equipment and from the sale of the property to someone else. Indeed, the property at that time might be more of a liability than an asset if the owner is then forced to spend money to restore some of its natural beauty or to reduce some hazard its abandonment represents to the community.

As units of the natural resource are removed, the loss of both capital investment and value of the property is known as depletion. Accounting for depletion is a process of amortizing the capital investment and value in a systematic manner over the useful life of the given property. In the sense of accounting periodically for loss of economic value, it is akin to accounting for depreciation. Assets that are being amortized by depletion accounting, however, are gradually being removed physically from a company and sold, whereas assets being amortized by charges for depreciation are not.

Hopefully, revenues from the sale of material removed from a natural resource area will be large enough to cover all costs, including depletion, and to provide a profit as well. To the extent that revenues are not adequate to provide for depletion as well as all other costs, then obviously, the capital invested in the natural resource will not be recovered.

... for Financial Reporting

The theory of depletion accounting for financial reporting purposes calls for the computation of a depletion cost per unit of the given natural resource. This unit cost is found by dividing the total capital invested in the property by the estimated number of recoverable units, such as barrels, pounds, tons, feet, or yards. The subsequent multiplication by this unit cost of the number of units removed in the given accounting period establishes the amount of depletion to be charged for that period.

The expense for depletion is sometimes shown as a separate item in the income statement. But, more often, it is merged with the charge for depreciation. The investment in the natural resource is not however reduced by this amount. Instead, an account for "accumulated depletion" is increased. The balance of this account at the close of the period is shown in the balance sheet as an offset to the asset.

The method of accounting for depletion just described is known as cost depletion in contrast to percentage depletion to be described later. With exceptions, also to be noted later, costs involved in exploration, purchase, or lease, and development of the property containing the natural resource are capitalized, i.e., entered in the accounts as assets, and amortized on a unit basis, as noted in the previous paragraph.

These costs, which are amortized as depletion, are of a type which for the most part could not be recovered if, as, or when the property was abandoned, in contrast to expenditures which could be salvaged to some extent. The actual drilling costs involved in drilling a productive oil well, for example, are amortized as depletion, whereas a truck used in the same oil field is subject to charges for depreciation, not depletion.

In times past, practice varied considerably between companies regarding the extent to which exploration and development costs involved in connection with natural resources were capitalized, versus being charged off immediately as expenses. This was particularly the case in oil and gas producing companies where practice ranged from the extremes of capitalizing all such costs, regardless of individual area or well successes or failures, to capitalizing only costs associated directly with successful wells. The first is known as "full costing" and the second as "successful efforts accounting."

We shall examine major aspects of these differences in practice and then discuss the Financial Accounting Standards Board's Statement No. 19 on accounting and reporting by oil and gas companies.

Full Cost Method.   Under the most extreme use of this method all costs incurred in acquiring, exploring, and developing properties within a large area, such as a country or continent, are capitalized as incurred. These are considered to be the costs of whatever oil or gas reserves are discovered and developed in the total area, even though some of the costs arise from exploration, and the drilling of exploratory wells, in sections of the total area where no oil or gas is found.

It is argued that the cost of a successful well includes the cost of searching and drilling unsuccessfully elsewhere, in the same sense as the cost of successful sales includes the cost of sales efforts along the way that were unsuccessful. Similarly, in a factory, good units must share the cost of units spoiled.

It is believed that capitalizing these costs is in keeping with the accounting principle of recording assets at their historical cost as acquired. Also, it is held that the amortization of these costs via cost depletion is in keeping with the accounting goal of a proper matching of costs and revenues.

The only proviso with respect to capitalizing these costs is that they must not in total exceed the total value of the oil and gas reserves discovered and developed.

Successful efforts accounting.   Under the most extreme use of this method only such costs as are directly connected with successful wells are capitalized as fixed assets. Costs of drilling, prior to knowing whether a well will be a success or failure, are capitalized as "construction-in-process." If the hole drilled proves to be dry, the accumulated costs on it are charged off immediately as expenses. If an oil or gas reserve is found, the costs incurred on the well are transferred from construction-in-process to a fixed asset account, provided that the estimated value of the oil or gas reserve discovered is in excess of these costs.

The principal argument for successful efforts accounting is that of conservatism in asset valuation for balance sheet purposes. The method also results in charging off some costs as expenses earlier than otherwise would be the case and thus results in more conservative income statements.

An argument against full costing, which by deduction leads one around to favoring successful efforts accounting, is that efforts involved in exploration and the drilling of exploratory wells, in areas in which no oil or gas is found, are too remote in time and place to have any bearing on the discovery and development of oil and gas reserves elsewhere. Thus there is no real cause and effect relationship between the cost of the one and the results of the other.

FASB Statement No. 19. Between the two extremes noted above there have been wide variations in practice. Some companies have used full costing by smaller areas (cost centers), such as fields, rather than by countries or continents. Many companies have differed in the handling of specific items of cost, either to be capitalized or written off as expenses when incurred. Some of these differences have resulted from differences in the perceived risks involved, some because of differences in accounting philosophy between managements, and some because of differences in beliefs as to the degree of conservatism that should be exercised in financial reporting.

Government officials, investment analysts, and others have complained that the differences in practice were so great as to affect materially the comparability of financial statements of oil and gas producing companies. They pressed the Financial Accounting Standards Board to narrow, if not eliminate, the free choice of accounting alternatives in this industry.

After careful study of the problem, including the use of draft proposals, position papers, and hearings on the issues involved, the FASB published its Statement No. 19, Financial Accounting and Reporting by Oil and Gas Producing Companies (December 1977). The major rulings of that statement are, in brief, as follows:

1. Initial exploratory costs, known as geological and geophysical costs, must be charged to expense, whether incurred before or after acquisition of the related property.
2. The costs of drilling all exploratory wells pending determination of success or failure (i.e., whether proved reserves of oil or

gas are found) should be capitalized as "construction-in-process."

3. If the drilling of an exploratory well results in the finding of proved reserves of oil or gas, the accumulated costs on it should be transferred from "construction-in-process" to a fixed asset account. If the drilling of an exploratory well results in a dry hole, the accumulated costs on it must be charged to expense.

4. After discovery of proved reserves of oil or gas, all costs incurred to build the producing system in the field within which the reserves are located are to be capitalized as part of the cost of that system. These costs include the costs of drilling unsuccessful development wells, and stratigraphic test wells, drilled in the proved area.

5. Capitalized acquisition, exploratory drilling, and development costs should be written off by unit-of-product amortization as depletion expense.

Definitions:

Development well . . . a well drilled within the proved area of an oil or gas reservoir to the depth of a stratigraphic horizon known to be productive.
Stratigraphic test well . . . a drilling effort, geologically directed to obtain information pertaining to a specific geologic condition.

It will be noted that the statement does not permit the capitalization of initial exploratory costs, nor the costs of exploratory wells that prove to be unsuccessful. Thus, to this extent, "full costing" is not permitted.

Once oil or gas has been discovered, however, all costs of building the productive system within the area of discovery are capitalized, including the costs of drilling any development wells that turn out to be unsuccessful, and test wells that are nonproductive. Thus, although it has been said that Statement No. 19 requires companies to practice "successful efforts accounting," this is not strictly true. Strict interpretation of successful efforts accounting would require that the costs of all unsuccessful efforts, including development of dry holes, be written off as expenses, not capitalized.

Statement No. 19 has eliminated extremes of both "full costing" and "successful efforts accounting" and so represents a reasonable compromise in the interest of eliminating wide variations of accounting practice in the oil and gas producing industry.

The following paragraph from the statement, however, is disturbing if taken as a generalization without further qualification:

> In the Board's judgment, when the same or similar facts and circumstances exist, as they do in the search for and development of oil and gas reserves, intercompany comparability requires a single method of accounting. Comparable reporting by companies competing for capital is, in the Board's judgment, in the public interest.

In the first place, "the same or similar facts and circumstances" do not always exist in the search for and development of oil and gas reserves. The risks and uncertainties can differ considerably between one location and another. For example, developing oil in a location that may be taken over at any time, either by militarists from the Right or the Left, is quite a different situation from conducting the same activities peacefully deep in the heart of Texas.

In the first example, it would be wise to charge off all expenditures possible against revenues until the entire investment had been recovered. In the second, it could be safe enough to capitalize all expenditures initially, providing that the company's holdings were, in general, sufficiently extensive and successful so that the value of its reserves of oil or gas were well in excess of the capitalized costs.

To establish an accounting requirement that came between the two would not satisfy either, and certainly would not make them comparable situations from an investment viewpoint.

In any industry where two companies are engaged in the same activities, even in similar locations, there can be important management differences between them that are revealed if alternative choices in accounting methods are available, and that would be hidden if practice was restricted to a single accounting method.

Availability of alternative accounting methods assists in revealing the degree of conservatism exercised by company management. It may also lead to an indication of a company's financial strength. Conservative managements tend to adopt conservative accounting policies. Generally speaking, such policies will also be followed by companies that are financially strong.

Indications of conservative management can be seen, for example, in the use of LIFO versus FIFO in inventory valuation; accelerated versus straight-line depreciation; and deferral versus flow-through in accounting for income tax investment credits.

As noted in Chapter 1, within the boundaries of a general principle, and even under the same circumstances, there are often several different but acceptable ways to reasonably account for an event. We should aim to reduce the swing of the pendulum of allowable practices, eliminating those that are less desirable, but retaining those for which reasonably substantial support can be given. Uniformity to a degree is highly desirable, but preoccupation with drastic reduction in available accounting alternatives can result in the presentation of financial statements that are less, rather than more, informative, and that have the appearance of comparability in situations that are not truly comparable.

. . . for Income Tax Purposes

Because of the contention surrounding it throughout its history, the allowance of depletion for income tax purposes can be a lengthy and emotional topic for discussion. We shall, however, restrict ourselves to a few of the major points.

In some companies, cost depletion rather than percentage depletion is sometimes used for income tax purposes, particularly in the early years of the life of a property, or for such other years as depletion computed on that basis proves to be higher than percentage depletion. A company's cost depletion for tax purposes would not necessarily be the same, however, as its cost depletion computed for financial reporting purposes in the same year.

For example, some development costs which had been capitalized for financial reporting purposes might have been expensed for income tax purposes. Therefore, the subsequent cost depletion would differ between the two on this account alone.

It should be noted also that if attempts to find and develop natural resources are unsuccessful, the costs involved will be written off as losses for both income tax and financial reporting purposes. However, such write-offs are not depletion charges; if no natural resources were discovered or those discovered could not be removed economically, there would be no depletion for which to account.

Discovery value depletion. The forerunner of percentage depletion for tax purposes was discovery value depletion. This approach essentially took the view that the value of a natural resource was what one should be willing to pay for it once the discovery had been made, regardless of the cost of finding it. The discovery value of the property was considered to be its value for income tax purposes, to be depleted on a per unit basis in the same manner as under cost depletion.

This approach was supported because it was believed that where, as normally would be the case, the discovery value was in excess of the finding costs an allowance of depletion based only on finding costs would result to some extent in the taxing of capital, not simply in the taxing of income.

There were the further considerations, particularly applicable to oil production, that the investment risks were heavy relative to other industries. Moreover, for the nation's welfare and defense, it was important to maintain and, even better, to expand the exploration and development of natural resources.

It was believed that the market value of a property in which a natural resource had been discovered would reflect reward for the risks involved, and that depletion allowances based on such a valuation would be sufficiently attractive to stimulate appropriately the exploration and development of the nation's natural resources.

However, the problem was that, short of an actual sale consummated after arm's-length bargaining, it was extremely difficult to arrive at a discovery value for a property with which all of the parties concerned would be happy. The inevitable results were frequent and expensive lawsuits, delays in tax settlements, and the expenditure of vast numbers of nonproductive hours by company and government officials, public accountants, and lawyers.

Percentage depletion. Faced with these difficulties, particularly in the petroleum industry — where finding and development costs are high, the chances of discovering a profitable well are low and the true amount of oil or gas (reserve) under ground in a discovered area uncertain — a simpler approach was sought which would meet the social and tax goals of the government and be fair to producers.

Studies in the petroleum industry showed that, under the practice of discovery value depletion, the depletion allowances amounted to roughly about one-third of the value of oil as it left the ground. It was then decided that depletion allowances could be computed with a reasonable degree of fairness by the application of an appropriate percentage to the company's direct sales of oil from a well, or to the market value of the oil when it moved from the well to another unit of the company for processing.

It should be remembered that the percentage allowance is applied to market value at the point of leaving the well, and not, as some people appear to believe, applied to the sales value of refined products or of oil or gas transportation. Moreover, the amount of depletion allowed on a given property in any given period cannot exceed 50% of its net income before depletion and income taxes.

In 1926, Congress wrote into the income tax law a depletion allowance of 27½% of the market value of oil and gas as it came from the well. This was a compromise figure, the House having voted for 25% and the Senate for 30%. The rate of 27½%, although debated off and on, continued in effect until 1971, when it was lowered to 22%.

In the Tax Reduction Act of 1975, effective January 1, 1975, percentage depletion for income tax purposes by oil and gas producers was repealed subject to two exceptions for domestic producers. One exempted certain well production while the other applied to small independent producers and royalty owners. For the companies coming under these exceptions, the percentage depletion rate of 22% was continued.

Oil and gas producers are allowed to use cost depletion for income tax purposes, as well as in their financial reporting to stockholders and others, but in most cases the depletion charges are much less than those previously allowed under percentage depletion.

Percentage depletion continues to be allowed to producers of other natural resources, but the percentages have ranged well below those for oil and gas because of differences in situations. In all cases, the maximum allowance has been 50% of the net income before depletion and income taxes.

It is difficult to understand, other than on emotional and political grounds, how it happened that the use of percentage depletion for tax purposes, which had been an important factor in encouraging exploration and development of oil and gas resources, was abandoned at a time when such efforts were so badly needed. However, perhaps as the need continues, there will be a return of interest in percentage depletion and, therefore, knowledge of the reasoning underlying it is still important.

I believe in the concept or principle of percentage depletion for income tax purposes, while recognizing that the exact percentage that should be allowed at any given time depends upon judgment as to the nation's needs for the finding and development of natural resources; the percentage depletion figure required to motivate sufficient exploration and development to meet these needs; and essential fairness in sharing the burden of taxation.

Percentage depletion has been criticized as a loophole for tax evasion. Although percentage depletion does provide a tax benefit, it is not fair to label it as a loophole. A loophole in a law is a means of escape that was overlooked when the law was drafted and passed. With all the debate that had centered on percentage depletion, its provision in the law could hardly be called an oversight. The word "loophole" is used appropriately in describing some means of getting around a law. It should not be applied to the legitimate use of provisions within it.

CHAPTER 11

The Balance Sheet:
Investment Credits

An accounting and reporting problem which has aroused great contention in recent years is that of the proper treatment of investment credits allowed for federal income tax purposes in connection with a company's purchase of certain types of depreciable assets. Investment credits could amount to as much as 7% of the cost of given types of depreciable assets acquired under specified conditions.

Investment credits were allowed by Section 38 of the Internal Revenue Code of 1954 and enacted by Congress in the revenue acts of 1962, 1964, and 1971. The purpose of the credits was to provide an incentive to private industry to make capital expenditures for modernization and growth, which would in turn bolster both employment and the general economy.

It should be noted that these were not outright gifts or grants but tax credits. Therefore, investment credits were available only to profitable companies having tax liabilities which could be credited.* They were gifts only in the sense that those companies which could, and did, take advantage of them had less income tax to pay than would otherwise have been the case.

Accounting Treatments

Throughout the history of investment tax credits, there has been contention as to how they should be accounted for and presented in financial reports. Major argument has centered on whether these credits

---

*The word "credited" here means credited theoretically in the government's books of account. A company's tax liability account is *debited* when it takes advantage of an investment credit as illustrated later in this chapter under "Accounting Examples."

should be accounted for 1. as contributions to the capital of the business; 2. as reductions in the income tax expense for the year during which the acquisitions were made, and therefore as increases in the net income of that year; or 3. spread out in one way or another over the lives of the depreciable assets acquired and thus affect the net income for each year of life instead of only the first year.

General agreement was reached rather early that the credits should not be accounted for as contributions of capital. However, sharp disagreement continued as to whether they should be treated as decreases in the tax expense for the year of acquisition or spread out over the years of useful lives of the depreciable assets acquired. There was no contention, of course, about the desirability of taking advantage of whatever investment credits were available to reduce the actual amount of income tax to be paid for the year of acquisition.

Current Situation

By an amendment to the Revenue Act of 1971, Congress ruled on what is considered to be acceptable practice in accounting for investment credits " . . . in Certain Financial Reports and Reports to Federal Agencies," under Act Section 101 as follows:

(1) In general . . . it was the intent of the Congress in enacting, in the Revenue Act of 1962, the investment credit allowed by Section 38 of the Internal Revenue Code of 1954, and it is the intent of the Congress in restoring the credit in this Act, to provide an incentive for modernization and growth of private industry. Accordingly, notwithstanding any other provision of law, on and after the date of the enactment of this act . . .

(A) No taxpayer shall be required to use, for purposes of financial reports subject to the jurisdiction of any federal agency or reports made to any federal agency, any particular method of accounting for the credit allowed by such Section 38,

(B) A taxpayer shall disclose, in any such report, the method of accounting for such credit used by him for purposes of such report, and

(C) A taxpayer shall use the same method of accounting for such credit in all such reports made by him, unless the Secretary of the Treasury or his delegate consents to a change to another method.

(2) Exceptions. Paragraph (1) shall not apply to taxpayers who are subject to the provisions of Section 46 (e) of the Internal Revenue Code of 1954 (as added by Section 105 (C) of this Act) or to Section 203 (e) of the Revenue Act of 1964 (as modified by Section 105 (e) of this Act).

For all practical purposes, this Congressional ruling means that industrial companies are now free either to treat investment tax credits as decreases in the tax expense for the year of acquisition, and thus as additions to the net income of that year; or to spread them out over the useful lives of the depreciable assets acquired, provided that they shall disclose the method used and follow it consistently.

Study of the background of the amendment to the Revenue Act of 1971 indicates that Congress adopted this ruling through fear that, unless such accounting freedom was allowed, businessmen might not be sufficiently motivated to purchase facilities to the extent desired by the Treasury Department in order to bolster employment and the general economy. While one can agree that jobs are of more immediate human and political importance than accounting entries, the ruling should be regarded as a matter of government expediency and not as a statement of accounting principle.

Thus it is still left for the management of each company having investment credits to decide whether such credits are to be reported to stockholders as gains resulting immediately from the purchase of facilities or as gains resulting from their use. While my views on the subject are admittedly biased, I regard this as being also a decision between expediency and accounting principle.

In any event, it is a matter on which the top managers of a company should come to a group conclusion, since they are to be held accountable for it, not simply their accounting and financial executives. It is therefore important for managers in general to understand the arguments related to each of the two major alternative practices — immediate reductions or spreading the effects.

The implications of the practice selected should also be understood clearly by anyone who is interested in analyzing the financial statements of companies reporting investment tax credits.

Accounting Examples

It is common practice for companies to estimate income tax expense each month based on income computed before deducting such an estimate and to record this estimated expense along with the liability connected with it. Thus:

Estimated Federal Income Tax Expense $1,261,520
   Liability for Federal Income Tax $1,261,520

In accounting for investment credits, the question is: Should a credit be entered in the accounts as an immediate reduction in the estimated income tax for the period already recorded (as just illustrated)? Or should it be deferred currently and taken gradually as reductions in estimated income tax expense over the life of the depreciable assets involved?

To illustrate, if investment credits amount to $150,000 for a period, on acquired assets having an estimated useful life of ten years, should they be accounted for as:

A. Liability for Federal Income Tax $150,000
    Estimated Federal Income Tax Expense $150,000

Or should they be acccounted for as:

B. Liability for Federal Income Tax $150,000
    Deferred Taxes $150,000

and to be followed each year of estimated useful life (assuming straight-line depreciation) by the entry:

Deferred Taxes $15,000
Estimated Federal Income Tax Expense $15,000

In each of the foregoing examples, it should be noted that the income tax liability, and thus the amount to be paid to the government, is reduced immediately by the amount of the investment credits. The only question is whether the $150,000 should be taken immediately as a reduction in the estimated income tax expense, and thus as an immediate increase of the same amount in the net income reported for the period, or spread out over the estimated life of the depreciable assets involved.

Arguments in Favor of Immediate Reductions

The principal argument in favor of treating an investment credit entirely as a reduction of the federal income tax for the year in which the credit arises is the belief that the intent underlying the treatment of these credits in the Revenue Acts of 1962, 1964, and 1971 was to provide a selective, immediate reduction in taxes to those who met certain stated requirements.

It is argued further that as a result of taking advantage of an investment credit a company is left at the end of the year with "money" to the extent of the credit which it would not otherwise have had. Thus this is obviously entirely a benefit of the year in which the credit is taken. The money in this case arises from a reduction in the outward flow of cash for the payment of income taxes.

It is also sometimes argued that if the credit is spread over the life of the acquired property, instead of being taken entirely into income of the year it arises, the deferred credit which must then appear on the liabilities side of the balance sheet is an anomaly, since it is neither a liability nor an ownership claim.

Arguments in Favor of Spreading the Effects

The principal argument for reflecting an investment credit in net income over the productive life of acquired property is the belief that income should be recognized when created by the use of property and not simply by its purchase.

Thus, in the same way that a purchasing agent is living up to his professional duty when he takes advantage of a saving connected with a purchase, the argument goes, so is a top management that takes advantage of investment tax credits in purchasing depreciable assets. A saving on a purchase should not be accounted for as income at the time of purchase. Whatever real profit (or loss) is to accrue to a company from a purchase will come in due time through the use or sale of the item purchased.

While the analogy is not perfect, suppose a company owed for materials already purchased and was told by the supplier that if it bought another lot during the current period it could reduce what it now owed him by an amount equal to 7% of the invoice price of the new lot. If the company took advantage of this offer and purchased an additional $100,000 of materials, how should it account for the $7,000 credit?

The debit would of course be to Accounts Payable. But, should the credit be treated as immediate income or as a reduction in the cost of the new lot of materials purchased? Surely, it should be the latter, since the offer was really for a discount on a new lot if purchased currently. The fact that the amount of the discount on the new purchase could be applied immediately as an offset to money already owed was simply a matter of making the financial terms in the timing of payments more attractive.

Somewhat similarly, in connection with investment tax credits, the government is saying that if a company will buy certain types of facilities it may apply (debit) an amount equal to a certain percentage of their costs as an offset to what it owes currently for income taxes.

The question then is: Should the credit matching this debit in the company's accounts be treated in net effect as immediate income, or in net effect as a reduction in the cost of the facilities acquired? I believe it should be the latter, as in the case of the purchase of materials just described.

Availability of Funds Provided

As we have noted, those who favor treating investment tax credits as immediate income hold that a company taking advantage of such credits is thereby left with money it otherwise would not have. Nonetheless, it is wise to go beyond this and recognize that for all practical purposes the money so provided is then tied up in the facilities whose purchase was stimulated by the availability of such credits.

In other words, the government offer was to assist companies indirectly to purchase certain facilities. And it should be assumed that the funds provided by investment tax credits have been used for this purpose. Certainly, this is a more rational assumption than that the intent was to provide money for immediate distribution to stockholders.

Thus the money saved through reduction of the current amount owed for taxes is not available for distribution to stockholders, even if the investment credits are accounted for as immediate reductions in tax expense and consequently as immediate increases in net income. Moreover, if the amount of an investment tax credit is passed along to customers in the form of lower prices for goods sold, or lower rates for services rendered, it never will become distributable income to the company or its stockholders.

The funds provided by investment tax credits are initially tied up in the facilities purchased with their assistance. Thus they will become available as distributable net income to stockholders only as they are recovered over the life of the property from the company's customers in the selling price for goods sold or services rendered.

Since these funds are not available to stockholders when first received, it is wiser in a conservative sense to take investment tax credits into income only over the life of the facilities as these recoveries take place rather than to take them entirely into income at the time the credits are granted.

In further explanation of this point, for income tax purposes a company is allowed to depreciate (over their useful lives) 100% of the cost of facilities to which investment tax credits are related, even though part of this cost was indirectly paid for by these credits.

Thus, if depreciation is recovered in full from customers over the life of the facilities purchased with the aid of these credits, the company will not only have recovered its own funds invested in the facilities, but also the funds provided by the credits as well. These funds will not be taxable and as they are received, the company will have earned the investment credits. Moreover, the money recovered from them will then represent income actually available either for distribution to stockholders or for reinvestment.

Accounting for Investment Grants

In recent years in Great Britain the government has made investment grants under specified conditions to companies which have constructed productive facilities in selected areas suffering from depressed economic conditions. These have been outright grants of money, i.e., not conditional on a company's income tax situation, as in the United States, which have amounted in some cases to 40% of the cost of facilities acquired.

Despite the fact that these grants have represented money in hand, they have not been accounted for as income at the time received. Instead, they have been treated as deferred items on the liabilities side of the balance sheet and brought into income over the estimated useful lives of the assets.

Thus British companies have been accounting for grants in the same way as the major alternative of spreading the tax expense effects we have been discussing in the accounting for investment tax credits.

In Great Britain, however, a company receiving an investment grant is allowed to depreciate for income tax purposes only such an amount as it has itself invested in the facilities involved.

Thus, if a company is profitable, the British government stands to recover in time through income taxes a substantial portion of the investment grants granted to it. The money thus recovered by the government will never at any time have been earned for the company as distributable income, even though the latter had the use of this money for the purchase of facilities.

The point is that when funds are provided for investment by either grants or investment credits, they will not represent income available for distribution to stockholders until recovered tax-free from customers in payment for goods sold or service rendered.

Businessmen's Views on Investment Credits . . .

For a number of years, I have asked businessmen for their opinions on how companies should account for and report investment tax credits. Our discussions have focused on the issues we have noted.

The majority of financial executives not directly connected with accounting have favored taking these credits into net income for the year in which they arise. This viewpoint appears to stem in part at least from the current emphasis on cash flow in financial circles.

The majority of nonfinancial executives, and those most directly connected with accounting, including public accountants, have favored amortization of the credits over the useful lives of the assets acquired.

When I have asked businessmen whether an investment tax credit up to 40% of the costs of assets acquired should be treated as income in the year received, the response from everyone has always been "No." It has then seemed evident to me that those who favored taking investment credits into income for the year in which they arise did so as a matter of opportunism limited only by the amount of money involved and not as a matter of principle.

The Future Trend

The amendment to the Revenue Act of 1971, the reader will recall, stated in part that "No taxpayer shall be required to use, for purposes of financial reports subject to the jurisdiction of any federal agency or reports made to any federal agency, any particular method of accounting for the credit allowed by such Section 38."

This ruling was in fact a victory for those people who believe that investment tax credits should be treated as immediate decreases in tax expense and thereby as increases in net income for the year of acquisition.

It was a victory for them because just prior to the adoption of this amendment the Accounting Principles Board was proposing to publish an opinion on the subject, the substance of which was that ". . . benefits arising from investment credits should be accounted for as reductions of income tax expense over the periods in which the cost of the related property is charged to income."

Had this opinion been put into effect, no other method of accounting for investment tax credits, including treating them as increases in net income for the year of acquisition, would have been permissible as a generally accepted accounting practice.

The amendment itself allows, if not encourages, those who have been treating investment tax credits as increases in net income for the year of acquisition to continue to do so. It does not necessarily encourage those who have been spreading out the effects of the investment credits over the lives of the assets acquired to switch to the much less conservative practice of taking them entirely into income in the year of acquisition.

However, the pressure on top managements of publicly held companies to show favorable earnings per share in order to stand up well in the marketplace for capital (stocks and bonds) is such that many companies have made this switch, particularly where competitors in the same industry had been following the less conservative practice. The passing of the amendment has assured that those who make such a switch will not, in the minds of Congress at least, be subject to censure for doing so.

Thus, in the future, it is still left for the management of each company to decide whether income tax credits should be reported as gains resulting immediately from the purchase of facilities or as gains realized over the useful lives of the facilities purchased. Nonetheless, the probability is that more and more companies will be reporting them as immediate gains.

Accounting Principles by Legislation

Although I believe that the trend just noted is regrettable, it is nowhere near so as the fact that in passing the amendment, Congress established a dangerous precedent by legislating for the first time what is to be allowed as acceptable practice in financial reporting for purposes other than taxation.

In taking this step, Congress preempted or undercut the authority of both the APB and the SEC to determine acceptable accounting practices. Moreover, it opened the gates for political changes in accounting practice to meet special interests.

Whatever the merits of the position taken by the Treasury Department, and supported by Congress, relative to the economic welfare of the nation, the passing of the amendment just discussed was a sorry event in the proper development of accounting principles.

Historical Background

Investment tax credits were provided for in the Revenue Act of 1962, as we have noted. In December 1962, in its Opinion on *Accounting for*

Investment Tax Credits, the APB stated: "We conclude that the allowable investment credit should be reflected in net income over the productive life of the acquired property and not in the year in which it is placed in service."[1]

This opinion was adopted by the assenting votes of fourteen members of the board, of whom one assented with qualification. Six members of the board dissented. The number of members of the board voting for and against this opinion is mentioned here to indicate the marked diversity of opinion, even among those professionals, as to the proper accounting for investment credits.

In January 1963, the Securities and Exchange Commission issued a release in which it noted, because of substantial diversity of opinion among responsible persons in the matter of accounting for the investment credit, that the commission would accept financial statements in which the credit was accounted for either in accordance with APB's Opinion No. 2 or as a reduction in taxes otherwise applicable to the year in which the credit arises.[2]

This ruling by the SEC effectively undercut the Accounting Principles Board's Opinion No. 2.

Under the pressure of the lack of general acceptance, the APB in March 1964 amended its Opinion No. 2, as indicated by the following statements:

> The Board, in light of events and developments occurring since the issuance of Opinion No. 2, has determined that its conclusions as there expressed have not attained the degree of acceptability which it believes necessary to make the Opinion effective.
>
> In the circumstances the Board believes that, while the method of accounting for the investment credit recommended in paragraph 13 of Opinion No. 2 should be considered to be preferable, the alternative method of treating the credit as a reduction of federal income taxes of the year in which the credit arises is also acceptable.[3]

Opinion No. 4 was adopted by the assenting votes of fifteen members of the board, of whom eight assented with qualification. Five members of the board dissented.

---

[1] APB Opinion No. 2, *Accounting for Investment Tax Credits* (New York: Accounting Principles Board, American Institute of Certified Public Accountants, December 1962), paragraph 13.

[2] See Accounting Series Release No. 96 (January 1963).

[3] APB Opinion No. 4, *Accounting for the Investment Credit* (March 1964), paragraphs 9 and 10.

APB Proposed Opinion in 1971

The Revenue Act of 1971, as first passed by the House on October 6, 1971, had made no provision as to the accounting treatment of investment tax credits.

Earlier, the APB had reviewed the problem as to the best method of accounting for investment tax credits. Then, after passage of the act by the House, the APB circulated approximately 100,000 copies of a proposed Opinion on the subject and invited written reactions to it.

The substance of this opinion, as we noted earlier, was that "benefits arising from investment tax credits should be accounted for as reductions of income tax expense over the periods in which the cost of the related property is charged to income." In other words, the investment tax credits should be accounted for over the years of useful life during which charges are made for depreciation on such property.

Thus in 1971, the APB had in mind returning to the position it had taken in Opinion No. 2 in 1962.

Senate Finance and Treasury Viewpoints

The report of the Senate Finance Committee on its version of the 1971 Revenue Act clearly suggested that companies should be free to think of the investment tax credits as a decrease in the price of the equipment purchased or as a selective tax rate reduction. Therefore, companies should be free either to spread the effect of the credits over the life of the facilities purchased or to flow them through to current income.

The Treasury Department strongly supported a continuation of the optional treatment. Both the Senate Finance Committee and the Treasury Department feared the adverse effect on the economy that might result from the elimination of the flow-through method and from the consequent drop in motivation to purchase facilities. The Treasury Department in particular feared that "any change in the pre-existing well-established financial accounting practice (flow-through) might operate to diminish the job-creating effect of the credit."

The Senate supported the view of its Finance Committee by adopting an amendment to the Revenue Bill, which with modifications became the amendment to the Revenue Act of 1971 quoted earlier in this chapter.[4]

---

[4] For an excellent summary of events leading up to this amendment, see Gilbert Simonetti, Jr., "Accounting for the Investment Credit," *The Journal of Accountancy,* February 1972.

TABLE 8
Investment Tax Credit*

	1976	1975	1974	1973	1972	1971	1970
Flow-through method	502	518	504	496	489	329	245
Deferral method	76	60	72	78	77	82	54
No reference to inv. cr.	22	22	24	26	34	189	301
	600	600	600	600	600	600	600

*Copyright ©1977 by the American Institute of Certified Public Accountants, Inc.

Opposition by Professional Societies

Before the amendment was passed, strong opposition to it was voiced by professional accountants and financial analysts through their professional societies. The strongest objections were against this precedent in legislating accounting principles. As the Financial Analysts Federation stated:

> ... we do not believe accounting and reporting standards should be established by legislation, especially without opportunity for hearing from investors who are affected by such standards. This provision undercuts the established authority of the Securities and Exchange Commission and the Accounting Principles Board for the determination of accounting standards. We fear that this action, if finally adopted by the Congress, will encourage special interest groups to attempt to bring about other changes in accounting standards through the legislative process. We believe this will result in a growing loss of confidence in corporate financial reporting to the detriment of investors.[5]

Recent Trends

Fortunately, in the years since 1971 the practice of establishing accounting principles through legislation has not increased. Some of our more severe critics of existing methods of accounting and financial reporting have continued to press for the tightening of accounting standards through government control, but not through the legislative process. They have called particularly for federal enforcement of uniformity in the development and application of accounting standards.

While the maximum possible investment tax credit available has been increased from 7 percent to 10 percent, there does not appear to have been much shifting between the use of the flow-through method

---

[5] *Ibid.*, p. 77.

and the deferral method in accounting for such credits since 1971. Proof of this is to be found in Table 8 from *Accounting Trends and Techniques* published by the research division of the American Institute of Certified Public Accountants. The table is a summary of information from the annual reports of 600 companies studied.

The table indicates a high preference for use of the flow-through method. Among those who use the deferral method, however, are companies such as General Electric, General Motors, and IBM. Thus, those who use this method, though outnumbered, are at least in rather good company.

CHAPTER 12

The Balance Sheet: Other Assets

The two final categories of assets appearing in balance sheets are those of intangible assets such as goodwill and deferred charges such as deferred advertising expense.

When a company incurs an unusually heavy expenditure, which is to benefit future accounting periods, it will commonly account for it initially as a deferred charge and amortize it over whatever number of periods seems reasonable. For example, heavy promotional expenditures connected with a new product might be accounted for in this way. Expenditures by an airline for retraining pilots, engineers, and ground crews upon the adoption of a new type of airplane is another example.

Treating such expenditures as deferred charges is in keeping with the concept of a proper matching of costs and revenues by accounting periods. To charge such expenditures immediately as expenses would result in a. an overstatement of expenses; b. an understatement of net income in the current period; and c. a reverse effect on stated expenses and net income of later periods benefiting from the expenditures.

Deferred charges are assets only in the sense that they are applications of funds of future benefit to the company and payment for them currently saves having to pay for them in the future. Obviously, they would not serve as collateral for a loan and would disappear in value if the company suddenly ceased operations. Such expenditures are, however, considered to be of continuing value under the concept of a going concern.

Accounting for Goodwill

All companies able to continue in operation presumably have some goodwill, in a layman's sense, attached to them. Goodwill appearing in a balance sheet, however, arises only in connection with the purchase of another company. This occurs when the total price paid is in excess of values that can be assigned to the net tangible assets and net identifiable intangible assets (such as patents) acquired.

For example, let us assume that $10 million is paid for a company and, by means of appraisals or other determinations, that $8 million of this was paid for tangible assets and identifiable intangible assets, net of the liabilities that also had to be taken over. In this case, the assumption would be that $2 million had been paid for goodwill.

For so long as the company acquired is not resold or abandoned, goodwill cannot be amortized as an expense or loss for income tax purposes. Thus to the extent that can be justified, the purchasing company in an acquisition assigns as much of the purchase price as possible to both tangible assets and identifiable intangible assets, which later can be treated as expenses, amortized, or depreciated for income tax purposes.

If an acquired company is later sold or abandoned, whatever goodwill had been paid for can then be taken into account for tax purposes in arriving at the gain or loss on disposal. Thus in recent years when General Mills phased out its grain business, the goodwill that had been involved earlier in the purchase of its grain subsidiaries could then be treated as losses for income tax purposes.

Amortization of Goodwill

In an earlier day, goodwill could, if a company saw fit to do so, be written off immediately against capital surplus or retained earnings. It would thus appear only briefly as an asset and never appear thereafter as part of either the asset or equity base against which one might measure return on investment. Moreover, although the goodwill might be lost in time, its loss would never appear as an element of expense or loss in the income statement.

Immediate write-offs of goodwill against capital surplus or retained earnings are not now considered to be acceptable accounting practices. Nor should it be written off or down to a nominal amount immediately after acquisition even though reported in the income statement as an extraordinary item of expense.

The Accounting Principles Board has expressed the opinion that goodwill should be amortized in a systematic manner over its estimated useful life, which should not however exceed 40 years.[1]

---

[1]APB Opinion No. 17, *Intangible Assets* (New York: Accounting Principles Board, American Institute of Certified Public Accountants, August 1970).

Straight-line amortization was assumed in this opinion to represent the most desirable systematic manner, unless it was clearly evident that some other pattern of amortization was more appropriate.

The APB concluded that few, if any, intangible assets last forever. Thus, as a practical matter, an arbitrary limit to the estimated useful life had to be established for accounting purposes.

Those who oppose this view hold that the useful life of an intangible asset, including goodwill, is dependent on individual circumstances. Therefore, estimates of this life should be made by responsible people who know the given situation instead of set or limited by an arbitrary rule.

Accounting for R & D Costs

In times past there were wide variations in practices among companies in accounting for research and development costs. The larger and financially stronger companies tended to write off such costs as expenses at the time they took place.

However, newer and less financially strong companies tended to account for such costs as deferred charges. These deferred charges were carried as assets until such time as their worth, or lack of it, could be established.

On the one hand, if it became evident that a given project was worthless, the costs deferred on it would then be charged off as expenses or losses. On the other hand, if a project proved to be of value — either to produce revenue in the accounting periods ahead or as something the entire rights to which could preferably be sold to someone else — an appropriate schedule would be worked out to amortize the accumulated costs against revenues as received.

In between these practices, some companies wrote off to expense basic research costs, or all research costs, but accounted for development costs as deferred charges. Research costs were expensed in these cases for two reasons.

The first reason was because of uncertainty as to whether the research projects on which they were expended would ever prove to be profitable, and the other, because the companies involved had tended to spend about the same amount of money on research each year. Thus they preferred to report these steady charges against income rather than the fluctuating charges that would come from the ever-shifting pattern of successes and failures in research.

In its Statement of Accounting Standards No. 2, October 1974, the FASB eliminated these options in accounting for research and development costs. With two exceptions, all such costs must now be charged to expense when incurred.

One of these exceptions is where the costs are for research and development activities for others under a contractual arrangement.

The other is for activities that are unique to enterprises in the extractive industries, such as prospecting, acquisition of mineral rights, exploration, drilling, mining, and related mineral development.

Some companies were not pleased with this ruling which forced them to expense all research and development costs as incurred. There was some feeling that all companies were being forced to follow this practice because a few companies that should have been following it had not done so.

Given a reasonably capable R & D organization, one can, of course, argue that expenditures on a project may justifiably be accounted for as deferred charges until evidence has been established that it is a lost cause. In such an organization, the total expenditures being deferred at any given time should represent expenditures on projects having a total potential of earnings far in excess of the total expenditures to date, even though a number of the projects on hand will in time prove to be failures.

The deferred charges in this instance might be likened to work-in-process in a factory at any given time, where good units must bear at least a fair share of the cost of the unfortunate units that have fallen along the way, and some units, although currently good, will never see the end of the finishing-room floor. Just because some units will not become marketable is no reason for writing off the entire lot.

The major argument for expensing R&D costs at the time they are incurred is that of conservatism because of the uncertainties connected with such projects. Conservatism is also part of the second reason given earlier; namely, where a company spends a fairly steady amount year by year on R&D costs and it is considered desirable to have these steady payments reflected in its income statement, rather than the fluctuations of successes and failures.

In addition to supporting conservatism in financial reporting, Statement No. 2 is a step in meeting a major objective of the board, namely, to reduce the number of alternative accounting practices presently followed.

The statement also aims at having companies supply more useful information about research and development costs. It does this by requiring that in the financial statements disclosure shall be made of the total research and development costs charged to expense in each period for which an income statement is presented.

However, conservatism in balance-sheet presentation is the dominant thrust of Statement No. 2, while the proper matching of costs and revenues in the income statement is made subordinate to it.

Accounting for Other Deferred Charges

In addition to deferring certain advertising expenses, promotional expenses, and retraining expenses, as mentioned at the outset of this chapter, a number of other types of expenditure are also accounted for as deferred charges to be amortized over future accounting periods.

Organization expenses, for example, as illustrated in Chapter 7, are commonly carried in the accounts and on the balance sheet as deferred charges until such time as there is revenue against which to amortize them. Similarly, heavy start-up costs on many different types of activity are first accounted for as deferred charges.

For several types of revenue and expense there are differences between what is considered appropriate financial accounting and reporting, and required practice for income tax purposes. The difference in mind here are differences in timing the recording and reporting of these types of revenue and expense and are often spoken of as differences in timing the recognition of a given type of revenue or expense. They will be discussed more fully in Chapter 16. For the moment we are concerned with their bearing on what shall be shown as deferred charges in the balance sheet.

Under proper accounting practice, for example, expenses are accrued in the financial accounts for such items as deferred compensation, bonuses, and vacation pay. But, these are not allowed as expenses for income tax purposes until paid. In the initial period of such a timing difference, therefore, there would be less expense, more taxable income, and a higher tax in reporting for tax purposes than would be computed on the smaller amount of income recorded in the company's accounts.

Similarly, there are some types of revenue that are accounted for later than required for income tax purposes. For example, rent received in advance must be reported as revenue for income tax purposes as of the time received, but would not be reported by a company as revenue until it had been earned in the time period for which it was paid. Here as in the previous example, in the initial period of the timing difference, the total income tax to be paid is greater than the tax computed on the income recorded in the company's accounts.

In both examples, increases in taxes currently payable because of differences between company accounting practice and required practice for income tax purposes are accounted for as deferred charges. In a later period or periods, the effects would be reversed and the initial deferred charges would be eliminated.

Commonly, these deferred charges are debited to an account titled Deferred Income Taxes. This same account is credited when revenue is recognized earlier in financial reporting than in income tax reporting (as in accounting for installment sales), and where expenses are deducted earlier for income tax purposes than for financial reporting (accelerated depreciation vs. straight-line depreciation). In most companies these deferred credits are likely to be greater than the deferred charges for any given period. Thus at the close of an accounting period, the balance in the Deferred Income Taxes account is likely to be a credit balance, which will be shown among the liabilities in the balance sheet, rather than a debit balance to be shown as one of the Other Assets. (See Chapter 13).

A final type of deferred charge we shall consider is that of bond discount and expense. When bonds are sold at a discount or premium, the issuing company records them at their face value and maintains a separate record of the premium, or discount and expense, involved in the issue. These separate amounts are then amortized over the life of the bonds, generally on a straight-line basis. Unamortized bond discount and expense are usually listed among the assets as deferred charges, while unamortized bond premium is listed as a separate item within the long-term debt classification.

CHAPTER 13

The Balance Sheet: Deferred Income Taxes, Long-Term Debt, and Owners' Equity

Deferred Income Taxes

The current liabilities, discussed in Chapter 8, are commonly followed in the balance sheet by the item *provision for deferred income taxes*.

As we noted in Chapter 10, when a company is reporting depreciation on an accelerated basis for income tax purposes and on the straight-line basis in reporting to stockholders and others, it is required under generally accepted accounting principles to report, for the latter purpose, the estimated income tax with depreciation computed on the straight-line basis.

The difference between this estimated income tax and the amount of tax actually owed to the government with depreciation computed on an accelerated basis is carried to a deferred income tax account. Many companies also include in this account as it appears in the balance sheet the then balance of investment credits being amortized over the useful lives of the depreciable assets for which such credits had been granted.

Many arguments have taken place as to the exact nature of the provision for deferred income taxes, i.e., as to whether it represents a liability, ownership claim, or deferred income. Some hold that it is none of these things and should not be allowed to exist. They believe that the income tax figure appearing in reports to stockholders and others should be only such amount as is actually owed to the government for any given period (in the income statement) and at any given time (in the balance sheet).

Along with many others who believe in the accounting procedures which involve the use of the provisions for deferred income taxes, I would be glad to see an end to this rather futile argumentation by general agreement that this provision is nothing more, or less, than a source of funds. If such an identification is not adequate, then surely man will in time be ingenious enough to develop a suitable classification of this item that will allow for its peaceful coexistence on the right-hand side of the balance sheet sandwiched comfortably between liabilities and capital.

Long-Term Debt

A major source of funds for many companies is some form of long-term indebtedness. For corporations, this indebtedness is commonly in the form of bonds paying interest at a specified rate. Although there are bonds of various types, each having particular features, the two major classifications are *mortgage bonds* and *debentures*.

Mortgage bonds are backed by specific stated properties which may be claimed by the bondholders if the terms of the indenture are not met and particularly if the issuing company passes out of existence.

Debentures have only a general claim on the assets of a company. However, where debentures are the only types of long-term indebtedness issued by a company, they are likely to contain provisions preventing the pledging of certain types of assets as security for other types of debt.

Bonds are commonly listed in a balance sheet as long-term liabilities and described as to type, rate of interest, and due date, e.g., First Mortgage 8% Bonds due 1988.

While bonds have a face value of a stated amount, usually $1,000 or multiples thereof, the actual price at which they sell is dependent on the rate of interest at the time of the sale considered appropriate by the buyer (or the bond market in general) for the class of bond being sold. Thus a bond paying interest at 8% of its face value may sell at a discount or premium and thereby yield the buyer a return on his investment which is greater or less than 8%. For example, if one were to buy such a bond having a face value of $1,000 for $941.18, the interest of $80 per year would provide a return on the investment of 8.5%, i.e., $80 \div \$941.18 = 8.5\%$.

If the issuing company sells bonds at a premium or discount, it records the bonds at their face value and maintains a separate record of the premium or discount and expense involved in the issue. These separate amounts are then amortized over the life of the bonds, generally on a straight-line basis.[1]

In a detailed balance sheet, unamortized bond discount and expense are usually listed among the assets as deferred charges, while unamortized bond premium is listed as a separate item within the long-term debt classification.

In a condensed balance sheet, long-term debt is shown net of unamortized discount, expense, and premium. There is much to be said for bringing these factors together even in a detailed balance sheet in order to show clearly the net liability for long-term debt as of the balance-sheet date.

Among the various types of bonds are those having a convertible feature by which they may, at the option of the holder, be converted to common stock of the issuing company at a specified price. These are classified in the balance sheet as long-term debt until such time as their conversion or retirement takes place.

Another type of bond carries with it detachable warrants to purchase stock. Here, the issuing company is expected to allocate the proceeds from the sale of the securities between the bonds and warrants in proportion to the fair value of each as of the time of issuance. The portion allocated to the bonds then appears in the balance sheet under the classification of long-term debt, while that proportion allocated to the warrants is classified as paid-in capital.[2]

Sinking Fund

Many bond indentures call for periodic payments into a sinking fund held by a trustee to be used to retire the bonds on or before their maturity.

The sinking fund eliminates the heavy drain on cash that would otherwise be called for at maturity or the necessity to refund the indebtedness at a time that might not be favorable. The gradual reduction of the indebtedness, where the sinking fund has been used to retire bonds before their maturity, tends to strengthen the support under the bonds still outstanding, in the sense that pressure on earnings in the future to meet interest payments and reduction of debt is thereby reduced.

---

[1] For the proper handling of the unamortized bond premium, discount, and expense at the time bonds are refunded, see Accounting Research Bulletin No. 43 (New York: American Institute of Certified Public Accountants, June 1953), Chapter 15.

[2] See APB Opinion No. 14, *Accounting for Convertible Debt and Debt Issued With Stock Purchase Warrants*, March 1969.

The requirement of a sinking fund is particularly appropriate where the funds received from the initial sale of the bonds are invested in assets subject to depreciation or depletion. In such cases, the funds to meet sinking fund requirements should come in large part from reimbursements by customers each period to cover the depreciation and depletion that has taken place. If the money so received is not put into a sinking fund, or used directly to retire bonds outstanding, but is used for some other purpose instead, it could well be that funds would not be available to meet the bond indebtedness at maturity, i.e., at the time it fell due.

For example, let us suppose that a company has borrowed $20 million by the sale of bonds in that amount that will mature in 20 years. Also, that it has invested this money in machinery and equipment having an economic life of 20 years. Thus, we assume that at the end of 20 years, the machinery and equipment will be worthless, while at the same time, the bond indebtedness for the full $20 million will fall due.

We would certainly hope that over the next 20 years, the company would receive enough from the sale of goods produced by this machinery and equipment to be reimbursed not only for the out-of-pocket costs involved, but also for the depreciation suffered by the machinery and equipment amounting to $1 million per year if computed on a straight-line basis. Of course we would hope that our company might make a reasonable profit in addition, but this is beside the point at the moment.

It is clear that unless the money received from customers as reimbursement for depreciation, in our case the $1 million per year, is put into a sinking fund or used directly to retire outstanding bonds, and instead is expended for some other purpose, the company may well face the embarrassment of not being able to meet its bond indebtedness when it falls due. Hence the desirability of having a sinking fund requirement in the bond indenture.

If the life of the bonds coincides exactly with, or is longer than, the useful life of the depreciable property in which the bond money is invested, and if revenues from customers are adequate to at least cover all costs including depreciation and depletion, it will not be necessary to draw on funds from earnings to meet sinking fund requirements.

However, if the life of the bonds is less than the useful life of the depreciable property in which the bond money is invested, or if the money recovered is invested in some asset which is permanent, such as an investment in a subsidiary company, or, like inventory, subject to turnover but not to depreciation or depletion, it will be necessary to draw upon funds provided by earnings to meet sinking fund requirements.

This assumes that funds provided by sources other than depreciation, depletion, and profit are committed to other uses; and, therefore, that these funds are not available to be put into the sinking fund.

Owners' Equity

Occasionally, the word capital is associated with the total resources (assets) of a business, as when someone asks, "How much money is tied up in that business?"

In financial circles, the words capital and capitalization usually refer to the combination of long-term debt and owners' equity. Thus it might be stated in a given case, for example, that a company's capitalization consists of 25% long-term debt and 75% owners' equity. Again, it is sometimes stated that the amount of a company's capital is found by subtracting total current liabilities from total assets.

The most common use of the word capital in accounting, however, is with reference to owners' equity, consisting of owners' claims to funds they have invested in the business and their claims to funds retained in the business that have come from earnings.

In a *single proprietorship*, the owner's equity is usually shown as a single balance sheet figure covering both the capital he has put into the business and net earnings he has left there. Since, from a creditor viewpoint, the owner's liability in this case is not limited to what he has put into the business, and since the published balance sheet of a single proprietorship is usually for the benefit of creditors, there is no particular point in attempting to distinguish between paid-in capital and retained earnings.

For the owner, however, useful information is provided by separating these matters in the accounts and also by maintaining a separate owner's salary or drawing account.

In a *partnership*, the owners' equity is usually shown in a balance sheet broken down by individual partners, unless it is a very large partnership. But the owners' equity is not separated by paid-in capital and retained earnings for the reasons stated with respect to the same matter in a single proprietorship. For internal management use, separate partners' accounts are usually maintained for such items as paid-in capital, share of net earnings retained, drawings, and for loans to or from the partnership.

In a corporation, the right-hand side of its balance sheet used to be titled "Liabilities and Capital." Today it is usually titled "Liabilities and Shareholders' Equity" or "Liabilities and Stockholders' Equity." The owners' equity (shareholders' or stockholders') is shown in at least two parts: "Capital Stock" (or "Paid-in Capital") and "Retained Earnings" (formerly often called "Surplus").

Where the capital stock is shown at a par or stated value, the difference between this value and the amount paid initially for the stock by stockholders, usually less costs connected with the issue, is shown as "Capital in Excess of Par or Stated Value," as "Paid-in Surplus," or as "Capital Surplus."

The ownership equity in paid-in capital, however shown, is kept separate from the ownership equity in retained earnings, both because the amount of paid-in capital is usually the limit of the amount of ownership in a company that a creditor can rely upon when granting credit to it, and because funds equal to the figure for retained earnings are legally available for dividends, even in cases where it is likely that they will be retained by the company permanently.

It is highly important for the lay reader of financial statements to grasp the fact that ownership equity, whether in the category of paid-in capital or retained earnings, represents a claim to funds and not the funds themselves. The funds entering a business either as paid-in capital, or earnings, are, if still on hand, among the assets listed on the other side of the balance sheet, inseparable from funds derived from other sources.

It will be recalled from our discussion of funds flow in Chapter 6 that, in accounting terms, paid-in capital and net income represent sources of funds and not funds in themselves. So too, we noted that the assets in a balance sheet show where the resources (funds) of the business are located as of the given date, by categories and monetary amounts, while the liability and ownership categories which are listed by amounts on the other side of the same balance sheet summarize the sources of these funds.

These matters are important, particularly since there are those who mistakenly think of retained earnings, which used to be called "surplus," as idle money which could better be paid out as wages, taxes, or dividends.

In many corporations, ownership equity will consist of preferred stock in addition to common stock, paid-in surplus, and retained earnings. In some cases, particularly in foreign countries, there are also reserves of one kind or another which, as of the balance-sheet date, represent ownership claims although subject to possible future loss.

Preferred Stock

This is a class of stock having a preferred claim over common stock as to dividends if a company is successful and as to recovery of investment if it is not. The owner of preferred stock is a shareholder in a business and not, like a bondholder, a creditor. Dividends paid to preferred stockholders are distributions of earnings of a business in contrast to interest payments to bondholders which are expenses of a business. Thus a bondholder is due payment of interest simply with the passing of time.

The obligation to pay dividends on preferred stock is first conditional upon a company's having earned a profit to provide funds which might be distributed and then upon a formal declaration of a dividend by the company's board of directors.

The amount of dividend that will be paid on a preferred stock, if one is to be paid, is stated on the stock certificates and in the balance-sheet description of the stock. The amount is stated either as a given number of dollars per share of stock or as a percentage of the par value of the stock. The description also states whether or not dividends are cumulative. If they are cumulative, the accumulated amount of any unpaid dividends must be declared and paid before any dividends can be declared and paid on common stock.

Since dividends on preferred stock are fixed in amount or percentage, the market value of the stock is dependent on how the return on it measures up to returns currently available from other forms of investment, with relative risks and expectations of business conditions in the future being taken into account. And since the amount to be received from dividends is fixed at best, and zero at worst, the growth potential in the market value of ordinary preferred stock is limited.

Although the analogy is a bit stretched, investing in such stocks is somewhat like betting to place, rather than to win or to show. The reasoning here is that they offer the potential of a return higher than the more certain interest of an investment in bonds, and less risk than an investment in common stock, in the same company.

Many investors seek the best of both worlds by investing in convertible preferred stock, a type of preferred stock which later can be converted to common stock at a given ratio at the option of the holder. Such an investment usually offers a good return, although not as high as it would be without the convertible feature, and also the possibility, if all goes well, of appreciation in the investment through the rising value of the common stock into which it is, or can be, converted.

Preferred stock does not usually have as complete voting rights as common stock. Generally, it does have the right to vote on proposals for increasing the number of shares of preferred stock or the sale of senior securities and full voting rights if the company gets into specified difficulties.

Par and No Par Preferred Stock

Preferred stock has either a par value assigned to it by the issuing company, or it is no par stock. Par value is an arbitrary amount assigned to a share of stock and has no necessary relationship to its market value at any given time. For accounting purposes, no par stock is assigned a stated value per share by the issuing company, and this is the basis on which the stock is presented in the balance sheet.

The excess price above either the par or stated value received at the time stock is sold initially is entered in an account entitled "Paid-in Surplus," "Capital Surplus," or "Capital in Excess of Par or Stated Value," the balance of which on the date of a balance sheet appears as a separate item in the capital section of that statement.

Theoretically, and in the eyes of the law, creditors rely on a company's stated capital (at par or stated value) when granting credit to it. Actually, to the extent that creditors pay attention to financial statements at all, they rely on their appraisal of a company's working capital condition as shown by its balance sheet and on how well that company is doing judged by their analysis of its income statement.

It is true, however, that if the par or stated value of either preferred or common stock outstanding has never been paid for in full, creditors can require that the stockholders make good the deficiency in the event that the company fails and is unable to pay off its debts. Moreover, creditors can still force payment for the deficiency, even though in selling stock at a discount the selling company might have assured the buyer in writing that as far as it was concerned the stock was fully paid and nonassessable.

As a practical matter, in this country the sale of a public issue of either preferred or common stock at a discount is no longer practiced, and it would be rare to find a private issue sold in this way. To be sure, because of the expenses involved in selling stock, a company does not end up with the full amount paid by an initial stockholder. But these expenses do not include a discount to him.

One way in which the danger to a stockholder of a possible later assessment has been avoided has been by selling preferred or common stock at a premium above its par or stated value. To effect this, the stock has been assigned a low par value, or it has been no par stock with a low stated value. The low par, or low stated, values have also been adopted in order to minimize the fees or taxes involved in the sale of the stock.

In this connection, it should be recognized that corporations are created, carry on their activities, are taxed, and are dissolved under state laws. Thus these statutes have a bearing on how a company reports ownership, as well as how it treats other matters in its balance sheet.

Stock Stated at Net Amount Received on Initial Sale

Leaving legal matters, taxation, and window-dressing aside, the most logical and forthright manner in which to display any type of stock in a balance sheet is at the amount received from its initial sale net of expenses connected with its issue. Some companies do this and thereby avoid the artificial separation of paid-in capital into a stated value and paid-in surplus. In such cases, the stock is shown at the amount paid by stockholders, and the costs connected with the issues are written-off as expenses. The main point, however, is that the split into capital stock and paid-in surplus is avoided.

Common Stock

If a corporation has only one type of stock outstanding, it is often shown in the balance sheet as "Capital Stock." If it has more than one type of stock, the major ownership classification will be that of "Common Stock"; and, in fact, in many companies even where there is only one type of stock outstanding it will be labeled common stock, presumably to distinguish it from some other type of stock which might be issued later.

Nonvoting common stock. At times in the past, some companies issued more than one class of stock, such as Class A and Class B stock, only one of which has had full voting rights. The objective here, of course, was to enable those who held the voting class of stock to control the company. Provided that the prospects of the given business appeared to be attractive enough, it was possible to sell nonvoting common stock to individuals who were eager to share in the profits of that business even though they would have no vote in it.

This practice, as far as the United States is concerned, has long since passed into disfavor because of the incongruity in labeling as a common shareholder one who has no vote in the corporation and because of general distaste with the idea of a publicly held company having voting rights restricted to a relatively small group among the owners. The major practical reason, however, has been that for many years now the New York Stock Exchange has refused to list stocks of companies that do not give full voting power to all of their common stock outstanding.

Par and no par common stock. The discussions earlier of par value and no par value for preferred stock, and stock stated at the net amount received on initial sale, are equally applicable to common stock.

Paid-In Surplus and Capital Surplus

For many years, the American Institute of Certified Public Accountants, the American Accounting Association, and others have argued against the use of the word "surplus" in the connection with either paid-in capital or retained earnings. Their reasoning is that many people who are not knowledgeable with respect to financial terms tend to picture the word as representing an accumulation of money or at least as an asset and not as an ownership claim.

In response, many companies are now recording premiums received on the initial sale of preferred or common stock as "Paid-In Capital Above Par or Stated Value," while earnings are recorded as "Retained Earnings" instead of as "Earned Surplus." Dropping the word surplus appears to gave gained more acceptance with respect to earnings, however, than with respect to paid-in capital.

Retained Earnings

In the past, it was not only common practice to record earnings as "Earned Surplus" but also to charge off unusual losses directly to this account. The argument was that if such losses were taken to "Profit and Loss" for the period, and included in the income statement, the reported net income would be distorted and the comparability of the statement with income statements of other periods destroyed.

For the information of readers of the given company's financial statements, it was common practice to present a "Surplus Reconciliation Statement" showing the changes that had taken place in earned surplus between the beginning and end of the accounting period. These were changes that had resulted from the profit or loss for the period, dividends declared, and unusual gains or losses entered in that account.

The difficulty was, however, that in judging a company's performance over a number of years, attention might be paid only to its earnings and earnings per share, as reflected in its income statements, while losses charged directly to surplus would be overlooked.

With this danger as the major reason, the APB recommended the use of an all inclusive income statement.[3] This form of statement,

---

[3] APB Opinion No. 9, *Reporting the Results of Operations* (December 1966).

which has become general practice, includes all items of income and expense, except for some most unusual prior period adjustments.[4]

Extraordinary items of income or expense (not prior period adjustments), adjusted for the applicable income tax, are shown separately in the income statement, however, so that income before, as well as after, taking these items into account may be clearly stated.

The former "Surplus Reconciliation Statement" has been replaced by the "Statement of Retained Earnings," which shows the retained earnings at the beginning of the period and adjustments to it for the profit or loss for the period, dividends declared, and items, if any, of the type stated in the preceding footnote. (See Exhibit 25 as an example of a statement of retained earnings.)

Minority Interests in Subsidiary Companies

Even though a parent company does not own 100% of the stock of one or more of its subsidiaries, the entire assets and liabilities of subsidiaries that are presented in consolidated statements are brought into the consolidated balance sheet. Where there are minority interests, the net assets of subsidiaries brought into the consolidated figures will be in excess of the parent company's claim to them.

Therefore it is necessary to show the amount of the minority interests in subsidiary companies as one of the ownership claims on the liabilities side of the consolidated balance sheet. Although this represents the minority interest in both the paid-in capital and retained earnings of subsidiaries, it is shown as a single figure and not broken down by these two elements.

Treasury Stock

Shares of a company's own stock which it has purchased and is holding for some purpose are accounted for as "Treasury Stock." At the time of purchase, they are recorded at their cost and carried at this valuation until sold or retired.

---

[4] Capital transactions were excluded from the determination of net income in the recommendations of the Board in Section 28 of Opinion No. 9, as follows: "The Board reaffirms the conclusion of the former committee on accounting procedure that the following should be excluded from the determination of net income or the results of operations under all circumstances: (a) adjustments or charges or credits resulting from transactions in the company's own capital stock, (b) transfers to and from accounts properly designated as appropriated retained earnings (such as general purpose contingency reserves or provisions for replacement costs of fixed assets) and (c) adjustments made pursuant to a quasi-reorganization."

EXHIBIT 25

P. M. Stanton's Statement of Retained Earnings

	For the Years Ended	
	Dec. 31, 1977	Dec. 31, 1976
Retained earnings at beginning of period	$ 486,524	$209,809
Net income for the period	555,824	276,715
	$1,042,348	$486,524
Common Stock dividend—5% (13,245 shares and $1,561 cash for fractional shares)	134,011	–
Retained earnings at end of period	$ 908,337	$486,524

Treasury stock is usually shown in the balance sheet as a deduction from the stockholders' equity, the type of stock and number of shares being stated. When it has been acquired for later resale to employees or others, it is considered permissible to show it as an asset when the reason for doing so is adequately disclosed in the balance sheet or footnote to it.

Regardless of where it is shown in the balance sheet, it is not stock outstanding in the sense of having voting power or being entitled to receive dividends as income.

In all states, although the wording of the law differs among them, treasury stock cannot be purchased if the company's legal capital would thereby become impaired. As we noted earlier, the law considers that a creditor has relied on a company's stated legal capital in granting credit to it. Under this concept, it would not be reasonable to allow a company to dissipate legal capital by the purchase of treasury stock.

The legal requirements of individual states alter to some extent the manner in which treasury stock affects balance sheet presentation and the accounting steps involved when treasury stock is retired after purchase. For our purposes here, however, it is not necessary for us to discuss these legal differences and their effect on financial accounting.

Reserves for Contingencies

Earlier in this chapter, mention was made that reserves of one kind or another are shown in some companies' balance sheets, particularly in foreign countries, which, as of the balance-sheet date, are really part of owners' equity.

In some foreign countries, companies are allowed to create such reserves by charges to income, and later to credit back to income amounts considered to be no longer necessary. In some cases these charges and credits are used to level-out reported earnings. These are government sanctioned adjustments, in the belief that steadiness in reported earnings is desirable for the nation's economy as well as for the companies involved. In some countries, whatever is reported as net income must be paid out to the owners. Under these conditions, the use of reserves created by charges to income enables funds to be retained and used in the business that otherwise would be withdrawn.

The practices described in the previous paragraph are not allowed in our country in reporting for income tax purposes, nor are they allowable in terms of generally accepted accounting principles. The major argument here is that a loss should not be charged against income until it takes place. In the meantime, if a company fears that an event in the future is likely to cause a loss, it is quite all right for it to appropriate a portion of retained earnings as a safeguard. It does this by debiting the retained earnings account and crediting a reserve for contingencies account in an amount considered reasonable. Later, if the feared-for loss takes place, it should be charged against income and not against the reserve for contingencies. Whatever amount had been set up in that reserve should then be returned to the retained earnings account by means of a reversing bookkeeping entry, except to the extent of estimated losses on loss contingencies that still remained.

The Financial Accounting Standards Board in its Statement No. 5, March 1975, provided guidelines on the proper accounting for contingencies. Examples of loss contingencies were shown as:

1. Collectibility of receivables.
2. Obligations related to product warranties and product defects.
3. Pending or threatened litigation.

The accounting requirements of Statement No. 5 are substantially those described briefly above. Particular stress is placed on the point that the reserve or appropriation for contingencies must be shown within the stockholders' equity section of the balance sheet and be clearly identified as an appropriation of retained earnings.

A minor point in the statement is that an estimated loss from a loss contingency shall be accrued by a charge to income if *both* of the following conditions are met.

a. Information available prior to issuance of the financial statements indicates that it is probable that an asset had been impaired or a liability had been incurred at the date of the financial statements. It is implicit in this condition that it must be probable that one or more future events will occur confirming the fact of the loss.

b. The amount of loss can be reasonably estimated.

In other words, this recognizes that it takes time to prepare financial statements for public presentation. During the elapsed time, it may be discovered that what had been thought to be only a loss contingency as of the end of the accounting period is now considered to have been a loss, and therefore an item that should have been charged against income for the period.

Another minor point in the statement is that contingencies that are expected to result in gains should not be brought into the accounts on the general grounds of not recognizing revenue prior to its realization.

The statement notes in this connection that adequate disclosure shall be made of contingencies that might result in gains, but care shall be exercised to avoid misleading implications as to the likelihood of realization.

CHAPTER 14

The Balance Sheet: Ratio Analysis

In common with other companies, P. M. Stanton presented balance-sheet figures for the previous year in a column alongside the column of figures in its balance sheet for the present year. This was to aid one of the steps in financial analysis, namely, a comparison of the figures of the current year with those of the past year. Since a comparison of this type is a primary function of the funds flow statement, we shall defer discussion of it until Chapter 15.

For the present, we shall examine the ratios commonly developed in connection with balance-sheet analysis. Ratios of this type are compared from year to year within the same company and with the ratios of other companies, particularly companies of the same size and nature in the same industry.

The figures with which we shall be dealing are those reported in the P. M. Stanton Company's financial statements. For internal purposes, this company, in common with others, can also make comparisons of actual results against budgeted figures in terms of both absolute figures and ratios.

Current Ratio

Earlier, I mentioned the desirability of maintaining a satisfactory ratio between current assets and current liabilities in order that current operations might be financed smoothly through the orderly rotation of each. We noted that current assets were financed to a considerable extent through incurring current liabilities, and current liabilities were in turn paid off in large part through the liquidation of current assets. I

EXHIBIT 26
P. M. Stanton's Comparative Balance Sheets

	Dec. 31, 1977	Dec. 31, 1976
Assets		
Current assets:		
Cash	$ 929,375	$ 930,250
Accounts receivable	1,067,737	765,162
Inventories at cost on the last-in, first-out basis	1,295,351	1,515,983
Prepaid assets	81,514	51,178
Total current assets	$3,373,977	$3,262,573
Property, plant, and equipment at cost less allowances for depreciation of $945,569 and $760,720	1,362,970	1,278,479
Investment in subsidiaries at cost	43,132	34,401
Deferred development expenses	80,069	116,878
	$4,860,148	$4,692,331
Liabilities		
Current liabilities:		
Bond sinking fund installment	$ —	$ 100,000
Accounts payable (trade)	332,200	153,220
Provision for pensions	163,500	177,300
Provision for federal income tax	417,300	226,675
Other accrued liabilities	246,800	224,974
Total current liabilities	$1,159,800	$ 882,169
Provision for deferred income tax	98,301	103,418
First Mortgage 6% Bonds due 1984 (note A)	—	800,000
Capital		
Common stock of $1 par value, 350,000 shares authorized, 295,371 and 268,022 shares issued and outstanding (notes B and C)	295,371	268,022
Paid-in surplus (note C)	2,398,339	2,152,198
Retained earnings, per accompanying statement	908,337	486,524
	$4,860,148	$4,692,331

Note A. On October 15, 1977, the Company retired the outstanding First Mortgage 6% Bonds by payment of $800,000 principal and $26,075 premium.

Note B. At December 31, 1977, options to purchase 1,447 shares at $10 per share (not less than 95% of the market price at the time of granting) were outstanding and exercisable. Options terminate in 1980 or when the employee leaves the Company. During the year, options for 14,104 shares were exercised and options for 1,092 shares lapsed.

Note C. During 1977, paid-in surplus was increased by $126,936 excess of option price over par value of 14,104 shares issued upon exercise of options and $119,205 excess of market value over par value of 13,245 shares issued as a stock dividend. There were no changes in paid-in surplus during 1976.

suggested that as a rough rule many companies believed it desirable to maintain a ratio of at least 2 to 1 of current assets to current liabilities.

For 1977 and 1976, the P. M. Stanton Company had the following current ratios:

	1977		1976	
Current assets	$3,373,977	= 2.91 to 1	$3,262,573	= 3.70 to 1
Current liabilities	$1,159,800		$ 882,169	

Although the current ratio dropped considerably from 1976 to 1977, it was still a strong ratio, particularly since the company carried inventories on a conservative last-in, first-out basis.

One should, in fact, question whether the company was using its assets as effectively as it might, i.e., sometimes a high current ratio indicates that a company is not doing so. In particular, here one might question the need of maintaining such a large cash balance and consider that some of the cash might better be temporarily placed in conservative investments so that at least some interest might be earned on it.

Quick Assets Ratio, Liquidity Ratio, or "Acid Test"

These three titles are applied to the ratio between the sum of a company's most liquid assets and its current liabilities. Some analysts have only cash and marketable securities as the assets in the ratio, while others include receivables. In the figures for P. M. Stanton, the liquid assets were cash and accounts receivable. Thus the company had the following quick assets ratio:

	1977		1976	
Quick assets	$1,997,112	= 1.72 to 1	$1,695,312	= 1.92 to 1
Current liabilities	$1,159,800		$ 882,169	

Here, as in the case of the current ratio, the ratio dropped from 1976 to 1977 but it was still strong in that a rough rule calls for a ratio here of at least 1 to 1. The company's cash position in this case was particularly strong since, even after paying off a sinking fund installment of $100,000 and $800,000 of First Mortgage Bonds in 1977, it was still left with a large cash balance of just about the same size as at the beginning of the year.

Accounts Receivable Turnover

A measure of efficiency in the use of funds invested in accounts receivable is to be found in the speed with which funds so invested turn over, usually as measured by the average number of days required for collection (the number of days' sales "on the books" as of the date of the balance sheet). This is a combined test of the quality of the accounts receivable and of the company's exercise of its credit policy.

For these figures to be most meaningful, one should know the terms of sale for both the company and the trade. And sales with payment on an installment basis should be separated from cash sales and regular sales on account.

In the case of P. M. Stanton, the only sales figures we have are the net sales of $9,990,486 for the year ended December 31, 1977 and $8,821,121 for the year ended December 31, 1976. Thus for both years, the accounts receivable turnover was as follows:

$$\frac{\text{Accounts Receivable}}{\text{Net sales}} \qquad \frac{1977}{\$1,067,737} = 10.7\% \qquad \frac{1976}{\$765,162} = 8.7\%$$

Assuming a 360-day year, as analysts commonly do, P. M. Stanton's accounts receivable for 1977 equaled 38.5 days' sales (10.7% × 360). At the close of 1976, the company's accounts receivable represented 31.3 days' sales (8.7% × 360).

These computations are probably a little harsh with respect to 1977, if we can assume that sales rose steadily during the year and that sales per day for the last month were much higher than for the earlier months of the year. Thus the number of days' sales on the books as of December 31, 1977 was probably somewhat less than 38.5 and the turnover of accounts receivable somewhat higher.

Another approach to the same type of ratio is that of first computing the average sales per day for the period and then dividing the accounts receivable figure by this average to find the number of days it represents, as follows:

$$\frac{\text{Net sales}}{\text{Period days}} \qquad \frac{1977}{\frac{\$9,990,486}{360}} = \$27,751 \text{ per day} \qquad \frac{1976}{\frac{\$8,821,121}{360}} = \$24,503 \text{ per day}$$

$$\frac{\text{Accounts receivable}}{\text{Average sales per day}} \qquad \frac{\$1,067,737}{\$27,751} = 38.5 \text{ days} \qquad \frac{\$765,162}{\$24,503} = 31.2 \text{ days}$$

Inventory Turnover

The efficient utilization of working capital calls for maintaining a proper relationship between inventories and the volume of operations as measured by both production and sales activity. The desire for a high rate of inventory turnover must be balanced with the need to maintain an adequate stock to serve customers properly, and — in a manufacturing plant — to avoid holding up production for the lack of some material or purchased part.

There are also considerations of purchasing and manufacturing in economic lot sizes, of forward buying when raw material prices appear to merit such action, and of maintaining steady production in order both to manufacture economically and to keep employees steadily employed.

One method of computing turnover is to divide net sales by the inventory as of the close of the accounting period. In P. M. Stanton's case, the results would be as follows:

	1977		1976	
Net sales	$9,990,486	= 7.7 times	$8,821,121	= 5.8 times
Ending inventory	$1,295,351		$1,515,983	

Since sales figures include profit margins and inventories do not, it is preferable to divide the cost of goods sold, rather than net sales, by the inventory. For P. M. Stanton, this computation for 1977 and 1976 would be as follows:

	1977		1976	
Cost of goods sold	$6,736,490	= 5.2 times	$6,360,782	= 4.2 times
Ending inventory	$1,295,351		$1,515,983	

The gross margins in this case were relatively high. Therefore, there is a substantial difference in the turnover figures when the cost of goods sold, rather than net sales, is used as the dividend.

Since P. M. Stanton's sales increased markedly in 1977, and inventories were much lower at the end of the year than at the beginning, it could well be that the inventory turnover figure just computed for 1977 is much higher than the company could hope to sustain in the coming year.

Here, as in many cases, a more suitable measure of inventory turnover is that computed by dividing the cost of goods sold for the

EXHIBIT 27
P. M. Stanton Company's 1977 Income Statement

	For the Years Ended	
	Dec. 31, 1977	Dec. 31, 1976
Net sales	$9,990,486	$8,821,121
Cost of goods sold	6,736,490	6,360,782
Gross margin	$3,253,996	$2,460,339
Selling expense	1,482,635	1,365,342
General and administrative expenses	595,605	538,517
Total selling, general and administrative expenses	2,078,240	1,903,859
Income from operations	1,175,756	556,480
Other income and other expense: Bond interest, 1977 bond redemption expenses (Note A) less other income ($13,444 and $29,228), net	66,523	26,522
Income before provision for taxes	1,109,233	529,958
Provision for federal income tax	487,864	219,744
Provision for state income tax	65,545	33,499
Net income	$ 555,824	$ 276,715
Net income per common share (Both years shown are based on 295,371 shares outstanding on December 31, 1977)	$ 1.88	$ 0.94

Note A. On October 15, 1977 the company retired the outstanding First Mortgage 6% Bonds by payment of $800,000 principal and $26,075 premium.

period by the average of the inventories at the beginning and end of the period. Thus the inventory turnover for P. M. Stanton for 1977 would be 4.8 times, computed as follows:

Beginning inventory	$1,515,983
Ending inventory	1,295,351
Total	$2,811,334 ÷ 2 = $1,405,667

$$\frac{\text{Cost of goods sold}}{\text{Average inventory}} = \frac{1977}{\$6,736,490} = 4.8 \text{ times}$$
$$\frac{\$6,736,490}{\$1,405,667} = 4.8 \text{ times}$$

Another approach in inventory analysis, again using P. M. Stanton's 1977 figures, is to compute average inventory as a percentage of sales:

$$\frac{\text{Average inventory}}{\text{Net sales}} \quad \frac{\$1,405,667}{\$9,990,486} = 14.1\%$$

Such a percentage is helpful in preparing a budget, i.e., given the expected sales for the period being budgeted, one can apply the inventory percentage to establish how much inventory might be on hand as of the close of the period.

It should be recognized, however, that the close of the year may be a time when a company's inventory is normally at a low point. Thus neither the inventory at that time as a percentage of sales, nor inventory turnover figures based on year-end inventories will be true indicators of what should be expected as inventory percentages and rates of turnover at other times of the year.

Moreover, in the present case with inventory carried at low LIFO valuations, the computed rate of turnover would expectedly be higher than that of other companies in the trade which use some other basis of valuation. Also, in this company as in all manufacturing companies, attention should be paid internally to the breakdown of inventory. This is particularly so in terms of raw material, work-in-process, and finished goods, and not restricted to an analysis of total inventory.

Turnover of Fixed Assets

A ratio that provides a rough indication of efficiency in the utilization of fixed assets relative to sales achievement is found by dividing net sales for the year by the investment in fixed assets.

In an expansion program, such a ratio can be helpful in checking whether additional investments in fixed assets have resulted in a proportionately desirable increase in sales. Also, the ratio provides a means of approximating the volume of increased sales that might be expected from a given increase in fixed assets.

In a broad sense, the ratio is an indicator of capital intensity, i.e., whether the company and industry are characterized by heavy or light investment in fixed assets in order to achieve a given volume of sales.

The question sometimes debated is whether the figure for fixed assets used in computing the ratio should be before or after deduction of accumulated depreciation and depletion. The argument for using the investment figure net of depreciation and depletion is that it is, after all, the only amount currently invested in fixed assets. And, therefore, it is the only proper figure for fixed assets against which to measure current sales realization and, even more importantly, against which to measure net income.

One argument for using the gross fixed asset figure is that, for reasons of conservatism and income taxation, the charges for depreciation and depletion are generally higher than the amount of depreciation and depletion that is actually taking place. Therefore, the fixed asset figure net of these accumulated figures is an understatement of the investment against which sales realization and net income should be measured.

Moreover, since companies vary considerably in their practices with respect to depreciation and depletion, ratios based on the relationship of sales to gross fixed assets are more comparable between them than ratios based on the relationship of sales to net fixed assets.

A further reason for using gross fixed assets in such a computation is that the ratio resulting is a more suitable base against which to judge the early results from the expansion of fixed assets, since but little depreciation or depletion would have been taken on them.

The comparable ratios for the turnover of the gross fixed assets of the P. M. Stanton Company were as follows:

	1977		1976	
$\dfrac{\text{Net sales}}{\text{Gross fixed assets}}$	$\dfrac{\$9,990,486}{\$2,308,539}$	$= 4.3$ times	$\dfrac{\$8,821,121}{\$2,039,199}$	$= 4.3$ times

Caution and common sense must be exercised in using ratios such as these. In the present case, for example, it appears as though the increase in sales in 1977 over 1976 resulted directly from the increase in gross fixed assets, since the ratio for 1976 was maintained in 1977.

While one would hope, and indeed expect, that an increase in fixed assets would result eventually in an appropriate increase in sales, the maintenance of exactly the same ratio for these two years is probably simply a coincidence, particularly since we know that the finished-goods inventory was drawn down substantially in achieving the sales figure for 1977.

Also, in comparing the ratio of one company with that of another, particularly if one is an old company and the other is relatively new, it should be recognized that fixed assets are carried in the accounts at their actual costs, which may be far different from the value of these assets at the time the ratios are computed.

Turnover of Total Assets

For the same reasons supporting the computation of the ratio of turn-over of fixed assets, many analysts compute the ratio of turnover of total assets. In the case of P. M. Santon, the computation would be as follows:

$$\frac{\text{Sales}}{\text{Total assets}}$$

	1977		*1976*	
	$\dfrac{\$9,990,486}{\$4,860,148} = 2.06$ times		$\dfrac{\$8,821,121}{\$4,692,331} = 1.88$ times	

As we noted in examining "ROI in assets" in Chapter 4, the turn-over ratio of total assets can be applied to net income as a percentage of sales to establish the percentage return on the investment in total assets. For P. M. Stanton, this would be as follows:

Net income as % of sales × Turnover of assets = Return on Assets

1977	5.5%	×	2.06	=	11.4%
1976	3.1%	×	1.88	=	5.8%

Turnover of Accounts Payable

Where a company's purchases are known, the average purchases per day can be found by dividing the figure by 360, in the same way as the average sales per day are found by dividing sales by 360. The accounts payable as of the close of the period divided by the computed average purchases per day then gives the figure for the number of days' purchases owed on the balance-sheet date. This is obviously information of interest to a creditor, and large creditors can usually get this ratio from companies to whom they have granted credit.

Published financial statements are, however, not usually published in such detail as to show a figure for purchases. In a merchandising business, a reasonably close approximation of the figure for purchases can be computed if the cost of goods sold is both shown and adjusted for the change that has taken place in the inventories between the beginning and end of the period.

However, in a manufacturing business, the cost of goods sold includes labor and manufacturing overhead as well as material. Thus the relationship of accounts payable to it may not be very meaningful. The trend of this relationship over time could nonetheless be meaningful.

For P. M. Stanton, the 1977 turnover of accounts payable ratio would be as follows:

$$\frac{\text{Accounts payable } \$332,200}{\text{Cost of goods sold, } \$6,736,490 - \text{Inventory change } \$320,632} = 5.2\%$$

Ratios of Liabilities and Capital

A ratio of interest to all who are concerned with a particular business is that of total debt to total assets. This indicates, on the one hand, the portion of assets which were provided by creditors; and, on the other hand, it gives some indication of the protection to creditors should the company get into difficulty.

Again for the P. M. Stanton Company, the debt ratios would be as follows:

	1977		1976	
Total liabilities	$1,258,101	= 25.9%	$1,785,587	= 38.1%
Total assets	$4,860,148		$4,692,331	

Thus the P. M. Stanton Company's creditors provided 38.1% of the recorded assets as of the end of 1976 but only 25.9% as of the end of 1977. The lower figure for 1977 reflects the retirement of the bond issue during the year.

Since the balance of the assets could be claimed by the owners of the business, their claim equaled 61.9% of the assets at the end of 1976 and 74.1% at the end of 1977. Thus as far as numbers are concerned, i.e., without regard to the quality of the assets involved, the position of the creditors was more protected at the end of 1977 than at the end of 1976.

Capitalization Ratios

Again, in terms of the question as to who has supplied the assets of the business and their relative claims to them, it is common to compute what are known as capitalization ratios. Capitalization means the composition of the long-term capital of a business.

For large companies, capitalization is commonly a combination of long-term debt, preferred stock, common stock, paid-in or capital surplus, and retained earnings. For all corporations, it will at least consist of common stock, and hopefully of retained earnings.

In the P. M. Stanton Company, the capitalization for 1977 was 100% owners' equity, consisting of common stock, paid-in surplus, and retained earnings. In 1976, it consisted of 21.5% long-term debt and 78.5% owners' equity.

Total and "Book Value" Per Share

The owners' equity in a business, called "stockholders' equity" or "shareholders' equity" in a corporation, consists of the par or stated value of both preferred and common stock, plus paid-in or capital surplus and retained earnings.

There is some interest on the part of stockholders and others in knowing the ownership equity per share of stock, called *book value per share.*

In the case of *preferred stock,* the so-called book value per share is found by dividing the assets, less liabilities, by the number of shares of this stock outstanding. This does not mean the share of ownership that each preferred stockholder actually has in the business. Rather, it means only that if the company got into difficulty but was able to convert all assets to cash at the amounts at which they were currently being carried in the books of account, and then paid off its creditors, the amount of cash available to meet the preferred stockholders' claims per share would be the book value computed, as we just noted.

As a practical matter, the call value or liquidation value, stated on the preferred stock certificate gives a more appropriate idea of the book value of preferred stock in terms of its real claim to assets in a going concern that is expected to keep on going successfully enough to at least meet its dividend requirements on the preferred stock.

The book value per share of *common stock* is found by dividing the assets net of liabilities, and less the stated or call value of any preferred stock outstanding, by the number of shares of common stock outstanding. For P. M. Stanton, the stockholders' equity and book value per share — based on 295,371 shares outstanding as of December 31, 1977, for comparability — were as follows:

	1977	1976
Stockholders' equity	$3,602,047	$2,906,744
Book value per share	$12.19	$9.84

Some analysts would subtract intangible assets, in this case the deferred development expenses, in establishing book value per share on the grounds that these expenses could not be recovered if the company were to be liquidated. The figures just shown were presented among the financial highlights in P. M. Stanton's 1977 annual report and included this intangible asset.

It should be recognized that there is no necessary relationship between book value per share and market value per share. Assets are carried in the accounts essentially at their historical cost, in the United States at least. On any given date, the market value of a company's shares of stock outstanding and the book value of its assets, less its liabilities, would only by the most unlikely chance be exactly the same.

Earnings Related to Owners' Equity

Net income as a percentage of owners' equity and earnings per share of common stock are figures of great interest to owners and managers of a business. The reader will recall that earnings per share and percentage return on owners' equity were examined at length in Chapter 4.

Limitations of Ratio Analysis

In closing this chapter, it is well to repeat a note of caution. Ratios do not explain what happened, nor do they necessarily serve as either suitable goals or measures of performance. Nonetheless, they are useful in spotting situations that merit investigation or bear watching. For this reason, they should be computed and studied by those interested in following the financial affairs of any given company.

CHAPTER 15

Construction of the Funds Flow Statement

With the increase in the number of companies that provide funds flow statements (Statements of Changes in Financial Position) in their annual reports, the need for either the professional or lay financial analyst to prepare such statements himself has greatly diminished. Nonetheless, knowledge of the major steps involved in the preparation of these statements is helpful to an understanding of them and enables one to prepare them in cases where they are not included in the financial reports of companies he wishes to study.

Funds Flow Work Sheet

Although a funds flow statement can be assembled by various means, a work sheet of the type illustrated in both Exhibit 28 and Exhibit 30 provides an orderly process for doing so and a complete picture of the construction once completed. Like all work sheets, since it is not a formal statement, it can be designed and carried out as best suits the user.

Balance Sheet Changes

Whether or not a complete work sheet is prepared in developing a funds flow statement, the first step in an orderly approach to the problem is to compute and list the changes that have taken place in balance sheet items between the beginning and end of the period under consideration. This is the same step that anyone takes, at least mentally, in comparing a balance sheet as of the end of an accounting period with a balance sheet as of the beginning of that period.

In Exhibit 28, the changes that took place in the balance sheet items of the P. M. Stanton Company between the beginning and end of 1977 are shown in columns 3 and 4. The reader will recall that a balance sheet can be viewed as a static picture of funds applied and their sources.

Asset items in the balance sheet depict where the funds of the business are then located, while liability and capital items indicate where these funds came from. Changes in the amounts of these items during a period result from financial transactions involving, for the most part, the flow of funds either within the enterprise or between the enterprise and parties external to it.

Each financial transaction involving the flow of funds has its dual aspects: Where the funds came from and where they went. The changes in the balance sheet items in Exhibit 28 have been separated into those which the initial analysis indicates to be applications of funds and those which appear to be the sources of the funds applied.

As should be expected, the total of the item changes assumed to be applications is matched by the total of those assumed to be sources, since both deal with the same funds; one indicating where they came from, and the other, where they have gone.

Changes representing applications of funds. To elaborate a bit, if—as we have assumed—the assets appearing in a balance sheet represent funds applied as they stand on that date, then a net increase in an asset for an accounting period would be a net application of funds for that item for the period. In the present case, for example, accounts receivable, prepaid assets, property, plant, and equipment, and the investment in subsidiaries have all increased during the period. Thus, as far as we can see at the moment, each represents a net application of funds for the period.

It is also easy to visualize the application of funds to reduce liabilities, as in the present case where a bond sinking fund installment has been paid and bonds retired. Also, the liability for payments to the pension fund and the provision for deferred income tax have been reduced. Again, as far as we can see at the moment, there were no reductions in the capital section of the balance sheet, which—had there been any—would have represented applications of funds.

At the top of column 3 in Exhibit 28, it is indicated that increases in assets (+A) and decreases in liabilities (−L) represent funds applied. But the (−L) is intended to mean that the column would show the decrease of any item on the liabilities side of the balance sheet. Therefore, it would include decreases in capital items as well as decreases in liabilities.

EXHIBIT 28
P. M. Stanton's Analyst's Work Sheet

	Dec. 31, 1976	Dec. 31, 1977	Applied +A or −L	Source −A or +L
Cash	930250	929375		875
Accounts receivable	765162	1067737	302575	
Inventories	1515983	1295351		220632
Prepaid assets	51178	81514	30336	
Property, plant, equipment	2039199	2308539	269340	
Allowance for depreciation	760720	945569		184849
Net fixed assets	1278479	1362970		
Investments in subsidiaries	34401	43132	8731	
Deferred development expenses	116878	80069		36809
	4692331	4860148		
Bond sinking fund installment	100000	—	100000	
Accounts payable, trade	153220	332200		178980
Provision for pensions	177300	163500	13800	
Provision for federal income tax	226675	417300		190625
Other accrued liabilities	224974	246800		21826
Provision for deferred income tax	103418	98301	5117	
First Mortgage, 6% Bonds	800000	—	800000	
Common stock	268022	295371		27349
Paid-in surplus	2152198	2398339		246141
Retained earnings	486524	908337		421813
	4692331	4860148	1529899	1529899

Dividend (cash for
  fractional shares)
Common stock options
  exercised
Net income
Decrease in working capital

EXHIBIT 28 (continued)

For the Year Ended December 31, 1977

Adjustments		Working Capital		Funds	
+A or –L	–A or +L	Increase	Decrease	Applied	Source
			875		
		302575			
			220632		
		30336			
				269340	
					184849
				8731	
					36809
		100000			
			178980		
		13800			
			190625		
			21826		
				5117	
				800000	
(a) 13245					
(b) 14104					
(a) 119205					
(b) 126936					
(c) 555824	(a) 134011				
(a) 1561				1561	
	(b) 141040				141040
	(c) 555824				555824
		166227			166227
830875	830875	612938	612938	1084749	1084749

Changes representing sources of funds.   If an increase in an asset represents an application of funds, then it can be assumed, as a generalization at least, that a decrease represents a source of funds.

In the present case, the reduction in cash and the liquidation of inventories certainly represent sources of funds. The increase in the allowance for depreciation is a decrease in an asset in one sense and a source of funds in another sense. Similarly, the reduction in the deferred development expense is a decrease in an asset and a source of funds in the same sense as depreciation.

Trade creditors, as we noted in an earlier chapter, are a source of funds. Thus an increase in the amount owed to them, as in the P. M. Stanton Company, indicates an increase in the amount of funds supplied. The increases in the provision for federal income tax and other accrued liabilities indicates that the company has had the use of funds in these amounts which otherwise might have been paid out to meet these debts at an earlier date.

As a generalization drawn from such examples, it can be stated that increases in liabilities represent sources of funds. Thus the capital section of the balance sheet for P. M. Stanton shows increases in capital stock, paid-in surplus, and retained earnings, all of which for the moment appear to be sources of funds. But we know from earlier information on this company that net income for 1977 was $555,824, not the $421,813 change in retained earnings shown in column 4 of Exhibit 28.

We know also that P. M. Stanton paid a stock dividend, and that some executives purchased shares of the company's stock through exercising stock options that had been granted to them in earlier years, both of which affected the items of common stock and paid-in surplus.

It is also evident that a more complete explanation of the changes that have taken place in the capital accounts, as listed in column 4 of Exhibit 28, could be made.

Changes representing changes in financial position.   It can be seen by inspecting columns 3 and 4 of Exhibit 28 that major changes in a company's financial position can be identified simply by studying changes that have taken place in its balance sheet items. In P. M. Stanton's case, the high net income for 1977, relative to the previous year, resulted in a substantial increase in retained earnings and assisted the company in maintaining a strong cash position despite the cash required to eliminate its long-term debt. The elimination of this debt was the outstanding financial event of the year, while the higher volumes of production and sales were responsible for marked increases in accounts receivable and accounts payable and a drop in inventories.

Inspection of balance sheet changes alone, however, does not provide as complete or accurate an analysis of changes in a company's financial position as is generally desirable. The funds flow statement is intended to supply this more complete and accurate analysis.

Adjustments to changes in establishing funds flow. Some of the changes that take place in balance sheet items during a period do not represent funds flow. The writing up or down of assets as a result of appraisals, for example, does not represent a flow of funds and thus should be eliminated (adjusted) in the construction of a funds flow statement.

However, not all of such changes are adjusted in many companies. For example, no such adjustment is made when inventories are written down from cost to a lower market value in the valuation of inventories at the lower of cost or market.

In the case of P. M. Stanton, a stock dividend was paid which was not included as an application of funds in the company's funds flow statement, even though the dividend involved a transfer from the retained earnings account to the accounts for common stock and paid-in surplus. The common stockholders' claims were not changed in total by the stock dividend, although to this extent the retained earnings had been converted to permanent capital.

In contrast, had the First Mortgage 6% Bonds been convertible bonds, and had they been converted to common stock, the conversion would have appeared as an item in the funds flow statement, even though no money had been involved in the exchange. This would have been a major financial event in which creditors' claims, substantial in amount, had been converted to ownership claims.

In the Exhibit 28 work sheet, in order to correct the figures for common stock, paid-in surplus, and retained earnings for the amounts by which the stock dividend affected them, adjustments are entered in columns 5 and 6. In effect, the amount of the dividend is put back into retained earnings (column 6) $134,011, while common stock (column 5) $13,245, and paid-in surplus (column 5) $119,205 are reduced.

The balancing item here is for the amount of the dividend paid in cash for fractional shares (column 5), which came to $1,561. Incidentally, the stock dividend was 5% of the shares outstanding, which came to 13,245 shares.

The market value at the time the dividend was declared was approximately $10 per share. This figure was used in determining the amount to be transferred from retained earnings (13,245 shares × $10 = $132,450 + $1,561 for fractional shares = $134,011).

Some adjustments are made in the work sheet simply to have

more accurate or informative classifications of sources and applications of funds. For example, in Exhibit 28, the common stock options exercised (column 5) were included with the stock dividend in the increases in common stock and increases in paid-in surplus. Adjustment (b) in column 5 removes the amount of common stock increase ($14,104) and the increase in paid-in surplus ($126,936), and combines them to show in column 6 the total figure for common stock options exercised, $141,040. This was the amount the managers and executives paid into the company at the rate of $10 per share for 14,104 shares.

Since adjustment (a) in the work sheet put the amount of the stock dividend back into retained earnings, the increase in retained earnings for the period then equals the net income for the period (see Exhibit 27, Chapter 14) amounting to $555,824. This amount is then removed from the retained earnings line by adjustment (c) and given a separate line in the work sheet so that it may be properly identified.

It should be understood that the adjustments we have been discussing are entered in the work sheet only, not in the accounting records. As a matter of fact, the work sheet designated as Exhibit 28 is intended to represent the kind of work sheet that a person outside of the P. M. Stanton Company might use in order to construct a funds flow statement if the given company has not presented him with one. It should be quite clear, therefore, that this work sheet would not affect the company's accounting records in any way.

Working Capital Changes

The next step in the use of the Exhibit 28 work sheet is to separate the changes that have taken place in working-capital items from changes in other items. This step is undertaken in columns 7 and 8 and provides the detail from which a statement of working capital changes may then be prepared (see Exhibit 18, Chapter 6) and the net change in working capital for the period (in this case a decrease of $166,227) as an item to be entered in the funds flow statement.

Funds Flow Identified by Applications and Sources

After having entered the working capital increases and decreases, the funds flow work sheet is then completed, as in Exhibit 28, by carrying across to columns 9 and 10 the remaining items in columns 3 and 4 (i.e., those other than working capital increases or decreases) adjusted by the data in columns 5 and 6.

In further explanation, it can be seen, as an example, that the two adjustments to common stock in column 5 representing decreases offset the increase in common stock shown in column 4, leaving nothing of this item to be carried across to columns 9 or 10.

The figures carried across to columns 9 and 10 can then be used as they stand, or combined to some degree for simplification, in drawing up a formal funds flow statement. This would be such a statement as drawn up by one who is outside of the business and has only the company's income statements, balance sheets, statement of retained earnings, and notes attached to these statements, as sources of information from which to construct it.

P. M. Stanton Company funds flow statement. The actual funds flow statement presented in the P. M. Stanton Company's Annual Report for 1977 is shown in Exhibit 29.

It is apparent from comparing the company's funds flow statement with the data in columns 9 and 10 of the work sheet (Exhibit 28) that in preparing this statement the company drew upon information not revealed completely by its balance sheets and income statements.

EXHIBIT 29
P. M. Stanton's Statement of Changes in Financial Position

	For the Years Ended	
	Dec. 31, 1977	*Dec. 31, 1976*
Source of funds:		
From operations:		
Net income	$ 555,824	$276,715
Depreciation	200,980	156,008
Amortization of deferred charges	50,275	65,685
Total	$ 807,079	$498,408
Common stock options exercised	141,040	—
Decrease in working capital	166,227	—
Miscellaneous	13,435	11,994
	$1,127,781	$510,402
Funds applied:		
Purchase of property, plant and equipment, less disposals	$ 285,471	$276,252
Redemption of long term debt	800,000	100,000
Deferred development expense	26,901	37,925
Increase in working capital	—	67,405
Miscellaneous	15,409	28,820
	$1,127,781	$510,402

The work sheet shown as Exhibit 30 is presented as an approximation of the work sheet the company itself would have used in constructing its funds flow statement. The first four columns of this work
sheet are, of course, the same as in Exhibit 28.

Adjustment for Depreciation

A company's "Allowance for Depreciation" (accumulated depreciation) account is affected by two major types of entries: 1. it is increased
by an amount equal to the depreciation expense for the period; and 2.
decreased by charges against it for the accumulated depreciation on
property, plant, or equipment that is sold or otherwise disposed of
during the period.

It has become common practice for companies to show the total
depreciation expense for a period either as a separate item in their
published income statements or as a footnote to them. This was not
the practice of the P. M. Stanton Company, although (as shown in
Exhibit 29) it did report its depreciation for the period in its *funds
flow statement.*

The actual amount of depreciation expense for 1977 ($200,980)
was more than was indicated in column 4 as being the increase for the
period in the "Allowance for Depreciation" ($184,849). Adjustment (a)
for $200,980 is entered in column 5 on the depreciation allowance line
to, in effect, remove this amount and bring it down below in column 6.
Thereby, it becomes an amount specifically identified as "Depreciation," to be listed in the funds flow statement as a source.

In Chapter 5, we noted the sense in which depreciation is considered as a source element in both cash flow and funds flow. We also
noted in particular that whatever amount of flow there might be in this
connection comes from customers in reimbursement for the depreciation identified with goods or services sold to them. The flow cannot
come merely from bookkeeping entries for depreciation.

In addition, it should be said that in a manufacturing business the
depreciation of productive facilities is typically charged to products as
an item in the burden rates (factory overhead) applied as production
takes place.

Depreciation is thus included in the cost valuation of inventories
of work-in-process and finished goods. If such inventories have been
built up during a period, customers will not, in fact, have reimbursed
the company for the full amount of the depreciation it shows as a
source of funds in its funds flow statement.

Similarly, if a net decrease in these inventories takes place, as it did in the case of the P. M. Stanton Company for 1977, the customers will have reimbursed the company for more than the amount of the depreciation for the period appearing in the funds flow statement.

As a practical matter, it would be more costly than the information would be worth to keep detailed records of depreciation as a separate element in inventories of work-in-process and finished goods in order to be able to show each period the extent to which depreciation had been absorbed or released in the net by these inventories.

Some companies, however, find it desirable for internal understanding of the inventory situation to maintain inventories by their cost elements of material, labor, variable burden, and fixed burden. Thereby, among other things, they are able to see the extent to which inventories have in the net absorbed or released fixed costs (which include depreciation charges).

Labor Input vs. Output in Cost of Goods Sold

In many manufacturing companies, it is even more important to monitor the relationship between the cost of labor expended during a period and the cost of labor in the goods sold during that period.

On the one hand, it is true that inventories will rise, and inventory turnover will slow down, if more direct labor is pumped into production than goes out through the shipping room door in the goods sold during the same period.

On the other hand, it is also true that a product must be made before it can be shipped. Thus preoccupation with maintaining a high rate of inventory turnover can lead to a loss of sales that might have been made, including the failure to expand operations as much as they might easily have been expanded.

Few companies have any records of sales lost because goods were not available when a customer wanted them. Therefore, few managers are held accountable for lost sales or for their failure to expand operations to the degree they might have been expanded. All levels of management monitor inventory turnover figures, however, and the pressure to maintain as good a turnover as in the previous period, if not to improve on it, is great indeed.

This is not to say that a satisfactory rate of inventory turnover is not important, but only that the rate should not be based purely on experience and that generally a build-up of inventory, and a consequent reduction in inventory turnover, has to precede the attainment of a higher level of sales volume.

EXHIBIT 30

P. M. Stanton's Assumed Company Work Sheet

			Applied Source	
	Dec. 31, 1976	Dec. 31, 1977	+A or –L	–A or +L
Cash	930250	929375		875
Accounts receivable	765162	1067737	302575	
Inventories	1515983	1295351		220632
Prepaid assets	51178	81514	30336	
Property, plant, equipment	2039199	2308539	269340	
Allowance for depreciation	760720	945569		184849
Net fixed assets	1278479	1362970		
Investments in subsidiaries	34401	43132	8731	
Deferred development expenses	116878	80069		36809
	4692331	4860148		
Bond sinking fund installment	100000	—	100000	
Accounts payable, trade	153220	332200		178980
Provision for pensions	177300	163500	13800	
Provision for federal income tax	226675	417300		190625
Other accrued liabilities	224974	246800		21826
Provision for deferred income tax	103418	98301	5117	
First Mortgage 6% Bonds	800000	—	800000	
Common stock	268022	295371		27349
Paid-in surplus	2152198	2398339		246141
Retained earnings	486524	908337		421813
	4692331	4860148	1529899	1529899

Depreciation
Amortization of deferred charges
Deferred development expense
Net income
Common stock options exercised
Miscellaneous applications
Miscellaneous applications
Miscellaneous applications
Miscellaneous sources
Decrease in working capital

EXHIBIT 30 (continued)

For the Year Ended, December 31, 1977

Adjustments		Working Capital		Funds	
Applications	Sources	Increase	Decrease	Applied	Source
			875		
		302575			
			220632		
		30336			
(b) 16131					285471
(a) 200980	(b) 16131				
	(h) 8731				
(j) 13435					
(c) 50275	(d) 26901				
		100000			
			178980		
		13800			
			190625		
			21826		
	(i) 5117				
					800000
(f) 14104					
(g) 13245					
(f) 126936					
(g) 119205					
(e) 555824	(g) 134011				
	(a) 200980				200980
	(c) 50275				50275
(d) 26901				26901	
	(e) 555824				555824
	(f) 141040				141040
(g) 1561					
(h) 8731				15409	
(i) 5117					
	(j) 13435				13435
		166227			166227
1152445	1152445	612938	612938	1127781	1127781

Adjustment for Property, Plant, and Equipment

We noted in Chapter 3, when discussing how one might establish the cost of goods sold for a given period, that an active balance sheet account is made up of four major parts as it stands at the end of a period: 1. its beginning balance; 2. what has come into the account; 3. what has gone out of the account; and 4. its ending balance. The bookkeeper who has maintained such an account can inspect it and find all four of these elements.

An outsider, given any three of the elements, can find the fourth by deduction. This is what a financial analyst does when constructing a funds flow statement in cases where a company has not provided such a statement but where he has access to the company's balance sheets as of the beginning and end of the period and its income statement for the period.

In the P. M. Stanton Company case, for example, if the analyst had been given the figure for the depreciation expense, either in the company's 1977 income statement or in a footnote to it, he could have made adjustment (a) shown in Exhibit 30 in his own funds flow work sheet.

He would then know the beginning balance of the allowance for depreciation, the amount that had been added to it, and the ending balance. Then, by deduction, he could find the amount he can assume had been removed from the account as the accumulated depreciation on property, plant, and equipment which had been sold or otherwise disposed of during the period. Thus his approximation of accumulated depreciation is as follows:

Beginning balance, January 1, 1977	$760,720
Depreciation added, 1977	200,980
	$961,700
Ending balance, December 31, 1977	945,569
Assumed removed from the account	$ 16,131

At the time items making up the $16,131 had been removed from the "Allowance for Depreciation" account, the "Property, Plant, and Equipment" account would have been reduced by the amounts at which these items had been carried in this account, presumably at their actual cost. If the analyst has not been given this figure, he can only assume that it was the same amount as removed from the depreciation allowance.

Since the reduction in these two accounts was brought about by bookkeeping entries not involving a flow of funds, he adjusts for this by, in effect, putting these amounts back into these accounts on his work sheet. This in fact is what has been done in adjustment (b) in Exhibit 30.

The analyst can then determine by deduction an approximation of the flow of funds into property, plant, and equipment for the period as follows:

Beginning balance, January 1, 1977	$2,039,199
Assumed reductions in this account	16,131
	$2,023,068
Ending balance, December 31, 1977	2,308,539
Apparent additions during the year	$ 285,471

A more complete analysis would reveal the flow of funds into the business from the disposal of property, plant, and equipment as a source, as well as the application of funds for the additions to this account. In the present case, presumably because the inward flow of funds from disposals was a minor amount, the company was content to show the purchase of property, plant, and equipment net of disposals in its funds flow statement ($285,471 in Exhibit 29).

In contrast, for 1970, the Mobil Oil Corporation showed $29.1 million book value of properties, plants, and equipment sold. This was clearly an item of sufficient importance to be shown separately by Mobil as a source of funds, rather than to be treated as a reduction in the figure for property, plant, and equipment acquired.

Adjustment for Amortization of Deferred Charges

In the absence of more information, a decrease in a deferred charges account would be assumed to represent a source of funds, as we assumed in Exhibit 28. This would be assumed to have been an amortization of deferred charges and, being the result of bookkeeping entries, would be a source of funds in the same sense that depreciation is a source of funds. Had there been a net increase for the period in this account, it would have been treated as an application of funds in the funds flow statement.

The P. M. Stanton Company, of course, knew the extent to which deferred charges had in fact been amortized for the period. The company also knew the amount which had been expended on development, and the portion of these expenditures which had been entered in the "Deferred Development Expenses" account.

Figures for these two items appeared in the funds flow statement (Exhibit 29). Here, we have entered them as adjustments (c) and (d) in our assumed company work sheet (Exhibit 30).

Other Adjustments

In Exhibit 30, adjustments (e), (f), and (g) are the same as adjustments (a), (b), and (c) in Exhibit 28. The exception is the dividend in cash for fractional shares ($1,561), which was merged by the company with other items under a "Miscellaneous Applications" caption in its funds flow statement.

These adjustments, the reader will recall, cancelled out the stock dividend since it did not represent a flow of funds and combined the common stock and paid-in surplus.

Adjustments (h) and (i) were to transfer the increase in investment in subsidiaries and the reduction in the provision for deferred income taxes to the "Miscellaneous Applications" category since they were relatively minor items.

Adjustment (j) has been entered in the work sheet to provide the figure for "Miscellaneous Sources" of funds that was listed in the company's funds flow statement. No explanation was given in the statement for this item, although it is clear that it came from the "Deferred Development Expenses" account since there was an unexplained balance in this account of the $13,435 in question.

One interpretation could be that because of the unusually profitable year the company saw fit to write off more of its deferred development expenses than provided by its normal amortization policy. It could also be, of course, that the loss had been taken because it had become evident that one or more projects whose costs had been treated as deferred expenses would never bear fruit.

Compilation of the Work Sheet

The columns for working capital increases and decreases in Exhibit 30 are the same as in Exhibit 28 since no adjustments were required for the items in them.

Columns 9 and 10 in Exhibit 30 provide the figures from which the formal statement of funds flow would be prepared. It can be seen that with the additional information at hand the company was able to draw up a more complete and, therefore, more accurate funds flow statement than the analyst would have been able to do on the basis of the information we assumed he had (Exhibit 28).

If the company had not in fact presented a funds flow statement in its annual report, it might nonetheless have provided information on its depreciation and amortization of deferred expenses for the year, as well as the notes it did provide on its stock dividend and common stock options exercised. If the company had done so, the analyst could have prepared a work sheet (as in Exhibit 30) and drawn up a funds flow statement exactly like the one the company did provide.

Analysis of Changes in Working Capital

P. M. Stanton, in common with most companies, presented the change in its working capital as a single item in its funds flow statement. However, I believe it desirable for a company to provide more detailed information than this by including in its annual report an analysis of changes in working capital as illustrated in Exhibit 18, Chapter 6.

Such an analysis is particularly applicable to the case of P. M. Stanton where changes in working capital items from period to period were often significant, as in 1977. The details for such a statement are provided by columns 7 and 8 of the work sheet for the funds flow statement, as illustrated in Exhibit 28 and Exhibit 30. These details could be included in the funds flow statement but they are presented more effectively in a separate statement.

Incidentally, the analysis of working capital changes just referred to is not the same as the statement of sources and uses of working capital illustrated in Exhibit 17, Chapter 6. The latter is one form of a funds flow statement, not a statement of working capital changes.

CHAPTER 16

Problems in Timing of Revenue and Expense

In earlier chapters, we noted that many accounting problems arise in the timing of revenue and expense. That is, problems in determining in what accounting periods given financial transactions should be accounted for as revenues or expenses.

For example, we discussed problems in determining at what time, and under what circumstances, it might be said that a sale had taken place. Similarly, we noted that to the layman the purchase of material would represent an expense at the time of purchase. However, to the businessman it would represent an item to be recorded in an inventory account as an asset at the time of purchase. Then, at some later time, possibly in a later accounting period, when used or sold it would be accounted for as an expense.

The most troublesome and controversial problems in the timing of revenue and expense are those in which financial transactions are recognized as revenue or expense a. in one accounting period for purposes of financial reporting to stockholders and others, and b. in a different accounting period in reporting to the government for income tax purposes.

The contention in the types of cases just mentioned is not with respect to whether there should or should not be differences in accounting treatment in reporting for these two different purposes. Rather, it is with respect to how the estimated income tax expense in financial reporting to stockholders and others should be computed under these circumstances.

In brief, some people believe that the amount of estimated income tax thus reported should be the same amount as the income tax computed in reporting to the government for income tax purposes for the same accounting period.

Others, however, believe that it should be the amount of income tax for which the company would have been liable had it reported for income tax purposes the pretax income it presented in its financial reporting. They hold also that the difference between this amount and the amount of tax the company computes in its income tax reporting for the same period should be accounted for and reported for financial reporting purposes as deferred taxes.

The latter views expressed are essentially those supported by the Accounting Principles Board in its Opinion No. 11, *Accounting for Income Taxes*, for the types of timing problems with which we shall be concerned in this chapter.

We shall return to these income tax matters after discussion of some basic considerations of revenue and expense determination.

Revenue and Expense Defined

In a funds flow statement, net income is shown as a source of funds. The funds thus provided have been applied in various ways, along with other funds. Thereby, they have served to increase assets or decrease liabilities and indirectly to provide or contribute to any dividends paid during the period.

As far as the balance sheet is concerned, net income results in increases in assets or decreases in liabilities balanced by an increase in owners' equity prior to the declaration of dividends.

Net income is gross income less expenses. Revenue is simply a term for gross income. Thus net income is revenue less expenses.

If net income results in increases in assets or decreases in liabilities with a corresponding increase in owners' equity, it can be appreciated that an item of revenue taken by itself results in a gross increase in assets or a gross decrease in liabilities with a corresponding increase in owners' equity.

In common terms, with each item of revenue, the owners of a business are for the moment that much better off. We are speaking here, of course, of the essential effect of such transactions and not of the bookkeeping procedures by which they are recorded.

It can be appreciated also that each item of expense taken by itself must have an effect opposite to that of an item of revenue. Thus such expense results in a gross decrease in assets or a gross increase in liabilities with a corresponding decrease in owners' equity. In other words, with the incurrence of each item of expense, the owners of a business are temporarily that much poorer.

The following definitions are in keeping with our discussion:

Revenue is a term for a financial transaction or event resulting in an increase in assets or a decrease in liabilities with a corresponding increase in owners' equity.

Expense is a term for a financial transaction or event resulting in a decrease in assets or an increase in liabilities with a corresponding decrease in owners' equity.

Again, let us be reminded that we are speaking here of the essential effect of transactions involving revenue or expense and not of the bookkeeping steps involved in recording them.

Revenue Recognition

In general, problems in determining revenue are not so numerous or so difficult as problems in determining expense. Sales of goods, products, and services constitute the major items of business revenue, along with the receipt of items such as interest, dividends, rent, commissions, royalties, and fees. Revenue also arises from the disposal of plant, equipment, and other assets in addition to the sale of goods and products.

Payments Received May Differ

The mere receipt of an asset, although usually a pleasant event, does not necessarily indicate that revenue has occurred at that time. Thus when a customer makes a payment on his account, cash is increased but accounts receivable are decreased for the same amount. There is, therefore, no net increase in assets, nor any change in owners' equity resulting from this transaction and hence no revenue is involved.

Similarly, when a customer, such as the government, makes a payment on a contract in advance, cash is increased but the company receiving it (not having yet done anything to earn it) does not account for it as revenue. Instead, it accounts for its liability to provide the products, or perform the services, for which the money was advanced.

Thus while there is an increase in assets, it is matched by an increase in liabilities. There is no change in owners' equity; hence no revenue is involved.

As performance takes place, the liability will be met and the revenue can be recognized since it will then have been earned. Thus gradually, there is a decrease in the liability and a corresponding increase in owners' equity resulting from this recognition of revenue in the accounts.

Other examples of payments received in advance, which are not considered to be revenue at the time received are rents, insurance premiums, and magazine subscriptions.

A Gift Is Not Revenue

An interesting type of asset increase to be accounted for arises from the receipt of a gift in the form of a grant. Thus, in Great Britain, it has sometimes been possible to receive money from the government in an amount up to 40% of the cost of buildings and equipment erected and installed in designated areas needing such economic development.

In one sense, the company receiving such a grant is thereby that much better off. Certainly, it is better off than it would be if it were to build the same plant and install the same equipment in the same location without such assistance.

However, the long-run economic justification for the investment may well be subject to uncertainty. In any event, the acceptance of such a grant carries with it the obligation to invest the money received in the property for which it was granted. (Since the actual receipt of the money is likely to be subject to some delay in connection with such grants, a company is likely to start building with its own or borrowed money, but this is a matter of detail and not of principle.)

The money thus invested will not then be available for any other purpose until it is recovered from customers who have paid enough for the goods produced by the plant and equipment to cover not only the out-of-pocket costs for such goods but also the depreciation on the plant and equipment as well.

For the reason just suggested, the customary accounting for grants of this type when received has been to increase (debit) the asset cash and to balance this with a credit to an investment grants account. The balance of this account at the close of a period is shown on the liabilities side of the balance sheet as a separate item.

It has been customary to amortize the amount of the investment grant over the estimated life of the property the grant assisted in financing. Essentially, this is a recognition of revenue over the economic life of the property. The investment grant account is thus debited each period, and in a roundabout way, the owners' equity is correspondingly increased.

Of course, if sales are not adequate enough in volume and price to cover the full costs of the products manufactured and sold, including depreciation on the plant and equipment used to make them, there will be no net increase in owners' equity. The reason for this is that whatever may have been recorded as revenues will have been more than eaten up by expenses.

Other types of gifts to encourage a company to locate in a certain area, or to help it get under way or expand, such as land or shares of the company's own stock, are also not considered to be revenue. These are accounted for as donated capital or as capital surplus. (In recent years, use of the term "surplus" has been frowned upon because its nature has been misunderstood by laymen. Nonetheless, it is still widely used for the purpose just noted since no appropriate short term has appeared as a satisfactory substitute.)

Thus, although assets are increased as the result of such gifts, the owners' equity is not changed as far as the accounts Retained Earnings or Earned Surplus are concerned.

Increases in Value Do Not by Themselves Constitute Revenue

In the United States, it is not yet considered necessary or desirable to increase the stated value of assets in a company's official accounts to reflect either a drop in the purchasing power of money or a rise in market value. Reasons for this viewpoint will be discussed at some length in Chapter 19 with respect to the valuation of property, plant, and equipment.

In the 1920s, a number of companies did write up their assets — particularly, property, plant, and equipment — to reflect appraisal values that were higher than the historical costs at which the assets had been carried in the accounts.

It was not considered sound, however, to regard these increases in assets as arising from revenues. Instead, they were balanced in the accounts by credits to an account commonly entitled "Appraisal Surplus."

Thus the owners' equity with respect to retained earnings, or "Earned Surplus," was not affected.

Similarly, although there are many people today who are urging that financial statements be restated to reflect changes in the purchasing power of money, and some who would like to have a company's official accounts reflect current market values, few believe that these increments should be accounted for as having arisen from revenues.

In a few cases, such as in the mining of gold and in the joint costing of some agricultural products, inventories are carried at market values and gains above cost are reflected as an increase in owners' equity. Thus, in these cases, revenue is considered to have been realized simply from the creation of value.

Fortunately, in the view of those who, like myself, see no real justification for such eagerness to reflect gains before the goods involved are sold, these cases are few in number.

Revenue Involves Performance and Exchange

The examples we have been discussing indicate that under conventional accounting revenue is not considered to have been realized simply by the receipt of something of value, nor simply by the increase in value of something already held.

To be realized, revenue must have been earned, and this involves performance of one kind or another. Moreover, the receipt of something for nothing is a gift and not revenue. Revenue involves an exchange of goods or services for whatever is received.

Similarly, revenue is not recognized while something being held is rising in value, but only at the time it is exchanged for something else with someone outside of the given accounting entity.

Problems in Timing Revenue Realization

Even though one may accept the concepts of revenue and revenue realization just discussed, there are still problems in determining in some cases what is the most appropriate timing with respect to the accounting recognition of revenue.

For example, we noted earlier that a sale and, therefore, revenue would normally be considered to have taken place upon the delivery of the goods sold, which in many cases would be when the goods involved were placed in the hands of a common carrier for delivery.

One might well question, however, whether goods which are delivered but not to be paid for except by installments over several months should be recognized as providing revenue at the time of delivery.

An example in the other direction is the case of an aircraft carrier that takes six years to build following the signing of the contract. In this case, it would seem appropriate to recognize revenue at some points prior to the physical delivery of the completed ship, as we shall discuss in a moment with respect to construction contracts.

Accounting decisons in such cases involve judgment, or what a layman would consider to be common sense. Moreover, they involve accounting principles, concepts, and conventions. In particular, they involve ideas and beliefs with respect to conservatism, materiality, consistency, comparability, and convenience.

Conservatism in Revenue Recognition

On the grounds of conservatism, one might decide to wait until sufficient installments had been received on a given installment sale to recover the cost of the goods involved before considering that any income had been realized from it. Or it might be considered desirable to treat each installment as being in part a recovery of the cost of the goods involved and, in part, a realization of a portion of gross income.

In fact, it used to be a matter of choice with respect to installment sales as to whether gross income would be recognized at the point of delivery, as payments were received, or only with final payments. The important provision was only that whatever method was adopted be followed consistently.

Comparability in Revenue Recognition

Since December 31, 1966, however, installment sales are supposed to be accounted for like any other sale "unless the circumstances are such that the collection of the sale price is not reasonably assured."[1]

The reasoning given is that the APB "believes that revenues should ordinarily be accounted for at the time a transaction is completed, with appropriate provision for uncollectible accounts."[2] This reasoning does not, however, get at the heart of the problem — namely, when should it be said that a transaction is completed?

For example, those who used to account for revenue on installment sales as installments were received, or only after the cost of the goods had been recovered, did not consider that the transaction had been completed merely upon delivery of the goods.

In any event, presumably the aim of the APB in outlawing the installment method of recognizing income was to bring about uniformity in accounting for sales, regardless of the timing of payments, as a step in improving the comparability of financial statements between companies.

Performance Is a Key Word

In the case of services, construction, and other work involving long-term contracts, delivery in the sense of performance is the key consideration in revenue recognition. The exact timing of the revenue recognition as far as bookkeeping and billing of customers are concerned is usually dependent on custom in the trade or the specific terms of the contract.

---

[1]APB Opinion No. 10, *Omnibus Opinion* (New York: Accounting Principles Board, American Institute of Certified Public Accountants, December 1966), paragraph 12.

[2]*Ibid.*

Thus, in the case of a service, it might be customary to bill customers once a month and to recognize income at the time of such billing. Similarly, a construction contract is likely to call for stated payments at the completion of specific stages of work, and it is at such times that billing takes place and revenue is recognized.

Consistency, Materiality, and Convenience

Consistency of practice in the timing of revenue recognition is, of course, a matter of importance in order to preserve the comparability of a company's financial statements from period to period. Moreover, the shifting of practice from period to period would represent a form of manipulation of earnings which should not be allowed.

For minor items of revenue, the exact timing is not important. The amounts involved are not material and, therefore, the timing of their accounting can well be a matter of convenience. Also, although some significant items of revenue may be "earned" daily, their recognition in the accounts will be made only at such times as are convenient or useful.

Thus, if a company has loaned money to others at interest, a proportionate amount of interest will have been earned as each day passes. The company is likely to account for interest income on the loans, however, only once each month in connection with the preparation of its financial statements.

Indeed, if the amount of interest income involved in all of its loans is very small compared with its revenues from other sources, the company may well account for interest income only at such times as it is received in cash.

Timing Differences in Financial Reporting Versus Income Tax Reporting

There are some items of revenue or gain which are, or can be, reported in one accounting period for financial reporting purposes and in another for income tax reporting purposes. Timing differences of the type with which we are concerned in this chapter originate in one accounting period and are reversed in one or more subsequent periods.

For example, revenue on an installment sale is recognized for financial reporting purposes but not for income tax reporting purposes in the accounting period in which the goods are delivered. For each period during which installments are received thereafter, revenue is recognized for income tax reporting purposes but not for financial reporting purposes. (We shall be dealing here only with some basic examples of timing differences in revenue recognition between financial reporting and reporting for income tax purposes.[3])

Financial Reporting Earlier Than For Income Tax Reporting

As we have noted, it is customary for financial reporting purposes to recognize revenue on installment sales at the time goods are delivered and on long-term contracts by stages as performance takes place. For income tax purposes, however, it is permissible to report revenue on installment sales as installments are received and on long-term contracts upon the completion of the contract.

Unless a substantial increase in income taxes is anticipated in the near future, it is natural for companies engaged in installment sales or long-term contracts to take advantage of the provision in the law for delaying the recognition of income on such transactions. Thus they have the use of money which otherwise would be paid to the government at an earlier date.

It should be clearly understood that this is a matter of taking advantage of a provision of the law and not of a loophole in it. A loophole, which is a matter that was overlooked or not provided for in the law, is a means of circumventing a law and not of operating within its provisions.

Financial Reporting Later Than For Income Tax Reporting

There are a number of items of revenue such as rents, fees, dues, and service contracts which are by custom paid in advance. As we noted earlier, conservatism in the recognition of income leads companies to defer revenue recognition of such items until whatever it was they were paid for has taken place or been performed. Thus they may be said to have been earned.

For income tax purposes, however, the government requires that such payments be reported as revenue at the time received, or more accurately as revenue of the taxable accounting period during which they were received. The logic of this requirement is not explained in the law, nor in the income tax regulations.

---

[3]For a study in detail of this area, see Homer A. Black, "Interperiod Allocation of Corporate Income Taxes," Accounting Research Study No. 9 (New York: American Institute of Certified Public Accountants, Inc., 1966); see also APB Opinion No. 11, *Accounting for Income Taxes* (December 1967).

One might assume, however, that since the company has actually received the money from such sources the government sees fit to have it included as revenue in arriving at the taxable income for the period. In contrast, with respect to revenue on installment sales and long-term contracts, the government is willing to wait until the company has the money in hand or at least until the amount of taxable income is assured.

For all practical purposes taxation is thus on a cash basis in the various examples mentioned, whereas the company is accounting for revenue on the accrual basis.

Expense Identification

Earlier, we noted that each item of expense has an effect on assets or liabilities, and on owners' equity, opposite to that of an item of revenue. It was suggested that expense is a term for a financial transaction or event resulting in a decrease in assets or an increase in liabilities with a corresponding decrease in owners' equity. These were noted as the essential effects of an expense, although the bookkeeping procedures are actually more indirect than these stated effects would imply.

The reduction of an asset does not by itself indicate that an expense has taken place. The result may have been simply to increase another asset or decrease a liability, with no change in owners' equity. Thus when raw material is moved from stores into the factory to be worked upon, the transfer should be accounted for as a transfer from the asset "Raw Material" to the asset "Goods-in-Process."

Similarly, when a company makes a payment to one of its creditors, it should be accounted for by a decrease in the asset "Cash" and a decrease in the liability "Accounts Payable."

Although the character of the company's resources has changed, neither of these transactions or events has resulted in the owners being either better off or worse off in an accounting sense.

When a liability is increased, the increase does not by itself indicate that an expense has taken place. The result may have been simply to decrease another liability, or the increase may have been balanced by an equal increase in some asset.

Thus when a company cannot pay an invoice as due, it may be permitted by the creditor to give a note for the time being on which interest would be payable. This would be accounted for as a reduction (debit) in "Accounts Payable" and an increase (credit) in "Notes Payable."

Similarly, when a merchant purchases goods on account, the asset "Merchandise Inventory" is increased (debited) and the liability "Accounts Payable" is increased (credited).

Neither of these transactions or events which would result in increases in liabilities would cause any change in the owners' equity.

Expenses Closely Identified with Revenues

The cost of goods sold, the cost of services sold, and the cost of assets other than goods sold are all expenses that can be closely identified with specific revenues each accounting period. The aim in identifying these expenses with specific revenues is to have a proper matching of costs and revenues in arriving at the net income to be recorded for the period.

Problems in accounting for costs by type of expense, by products, and by periods will be considered at some length in chapters to follow.

There are a number of expenses under the headings of selling expenses and administrative expenses which can also be directly related to the goods or assets sold, or services rendered, during a given period. Thus when charged as expenses of that period, these can be said to have been so charged in order to have a proper matching of costs and revenues.

Expenses Not Closely Identified with Revenues

Some selling expenses, however, are not directly related to the goods or services sold during a given period. Some of these will result in sales in future periods and some will not further the sales of any period.

Similarly, most administrative expenses are not directly related to the sales of any given period. These selling and administrative expenses fit into the concept of a proper matching of costs and revenues in an income statement only in the sense that expenses, which seem appropriately to be charged to a given period, are matched against revenues, which seem appropriately to be credited to that period, in arriving at net income for the period.

Many of these expenses not closely identified with revenues are charged to a given period either because it would not be conservative accounting to defer their recognition to a later period or simply because there is no better way to account for them.

Losses and Declines in Value Treated as Expenses

Losses from accidents, fires, and theft are accounted for as expenses of the periods in which they take place.

On the grounds of conservatism, inventories are written down to market value when that value is below their costs. It is considered sound practice to take the loss during the period in which the market value (replacement cost) drops below cost, rather than to defer the loss to the period in which the materials or goods involved are sold. This practice departs from the convention of consistency, since inventories are not written up to the market when their market value is above their cost.

Expenses for Financial Reporting

As a matter of conservatism, and in keeping with what is considered to be a proper matching of costs and revenues, many types of expense are accounted for earlier for financial reporting purposes than are allowed for income tax purposes.

Some of these are cases of accruing the expense in financial reporting, while having to report on a cash basis in tax returns. For example, pension costs are accrued in the financial accounts and reports. But these are not allowed as a deduction for tax purposes until paid into a pension fund or paid to a pensioner.

Similarly, expenses are accrued in the financial accounts for deferred compensation, profit-sharing, bonuses, and vacation pay. But, again, these are not allowed as expenses for tax purposes until paid.

In other cases, a company considers it wise to anticipate a loss but the government will not permit the item to be treated as an expense for tax purposes until it can be established that the loss has taken place. Thus a company will set up a reserve for some contingency, such as an inventory loss, but it cannot take the loss for tax purposes until actually suffered.

Similarly, a company will charge itself some amount each period as a current expense for self-insurance, with a corresponding credit to a reserve account, but it can only deduct for income tax purposes the cost of actual losses as they take place. Again, when a company decides to abandon some phase of its business or dispose of major facilities, it is likely to anticipate the loss in its own financial accounting, but it cannot do so for income tax purposes.

Although a company is allowed to anticipate a reasonable amount for loss on bad debts, based on experience, it is not allowed to deduct anticipated costs of guarantees and warranties. Many companies do however make provision for such expected costs in their own financial accounting and reporting.

A final type of difference in the timing of expense between financial reporting and income tax reporting is found in cases where a company is more conservative in accounting for a given expense than it is allowed to be for tax purposes. Not infrequently, for example, a company will depreciate machinery and equipment over shorter estimated economic lives than allowed for tax purposes. Similarly, it will write off organization costs or other expenditures immediately that must be amortized over several periods for income tax purposes.

Expenses Deducted for Income Tax Reporting

The principal examples in timing the recognition of expenses earlier for tax purposes than in financial reporting are the use of accelerated depreciation for tax purposes while using straight-line depreciation in financial reporting and the deduction of R&D and other costs when incurred while amortizing such costs in financial reporting.

The major reason for such differences in timing is, of course, to enable a deferring of income tax to the degree permissible under the law, and thus to have the use of money that would otherwise go to the government at an earlier date.

One might then well wonder why the same procedures should not be used for financial reporting purposes as for tax purposes. Some companies do, in fact, follow the same practices for these two types of reporting, either because it is simpler to do so or because it can be easier to support a practice for tax purposes if a company follows the same practice in its own accounting.

Those companies, which account differently for these expenses in their own accounting and financial reporting than in their tax reporting, either do so as a matter of principle or because the higher net income they are able to report in their financial reporting makes them appear more favorable to stockholders and others.

Not infrequently, although a company might like to present a more conservative statement of income, it believes itself forced to follow less conservative practices because this is what others in the given trade are doing. In other words, there are situations in which uniformity in practice will lead to less conservative financial reporting.

The fact that a company reports differently for financial reporting purposes than for income tax purposes should not be held against it. The tax laws and regulations are geared to the financial needs of the government and to problems in managing or stimulating the economy. Therefore, on many points, these are not in keeping with the best of accounting principles.

Moreover, the laws and regulations either change exceedingly slowly, and thus hamper the development of better accounting practice, or they change overnight in some respect to meet some government financial problem, without any reference to sound accounting principles.

Fortunately, to date income tax reporting requirements do not set the standard for what may be followed in financial reporting, except in the use of the LIFO method of inventory valuation. I hope that this will always be so. But there are some who keep advancing the idea that companies should be forced to report to their stockholders in the same way they report for income tax purposes.

Interperiod Tax Allocation

In our discussion, we have noted timing differences in the reporting of revenue and expense for financial reporting purposes versus income tax purposes. Although there may be differences of opinion on individual items, it seems evident that there are a number of areas where timing differences between financial reporting and requirements for income tax purposes can be justified. This view is generally recognized and accepted.

The real problems with respect to these timing differences lie in the question: How should the income tax be computed and shown in the financial reporting where these timing differences exist?

A few people still contend that the amount of estimated tax expense reported for a period in financial reporting should be the same as that computed in the tax return for the same period.

The great majority, however, believe that the estimated income tax in financial reporting should be the amount of tax based on the pretax income reported. For a company to report instead the amount of tax computed in its tax return on a different amount of income would be to report its income tax expense essentially on a cash basis, whereas the pretax income reported is on the accrual basis. Presenting the estimated income tax based on the pretax income of financial reporting is known as interperiod tax allocation.

Deferred method of interperiod tax allocation. Although there are different methods of interperiod tax allocation, we shall be concerned here only with the deferred method. According to the APB, the deferred method of interperiod tax allocation is:

> ... a procedure whereby the tax effects of current timing differences are deferred currently and allocated to income tax expense of future periods when the timing differences reverse. The deferred method emphasizes the tax effects of timing differences on income of the period in which the differences originate. The deferred taxes are determined on the basis of the tax rates in effect at the time the timing differences originate and are not adjusted for subsequent changes in tax rates or to reflect the imposition of new taxes. The tax effects of transactions which reduce taxes currently payable are treated as deferred credits; the tax effects of transactions which increase taxes currently payable are treated as deferred charges.[4]

Thus where revenue is recognized earlier in financial reporting than in income tax reporting (as in accounting for installment sales and long-term contracts), and where expenses are deducted earlier for income tax purposes than for financial reporting (accelerated depreciation vs. straight-line depreciation), the total taxes to be paid are less than those computed for financial reporting purposes in the period of initial timing differences. The difference is thus accounted for as a deferred credit.

The treatment in the accounts may be illustrated in round numbers as follows:

For a period of initial timing differences:

Estimated Income Tax Expense	$100,000	
Income Tax Liability		$80,000
Deferred Income Taxes		20,000

The difference between the estimated income tax expense and the income tax liability is the difference between the amount of tax estimated for financial reporting purposes ($100,000) and the tax estimated for income tax reporting ($80,000).

In later accounting periods, more income will be reported for income tax purposes than for financial reporting, and the deferred income tax account will be debited. When the timing differences have completely reversed, the initial credit to deferred taxes will have been used up.

---

[4] APB Opinion No. 11, *op. cit.*, paragraph 19.

Where expenses are accounted for earlier in financial reporting than in income tax reporting (such as in accounting for pension costs, self-insurance, and warranties), and where revenue is recognized later in financial reporting than is allowed for income tax reporting (as in the case of prepaid rent), the total taxes to be paid are more than those computed for purposes of financial reporting in the period of initial timing differences. The difference is thus accounted for as a deferred charge.

The treatment in the accounts may be illustrated in round numbers as follows:

For a period of initial timing differences:
Estimated Income Tax Expense	$80,000	
Deferred Income Taxes	20,000	
Income Tax Liability		$100,000

In these cases, the differences which increase the taxes currently payable are accounted for as deferred charges. In a later period or periods, the effects would be reversed and the initial deferred charges would thereby be eliminated.

Partial interperiod tax allocation. Although the great majority of people concerned in the matter believe in interperiod tax allocation, some believe in having only partial allocation. That is, they believe it to be unnecessary or undesirable to have tax allocation of all tax differences, particularly of those that will be postponed indefinitely.

The cases in which major contention arises are those where a company is reporting depreciation on an accelerated basis for tax purposes and on a straight-line basis in its financial reporting. Those who believe in partial allocation hold that where a company maintains a stable investment in fixed assets, or is growing with respect to fixed assets, the taxes that would be deferred under interperiod tax allocation will never be called upon for payment.

Thus, under these conditions, income is understated and an item of deferred taxes is shown in the balance sheet as a liability when, in fact, it is not an amount for which the company is, or is ever likely to be, liable.

Comprehensive interperiod tax allocation. Those supporting complete (comprehensive) interperiod tax allocation believe that the tax effects of timing differences should be recognized and accounted for when they first take place and that the differences in taxes should be deferred and allocated to the periods in which the timing differences reverse. They believe that partial allocation, which emphasizes cash outlays for taxes, is not in keeping with the remainder of a company's accounting, which is on the accrual basis.

Comprehensive interperiod tax allocation is supported by the APB in its Opinion No. 11, which also concluded that the allocation should be carried out by the deferred method. This Opinion was adopted by the assenting votes of fourteen out of twenty members of the Board.

Those on the Board dissenting did so, essentially, because they believe that in cases involving timing differences of the type we have been discussing, i.e., those that reverse themselves in a later period or periods, income tax expense should be determined on the basis of partial allocation.

It is clear that the use of accelerated depreciation, rather than straight-line depreciation, for tax purposes enables a company to have the use of money in the early years of the life of depreciable property which otherwise it would have to pay to the government at an earlier date. In doing so, it has given up a portion of the tax shield that would otherwise be available to it in the future.

In reporting to its stockholders and others on a straight-line basis of depreciation, a company is enabled to show higher profits in the early years of the life of depreciable property than would be the case if it used accelerated depreciation.

If it is going to do this, however, it seemed to the majority of the members of the APB, and incidentally to me, that it should estimate its income based on the pretax income reported.

To compute its income tax on the smaller amount of income reported for tax purposes not only places this expense on a cash basis, whereas all other expenses are reported on an accrual basis, but it also fails to acknowledge the amount of tax shield given up.

Unfortunately, there has been much contention over the nature of a deferred tax account. Those who believe in partial allocation, instead of comprehensive allocation, hold that in a growing company, or one maintaining a stable situation with respect to depreciable property, a credit balance in a deferred tax account would never represent a liability since it was never owed and never would have to be paid.

It is certainly clear, however, that this difference represents an amount of funds left with the company by the use of accelerated depreciation, or by some other different method of accounting in its income tax reporting, than in its financial reporting. It would be much better if there could be general agreement that a credit balance in the deferred tax account simply represents a source of funds, rather than argue whether it does or does not represent a liability.

The argument that in a growing or stable company the deferred tax credit would never have to be met, because credits used up on older items of property would be replaced by credits on newer properties purchased for replacement or expansion, is shortsighted and dangerous. It is argumentation along these lines that encourages a company, or a government, or an individual to maximize today's benefits or appearance, regardless of what may happen tomorrow.

For example, for many years it was argued that railroads and public utilities did not have to account for depreciation as did other industries because they would always be growing. The only responsibility the then owners and managers had was to maintain the property in as good condition as when it was received by them.

Thus it was considered necessary for them to make provision only for the property that would shortly have to be replaced. The resulting understatement of depreciation expense resulted in gross overstatements of net income.

Fortunately, this so-called retirement accounting theory has long since been outlawed. Nonetheless, much the same type of reasoning has been advanced by those who favor partial allocation over comprehensive allocation of taxes in connection with timing differences which reverse.

The following comments from the Accounting Principles Board summarize the views (of those who support comprehensive allocation) with respect to the point that the effect of the reverse of initial differences is offset by initial differences on new property purchased for expansion or replacement:

> Those supporting comprehensive allocation believe that the tax effects of initial timing differences should be recognized and that the tax effects should be matched with or allocated to those periods in which the initial differences reverse. The fact that when the initial differences reverse other initial differences may offset any effect on the amount of taxable income does not, in their opinion, nullify the fact of the reversal. The offsetting relationships do not mean that the tax effects of the differences cannot be recognized and measured. Those supporting comprehensive allocation state that the makeup of the balances of certain deferred tax amounts "revolve" as the related differences reverse and are replaced by similar differences. These initial differences do reverse, and the tax effects thereof can be identified as readily as can those

of other timing differences. While new differences may have an offsetting effect, this does not alter the fact of the reversal; without the reversal there would be different tax consequences. Accounting principles cannot be predicated on reliance that offsets will continue. Those supporting comprehensive allocation conclude that the fact that the tax effects of two transactions happen to go in opposite directions does not invalidate the necessity of recognizing separately the tax effects of the transactions as they occur.[5]

---

[5]APB Opinion No. 11, *op. cit.*, paragraph 29.

CHAPTER 17

Inventory Valuation: Cost Methods

Under ordinary circumstances, inventories are priced (valued) at some form of cost. Problems of inventory valuation are largely concerned with determining what costs are to be identified with inventories in a given situation. Having determined this, the remaining costs under consideration are allowed to become period costs by deduction. Period costs, as defined in this connection, include costs within the title "Cost of Goods Sold."

Actually, the impact of the resulting period costs on the profit computed for a period is usually of greater significance than the particular valuation placed on inventories. The reason for this is that the various parties interested in a business are generally more concerned about the profitability of that business than about the value of its current assets.

In keeping with this viewpoint, our major concern with inventory valuation will be in its role as a critical determinant of profit. We shall therefore be more concerned with problems in developing a proper matching of costs and revenues by accounting periods than with current asset valuation for balance sheet purposes.

Importance of Inventory Valuation

Many companies have no inventory valuation problems, either because they have little or no inventory, or because the inventory is so small relative to total operations that its valuation on one basis versus another would have no significant effect on reported net income or on stated assets.

Companies that have highly seasonal characteristics, such as many processors of agricultural products, may have serious inventory valuation problems for purposes of monthly financial statements at certain times of the year. But these companies are likely to have worked the inventory down to a low enough point just prior to a new season so that its valuation on one basis versus another will have no significant effect on fiscal-year financial statements prepared at that time.

Of course, if such a company is caught with a substantial carry-over inventory at such a time, it then does have an inventory valuation problem. The seriousness of this problem, however, is likely to be overshadowed by operating and financial problems of even greater concern.

For the great majority of merchandising and manufacturing companies, inventory valuation is an important matter, varying in degree of importance between companies and within companies from time to time. Not only are the inventories of such companies relatively large but they are also subject to significant fluctuations from period to period in size and mix and in prices, costs, and values.

Under these conditions, the particular policies and practices adopted for inventory valuation can have a significant effect on the inventory and working capital condition presented in a company's balance sheets and on the expenses, income tax, and net income reported in its operating statements.

Short-run vs. Long-run Effects

Some people may argue that inventory valuation is only a short-run problem. They believe that its effect on the computation of profit will average out in time. Thus their proposition is that over the long run a company's net income will be the same regardless of the particular inventory valuation policies and practices followed in the interim, assuming that its income tax rate remains unchanged.

Certainly, it is possible to construct hypothetical examples in which the arithmetic will support this proposition. It is also possible to reconstruct the operating results of an actual company over several years by substituting different bases of inventory valuation from those actually used and, with the right example, to note that the total net income over the years selected would have been approximately the same regardless of the basis of inventory valuation adopted.

The fallacy in both types of examples, however, is that they are dependent for their validity on the assumption that "all other things remain equal"; a state which is rarely found in actual practice.

Motivational Aspects

Examples of the type suggested do not take into account the human or motivational aspects of the inventory valuation problem. The attitudes, opinions, and actions of the various parties interested in a company are affected in varying degrees by the results revealed in its financial statements. Inasmuch as different policies and practices with respect to inventory valuation can have significantly different effects on reported financial results, they are likely to cause differences in peoples' attitudes, opinions, and actions relative to the company involved.

These human or motivational aspects should not be taken lightly since they involve attitudes and actions on such matters as the buying, holding, or selling of stock in the company by stockholders and prospective stockholders; the granting or withholding of credit by creditors; and the hopes, expectations, and demands of employees relative to wages and salaries, profit sharing, and bonuses.

The motivational aspects also involve attitudes of optimism or pessimism regarding the company's condition and prospects for the future. These, in turn, affect management decisions on such matters as expanding or contracting operations, the pricing of products, shifting sales effort from one product line to another, dividend distribution, profit sharing, and the granting of wage and salary increases and bonuses.

While the human reactions suggested will vary in significance from case to case, they are matters of sufficient importance to merit concern when adopting inventory valuation policies and practices and to be kept in mind when studying problems of inventory valuation. In particular, it should be recognized that an inventory valuation problem is more than a simple problem of arithmetic, the effects of which are expected to balance out in due time.

Dishonest Practices

It might also be noted, with regret, that the important effect of inventory valuation on reported profit offers a tempting field for dishonest practices. Some businessmen who have succumbed to such temptation have understated their inventories, thus overstating their period costs and understating their profit in order to reduce, temporarily at least, their income tax.

Others have practiced the reverse of this procedure in order to report to stockholders and others profits greater than their companies have actually realized. In fact, some of the outstanding embezzlers of the past fifty years did not stop at simply overstating inventory values but developed devious methods for reporting inventories that were physically nonexistent.

While the public accountant is well aware of the danger of false statements of inventory, he is not in a position to certify as to the correctness of inventory figures except in a very limited sense. His audit includes a review of the company's system of internal checks and controls, including its inventory record keeping and inventory control procedures, to assure appropriateness, adequacy, and consistency in these areas. He advises on and reviews the company's methods of taking physical inventories and spot-checks representative items against book records from time to time.

However, the public accountant does not have a large enough staff to regularly supervise the taking of physical inventories, particularly since so many of his clients are on a calendar-year reporting basis and are therefore taking their physical inventories at the same time.

Moreover, the public accountant's staff does not have the expertise to properly identify many of the items inventoried by a wide variety of clients. For example, it would take an expert to determine whether a barrel of white powder labeled as some new wonder drug was in fact that or simply a barrel of common aspirin unpilled.

All in all, the public accountant simply cannot verify inventory figures beyond the limited steps just described. Whatever is reported for inventories is therefore primarily a management report and a management responsibility.

Income Tax Considerations

Quite apart from any question of dishonesty, there is no doubt that the pressure of income taxes tends to motivate management to adopt conservative inventory valuation policies and practices. Whether or not the resulting tax savings remain more or less permanent depends on the individual situation.

Such savings may represent the current avoidance of taxes on inventory gains which otherwise would be followed by inventory losses and corresponding tax reductions. Or they may simply represent a deferring of taxes that will have to be met sometime in the future. Under conditions of continued inflation, if inventories are held constant or expanded in physical terms, tax savings through conservative inventory valuation practices will be maintained and could become permanent.

Whether or not the tax savings are permanent, the important point at the moment is that a profitable company following conservative inventory valuation practices has the use of money which, under less conservative practices, would have been paid to the government as taxes at an earlier date. Moreover, the lower stated profits from conservative inventory practices allow a company to retain and use money which otherwise might have to be paid out as additional bonuses, profit sharing, or dividends.

These various cash-flow considerations tend to motivate management to adopt conservative inventory valuation policies and practices.

Influence of Other Pressures

In contrast to this viewpoint, a management that is under pressure to maintain or improve earnings per share under difficult operating conditions could be motivated to adopt inventory valuation policies and practices that were not conservative. In fact, if it were not for the common application of the generally accepted accounting principle of consistency to this area, a management might be motivated to change its inventory valuation policies and practices from year to year to assist in leveling stated profits or in maintaining a desired upward profit trend.

This is a matter of particular concern to the public accountant who must certify as to his clients' consistency in practice or state specifically what changes in practice have been made that are of material significance. Under the convention of full disclosure, a major change in practice is not taken lightly since a reasonable explanation must be stated for the change. And this puts a damper on opportunism with respect to inventory valuation.

On the other hand, while consistency in method is important in maintaining comparability of reported figures from period to period, there is no virtue in being consistently wrong. If, because of changed conditions or further enlightenment in the given area, it is evident that some other method would be more appropriate when followed consistently, it is reasonable to make a change. Full disclosure of such a change should, of course, be made if the change has a material effect on the figures reported.

In this connection, one should be aware of the possible effect of a change in method when one company is acquired by another. If, for example, the acquired company has been following a conservative inventory valuation policy which is changed to a less conservative policy after the acquisition, on the grounds of bringing it into line with uniform policy for the company as a whole, an inventory profit will arise which will of course not be repeated. This "instant profit" could make the acquisition appear to be more attractive than it had in fact been from an operating viewpoint.

Invoice Prices Relative to Inventory Valuation

In the valuation of materials (meaning raw materials and purchased parts or goods) at cost, it must be decided whether to: a. identify materials by specific lots related to specific invoices; b. assume that purchases of the same types and grades of materials have been mixed in storage and drawn on as a mixture at average cost; c. assume that materials have been withdrawn in the order in which they were purchased — that is, first-in, first-out; d. assume that for costing purposes materials have been withdrawn from the more recent purchases — that is, last-in, first-out; or e., assume that inventories, withdrawals, or both will be costed at standard cost.

Materials: cost of specific lot. In some situations, it is desirable to maintain the identity of specific lots and to cost them by reference to their related invoices. For example, if certain job lots of raw materials have been bought at unusually favorable prices and are to be made up into goods to be sold at a special price, it is desirable to maintain their identity and carry their actual cost to the point of sale.

Otherwise, their cost will be averaged with the cost of other goods using the same type of material. Or, under some other method of valuation, their cost might be charged entirely to other goods.

Ordinarily, however, there is little point in maintaining the identity of specific lots for costing purposes as long as materials can be identified and stored by type and grade. It is preferable to use some other basis so that the costs assigned to inventories or transfers of materials are not dependent on the manner in which, by accident or design, the specific lots have been handled in the storeroom.

Materials: average cost. Many companies use average cost in the valuation of their materials inventory. For this purpose, the average should be weighted by the quantities purchased, rather than by simple average of purchase prices.

Typically, in these companies, inventory records are maintained on a moving weighted-average basis in order to keep the average cost of each item up to date. That is, a new weighted average cost per unit is computed for a given material each time a new lot is purchased. Withdrawals are credited to the inventory records at the weighted-average unit cost in effect at the time of withdrawal.

Those who use average cost in the valuation of material inventories, and in computing the cost of materials used, do so because they are more concerned about average performance, average cost, and average profit than they are about the specific performance, the specific cost, and the specific profit on individual lots of product. The use of average cost tends to spread the effects of short-run price changes and to some degree assists in leveling out profits, particularly in industries where raw material prices are more volatile than finished goods prices.

However, the leveling of profit in this way may prove to be a mixed blessing. On the one hand, it is possibly good to the extent that it dampens undue optimism as prices rise. On the other hand, it is possibly harmful to the extent that it prolongs the effect of inventory losses as prices fall and thereby slows down the recovery of both optimism and profit.

Materials: standard cost. Materials in many companies are recorded at predetermined unit prices (standard costs) at time of purchase. The difference between the actual cost of these items and their standard cost is entered as a gain or loss in a purchase price variance account.

A major purpose of carrying material inventories at standard cost is to enable management to note, through reported purchase price variances, the extent to which actual material costs have differed from predetermined estimates. Timely information of this sort is useful a. in checking the purchasing activity and, where variances are unfavorable, in stimulating search for substitute materials or other cost reductions, and b. in adjusting selling prices where possible.

The use of standard costs also simplifies the keeping of detailed perpetual inventory records. Such records can then be kept in quantities only, with the standard cost per unit entered in an appropriate place on each card. Where the records are kept in both quantities and dollars, the use of standard costs obviates the necessity of arriving at a new average cost with each purchase.

Ideally, under standard costing procedure, the net purchase price variance for an accounting period should be taken as a gain or loss for that period. The theory here is that such gains or losses take place at the time of purchase. Therefore, standard costs only should be carried forward to the time of sale.

This is a common practice for purposes of monthly financial statements. But, at the close of the year, unless standard costs are reasonably close to actual costs, it is customary to adjust the standard cost valuations of materials to an approximation of their actual cost with a corresponding adjustment to the purchase price variance account.

If similar adjustments are made to bring the standard material cost in year-end inventories of work-in-process and finished goods to an approximation of their actual costs, the net purchase price variance remaining to be taken as a gain or loss for the year is approximately the purchase price gain or loss on materials in the goods sold during the year.

Materials: FIFO. In keeping with the common practice of using materials in the order of their acquisition to minimize losses from deterioration, many companies value their inventories of materials on a first-in, first-out (FIFO) basis. Although the method does assume for costing purposes that material is withdrawn from stores in the order acquired, it is actually not necessary to identify lots or to require that lots shall in fact be physically stored and withdrawn in the exact order of purchase.

While FIFO is known as a method of inventory valuation, the title actually refers to the assumption on which materials leaving the storeroom are costed, not to the inventory remaining. Under this method, the materials on hand in inventory are assumed to have come from the most recent purchases or, in other words, from the last goods that came in.

In situations where continuous inventory records are maintained for each material in both quantities and dollars, the FIFO procedure is to cost withdrawals in the order of their purchase. The inventory is automatically updated with each receipt or withdrawal of material when a computer or other appropriate equipment is used for inventory accounting and control.

If the inventory is not continually updated, it can be found by deduction at the close of a period by subtracting the costed figure for withdrawals from the sum of the recorded beginning inventory and purchases. The latter procedure is also followed where there are continuous inventory card records on each type of material for control purposes in the storeroom but no convenient way of summarizing these cards to establish inventory figures monthly for accounting purposes.

Whatever the system of inventory accounting and control, it is common practice to make physical counts of inventory periodically and thereby to correct the accounting and storeroom records and to bring them into line with the physical situation.

In cases where continuous inventory records are not maintained and a physical count must be taken to establish quantities on hand at the close of each accounting period, or where continuous inventory records are for quantities only, the FIFO procedure is to establish the cost of inventory by working back from prices on the most recent purchases until the quantity on hand has been covered. The cost of materials withdrawn is then established by subtracting this ending inventory figure from the sum of the recorded beginning inventory and purchases.

The principal argument for FIFO is that for all practical purposes the accounting for withdrawals from the storeroom parallels the physical handling of materials. Thus both the materials withdrawn and those remaining in inventory can be said to have been accounted for at their actual cost. We shall see an example of the FIFO method of inventory valuation a little further on in this chapter.

Materials: LIFO.   Under the last-in, first-out (LIFO) method of inventory valuation, it is assumed for costing purposes that the last materials coming into a company are the first to leave the storage room for use or sale during the given accounting period. As far as the cost of goods sold is concerned, this results essentially in the use of replacement cost for material rather than actual historical cost and enables to this extent a matching of costs and revenues for the period at approximately the same price level.

The LIFO method can therefore be regarded as a method for effecting a price-level adjustment for at least the material content of the cost of goods sold.

It should be understood that this is a matter of costing and not a matter of the way in which goods are handled physically. Presumably, for reasons mentioned earlier, physical movement will normally involve the use of the oldest materials first, regardless of the method of inventory valuation.

The mechanics of LIFO involve establishing at the end of an accounting period the ending inventory quantities by categories and pricing them by reference to beginning inventory unit valuations to the extent that the same quantities are on hand at the end of the period as were on hand at the beginning of that period.

Increments, if any, are priced as having come from the purchases of the period. The total LIFO inventory as then established is subtracted from the sum of the beginning inventory and purchases to arrive at the cost of withdrawals.

In effect, under LIFO when the type and physical size of the inventory remain unchanged, i.e., when there are no inventory increments or decrements, the cost of replacing inventories as they are used enters the "Cost of Goods Sold" account as though the inventory itself had not been touched.

The situation may be likened to that of a pipeline for oil, which must always remain filled even though oil is continually flowing through it. The amount the pipe must hold continually to maintain the flow is priced at the same amount all of the time. The cost of the oil entering the pipeline during an accounting period becomes the cost of oil sold out of the pipeline during that period as though the oil in the pipe itself had not been touched.

Examples of LIFO and FIFO

Let us assume that we have on hand at the beginning of the accounting period in which we adopt LIFO 100 units of a given article that cost us $2.00 per unit and that we have been selling similar articles for $2.50 with a resulting gross margin of $0.50 per unit.

Let us assume further a. that in the current accounting period the replacement cost of this article has risen to $2.25; b. that, in line with this, we have raised our selling price to $2.75; and c. that we have sold 500 units at $2.75 per unit and purchased 500 units at $2.25 per unit.

The computed cost of goods sold and gross margin under LIFO would be as follows:

Beginning inventory 100 units @ $2.00	$ 200
Purchases 500 units @ $2.25	1,125
	$1,325
Less: ending inventory 100 units @ $2.00	200
Cost of goods sold 500 units @ $2.25	$1,125
Sales 500 units @ $2.75	$1,375
Cost of goods sold 500 units @ $2.25	1,125
Gross margin 500 units @ $0.50	$ 250

Note: a. that the closing inventory is the same physical size as the beginning inventory and has been "valued" at the same $2.00 per unit; b. that the cost of goods sold has been stated at its replacement cost; and c. that the resulting gross margin is at the normal operating margin of $0.50 per unit. Of course, if the selling price had not been raised in an amount to exactly offset the increase in replacement cost, the margin would have been correspondingly less or greater than normal.

The example is intended to illustrate the use of LIFO in industries in which current selling prices for finished goods are strongly influenced by their replacement cost, since LIFO is most applicable to such industries.

Let us now take the same situation but assume inventory valuation under the first-in, first-out method. To avoid further complications, we shall assume that the beginning FIFO inventory is at the same cost of $2.00 as in the LIFO example and that the selling price per unit, replacement cost per unit, and quantities purchased and sold are the same.

The computed cost of goods sold and gross margin under FIFO would then be as follows:

Beginning inventory 100 units @ $2.00		$ 200
Purchases 500 units @ $2.25		1,125
		$1,325
Less: ending inventory 100 units @ $2.25		225
Cost of goods sold		$1,100
100 units @ $2.00	$ 200	
400 units @ 2.25	900	
500 units	$1,100	
Sales 500 units @ $2.75		$1,375
Cost of goods sold		1,100
Gross margin		$ 275
100 units @ $0.75	$ 75	
400 units @ 0.50	200	
500	$ 275	

Note that the 100 units of beginning inventory carried at $2.00 have been replaced by 100 units at their cost of $2.25. Assuming, as was doubtless true, that the oldest units were actually sold first, there is no question but what the 100 units physically on hand at the close of the period actually cost $2.25 each.

Thus, if one believes that inventory should be carried at actual cost, this is the figure which should be used in this case. This belief would support FIFO, not LIFO.

Some defenders of LIFO have argued that where materials upon purchase are placed in common storage with units of like kind and thereby lose their identity, it is just as logical to assume that the last units to come in were the first to be used as it is to assume the reverse. Thus they would argue that in this example $2.00 could in fact represent the actual cost of each unit on hand at the close of the period. This is a petty argument, however, and hardly one on which the defense of LIFO should rest.

Since, under FIFO the ending inventory has been valued in our example at $2.25, the beginning inventory at $2.00 has been moved along to become part of the cost of goods sold. Having been sold at $2.75, the gross margin accounted for on the inventory sold was $0.75 per unit which therefore included an "inventory profit" of $0.25 per unit in addition to the normal profit of $0.50 per unit.

In the view of those who believe in FIFO, this pairing of actual cost against sales realization represents a proper matching of costs and revenues. Those who believe in LIFO, however, hold that in this type of situation, where items sold out of inventory must be replaced if the company is to remain in business, the replacement costs involved should be taken into account in determining the profit realized on sales made during a given accounting period.

In their view, therefore, the pairing of the cost of replacing the items sold against sales realization represents a proper matching of costs and revenues.

Turning back to the figures in the example, it can be seen that the difference of $25 in gross margin between the two methods is the difference in cost of goods sold between using the actual cost of the beginning inventory that was sold (under FIFO) and using the cost incurred to replace that inventory (under LIFO).

If the example had been continued beyond the gross margin stage to include selling and administrative expenses and any other items of income and expense, the net income before income taxes would have shown the same difference in results between the two methods as appeared at the gross margin stage.

If the example had been continued to include estimated income taxes and net income after tax, the estimated income taxes would of course have been different between the two methods. The reason for this is that the net income before income taxes would have been different because of the difference in the cost of goods sold.

Problem of Distributable Profit

Assuming that the customers paid us immediately in cash for the goods sold in our examples, how would we have made out in terms of cash available for some use? If we had sold one of the beginning inventory units that had cost us $2.00, and had then gone out of business, we would have had cash on hand of $2.75 and a realized gross margin of $0.75 on the unit sold.

Assuming that we had stayed in business after that sale, however, and in order to do so that we had to immediately replace the item sold, we would have had to pay out $2.25 to meet this requirement and would be left with only $0.50 of the $2.75 received. The $0.50 is all that would be left to cover selling and administrative expenses, and to provide income, if any, for profit sharing, income taxes, and net profit.

The reader will note that the computed profit under LIFO matches this figure, whereas the $0.75 reported under FIFO is not all available for these purposes since $0.25 of it has had to be used to replace at a higher price the item that had been sold. The fact that LIFO enables a reporting of profit that is closer to actual distributable profit than other methods of inventory valuation is the major theoretical argument in its favor.

Income Tax Aspects of LIFO

Regardless of the theoretical arguments for or against the LIFO concept, however, there is no question but that the effect on income taxes has been the major factor that has led to its widespread adoption.

The original impetus came in the late 1930s after the federal government had in 1936 enacted an undistributed profit tax law. Under it, essentially, that portion of the earnings for the year after ordinary taxes which was not distributed to stockholders as dividends was subject to an additional tax.

At that time, prices in general were rising from their depression depths and all companies of the types with which we are concerned were experiencing inventory profits such as just illustrated. It can be appreciated in this example that the $25 of inventory profit was not distributable to stockholders as dividends, let alone being distributable to the government as taxes, since it had to be used to replace the inventory at a higher cost per unit.

As might be expected, industry was aroused by the situation and while primary efforts were directed toward repeal of the undistributed profits tax, considerable interest developed in the LIFO concept. Those most interested pressed the Treasury Department and Congress for permission to use LIFO for tax purposes.

Prior to the late 1930s, LIFO had not been used, although a few companies had adopted its major concept in their own accounting by practicing what is known as the *base-stock* or *normal-stock* method. In this method, the basic inventory quantity is carried at a fixed unit price, while quantities in excess of this are carried at FIFO or average cost.

Permission to use the LIFO method rather than the base-stock method was sought in the late 1930s because the use of the base-stock method for tax purposes had previously been denied in a number of cases, which culminated in a Supreme Court decision on the matter in *Lucas* v. *Kansas City Structural Steel Company*, 281 U.S. 264 (1930).

The major argument denying the use of the base-stock method for tax purposes had been that it was not used by enough companies to be considered as "a common practice in the trade." Therefore, to allow its use by the few who sought to use it would give them a tax advantage over the many who did not.

Although this argument is logical, unfortunately a major reason why the method had not become common practice was that it had not been allowed for tax purposes. The fact that relatively few companies had adopted the method was a prime example of an idea being stifled, given inadequate consideration, or considered faulty because it did not happen to fall within permissive procedures under the current tax law.

It also illustrated that a government edict, no matter how logical at the time issued, may hamper the evolutionary development of accounting practice and in time require revolutionary steps in order to effect progress.

In 1938, permission was granted certain industries to adopt LIFO under the nondescript title of "the elective method." There was no rush by companies to adopt the method, however, possibly because one of the requirements in being allowed to do so for tax purposes was that the same method also had to be used in all financial reporting to stockholders and others. This was, and still is, the only such requirement in the entire income tax law.

Since 1938, permission to use LIFO has been so broadened that practically any company having an inventory of materials or goods, as distinct from such items as stocks or bonds, is free to elect the method. To some degree, the elimination of the undistributed profits tax in 1938 and provisions instituted in 1942 for carry-back and carry-forward of losses reduced the attractiveness of LIFO, particularly for those who viewed it only as a tax-saving device.

However, with the advent of higher taxes during World War II, and particularly under the excess profits taxes during the war, interest in LIFO quickened. And, under the inflation and high taxes since then, interest has been maintained.

LIFO and Balance-Sheet Interpretation

It can be appreciated that under conditions of rising prices the LIFO valuation of inventories will in time be well below current market value or replacement cost. Thus LIFO will not provide a sound valuation of inventory as a current asset or a proper measure of this factor in judging a company's working capital position.

LIFO is more concerned with what its adherents believe to be proper profit determination, while balance-sheet considerations are made subservient to this goal. In contrast, traditional methods of valuation, such as average cost and FIFO, with valuation at market if market falls below cost, represent primarily a balance sheet viewpoint and profit determination is made subservient to it.

As a footnote to their balance sheets, companies practicing LIFO do, or should, provide an estimate of the market value by showing average cost or FIFO valuation of inventories to assist in interpreting these statements.

LIFO and Falling Prices

The examples used in comparing LIFO and FIFO served to illustrate the differences in results under conditions of rising prices. Let us assume now that in the next accounting period following our examples price conditions were reversed although the same number of units of inventory, purchases, and sales were involved. A comparison of results under LIFO and FIFO would then be as follows:

		LIFO		FIFO
Beginning inventory	100 units @ $2.00	$ 200	@ $2.25	$ 225
Purchases	500 units @ $2.00	1,000	@ $2.00	1,000
		$1,200		$1,225
Less: ending inventory	100 units @ $2.00	200	@ $2.00	200
Cost of goods sold	500 units @ $2.00	$1,000		$1,025
		100 units	@ $2.25	$ 225
		400 units	@ $2.00	$ 800
				$1,025

		LIFO	FIFO
Sales	500 units @ $2.50	$1,250	$1,250
Cost of goods sold		1,000	1,025
Gross margin		$ 250	$ 225

500 units @ $0.50 = $250 100 units @ $0.25 = $ 25
                                        400 units @ $0.50 = $ 200
                                                                       $ 225

Note that under LIFO the cost of goods sold has been stated at replacement cost and the resulting gross margin of $250 is at the normal operating rate of $0.50 per unit. In contrast, the gross margin of $225 under FIFO has suffered from an inventory loss of $25 which is exactly equal to the inventory gain taken in the previous period.

In terms of distributable profit, there was actually $250 in cash available at the gross margin stage regardless of the method of inventory valuation. The reason for this is that only $1,000 out of the $1,250 received through sales was required to replace goods as they were sold. This situation was reflected under LIFO, whereas under FIFO the gross margin accounted for was only $225, even though $250 was available.

As evidenced by this example, LIFO enables the denial of short-run gains on basic inventory as prices rise. This is considered desirable by LIFO advocates because such gains are not available for profit sharing, dividends, taxes, or any other purposes. Instead, they must be used to cover the increase in replacement costs of the units removed and sold from that inventory.

Similarly, LIFO results in the denial of short-run losses on basic inventory as prices fall. This is considered proper because units removed and sold from that inventory are replaced at a correspondingly lower cash outlay. Moreover, short-run gains on the basic inventory, which are denied by LIFO but reported under FIFO, are in time exactly balanced out by short-run losses as prices fall.

LIFO adherents hold, therefore, that these short-run inventory gains as reported under FIFO are false profits which should not be recognized since they are not available, and will not be available, for as long as the basic inventory is maintained.

To report short-run gains as profits not only creates problems in profit sharing, dividend policy, and income taxes, but also stimulates undue gratification with a company's reported results and apparent prospects for the future as prices rise and the reverse as prices fall.

Long-run LIFO Considerations

Under long-run inflation, a company adopting LIFO will find after a time that prices on items in its basic inventory will not drop back during business recessions to the levels at which they stood when this method was adopted. In these circumstances, there is at any given time a net inventory gain which would have been included in reported profits under FIFO, but denied under LIFO.

While it can be argued that one should surely recognize as income any gain that is permanent, the LIFO concept would hold that it is impossible to determine how much of the gain on the basic inventory at any given time will prove to be permanent. And, in any event, none of it is in a distributable form since it is tied up as a part of the investment in that inventory.

The net longer-run gain at any given time is no different in this respect than a short-run gain on the basic inventory. Therefore, from a LIFO viewpoint, it should not be recognized as income.

Under the circumstances just stated, a company using LIFO would enjoy a permanent tax advantage over the use of FIFO. That is, permanent to the extent that the basic inventory was maintained and inflation continued. Some people would hold that this provides an unfair tax advantage to LIFO users.

From a LIFO viewpoint, however, this is not a special privilege. The so-called inventory gain quite properly should not be taxed since it is not available for taxes or anything else other than maintenance of the basic inventory.

Accounting for the Initial LIFO Inventory

In a new company starting from scratch, there is, of course, no beginning inventory. The initial LIFO inventory for tax purposes in such a case will be the inventory at the end of the first taxable accountng period. Logically, to fit the name of the method, the units on hand at that time should be priced as though they had been the earliest units to enter the company.

As a matter of convenience, however, a company in this situation is allowed the options of pricing its initial LIFO inventory on a LIFO assumption, FIFO assumption, or at average cost. Having made the selection, the unit values selected will be used from that point on in the valuation of whatever quantities of the initial LIFO inventory remain conceptually in hand at any given time.

When a company changes to LIFO from some other basis of inventory valuation, the total value for the beginning inventory of the period in which the adoption takes place is generally whatever value had been assigned to the ending inventory of the previous period by the method then in use. However, it is desirable to reclassify or regroup inventories into as few categories as practicable for LIFO purposes, for reasons to be discussed shortly.

Accounting for inventory increments and decrements.   At the end of an accounting period under LIFO, if the physical quantities of materials or goods on hand are, by chance or design, exactly equal to the physical quantities on hand at the beginning of that period, the ending inventory will be given the same valuation as the beginning inventory. In other words, the accounting treatment is the same as though the items involved had not been touched, even though turnover has actually taken place.

If the physical quantities in any category on hand at the end of the period under LIFO are more than at the beginning of the period, the amount equal to the beginning inventory quantities will be given the same valuation as the beginning inventory. The increment in each category should theoretically be priced as having come from the first purchases of the period.

It is permissible for tax purposes, however, to price an increment as having come from the earliest purchases, the latest purchases, or at average cost for the period, whichever is most convenient. The unit values selected must be used from that point on in the valuation of whatever portion of the given increment remains conceptually on hand at any given time.

In an expanding company, there would be additional increments to be priced each year. Assuming that the inventory had never dropped below the quantity on hand at the time LIFO was adopted, and that expansion had taken place each year, the total inventory at any given time would consist of the original quantity priced as it was at the time LIFO was adopted, plus a series of increments identified by category and by year of acquisition and priced accordingly.

If the physical quantities in any category on hand at the end of the period under LIFO are less than at the beginning of the period, the decrement will be assumed to have come from the latest increment in keeping with the last-in, first-out concept.

If no increments are left, or if there never were any increments, a decrement involves a decrease in the original LIFO inventory. When a decrement takes place, the cost valuations on the quantities removed from inventory are lost for all time.

(An exception to this is made when decrements are caused by wartime, strikes, or other conditions beyond the control of the given company which prevent it from replacing materials as they are withdrawn from inventory. Under these conditions, a company is allowed by income tax regulations to replace the inventory, when it can do so, at the LIFO valuations previously carried, and to write off as a loss the difference between these valuations and the higher prices paid for the replacements.)

In our LIFO example, if the inventory at the end of the first period had dropped to 90 units, the $2.00 per unit valuation on the 10 units released would be gone. If the inventory were built up to 100 units again sometime in the future, the 10 units acquired would be accounted for as an increment.

To avoid the loss of low inventory prices under LIFO, it is very important for a company to get its inventory quantities at the end of the accounting period in line with quantities as they stood at the beginning of the period or at least to have increments rather than decrements. As an aid in this connection, it is desirable to carry the inventory in as few categories as practicable, since shortages on some items within a category can be offset by overages in others, thereby easing the problem of maintaining the inventory position for each category as a whole.

It is generally also important to practice LIFO on an annual basis only, and to use standard costs for monthly purposes in costing materials used and sold. The reason for this is that seasonal variations can cause marked shifts in monthly inventory quantities of individual items, whereas year-end inventory quantities are not likely to fluctuate so markedly from period to period.

LIFO and Inventory Speculation

Although LIFO is a conservative method of inventory valuation, it should not be regarded as a method which prevents inventory speculation, nor is it a substitute for hedging. To the extent that a company using LIFO must maintain an inventory in order to remain in business and, therefore, purchases simultaneously with sales in order to maintain its inventory position, short-run price gains on inventory will not have to be taken, as we noted previously.

However, to the extent that a company using LIFO does not simultaneously match purchases and sales and, therefore, temporarily goes either short or long on inventory relative to its basic requirements, it is taking a speculative position and eventually will gain or suffer thereby. As a matter of fact, if a company is not simultaneously matching purchase and sales quantities, or hedging through trading in futures, it is engaging in inventory speculation no matter what method of inventory valuation it may be using.

Industry Characteristics Best Suited to LIFO

Although LIFO is practiced by companies in a variety of industries, the method can best be justified for those industries in which material costs are a significant part of the total cost of finished products; and where material prices and finished goods prices tend to move up and down together seasonally, cyclically, and over longer periods of time.

Under these conditions, LIFO not only enables the reporting of income in terms of distributable profit but also assists in leveling the profit per unit on items sold. While the profit for an accounting period is dependent on the volume of units sold as well as on the profit per unit, nonetheless, a leveling of the profit per unit can be helpful to a company and industry by dampening optimism to some extent under conditions of rising prices and by tempering pessimism under conditions of falling prices.

Exhibit 31 illustrates a situation in which the finished goods and raw material prices per unit move up and down together over the passage of time. Thus the spread between the two is uniform for the time periods illustrated.

Here, let us assume that material purchased at time A was made up into goods which were sold at time B, and that the material thereby withdrawn from inventory was replaced by the purchase of an equal quantity at time B. In this case, the use of FIFO would result in accounting for DF as the spread between the material cost incurred and the finished goods price received, and this spread would include an inventory profit EF.

There would, of course, be many other costs to be subtracted from the spread before arriving at net profit. But these other costs would be the same regardless of the method of inventory valuation in use. Therefore, they have not been included in the exhibit.

The use of LIFO in this situation would result at time B in accounting for DE as the spread between the material cost incurred and the finished goods price received. It would not, of course, include any inventory profit.

EXHIBIT 31

A Situation Where Material and Finished Goods' Prices Move Up and Down Together

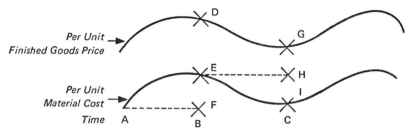

Let us assume further that material purchased at time B was made up into goods which were sold at time C, and that the material thereby withdrawn from inventory was replaced by the purchase of an equal quantity at time C. In this case, the use of FIFO would result in accounting for GH as the spread between the material cost incurred and the finished goods price received, and this spread would have suffered from an inventory loss equal to HI.

The use of LIFO, on the other hand, would result in accounting for GI as the spread between the material cost incurred and the finished goods price received. It would not, of course, include any inventory loss.

In summary, Exhibit 31 illustrates that in situations where material and finished goods prices move up and down together over time, and where substantial inventory quantities must be maintained at all times, the use of LIFO not only enables accounting for profit on a distributable basis but also assists in a leveling of profit from period to period.

Exhibit 32 illustrates a situation in which materials are subject to marked seasonal and cyclical fluctuations but finished goods prices are much less volatile.

Here, the use of LIFO enables accounting for profit on a distributable basis but does nothing to assist in leveling profit from period to period. The latter can be effected only through the valuation of inventories at average cost, a practice that is common in the tobacco industry among those companies not using LIFO.

The use of LIFO in this situation would result in accounting for DE at time B as the spread between the material cost incurred and the finished goods price received. It would not, of course, include the inventory profit EF that would be accounted for under FIFO in the spread DF.

The profit under LIFO would be relatively low, however, since finished goods prices would not have risen in line with the increase in

EXHIBIT 32

A Situation Where Materials Are Subject to Seasonal and Cyclical
Fluctuations

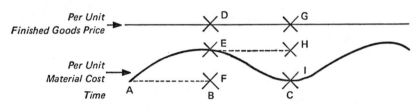

the replacement cost of materials. Similarly, at time C, the spread GI
reported under LIFO would not be affected by the inventory loss HI, as
would be the case in accounting for the spread GH under FIFO.

The profit under LIFO would be relatively high, however, since
finished goods prices would not have dropped in line with the decrease
in the replacement cost of materials.

Although LIFO does not assist in the leveling of profit from period
to period, in this case it is beneficial to some extent in reflecting more
promptly than FIFO the effect on profit of changes in material costs.
This is in addition to the benefit of LIFO in enabling accounting for
profit on a distributable basis.

A third type of situation might be illustrated in which finished
goods prices fluctuate with demand from period to period, while material prices remain relatively constant. However, there is no point in
spending time on this because, if material is assumed to have a constant cost, the cost per unit will be the same whether a given company
is practicing LIFO, FIFO, or average cost. Therefore, there will be no
difference in the effect of using one method versus another.

As we have noted, LIFO is most applicable to industries in which
material represents a significant part of the total cost of a product and
where material prices and finished goods prices tend to move up and
down together. The method can also be attractive to industries in
which finished goods prices are less volatile than material prices.

In both types of industries, the inventories must, of course, con-
stantly be of such a size as to make their valuation on one basis versus
another a significant matter. Otherwise, there is really no inventory valuation problem to be considered.

LIFO and Inventory Turnover

It has sometimes been stated that the rate of inventory turnover is a
factor to be taken into account in judging the appropriateness of LIFO

in a given situation. This is correct only to the extent that rate of turnover gives an indication of the size of the inventory relative to total operations.

The presumption is that the lower the turnover the larger the inventory relative to total operations and, therefore, the greater the difference in computed income from using one basis of valuation versus another. The important point is not the rate of turnover but whether the valuation of inventory on one basis versus another has a significant effect on computed income.

For example, some meat packers, even though having a high rate of inventory turnover relative to many other industries, have found it advantageous to adopt LIFO. Their material costs and finished goods prices certainly move up and down together. Although inventories are low relative to their sales volume, their profit per sales unit is low and inventories are sufficiently high so that computed income in the short run is markedly affected by the basis of inventory valuation used.

It is sometimes mistakenly thought that LIFO should be particularly appropriate in an industry characterized by low turnover. The reasoning here is that materials and goods are held for longer periods of time in such industries and, therefore, these are more subject to gains and losses from price fluctuations between the time of purchase and time of sale.

It should be remembered, however, that LIFO is not concerned with inventory gains or losses on goods sold; it is concerned with avoiding the taking of gains or losses on inventory *not* sold. Essentially, it aims to avoid taking inventory gains and losses on its basic inventory.

Assuming that once having started LIFO the replacement cost of the inventory has not dropped below its LIFO valuation, the amount of profit avoided on the basic inventory as of any given time would be essentially the same regardless of the number of times the inventory had turned over since LIFO was started.

Let us assume that we adopt LIFO at a time when we have on hand 500,000 pounds of a given item costing $0.50 per pound: total valuation $250,000. Let us assume further that over time the replacement cost of this item rises to $0.60 per pound and that throughout this period we have maintained the same inventory quantity by replacing immediately through purchase whatever pounds were sold.

At the end of this time period, assuming that the inventory has turned over at least once while the replacement cost is at $0.60, the valuation of the inventory under LIFO would still be $250,000, whereas under FIFO it would be $300,000. The difference of $50,000 in

EXHIBIT 33
Inventory Valuation Under FIFO

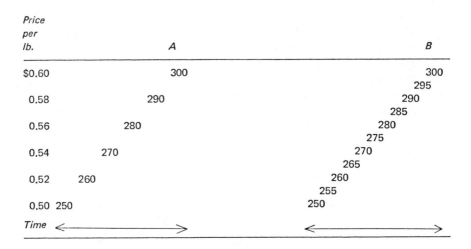

Price per lb.	A	B
$0.60	300	300
		295
0.58	290	290
		285
0.56	280	280
		275
0.54	270	270
		265
0.52	260	260
		255
0.50	250	250
Time		

inventory and computed profit between the two methods will be the same regardless of the number of times the inventory has turned over.

To illustrate the point, in Exhibit 33 the assumption under A is that during the time period under consideration the inventory has turned over five times, whereas the assumption under B is that the inventory has turned over ten times during the same period. The $50,000 difference in inventory and computed profit between LIFO and FIFO is the same at the end of the period whether the turnover during the period is five or ten times.

Turnover is not, therefore, of significance with respect to the amount of profit denied under LIFO and reported under FIFO. The significant difference between A and B is that the volume of operations in B is double that of A, although inventories are the same in size.

LIFO is more important to A because the inventory, although the same size as in B, is larger percentagewise relative to sales volume. Thus the $50,000 difference in inventory valuation and computed profit is, of course, more significant to A than to B since the sales volume is only half that of B.

LIFO and Multiple Inventories

In addition to the qualifications already discussed, it was believed at one time that LIFO was appropriate only in companies where the inventory consisted largely of a few basic materials and where goods at all stages of production could be converted into terms of units of these materials. Moreover, it was considered necessary to maintain identical quantities of such units if the LIFO position was to be maintained.

These restrictions ruled out LIFO as a practical method for wholesalers, retailers, or manufacturers of multiple products since thousands of different items are involved in such businesses and inventories are continually changing in detail. To meet this problem, a number of retailers developed and used in their own accounting what became known as the dollar-value method of LIFO, and they sought permission to use this method for tax purposes. Such permission was granted to retailers in 1948, and later for general use.[1]

Dollar-Value Method of LIFO

Under this method, the inventory is regarded as consisting of an investment in terms of base dollars, adjusted by increments or decrements as time passes. The base dollar represents a dollar of investment in a given category of inventory at the level of prices for materials or goods within that category in effect at the time LIFO is started.

Base dollars by inventory categories are used as common denominators like pounds to combine items that are otherwise dissimilar and to enable measurement of, and changes in, physical size of the inventory from period to period.

The dollar-value method of LIFO may be illustrated briefly. Let us assume that at the beginning of the period in which we start the method, we have on hand an assortment of goods which cost us $200,000 and which can be combined into one inventory category, since the items involved are subject to the same pattern of price fluctuations even though differing in physical characteristics.

Let us assume further that at the end of the first period under this method, a physical inventory is taken and the goods then on hand are priced at their replacement cost totaling $231,000. An appropriate price index for the type of goods in question shows replacement costs at the end of the period to be 110% of costs as they stood at the beginning of the period. Dividing $231,000 by 110% tells us that the ending inventory is $210,000 expressed in base dollars. There has therefore been a physical increase in inventory of 5% ($10,000 ÷ $200,000).

As a matter of convenience, this increment would be priced by applying the price index at the end of the period to its base-dollar value,

---

[1] Amendment to Section 29.22(d)-1 of the Income Tax Regulations in Treasury Decision 5756, November 2, 1949.

the base dollars in this case having been assigned a price index of 100. Thus $10,000 × 110% gives us an $11,000 LIFO valuation for the increment.

The total LIFO valuation at the end of the period would then be $200,000 base inventory, as though the beginning inventory had not been touched. In fact, it doubtless has not only turned over but has also changed with respect to mix of items and may include items of a type that had not even been in the beginning inventory, plus the increment of $11,000 making the total valuation $211,000.

Thus the summary of inventory at the close of the first period can be illustrated as follows:

	Base Dollars	Price Ratio	Total
Beginning LIFO inventory	$200,000	100%	$200,000
Increment first period	10,000	110	11,000
Ending LIFO inventory	$210,000		$211,000

The price index used in connection with the dollar-value method of LIFO, subject to approval by the Internal Revenue Service, may either be developed by the given company from appropriate industry and company data, or it may be selected from published government price indexes.

CHAPTER 18

Inventory Valuation: Other Materials' Costs and Market Valuations

There are a variety of costs other than invoice prices of materials purchased involved in the acquisition, storing, and handling of materials. Decisions must be made as to whether such costs are to be included in the valuation of inventories or whether they are to be charged off completely as period costs in the period in which they are incurred.

One might argue that where materials are to be valued at cost, any cost incurred in connection with them, which would not therefore have been incurred without them, should be included in their valuation. The problem, however, is not so simple as this.

There are practical difficulties involved in making sound allocations of such costs to inventory items. Moreover, the cost of detailed accounting by such items may be prohibitive relative to any gains from having more accurate or more correct cost valuations. Under these conditions, common sense, not blind rules, should guide decisions in these areas.

Costs Other Than Invoice Prices

If inventories remained exactly the same in physical terms from period to period, there would be no problems in accounting for these other costs. For all practical purposes, the amount of such costs applicable to the ending inventory would be the same as the amount applicable to the beginning inventory. Thus the costs incurred for the period would all become period costs as though the inventory had not been touched.

The fact is, of course, that inventories do change in physical terms from period to period. Therefore, problems in accounting appropriately for such costs must be faced and decisions made with respect to them.

Inward Freight and Trucking

Transportation provides a place utility that is indispensable, and inward transportation costs are clearly identifiable with materials purchased. On these grounds, it is reasonable to charge such costs to materials purchased and thus include them as part of the valuation of inventories at cost. Many companies follow this practice.

Other companies, however, particularly where transportation costs are small relative to the purchase price of materials, charge them off as period costs on the grounds that charging them to materials purchased and including them in inventory valuations would not be worth the bother and bookkeeping expense.

As an example, they would not consider it worthwhile to allocate a freight bill of $12.29 on an incoming shipment of eight items differing in size, weight, and cost packed in one box.

Generally, a compromise is called for in this area, such as identifying and charging inward transportation costs only to purchases of major raw materials and to other major items such as equipment and charging off all other inward transportation costs as period costs.

In many companies, inward transportation costs on materials purchased are accumulated in what is essentially an "Inward Freight and Truckage Inventory" account. At the end of each month, the accumulated costs are split in proportion to material costs in inventories and material costs in "Cost of Goods Sold." The portion applicable to inventories is carried forward in the "Inward Freight and Truckage Inventory" account and the other portion is accounted for as a period cost included in "Cost of Goods Sold."

Trade Discounts

In many industries, it is common practice to establish catalogue or list prices which often remain unchanged for long periods of time. The actual price at any given time, and for any given class of buyer, is determined by the application of current discounts to the catalogue or list prices. Such discounts are changed from time to time in the light of changes in cost and market conditions.

The catalogue or list prices are thus simply basing points for pricing purposes. They never represent either selling prices for the seller or costs to the buyer. Therefore, the "cost" of material for inventory valuation purposes should be net of trade discounts.

Cash Discounts

The question as to whether cash discounts should be treated as reductions in the cost of goods purchased or as financial income has been debated for many years.

Those who believe that cash discounts should be treated as financial income hold that the true cost of the goods is the gross price. The cash discount is offered as a reward for prompt payment, and discounts taken should be reflected as financial income, since they result from the financial ability to pay for purchases before final payment on them is due.

Similarly, with respect to the seller, it is held that cash discounts offered and taken should be treated as financial expense. They are not reductions in selling price, since they represent a financial sacrifice in order to receive and have the use of money from customers earlier than would otherwise be the case.

Those who believe that cash discounts should be treated as deductions from sales by the seller, and as reductions in the cost of goods purchased by the buyer, hold that prompt payment is the normal expectation. Therefore, the price net of the cash discount is the normal or true price. If the gross price has to be paid, it is the result of financial inability to pay on time. Some go so far as to enter all purchases at the net price and to charge as a financial expense any cash discounts not taken.

Many companies, regardless of theory, treat cash discounts received as financial income. This is the simplest procedure, particularly where perpetual inventory records are maintained in dollars as well as in quantities and where treating cash discounts as a reduction in cost would involve recomputing the cost of every item on every invoice when posting to the inventory records.

Interest on Investment in Inventories

In some industries, such as tobacco and liquor, it is the practice to carry inventory for several months or years while it undergoes an aging process. Whether or not it is computed, part of the cost of undertaking this process is the return foregone by investing in inventory that could have been realized if the same amount of money had been invested elsewhere.

Moreover, as an alternative to buying raw material and aging it, it is possible in industries of this type to buy aged material, the price of which, other things being equal, includes a return on the investment to the company that undertook the aging process.

Whether one considers that alternative revenue has been lost, or that alternative cost has been avoided, it can be argued that a company which does its own aging of materials should include interest on the investment in these materials in establishing their valuation on a cost basis.

If such a company has actually borrowed money to finance inventories under these conditions, it is logical to consider interest paid on such borrowings as part of the cost of the aging process. Moreover, in order to have a proper matching of costs and revenues, it can be argued that this cost should be added to the valuation of inventory and carried forward to the point in time when the goods so costed are sold and thus be included as part of the cost of goods sold at that time.

Some companies in this type of situation do follow this practice, while the remainder, largely on grounds of conservatism, treat interest on such borrowings as period costs, even though the aging process has in fact increased the value of the inventories as well as their cost.

Where the aging process takes place over several years and the inventory, although subject to some seasonal fluctuation is substantial at all times, the bulk of the inventory is financed by stockholders' equity or by a combination of equity and long-term loans which together finance other assets as well as inventories.

Under the latter conditions, interest is treated as a period cost. It would be arbitrary, and rather fruitless, to attempt to identify the extent to which any given asset has been financed by long-term borrowing versus stockholders' equity and, thereby, to determine how much of the interest paid in any given period should be charged against the investment in any given asset.

In a company using only stockholders' equity to finance inventory during an aging process, it could be helpful for certain decisions to make side estimates of the cost of the funds so used. Such estimates can aid decisions as to whether to age material or to buy it aged. They may also be helpful in judging the profitability of a given product line and possibly be of use in pricing.

The reason for not entering such cost estimates in the books of account is that if a company were to charge itself interest through a charge to inventory it would also have to give itself credit for interest income. The interest income presumably would be recorded as income for the period for which it was computed, since it would have been earned during that period.

The cost side of the computation would be passed along in the inventory from period to period until the goods to which it was attached were sold. This would be taking credit for interest income which, at best, would not be recovered from customers until some future accounting period. Such a procedure would be lacking the usual degree of conservatism associated with income determination.

Inventories that do not go through an aging process are subject to more rapid turnover and, even though they may require a relatively large investment, any interest payments involved in financing them are charged off as period expenses. This is a matter of conservatism supported by the point that, while interest payments are part of the cost of carrying such assets, the materials themselves do not increase in value merely by storage.

The fact that these assets require financing, and financing involves interest, does not necessarily mean that such interest should be included in their valuation any more than in the valuation of any other asset. In order to carry accounts receivable, for example, it is often necessary for a company to borrow money and pay interest thereon. But this does not mean that such interest should be added to the valuation of customers' accounts.

Purchasing, Handling, Storing, and Accounting for Materials

Although these costs can be identified with the acquisition and carrying of specific materials, this does not mean that they must necessarily be included in the cost valuation of materials on hand, any more than in the case of interest as noted in the previous paragraph. Generally speaking, materials are not enhanced in value by being purchased, handled, or accounted for, nor are they enhanced by being stored.

In manufacturing companies, such costs are not included in the cost valuation of materials, except where an aging process is involved. As a matter of convenience, as well as conservatism, many manufacturing companies treat such costs as period costs.

Others, in order to carry out more complete product-costing, include these costs as part of the overhead costs charged to work in process and finished goods. They do not include them in the cost valuation of raw materials or purchased parts.

In the case of nonmanufacturing businesses, the costs of purchasing, handling, storing, and accounting for goods and supplies are treated as period costs and not included in the valuation of inventories.

Costs in Work in Process and Finished Goods

The cost valuation of the material element of work in process and finished goods inventories will, in the majority of cases, be dependent upon the manner in which the specific company has applied costs in the valuation of its raw material inventories. The selection of cost of specific lot, average cost, FIFO, LIFO, or standard cost — as we saw in Chapter 17 — and the accounting treatment accorded other costs, set the pattern which will be followed in valuing the material element of work in process and finished goods.

Some companies, however, carry raw material inventories at actual cost (specific lot, average, FIFO, or LIFO) but carry inventories of work in process and finished goods at standard cost. The difference between the actual cost and the standard cost of the raw material entering production during a period is siphoned off as a price variance and treated, preferably, as a separate loss or gain for the period rather than as an adjustment to the cost of goods sold during the period.

Here, it is considered that a proper matching of costs and revenues is achieved by matching the standard cost of products against their sales revenue. All variances between the actual costs and standard costs of products are considered to be accounted for appropriately as operating gains or losses each period during the course of their production.

A common practice is to use standard costs for purposes of monthly internal operating statements, but to convert year-end inventories of work in process and finished goods to approximations of actual cost.

Here, inventories which have first been established at standard costs are adjusted to approximations of actual cost by allocating to them what is considered to be a proper share of the cost variances that have taken place during the year. The cost variances not allocated to inventories are allocated to "Cost of Goods Sold" to bring it to an approximation of actual cost.

Labor Cost

The application of labor cost to inventories of work in process and finished goods is dependent on the specific company's methods of wage payment, the nature of its production processes, and its system of cost accounting. Accounting for labor cost as part of a cost system will be discussed in a later chapter.

For the moment, let us note simply that practice ranges from detailed and accurate accounting for labor cost applied by each individual to a product or batch of products to rather arbitrary allocations of labor costs to inventories of work in process and finished goods and to goods sold, generally within a product-line classification.

Also, as in the case of raw material, many companies apply standard rather than actual costs in valuing the labor-cost element of work in process and finished goods. And they close out variances between actual and standard costs as expenses of the period in which they took place.

In addition to problems in determining the appropriate accounting for direct labor costs as such, there are problems in accounting for allied costs such as overtime payments, night-shift premiums, and fringe benefits. Similarly, there are problems in determining the appropriate accounting for labor paid during machine breakdowns, while waiting for work, and for meeting guaranteed minimum wages when piece-rate earnings do not reach the minimums.

Solutions to some of these problems have evolved as generally accepted procedures but many of them call for judgment in the light of individual circumstances. In particular, judgment is called for in determining on an incremental basis whether in the specific instance more detailed and accurate cost data will be worth its incremental accounting cost.

It is true that within the statement "Inventories of work in process and finished goods have been valued at cost," it is possible to have substantially different valuations depending upon the methods by which labor costs, and costs allied with them, are computed and applied. Generally speaking, however, these differences arise from practical considerations and not from ignorance, caprice, or a desire to make a better appearance.

Here, as in other areas, the requirement of consistency in practice from period to period is a major protection against differences which might otherwise be manipulated through frequent changes in practice.

Material Overhead

As noted earlier, except where an aging process is involved, the costs of purchasing, handling, storing, and accounting for materials are not included in the cost valuation of raw materials and purchased parts. In some cases, all or parts of these costs are treated as period costs and appear in an operating statement as items within the general classification of administrative expenses.

In other cases, a standard charge for material-handling costs is made at the time raw materials or purchased parts are moved into production. In this way, these costs enter the valuation of inventories of work in process and finished goods. Such standard charges are commonly developed as a percentage of material cost, or as a rate of so much per 100 pounds or other physical unit. The difference between the costs absorbed by the application of these standard charges and the actual costs incurred during a period is treated as a gain or loss for the period.

Companies using this procedure believe that costs of this type are identifiable with materials and should be charged on a material cost or unit basis. These companies do not believe that such costs should be combined with other factory burden and allocated to products on some other basis having little or no relationship with material handling costs.

A third approach is the one just suggested — namely, to merge these material-handling costs with other items of factory burden and to allocate them to products by means of a burden rate or rates. This is a relatively simple, although not too accurate, method for charging such costs to products if a single plant-wide burden rate is used. This approach is more complicated, but no more accurate, if separate cost-center or department rates are used and material-handling costs must be fitted into this rate structure.

Factory Burden

All production costs other than direct labor, raw materials and containers, and purchased parts are classified as "factory burden," "factory overhead," or "manufacturing expenses." These costs include variable or semivariable costs such as supervision, indirect labor, heat, light, and power, supplies, and repairs and maintenance. Factory burden also includes fixed costs such as depreciation, property taxes, and fire insurance.

As we noted in the previous section, some companies treat some of these costs separately as material-handling costs or as material overhead.

The accounting for and control of factory burden will be considered later in detail. For present purposes, the first point to note is that there can be significant differences in the cost valuation of inventories of work in process and finished goods, depending upon the methods used in charging factory burden to products.

At one extreme, products, including those in inventories of work in process and finished goods, are not charged with any factory burden. They are charged with prime costs only, i.e., material and labor costs, while all items of factory burden are treated as period costs.

At the other extreme, all factory burden is prorated equitably to the products completed and partially completed each period, regardless of fluctuations in production volume from period to period.

Between these extremes, there are a variety of practices with respect to the factory burden items to be included in inventory cost valuations and those to be treated as costs of the period. One of the more clearly defined practices in this area is the use of direct costing, under which goods in inventory are charged with their variable factory burden costs but all fixed costs are charged to the period. Another clearly defined practice is the use of standard costs, including a share of fixed factory burden costs, for inventory valuation purposes, while variances between actual and standard costs are treated as period gains or losses.

Prime Costs

Those who use prime costs only in the valuation of inventories of work in process and finished goods do so either for the sake of conservatism or because this has always been common practice in the trade in which they are engaged, or for both reasons. The practice stems from mercantile accounting, and its use in a few manufacturing industries goes back to the days before the industrial revolution, when factory burden was a relatively minor part of the cost of operations.

For internal management accounting purposes, a company can, of course, value inventories on any basis it sees fit, including the valuation of work in process and finished goods at prime costs only.

For income tax purposes, however, inventory valuation at prime costs only has been restricted to a few industries, such as the clothing trade, where the practice was traditional long before income taxes were ever instituted.

For financial reporting purposes to stockholders and others, generally accepted accounting practice is opposed to the exclusion of all overheads from inventory values. This viewpoint rules out valuation at prime costs only but still leaves plenty of room for differences of opinion and practice as to what is, or should be, included for factory burden in inventory values.

Viewpoint of public accountants.   The following excerpt is a more complete statement of the viewpoint expressed in the previous paragraph:

> Although principles for the determination of inventory costs may be easily stated, their application, particularly to such inventory items as work in process and finished goods, is difficult because of the variety of problems encountered in the allocation of costs and charges. For example, under some circumstances, items such as idle facility expense, excessive spoilage, double freight, and rehandling costs may be so abnormal as to require treatment as current period charges rather than as a portion of inventory cost. Also, general and administrative expenses should be included as period charges, except for the portion of such expenses that may be clearly related to production and thus constitute a part of inventory costs (product charges). Selling expenses constitute no part of inventory costs. It should also be recognized that the exclusion of all overheads from inventory costs does not constitute an accepted accounting procedure. The exercise of judgment in an individual situation involves a consideration of the adequacy of the procedures of the cost accounting system in use, the soundness of the principles thereof, and their consistent application.[1]

Direct Costing

The practice of direct costing has been a popular topic for discussion in accounting articles and meetings for many years. Under this practice, products are charged only for such costs as are directly involved in their production (including items of variable burden), leaving all other manufacturing costs to be treated as period costs.

The major area of contention is in the valuation of inventories at direct costs only and the consequent effect of this practice on income determination. Our present discussion will be restricted to this area, leaving the analysis of direct costs for other purposes to later chapters.

As just noted in the quotation from *Accounting Research Bulletin 43*, "the exclusion of all overheads from inventory costs does not constitute an accepted accounting procedure." This statement rules out direct costing as an acceptable accounting practice in public financial reporting.

---

[1]Accounting Research Bulletin 43, *Restatement and Revision of Accounting Research Bulletins* (New York: American Institute of Certified Public Accountants, 1953) Chapter 4, Statement 3, Discussion 5.

For internal management purposes, however, a company is not required to follow generally accepted accounting principles. Therefore, it can practice direct costing for these purposes if it sees fit to do so. Since many companies do, in fact, practice direct costing for internal management purposes, it is appropriate to study the merits of this practice.

Moreover, many who are most enthusiastic about the use of direct costing are quite vocal in their enthusiasm and are persistent in promoting its general acceptance. Since these promotional efforts are likely to continue, and may be expanded in the future, businessmen who are not using direct costing should at least understand the practice and come to their own conclusions about it.

Inventory changes key factor in the controversy. If inventories of work in process and finished goods remained constant in physical terms from period to period, and if — under "full" or "absorption" costing — indirect costs were charged to products at standard rates, there would be no controversy over direct costing. Constant sized inventories of work in process and finished goods under full costing would contain substantially the same amount of absorbed indirect costs from period to period.

Inventories under such conditions would remain in effect untouched, and the costs accounted for during the period would essentially become charges against the revenues of that period. Thus indirect costs would be charged to the period, and the net profit would be the same whether the company practiced direct costing or full costing.

While inventories would always show lower values under direct costing than under full costing for the same company, which could be a matter of concern from a creditor's viewpoint, this direct costing practice would not be likely to arouse more general concern.

The fact is, of course, that inventories of work in process and finished goods do change from period to period, and the change is often substantial. Under conventional methods, when these inventories are increased they absorb proportionately more indirect manufacturing costs, which would be charged to the period under direct costing. Thus the stated profit is correspondingly increased relative to what would be reported under direct costing.

When these inventories are decreased, the absorbed indirect manufacturing costs carried over from the previous period in the valuation of the units decreased results in a charge against revenue, which would not be present under direct costing. Correspondingly, there is a decrease in the relative stated profit.

In contrast to conventional practice, the use of direct costing results in a more conservative statement of income for periods in which there is a net increase in the size of work in process and finished goods inventories. At the same time, direct costing results in a less conservative statement of income for periods in which there is a net decrease in the size of these inventories.

Changes in the size of these inventories occur when production and sales volumes are not equal during the given period. Thus direct costing results in a more conservative statement of income for periods in which production volume is greater than shipping volume and a less conservative statement of income for periods in which the reverse condition exists.

An important point to keep in mind is that stated net income under conventional practice is dependent not only upon the sales volume for the given period, but also upon production volume, with its consequent absorption of indirect manufacturing costs.

In contrast, the stated net income for a period under direct costing is highly dependent upon the sales volume for that period. But it is not directly influenced by production volume, since the indirect manufacturing costs are all charged to the period regardless of what is produced.

Most manufacturing companies try to maintain relatively steady production in order to produce economically, whereas the timing of sales (shipments) is dependent on external factors largely beyond the control of the manufacturer. Thus the general tendency is for sales volume to show greater fluctuations than production volume from period to period.

Generally speaking, it follows from this that net income will fluctuate more from period to period if a company is practicing direct costing than it will if it is practicing full or absorption costing.

Major arguments for direct costing.   Those who favor this practice hold that direct costs are the current costs of making goods. Thus direct costs are the only costs that should be identified with current costs for inventory valuation and profit determination.

Indirect manufacturing costs are largely the result of past management decisions and, in any event, are not directly dependent in amount on the particular type or quantity of goods produced during a period. Thus, being more closely related to time than to products, they should be charged as period costs rather than product costs. Furthermore, to charge products with indirect manufacturing costs involves arbitrary, time-consuming, and expensive cost allocations.

It follows from the foregoing that under direct costing there should be savings in clerical cost which would otherwise be spent in making computations, allocations, and entries of indirect costs on cost records and in detail on the books of account. Such savings would, of course, be offset by whatever time was spent on the same activity apart from these records in order to provide management with a knowledge of full costs for purposes other than inventory valuation.

Major benefits claimed for direct costing are its psychological and educational effects on management. In companies that have adopted direct costing, the attention of management has obviously been focused thereby on direct costs. And this has apparently been helpful in situations where executives have previously been preoccupied with full costs.

In other cases, the adoption of direct costing has clarified the company's product-cost situation and made executives more aware of the differences in the nature of its various costs. In such cases, the treating of fixed costs as period costs has made managers at various levels in an organization more keenly aware of the size and importance of such costs.

Beyond the points just mentioned, it is the belief of those who favor direct costing that, in contrast to conventional practice, this approach provides a more correct statement of the operating profit or loss for an accounting period. Concurrently, inventories of work in process and finished goods are more properly stated when charged only for such costs as are directly involved in their production.

With respect to profit or loss, the belief is that the major determinants of operating income should be revenue from shipments matched by the direct costs of the goods shipped and the full indirect manufacturing costs of the period during which the shipments took place. It is also considered to be an advantage that inventories under direct costing are stated more conservatively than under full costing.

Major arguments for inclusion of indirect costs. The purpose underlying the incurrence of indirect manufacturing costs is the production of goods, regardless of when the costs are incurred. Thus the conventional view holds that a fair charge for such costs is just as much a part of the cost of a product as is the labor expended upon it and the material from which it was fashioned. Therefore, if inventories are to be valued at cost, the valuation should include a fair share of indirect costs.

From this viewpoint, it is not sensible to hold that the cost of machine operations performed on a product are not product costs, while the same operations, if performed by hand, would be accounted for as product costs without question.

Similarly, if a company suddenly adopted a guaranteed annual wage for all of its employees, so that wages would become essentially fixed costs, this should not mean that labor actually expended on products should no longer be identified as part of their costs.

Although it is true that the application of indirect costs to products does involve allocations, which are to some extent both arbitrary and time-consuming, this does not mean that they are undertaken capriciously or at exorbitant expense. Arbitrary does not mean illogical, nor the abandonment of common sense. While the cost of getting information should always be taken into account in developing an information system, the aim should be to get useful information at a reasonable cost, not simply to develop an inexpensive system.

The conventional view holds that in a manufacturing business both production and sales volumes are significant factors bearing on profit realization, not sales volume alone. Thus the impact of production volume through absorption of indirect manufacturing costs should be reflected in financial statements.

Manufacturing businesses in general obviously involve more complicated operations than merchandising businesses. In particular, their success or failure is dependent on production activity, as well as on selling and shipping activity.

From the conventional viewpoint, to practice direct costing in such businesses, and thereby to allow shipping to be the only volume factor reflected in financial reports, is an oversimplification of the true situation and results in the presentation of incorrect financial statements.

Beyond these points, it is believed by some who oppose direct costing that the emphasis on direct costs for inventory valuation, along with the emphasis on pricing and control, may lead executives to overlook or minimize the importance of indirect manufacturing costs. At the very least, these executives may not feel any responsibility in connection with such costs despite their impact on a company's profit or loss situation.

This situation is particularly distressing to some who note that with increasing automation the indirect manufacturing costs are becoming the critical costs in their industries, while direct costs are becoming relatively less important.

In rebuttal, those who believe in direct costing argue, as we noted earlier, that as far as income statements are concerned direct costing does emphasize indirect manufacturing costs. In fact, the emphasis is even more pronounced here than in conventional practice, because direct costing shows the full amounts of indirect manufacturing costs as expenses each accounting period.

Full Costing

At the extreme opposite of direct costing, all of the actual indirect manufacturing costs incurred during each accounting period are apportioned among goods sold and ending inventories of work in process and finished goods, presumably on rational bases. This practice is a literal interpretation of full costing and, under it, one can state without much argument that inventories are valued at their full manufacturing cost.

Full costing causes no problems, except to firm believers in direct costing, in situations where production volume varies but little from month to month and where gradual increases in production volume are matched by gradual increases in indirect manufacturing costs. Under these conditions, there are no significant short-run changes in production volume or in direct manufacturing costs to cause fluctuations in product-unit costs.

In situations where there are seasonal and/or cyclical changes in production volume, however, this approach can be unsatisfactory. Presumably, in such cases, it is not completely possible to maintain level production and to meet fluctuating sales demands by alternately building up and drawing upon inventory.

Presumably also, it is not strategically desirable, and may not in fact be possible, to build and maintain only such manufacturing capacity as would meet the minimum seasonal or cyclical demand in the hope of being able to maintain capacity production at all times. In other words, in these situations some seasonal and cyclical idleness in the use of facilities is to be expected.

If the actual indirect manufacturing costs each period are simply charged to whatever goods are produced, the product-unit charges will be unfairly high during periods of low activity and unfairly low during periods of high activity. These charges will be unfair to the goods produced in periods of low activity because it would have been known in advance that the facilities would not be used completely during such periods and the extra capacity had been built and maintained to take care of the demand in more active periods.

Similarly, the product-unit charges will not be fair in periods of high activity because they will not allow for the fact that in order to have the facilities for such high activity other periods have been forced to incur costs for idle capacity.

Full costing with indirect manufacturing costs charged at standard rates. To avoid the problems just stated, and as a matter of convenience, the great majority of manufacturing companies apply manufacturing costs (factory burden) to products by means of predetermined (standard) burden rates.

In such companies, the valuation of goods in process and finished goods at their full actual cost means valuation at the actual cost of material and labor involved in their production, plus manufacturing costs applied by burden rates. The development of various types of rates will be considered in detail in a later chapter.

For the moment, let us take one type — namely, a labor-hour rate, — as an example. A common approach here is to divide the expected manufacturing costs of a given section of the plant, or of the plant as a whole, for either six months or one year ahead, by the expected number of direct labor hours for the period and area selected.

Another common approach is used in companies where production volume fluctuates markedly from year to year. This method establishes burden rates based on the average or "normal" expected volume of operations per year and expected costs at that level, rather than on the expected volume and costs for a specific period of six months or one year ahead.

Rates developed under either of these approaches are applied to the actual labor hours expended on work in process and finished goods inventories in establishing their valuation at full actual cost. Thus the burden cost in this instance means the actual time expended priced at standard rates.

The major justification for the use of such rates, apart from convenience, is that each product is thereby charged in proportion to the time it uses the facilities involving manufacturing costs. Thus each product is made to bear its fair share of the fixed costs therein. But it is not made to suffer for, nor benefit from, having been produced in a period of lower or higher than average expected volume.

Burden rates based on the expected volume for a period of six months or one year ahead are aimed essentially at spreading the cost of seasonal idleness fairly to all products. Similarly, rates based on expected average or normal volume are aimed essentially at spreading the cost of cyclical, as well as seasonal, idleness fairly to all products.

When burden rates are used for product costing, it would be rare indeed if the total amounts charged to products during a period exactly equaled the manufacturing costs incurred during that period. The amount of burden under- or overabsorbed each period is commonly accounted for as a period gain or loss. Thus period results suffer when the production volume is below that of the average volume assumed per period at the time the rates were developed. Conversely, period results benefit when production volume is above this average.

In some companies, burden under- or overabsorbed as a result of fluctuations in volume are not closed out each month. Instead, they are carried forward in the hope, if not the expectation, that amounts under-absorbed during months of low production will be offset at year end by overabsorbed cost during months of high production.

Full costing at standard costs. Discussion in the previous section involved the determination of product manufacturing costs by the application of burden rates to some measure of actual activity, such as labor hours, expended on the product being costed.

An extension of this practice is to value the burden element in inventories of work in process and finished goods at standard cost. In situations where burden can most appropriately be identified with labor hours, for example, this means the application of standard burden rates to the standard number of hours that should have been spent on a product, rather than to the hours actually expended on it.

The difference between the hours actually spent and the hours that should have been spent is, of course, an efficiency variance. Valuations of inventories at standard manufacturing costs assumes that efficiency losses or gains, along with losses or gains arising from fluctuations in production volume, should be treated as period losses or gains.

I favor the inclusion of both fixed and variable burden at standard costs in inventories of work in process and finished goods. The standard costs should be reasonably up to date with respect to price and efficiency factors, and they should be based on the normal volume of operations.

To the extent that fixed costs are included in the standard burden cost, the theory, again, is that each unit of product should bear its fair share of fixed costs and not suffer or benefit as a result of unusually low or high volumes of production activity currently experienced. Therefore, under- or overabsorbed fixed costs are properly charged or credited to the period as reflections of the experience of that period.

Similarly, price and efficiency variances from standard costs are charged or credited to the period. These variances represent current departures from expected performance and, as such, should be taken into account in determining the profit or loss for the period. Inventories are then carried forward from one period to another at their standard cost.

Selling and Administrative Expenses

Except for such administrative expenses as are identifiable with production activity, selling and administrative expenses are rarely included in the cost valuation of work-in-process and finished goods inventories.

Articles have been written from time to time that advocate capitalizing the cost of getting an order and carrying it forward to the time of shipment as part of a proper matching of costs and revenues. However, few companies appear to have adopted the suggestion. Conservatism in inventory valuation, and maintaining consistency with income tax treatment of these costs as period expenses, are reasons for not following such a policy.

Another point is that current selling and administrative expenses are generally not sufficiently closely allied to the specific goods on hand, either in process or finished, to make it possible to say that they have added to either the cost or value of these goods.

The selling expenses of an accounting period are in large part incurred to procure orders for future production and shipment. Thus they are not directly related to goods on hand. Nor can they be identified easily with specific orders in any event, because part of the costs of the order landed are the expenditures involved in fruitless efforts.

Similarly, the majority of general administrative expenses are neither directly related to nor easily identified with current production. Under these circumstances, it seems reasonable to treat selling and administrative expenses as period costs, and therefore, to omit them in inventory valuation.

Cost vs. Market Valuation

It should be remembered that the alternative procedures we have been discussing, both here and in the preceding chapter — namely, cost of specific lot, average cost, FIFO, LIFO, and standard cost — as well as the different types of cost to be included or excluded from inventory valuation are matters connected with the valuation of inventories at cost.

Shortly, we shall examine the valuation of the various classes of inventory at market and note the desirability of using valuation at the lower of cost or market. If the latter practice is followed, then no matter what definition of cost is adopted, the inventory will at least never be stated above its market value.

The foregoing statement is not intended to mean that the selection of one definition of cost versus another is a matter of indifference. Rather, it means only that under these conditions market sets a ceiling on the valuation no matter what definition of cost is used.

Summary on Valuation at Cost

To the layman, cost is a simple concept. It is the price he pays for some article or service that he buys. One man's selling price is another man's cost.

For the businessman, however, and especially for the manufacturer, cost is not a simple concept, particularly in the valuation of inventories. Here, a decision must be made regarding the order in which it is to be assumed, for costing purposes, that materials move out of storage and through the plant.

A variety of problems also arise in determining the accounting treatment to be accorded costs of purchasing, receiving, storing, accounting for, and handling of materials, as well as the costs of labor and factory burden involved in working upon these materials. Many of these costs cannot be directly identified with specific lots of material. Therefore, they must be allocated to products on some predetermined basis, the selection of which is a matter of judgment.

The valuation of inventories at cost involves accounting convention to some extent. But, to an even greater degree, it involves judgment in determining, in the light of individual circumstances, the most suitable accounting treatment of a wide variety of costs. Thus within the statement that "inventories have been valued at cost," there can be significant differences in practice between one company and another which will be reflected in their respective financial statements.

Major differences occur, of course, when the bases of valuation are markedly different, as where one company is practicing LIFO and another FIFO, or where one is practicing direct costing and another full costing. Other differences average out over a few years and are relatively minor even in the short run.

Valuation of Inventories at Market

The valuation of raw materials and purchased parts or goods at market in a going concern commonly means their valuation at estimated replacement cost; that is, what it would cost to replace the inventory on the date of the valuation at prices then in effect for purchases from the regular sources of supply in lot sizes commonly purchased. In contrast, obsolete materials are commonly valued at prices at which it is estimated they can be disposed of in liquidation.

For example, if a company includes freight-in and other costs in addition to invoice price, then it should logically include such costs in the valuation of materials at market in terms of replacement cost. Here, however, unless such costs are highly significant, they are generally omitted for the sake of simplicity in valuation, as well as of conservatism.

Furthermore, materials in manufacturing companies are bought for production and not for resale in their purchased condition. Nonetheless, many manufacturers, who are possibly influenced by the attitude of commercial bankers on the subject, wish to show what these materials would fetch as such, in orderly liquidation, at prices in effect on the date of the balance sheet.

Under these conditions, they could not in all probability hope to recover freight-in or other costs except invoice prices exclusive of freight-in. The prices selected for market valuation would then be replacement cost in terms only of invoice price currently quoted by regular sources of supply and in lot sizes commonly purchased.

Work in Process at Market

Some goods are in salable form at certain stages during their processing, and a going market value can be established for them at these stages. In a woolen textile mill, for example, yarn that has been spun is in a salable form, even though the intention is to convert it further by weaving it into cloth.

Most work in process, however, is not in salable form except as scrap. Hence, since there is no market, there are no market prices for these goods in the usual sense. The valuation of work-in-process inventories at market under such conditions commonly involves the use of replacement cost. That is, market means what it would cost to replace the material, labor, and burden in the goods at prices and rates in effect as of the date of the balance sheet.

In many companies, this would involve so much clerical work that no attempt is made to value work in process at market. Rather, such inventories are carried either at actual or standard cost.

In other companies, replacement cost is computed for the material element of the work in process. Here, labor and burden are carried in the inventory at either actual or standard cost. If work in process does not vary significantly from period to period in physical size or nature, there is not too much point in worrying about refinements in its valuation.

In fact, one can argue for keeping work in process at a constant valuation under these conditions, thereby allowing the production costs incurred during a period to become the cost of goods completed during that period. This procedure can be supported strongly for the valuation of goods in process in continuous process industries.

Sometimes work in process has been committed to the production of certain types or styles of product for which demand has fallen and the selling price of finished goods has dropped, although raw material prices have remained firm. In such cases, it is usually desirable to establish a market value by working backward from finished goods price.

Thus the estimated selling and administrative expenses and the estimated remaining conversion costs are subtracted from the current finished goods price to arrive at a market value for the work in process. The purpose, of course, is to charge off to the current period losses arising from a fall in the demand for products for which the company has already committed itself.

Some companies also subtract an allowance for profit, thereby allowing the period of sale to make this profit on these goods. The provision here, of course, is that selling prices do not change further, and that the remaining conversion costs and the selling and administrative expenses turn out as estimated.

Finished Goods at Market

The same concepts of market in terms of replacement cost or finished goods' selling price, as just described for inventories of work in process, are found in the valuation of finished goods' inventories. For finished goods, however, the replacement cost would cover all costs of completion.

Also, in working back from the finished goods' selling price, there would be no remaining conversion costs to be subtracted, as would be the case with work in process.

Valuation at the Lower of Cost or Market

This method first involves the valuation of each item at both cost and market, on the basis of the definitions of cost and market adopted, and then the selection of the lower of the two, item by item. The reader should note that this is not the same as the lower of the total inventory at cost and the total inventory at market.

Valuation at the lower of cost or market is supported on grounds of conservatism. It is allowed for tax purposes as a consistent method, although it actually lacks consistency in that it anticipates losses but does not anticipate gains.

Furthermore, it lacks consistency in the degree of conservatism with which inventories are stated when market is above cost. That is, at times market value will be well above cost, and inventory valued at cost will be stated very conservatively; at other times, it will be the same as cost, or only slightly above, and valuation at cost will be relatively less conservative.

Despite these inconsistencies, the valuation of inventories at the lower of cost or market is a common practice.

Valuation at Market Above Cost

The Securities and Exchange Commission has in recent years required larger companies to present in their Form 10-K reports 1. the estimated replacement cost, as of the end of the fiscal year, of property, plant, and equipment, and inventories and 2. the calculated effect of the estimated replacement costs on the cost of goods sold and depreciation expense. Figures must be presented for the previous year as well as for the year being reported.

Both the SEC and the companies reporting this replacement cost information have cautioned against simplistic use of this data, particularly to restate net income. The required information is not precise and does not give a complete or balanced presentation of the impact of inflation.

Price-level adjustments will be discussed more fully in the next chapter on accounting for property, plant, and equipment. For the moment we are concerned only with the question of valuing inventory at market (or replacement cost) which is above the amount at which it is being carried in the accounts.

In Chapter 3, we noted that it has long been an accepted rule among businesses not to value inventories above their costs and, therefore, not to recognize revenue on materials or goods until they have been sold. Also, in Chapter 17, we noted that when LIFO is used under conditions of inflation, the figures at which inventories are being carried are in time likely to be well below replacement costs. Having these points in mind, it is understandable that businessmen in general,

TABLE 9

($ thousands)	1977		1976	
	Historical Cost from Balance Sheet	Estimated Replacement Cost	Historical Cost from Balance Sheet	Estimated Replacement Cost
Inventory	$ 168,743	$ 232,754	$157,554	$214,000
Cost of Sales (excluding depreciation)	$1,064,349	$1,066,131	$919,954	$921,000
Depreciation expense	$ 40,136	$ 87,000	$ 35,198	$ 75,000

and LIFO users in particular, have expressed concern that the replacement cost data on inventories required by the SEC may be used incorrectly to adjust reported net income.

The figures from the annual report of Koppers Company, Inc. (Table 9) are an example of supplementary replacement cost information on inventory, cost of goods sold, and depreciation expense. The company also provided replacement cost information on machinery, equipment, and buildings, with which we are not concerned at the moment.

For balance sheet purposes, inventories are valued at the lower of cost or market. Cost for substantially all domestic inventories of Koppers Company, Inc. is determined by the LIFO method. Cost for the remainder of the inventories represents average costs or standard costs which approximate actual on the first-in, first-out basis. Market is replacement cost for raw materials and net realizable value for work-in-process and finished goods.

With respect to the inventory replacement cost information Koppers reported on Form 10-K, the estimated replacement cost of raw material was based on standard cost which approximated current cost. Finished goods and work-in-process inventories were estimated on the basis of standard costs that approximated current costs and included current material, labor, and overhead variances as well as an allocation of replacement cost depreciation of buildings, machinery, and equipment determined on a straight-line basis.

For those inventories accounted for on a LIFO basis, the estimated replacement cost of sales, exclusive of depreciation, was based on applying the LIFO method of costing ending inventories adjusted for any decrements during the year. The turnover rate of inventories accounted for on a FIFO basis was considered to be fast enough to approximate replacement cost.

It can be seen in the figures that the difference in the valuation of the inventories at historical cost and their estimated replacement cost was substantial. The difference arose in large part through the use of

LIFO for balance-sheet purposes. If someone reading this information were to apply this difference as an increase in net income before taxes, he would not only be nullifying the benefit the company sought in adopting LIFO but would be assuming a profit on inventory before the materials or goods involved were sold.

It will also be noticed that because of the use of LIFO for the bulk of its inventories, the cost of goods sold as reported in the company's financial statements was approximately the same as its replacement cost. The fact that the use of LIFO does result in putting the cost of goods sold on a replacement cost basis, for all practical purposes, is, of course, a major reason for its use.

In conclusion, supplementary information on the replacement cost of inventories, when that cost is above its historical cost, may be helpful in arriving at a more accurate valuation of a company's current assets, but can be harmful if it is used incorrectly as an adjustment to net income.

Accounting for Property, Plant, and Equipment

Among the most critical accounting problems faced by the great majority of companies are those that involve property, plant, and equipment. The problems that arise here are of three types: 1. problems in determining the cost of depreciable assets acquired; 2. problems in estimating the probable useful life of these assets; and 3. problems in selecting the most appropriate manner in which to amortize the cost of any given depreciable asset over its estimated useful life.

Decisions in handling these problems require the exercise of judgment, aided by experience, and tempered by the degree of conservatism viewed as being appropriate in the given situation by those making the decisions.

Also, because of continuing inflation, the question being discussed more and more seriously is: Should the amounts carried in the accounts for property, plant, and equipment, and reported in financial statements, be restated periodically to reflect changes in the general purchasing power of money, either as supplementary information or as a substitute for the use of historical cost?

Indeed, the question is also being discussed seriously whether or not management should be expected, or required, to provide an opinion on the current market value or replacement cost of these assets in its report to stockholders.

In fact, in an effort to determine the possible usefulness of such information, and the difficulties and expense involved in getting it, the SEC has for some years now required large companies to furnish an estimate of the replacement cost of their property, plant, and equipment in their Form 10-K annual reports to the commission.

Problems in accounting for property, plant, and equipment are critical since the way in which they are handled can have significant effects on the data presented in balance sheets and income statements. Amounts invested in these assets are high relative to funds invested in other assets taken individually. Their valuation on one basis versus another can, therefore, have a significant balance-sheet effect.

Likewise, depreciation on these fixed assets is a heavy expense relative to many other expenses. Therefore, differences in accounting treatment affecting the amount of depreciation computed for a given period can have a significant effect on the amount of both net income before taxes reported in an income statement and income taxes to be paid.

Depreciable Assets Acquired

An obvious rule can be followed up to a point in accounting for the cost of many assets. Namely, that all costs incurred which would not have been incurred had a given asset not been acquired should be accounted for as costs of that asset.

Thus, in connection with the purchase of a machine, the price paid, as evidenced by the invoice covering the purchase, would normally be accounted for as its major cost, with freight and delivery costs added. There are other costs, however, related to such a purchase that would not normally be added to the recorded cost of the asset purchased. Instead, these would be charged as expenses of the period.

This accounting treatment is spoken of as "expensing" such costs, rather than as "capitalizing" them. While it might be argued, for example, that time and expenses incurred by an engineer in investigating and selecting the particular machine purchased should be accounted for as part of its cost, this is not normally done.

Similarly, the cost of the machine is not charged for the time and expenses of other individuals such as the purchasing agent, or someone in his department, who orders the machine; the receiving clerk who receives it; the bookkeeper who accounts for it; and the treasurer or cashier who pays for it. These expenses are defined broadly as overhead expenses. They are relatively minor with respect to an individual purchase. For this reason, if for no other, they are not accounted for as part of the acquisition costs of an asset.

Installation costs, however, and the cost of trial runs if material in amount, are commonly accounted for as part of the cost of the machine acquired. This includes the fees, travel, and living expenses of people brought in to supervise, or assist in, the installation.

Now and then, there are borderline situations, as when the floor where a new machine is to be placed has to be strengthened because of the weight of the machine. Here, it can be argued that it was this particular machine which required the extra cost. Therefore, it should be accounted for as part of the cost of the machine to be amortized over the machine's useful life.

It could however be argued, presumably with as much logic, that the floor had not been constructed properly to house machinery and that the strengthening of it really changed the character of the building, making it more valuable for the future as well as for its current use by the new machine. The cost should therefore be regarded as a cost to be added to the cost of the building and to be depreciated, along with the other costs of the building, over its estimated remaining useful life.

Finally, instead of either of these approaches, it might be argued that the cost of strengthening the floor should be charged to the period as a maintenance expense because the floor had weakened and bolstering it would simply enable it to fulfill the useful life that had been estimated for it at the time it had been constructed. The decision here depends upon one's interpretation of the facts of the case and a common-sense weighting of the alternatives.

The point is that in situations such as this there is no one clear answer, and there are alternatives to the method selected which might be defended equally well. Wise decisions here depend on the exercise of judgment, not on narrow dogma.

The invoice price of a machine should not in every case be considered as its true purchase price. When payment includes something other than cash, for instance, both the invoice price and the value placed on what was given in payment may be inflated.

For example, in a business where the typical purchase of a new machine involves the trading-in of an old one in partial payment, the amount allowed on the trade-in unit is likely to be generous, even after bargaining, in order to please the buyer. Thus the invoice price on the new unit is likely to be correspondingly generous the other way in order to please the seller.

A more appropriate figure to be recorded for the cost of the unit purchased is the amount that would be paid if it were purchased for cash with no trade-in. It should usually be possible for a buyer to find out what this figure would be and to use it as the cost of the asset acquired, with a corresponding reduction in the credit for the old unit traded in.

Depreciable Assets Produced

When a company produces a machine or piece of equipment for its own use, there should be no difficulty in keeping track of the cost of material and labor used. But there may well be problems in determining what and how much indirect manufacturing cost and overhead, if any, should be charged as part of the cost of the item produced.

In such a case, some people hold that since the company is making the machine or equipment for itself, it should not charge any indirect or overhead expenses to it, or at least should charge only for such additional expenses as would not have been incurred had the machine or equipment not been made. Accordingly, they omit most, if not all, indirect or overhead expenses in arriving at its cost.

There are others, however, who do not agree with this purely incremental cost approach. They fail to see why an item made for oneself should be costed any differently than the same item would be costed if it were made for someone else.

Assuming that a company's own costs are not badly out of line with what it would cost someone else to make the item, there is no reason why it should be recorded at its direct costs only. After all, if it were bought outside the price would presumably include a profit to the seller as well as reimbursement for his full costs.

Those who do not agree with the incremental approach, therefore, account for the full cost of the machine, including indirect or overhead expenses.

Under the profit center concept, if one division of a company manufactures machines for sale to customers outside of the company as its major activity, it seems logical to me that when it does sell a machine to some other division within the company the price charged should be the same as would be charged to an outsider.

Conversely, if it installed one of its own machines for its own use, it should not charge itself the full price and thereby capitalize its own profit as well as selling and administrative expenses which would not, in fact, have been incurred. Instead, it should record the machine at its full cost to manufacture.

Whatever benefits are to come from the subsequent use of the machine will be increased because of the lower depreciation charges on it, since it would have been entered in the accounts at less than its full selling price. The full manufacturing costs to be accounted for, however, would be the same as those accounted for on a machine produced for sale. These would include indirect manufacturing costs and such overhead expenses as can clearly be identified with the production function.

If a machine or piece of equipment produced internally is not one of the usual items of the producing unit, the computing of appropriate indirect manufacturing costs and production overhead costs may be more difficult.

For example, if the company uses a plant-wide overhead rate in costing its regular products, such a rate is not likely to be appropriate for the production of a machine or piece of equipment that would not be passing through the same departments or operations as regular products.

However, if each shop in which some part of the machine or equipment is made or assembled has a rational overhead rate for work performed within it, the cost accounting utilizing these rates should be appropriate in costing the machine or equipment produced.

The main point is that judgment is called for in determining how best to account for the indirect manufacturing and production overhead costs on an item that is not part of a company's regular production.

The first model of a new machine a company builds for its own use is likely to involve research, development, and experimental costs that are far higher than will have to be spent on subsequent models. Some people favor writing off these costs as operating expenses when incurred, both on the grounds of conservatism and to avoid penalizing the first model by charging it for costs that will also benefit subsequent models.

If it is known that later models will, in fact, be built, a case can be supported for charging a portion of these costs to the first model and deferring the remainder to be charged to later models. However, if the first model is the one and only machine of its kind that will ever be built, then surely all of the research, development, and experimental costs connected with it are part of its cost, no matter how high they may be.

Relocating a Machine

Not infrequently machines are moved from one part of a plant to another, or are realigned, hopefully to improve productivity. Although some sort of record of such costs should be kept, and questions raised later as to whether the moves had paid off, the costs should be expensed as incurred, not capitalized.

This is in part a matter of conservatism because of uncertainty as to the benefits to be gained from any given move. Beyond this, since a machine is usually charged for its initial installation costs, the benefits from which would be lost by the move, it should not have another installation charge added to it.

While one might argue that the initial installation costs should be removed and charged against the accumulated depreciation and the moving costs should be capitalized in their place, this involves more bookkeeping than seems worthwhile. Or, one might say that treating the moving costs as an expense is for all practical purposes a recognition of the loss of the initial installation cost that has suddenly taken place.

Demolition Costs

It often happens, particularly in cities, that a site is purchased containing old buildings currently in use which will be demolished in order to clear the land for the construction of a new building. Here, the seller, who is using the old buildings, presumably would expect to be compensated for them as well as for the land on which they stand.

The buyer, however, who has no use for the old buildings, has to consider that whatever he pays for the property as a whole is the price he is paying for the land. Moreover, the cost of demolishing the old buildings and leveling the land thereafter are also costs of the land to him.

If the owner of the property described in the previous paragraph instead of selling it decided to have the old buildings demolished, and a new building built himself, the end result could be somewhat different. It could be argued, for example, that the old buildings had become obsolete.

Therefore, if any undepreciated cost remained for them in the accounts, it was because the depreciation rates used had not provided adequately for the factor of obsolescence. Their only current value would lie in the income tax benefit to come from writing them off at the time they were demolished.

At such a time, the after-tax loss would be accounted for as an extraordinary loss charged to the period, instead of being added to the cost of the land for the new use.

Then, again, the circumstances might well be that the old buildings were not completely obsolete and might in fact be far from it. The owner might believe, however, that he could do much better if the land were put to a different use, i.e., if a new building were put on it for some other purpose than that being currently served by the present buildings.

In this case, part of the cost of the decision to put up a new building would be the value of the old buildings destroyed. Thus the owner would be in the same position as an outside buyer in the sense that he would be willing to suffer this loss (or undergo this cost) in order to have the land.

The net result would probably still be somewhat different than that of an outside buyer. In the case of the latter, the purchase price and the cost of demolition would be the cost of the land acquired. In the case of the owner, it would be his original cost of the land, the net after-tax loss from writing off the undepreciated cost of the old buildings, and the demolition costs.

New Buildings

As a general rule, all of the costs involved in connection with the construction of a building up to the point of occupancy are accounted for as its costs. These costs include items such as architect's fees, permits, and the wages of guards as well as items involved in the physical construction of the building.

Assuming that the construction is not on a fixed-price basis, the total cost would also include the costs of errors and delays, since no building was ever built without them. As a matter of fact, a fixed price would have an allowance built into it in expectation of such additional costs.

Repairs and Maintenance

Expenditures for minor repairs and ordinary maintenance which do not prolong the useful life of property beyond that anticipated when it was purchased or constructed should be charged as expenses at the time they take place. Major repairs which do prolong life should be capitalized.

Similarly, attachments or alterations which increase the usefulness of the property or change it in some way, even though not increasing its life, should be capitalized and written off over its estimated remaining useful life.

A difficult problem arises in this area when a substantial part of a property is removed and replaced. The problem is to decide how much of the original cost should be deducted from the asset account and written off against accumulated depreciation.

For example, when steamships were converted from coal burning to oil burning equipment, the problem was to determine how much of the original cost of a ship could be said to have been paid for the coal burning equipment, since the ship had been bought as a whole and not by its parts.

Similarly, because of storms wooden poles for supporting telephone or electrical lines in some parts of the country deteriorate more rapidly in their upper parts than in their lower parts. It is thus less expensive to make one replacement of the tops, rather than to put in whole new poles. The problem is, however, to decide how much of the original cost of a pole and its installation should be removed and charged against accumulated depreciation at the time its top is replaced.

It must be admitted that income taxes have some bearing on whether a given repair or maintenance expenditure is capitalized or expensed. From a tax viewpoint, the general policy is to expense an item if there is any possible justification for doing so.

The tendency to expense rather than to capitalize repair and maintenance expenditures has increased in recent years. For example, many a maintenance man now complains that the accounting department has raised havoc with his ability to meet his budget by expensing items of cost which were formerly capitalized.

Estimating Useful Asset Lives

Property, plant, and equipment except for most land are subject to limited life through physical wear and tear and obsolescence. Physical depreciation can be estimated with some degree of accuracy, but not obsolescence which does not necessarily follow any historical pattern.

Guidelines established by the Internal Revenue Service for income tax purposes are helpful in estimating probable useful lives for various types of property, plant, and equipment and, in my opinion, these are reasonably generous. There can be many an exception, however, and even with the guidelines management has to exercise judgment in deciding on the probable useful lives of individual items, particularly on new types of machinery or equipment.

One of the problems in estimating useful life is the selection of the unit to be depreciated. For example, if a machine has an individual drive, should it be depreciated as a whole? Or should the motor, having a shorter life than the rest of the machine, be depreciated separately?

Similarly, should a building be depreciated as a whole? Or should it be broken down to units such as roof, frame, floors, wiring, plumbing, windows, doors, partitions, and elevators?

Reasonable answers to problems such as these are best arrived at by the exercise of common sense, rather than by rules. In some cases, detailed unit depreciation accounting may be more trouble than it is worth. In others, it may result in period cost computations that are sufficiently more accurate as to be worthwhile.

Elevators in an office building, for example, are costly items subject to relatively rapid obsolescence in addition to physical depreciation. On these grounds, they should be costed and depreciated separately, whereas there would not be as strong a case for the separate treatment of freight elevators in a factory.

Composite Depreciation

Another problem in determining the unit to be depreciated is that of deciding whether the unit should be a single item, e.g., a particular machine, or a group of like items. Depreciation on the latter basis is known as composite, or group account, depreciation.

When an item being depreciated on an individual basis comes to the end of its actual useful life, its cost is removed from the asset account, the accumulated depreciation on it is removed from the accumulated depreciation account, the cash account is increased for any cash received from the sale of the item, and a loss or gain is accounted for on the disposal.

When an item that has been depreciated on a composite basis reaches the end of its useful life, however, its cost is removed from the asset account and charged completely to the accumulated depreciation account except for any cash that is received on disposal.

Composite depreciation charges per period are based on an assumed average useful life. Some individual items in a group will last longer than others. Thus charging them off to the accumulated depreciation account on retirement results in the averaging of experience. Over time, experience may prove the assumed useful life to have been incorrect, in which case the depreciation rate charged on the group is changed to one thought to be more appropriate.

Accounting for depreciation on individual items of machinery and equipment is much more time-consuming and expensive than on a composite or group basis in cases where a computer is not available for the purpose. Since it does deal with the expected and actual lives of individual items, however, it is likely to result in more accurate accounting for depreciation each accounting period.

This may not be a significant point because the accuracy of depreciation accounting is far more dependent on the ability to estimate years of useful life than on the selection of individual item depreciation versus composite or group depreciation.

With the aid of a computer, the cost of accounting for depreciation on an individual item basis should be but little higher than accounting on a composite or group basis. Under these circumstances, the argument for composite or group depreciation narrows down to the benefit, if any, of having depreciation expense for any given period reflect average experience by groups of depreciable property, rather than the experience on individual units.

Accounting for Depreciation

For present purposes, it will be helpful to recall that "depreciation accounting is a system of accounting which aims to distribute the cost or other basic value of tangible capital assets, less salvage (if any), over the estimated useful life of the unit (which may be a group of assets) in a systematic and rational manner. It is a process of allocation, not of valuation."[1]

The last sentence is particularly important in contrast to the rather common belief that depreciation represents a "fall in value," and that accumulated depreciation when subtracted from the figure for property, plant, and equipment in the balance sheet thereby "places a value on" those assets.

Views on Depreciation and Purposes in Accounting for It

There are, in fact, a variety of interesting ideas about depreciation, and reasons for accounting for it, that are not in agreement with accounting practice.

There is the view, for example, that depreciation is simply a tax matter, i.e., the only thing of interest about depreciation is its ability to reduce income taxes. This view emphasizes that depreciation is a fixed cost resulting from past decisions and a matter of no importance in the current management of a business, other than with respect to income taxes. Those who hold this belief obviously have a limited view of a manager's responsibilities.

Another theory of depreciation is that of the recovery or maintenance of productive capacity. One version of this view is that as long as productive capacity is maintained no depreciation has taken place. Therefore, no depreciation expense need be charged until it is evident that funds must be withheld from revenues in order to replace units of property, plant, or equipment that are approaching the end of their useful lives.

Unfortunately, this was a common view among railroads and public utilities for many years and led to gross understatements of costs and overstatements of net income for many companies in these two industries. It was not until around the start of World War II that these

---

[1]*Accounting Terminology Bulletin No. 1* (New York: American Institute of Certified Public Accountants, August 1953), paragraph 56; see also Chapter 10, pp. 192–204, where methods of accounting for depreciation are illustrated and discussed.

companies were forced to change from "retirement accounting" to depreciation accounting, as commonly practiced by other industries.

This change to depreciation accounting was one of the most important changes in accounting practice to have taken place in many years, although its significance was overshadowed by the many accounting problems that arose under wartime conditions.

Even today, the ratio of accumulated depreciation to the total cost of depreciable assets is less for railroads and public utilities than for most industrial companies that have been in operation for twenty-five years or more. In part, to be sure, this is because of the relatively longer lives of public utility plant and equipment, and the rapid growth of public utility companies in recent years, with consequent new heavy investments in fixed assets. But these two factors do not fully account for the difference. Certainly, they have not been factors that would explain the difference for the railroad industry.

Another version of this view of depreciation accounting, as the means of recovering or maintaining productive capacity, accepts the idea of cost allocation over the useful lives of the assets being depreciated, but stresses the purpose as having the funds to replace specific assets when they wear out.

An extension of this view holds that the aim of depreciation accounting should be the maintenance of a company's competitive position by charging enough against revenues so as to have funds with which to purchase better, and presumably more expensive, facilities as present facilities wear out or become obsolete.

Finally, another view of depreciation gaining momentum in discussion, although not in practice, is that the purpose of accounting for depreciation should be to recover the purchasing power of the capital lost through depreciation.

Under conditions of inflation, this means, of course, that amounts recovered through depreciation charges should be greater than the actual cost (historical cost) of the items being depreciated. This used to be discussed sometimes as "depreciation based on replacement cost."

But the replacement cost of a particular item does not necessarily reflect accurately a change in the general purchasing power of money. Moreover, given a choice, companies probably would not care to replace exactly the same units being depreciated. They would buy better or at least somewhat different ones.

Current interest lies, for the most part, not in abandoning depreciation based on the allocation of historical costs. Rather, the interest rests in supplementing the financial statements in which depreciation appears with the same depreciation information restated to reflect changes in the general purchasing power of money.

Allocation of Historical Cost

Regardless of these various views as to what depreciation is, or should be, in actual practice it is an allocation of historical cost over the estimated useful life of the item, or group of like items, being depreciated. Differences in practice among companies lie in the number of years of life estimated for each type of fixed asset; the selection of the method of depreciation, i.e., straight-line or an accelerated method; and depreciating individual items versus groups of like items.

The allocation of historical cost over estimated useful life fits into the concept of a proper matching of costs and revenues by time periods. In manufacturing companies, depreciation of manufacturing facilities is not only accounted for by time periods, but it is also commonly charged to goods produced within each period as an element in the manufacturing overhead charged to them. Here, the aim is to have each product bear its "fair share" of this cost.

Recovery of Capital Invested

Depreciation, whether in terms of wear and tear or obsolescence, may be thought of as a loss of the capital invested in the facility subject to it. Although it does not involve an outlay of cash at the time computed, nonetheless, it is if anything a more important cost than many out-of-pocket costs. Certainly, revenue must be adequate to cover depreciation, as well as all other costs, before a profit can be said to have been realized.

There may be times when a company cannot receive full reimbursement for costs incurred, and thus it has to settle for recovery of its out-of-pocket costs and some contribution toward fixed costs. Nonetheless, this situation cannot continue indefinitely since under it the loss of capital through depreciation is not being fully recovered and the company is thereby slowly and quietly going through liquidation.

Accounting adequately for depreciation, as well as for all other costs, will not by itself ensure that the loss of capital through depreciation will be recovered. But it will ensure that no profit will be reported until such recovery has taken place.

The only way to ensure that the loss of capital through depreciation will be recovered is to see to it that revenue for goods or services sold is at least adequate to cover all costs including depreciation. This is a management responsibility which cannot be shrugged off by holding that depreciation is simply a bookkeeping entry or an income tax shield.

Replacement of Facilities

The purpose of depreciation accounting as currently practiced, as we have noted, is to allocate the historical cost of depreciable assets over their useful lives. Companies should try to see to it that revenues are adequate to cover all costs, including depreciation, and to provide a reasonable profit as well. But this is a management responsibility and not an accounting problem.

Or perhaps it would be more accurate to say that accounting properly for depreciation is a combined management and accounting problem, whereas collecting reimbursement for depreciation from a customer is a management responsibility alone.

Assuming that revenues have been adequate to at least cover all costs, there has then been a recovery of the capital lost through depreciation. It is this recovery of capital that is of primary concern. What shall be done with the funds so recovered is another management problem, although a relatively pleasant one.

As we noted earlier, one view of the purpose of accounting for depreciation is to provide for the replacement of current facilities when they wear out. It is rarely the case, however, that exactly the same facilities are in fact replaced, and sometimes old facilities are demolished or sold and not replaced at all.

If one wishes to think of depreciation charges as providing anything, it is better to think of them as providing a recovery of capital, rather than as providing for the replacement of current facilities when they wear out. It is even better to remember, as I have suggested several times, that whatever funds are recovered from depreciation which has taken place will in fact come from customers and not from bookkeeping entries for depreciation.

Allowance for the purchase of better facilities. There are some people who have held that the purpose of depreciation charges should be to ensure that a company is able to maintain its competitive position by providing funds with which to purchase better, and presumably more expensive, facilities when the present facilities are worn out or become obsolete.

I have tried to stress that whatever reimbursement a company is to get for depreciation (other than a capital loss taken for tax purposes) has to come from customers. This was not meant to imply that a customer should be expected to pay for better facilities than were actually used in making the goods or in providing the service he bought.

For example, if one took a ride in a Chevrolet taxi and was told upon arrival at his destination that he was going to be charged a higher fare because the driver wanted to be able to buy a Cadillac when his present cab wore out, one would certainly demur, to put it mildly.

Pricing can be a highly complicated matter and I have no wish to pretend otherwise. Certainly, there is usually more to it than simply adding up costs for which reimbursement is expected, together with what is considered to be a reasonable profit.

For our present discussion, however, if we visualize pricing in this simple way, it becomes even more obvious that a customer should not be expected to pay for better facilities than were used in making the goods or in providing the service he bought. He should not be expected to pay either a higher amount for cost reimbursement or a higher amount of profit.

If funds are to be reserved from revenues in order to buy better facilities when the present facilities wear out or become obsolete, the source of the extra amount needed will have to be the seller's ordinary profit. In other words, funds derived from ordinary profit will have to be used for this purpose, rather than for the payment of dividends or some other purpose.

If there is no profit with costs computed on an historical basis, there will be no funds available from revenues to buy better facilities, no matter what additional bookkeeping entries are made.

The problem of providing for the purchase of better facilities is a financial one, although accounting can be of assistance. The financial problem is one of seeing to it that the necessary money is on hand when it comes time to purchase the new facilities, and this does not necessarily involve any additional accounting entries. It requires control over cash expenditures and being sure that an adequate amount of retained earnings is in fact retained in the business and not paid out as dividends.

If accounting entries are to be made to assist this process, they are not entries for depreciation. Instead, they are charges against income for the purpose of creating reserves for the purchase of facilities. Reserves of this type appear on the liabilities side of the balance sheet. They are claims to funds and not funds in themselves. They are simply earnings earmarked as reserves and, as such, they are a part of ownership equity.

Once the new facilities have been purchased by funds from the other side of the balance sheet, the reserves are no longer needed. Thus they can be transferred through the income account for the period to retained earnings.

Price-Level Adjustments

For years, many individuals have written about, lectured on, and debated the desirability of adjusting property, plant, and equipment and other accounts to reflect changes in the purchasing power of money, as has been done in other countries where inflation has been more severe. Such adjustments at present neither fall within accepted accounting practice in the United States nor are they allowed for income tax purposes here.

It is the contention of those who favor the use of price-level adjustments that, under conditions of inflation or deflation, financial statements based on historical costs are so far removed from economic reality as to be incorrect and misleading representations of a company's financial condition and result of its operations.

This, they believe, is particularly true of accounts for property, plant, and equipment that for most companies cover items purchased over several years, in varying amounts per year, and at different price levels. These accounts are considered to be incorrect and misleading as reported in the balance sheet on any given date. Likewise depreciation charges based on them, representing amortizations of historical cost, are considered to be incorrect. The result is an improper matching of costs and revenues and, therefore, an incorrect and misleading statement of net income or loss each period.

Furthermore, financial statements based on historical cost are not considered to be comparable from period to period within the same company, even though it has maintained consistency in accounting practice. The same consideration is true in making comparisons with other companies, even though all of them might have maintained uniformity as well as consistency in accounting practice.

One line of argument for price-level adjustments starts with the comment that corporate financial accounting based on historical costs assumes that the monetary unit is stable or, more specifically, that the continued valuation of assets at their historical cost is an assumption that the monetary unit is stable.

The argument then proceeds to demonstrate in one way or another that the monetary unit is not in fact stable. Demonstration of this point appears to be all that is considered necessary to prove that financial statements should be adjusted for price-level changes.

However, neither this approach nor many others specify as to exactly how one is expected to benefit from such adjusted financial statements.

Studies by professional accounting associations.   Over many years, various committees, research staffs, and individual members of professional accounting associations have studied problems of price-level adjustments in financial reporting, and they have presented their findings in articles, pamphlets, and books. The American Accounting Association and the American Institute of Certified Public Accountants have been particularly active in this connection. As might be expected, there has been more general agreement in these studies that something should be done in this area than on what should be done and how it should be accomplished.

A few members of these societies have urged the abandonment of the valuation of assets at historical cost other than at the time of acquisition and the substitution of market value. However, the majority of those interested in bringing about some form of price-level adjustments have neither sought for the present at least the abandonment of financial statements based on historical cost nor the substitution of market values.

Instead, the majority have favored the preparation and presentation by publicly held companies of supplementary financial statements in which the effects of general price-level changes are reflected. The types of supplementary financial statements recommended are historical-cost statements adjusted by the application of a general price index which reflects changes from period to period in the purchasing power of money.

Financial statements of the Indiana Telephone Corporation, taken by permission from the Corporation's Annual Report for 1971, are presented as Exhibit 34, Exhibit 35, Exhibit 36, and Exhibit 37, with accompanying notes. These are examples of financial statements at historical cost restated for changes in the purchasing power of the dollar. Notes 1 and 2 present arguments in support of the restatements as well as explanations of them. Exhibit 37 includes the auditors' opinion on these statements.

Recommendations of the APB.   In the first paragraph of its recommendations on general price-level financial statements, the APB states the following beliefs:

> The Board believes that general price-level financial statements or pertinent information extracted from them present useful information not available from basic historical-dollar financial statements. General price-level information may be presented in addition to the basic historical-dollar financial statements, but

general price-level statements should not be presented as the basic statements. The Board believes that general price-level information is not required at this time for fair presentation of financial position and results of operations in conformity with generally accepted accounting principles in the United States.[2]

In December 1947, the Committee on Accounting Procedure (later superseded by the APB) of the American Institute of Certified Public Accountants issued a research bulletin dealing with the subject of depreciation and high costs.[3] In October 1948, the committee published a letter to the membership reaffirming the opinion expressed in the bulletin. This letter read as follows:

> The Committee on accounting procedure has reached the conclusion that no basic change in the accounting treatment of depreciation of plant and equipment is practicable or desirable under present conditions to meet the problem created by the decline in the purchasing power of the dollar.
>
> The committee has given intensive study to this problem and has examined and discussed various suggestions which have been made to meet it. It has solicited and considered hundreds of opinions on this subject expressed by businessmen, bankers, economists, labor leaders, and others. While there are differences of opinion, the prevailing sentiment in these groups is against any basic change in present accounting procedures. The committee believes that such a change would confuse readers of financial statements and nullify many of the gains that have been made toward clearer presentation of corporate finances.
>
> Should inflation proceed so far that original dollar costs lose their practical significance, it might become necessary to restate all assets in terms of the depreciated currency, as has been done in some countries. But it does not seem to the committee that such action should be recommended now if financial statements are to have maximum usefulness to the greatest number of users.
>
> The committee, therefore, reaffirms the opinion it expressed in Accounting Research Bulletin No. 33, December 1947.
>
> Any basic change in the accounting treatment of depreciation should await further study of the nature and concept of business income.

---

[2]APB Statement No. 3, *Financial Statements Restated for General Price-Level Changes*, paragraph 25. Note: Statements are not the same as opinions by the board. They are issued for information and assistance to those interested in the given subject but practice relative to recommendations in them is not mandatory.

[3]Accounting Research Bulletin, No. 33.

EXHIBIT 34

Indiana Telephone's Statement of Assets, December 31, 1971

	Column A Historical Cost	Column B Historical Cost Restated for Changes in Purchasing Power of Dollar
Telephone plant, at original cost (Note 1):		
In service	$32,681,923	$41,791,787
Less—accumulated depreciation	10,598,883	14,354,244
	22,083,040	27,437,543
Plant under construction	1,568,243	1,580,428
	23,651,283	29,017,971
Working capital:		
Current assets—		
Cash	679,475	679,475
Temporary cash investments accumulated for construction—at cost, which approximates market	3,074,351	3,074,351
Accounts receivable, less reserve	1,220,555	1,220,555
Materials and supplies	531,855	536,583
Prepayments	71,059	71,611
	5,577,295	5,582,575
Current liabilities—		
Sinking fund obligations (Note 4)	162,000	162,000
Accounts payable	635,552	635,552
Advance billings	315,647	315,647
Dividends payable	23,886	23,886
Federal income taxes (Note 2)	242,393	242,393
Other accrued taxes	600,190	600,190
Other current liabilities	713,455	713,455
	2,693,123	2,693,123
Net working capital	2,884,172	2,889,452
Other:		
Debt expense being amortized	201,810	260,266
Other deferred charges	49,616	57,566
Deferred Federal income taxes (Note 2)	(1,273,254)	(1,390,176)
Unamortized investment tax credit being amortized over the useful lives of related property	(391,778)	(472,321)
	(1,413,606)	(1,544,665)
Total investment in telephone business	$25,121,849	$30,362,758

The accompanying notes are an integral part of this statement.

EXHIBIT 35
Indiana Telephone's Statement of Capital, December 31, 1971

	Column A Historical Cost		Column B Historical Cost Restated for Changes in Purchasing Power of Dollar	
	Amount	Ratio	Amount	Ratio
First mortgage sinking fund bonds:				
Series 1, 3% due June 1, 1977	$ 770,000		$ 770,000	
Series 2, 3 3/8% due June 1, 1977	390,000		390,000	
Series 3, 3 7/8% due June 1, 1977	410,000		410,000	
Series 4, 3 3/4% due June 1, 1984	935,000		935,000	
Series 5, 4 1/4% due September 1, 1986	870,000		870,000	
Series 6, 5 3/8% due September 1, 1991	1,840,000		1,840,000	
Series 7, 4 3/4% due May 1, 1994	1,995,000		1,995,000	
Series 8, 4 3/4% due July 1, 2005	2,910,000		2,910,000	
Series 9, 6 1/2% due October 1, 2007	2,940,000		2,940,000	
Less—Current sinking funds (Note 4)	(142,000)		(142,000)	
Total first mortgage sinking fund bonds	12,918,000	51%	12,918,000	43%
Preferred stock (no maturity):				
Cumulative, sinking fund, par value $100 per share, 30,000 shares authorized of which 10,000 are unissued:				
1950 Series 4.80%	240,000		240,000	
1951 Series 4.80%	242,900		242,900	
1954 Series 5 1/4%	333,400		333,400	
1956 Series 5%	256,900		256,900	
1967 Series 6 1/8%	686,000		686,000	
Less—Current sinking funds (Note 4)	(20,000)		(20,000)	
Total preferred stock	1,739,200	7%	1,739,200	6%
Common shareholders' interest:				
Common stock, no par value, authorized 500,000 shares, issued 492,086 shares	4,251,785		6,474,592	
Retained earnings (Note 5)	6,295,365		3,500,069	
	10,547,150		9,974,661	
Less—Treasury stock, 4,336 shares, at cost	(5,192)		(7,882)	
Stock discount and expense	(77,309)		(121,103)	
Total common shareholders' interest	10,464,649	42%	9,845,676	32%
Unrealized effects of price level changes (Note 1)	–	–	5,859,882	19%
Total investment in telephone business	$25,121,849	100%	$30,362,758	100%

The accompanying notes are an integral part of this statement.

EXHIBIT 36
Indiana Telephone's Statement of Income

Operating revenues:
  Local service
  Toll service
  Miscellaneous
    Total operating revenues
Operating expenses:
  Depreciation provision (Note 2)
  Maintenance
  Traffic
  Commercial
  General and administrative
  State, local and miscellaneous Federal taxes
  Federal income taxes (Note 2)
    Currently payable
    Deferred until future years
    Deferred investment tax credit (net)
    Total operating expenses
Operating income
Income deductions:
  Interest on funded debt
  Other deductions
  Interest charged to construction (credit)
  Other income (credit)
  Gain from retirement of long-term debt through
    operation of sinking fund (credit)
  Price level gain from retirement of long-term debt
    (credit) (Note 1)
  Gain from retirement of preferred stock through
    operation of sinking fund (credit) (Note 1)
  Price level gain from retirement of preferred
    stock (credit) (Note 1)
  Price level loss from other monetary items
    Total income deductions
Net income (Note 1)
  Preferred stock dividends applicable to the period
Earnings applicable to common stock
Earnings per common share
Book value per share
Stations in service at end of year

The accompanying notes are an integral part of this statement.

EXHIBIT 36 (continued)

Column A Historical Cost		Column B Historical Cost Restated for Changes in Purchasing Power of Dollar	
1971	1970	1971	1970
$ 5,744,356	$5,384,154	$ 5,788,990	$ 5,695,270
4,852,156	4,350,496	4,889,858	4,601,883
304,522	234,979	306,888	248,557
10,901,034	9,969,629	10,985,736	10,545,710
1,943,551	1,541,560	2,497,078	2,026,211
1,486,495	1,427,487	1,505,457	1,523,311
1,226,906	1,157,565	1,237,139	1,224,453
511,661	449,104	515,637	475,054
1,055,318	1,170,198	1,068,682	1,278,407
912,601	648,996	919,692	686,497
1,132,500	1,127,087	1,141,300	1,192,215
315,800	295,000	318,254	312,047
9,708	(14,997)	3,262	(21,018)
8,594,540	7,802,000	9,206,501	8,697,177
2,306,494	2,167,629	1,779,235	1,848,533
651,195	659,567	656,255	697,679
36,828	21,355	40,229	24,583
(63,905)	(30,442)	(64,402)	(32,201)
(95,974)	(98,759)	(96,720)	(104,466)
(15,192)	(15,865)	(15,310)	(16,781)
—	—	(61,137)	(55,175)
(5,055)	(5,515)	(5,094)	(5,834)
—	—	(12,908)	(12,029)
—	—	87,508	118,125
507,897	530,341	528,421	613,901
1,798,597	1,637,288	1,250,814	1,234,632
96,209	97,541	96,957	103,178
$ 1,702,388	$1,539,747	$ 1,153,857	$ 1,131,454
$ 3.49	$ 3.16	$ 2.37	$ 2.32
$ 21.45	$ 18.29	$ 20.19	$ 18.14
75,015	72,569	75,015	72,569

EXHIBIT 37
Indiana Telephone's Statement of Retained Earnings for the Year 1971

	Column A Historical Cost	Column B Historical Cost Restated for Changes in Purchasing Power of Dollar
Balance, December 31, 1970	$4,751,675	$2,506,142
Net income	1,798,597	1,250,814
	6,550,272	3,756,956
Deduct:		
Cash dividends declared—		
Common stock, annual rate—$.50 per share	182,906	184,327
Preferred stock	72,001	72,560
	254,907	256,887
Balance, December 31, 1971 (Note 5)	$6,295,365	$3,500,069

The accompanying notes are an integral part of this statement.

AUDITORS' REPORT

To the Shareholders of Indiana Telephone Corporation:

We have examined the statements of assets and capital of Indiana Telephone Corporation (an Indiana corporation) as of December 31, 1971, and the related statements of income, retained earnings, and changes in financial position for the year then ended. Our examination was made in accordance with generally accepted auditing standards and accordingly included such tests of the accounting records and such other auditing procedures as we considered necessary in the circumstances. We have previously examined and reported on the financial statements for the preceding year.

In our opinion, the accompanying financial statements shown under Column A present fairly the financial position of the Corporation as of December 31, 1971, and the results of its operations and changes in financial position for the year then ended, in conformity with generally accepted accounting principles applied on a basis consistent with that of the preceding year.

In our opinion, however, the accompanying financial statements shown under Column B more fairly present the financial position of the Corporation as of December 31, 1971, and the results of its operations for the year then ended, as recognition has been given to changes in the purchasing power of the dollar, as explained in Note 1.

Arthur Anderson & Co.

Indianapolis, Indiana,
March 1, 1972.

Notes to Indiana Telephone's Financial Statements (Exhibits 34, 35, 36, 37)

1. Explanation of financial statements

In the accompanying financial statements, costs measured by the dollars disbursed at the time of the expenditure are shown in "Column A—Historical Cost." In "Column B—Historical Cost Restated For Changes in Purchasing Power of Dollar" (where the amounts in A and B differ), these dollars of cost have been restated in terms of the price level at December 31, 1971, as measured by the Gross National Product Implicit Price Deflator. Since 1954, the Corporation has presented supplemental financial information recognizing the effect of the change in the purchasing power of the dollar relating to telephone plant and depreciation expense in the annual report to shareholders.

In computing the amounts set forth in Column B of the accompanying financial statements, the Corporation has followed the methods set forth in Statement No. 3 released in June, 1969, by the Accounting Principles Board of the American Institute of Certified Public Accountants, except that, contrary to Statement No. 3, the effects of price level changes on long-term debt and preferred stock have been reflected as income in the year in which the debt and preferred stock are retired (as required by the specific instruments under which they were issued) and not refinanced. The Accounting Principles Board has tentatively taken the position that all such amounts should be taken into income in the year of price level change. In the opinion of the Corporation's management and of its independent public accountants, such tentative viewpoint of the Accounting Principles Board does not result in a proper determination of income for the period. "Unrealized Effects of Price Level Changes" recognizes the excess of adjustments on the Statement of Assets over the adjustments of Common Stock and Retained Earnings.

Dollars are a means of expressing purchasing power at the time of their use. Conversion or restatement of dollars of differing purchasing power to the purchasing power of the dollar at the date of conversion results in all the dollars being treated as mathematical likes for the purpose of significant data. The resulting financial statements recognize the change in price levels between the periods of expenditure of funds and the periods of use of property. Accordingly, the earnings, results of operations, assets and other data available for use by management and other readers of financial statements provide important information and comparisons not otherwise available.

No one would attempt to add, subtract, multiply, or divide marks, dollars and pounds. The failure to change the title of the monetary unit may be partially responsible for this violation of mathematical principle. This conceals the fact that mathematical unlikes are being used and therefore unfortunate results have been produced by generally accepted accounting methods.

2. Recovery of capital and return on capital

Under the law of Indiana, the Corporation is entitled to recover the fair value of its property used and useful in public service by accruing depreciation based on the "fair value" thereof and is entitled to earn a fair return on such "fair value." The amount shown in Column B for telephone plant approximates the fair value of the property as determined based on the principles followed by the Public Service Commission of Indiana in an order dated September 1, 1967, authorizing the Corporation to increase its subscriber rates.

In the accompanying financial statements, Column A includes depreciation expense based on historical cost and Column B includes depreciation expense, as well as other expenses, on the basis of historical cost repriced in current dollars to reflect the changes in the purchasing power of the dollar, Also, the annual reports to the Indiana Commission are in the same basic form shown herein.

EXHIBIT 37 (continued)

It must be kept in mind that this determination of depreciation expense is a year-to-year estimate and there are involved the questions of obsolescence, foresight, and judgment giving due consideration to maintenance but the regulatory process does not adjust even to this accurately.

If use of property, obsolescence and current denominators (in the case of monetary inflation) are used accurately by way of keeping the allowable expense of depreciation current and rates sufficient to return it along with a fair return, and the proceeds are immediately invested in property used and useful in the public service, there more likely will be a real return of capital and a fair return thereon. However, if monetary inflation continues, as it usually does, purchasing power of capital is unlikely ever to be truly returned. It must be observed there is a substantial lag in the regulatory process. In rate making there is no guarantee of recovery of capital or of an adequate rate of return to the Corporation. This is an added risk which should be considered in estimating a fair return.

Since the present Internal Revenue Code does not recognize the costs measured in current dollars, they are not deductible for computing Federal income tax payments, and the Corporation in fact pays taxes on alleged earnings which do not exist in true purchasing power. If they were deductible, as they should be, reductions in Federal income taxes as shown in Column B of $266,000 in 1971 and $252,000 in 1970 would result. By requiring the use of the Uniform System of Accounts for utility accounting and by virtue of the Internal Revenue Code, the Government has condemned and confiscated during the last 7 years over $1 million (in terms of the dollars of the years in which they were paid) of the assets of this Corporation through taxation of overstated earnings. This is true to a greater or lesser extent in each case where we have been able to ascertain the facts. We do not understand why this is currently concealed by management and accountants —to their detriment.

For book and financial reporting purposes, the Corporation provides for depreciation on a straight-line basis over the average service lives of the various classes of depreciable plant. In 1971, the overall rate was 6.3%. For Federal income tax purposes, beginning in 1967, an accelerated depreciation method is used and a provision is made in the Statement of Income for the taxes deferred as a result thereof.

3. Credit agreement

The Corporation has entered into a credit agreement which provides for the Corporation to issue unsecured notes not to exceed $3,000,000, bearing interest at 1/2 of 1% above the lowest prime rate charged by The Indiana National Bank or by Continental Illinois National Bank and Trust Company of Chicago, but not less than 6% or more than 7 1/2%. Such notes may be issued at any time until April 30, 1973, and will be payable in installments to December 31, 1977.

4. Sinking funds

The aggregate annual sinking fund requirement on First Mortgage Sinking Fund Bonds is $142,000 (of which $41,000 relates to Series 1 through 5, proposed to be refinanced as discussed in Note 5). At respective maturity dates, after all required sinking fund payments, including repayments of an assumed borrowing under the bank credit agreement, the remaining balance to be paid will be as follows:

Series	Maturity Date	Balance to be Paid
Bank Note (Note)	12/31/73	$ 150,000
Bank Note (Note)	12/31/74	240,000
Bank Note (Note)	12/31/75	450,000
Bank Note (Note)	12/31/76	750,000
1, 2, & 3	6/1/77	1,470,000
Bank Note (Note)	12/31/77	1,410,000
4	6/1/84	803,000
5	9/1/86	730,000
6	9/1/91	1,460,000
7	5/1/94	1,533,000
8	7/1/2005	1,950,000
9	10/2/2007	1,890,000

EXHIBIT 37 (continued)

Note: Assumes $3 million is borrowed from bank.

To the annual sinking funds aggregating $142,000 on bonds should be added the annual sinking fund requirement on preferred stock of $20,000. For the year 1972 and thereafter, the total annual sinking fund requirement, exclusive of repayments under the credit agreement (Note 3), on both preferred stock and bonds is $162,000.

5. Proposed financing

The Corporation has agreed, subject to the approval of the Public Service Commission of Indiana, to issue $4,875,000 principal amount of First Mortgage Sinking Fund Bonds, Series 10, 7 3/4% due 2008. The bonds are to require sinking fund payments of $48,750 annually, starting in 1975.

The agreement provides that $3,375,000 will be used to refinance the outstanding balance of First Mortgage Sinking Fund Bonds, Series 1, 2, 3, 4 and 5. The remaining $1,500,000 is to be used for proper corporate purposes. Thus, the total amount of bonds outstanding will increase $1,500,000 with no maturities until 1991. The agreement also provides that cash dividends on common stock and purchases of common stock are limited to earnings after December 31, 1971, plus $600,000. Under the agreement the transaction is to be completed on or before May 23, 1972.

6. Retirement plan

The Corporation maintains a noncontributory money purchase retirement plan which covers all employees who meet the eligibility requirements based primarily on length of service. The cost under the plan, which is fully funded each year, was $87,000 and $99,000 for the years ended December 31, 1971 and 1970, respectively.

7. Construction commitments

Construction expenditures for the year 1972 are estimated at $6,973,000. Substantial commitments have been made in connection therewith.

The immediate problem can and should be met by financial management. The committee recognizes that the common forms of financial statements may permit misunderstanding as to the amount which a corporation has available for distribution in the form of dividends, higher wages, or lower prices for the company's products. When prices have risen appreciably since original investments in plant and facilities were made, a substantial proportion of net income as currently reported must be reinvested in the business in order to maintain assets at the same level of productivity at the end of a year as at the beginning.

Stockholders, employees, and the general public should be informed that a business must be able to retain out of profits amounts sufficient to replace productive facilities at current prices if it is to stay in business. The committee therefore gives its full support to the use of supplementary financial schedules, explanations or footnotes by which management may explain the need for retention of earnings.

Six years later, this letter, along with Bulletin No. 33, was reprinted in Accounting Research Bulletin No. 43, *Restatement and Revision of Accounting Research Bulletins.*[4] The views expressed earlier were thereby reaffirmed in writing at this time.

Again, in APB Opinion No. 6, *Status of Accounting Research Bulletins,* there being no suggestion by the board for revision of Bulletin No. 43, it was assumed by the opinion that this section continued to be "in full force and effect without change."[5]

Thus the official view of the Accounting Principles Board still supports the valuation of property, plant, and equipment on an historical cost basis, with depreciation based on the allocation of such costs over the estimated useful lives of the items subject to depreciation.

Company response to suggestions for restating financial statements. Despite all of the studies, writings, and discussions that have taken place on the need to recognize price-level changes in financial reporting, and in spite of continued inflation, the response by companies as of the present writing has been practically nil.

For example, the financial statements of the Indiana Telephone Corporation shown earlier, which reflected changes in the purchasing power of the dollar, were the only such statements I was able to find in a study of the annual reports of 385 leading United States corporations.

---

[4]Chapter 9, Section A, "Depreciation and High Costs" (ARB No. 43, June 1953).
[5]APB Opinion No. 6, October 1965.

The typical annual report contains a few comments on the economic situation. It stresses primarily, as far as inflation is concerned, rising costs, the inability to increase selling prices rapidly enough to offset rising costs, and the resulting profit squeeze. Mention is also made of the need to retain earnings not only for purposes of expansion but also for the replacement at inevitably higher costs of existing facilities as they wear out or become obsolete.

These comments are of some help in interpreting the financial results of operations for the given period and in explaining the company's dividend policy. But they fall far short of meeting suggestions for the presentation of supplementary financial statements restated for general price-level changes.

Some enthusiasts for price-level adjustments believe that this lack of management response must be met by increased educational efforts. Their argument is that if executives really understood the economic effects of price-level changes they could not help but see the need for such accounting adjustments and the benefits to be derived from them. Therefore, executives should be willing to support such steps in their own companies; certainly, on a supplementary basis at least.

Surely, after all of the writing and discussion in this area over the past fifty years, and intensified in recent years, the top managers of companies of any size in this country are well aware of what is involved. They do not need more education in the sense of awareness and understanding.

If the presidents or directors of such companies have not read extensively in this area, their financial executives and public accountants would have done so. And the latter would have raised questions and expressed their opinions as to what action, if any, should be taken with respect to it.

It may well be that greater exhortation is needed to get managements to present financial statements restated for price-level changes, even on a purely supplementary basis. If enough of our leading companies led the way, many other company managements might be stimulated to do so.

But education alone, in the sense of becoming informed about the shortcomings of historical-dollar statements, quite evidently is not enough to get management action in this direction.

Or perhaps, it has in fact been education gained by experience, as well as by reading and discussion, that has led the managements of our leading companies to conclude up to now that the preparation and presentation of such information either would not be worth the effort or would not be to their companies' best interests.

In presenting financial statements to their stockholders on an historical-cost basis, they surely are not themselves assuming that the monetary unit is stable. Nor is it fair to hold that despite this knowledge they are pretending the monetary unit is stable in their financial reporting. The fact of the matter is that they are simply assuming, or concluding, that the use of historical cost in financial reporting is preferable to the use of some alternative basis of valuation.

Arguments in support of the use of historical cost.   The traditional arguments for the use of historical cost in the valuation of fixed assets note that such assets are purchased for use and not for resale. Since it is not the intention to dispose of them in the near future, there is no particular point in showing them in such a statement at other than their remaining unamortized investment cost, i.e., at acquisition cost less depreciation taken.

Moreover, the historical cost of property, plant, and equipment, as well as of other assets, represents fact supportable by documentary evidence and verifiable by audit. It provides for a proper accounting by management of the stewardship of funds for which it is held responsible. The balance sheet, with assets stated at historical cost, shows to a penny where the company's funds are then located and where they came from.

Other arguments are commonly advanced against the abandonment of historical-cost statements, and to a lesser extent against the presentation of supplementary statements adjusted for general price-level changes. These arguments — ten of them in all — are as follows:

1. Inflation to date in the United States has not been so severe as to require either the abandonment of historical-cost statements or to justify the time and effort to prepare supplementary statements adjusted for price-level changes.
2. There are no income tax benefits to be gained from such a change in practice, since financial statements adjusted for price-level changes are not permitted for income tax purposes.
3. The Accounting Principles Board "believes that general price-level information is not required at this time for fair presentation of financial position and results of operations in conformity with generally accepted accounting principles in the United States."[6]

---

[6]APB Statement No. 3, *Financial Statements Restated for General Price-Level Changes* (June 1969), paragraph 25.

4. The Securities and Exchange Commission has not required, supported, or urged the preparation of financial statements adjusted for price-level changes, even on a supplementary basis.
5. Because of rapid technological changes since World War II, which quickened obsolescence of machinery and equipment, and because of the high rate of expansion of manufacturing capacity since that time, a high proportion of the fixed assets of most manufacturing companies are reasonably modern. Therefore, these fixed assets are being stated at figures which come close enough to current dollars of purchasing power for all practical purposes.
6. The use of conservative estimates of the economic life of depreciable assets; accelerated depreciation; investment tax credits; and LIFO have cushioned the effect of price-level changes as far as income taxes are concerned. And these conservative estimates have offset, to a considerable degree at least, inflationary profit in income reported to stockholders.
7. Much of the potential effect of price-level changes has been offset by financing the purchase of property, plant, and equipment through long-term debt at fixed interest rates.
8. Experience of the 1920s in writing up properties was believed by many to have contributed psychologically to an acceleration of inflation. Thus any form of upward price-level adjustments of properties should be avoided. Moreover, there are still men in top management positions who remember the bitterness of having to write down properties in the 1930s after having written them up in the 1920s.
9. Although it is often stated that management, stockholders, and others will benefit from financial statements adjusted for price-level changes, the supposed benefits are never specified.
10. Financial statements adjusted for price-level changes, whether presented alone or as supplementary information:
   a. Would involve tedious and expensive clerical and supervisory effort, the benefits of which would be questionable.
   b. Would not be understood by most readers of financial statements.
   c. Would inevitably show higher depreciation costs, and resulting lower profits, for manufacturing businesses under inflation conditions. Therefore, these adjustments could not be presented by a company acting alone without running the risk of being regarded unfavorably by its stockholders, its creditors, and the financial community in general, relative to its competitors and other companies not supplying similar information.

    d. Would tend to cater to those who had a short-run or specu-
lative interest in a company which might not be to the
best interests of the long-run stockholder, or to the long-
run best interest of the company.

The arguments just listed have been gathered from various sources
and do not therefore represent a logical or cohesive whole. Moreover,
they are largely arguments for the continued use of historical-cost (described also as historical-dollar) statements as the basis for financial
reporting and not against the presentation of general price-level financial statements as supplementary information.

I share the belief that until inflation becomes more pronounced
than it is at the present time in the United States, historical-dollar
financial statements should continue to be presented as the basic
statements of financial position and results of operations. Since the
rate of inflation is accelerating, however, I would urge that companies
now start furnishing their stockholders with supplementary historical
cost statements restated for changes in general purchasing power. Such
statements should be prepared along the lines recommended by the
APB in its Statement No. 3, *Financial Statements Restated for General Price-Level Changes,* to which reference has been made.

These statements would become more and more significant in
measuring performance as inflation increased. For internal management purposes they would raise points to be considered in decisions
involving such matters as pricing, dividends, salaries and wages,
bonuses, and the expansion or contraction of operations.

For reporting purposes, when compared side by side with
historical-cost statements, they should provide stockholders and
others, including government, with a better understanding of the impact of inflation on the given company's affairs. They would therefore
be important vehicles for management communication on this matter
as well as statements of importance to the recipients relative to investment decisions and other economic considerations.

Under conditions of marked inflation it could be highly beneficial
to companies having heavy investments in property, plant, and
equipment if such general price-level financial statements were to be
allowed in reporting for income-tax and rate-making purposes. Gov-
ernments in other countries have made similar concessions under conditions of heavy inflation.

However, for so long as companies in our country do not consider
that the effects of inflation on operating results are serious enough to
furnish their own stockholders with such information on a purely

supplementary basis, it is difficult to see what arguments they might reasonably use to move government to make such concessions here.

Nature of financial statements restated for general price-level changes. It should be understood that the supplementary statements recommended by the APB are historical-cost statements adjusted by the application of a general price index to reflect the general purchasing power of the dollar at the latest balance sheet date. The index recommended by the APB as being the most comprehensive indicator of the general price level in the United States is the Gross National Product Implicit Price Deflator (GNP Deflator).[7]

In adjusting amounts of property, plant, and equipment for presentation in general price-level financial statements, items are first listed at their historical cost by year of acquisition. The price index is then used to convert these costs into the current amount of money it would take to represent the same amount of purchasing power as the costs represented in their years of acquisition.

Under conditions of inflation, the total of the adjusted figures would, of course, be greater than the total historical cost of the items being adjusted.

Similarly, the current amount of accumulated depreciation based on historical cost is broken down by the years that the assets to which it is related were acquired. The price index is then used to adjust these figures to reflect the amount of depreciation taken to date, expressed in terms of the current purchasing power of money.

Under conditions of inflation, the total of the adjusted figures for accumulated depreciation would of course be greater than the total of the accumulated depreciation based on historical cost.

When the accumulated depreciation expressed in terms of the current purchasing power of money is subtracted from the adjusted cost of property, plant, and equipment, the result — as far as depreciable assets are concerned — represents the remaining cost to be depreciated over the remaining life of these assets but expressed in terms of the current purchasing power of money. Thus the net adjusted figure is simply historical cost, net of depreciation taken, adjusted for general price-level changes. It does not represent replacement cost, appraisal value, market value, or any other type of cost or value.

Just as property, plant, and equipment, and accumulated depreciation are adjusted by the use of a price index in connection with the

---

[7]Issued quarterly by the Office of Business Economics, U.S. Department of Commerce.

preparation of a balance sheet adjusted for general price-level changes, so too depreciation expense is adjusted to terms of current purchasing power by the use of the same price index in connection with the preparation of an income statement adjusted for general price-level changes.

For this purpose, the depreciation for the period covered by the income statement, based on historical cost, is broken down by year of acquisition of the assets to which it applies. These amounts are then adjusted by the use of the price index to their equivalents in terms of the purchasing power of money at the close of the period under consideration.

It can be realized that during times of inflation the adjusted figure for depreciation would be larger than depreciation based on historical cost, and the computed operating profit for the period would be correspondingly less.

The revealing of this higher computed cost of depreciation and subsequent lower operating profit under conditions of inflation is a major reason, if not the major reason, for the preparation of financial statements restated for general price-level changes.

Adjustments for items other than fixed assets and depreciation. The supplementary financial statements recommended by the Accounting Principles Board in Statement No. 3 are complete balance sheets and income statements. Thus they go well beyond the concerns of ARB No. 33, ARB No. 43, and APB Opinion No. 6. All of these, with respect to price-level changes, were restricted to the problem as to a. whether any basic change should be recommended in the accounting treatment of depreciation of plant and equipment in view of the decline in the purchasing power of the dollar; and b. the desirability of having management, in one way or another, explain to stockholders, employees, and general public: "... that a business must be able to retain out of profits amounts sufficient to replace productive facilities at current prices if it is to stay in business."

Since our concern in the present chapter is that of accounting for property, plant, and equipment, we shall not attempt at this point to examine the treatment of other items in the supplementary financial statements restated for general price-level changes recommended by the Accounting Principles Board.

Dollars of current purchasing power related to replacement costs. It should be made clear that even if depreciation were to be accounted for in terms of historical cost adjusted to the current purchasing power of money this would be no guarantee that enough money would be on hand to replace any given asset when it wore out, at the replacement cost then in effect.

As we have noted earlier, merely making a higher bookkeeping charge for depreciation does not necessarily mean that it is going to be possible to recover the extra amount from customers. Also, even if funds are recovered on a given item, they may not be available when the time comes to replace it because of having been expended on something else.

The major point, however, is that if costs are rising each year, the amount collected in total — even if depreciation is recomputed each year for the drop in the purchasing power of money and is actually recovered from customers — will not be adequate to replace assets at costs in effect at the time replacement is required.

In order to have the necessary funds in total, the amounts recovered via the adjusted depreciation each year would have to be invested in something, such as common stock, which would rise in dollar valuation with inflation. Such funds could be invested in property, plant, and equipment in order to maintain their purchasing power under inflation. But, if so, the funds would not be readily available for the replacement of the specific assets for which they were recovered.

While these are important considerations, they are problems of financial management and not problems in accounting properly for property, plant, and equipment.

Market Valuation of Property, Plant, and Equipment

Some people believe that financial statements should not simply be restated for general price-level changes but also to reflect current market values. Of these, some would abandon historical-dollar financial statements completely and substitute statements adjusted for estimated current values. Others would continue to use historical-dollar statements as the basic statements and have the adjusted statements presented as supplementary information.

The idea of having a statement which tells what a business is currently worth is certainly appealing. Moreover, it can be acknowledged that historical-dollar statements by definition reflect the past, whereas stockholders, creditors, and others interested in a company are largely interested in how a business stands today, and how it is likely to stand tomorrow.

Some people would like to be able to measure and judge performance with respect to how well management is using the resources of the company relative to the current value of these resources rather than to their historical cost.

The problem, of course, is that in the absence of an actual sale it is usually very difficult to determine how much any item is worth. An appraisal calls for the exercise of judgment, estimates based on experience, and conjecture.

When done well, it is expensive because it is time-consuming and calls for the work of experts. When given to well-meaning but incompetent people, it is an impossible task.

And when undertaken by those who are competent but unscrupulous, or under heavy pressure to show an upward trend in earnings per share or to provide other evidence of successful operations, it presents a dangerous opportunity or temptation for manipulation.

The valuation of property, plant, and equipment at current market values is only one part, but a most important one, of the question of the desirability of valuing all resources at their current market values. An easy way to dismiss the problem is to note that the valuation of these assets at a market figure above their historical cost is not a generally accepted accounting principle.

Proof on this point is to be found in the following sentence from Accounting Principles Board Opinion No. 6:

> The Board is of the opinion that property, plant, and equipment should not be written up by an entity to reflect appraisal, market or current values which are above cost to the entity.[8]

This applies to financial statements as currently prepared. It does not rule out the desirability of stating the appraisal, market, or current value of property, plant, and equipment as supplementary information. Nor does it, of course, rule out the possibility that current practice should be changed.

Where significant land values are involved, it should be possible to get from experts appraisal figures that are reasonably reliable and that might be useful information.

For other properties, such as machinery, there are very real problems in determining meaningful figures for current value. The estimated replacement cost of such items is a useful figure for insurance purposes but a dubious figure of current value for a going concern, particularly where, if given the choice, the company would not replace the items it now has. What the items might fetch if sold is anyone's

---

[8]APB Opinion No. 6, *Status of Accounting Research Bulletins,* paragraph 17.

guess and not particularly meaningful if the company has no intention of selling them.

Current value in terms of earning power can be computed for the company as a whole by multiplying current yearly earnings by a figure such as 10, on the theory that the business should be able to earn 10% per year. But this is arbitrary, and anyway it can be computed easily by a stockholder using whatever number he pleases. To determine the current value of individual items of property, plant, and equipment in terms of earning power is at best difficult if not impossible.

Except for land values, it seems to me that the possibilities of being able to get meaningful and reliable figures of market value, or current value, of vast numbers of items of property, plant, and equipment are not good. This is not to say that it is impossible to restate historical costs to take into account changes in the purchasing power of money or to compute replacement costs. Nonetheless, neither of these is a true statement of market value or current value of items on hand.

On occasion, individual items of plant and equipment have been written down when it has become apparent that it is not going to be possible to recover in the future the full remaining undepreciated costs. In a sense, this is writing such assets down to a market value lower than cost.

Such a policy is not consistent with the policy of not writing up assets when their market values are above their cost but this practice is defended on the grounds of conservatism. In many other cases, obsolescence sets in at a faster rate than was originally anticipated and so depreciation rates are increased but no immediate write-down is taken.

Replacement Cost Data Prepared for the SEC

Earlier in this chapter it was noted that in an effort to determine the possible usefulness of replacement cost information, and the difficulties and expense in getting it, the SEC has required large companies to furnish an estimate of the replacement cost of property, plant, and equipment in the Form 10-K annual report to the commission.

The SEC has also required estimated replacement cost data on inventories, and calculations of the effect of the estimated replacement costs on cost of goods sold and depreciation expense, as noted in Chapter 18.

The note from the Form 10-K annual report filed by the General Electric Company for the fiscal year ended December 31, 1977 is a good

EXHIBIT 38
General Electric Company and Consolidated Affiliates
Unaudited Notes to Financial Statements

B. Estimated Current Replacement Cost of Certain Assets and Certain Costs and Expenses (Unaudited)

In accordance with regulations issued by the Securities and Exchange Commission (SEC), the Company has (1) estimated replacement cost, as of December 31, 1977 and 1976, of property, plant and equipment and inventories and (2) calculated the effect of the estimated replacement costs on 1977 and 1976 cost of goods sold and depreciation expense.

The SEC has noted that the information required must be estimated on the basis of numerous assumptions and untested techniques which may not have been developed fully. Recognizing the experimental character of this requirement, the SEC has cautioned against simplistic use of the data presented, especially the conversion of the estimated replacement cost of sales and depreciation expense to a net income basis.

Amounts tabulated below represent Company management's efforts to comply with the SEC requirements.

	1977		1976(a)	
	SEC Replacement Cost Data	Historical Cost	SEC Replacement Cost Data	Historical Cost
	(Amounts in millions)			
At December 31				
Inventories	$ 4,000	$ 2,604.3	$ 3,540	$ 2,265.4
Property, plant and equipment	$15,500	$ 7,294.7	$12,550	$ 5,761.0
Less accumulated depreciation	(9,200)	(3,917.8)	(7,700)	(3,343.5)
	$ 6,300	$ 3,376.9	$ 4,850	$ 2,417.5
For the years ended December 31				
Cost of goods sold	$13,070	$12,744.4	$11,110	$10,851.6
Depreciation expense				
In cost of goods sold	$ 710	$ 456.7	$ 570	$ 365.4
In selling, general and administrative expenses	100	65.4	80	53.3
	$ 810	$ 522.1	$ 650	$ 418.7

(a) Excludes Utah International Inc.

Procedures developed by the Company in determining replacement cost data are described in the following paragraphs.

Inventories—For inventories valued on a LIFO basis (principally in the United States) it was generally assumed that adjustment of acquisition costs by application of LIFO

EXHIBIT 38 (continued)

indices resulted in a reasonable estimate of current replacement costs. For remaining inventories (principally outside the United States) published inflation indices were used, where available, or specific sample indices were developed to estimate current replacement cost by adjustment of acquisition cost data.

Property, plant and equipment—With respect to buildings, several techniques were used to estimate replacement costs. These included use of (1) planning data (adjusted to present productive capacity) in those instances in which plans actually existed for replacement; (2) "reference plants" where an existing design might be usable whenever replacement becomes necessary; (3) insurance appraisal data where the replacement facility would be substantially similar to an existing facility; and (4) engineering estimates of replacements for other facilities which it is probable would not be replaced in kind.

With respect to most machinery and equipment, restatement indices were developed from a sample of the Company's major machinery and equipment accounts and applied to historical costs by year of addition. Planned costs were used where available and specially prepared estimates were utilized where machinery and equipment would not be replaced substantially in kind.

Costs applicable to (1) mining lands, leases, and development costs and (2) oil and gas properties were included in current replacement cost data at historical cost amounts. Estimated replacement cost data for such assets are not required by current SEC regulations.

Accumulated depreciation—Accumulated depreciation as of year end and replacement cost *depreciation expense* for each year were determined using the service lives used for financial accounting purposes. In accordance with the SEC regulation, replacement cost depreciation was calculated using the "straight-line" method rather than the accelerated methods generally used by the Company in its financial statements.

Cost of goods sold—With respect to the inventory-related portion of cost of goods sold, no adjustment was generally deemed necessary for LIFO-valued inventories. Cost of goods sold for non-LIFO valued inventories was adjusted to estimated replacement cost at time of sale. The depreciation portion of cost of goods sold was calculated as discussed above.

Limitations—Despite the inherent imprecisions involved in determining the replacement cost of the Company's productive capacity, it is management's view that the data shown in the preceding tabulation have been reasonably estimated. It should be recognized, however, that actual replacement of property, plant and equipment occurs in the normal course of business over many years, rather than at a specific point in time. Furthermore, no attempt has been made to estimate the theoretical improvements in operating costs, such as increased labor productivity and reduced maintenance expense, which normally are associated with replacing productive equipment. Finally, in the continued evolution of the Company's strategic planning activities, some fixed assets designated as subject to replacement in current estimates might not be replaced at the end of their useful lives.

example of the presentation of this type of information. The SEC and companies reporting this replacement cost information have cautioned against simplistic use of this data, particularly to restate net income. The required information is not precise and does not give a complete or balanced presentation of the impact of inflation.

Accounting for Leases

The practice of leasing property, rather than purchasing it, as a means of spreading out or delaying payment for property purchased, has grown markedly in recent years.

A lease is defined as an agreement conveying the right to use property, plant, or equipment, usually for a stated period of time.

In some cases, the purpose of leasing from the viewpoint of the lessee is to eliminate minor management problems that are a nuisance, such as those connected with the purchase, maintenance, and trade-in of automobiles provided to salesmen who are scattered all over the country.

In other cases, the aim has been to avoid the risks of obsolescence and also to have the benefit of the latest technical developments, as in the leasing of computers.

In still other cases, the reasons for leasing have been largely financial. Here, a given company has either not had the money to purchase the property in question or has believed it to be wiser to use its own money, or money it might borrow from other sources, for other purposes.

In some of these cases, payments under a lease have continued throughout the years the lessee has had the use of the property. In other cases, legal title to the property has eventually passed to the lessee and payments under the lease have really represented the purchase of the property over time, plus interest on the declining balance of the purchase price as payments were made.

Although there are many variations in leases, and in the terms connected with them, they are identified for accounting purposes by the two major types described in the previous paragraph. The first of these types is known as an operating lease, and the second, as a capital lease.

The Financial Accounting Standards Board has published a clear set of rulings in its Statement No. 13, Accounting for Leases (November 1976). The statement contains not only the rulings but also explanations of how they were determined, and the reasoning underlying them, as well as examples of accounting for leases by both lessees and lessors. In view of this availability of information we shall deal here only with the major requirements for lessees in accounting for their leases.

The accounting requirements for operating leases are quite simple. Rental payments are to be charged to expense over the lease term as they become payable. Rental expense is to be reported separately each period for which an income statement is presented.

Disclosure is to be made in the balance sheet, or footnote thereof, of future payments required as of the balance-sheet date, in the aggregate and for each of the five succeeding years.

Accounting for capital leases is more involved. The requirements are summarized briefly in Statement No. 13 as follows: "A lease that transfers substantially all of the benefits and risks of property ownership should be accounted for as the acquisition of an asset and the incurrence of an obligation by the lessee and as a sale or financing by the lessor."

The property involved is recorded and stated in the balance sheet as an asset at the discounted amount of the required future payments on it under the lease agreement. At the time of recording, the amount recorded as an asset is balanced by recording the same amount as a liability for future principal payments for leased facilities.

The method of discounting the future payments is the discounted cash flow method described in Chapter 27 of this book. The discount rate (interest rate) to be used in the computation by the lessee is, essentially, the rate he would have to pay currently for loans. If he can learn the implicit rate computed by the lessor and that proves to be less than his (the lessee's) borrowing rate, then he should use the lower rate.

If it happens that the discounted amount of the required future payments is more than the fair value of the property at the inception of the lease (the amount for which it would be sold rather than leased), the amount to be recorded as the asset and obligation is the fair value.

Except for certain cases requiring modifications, the asset is amortized in a manner consistent with the lessee's normal depreciation policy for owned assets. The amortization can be included with the depreciation expense of other assets but, if so, its amount must be separately disclosed in the financial statements or footnotes thereto.

As each payment on the lease takes place, cash, of course, is credited. The debit side of the recorded transaction is split between a reduction in the liability for future principal payments and interest expense. The accounting is like accounting for the payment on a mortgage, where the same rate of interest is applied consistently to the

EXHIBIT 39
Litton Industries, Inc.

NOTE D: LEASES

Property, plant and equipment includes the following amounts for capital leases as defined by Statement of Financial Accounting Standards No. 13—Accounting for Leases:

	July 31,	
	1977	1976
	(thousands of dollars)	
Property, plant and equipment, at cost:		
Land	$ 1,044	$ 1,026
Buildings	109,615	107,561
Machinery and equipment	43,802	44,226
	154,461	152,813
Less accumulated depreciation	(60,390)	(52,101)
Net property, plant and equipment	$ 94,071	$100,712

Depreciation of these assets was included in depreciation expense.

The significant capital land and plant lease relates to the shipyard facility at Pascagoula, Mississippi which may be acquired by the Company under certain conditions. Other capital leases also contain provisions for acquiring the facilities.

The obligation related to future principal payments under capital leases at July 31, 1977 was $4,355,000 payable in fiscal 1978 and $134,700,000 due thereafter. Comparable amounts at July 31, 1976 were $4,044,000 and $136,927,000, respectively.

As of July 31, 1977, minimum rental commitments under capital and noncancellable operating leases were:

Year Ended July 31,	Capital Leases	Operating Leases
	(thousands of dollars)	
1978	$ 11,308	$ 28,577
1979	11,318	19,681
1980	11,289	13,469
1981	11,291	11,036
1982	11,189	8,570
Thereafter	166,562	21,122
Total minimum lease payments	222,957	$102,455
Amounts representing interest	(83,902)	
Present value of net minimum lease payments	$139,055	

Rental expense from noncancellable operating leases, including amounts for short-term leases with nominal, if any, future rental commitments, was $43,816,000 and $47,289,000 for the years ended July 31, 1977 and 1976, respectively. The minimum future rentals receivable under subleases and the contingent rental expenses were not significant.

declining balance of the obligation. Thus, as time passes, while the lease payments per period remain the same, the amount covering interest is reduced and the amount for payment of principal correspondingly increased.

With respect to disclosure in the balance sheet, or footnotes thereto, the major points are that the gross amount of assets under capital leases, and accumulated depreciation, shall be presented by major classes according to nature or function. On the liabilities side, the obligation as of the balance-sheet date, related to future principal, payments under capital leases, must be shown. Also, future minimum lease payments as of the date of the balance sheet must be presented in the aggregate and for each of the five succeeding fiscal years, with certain deductions, the major item of which is the amount of imputed interest necessary to reduce the net minimum lease payments to present value.

The application of the disclosure requirements in accounting for leasing is illustrated in the note (Exhibit 39) from the annual report of Litton Industries, Inc. and Subsidiary Companies for the fiscal year 1977.

CHAPTER 20

Accounting for Business Combinations

In Chapter 9, we examined the nature of investments in subsidiaries, particularly with reference to accounting for such investments under the equity method versus historical cost. Now, in this chapter, we shall go beyond that type of investment and examine what has become identified as a "business combination."

A business combination results from financial transactions by which an existing corporation and one or more existing incorporated or unincorporated businesses are combined under one accounting entity to carry on essentially the same activities each had previously carried on independently. In an earlier day, these kinds of business combinations were known as mergers, consolidations, or amalgamations.

A business combination is accounted for under one of two methods: as a purchase or as a pooling of interests. We shall examine only the highlights of these methods. Further information on them is to be found in APB Opinion No. 16, *Business Combinations*.[1]

Purchase Method

Use of the purchase method implies that the given business combination has resulted from the acquisition of one company by another through purchasing its assets and assuming its liabilities.

The assets acquired are entered in the records of the acquiring company at their cost to it. Since the amount paid for the company

---

[1] APB Opinion No. 16, *Business Combinations* (New York: American Institute of Certified Public Accountants, August 1970).

acquired is net of the liabilities assumed, the total cost of the assets acquired is the net amount paid for the company plus the amount of the liabilities assumed.

This total cost is bound to be different from the total of the historical costs at which these assets had been carried in the accounts of the company acquired, particularly if they had been held for some time by that company. It is necessary, therefore, to apportion the total cost on some rational basis to each classification of assets acquired.

To do this, the tangible and identifiable intangible assets acquired are entered at their fair value as of the date of the acquisition as determined by appraisal or otherwise.

Where the total cost of the assets is in excess of the fair value entered for the classifications of tangible and identifiable intangible assets acquired, the excess should be entered as an asset classified as "goodwill."

Where the total cost of the assets is less than the fair value calculated for the classifications of tangible and identifiable intangible assets acquired, it is the opinion of the Accounting Principles Board that the fair values ascertained for the noncurrent assets acquired should be scaled down accordingly to avoid having to record "negative goodwill."[2]

Goodwill neither should be written off immediately nor should it be charged against either retained earnings or capital surplus. Instead, it should be amortized on a straight-line basis over a reasonable period not in excess of forty years.[3]

Pooling of Interests

As suggested by its title, a business combination effected by the pooling of interests method implies that there has not only been a combining of the assets and liabilities of two or more existing companies but, more importantly, a combining of the interests (claims) and risks of the existing stockholders of these companies.

Indeed, some who support the use of the pooling of interests method argue that in the types of business combinations where the use of this method is appropriate, it is the stockholder groups involved who determine whether or not to combine their interests and thus bring about the business combination. A combination results when, in effect, these stockholder groups "exchange voting common stock in a

---

[2] *Ibid.*, paragraph 87.
[3] APB Opinion No. 17, *Intangible Assets* (August 1970), paragraphs 27 to 31.

ratio that determines their respective interests in the combined corporation."[4]

Under the pooling of interests method, the assets and liabilities of the combining companies are recorded by the combined corporation at the amounts at which they stand on the date of combination in the accounts of the separate companies. There is, therefore, no necessity to record any appraisal or other measure of current value for the assets thus joined. Nor is there a necessity to account for whatever goodwill may have been involved in the transaction. (A minor point here is that the account may be adjusted to effect uniformity in accounting methods.)

In bringing about the type of business combination which is accounted for under the pooling of interests method, one of the combining companies, known as "the issuing corporation," issues voting common stock in exchange for at least 90% of the then outstanding voting common stock of the other combining company or companies.

The remaining 10% or less, usually held by dissenting shareholders, may be settled by payment of cash, for some other consideration, or left outstanding as a minority interest without preventing accounting for the combination as a pooling of interests.

We have noted that under a pooling of interests the assets and liabilities of the combining companies are recorded by the combined corporation essentially at amounts as they stand in the accounts of the separate companies. To balance these amounts, the stockholders' equities in the separate companies must also be combined.

To accomplish this requires some adjustments. The reason is that the capital stock issued to effect the combination is not, in all probability, to be carried at the same par or stated value as the stock for which it was issued.

Thus, while the total stockholders' equity in the combined corporation will be the same as the total of the equities in the separate companies on the date of the combination, the amounts assigned to capital stock, capital in excess of par or stated value (capital surplus), and retained earnings will differ. More will be said on this point later.

Exchange of Voting Common Stock

The most essential condition for using the pooling of interests method in accounting for a business combination is that the combination shall have been effected by the exchange of voting common stock. Where

---

[4] APB Opinion No. 16, *op. cit.*, paragraph 45.

cash or some consideration other than the exchange of voting common stock is involved, it is obvious that one company has, in fact, acquired another and a purchase rather than a pooling of interests has taken place.

In terms of ownership claims, one group has sold at least part, if not all, of its interests (rights) to another. Therefore, it cannot be said that all of the previous separate interests have been combined.

Other Considerations

In addition to the requirement of an exchange of voting common stock, there are a number of other conditions that must be met if a business combination is to be accounted for as a pooling of interests.

One of these is that each of the combining companies must have been independent of the other combining companies prior to the combination. Where the intercorporate investments are in excess of 10% of the outstanding voting common stock of a combining company, there has, of course, already been a purchase rather than a pooling of interests to this extent.

Moreover, when voting common stock is issued for the remaining outstanding voting common stock of that combining company, there is a shift in proportional ownership and in relative voting rights. This is, therefore, not in conformance with the idea of a pooling of existing stockholder interests.

Another set of conditions has to do with actions after the combination has been effected.

For example, a pooling of interests would be nullified if the combined corporation retired or reacquired voting common stock that had been issued to effect the combination. To be sure, individual stockholders who have received such stock are free to sell their shares to other individuals but this is not the same as selling them to the combined corporation. Selling to other individuals means that outstanding stockholder interests will be maintained, even though the individuals involved will change.

Moreover, since most combinations with which we are concerned require the approval of existing stockholders, it is likely that the great majority of them will hold their stock for some time after the combination has been effected.

Another important condition with respect to action after a pooling of interests has taken place is that there must not be any significant disposal of the assets of the combined corporation within two years after the date of the combination. Duplicate facilities may be eliminated and normal replacements may be made, but a substantial disposal of assets would be contrary to the concept of carrying on in combination activities which had previously been carried on by the separate companies.

Moreover, the argument for bringing assets into the combination at the amounts as they stand in the records of the separate companies is that their use is to be continued. If the intention is to dispose of them, they should be recognized as having been purchased and thus brought into the records of the combined company at their fair market value as of the date of the combination.

A final major condition relative to action after a pooling of interests has been effected is that there shall be no financial arrangements or adjustments with former stockholders after the combination that would defeat the purpose underlying the exchange of equity securities.

Purchase vs. Pooling of Interests

It should be recognized from the foregoing that other conditions, as well as the requirement of an exchange of voting common stock, determine whether a business combination shall be accounted for as a pooling of interests. In fact, if all of the conditions are met, a given business combination must be accounted for as a pooling of interests.[5] Otherwise, it must be accounted for as a purchase.

It has long been a practice to exchange voting common stock in bringing about a business combination. This obviously allows the issuing corporation to bring the companies together without payment of cash or other consideration. Those who have received stock in exchange for stock given up have not been required to report for federal income tax purposes any gain on the exchange. If they sold this stock later, a taxable gain or loss had to be reported.

Where the exchange of stock has been a tax-free exchange, the tax basis of the assets combined remains unchanged by the transfer. Depreciation charges, for example, remain the same.

Thus, in major respects, for tax purposes the exchange is accounted for as a pooling of interests. However, as we have noted previously, except for LIFO there is no requirement that a company's financial accounting and reporting shall conform to its accounting to the government for tax purposes.

---

[5] APB Opinion No. 16, *op. cit.*, paragraph 8.

Example of Business Combination Accounting

To clarify the two different ways of accounting for a business combination, let us assume that two companies, which are to be combined to carry on the operations of both companies as a single accounting entity, show the following condensed financial positions on the date of combination:

	(In $ thousands)	
	Alpha, Inc.	Omega, Inc.
Current assets	$163,086	$ 4,601
Property, plant, and equipment (net)	241,797	3,034
Other assets and deferred charges	14,043	2,589
Total	$418,926	$10,224
Current liabilities	$ 51,086	$ 1,232
Long-term debt	90,582	—
Minority interest	19	—
Stockholders' equity:		
Preferred stock	11,931	—
Common stock:		
Alpha, Inc. ($5 par value)	47,500	—
Omega, Inc. ($5 par value)	—	700
Capital above par value	64,748	19
Retained earnings	153,060	8,273
Total stockholders' equity	$277,239	$ 8,992
Total	$418,926	$10,224

After negotiation, the 140,000 outstanding shares of Omega, Inc., voting common stock are exchanged for 280,000 shares of Alpha, Inc., voting common stock. At the time of the exchange, the market value of Alpha's stock is $40 per share. The total fair market value of Apha's stock in the exchange is therefore $11,200,000.

Combination as a Purchase

Let us first assume that, although the combination has been effected by the exchange of voting common stock, certain other conditions necessary for the combination to be accounted for as a pooling of interests have not been met. Accordingly, we shall account for it as purchase of Omega, Inc., by Alpha, Inc.

To simplify the example, we shall assume that Omega's current assets, other assets, and deferred charges just listed are close enough representations of current market values to be brought into the records of the Alpha company as they stand. Similarly, we shall bring in the same figure for Omega's current liabilities as just shown.

We shall also assume that Omega's items of property, plant, and equipment have been appraised and that their fair market value on the date of the purchase, net of accumulated depreciation, is considered to be $4,442,000.

The tangible and identifiable intangible assets purchased would then be valued for the combination as follows:

Current assets	$ 4,601,000
Property, plant, and equipment (net)	4,442,000
Other assets and deferred charges	2,589,000
	$11,632,000

At the same time, current liabilities would be assumed of $1,232,000, leaving $10,400,000 as the fair market value of net tangible and identifiable intangible assets acquired.

As we noted earlier, however, the fair market value of the Alpha, Inc., stock exchanged to acquire Omega was $11,200,000. The $800,000 difference between this amount and the $10,400,000 for the net tangible and identifiable intangible assets acquired is assumed to be the amount paid for the intangible asset called goodwill.

The journal entry to record the purchase of Omega by Alpha would then be substantially as follows:

Current assets	$4,601,000	
Property, plant, and equipment (net)	4,442,000	
Other assets and deferred charges	2,589,000	
Goodwill	800,000	
Current liabilities		$1,232,000
Common stock:		
Alpha, Inc. ($5 par value)		1,400,000
Capital above par value		9,800,000

Note that the 280,000 shares of common stock issued in the exchange have been entered in the records at $5 par value per share, while the market value above $5 per share for the shares issued has been entered as capital above par value. The total of the two figures, amounting to $11,200,000, is the price paid for the assets listed, net of the current liabilities assumed.

After Alpha's purchase of Omega, the figures for the combined company would be as follows:

	(In $ thousands)
Current assets	$167,687
Property, plant, and equipment (net)	246,239
Other assets and deferred charges	16,632
Goodwill	800
Total	$431,358
Current liabilities	$ 52,318
Long-term debt	90,582
Minority interest	19
Stockholders' equity:	
Preferred stock	11,931
Common stock:	
Alpha, Inc. ($5 par value)	48,900
Capital above par value	74,548
Retained earnings	153,060
Total stockholders' equity	288,439
Total	$431,358

Combination as a Pooling of Interests

Let us now change our assumption so that the combination is to be accounted for as a pooling of interests.

For this purpose, the assets, liabilities, and retained earnings of Omega, Inc., just listed would be brought into the records of Alpha, Inc., as they stand. Adjustments would be made with respect to the accounts for capital stock and capital above par value.

Thus the journal entry to record the combination as a pooling of interests would be substantially as follows:

Current assets	$4,601,000	
Property, plant, and equipment (net)	3,034,000	
Other assets and deferred charges	2,589,000	
Capital above par value	681,000	
Current liabilities		$1,232,000
Common stock:		
Alpha, Inc. ($5 par value)		1,400,000
Retained earnings		8,273,000

After accounting for the combination as a pooling of interests, the figures for the combined company would be as follows:

	(In $ thousands)
Current assets	$167,687
Property, plant, and equipment (net)	244,831
Other assets and deferred charges	16,632
Total	$429,150
Current liabilities	$ 52,318
Long-term debt	90,582
Minority interest	19
Stockholders' equity:	
Preferred stock	11,931
Common stock:	
Alpha, Inc. ($5 par value)	48,900
Capital above par value	64,067
Retained earnings	161,333
Total stockholders' equity	$286,231
Total	$429,150

Major elements.   The figures we have just seen illustrate that under the pooling of interests method of accounting for a business combination assets are brought into the combination as they stand in the accounts of the separate companies on the date they are combined. Therefore, it is not necessary to record them at appraisal value or other measure of their current worth. Nor is it necessary to record any figure for goodwill.

Similarly, the liabilities, preferred stock, and retained earnings of the combining companies are merged as they stand in the accounts on the date the companies are combined.

Finally, the common stock issued in the exchange is recorded at its par value. And the difference between this amount and the par value of the stock for which it was exchanged is charged against the account for capital above par value. In our example, the difference was $700,000.

This amount, less the $19,000 of capital above par value brought over from Omega, called for a debit to "Capital Above Par Value" of $681,000. If this account had not been adequate to absorb this adjustment, it would have been necessary to charge the balance against the "Retained Earnings" account.

The reader will note that under the pooling of interests method the total stockholders' equity in the combined corporation, amounting to $286,231, is the same as the sum of the stockholders' equity in the two companies at the time they were combined ($277,239 + $8,992 = $286,231). The detail with respect to common stock and capital above par value, however, is different.

Since the assets and the liabilities of the two companies as they stand on the date of the combination are combined, it is only natural that the combined stockholders' equity shall equal the total of separate stockholders' equities as they stood on the date of the combination.

Major advantages. Use of the pooling of interests method not only avoids having to determine and defend appraisal or other values placed on assets acquired by the combined corporation, but it also avoids having to account for goodwill. The major benefit from these avoidances is that costs after the combination are lower than they would be if the combination had been accounted for as a purchase. Management is thereby able to report correspondingly higher net income and higher earnings per share.

Under the purchase method, where depreciable assets acquired would normally be written up, as in our present example, the depreciation expense after the combination is higher per period than under the pooling of interests method. Also, the goodwill arising under the purchase treatment must be amortized over a period not in excess of forty years. This increases costs per period and reduces net income and earnings per share accordingly.

Not only are the computed earnings likely to be higher for the combined corporation using the pooling of interests method rather than the purchase method, but also the reported assets are likely to be lower. Thus, on both counts, the computed percentage return on investment will be more favorable.

Neither the "true" cost of operation nor revenues are likely to be affected by the selection of one versus the other of these two methods of accounting for a business combination. Thus the benefits of the higher reported earnings under the pooling of interest method to stockholders who maintain their holdings in the combined corporation are problematical.

With the emphasis that stockholders place on earnings figures, however, these higher reported earnings will at least provide such stockholders with emotional satisfaction. And these higher reported earnings will enhance the reputations of the managers who made the decision to recommend to the stockholders of the combining companies that there be a pooling of interests.

To be sure, if the combined corporation has a generous dividend policy, a stockholder may receive a more immediate benefit from a business combination accounted for as a pooling of interests rather than as a purchase. Dividends paid might be higher both because the reported earnings under the pooling of interests method will be higher and because under that method the retained earnings figure for the company acquired will be brought into the combined company as such and not as capital.

This more immediate benefit of higher dividends to stockholders will not be realized in cases of "growth" companies accounting for business combinations under the pooling of interests method. The reason is that they pay out little, or nothing, in the way of dividends.

The higher earnings reported under the pooling of interests method should of course have a favorable effect on the market value of the given company's common stock. This again, however, usually provides only emotional satisfaction to the stockholder who does not intend to sell his stock. However, he may benefit indirectly if the company is thereby enabled, as part of its expansion policy, to sell additional stock in the open market at a higher price than it otherwise would have received.

Past objectionable practices.   In times past, a number of objectionable practices arose in accounting for business combinations under the pooling of interests method. We shall not dwell upon them since they are now outlawed in terms of accepted accounting practices. I shall mention a few of them, however, as historical examples of unacceptable practices.

One example is that many of the pooled assets did not remain pooled. Instead, they were sold at much higher figures than the low historical costs at which they had been brought into the books of the combined corporation. These "instant" profits were false in that the true cost of the assets sold had not been taken into account in computing them.

Under present rulings, a business combination cannot be accounted for as a pooling of interests if assets brought into the combination are sold within two years after the date of the combination, other than minor sales where there are duplicate facilities or sales made in connection with the normal replacement of facilities. This ruling is certainly reasonable since a given business combination could hardly be called a genuine pooling of interests if substantial assets that had been pooled were sold shortly thereafter.

Another objectionable practice (now outlawed) was where the combination was effected, at least in part, by the exchange of something other than voting common stock, such as debentures, preferred stock, or cash. This was, therefore, not a complete pooling of interests since previous proportional ownerships were not maintained.

In many cases, the result was that, even though the earnings in total might remain the same as the total of the earnings of the combining companies before the combination, the earnings per share of the combined corporation would rise because proportional ownership had not been maintained. In other words, there was not a true pooling of ownership interests.

A similar objectionable practice (also outlawed) took place when a combined corporation in one way or another later retired or reacquired voting common stock that had been issued to effect the combination.

A third example of objectionable practice was where a business combination was effected toward the close of a year or even after the close of the year, but before the annual reports were published. Thus the combined operations were reported as though the separate companies had in fact been combined for that year in full. This practice often took place where the acquiring company wished to improve its reported earnings per share and did so by acquiring a company that had enjoyed a highly profitable year.

The solution for this type of problem has been found in requiring full disclosure of the financial results of the various divisions of a business. This enables the reader of a company's financial statements to see the various sources and amounts contributing to total earnings per share.

While accounting under the pooling of interests method is by no means currently without its problems, and there are many who believe it should not be allowed at all, the major objectionable practices, or what some considered to be "abuses," have been eliminated.

Purchase arguments. In the minds of those who believe that most, if not all, business combinations should be accounted for as purchases, the major argument in favor of such treatment is that it simply records the truth of these events. To them, the concept that the stockholders of the combining companies have agreed among themselves to exchange stock, and thus to pool their interests independently of their companies as separate entities, is a myth. They hold that in practically all cases one company does in fact acquire another. Thus where voting common stock is used to effect the purchase, it is simply the medium of exchange used and does not affect the basic nature of the transaction.

To bring the assets of an acquired company into the records of the combined corporation at figures as they stand in the records of the acquired company fails to record them at their true cost to the combined corporation. This is not only a departure from the well-established accounting principle of recording assets at cost as of the date of their acquisition, but it also fails to record the true amount of the investment made for which the management of the combined corporation should be held accountable.

It is the latter point which is most disturbing to many and leads them to favor accounting for all business combinations as purchases. Some who share this viewpoint believe that an exception could be made in the relatively few cases where each of the combining companies is sufficiently equal in size so that their combining might truly represent a mutual sharing of ownership risks and benefits.

CHAPTER 21

Elements of
Cost Accounting

In the early stages of its development, cost accounting dealt with factory costs for use in inventory valuation, profit determination, and pricing. These are still important aspects of cost accounting but the field has been expanded in areas such as cost control, budgeting, and cost determination for a variety of managerial uses, and the field has also been broadened to include administrative, selling, and distribution costs, and the cost and control problems of nonmanufacturing businesses.

Cost accounting routines necessarily involve accumulating, recording, and reporting costs by type of expense, by area of responsibility, and by products and services. However, managerial interest lies in the use of cost information in planning and controlling the operations of a business and in arriving at decisions in a variety of business problems.

Effective use of information supplied by cost accounting involves both an understanding, on the part of the supplier of information, of the purpose for which the information is to be used and an understanding of the way it can and will be used for this purpose. Effective use also involves an understanding, on the part of the user, of the basis and possible limitations of the information supplied, as well as of the way it can and should be used for a given purpose.

The useful cost accountant, therefore, is not only an "expert accountant," but he is also well versed in the basic operations and operating problems of his company. In turn, executives who use information supplied by cost accounting are able to do so more effectively if they have a basic understanding of this area of accounting. Such understanding should also enable them to discuss their informational needs more effectively with accountants.

In this chapter, we shall be concerned largely with accumulating, classifying, and recording cost data. Our interest in such matters is in keeping with an earlier observation that in order to understand the information which comes out of an accounting system one should understand the information that goes into it.

Although executives are more concerned with the nature of cost information and its use than with the mechanics of its assembly, the ways in which cost data are assembled do affect the nature of the cost information reported. For this reason, they are of managerial importance.

As work progresses within a manufacturing plant and as goods are completed and sold, the costs involved in their production flow from cost categories into inventory classifications, then out again into further cost categories, and so on. What is a cost or expense at one moment becomes an asset in the next, and vice versa. This process is substantially as pictured in Exhibit 40.

EXHIBIT 40
Illustration of the Cost-Flow Process

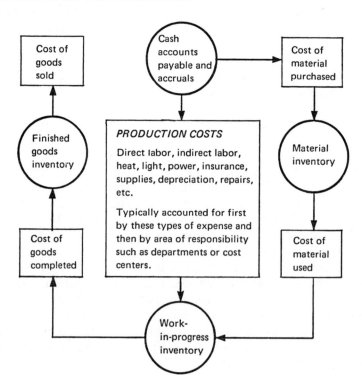

In terms of debit and credit, the reader will recall that an expense or cost account is debited when a cost is incurred. Similarly, inventory accounts are asset accounts and are debited for increases. Thus when a cost moves into inventory, the inventory account is debited and the cost account credited. When an item leaves an inventory account and becomes a cost, the cost account is debited and the inventory account credited.

At the close of an accounting period, those costs which are not impounded in inventories, or treated as prepaid expenses or deferred charges, move on to become the cost of goods sold or other categories of expense in the income statement, as illustrated in Exhibit 41.

Major Cost Classifications

In order to be most useful for the costing of products and services, for cost control, and for a variety of other purposes, costs should be accumulated under three major classifications: by type of expense; by department or cost center; and by job, process, or service.

Account classifications of costs by type of *expense* for the company as a whole and by its major divisions can provide information by time periods on individual operating costs, such as the amount spent for a given period on direct labor or repairs. This type of information is both helpful to executives by enabling them to keep in touch with current activities and useful for control purposes in a broad sense when compared with past costs for a similar time period or with estimated costs of a financial budget.

For budgetary purposes, as well as other forms of cost control, it is further desirable to identify costs by type of expense within specific *departments* or *cost centers*. Thus the individuals at these levels of management may have this information for control purposes and be held accountable for cost performance.

The identification of costs with individuals responsible for them is the essence of what is known as responsibility accounting, which also extends beyond the factory to sales, administrative, and other departments, and in summary form to profit centers or other divisions of a business. Thus costs are identified not simply with departments or functions but with people.

Finally, for purposes of cost control, inventory valuation, profit determination, financial budgeting, determining where effort should be applied or shifted, and often for pricing decisions, it is desirable to identify costs by type of expense incurred on specific *jobs, processes,* or *services*. In other words, it is desirable to identify costs by products.

EXHIBIT 41
Major Accounts in Factory Costing

Costs

Raw Material Used

Debit	Credit
1. Material used—as determined by cost records	1. Closed to Work in Process

Factory Labor

Debit	Credit
1. Labor cost as determined by payroll records	1. Labor cost as determined by cost records and charged to Work in Process

Factory Burden

Debit	Credit
1. Burden costs closed from various accounts: Depreciation, Power, Indirect Labor, etc.	1. Burden absorbed by production, as determined by cost records and charged to Work in Process

Balance overabsorbed or underabsorbed closed to profit and loss

Inventories

Raw Material

Debit	Credit
1. Opening inventory 2. Purchases	1. Credit for raw material used 2. Balance closing inventory

Work in Process

Debit	Credit
1. Opening inventory 2. Raw material used 3. Factory labor 4. Factory burden	1. Cost of goods completed as determined by cost records and transferred to Finished Goods 2. Balance closing inventory

Finished Goods

Debit	Credit
1. Opening inventory 2. Goods completed and transferred from Work in Process	1. Cost of goods sold as determined by cost records 2. Balance closing inventory

Cost of Goods Sold

Debit	Credit
1. Cost of goods sold as determined by cost records	1. Closed to Profit and Loss

Note: In actual practice, of course, many more accounts are used than those pictured. For example, a separate account would be kept for each type of expense as well as accounts for both direct departments and service departments, with costs broken down by type of expense within them.

Account Classifications

The number of accounts into which costs are classified can, of course, be many or few. The number selected is dependent on their usefulness as well as on the cost in time and money to maintain the records involved. Judgment is called for in order to avoid developing, on the one hand, a system with so much detail that the classifications will be more confusing than informative or more costly than worthwhile; or, on the other hand, a system whose only virtue lies in its simplicity.

If one must err here, it is better to err on the side of too much detail rather than too little. Information which can be collected in detail relatively inexpensively as a matter of orderly routine bookkeeping is time-consuming and costly to establish when it is necessary to work backward from summary accounts to original documents.

Moreover, some information, if not kept in detail, will never be available. For example, it is impossible to establish the cost of spoilage in production for a given time period broken down by major causes unless a record is made of each item spoiled, identified as to cause, at the time spoilage takes place or shortly thereafter.

This does not mean that management reports need be burdened with detail. The detail can be kept in the accounting records and monitored by the accounting department for the spotting of significant items that should be brought to management's attention.

There is a popular notion that considerable savings in bookkeeping can be realized by reducing the number of accounts in which information is to be recorded. Doubtless some savings can be realized in this way. But the reader will recall from earlier discussion that each financial event must be duly recorded with respect to its debit and credit effects, whether the accounts are many or few. Thus it should be evident that the cost of bookkeeping is far more dependent on the volume of financial transactions involved than on the number of accounts or pigeonholes in which information is to be stored.

The main question, of course, is whether savings realized through reducing the number of accounts would be adequate to compensate for the resulting loss of information. This is a hard question to answer for two reasons. One, because it is difficult to measure what, and how much, is saved when an account is eliminated. The other, because it is difficult to measure what the absence of the information the account provided might cost sometime in the future.

In some companies, uncertainty here may well mean that few accounts are ever eliminated. In this type of situation, management consultants can help companies to realize savings through judicious account simplification.

Variations in Costing Practice

Procedures for accumulating cost data vary from company to company and for different types of expense within companies.

For example, in many companies the primary accounting is by type of expense, followed by allocations of these expenses to departments or cost centers and then to work processed.

In others, some costs are first accumulated by jobs by types of expense, then summarized by departments and cost centers by type of expense.

In still other companies, different clerks are provided with copies of the same basic cost documents for certain costs, e.g., direct labor, so that costing by type of expense for the division or company as a whole, by departments and cost centers, and by jobs can be carried on simultaneously.

In addition to detailed records covering costs of specific jobs, processes, or services, it is common practice to maintain special cost journals and ledgers in which to record expenses. As with other records, the details may actually be stored on cards, tapes, or in some type of information storage connected with a computer.

In educational discussions, the basic accounting records are spoken of as "books of account" and in a great many companies these are in fact loose-leaf record books. Such special books, used in addition to the general journal and general ledger, result in a division of bookkeeping labor, as each plant or other operating unit has in effect a "set of books" of its own.

Owing to many variables such as size of organization, nature of manufacturing processes, and types of product being manufactured, there are considerable differences among companies with regard to details of procedure in accounting for jobs, processes, and services.

However, there are two common basic systems of cost accumulation, the one known as "job costing" and the other as "process costing." Under each of these systems, it is possible to account for either or both actual costs or "standard costs."

Job Costing

As its name implies, under job costing the costs are collected on each job or production lot regardless of the time periods involved. Some jobs, for example, may be completed in a short time, whereas others may extend over several months.

Typically, either a "job cost sheet" or a "lot cost sheet" form is used on which costs are accumulated for each job or lot as work progresses. This form is similar to the type a garage uses for collecting costs and billing a customer for automobile repairs. Large jobs or projects are generally broken down into segments, not simply for accounting purposes but to facilitate the assignment and control of work. For identification purposes, jobs are given numbers in rotation.

Materials are bought or requisitioned from stock separately for each job. The cost of these materials is posted from suppliers' invoices or from detailed inventory records to copies of purchase or material requisitions. These, in turn, serve as the basis for material cost entries on job sheets.

Labor costs are recorded on work cards, books, or chits, identified by job number as well as by employee, and posted from this source to job cost sheets.

Factory burden, consisting of all manufacturing costs except direct materials and direct labor, is generally charged to jobs by means of burden (overhead) rates. A little further on, I shall discuss the manner in which such rates are established.

For present purposes, the use of these rates may be visualized as factory overhead expenses charged to a job either as a percentage of the direct labor cost incurred or at predetermined rates per hour for the labor hours or machine hours expended. Factory burden not absorbed, or overabsorbed, by these charges to jobs is closed at the end of an accounting period to "Profit and Loss" or, as in some companies, to "Cost of Goods Sold."

At the close of each accounting period, a summary of the costs on job cost sheets for jobs still in process should equal the inventory of "Work-in-Process" in the books of account. In fact, these job cost sheets serve as a subsidiary ledger in this connection.

Thus the total of the costs on job cost sheets covering jobs completed during the period provides the figure for recording the transfer from "Work-in-Process" to "Finished Goods" for the period. In cases where goods are shipped immediately upon completion, the transfer is to the "Cost of Goods Sold" rather than to "Finished Goods."

Process Costing

Under process costing, the costs are entered as they take place, or summarized at appropriate intervals, in cost sheets by type of expense for each department or cost center rather than by job or lot, and accumulated for a specific period of time, commonly one month. Records of physical units are also maintained by these same production areas. And unit costs are established by dividing the costs for a given period by the number of units processed during that period.

Unit costs established in this way are, of course, most accurate if the products are all alike and the manufacturing process is therefore applied uniformly to them. However, it is possible to make reasonably equitable prorations of cost, even though nonuniform units are being processed, if factors or weights developed by careful study are used.

The weakness of using such prorations to determine costs per unit is that at times some types of product may in fact be produced more or less efficiently than allowed for in the standard factors or weights. Thus all products will be made to bear either more or less than their proper share of the costs incurred for the period.

Whether or not the problem is serious depends upon the magnitude of the effect on the costs of each product resulting from these fluctuations in production efficiency. Where the efficiency of operation for a process is primarily a matter of labor or machine efficiency, and not a matter of the particular product being processed at any given time, the use of standard factors or weights for cost allocations to products can be most appropriate.

Good or bad experiences are thereby shared by all goods produced during a period. Thus these variances are not charged or credited to the goods which, by chance, were being worked upon when these departures from normal performance took place.

Cost allocation of partially completed units. Under process costing, unless all product units are completed at the end of a period for a given department or cost center, there is the problem of allocating costs between units fully completed during the period and those only partially completed. Typically, this is handled by estimating the degree of completion of the closing inventory of work-in-process, computing the quantity of this inventory in terms of its work equivalent in finished units, and adding this quantity to the quantity of units fully completed to establish a common denominator for arriving at unit costs.

For a continuous process, a common assumption is that work-in-process is one half complete as far as labor and factory overhead for the given process are concerned. Thus 10,000 units of work-in-process would be the work equivalent of 5,000 finished units.

The measure of degree of completion is different for material costs than for labor and overhead costs. The reason for this is that the bulk of material usually enters production at the outset of the first process in the type of production for which process costing is appropriate.

A simple example involving labor costs only may be helpful to an understanding of cost allocation between partially completed and fully completed units under process costing. Consider:

Direct Labor Costs

	Actual Units	Amount
Beginning work-in-process	8,000	$ 4,000
Input	102,000	101,000
Total	110,000	105,000
Goods completed	100,000	100,000
Ending work-in-process	10,000	$ 5,000

In these figures, the cost center started with a beginning inventory of 8,000 units which were assumed to be one half complete. Thus they were the work equivalent of 4,000 units fully completed. The cost assigned to this inventory was $4,000 and thus represented a cost of $1.00 per unit in terms of finished units, or $.50 per unit in terms of work-in-process units.

During the period, 102,000 units entered production, making the total units to be accounted for 110,000; and 100,000 units were completed, leaving 10,000 units in process at the end. The cost of labor for the period was $101,000 to be allocated between the 100,000 units completed and the 10,000 units left in process.

Completed units and partially completed units have obviously had different amounts of labor applied to them. Therefore, they cannot be added together to arrive at a common denominator for establishing unit labor costs.

For example, on the assumption that work-in-process is one half complete, the closing inventory of 10,000 units in process is the work equivalent of 5,000 finished units. This figure can be added to the 100,000 units completed and the output for the period as far as labor is concerned can be stated as being the equivalent of 105,000 finished units.

The $105,000 labor cost when divided by this common denominator shows the unit cost of a completed unit to be $1.00, and the cost of a unit still in process would of course be one half of this, or $.50. These unit costs can then be applied to arrive at the cost of goods completed for the period ($100,000) and the cost of the closing inventory in process ($5,000).

Incidentally, the $101,000 of input costs may be regarded as having been spent as follows:

Labor applied to complete beginning inventory	8,000 × $0.50	$ 4,000
Labor applied to units started and fully completed	92,000 × 1.00	92,000
Labor applied to units of ending inventory	10,000 × 0.50	5,000
		$101,000

Where the amount of work actually in process within a department or cost center at the end of a period is small in relation to throughput for the period and is fairly consistent from period to period, it is commonly ignored or assigned a constant value. The reasoning here is that, for all practical purposes, the costs of the department or cost center for a period are also the costs of the goods completed by that operating unit for the period.

Similarly, in companies where there are a number of processes but only a few points in the plant where goods in process accumulate to any degree, cost reports will be prepared by type of expense for each process for control purposes but product costs will be established by combining processing costs at appropriate inventory points.

Material costs under process costing. In process cost situations, the bulk of raw material used typically enters the first department or process, and then moves on from department to department for further processing with smaller amounts of supplementary materials added from time to time. Materials are likely to enter processing on the basis of production schedules rather than through material requisitions as used on job costing.

Records of quantities used will be maintained, commonly at the point of use. These materials will be costed later by the accounting department by reference to perpetual inventory records.

Under some process cost systems, the output of one department or process, including the labor and burden expended on it as well as its material cost, becomes the cost of material to the next department or process in line. While this simplifies accounting procedure, it does not reveal the total material cost, total labor cost, and total burden cost for the product as a whole.

Other systems provide for this more complete information a. by keeping separate the material costs, labor costs, and burden costs as transferred from one department to another; and b. by maintaining this separation throughout process costing.

Labor and burden costs under process costing. Labor costs under process costing need simply be identified with the department or process in which the work is performed. These can usually be obtained from payroll records without the need for the detailed work cards or chits required in job costing. Complications arise when labor is transferred between departments during a period, to keep people employed or to overcome bottleneck situations, but these transfers can also be accounted for as part of the payroll procedure.

Similarly, factory burden by type of expense can be identified by department or process, or allocated thereto, without having to use burden rates as required in job costing. Many of these costs, and particularly depreciation, are fixed for a period regardless of the quantity of goods processed. Thus the practice of charging the total burden for a period to whatever goods are produced in that period can result in marked changes in unit costs from period to period as volume fluctuates over the year and from year to year.

To avoid such fluctuations in unit costs, and in particular to avoid the lack of conservative valuation of inventories that could result when volume was low, some companies apply burden to process cost sheets at a standard percentage of direct labor cost for the period or at standard rates per labor-hour, per machine-hour, or per unit of product. Burden under- or overabsorbed by these charges is closed to "Profit and Loss," or to "Cost of Goods Sold," at the end of an accounting period.

Other Systems of Cost Accumulation

Many companies do not consider it either desirable or worthwhile to maintain continuous records of product costs as required typically under either job costing or process costing. Some of these cases are simply examples of inadequacy in accounting procedures. In many other cases, however, the matter has been weighed carefully to come to a reasoned conclusion.

In some situations, complete job costing would be far more expensive to maintain than the benefits that might come from it, while the wide variety of products being manufactured, and the many variations in the work performed on each, prohibit process costing.

It is the practice in some of these cases to account for jobs in terms of physical quantities of material, labor hours, and machine hours. For control purposes, these figures are then checked against predetermined standards. The avoidance of dollar calculations saves clerical time and cost, yet the physical data assist in the control of operations.

Under such a system, costs can be established, if wanted for some special purpose, by the application of standard rates to the records of physical performance. This is often done on the first run of a product.

In other cases cost accounting is concentrated on identifying costs by type of expense with departments or cost centers and on comparing these figures with budgeted figures for control purposes. Any continuous accounting for products is in physical terms — that is, measuring the flow of goods by major type and quantity per hour, per day, per week, and so on in relation to standards or production schedules, and recording such factors as yield and spoilage.

The general philosophy here is that if goods are produced according to schedule by standard crews at standard speeds, and with standard yield and spoilage, they will be produced at satisfactory costs, assuming also that variable burden costs are under control by such means as variable budgeting. It is believed that detailed product costing would not further this control process to a degree worth the additional accounting cost that would be involved.

Estimated Product Costs

Such product costing as is undertaken in systems of the type just mentioned lies in the preparation of cost estimates on each type of product, checked possibly by occasional detailed accounting on test runs. In the preparation of these estimates, reference is made to material and labor specifications and to machine routings established by the engineering department and checked periodically from experience.

Material prices to be applied to material specifications are obtained from perpetual inventory records, price lists, or by reference to suppliers' invoices. Known labor rates by classifications of skills in each department are applied to specified labor times for required operations. And burden is computed as a standard percentage of direct labor cost or at predetermined rates per man-hour or machine-hour.

These product cost estimates, checked from time to time with changes in material costs, labor rates, yield, and manufacturing processes, are considered sufficiently accurate for purposes of inventory valuation, profit determination, and pricing. As suggested earlier, it is considered that costs can be controlled adequately by means other than through detailed product costing.

Under systems of this type involving the use of estimated costs, costs incurred during an accounting period, identified by type of expense and by department or cost center for informational and control purposes, are closed at the end of the period to one or more clearing accounts, along with the beginning inventories of work-in-process and finished goods. Closing inventory quantities of work-in-process and finished goods, established by physical count or by the maintenance of records on physical quantities, are priced by reference to the file of product cost estimates and removed from these clearing accounts.

In cases where there are hundreds, and even thousands, of inventory items in process and finished, it is often the practice to summarize inventory quantities by major categories and to select one product in each group as being representative of the group. The quantity in each group is then multiplied by the estimated cost of its representative item to establish its valuation at cost.

A typical internal profit and loss statement, utilizing estimated or standard costs for inventory valuation purposes, as just described, shows costs for the period listed by type of expense. The total of these is then adjusted for the difference between the beginning and ending inventories of work in process and finished goods for that period to arrive at the cost of goods sold.

Disadvantages of limited product costing. A system along the lines just described may well represent the only practical approach in complicated situations or in those in which the cost of accounting, along with other costs, must be kept at a minimum because the company is struggling for survival.

Then again, since the product cost information supplied by such a system is fragmentary in nature, it is probably not so accurate as that produced by more complete product cost accounting systems. From a control viewpoint, while it is true that the proper control of the physical factors of production should also control costs, there is something to be said for bringing the dollars involved to the attention of line supervisors, if not to operators.

For example, a drop in yield expressed in physical terms is not likely to be so impressive as a statement of the dollar value (or cost) of product lost. Knowledge of the cost or value of goods being handled should be helpful in bringing home a realization of the importance of processing them efficiently and with minimum waste.

Certainly, it can be said that companies which are doing less than complete product costing should at least review the matter from time to time to determine whether specific additional costing might be worth more than the incremental accounting cost involved. In this connection, the development of highspeed office equipment of various types opens the possibility of undertaking phases of product costing previously considered to be too difficult, too time-consuming, or too costly to handle.

For example, material requisitions and labor time chits prepared for machine or electronic handling in connecton with perpetual inventory records and payrolls can, with but little additional cost, be identified with jobs or individual products. Thus they can be used for establishing product costs promptly and in detail.

Basic Cost Data

Whatever system of cost accumulation is followed, it is clear that a variety of basic data must be gathered for the three segments — material, labor, and burden — that make up the overall manufacturing cost of a product.

In the sections to follow, I shall discuss the major records and procedures by which the cost of each of these segments is established.

Material Costs

The practice of maintaining perpetual inventory records for raw materials has long been followed. These records may be in the form of cards for each type of material that are maintained either by hand posting or by the use of bookkeeping machines. Or these records may be in the form of punched cards, tapes, or drums that are maintained by the use of tabulating or electronic equipment of various types.

The records store and provide information on each item for quantities on hand, ordered, received, and issued. In some cases, records are also kept of quantities allotted but not yet issued to scheduled work. Thus not only will material for the scheduled work be provided for, but also the amount of material actually available for new orders will be known.

If the given company uses actual costs for purposes of inventory valuation and product costing, the records will provide actual cost data for quantities on hand, received, and issued. If it accounts for product costs on both an actual and a standard cost basis, the records will provide the unit standard cost for the item in addition to actual quantities and actual costs.

However, if purchase price variances are segregated at the time materials are purchased; shown in the balance sheet; and charged into production at standard cost only, the records will provide only quantities. The standard cost per unit will nonetheless be shown in a prominent place on the card, if a card record is used, or it will be available elsewhere.

For control and assistance in purchasing, the record for an item usually provides figures for the minimum quantity to which it should be allowed to drop before being reordered, the maximum quantity to be allowed as a combination of items on hand and ordered, and the size of lot commonly purchased. Generally, the size of the lot is that of a purchase lot, or multiples thereof, common in the trade. In other words, the size of the lot is such a quantity as must be ordered to take advantage of available discounts.

Perpetual inventory records can generally be justified for control purposes alone. But, in addition to this, they provide the cost information necessary to account for the cost of material entering production and, in turn, the material cost figures for product costing.

To be sure, the original and basic documentary evidence for material cost is the supplier's invoice. Nonetheless, this is an awkward record to which to refer when trying to establish the cost of materials issued to production. The reason is that one invoice from a supplier may cover several types of material, or the same type of material may have been bought from more than one supplier. Moreover, purchase invoices are commonly filed alphabetically by suppliers' names, not by type of material purchased.

The same types of perpetual inventory cards in general are used for recording and controlling purchased parts as well as parts manufactured within the company which are stored for later use in production.

Material requisitions. Some documents which provide cost data serve more than one purpose and would probably be used even if no cost accounting for products was involved. For example, since materials should be issued from the storeroom only with proper authorization, a material requisition, signed by the proper authority or his delegate, is usually presented to the storekeeper when material is required for production.

After the materials have been issued, a copy of the requisition is sent to the clerks maintaining the raw material and manufactured or purchased parts' perpetual inventory records, where it is used as the basis for recording issues.

The perpetual inventory clerks then enter on the copy of the requisition the cost of the items issued. Thus the requisition in this form becomes the basic document furnished to the cost clerks for use in accounting for material costs.

Summaries of these requisitions are posted to job or process cost sheets, and further summaries are commonly used as the basic figures for entries in the books of account when transferring costs from "Raw

Material" and "Parts" to "Work-in-Process" accounts. They can also be used for statistical data on stores issued by type of material, both as one picture of operations for a period and as a summary of materials used for review by the purchasing department.

If the data on requisitions are put on tabulating cards or tapes at an early stage, they can of course be used still more easily for a variety of purposes along the lines indicated. It is of some importance to note the variety of purposes served by the material requisition and its summaries, since product costing alone is often blamed for the volume of clerical work and accounting involved.

Summary on material costing. The accumulation of material costs requires the use of a variety of supplementary forms or records in addition to the regular books of account. Key forms and records in this connection are, typically, the supplier's invoice; the perpetual inventory record for raw material and for purchased and manufactured parts; the material requisition; and the job or process cost sheet, or the departmental cost summary. The specific titles of these forms and records differ among companies. But whatever the labels, the functions of the forms and records are the same.

Labor Costs

Here again, as for material costing, I shall discuss only key records and procedures for collecting labor costs.

Depending upon the company's method of wage payment, it will maintain files or books of basic hourly wage rates for various types of work, piece rates paid for all operations on piecework, and standard minutes allowed for all operations under incentive wages.

In addition, there will be a record of each factory employee's base wage rate per hour. This, of course, is not only the regular rate of pay for an employee working on an hourly rate basis, but it is also the base rate to be paid for any hourly work done by an employee who is normally paid on a piecework or a wage-incentive basis, i.e., when such an employee is required to perform nonstandard work for which piece rates or standard minutes have not been computed.

An employee's base pay rate is also used in computing his pay for idle time beyond his control, as when a machine breaks down or he is forced to wait for work. And his base pay is used in computing his earnings for the minutes or points he has earned under a wage incentive plan and his guaranteed minimum pay, if the plan includes such a guarantee.

Typically, two basic documents underlie the accumulation of labor costs. One, the clock card, is an attendance record for each employee on which the time is recorded whenever he enters or leaves the plant. The other is in the form of one or more work cards or chits, or a book maintained by the foreman, on which is recorded the work each employee has performed each day, in terms of the time spent, the pieces produced, or the minutes earned on each job or process on which he has worked.

The records of work performed by each employee are checked against his clock card to account for all his time spent in the plant. Wage rates are then applied to the work done to establish its labor cost.

From this primary record, the payroll is established and labor charges entered on job or process cost sheets or on departmental cost summaries. These steps also provide the data for entering the cost of labor in the books of account, which is later transferred to "Work-in-Process."

As in the case of material costing, much of the detail of labor costing would be required whether or not a company undertook product costing. In fact, labor costing of products might well be considered a by-product of payroll accounting.

Summary on labor costing. Whatever other labor records individual companies may have, the key records in addition to the books of account for purposes of cost accumulation are, a. a file or catalogue of hourly rates, piece rates, or standard allowed minutes for various classes of work; b. a record of the base hourly rate of pay for each worker; c. a clock card for recording employee attendance; d. a work card, book, or chit to identify the work performed by each worker on each job or process in each department; e. a payroll record; and f. the job or process cost sheet, or the departmental cost summary, for accumulating labor costs identified by products.

These forms and records may of course be prepared and maintained by hand or by the use of a variety of mechanical, electrical, or electronic equipment.

Burden Costs

Factory burden consists of all manufacturing costs except those for materials and labor applied directly to goods manufactured. Typical items of a factory burden are indirect labor; manufacturing supplies; heat, light, and power; repairs and maintenance; depreciation; property taxes; and insurance.

In addition to the difficulty of accounting for a large number of different kinds of expense, accounting for factory burden by operating units and by products or product lines involves many cost allocations. Some costs can be clearly identified with specific departments or cost centers. But other costs must be allocated to such operating units on some equitable basis.

Furthermore, in factories of any size, there are service departments such as maintenance, personnel, medical, cafeteria, and power plant whose costs must be prorated equitably to direct producing departments if the complete costs of goods produced by the latter departments are to be computed.

Finally, when a variety of products is being manufactured within each direct producing department, it is generally impossible to identify specific actual burden costs with specific goods produced. Therefore, it is necessary to compute the burden cost of products by the use of some sort of burden rate or combination of rates.

Burden rates. In further explanation of the previous sentence, it would be impossible to determine for one job among many being worked upon in a department the exact amount of indirect labor, depreciation, maintenance, and other indirect costs that had been expended on that job. If, however, it is believed that these costs are identifiable with time expended, hourly or daily rates can be developed and applied to the time worked upon jobs to arrive at fair allocations of burden costs to them.

Thus, if reasonably current experience shows that the factory burden in a department averages approximately $5 per direct labor hour (total burden costs for a trial period divided by total direct labor hours for that period), a reasonable burden charge to a given job could be made if the labor hours spent on it were multiplied by a burden rate of $5 per hour. While this would not be literally the burden cost of that job, it should be a reasonable approximation. And it would be actual in the sense that the given job, in relation to others, would be charged in proportion to the actual time spent on it.

In some departments, machine hours are a more significant measure of burden application than labor hours. Therefore, machine-hour rates rather than labor-hour rates are used for burden charges to jobs.

In many companies, burden is applied to jobs as a percentage of the accumulated labor cost of the job. Thus the percentage is established by relating total burden for the department to the total direct labor cost of that department for a representative accounting period.

In some situations, a machine rate per hour or per day is used which includes the pay of the operator and operating expenses as well as overhead. In accounting for the costs of construction, for example, a job would be charged at rates of this type for the use of trucks, bulldozers, and portable cranes.

Some companies use a single rate for the factory as a whole, while others use a separate rate for each department or cost center. While the use of a single plant-wide rate simplifies accounting procedure, it obviously does not produce results that are as accurate as those reached by the use of individual departmental rates. This is particularly true when departmental rates differ markedly from one another and when products differ significantly in the proportion of time spent in one department versus another.

Also, where there are marked shifts from period to period in the quantities of work in process at various stages, the use of departmental rates rather than a single plant-wide rate can make a significant difference in the valuation of inventories and in the net income reported for any given period.

Example of burden distribution. It has been found useful to summarize on a burden distribution sheet the allocations of burden costs to both direct and service departments and the reallocation of the service department costs. A simplified version of such a sheet is presented in Exhibit 42. A description of the basis of distribution of the various burden items and allocation of the costs of the service departments on this Bond Manufacturing Company sheet follows:

Supervisory Salaries and Indirect Labor: Charged to departments as summarized from payroll records. Where supervisors or indirect workers served more than one department, they reported each week the approximate portions of their time spent in each department.

Fuel and Purchased Power: Charged to the power department.

Water: Allocated between Heat and Light and Power on the basis of an estimate by the chief engineer as to its use.

Supplies: Charged to each department on the basis of actual requisitions processed.

Real Estate Taxes: Distributed according to the percentage of floor space occupied by each department.

Insurance: The cost of insurance was first divided between buildings and machinery in proportion to the cost of each before allowing for depreciation. The portion assumed to apply to buildings was then allocated to departments in proportion to floor space occupied. The remaining portion applying to machinery was allocated to departments on the basis of investment in machinery. For example, in Exhibit 42, the insurance cost of $2,700 was divided in the ratio of 1:3 and 2:3 to

EXHIBIT 42
Bond Manufacturing Company, Burden Distribution Sheet —
Six Months Ending June 30, 19—

| | | Productive Departments | | | | | Service Departments | | | |
	Total	Dept. 1	Dept. 2	Dept. 3	Dept. 4	Dept. 5	Heat & Lgt.	Power	Maint. & Repairs	Packing & Shipping
Supervisory Salaries	25,200	6,300	4,800	2,700	1,800	3,300	1,500	1,500	1,500	1,800
Indirect Labor	28,800	7,200	6,000	3,300	2,400	2,700	2,100	1,500	2,400	1,200
Fuel	16,500							16,500		
Purchased Power	7,500							7,500		
Water	2,700						300	2,400		
Supplies	14,400	3,300	2,700	2,400	2,100	900	600	300	600	1,500
Real Estate Taxes	6,000	1,500	1,200	840	600	720	360	420	120	240
Insurance	2,700	585	450	306	306	234	342	315	72	90
Depreciation—Building	6,000	1,500	1,200	840	600	720	360	420	120	240
Depreciation—Machinery	30,000	6,000	4,500	3,000	3,600	2,100	4,800	4,200	900	900
Totals	139,800	26,385	20,850	13,386	11,406	10,674	10,362	35,055	5,712	5,970

EXHIBIT 42 (continued)

							Heat & Light	Power	Maint. & Repairs	Packing & Shipping
Cross Allocations:										
Steam to Heat & Light							8,100	(8,100)		
Maint. & Rep. to Service							300	570	(1,020)	150
Reallocations Service Depts.:										
Heat and Light		5,066	3,940	2,814	2,064	2,439	(18,762)	1,313	375	751
Power		8,658	7,206	3,456	5,761	2,315		(28,838)	865	577
Maintenance & Repairs		1,483	1,009	949	1,127	1,364			(5,932)	
Packing and Shipping				1,482		5,966				(7,448)
Total Burden Productive Depts.	139,800	41,592	33,005	20,605	21,840	22,758				
Direct Labor Expense	84,500	21,125	14,365	13,520	16,055	19,435				
Per Cent		25%	17%	16%	19%	23%				
Burden Rates		197%	230%	152%	136%	117%				
Floor Space—Per Cent		25%	20%	14%	10%	12%	6%	7%	2%	4%
Machinery Cost—Per Cent		20%	15%	10%	12%	7%	16%	14%	3%	3%
Power Consumption—Per Cent		30%	25%	12%	20%	8%	—	—	3%	2%

buildings ($900) and machinery ($1,800). The cost of insurance for Department 1 was then computed as ($900 × 25%) Floor Space = $225, this + ($1,800 × 20% Machinery Cost = $360) = $585. (Percentages used are shown at the bottom of Exhibit 42.)

Depreciation on Buildings: Distributed to each department on the basis of floor space occupied.

Depreciation on Machinery: Distributed on the basis of the cost of machinery in each department.

Exhibit 42 shows that after the foregoing steps have been taken, all the burden items by type of expense have been distributed to both productive and service departments.

The next step required an addition to the expenses of the productive departments for the costs of services provided to them by the service departments. Since some of the service departments also served the other departments, it was first necessary to make cost allocations between them.

Thus upon the basis of an estimate by the chief engineer the cost of exhaust steam was transferred from the power department, where it was made, to the heat and light department, where it was used. Also, on the basis of a combined estimate by the heads of the maintenance and accounting departments, the amounts chargeable for "Maintenance & Repairs" were allocated to the three other service departments and credited to "Maintenance & Repairs."

The remaining expenses of the service departments were then allocated to the productive departments as follows:

Heat & Light: On the basis of floor space occupied, omitting its own.

Power: On the basis of rated horsepower in each department tempered by known shifts in productive activity between departments.

Maintenance & Repairs: According to the percentages of direct labor expense in the productive departments. It was recognized that more accurate results could be obtained by accumulating job cost records on maintenance and repairs but the company did not wish to incur this additional clerical expense. It was believed that over a period of time maintenance and repairs would be proportional to direct labor in all productive departments and therefore this basis of allocation was considered satisfactory.

Packing & Shipping: Divided between Departments 4 and 5 on the basis of the dollar value of the shipments made from each of those departments.

After the foregoing allocations, the total burden expense of each productive department was available, and burden rates could be computed by dividing the burden of each department by the direct labor expense of that department.

These rates were used by the company for pricing the burden content of work-in-process and finished goods inventories at the end of the six-month period for which they were computed. These rates also served for cost estimation purposes for the next six months. It was the company's practice to prepare financial statements only semiannually. However, costs by type of expense were reported to management each month, and daily, weekly, and monthly production, sales, and financial data were reported for control purposes.

Uses of burden distribution sheet.   A burden sheet along the lines of Exhibit 42 is prepared by many companies at the close of each month to serve as the basis for journal entries charging both direct and service departments for what are considered to be their shares of the various burden costs for control purposes.

The burden distribution sheet is also used as the basis for journal entries which allocate the costs of service departments to other departments, resulting finally in having all burden costs for the period assigned to direct departments.

In some companies, as in the Bond Manufacturing Company, this actual cost data is also used in establishing burden rates by means of which the actual burden costs for the period are charged to jobs or processes and thus to goods produced.

It is far more common, however, to establish burden rates based on projections of burden costs for a coming period of six months or a year rather than on actual costs incurred. It is also common to base the volume factor (such as quantity of machine hours or labor hours) on an expected average or normal volume rather than on the expected actual volume, a matter which I shall discuss in Chapter 22, "Standard Costs."

If burden rates based on actual experience are to be used, as in the case of Bond Manufacturing Company, it is necessary to delay this aspect of product costing until the close of the period. The use of predetermined rates avoids this delay and also provides the means for making estimates on product costs for use in budgeting, inventory valuation, and pricing.

If the predetermined rates are based on the expected costs and expected volume of operations for the coming period of six months or year, a burden distribution sheet used as an aid in arriving at the rates represents in essence a budget of burden costs for that period.

Burden not absorbed or overabsorbed. The matter of burden not being fully absorbed, or being overabsorbed, seems to confuse some executives. Thus I shall try to overcome some of the confusion at this point.

It should be easy to understand that if, on the one hand, all of the actual burden costs shown in Exhibit 42, which ended by being charged to the productive departments of the Bond Manufacturing Company, were in turn charged to the goods produced that period by means of the burden rates noted in the exhibit, all of the burden incurred would thereby be absorbed by the goods produced that period and there would be no burden not absorbed or overabsorbed.

If, on the other hand, the productive departments were charged for actual burden as illustrated in Exhibit 42, but the products were charged and the productive departments were credited for burden costs at predetermined rates, it would only be by the rarest of circumstances that these two amounts would balance. Therefore, inevitably some amount of burden would not be absorbed or would be overabsorbed for the period.

For the moment, let us simply note that when burden is not fully absorbed or is overabsorbed for a period, the company in which this occurs is using predetermined or standard burden rates in charging burden costs to products instead of charging them for the total actual burden costs incurred.

I shall leave until later a discussion as to why such predetermined or standard rates are used and how one can analyze the variance between actual costs and costs absorbed.

Factory burden not absorbed or overabsorbed by the application of predetermined rates to goods produced is closed at the end of an accounting period to "Profit and Loss" or to "Cost of Goods Sold." To amplify this point, the amount involved does not apply to some of the goods shipped during the period, since they have been manufactured in previous periods, and part of it applies to goods in process or completed and still on hand.

Therefore, it is more logical to close the variance to "Profit and Loss," to be shown in the income statement as a separate item of gain or loss for the period, than to "Cost of Goods Sold" as though the variance applied only to the goods shipped during the period.

In some companies, factory burden under- or overabsorbed, or at least that portion of it resulting from volume variances, is carried forward from month to month and closed out at the end of the year. In this way, seasonal and minor random variances are given a chance to balance out.

During a year in which it becomes evident as the year progresses that accumulated burden not absorbed to date is not likely to be balanced out by burden overabsorbed during the remaining months of the year, it is incumbent upon the accounting department to warn executives about an unfavorable write-off that will have to be taken at year end.

Summary on burden costing. The accumulation of factory burden costs typically involves six major steps:

1. The accumulation of costs by type of expense, e.g., indirect labor, depreciation, insurance, for the plant, division, and company as a whole.
2. The charging, or allocation, of these expenses on various bases to both direct and service departments.
3. The charging, or allocation, of service department costs to direct departments on equitable bases.
4. The development of burden rates based on either actual or estimated burden costs for a given period of time related to the actual, expected, or normal volume of operations for such a period expressed in terms of labor hours, machine hours, or direct labor cost.
5. The charging of burden to jobs or processes by the use of the burden rates established.
6. The closing to "Profit and Loss" of the amount of burden under- or overabsorbed by charges to jobs or goods produced during the period.

These major steps, as well as key forms and records for accumulating material, labor, and burden costs, are illustrated in Exhibit 43.

Selling and Administrative Expenses

The costs we have just been examining are all related to products or services produced. We noted also the desirability of identifying these costs by type of expense and by area of responsibility for purposes of budgeting, cost control, and financial analysis.

In addition, of course, there are selling and administrative expenses to be accounted for, also by type of expense and by area of responsibility, in much the same way as manufacturing costs. These expenses, however, are known as "period costs," rather than "product costs" or "inventory costs," in that they are charged off as expenses each period in the books of account. They are not identified with

EXHIBIT 43
Major Steps in Accumulation of Factory Costs

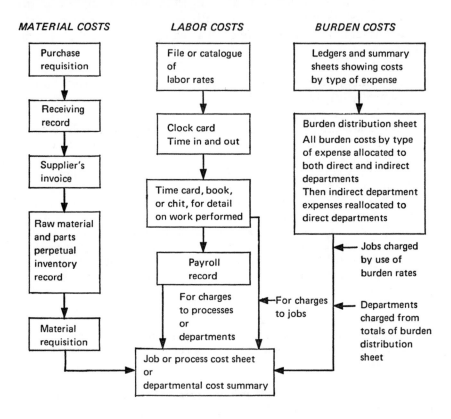

specific jobs or goods produced, nor included in the valuation of inventories. The distinction between product costs and period costs is illustrated in Exhibit 44.

Although selling and administrative expenses are accounted for as period costs, they are often identified with specific product lines in detailed income statements and even with specific products on cost sheets or estimates apart from the books of account. The identification of these expenses with product lines is in keeping with the concept of a proper matching of costs and revenues. And it provides the means of measuring and judging the profitability of each product line.

Estimates of the selling and administrative expenses thought to be associated with specific products, or reasonably to be borne by them,

EXHIBIT 44
Distinction Between Product Costs and Period Costs

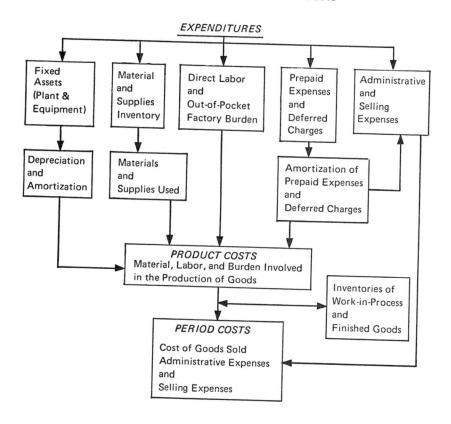

EXPENDITURES

| Fixed Assets (Plant & Equipment) | Material and Supplies Inventory | Direct Labor and Out-of-Pocket Factory Burden | Prepaid Expenses and Deferred Charges | Administrative and Selling Expenses |

Depreciation and Amortization

Materials and Supplies Used

Amortization of Prepaid Expenses and Deferred Charges

PRODUCT COSTS
Material, Labor, and Burden Involved in the Production of Goods

Inventories of Work-in-Process and Finished Goods

PERIOD COSTS

Cost of Goods Sold
Administrative Expenses
and
Selling Expenses

are considered useful in pricing; in determining whether to produce or handle an item, given its selling price; and in deciding where to spend or concentrate sales or production effort at any given time.

For example, the available margin or revenue above the material, labor, and factory burden costs per unit of a given product might appear attractive and seem to warrant the expenditure of money and effort to sell it. Care must be taken, however, for if each customer purchased only a tiny quantity of this product per year a study would probably reveal that the cost of selling to such customers directly would more than eat up the gross margin available.

In Summary

In this chapter, we have been concerned largely with cost accounting routines for accumulating, recording, and reporting costs by type of expense, by area of responsibility, and by products and services.

Accounting for costs by type of expense, in addition to its function of accounting for the stewardship of funds, provides important data for use in operating reports and income statements for the company as a whole and for its major subdivisions.

Accounting for costs by type of expense, by areas of responsibility such as profit centers, cost centers, and departments, identifies costs with the individuals held accountable for them. The cost data recorded are reported to the individuals in charge of the areas in which the costs were incurred and to higher echelons of management also held accountable for these costs.

Accounting for costs by products and services provides data for inventory valuation and for determining the cost of goods and services sold during a period. These costs thus have an important bearing on the amount of net income computed and reported. Product cost information is also useful in budgeting, in pricing, and in determining where production or sales effort should be applied or shifted.

For control purposes, actual costs by type of expense, by area of responsibility, and by type of product, are commonly compared with similar actual costs for previous time periods or for units of the same type of product made previously. This practice is frowned upon by control experts because actual costs of the past may well not be valid or desirable standards for the future.

Nonetheless, many executives follow this practice and maintain files of experience to which they will refer if current reports on operations do not include data from the past. Such comparisons are at least beneficial in spotting areas that are out of line with the past, either favorably or unfavorably, and that therefore merit investigation.

It is generally more important to spot major variances by cause as a guide to action in the future than it is to have an exact measurement of current performance against some ideal standard. Of course, it is all the better if one can have both.

For planning purposes and for the measurement and control of performance, it is common practice for companies to prepare budgets and to compare actual performance against them. With respect to costs, the budgets represent estimated costs by type of expense and by areas of responsibility for given time periods in the future, or for various volumes of production or sales within the expected range of operations.

The cost classifications for budgeting purposes are kept essentially the same as the account classifications for cost accounting. Thus the actual costs to be compared against budgeted figures will be those accumulated in the regular accounting system and duplication of effort will be avoided.

For control purposes, pricing, budgeting, and in some cases for inventory valuation and for computing the cost of goods sold, many manufacturing companies make use of standard costs in accounting for the cost of their products. This is an important area that I shall discuss in the next chapter.

CHAPTER 22

Standard Costs

A standard cost is a predetermined cost usually associated with a manufactured product, thus standard costing is a procedure under which predetermined costs are used by manufacturing companies for establishing cost goals and measuring performance against them and for purposes of inventory valuation, profit determination, budgeting, and pricing.

Although it may seem a paradox, standard cost systems are not uniform systems. While many features are common to all such systems, there are significant differences in practice. Thus when one states that a company has a standard cost system, he is revealing only that it is making some use of standard costs.

Standard Product Costs

In a standard system, costs are established for the material, labor, and burden cost elements of a product. Many companies also estimate the amount of selling and administrative expenses that a product should be expected to bear in addition to the costs of its production.

The standard costs of a product, per unit or per normal production lot, consist of quantitative factors such as standard pounds of given materials, standard labor hours for specified operations, and standard machine hours for the scheduled machines to be used; and price factors such as standard cost per pound and per hour, by which the standard quantities are converted to the standard product costs.

The quantitative factors are based on engineered specifications tempered by experience, and vice versa. Prices used are typically those which are expected to be representative of actual prices during the period for which the standard product costs are being established.

It is common practice to maintain a file of standard cost cards or sheets on which the standard quantitative and cost data for each product are summarized. In cases where large numbers of products are involved, the preparation of standard cost cards or sheets is commonly restricted to a relatively small number of representative products.

Later, if the standard cost is wanted on some other item, it can be computed easily by applying adjustments to the standard cost of a representative or base model. An example of a simple standard sheet is presented as Exhibit 45.

In many situations, much of the cost of an end product consists of the costs of components manufactured and used by the same company for other products as well. Or the cost involves the use of material formulas common to a variety of products.

EXHIBIT 45

Standard-unit Cost Sheet

Unit _____   Dept. _____   Article _____
                                           Date Estimated _____

	Material	Labor	Mfg. Overhead	Total	Cost per Unit
Materials					
Labor					
Mfg. overhead at ___% labor					
Total Cost Molding					
Materials					
Labor					
Mfg. overhead at ___% labor					
Total cost packing					
Printing					
Total mfg. cost					
Selling and admin. cost ___% mfg. cost					
Commission					
Royalties					
Freight					
Total cost				%	
Net profit				%	
Selling price				%	

In a rubber company, for example, the same mixture of rubber and chemicals is appropriate for use in manufacturing the soles of a variety of footwear. In such cases, standard cost details are developed on cards or sheets for the components and mixes, identified by number. In developing the standard cost of the end product, reference is then made to the cost card for a given component or mix to be used. Thus, at such a time, the costs of such components and mixes do not have to be recomputed.

Standard Material Cost

As noted earlier, the material cost of a product has two elements, quantity and price, and both must be taken into account in arriving at the standard material cost of a product.

Material quantities per unit, lot, or batch of product used in computing standard costs are based on material specifications established in connection with production operations. Therefore, the quantities should be available for standard costing without extra effort.

In establishing the standard material quantities, due allowance must be made for normal shrinkage or waste. For example, if a circular piece is to be cut from a square of material, the standard quantity called for is the amount needed for the square, not that needed for the circle alone. Should there be any significant value in the recoverable scrap, a standard credit can be made when figuring the standard cost of the product.

In addition to normal shrinkage, a normal amount of spoilage and off-standard goods or "seconds" are expected. Standard amounts for losses of this type can be allowed for in the standard material and labor costs of a product. However, many companies prefer to treat such losses either as a separate element in the cost of a product or as an element of factory burden charged to it. The main point is that good units should bear the costs of the normal number of their unfortunate brothers who fail along the way.

In establishing the price factor of a standard material cost, a list, file, or catalogue is developed which shows standard prices of all materials commonly used, expressed in terms of cost per unit in the size of lot commonly purchased. The prices should be the average expected during the period for which the standards are being set, usually six months or a year.

Some companies, however, through inertia allow longer periods to elapse before changing standard prices, while others change them with every significant shift in market prices.

Standard quantities recorded on cost cards or sheets are priced by reference to the list, file, or catalogue of standard material prices. The cost card or sheet for a product then shows the standard cost of the standard quantity of each type of material required to produce it.

Standard Labor Cost

As with material costs, the cost of labor in a product involves the two factors of quantity and price, with the time needed to perform each operation as the basic quantity factor and wage rates as the basic price factor.

In establishing the quantity factor, the cost accountant refers to manufacturing specifications set up by either the production or engineering department. These specifications state the required operations to be performed on each type of product and the standard time for each operation, as developed from either or both time-studies and experience.

In determining the standard labor cost of products, the company's method of wage payment must, of course, be taken into account. If a wage-incentive plan is in operation and standard minutes (or points) have been established for each operation as a basis for computing wage payments, such standard minutes can be used when establishing the standard time to perform each operation on a given product.

In a company where a piece-rate system is used, the piece rate for an operation is also the standard cost of that operation. If straight day wages are paid, the quantity factor is established, as suggested earlier, by time study or from records of experience for each operation, and a standard wage rate per hour for the degree of skill required is applied.

In establishing the price factor, a list, file, or catalogue is developed of the basic hourly wage rates and piece rates for the various kinds of work involved in the manufacturing process. Then, to arrive at the standard labor cost of each operation on a product, the appropriate hourly rates or piece rates are applied to the quantity factors as just noted. The cost sheet then shows the standard cost of the standard quantity of each type of labor required for the product.

Standard Burden Cost

The reader will recall that the burden rates, which we examined in an earlier chapter, commonly used are labor-dollar rates, labor-hour rates, and machine-hour rates. We also noted that some companies use a single plant-wide rate, whereas other companies seek greater accuracy by the development and use of departmental or cost-center rates.

We noted further that in some cases in an "actual" cost system the burden rates are based on actual costs and volumes of production, as measured by actual labor dollars, labor hours, or machine hours. More often, however, the burden rates used in an actual cost system are predetermined or standard rates based upon expected costs at either the expected or "normal" volume of operations.

In either case, the burden applicable to products is computed by applying the rates to the actual cost of labor, the actual labor hours, or the actual machine hours expended in their production during a given period.

Under standard costing, burden rates of the second type just described are used, i.e., rates based on costs expected in the future at either the expected or normal volume of operations. The standard burden cost of a product is computed by applying these burden rates to the cost of labor; to the number of labor hours; or to the number of machine hours required to produce it according to production or engineering specifications.

In companies making only one or a few products, it is possible and often desirable to establish burden rates directly on a product unit basis, rather than to use labor-dollar, labor-hour, or machine-hour rates. The product may be literally one item, or it may be a ton, a gallon, 100 pounds, or some other common physical unit of measurement.

Standard Gross Margin and Selling Price

After establishing standard material, labor, and burden costs, many companies also compute a standard gross margin (gross profit) and a standard selling price for each product for entry on the standard cost sheet. The selling price recorded is not necessarily the best price that can be obtained or the actual price that will be obtained. But, at least, it is a starting point for pricing purposes.

On the one hand, in situations where the selling price of a product is fixed by market conditions, this obviously is the product's standard selling price. Its standard gross margin is then found simply by subtracting its standard material, labor, and burden costs from this standard selling price.

On the other hand, in situations where the individual producer has some leeway in setting prices, the standard selling price and standard gross margin on a product can be established in a number of different ways. One approach is to determine from experience the percentage of gross margin that seems to be necessary to cover selling, distribution, and administrative expenses, and to provide a reasonable net profit for each product line taken by itself.

For example, if the gross margin percentage is determined to be 40% of selling price for a given product line, the total of material, labor, and burden for the line is then assumed to represent 60% of selling price. Dividing the total standard cost of material, labor, and burden for a given product within this product line by 60 and multiplying the result by 100 establishes its standard selling price.

The dollar amount of standard gross margin for the product then, of course, can be computed by applying 40% to the standard selling price, or by subtracting the sum of its standard material, labor, and burden costs from its selling price.

Standard Selling and Administrative Expenses and Net Profit

In cases where a standard selling price and standard gross margin are established for each type of product within a group of products, it is also common practice to enter on each cost sheet a standard cost for selling expenses and another for administrative expenses. These expenses are then subtracted from the standard gross margin to establish a standard net profit for the given product.

Typically, the standard cost for selling expenses is based on a predetermined standard percentage relationship between sales dollars (selling price) and selling expenses. It is generally sound practice to establish this relationship by lines of product, rather than to use a single percentage relationship for all products, since selling costs often vary considerably between product lines.

In some companies, the standard cost for administrative expenses is also based on a predetermined percentage relationship to sales dollars. In others, it is based on a predetermined relationship to manufacturing cost (material, labor, and burden) or to labor cost alone. The base selected should be that factor which best measures the relative amount of administrative effort or concern required for the given product versus other products.

Income Statement Under Standard Costing

It should be understood clearly that an income statement under a complete standard cost system is not just a simple matching of costs and revenues. That is, it does not attempt to pair the actual cost of goods sold with sales, as is done under actual costing where the theory is that actual costs, even though possibly abnormal, should be identified with specific goods and charged against income at the point of sale. Under this theory, inventories are, of course, carried into the next accounting period at their accumulated actual costs.

In contrast, under standard costing, the income statement shows the inward flow of revenue from the sale of goods during the period and the matching of the standard cost of those goods to arrive at their gross margin contribution for the period.

In some income statements, this figure is entitled "Standard Gross Profit." But this is a misnomer, not because the word "profit" instead of "margin" is used, but because it is not the standard gross profit. Rather, it is the gross margin or profit resulting from the subtraction of the standard cost of goods sold from the actual revenue realized on those goods.

A figure for standard gross profit could be useful information if the sales figure were first compared with the revenue that would have been realized had the goods been sold at their standard selling prices. Nonetheless, I have never seen this done in practice.

Following the gross margin figure, the income statement under standard costing then commonly shows the manufacturing gains or losses between actual costs and standard costs which took place during the period. The theory here is that such gains or losses should be taken into account in the period in which they took place and should not therefore be deferred to the time of shipment of the goods on which the variances were incurred.

Part of this same theory is that closing inventories of work in process and finished goods should be passed on to the new period at standard cost, since the new period should not be penalized for, or benefit from, cost variances which took place in prior periods. This viewpoint emphasizes period profitability, rather than product profitability.

Nonetheless, cost variances can be associated with product lines in product-line income statements, and variances can also be identified with individual jobs and processes, as we shall see later.

The reader should also recall that in the typical income statement neither selling nor administrative expenses are necessarily directly related to the sales of the period. Particularly if goods are made to order, and the production cycle is a long one, the selling expenses, and to a lesser degree the administrative expenses, shown in an income statement have been incurred for bringing in business which will not appear as sales in an income statement for months to come.

Selling and administrative expenses under these circumstances are not directly related to sales, nor are many of the manufacturing losses and gains that appear in an income statement. Therefore, it is not correct to assume, when these costs are subtracted from the gross margin, that the resulting net operating income is *the* net operating income on the specific goods represented by the sales figure for the period.

Rather, it is the computed net operating income for the *period*. Under a complete standard cost system, this takes into account the flow of revenue from shipments matched with the standard cost of the goods shipped; the manufacturing gains or losses for the period on goods produced, whether or not those goods have been shipped; and the selling and administrative expenses, which have been treated as period costs.

A condensed income statement for a company having a complete standard cost system is presented in Exhibit 46.

EXHIBIT 46
Condensed Income Statement Under Standard Costing

	Loss	Gain		
Sales				$275,000
Cost of goods sold (at standard cost)				190,000
Gross margin				$ 85,000
Manufacturing losses and gains.				
Material:				
Price variance	$ 3,000			
Yield variance		$1,000		
Labor:				
Price variance	4,000			
Efficiency variance		2,000		
Burden:				
Spending variance	2,000			
Volume variance	3,000			
Efficiency variance		4,000		
	$12,000	$7,000		5,000
Adjusted gross margin				$ 80,000
Selling expenses			$40,000	
Administrative expenses			18,000	58,000
Net profit before income tax				$ 22,000

Use of Standard Costs in Inventory Valuation

Valuation of inventories at standard cost simplifies the pricing of inventory, provides a basis of consistent practice, and charges or credits operating losses and gains to the accounting period in which they took place.

If perpetual inventory records of raw material, work-in-process, and finished goods are kept at standard cost, it is simply necessary to show the unit standard cost in a conspicuous place on each inventory card and to keep the record in terms of units only. Thus the unit standard cost is available whenever needed for inventory valuation and the pricing of stores issues.

All dollar entries, additions, and subtractions are eliminated. And it is not, of course, necessary to compute a new average unit price with each input entry, as is the case when perpetual inventory records are maintained at actual cost.

The valuation of inventories at standard cost and consequent presentation of cost variances from standard in internal operating statements assists executives in analyzing and interpreting operating results. In complete standard cost systems, these variances are identified in detail by type, cause, and location.

Use of Standard Costs in Budgetary Planning and Control

The knowledge of cost relationships gained through study while establishing the standards is useful in both budgetary planning and control. For these purposes, of course, it is highly desirable to adjust the cost standards for any significant changes in operating conditions and prices expected in the period being budgeted.

However, in some cases, it is possible to maintain the original standards and to make allowance in the budget for expected changes as allowable variances from standard.

Standard costs developed on each product can be used to convert sales estimates (budgeted sales) to the estimated costs (material, labor, and burden) of the goods expected to be sold. Similarly, standard product costs are of assistance in making projections of the production costs to meet sales requirements, having in mind the extent to which inventories are to be built up or reduced during the period.

In situations where a wide variety of products are involved, it is possible to select and use the standard costs on a few products representative of larger groups, or by analysis to develop representative proportions of material, labor, and other costs by product lines.

As an example of the latter point, it might be found that the typical manufacturing cost proportions for a given product line are 55% material, 25% direct labor, and 20% burden. It might also be found that these costs represented on the average about 75% of selling price and, therefore, the product line showed a normal gross margin of 25%.

While the standard costs developed on each product might include data on selling and administrative expenses, which could be helpful in budgeting such expenses, the budgetary process for them is normally independent of standard costing of products. The heads of the various sales and administrative departments are called upon to develop their budgets by other means. Over time, these expenses are expected to bear a reasonable relationship to sales achieved. But this is not considered to be a matter of product costing.

Similarly, through studies underlying the development of departmental or cost-center burden rates, and in turn the burden cost of products, it is possible also to note the relationship between each type of expense and some appropriate measure of volume of activity such as direct labor hours. This provides a basis for determining what these expenses should be in the future for any given volume of activity within the practical range of operations for each department or cost center, as well as what they should have been for the actual volume of activity experienced in a period just past.

Although these are certainly cost standards, they are not usually thought of as standard costs. They are costs by type of expense related to the volume of activity of a department or cost-center. In terms of control mechanisms, these costs are controlled by what are known as variable or flexible budgets and not by standard costs.

Use of Standard Costs in Pricing

The subject of pricing will be discussed later at greater length. For the moment, let us note that the standard cost of a product can be useful as one of many factors to be taken into account in pricing. Standard costs, which have been kept reasonably up to date, are based on costs expected currently and for the near future. Thus they are at least more appropriate for this purpose than are actual costs based entirely on the past.

The full standard cost of a product is a useful starting point in pricing, particularly where the adopted price is to be maintained for some time. It provides a warning that unless this amount, and something more for profit, is recovered in the selling price, the product will not be really profitable.

When competitive conditions are such that full cost reimbursement cannot be realized in the selling price, the detailed knowledge of costs gained in setting the standards should make it possible to establish the fixed and variable costs involved.

This knowledge should also make it possible to provide the entire cost picture of a product, ranging from its out-of-pocket costs to its full costs. It is then possible to determine the extent to which what is thought to be an available price will cover out-of-pocket costs and contribute to fixed costs.

If the standard selling price, standard gross margin, and standard net profit are used as aids in pricing or in judging the profitability of individual products, the assumptions on which they are based should always be taken into account. In particular, one should pay attention to the assumed volume of operations; if the actual volume realized differs from this, it is highly probable that the actual unit costs for manufacturing, selling, and administration will differ also, as will the actual gross margin and net profit per unit.

In some cases, standard costing has fostered unfortunate rigidity in pricing. One form of such rigidity is the refusal to accept any price which does not at least recover full standard cost. This has of course been coupled with the failure to recognize that, in terms of overall results, it may be better at times to accept some business at less than full cost recovery, rather than to lose this business completely, since it contributes toward covering fixed costs which must be met in any event.

Perhaps of even greater importance for the seller, rigid adherence to pricing based on standard costs has at times resulted in prices that have been lower than necessary in relation to the existing demand situation. It is well, therefore, to stress that standard cost — or for that matter any cost, however computed — is only one of many factors that should be considered in pricing.

Use of Standard Costs in Cost Control

The use of standard costs in budgetary control has already been mentioned. Also, the presentation of cost variances in the internal income statement, as illustrated in Exhibit 46, provides a form of cost control in the sense of a checkup on operations by major types of expense, although it is really more of an explanation of causes of profits or losses than a tool of cost control.

Therefore, the most effective use of standard costs for purposes of cost control lies in detailed costing by jobs and processes.

Cost control under job costing. In many companies using job costing, both the actual costs and the standard costs of material, labor, and burden are computed for each job or product lot as it proceeds through the plant. Significant discrepancies between actual and standard cost at any production stage can thus be brought to the attention of operating people, so that corrective action can be taken.

To be sure, such disclosures are historical and cannot correct costs that have already been incurred. If reported quickly enough, however, they indicate operating conditions that are getting out of line in time to correct the situation on other work coming through. The objective, then, is to control the cost of operations and thus, indirectly, the cost of individual jobs.

Beyond this, prompt information when costs are out of line in the early stages of large jobs may lead to extra effort to reduce costs on remaining work, so that in total the work on these jobs may be produced within standard cost allowances. On all jobs, the knowledge that a step-by-step check on performance is in operation should in itself be a stimulus to keep performance up to standard.

Where one type of product consistently causes more trouble than another, summaries of jobs or lots will reveal this and arouse efforts to improve the performance of the troublemakers, or perhaps to change the standards on them, or to have the sales department shift its efforts to other products.

These differences between products would not be brought to light in the absence of detailed records, i.e., if records were kept only on costs by department or cost center and not by jobs or product lots.

Cost control under process costing. In situations where products are being made on a continuous-process basis, some companies believe that, since actual costs can be established relatively easily for such production, standard costing is not necessary in the accounting process, although it might be useful as a side computation for pricing purposes.

This is true if standard costs are thought of only as convenient substitutes for actual costs when the latter can be ascertained only with considerable difficulty or at a high clerical cost.

The fact is that in a typical process cost system both actual costs and standard costs can be established relatively easily, although a few problems may be faced in the allocation of joint costs. The use of standard costs along with actual costs provides measures of performance for control purposes that are lacking when actual costs only are provided.

Recording Standard Costs

In some cases, standard costs are developed as supplementary data, apart from the books of account. Standard cost cards or sheets are prepared for each product or representative products to be used for purposes of pricing and budgeting. To some extent, these are also used for cost control, but not for inventory valuation or profit determination, since standard costs are not brought into the accounting records.

Cost of Goods Sold Computed at Standard Cost

The least expensive, and least effective, standard cost system involving the books of account is one in which the only application of standard costs each month is to the units of product sold. Such a system does require the preparation of standard cost cards or sheets for each product or representative products, and a record of the number of units sold.

But, except for computing the cost of goods sold at standard cost, cost accounting is restricted to accounting for costs by type of expense for the company as a whole and possibly for its departments or cost centers.

To simplify such a system further, some companies combine the inventories of raw material, work-in-process, and finished goods into one account. Therefore, they do not have to bother to account for transfers among them.

The accounting process affecting this one inventory account is known in some quarters as "basket accounting." The beginning inventories, material purchases, labor costs, and other manufacturing expenses are all put into the inventory "basket." The units sold each month are costed at their standard cost and removed in total from the inventory account and charged to "Cost of Goods Sold." Thus the cost of goods sold figure appearing in the income statement is at standard cost.

The balance remaining in the inventory account, and as presented in the balance sheet, is a hodgepodge of inventories and accumulated variances between actual and standard costs. At the close of each six months a physical inventory is taken. Both the cost of goods sold and inventories are then costed at standard cost, and the accumulated figure for variances between actual and standard costs is removed from the inventory and charged or credited as a gain or loss.

An improvement on the system just described is illustrated in Exhibit 47. Here, separate inventories are maintained for raw material, work-in-process, and finished goods. Raw materials are transferred to

EXHIBIT 47
Standard Cost System Accounts

Work-in-Process

1. Beginning inventory established on the same basis as shown for the closing inventory under item 2 on the credit side of this account. 2. Actual cost of material put into production during the period. 3. Actual labor costs. 4. Burden absorbed by the application of burden rates.	1. Cost of goods manufactured. Computed by applying standard unit costs to the actual quantity of goods completed during the period. 2. Closing inventory established at the end of each six months or year by physical count priced at standard cost. Computed at the close of each month within the six months or year by subtracting the cost of goods manufactured (1 above) from the total of the debit entries.

1. Beginning inventory.
   The debit or credit balance remaining in the account after the above entries at the close of six months or year representing variances between actual and standard costs would be closed to Cost of Goods Sold or to Profit and Loss.

Finished Goods

1. Beginning inventory at standard cost. 2. Cost of goods manufactured at standard cost.	1. Cost of goods sold at standard cost. 2. Closing inventory at standard cost.

1. Beginning inventory at standard cost.

Cost of Goods Sold

1. Cost of goods sold at standard cost. Debit or credit also for cost variances at close of six months or year unless these are closed to profit and loss.	

"Work-in-Process" at their actual cost (FIFO, LIFO, or Average). Goods completed are transferred from "Work-in-Process" to "Finished Goods" to "Cost of Goods Sold" at their standard cost.

Variances are accumulated along with inventory in the work-in-process account and are closed out at the end of each six months when a physical inventory is taken and costed at standard cost. In this system, burden is charged in "Work-in-Process" by the application of burden rates. The difference between the amount of burden absorbed in this way and the total actual cost of burden is closed out each month. The result is that the amount of accumulated variance between actual and standard costs is not as large as in the system previously described.

Nonetheless, one of the weaknesses of both of these systems is that monthly results may appear to be satisfactory, whereas serious

EXHIBIT 48
Standard Cost System Accounts

Work-in-Process

1. Beginning inventory at standard cost.	1. Closing inventory at standard cost.
2. Actual cost of material put into production during the period.	2. Cost of goods manufactured. Computed by subtracting the closing inventory at standard cost from the total of the debit entries.
3. Actual labor costs.	
4. Burden absorbed by the application of burden rates.	
1. Beginning inventory at standard cost.	

Finished Goods

1. Beginning inventory at standard cost.	1. Closing inventory at standard cost.
2. Cost of goods completed during the period as found by deduction in the work-in-process account above.	2. Cost of goods sold. Computed by subtracting the closing inventory at standard cost from the total of the debit entries.
1. Beginning inventory at standard cost.	

Cost of Goods Sold

1. Cost of goods sold computed as indicated in the finished goods account above.	

losses may be building up which will not be revealed until the close of the current six-month period.

Inventories Computed at Standard Cost

Another type of relatively inexpensive standard cost system is one in which inventories at the close of each month, established by physical count or by records of physical quantities, are costed by standard costs, while costs that are not thus impounded flow on to become the cost of goods sold. Such a system is illustrated in Exhibit 48.

Typically, under such a system, there is no detailed accounting for the actual costs of products other than for the raw materials entering production. This procedure has the advantage of simplicity.

However, its weaknesses are that the actual cost of individual products or product lots is unknown, and the cost of goods sold has buried in it cost variances on goods which have not yet been sold. That is, it includes all the variances incurred during the period, whether or not they are in fact applicable to the specific goods sold during that period.

In fairness, it should be admitted that under a system of this type inventories are stated in the balance sheet on a rational basis; that is, provided standard costs have been kept reasonably up to date. Net income computed each month is not likely to be distorted as under the two systems previously described.

Furthermore, costs can be controlled by type of expense, by area of responsibility, in major respects without undertaking product costing. The decision to go beyond this and account for both the actual and standard cost of products should be dependent on whether the incremental information and cost control to be gained would thereby be considered worth the incremental cost of the accounting involved.

Combined Approaches

In a really complete standard cost system, in which all products are accounted for at both actual and standard costs under either job costing or process costing, it is possible to combine the approaches illustrated in Exhibit 47 and Exhibit 48.

Thus the cost of goods produced, the cost of goods sold, and inventories can all be costed at standard cost, and variances between actual and standard costs are presented in the income statement in arriving at net income each month as illustrated in Exhibit 46.

Of course, the analyses of and comparisons between actual cost and standard costs by jobs or processes are made apart from the books of account, in connection with the control of operations.

CHAPTER 23

Variance Analysis

The extent to which the causes of variances between actual and standard costs are established is governed by the amount of time, effort, and money that a company is willing to spend in accumulating data as variances take place. It is relatively simple and inexpensive to establish variances by major causes. However, the more detailed the accounting for causes becomes, the more expensive the accounting procedure is.

One of the difficulties in deciding how far to go in this connection is that certain information considered highly desirable at one time may not be so important or useful at another. Furthermore, it is not always possible to estimate in advance just how valuable a detailed analysis of variances by causes will prove to be.

It is important to remember, however, that unless information on variances by causes is accumulated regularly and consistently in some detail, it is either impossible or too costly to assemble the detail at a later date. When in doubt, therefore, it is best to lean toward collecting data in greater detail than may seem to be really necessary.

Establishing detailed information on variances by causes involves the time of operating people as well as of accounting clerks. Operating people are on the spot as variances take place, since they are often required to record the events involved such as downtime or spoilage and to explain why the variances took place.

This sometimes results in conflicts. People at the operating level blame the accounting system or the accounting department for red tape. At the same time, managers above them are demanding detailed information on operating results.

It should be borne in mind that an accounting system, like a machine used in production, can turn out in a finished product only such material as is fed into it. The form of the material will be changed by the process or system in use, but the content is established at the point of input.

Analysis of Variances for Material, Labor, and Burden Costs

Under a system of job costing where standard costs for the materials to be used and the operations to be performed on a product have been established in detail, it is possible to match standard costs against actual costs as work takes place and to analyze the variances between them as to causes. This is considered to be particularly helpful in the control of material and labor costs.

Nothing, of course, can be done about the actual costs that have taken place, other than to berate those responsible for unfavorable figures and to congratulate those whose performance is to their credit. The point is that such checks help to spot operating areas needing correction, so that work coming along will be handled within standards. Moreover, the constant knowledge that actual costs are to be checked against standards is considered to have a salutary effect on performance.

Under a system of process costing utilizing standard costs, variances between actual and standard costs are established at each of the process points for which costs are accumulated, for the time period covered by process cost sheets. Such sheets have to be prepared monthly for use in the preparation of monthly income statements. From a control point of view, they should also be prepared daily and weekly, so that variances from standard, particularly on material and labor costs, can be noted and action taken to correct the operating situation without delay.

Conceptually, the analysis of variances by jobs, processes, and departments or cost centers is much the same. To simplify the discussion, I shall illustrate the analysis of variances for material, labor, and burden costs through an assumed process involving the manufacture of only one type of product.

Material Cost Variances

Since the cost of material in a product is based on the two factors quantity and price, the actual cost can differ from the standard in two respects: 1. because the actual price of the material used differed from its standard; and 2. because either a larger or smaller quantity of material was used than called for, or a better or poorer yield than standard was realized from the material used. The total material cost variance is thus a combination of a price and quantity variance. Computation of these variances may be illustrated as follows:

Assumed standard specifications and costs:

1.	100 pounds of raw material input	100
2.	At a standard cost of $1.60 per pound	× $1.60
3.	Should produce 80 pounds of product	80/$160.00
4.	At a standard cost of $2 per lb. of finished product	$2.00

Assumed actual results for the period:

1. 200,000 pounds of raw material input
2. At an actual cost of $340,000
3. Resulting in the production of 165,000 lb. of finished product

Computation of total material variance:

Actual cost of raw material input	$340,000
Standard material cost of finished product	
output (165,000 lb. × $2)	330,000
Total material variance (loss)	$ 10,000

Computation of material price variance:

Actual cost of raw material input	$340,000
Standard cost of raw material input	
(200,000 lb. × $1.60)	320,000
Material price variance (loss)	$ 20,000

Computation of material quantity variance:

Standard cost of raw material input	$320,000
Standard material cost of finished product output	330,000
Material quantity variance (gain)	$ 10,000

Summary:

Material price variance (loss)	$ 20,000
Material quantity variance (gain)	10,000
Total material variance (loss)	$ 10,000

Total material variance.   This variance shown first in the foregoing
example is the difference between the actual cost of the actual quantity
of material entering the process and the standard cost (or what some
call the "standard value") of the actual quantity of goods produced. The
summary of the material price variance and the material quantity variance at the close of the example is simply a check on the $10,000 total
material variance computed earlier.

Material price variance.   This variance represents the difference between the price paid for materials and a predetermined standard cost
for them. In the foregoing example, the loss of $20,000 shown could
also be computed as follows: The actual cost of the material used was
$1.70 per pound compared with the standard cost of $1.60 per pound.
The price variance was therefore a higher cost of 10 cents per pound ×
200,000 input pounds, or $20,000 (loss).

Timing of a material price gain or loss.   In the example just given, the
material price variance was computed for the period in which material
entered production. Under such a practice, materials enter the accounting records at actual cost as of the time of purchase, and they are
carried in inventory at actual cost until used in production.
  This practice makes it possible to establish the actual cost, as well
as standard cost of materials used for specific products or product lines.
Thereby, it is possible to compute material price variances on them
under a complete standard cost system of job or process costing.
  Such a procedure does involve a considerable amount of clerical
work in maintaining perpetual inventory records for actual costs as
well as quantities; in recording in detail the actual cost of materials
issued to production; and in computing material price variances by job,
batch, or daily run.
  In many companies, the price variance is computed at the time
each lot of materials is purchased. Thus the raw material inventory is
charged at standard cost and a material purchase price variance account is debited or credited for the amount of the variance. At the close
of the month, the net accumulation of price variances is treated as an
operating gain or loss for the period.
  Where purchases are not on a hand-to-mouth basis and thus
closely allied to production and sales volume, purchase price variances
when taken as gains or losses for the month of purchase can cause
distortions in the operating results reported. In recognition of this, in
many companies where the material price variance is separated at the
time of purchase, the accumulated variance at the close of a period is

apportioned between the cost of goods sold for the period and the ending inventories in proportion to the estimated amount of standard material cost in each.

The aim here, of course, is to have both the ending inventories and the cost of goods sold reported at an approximation of actual cost as far as material content is concerned.

The separation of the material price variance at the time of purchase simplifies detailed record keeping under a perpetual inventory system. The reason for this is that the records can then be kept in terms of quantities only, with the standard-unit cost for each item indicated in an appropriate spot on the inventory card.

In situations where materials are issued to production in lots of standard amounts, it is possible to use printed specification forms or pre-punched tabulating cards. This procedure saves the clerical work otherwise involved in making out and computing costs on material requisitions.

Even if materials are not issued in standard amounts, segregating the price variance at the time of purchase not only saves clerical effort in keeping inventory records, but it also avoids having to account for the material price variance on each job, batch, or daily run of product. At the same time, however, such a procedure makes it impossible to determine the exact actual material cost of any given job, batch, or run of product. An approximation can however be made at any time by applying costs from current invoices to the quantities called for under standard product specifications.

Accounting for the material price variance at the time of purchase is clearly the less expensive of the two procedures described. The decision whether to delay computing the material price variance until material enters production is largely dependent on whether or not it is believed that the information on actual costs and material price variances by job, batch, or run of product is worth the clerical cost to have it.

Material quantity variance.   The quantity or yield variance ($10,000 gain) in the foregoing illustration was, of course, found by deduction. That is, it was simply the difference between the standard cost of the material that entered production for the period under consideration and the standard cost (or standard value) of the pounds of finished product produced from the material.

The same result could have been computed as follows: 200,000 pounds of raw material input, at a standard yield factor of 80%, should have resulted in 160,000 pounds of finished product. The actual output was 165,000 pounds. The gain of 5,000 pounds × $2.00 standard cost (or standard value) per pound shows a material quantity variance of $10,000 gain.

The computation of such a figure, and its inclusion as a separate item in the income statement, is helpful to an understanding of the financial results for the period, but it does not indicate the cause of the variance. If the variance were significant in amount, one would wish to know where to turn to do something about it with respect to the future.

For example, if it were found that the favorable quantity variance in the present case was the result of the use of a better quality of raw material than normal, it might be decided to continue to buy the higher grade. Then again, if it were found that a given supplier consistently supplied higher quality material than others of a supposedly standard grade, it might be decided to continue to buy from the same supplier.

In the foregoing illustration, we note that there was an unfavorable price variance of $20,000. If this were due to the fact that a better grade of raw material than standard had been used, it could be that a premium of $20,000 had been paid to get a $10,000 better yield. Obviously, this is a policy which should not be continued unless it were to result in a superior product which could command a sufficiently better price than normal or which could hold a market that might otherwise be lost.

A material quantity variance can arise in this, and other cases, from a variety of causes other than the quality of the raw material used. For example, spoilage or yield may be greater or less than normally expected because either men or machines are not operating at standard efficiency. Indeed, when men or machines are more efficient than normal, in the sense of producing more work per hour, it is quite likely that the percentage of spoilage will increase and cause an unfavorable material quantity variance.

It is important to remember that unless records are built up of spoilage by cause as it takes place — and in process industries of yields per hour, day, and week, with explanations when yields are out of line — it will not be possible for management to know where to take action to overcome material quantity variances from day to day. Nor will it be possible to summarize material quantity variances by cause, by months or longer periods, as explanations of operating results or indicators of trouble spots to which major attention should be given.

EXHIBIT 49
Material Costs — Actual Measured Against Standard

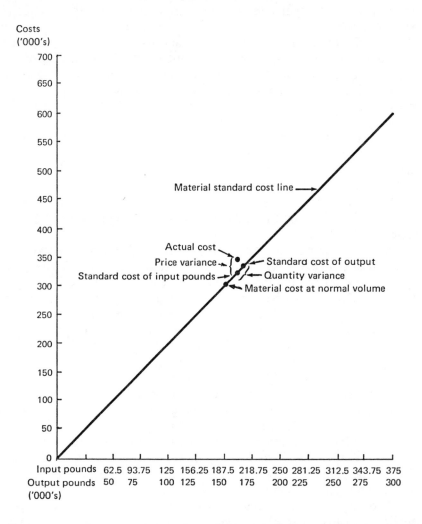

Illustration of material cost variances. A diagram illustrating the variances we have been examining is presented in Exhibit 49. Most actual situations are too complicated to permit the use of such diagrams for analytical purposes. But they are useful for educational purposes when relatively simple figures are involved, as in the present case.

Direct Labor Cost Variances

Since the direct labor cost of a product is based on the two factors price and quantity, the actual labor cost of a product can differ from its standard cost in two respects: because the actual rates of pay differ from standard; and because more or less time than standard has been taken to make it. Also, the yield or spoilage may differ from standard as another factor causing a quantity variance.

The total labor cost variance is thus a combination of a price and a quantity or efficiency variance. The steps involved in computing these variances, also quite similar to those shown in the earlier illustration of material variances, may be illustrated as follows:

Assumed standard specifications and costs:

1. Standard labor costs are computed for the same product units as the standard material costs in the earlier illustration — namely, 100 lb. of raw material having a standard yield of 80 lb. of finished product.
2. To convert 100 lb. of raw material into 80 lb. of finished product should require 32 hr. of direct labor   32
3. At a standard direct labor rate of $4.20 per hr.   × $4.20
4. Resulting in a standard direct labor cost of $134.40   80/$134.40
5. And a standard direct labor cost per finished lb. of $1.68 $ 1.68
6. Standard minutes per finished lb. (32 hr. × 60 min. ÷ 80 lb.)   24 min.

Assumed actual results for the period:

1. 200,000 lb. of raw material put into production
2. Resulting in 165,000 lb. of finished product
3. Actual direct labor hours worked: 64,500 hr.
4. Actual direct labor cost: $277,350.
5. To simplify the present illustration, it is assumed that each unit of product is fully completed by the end of the period and, therefore, that there are no beginning or ending goods in process partially completed, the degree of completion of which would otherwise have to be taken into account.

Computation of total direct labor variance:

Actual direct labor cost input	$277,350
Standard labor cost of finished product output (165,000 lb. × $1.68)	277,200
Total direct labor variance (loss)	$ 150

Computation of direct labor price variance:

Actual direct labor cost input	$277,350
Standard labor cost of hours worked (64,500 hr. × $4.20)	270,900
Direct labor price variance (loss)	$ 6,450

Computation of direct labor quantity, or efficiency, variance:

Standard cost of hours worked	$270,900
Standard labor cost of finished product output (165,000 lb. × $1.68)	277,200
Direct labor quantity, or efficiency, variance (gain)	$ 6,300

Summary

Direct labor price variance (loss)	$ 6,450
Direct labor quantity, or efficiency, variance (gain)	6,300
Total direct labor variance (loss)	$ 150

As can be seen in the first computation, the total direct labor variance between the actual direct labor cost of $277,350 and the standard direct labor cost of goods produced during the period, $277,200, amounted to a small loss of $150. If the analysis stopped here, one could assume that the labor cost for the period had approximated standard expectations.

Further analysis shows, however, that there was an unfavorable price variance of $6,450 offset for the most part by a favorable quantity or efficiency variance of $6,300 to arrive at the total or net direct labor variance of $150. These two variances were of sufficient size to warrant management attention, and thus the additional analysis involved was certainly justified.

Direct labor price variance. The price variance here could result from a number of different causes. But, as we noted in connection with material variances, unless detailed variances by cause are recorded during the period, it is likely to be impossible at the end of the period to determine the exact causes of the variance.

The reader will note that the average rate per hour for the actual direct labor costs was $4.30 ($277,350 ÷ 64,500 hr.) compared with the standard rate of $4.20 per hour. This variance of $0.10 per hour might simply be the result of a blanket wage increase of this amount without a corresponding adjustment in the standard costs.

However, other possible causes might be extra pay for overtime which was not accounted for separately as such, the use of more expensive grades of help than called for in the standards, or extra allowances granted for nonstandard operating conditions.

In fact, there might be a long list of variances by causes if it were considered desirable to account for these matters in detail. However, if the company has various safeguards for controlling price variances, or if the price factor is beyond the control of the operating people at the point of expenditure, knowledge of the total price variance only might be sufficient. It could then be isolated before computing controllable variances or used to advantage when interpreting the net operating income for the period.

Direct labor quantity variance. After having eliminated the price variance, the remaining difference between the total actual direct labor cost for the period and the standard cost of the good units produced is, of course, the result of quantitative factors.

Here, as noted for other variances, it is difficult if not impossible to determine the amount of quantity of efficiency variance by specific causes unless detailed records of variance by cause have been maintained during the period. Even without such detailed records, however, the direct labor quantity variance can often be broken down to major aspects of speed and yield or spoilage.

That is, direct labor quantity variance arises partly because men or machines work faster or slower than standard and partly because the yield or spoilage of product is greater or less than standard. Such a breakdown of the variance will be illustrated shortly for the reader who wishes to explore variance analysis in somewhat greater depth.

The quantity variance can be computed in terms of direct labor hours as follows:

1. 165,000 lb. × 24 min. ÷ 60 = 66,000 earned hours
2. 66,000 earned hours − 64,500 actual hours = 1,500 hours gained
3. 1,500 hours gained × $4.20 per hr. = $6,300 quantity variance

Quantity variance at standard vs. actual costs.   Some people enjoy debating whether labor hours gained or lost should be costed at standard or at actual cost per hour. This is sometimes called "the gray area" in variance analysis.

As a practical matter, computing and removing the price variance as the first step simplifies variance analysis, whether for the costs of labor, material, or factory burden. Moreover, assuming that standard costs are kept reasonably up to date, the difference between the quantity variance for labor computed at current actual cost per hour versus standard cost per hour is not likely to be great enough to change in any respect any corrective action taken relative to the variance.

For these reasons alone, I favor the costing of labor hours gained or lost at standard cost.

Illustration of direct labor variances.   A diagram illustrating the labor variances we have been discussing is presented in Exhibit 50. For this purpose, labor hours, rather than pounds, have been used as a measure of volume.

Burden Cost Variances

Although burden cost is based on the same two factors — price and quantity — as are material and labor costs, the resultant variances are considerably more involved unless one is content with only a broad-brush analysis. The quantity variance for burden is similar in character to that for direct labor.

But what is called a "price variance" in the case of material and labor costs is a much more complicated variance in the case of burden. The reason for this is that it involves factors of volume and of efficiency in spending, as well as price.

Moreover, burden is composed of a variety of costs such as supervision, indirect labor, supplies, maintenance and repairs, heat, light and power, and depreciation. These burden costs are obviously less homogeneous than material costs or direct labor costs taken by themselves.

EXHIBIT 50
Labor Costs — Actual Measured Against Standard

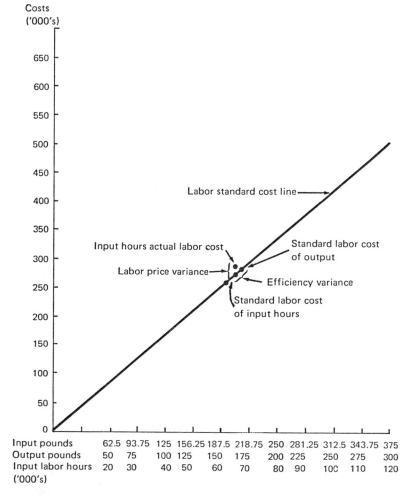

At the outset, I shall illustrate the computation of burden variances in the same manner as I used earlier in illustrating material and labor variances. Then later, I shall illustrate a somewhat more informative type of burden variance analysis. Consider:

Assumed standard specifications and costs:

1. Standard burden costs are computed for the same product units as standard material and labor costs — namely, 100 lb. of raw material having a standard yield of 80 lb. of finished product.

2. Standard burden is applied to products on a direct labor-hour basis at a rate of $8 per hr. computed as follows:
   a. Normal burden cost per period: $480,000
   b. Normal direct labor hours per period: 60,000 hr.
   c. Burden rate: Normal cost $480,000 ÷ normal hours 60,000 = $8 per hr.
3. To convert 100 lb. of raw material into 80 lb. of finished product should require 32 hr. of direct labor   32 hr.
4. At a standard burden cost of $8 per hr.   × $8
5. Results in a burden cost of $256   80/$256
6. And a standard cost per finished lb. of $3.20 $3.20

Assumed actual results for the period:

1. 200,000 lb. of raw material put into production
2. Resulting in 165,000 lb. of finished product
3. Actual direct labor hours worked: 64,500
4. Actual burden cost: $504,650
5. All units of product assumed to be fully completed, and it is assumed that there are no beginning or ending inventories of goods in process for the accounting period under consideration.

Computation of total burden variance:

Actual burden cost for the period	$504,650
Standard burden cost of finished product	
output (165,000 lb. × $3.20)	528,000
Total burden variance (gain)	$ 23,350

Computation of combined price, spending, and volume burden variance (representing the difference between the actual burden cost for the period and the burden absorbed on the basis of the actual hours worked):

Actual burden for the period	$504,650
Standard burden cost of hours worked	
(64,500 hr. × $8)	516,000
Combined price, spending, and volume burden variance (gain)	$ 11,350

Computation of burden quantity or efficiency variance:

Standard burden cost of hours worked	$516,000
Standard burden cost of finished product	
output (165,000 lb. × $3.20)	528,000
Burden quantity or efficiency variance (gain)	$ 12,000

Summary:

Burden combined price, spending, and volume	
variance (gain)	$11,350
Burden quantity or efficiency variance (gain)	12,000
Total burden variance (gain)	$ 23,350

Total burden variance. As can be seen in the first computation, the total burden variance is the difference between the actual burden cost for the period and the amount of burden absorbed by the good units of product produced during the period. This variance is often shown in an internal income statement as a separate item under the title "Burden Over- or Underabsorbed."

For the current period in our illustration, the total burden variance was a gain and thus represented burden overabsorbed. This means simply that the standard cost (or what some call the "standard value") of the goods produced during the period was in excess of the actual burden cost for the period.

Burden price variance. As mentioned earlier, the figure computed in the same manner as the price variances for material and direct labor costs is not only a price variance but contains spending and volume variances as well, a matter which I shall discuss shortly.

Burden quantity variance. This variance is a reflection of the material and labor quantity variances. For example, we noted with respect to the labor quantity variance that 165,000 pounds of output could be expressed as 66,000 "hours-worth" of direct labor. Since only 64,500 hours of labor were expended, there was a gain of 1,500 hours.

So too, with respect to burden. The same 1,500 labor hours multiplied by the standard burden cost of $8 shows the quantity variance to be $12,000 (gain), which is the same as computed in the foregoing illustration. Later, I shall break this variance down to its speed and yield factors. But, for the moment, let us be content to have the single figure of $12,000 (gain) for the quantity variance.

Burden costs combining use of variable budget.   In a later chapter, we shall examine the variable budget, but I wish also to bring it into the discussion at the moment for its use in variance analysis.

Briefly, a variable budget provides the means for knowing in advance what the cost should be, by individual items and in total, for a given department or other organizational unit for a stated length of time at any volume within the practical range of operations for that unit. This is in contrast to the ordinary or fixed budget which shows, so far as costs are concerned, what the costs should be, individually and in total, for a given department or other organizational unit for a stated period of time at a stated volume of operations.

In essence, the variable budget tells what costs should be for any volume of operations likely to be experienced, while the ordinary or fixed budget tells what the costs should be for one given volume of operations.

The variable budget, known also as the flexible budget, may be stated as a formula, shown as a graph, or presented as a table of cost allowances. We shall make use of both a formula and a graph in our examination. We shall break down burden to its major components of fixed and variable costs, but to simplify matters, we shall not attempt at this point to carry the analysis to individual types of expense within these two broad categories.

By fixed costs we mean costs which are, or should be, essentially fixed in amount each period regardless of the volume of operations. Depreciation, real estate taxes, and insurance are examples of such costs.

By variable costs we mean costs which are subject to change with a change in the volume of operations. Supplies, repairs, and power are examples of such costs. We shall assume in our example that the total amount of variable costs each period is expected to change directly in proportion to a change in the volume of operations.

Variable budget formula.   Among the figures with which we were dealing, the normal burden cost per period was shown as $480,000. Let us now assume that this consists of $288,000 of fixed costs and $192,000 of variable costs.

We shall assume further that direct labor hours worked, i.e., input labor hours, represent a suitable measuring stick of the volume of activity and, therefore, that total variable costs should rise or fall from period to period in proportion to changes in hours worked.

As we just noted, variable costs are assumed to be $192,000 for a normal period, and reference to the figures in the foregoing illustration shows the normal direct labor hours for such a period to be 60,000. Thus dividing the dollars by the hours shows variable costs per hour to be $3.20.

Combining the knowledge of expected fixed costs per period with the knowledge of expected variable costs per direct labor hour provides a formula for determining the total expected burden costs for any given period for which the direct labor hours are known. This formula is one form of a variable budget and in our example would be computed as follows:

$288,000 of fixed costs + ($3.20 variable costs per hour × labor hours)

Thus in the present illustration where the actual labor hours were 64,500, one would have expected the total burden costs to have been $494,400 computed as follows:

$288,000 fixed costs + ($3.20 variable costs per hr. × 64,500 hours)
$288,000 fixed costs + $206,400 variable costs = $494,400 total costs

Let us now work these figures into our variance analysis.

Burden price and spending variance. In order to break the burden variances down to their fixed and variable components in addition to their totals, we shall assume that the actual costs of $504,650 consisted of $291,000 fixed costs and $213,650 variable costs. The computation of the burden price and spending variance is then as follows:

	Fixed Costs	Variable Costs	Total
Actual burden cost for the period	$291,000	$213,650	$504,650
Burden variable budget allowance	288,000	206,400	494,400
Burden price and spending variance	$3,000 loss	$7,250 loss	$10,250 loss

This loss of $10,250 is quite a contrast to the $11,350 gain previously computed where the analysis combined the volume variance with the price and spending variance. The introduction of the variable budget allowance enables the separation of the variance, first to its price and spending component, and then, as we shall see in a moment, to its volume component.

It might appear that fixed costs, by definition, should remain fixed and therefore that there should be no variances connected with them. The term fixed costs as used in variable budgeting, however, means costs that are fixed relative to changes in the volume of activity from period to period. In our example, these costs are expected to remain at $288,000 per period whether or not the volume of activity, as measured here by input labor hours, differs from the normal operation of 60,000 hours.

The budgeted figure of $288,000 per period is a predetermined figure which is likely to remain in use for a year. As actual periods go by, the cost of items such as insurance is likely to change somewhat from the figure estimated for it in the budget, hence the price or spending variance, which in our example amounted to a loss of $3,000 for the given period.

Variable costs, in contrast to fixed costs, are expected to vary as the volume of activity changes, and, in our example, are expected to change in total directly in proportion to changes in volume as measured by input labor hours. They failed to do this, however, for the given period and showed a loss here of $7,250.

Computing these losses, as we have, can be helpful in explaining the financial results of the period, but sufficient detail is not available for use in correcting the situation so that losses will not continue. For the latter purpose, the variable budget broken down by type of expense, for each department or cost center, is particularly helpful and will be discussed later in the chapters on budgeting.

To the extent that the price and spending variance can be determined to represent price increases beyond the control of those who have incurred the expenses, they would not be held accountable. They would however be held accountable otherwise for having spent more than warranted by the budget.

Burden volume variance. A burden volume variance gain occurred in this period because the volume of operations, as measured by the 64,500 actual direct labor hours, was 4,500 hours above the normal hours of 60,000 per period. If the normal hours are in fact the average hours to be expected per period, then, over time, volume variance gains and losses should balance out.

The monetary amount of the burden volume variance is based on the standard fixed costs per unit for whatever unit is used to measure volume of activity. In our example, volume of activity is measured by input labor hours. Fixed costs are assumed to be $288,000 per period, and normal labor hours to be 60,000, which means that the standard fixed costs per hour are $4.80. The monetary amount of the burden volume variance in our example would therefore be 4,500 hours × $4.80 = $21,600 gain.

The analysis can also be computed as the difference between the standard burden cost of the 64,500 hours worked and the burden variable budget allowance for this same number of hours as follows:

	Fixed Costs	Variable Costs	Total
Burden variable budget allowance	$288,000	$206,400	$494,400
Standard burden cost of hours worked	309,600	206,400	516,000
Burden volume variance	$21,600 gain	0	$21,600 gain

Note that the volume variance has to do entirely with fixed costs. One way of looking at this is to picture the period as having been charged $8 per hour for operating time spent involving the use of facilities and expenses identified as burden costs. Of this, $4.80 per hour is for fixed costs, and $3.20 for variable costs. The variable budget allowance and standard cost of hours worked are identical for variable costs, both being based on 64,500 hours worked at $3.20 per hour. The variable budget allowance for fixed costs is, however, set at $288,000 per period regardless of the number of hours operated, whereas the standard cost of hours worked for fixed costs is based on the 64,500 hours worked at $4.80 per hour.

The 64,500 hours was 4,500 hours greater than the normal volume of 60,000 hours on which the standard cost per hour of $4.80 was based. Where this is a volume gain, as in this case, the period is said to have "overabsorbed" its fixed costs. In a period when the volume of activity was below 60,000 hours there would be an unfavorable volume variance and the period would be said to have "underabsorbed" its fixed costs. In time, if the hours operated have averaged the projected 60,000 per period the "overabsorbed" and "underabsorbed" fixed costs will balance out.

Accountability for a volume variance depends on the facts in each case, including the fact that the estimated normal hours of operation may have been a poor estimate. An unfavorable variance, for example, might result from unfavorable general business conditions over which no one in the company had any control. There could be a number of reasons, such as failure on the part of the sales organization to meet budgeted sales quotas, or a shutdown of some part of the plant because of inadequate preventive maintenance by production people. In general, however, as far as the production organization is concerned, volume variances are not subject to the degree of responsibility or control as either spending variances or efficiency variances.

Burden quantity or efficiency variance. Though the production organization might, or might not, be held accountable for such volume
variances as take place, it should be held accountable for the efficiency
of time spent. In our example, this means that since they put in 64,500
labor hours the operating people are expected to show 64,500 hours-
worth of product coming out. As we know from the earlier computations, they actually produced 66,000 hours-worth of product. Thus
they had a favorable quantity or efficiency variance of 1,500 hours.
Since the standard burden cost here is $8 per hour the quantity or
efficiency variance amounted to a gain of $12,000.

The analysis can also be computed as the difference between the
standard burden cost of the 64,500 hours worked and the standard
burden cost of hours-worth of goods produced as follows:

	Fixed Costs	Variable Costs	Total
Standard burden cost of hours worked	$309,600	$206,400	$516,000
Standard burden of goods produced	316,800	211,200	528,000
Burden quantity or efficiency variance	$7,200 gain	$4,800 gain	$12,000 gain

Total burden variance. With the introduction of the variable budget
allowance in our calculations the variances may be summarized as
follows:

Burden price and spending variance (loss)	$10,250
Burden volume variance (gain)	21,600
Burden quantity or efficiency variance (gain)	12,000
Total burden variance (gain)	$23,350

The total burden variance can also be computed as the difference
between the actual burden costs for the period and the standard burden
cost valuation of the goods produced as follows:

	Fixed Costs	Variable Costs	Total
Actual burden costs	$291,000	$213,650	$504,650
Standard burden cost of goods produced	316,800	211,200	528,000
Total burden variance	$25,800 gain	$2,450 loss	$23,350 gain

EXHIBIT 51

Burden Costs — Actual Measured Against Variable Budget and
Standard

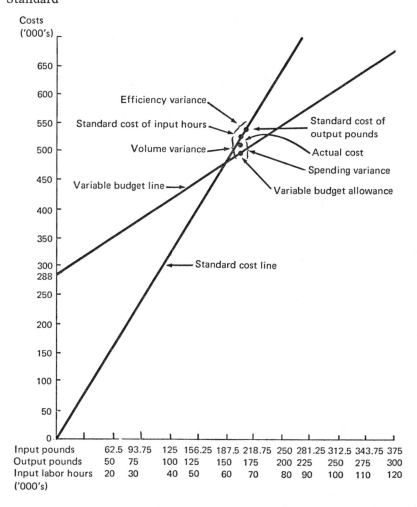

Illustration of burden cost variances. A diagram illustrating burden
cost variances is presented in Exhibit 51. Note that the variable budget
line combines fixed and variable costs. Note also that the standard cost
line and the variable budget line meet at 60,000 hours of volume,
which is considered to be the normal volume of operations. Above this
point, fixed burden costs are overabsorbed, while below it they are
underabsorbed until at zero volume the underabsorbed burden is, of
course, exactly equal to the fixed costs.

Refinements of Variance Analysis

The material I have been discussing up to this point covers the basics of variance analysis. If the reader wishes to go further, here are a few additional points which I shall now discuss.

Price Variances by Type of Material and Mix Variances

Many products call for the use of more than one type of raw material. Thus it is often considered desirable to establish a separate price variance for each major type of material used. When more than one raw material is used, it is also possible in many instances to vary somewhat the relative quantities of each of the materials used. This results in a mix variance in addition to the material price and quantity variances already discussed.

A mix variance is often found in situations a. where a given mix or batch of materials is supposed to meet certain chemical or physical specifications or characteristics, but b. where factors such as temperature, humidity, and minor variations in the materials used either require or allow a somewhat different combination of materials than called for under the assumed normal specifications.

In the manufacture of woolen textiles, for example, where various types of wool are combined to obtain a desired end result, it is often possible to produce a cloth that will meet standard specifications from a blend which differs from the normal combination of wools. Where this is done, the aim is of course to produce the desired quality of cloth from a cheaper blend of wools.

There are, however, many situations in which a change in the mix of raw materials may affect the yield of finished product. Where this is the case, care must be taken that efforts aimed at achieving favorable mix variances are not more than offset by unfavorable yield variances.

One way of keeping price, mix, and quantity or yield variances separate in the mind is to think of the functions of buying, mixing, and producing as being carried out by three different individuals.

The buyer tries to buy materials at or better than standard prices established for them. Price variances indicate how close he actually came to meeting these goals, even though such variances are often not within his control. The mixer is furnished with materials at their standard cost. He mixes them so as to at least match the standard mix and even better to come out with some gain. The producer then takes the mixed material at its standard cost as a mixture and attempts to produce goods at minimally the standard yield and within the standard time allowed.

To illustrate the development of a separate price variance for each of several types of material used, as well as a mix variance, the illustration presented earlier will be expanded as follows:

Assumed standard specifications and costs:

1. 60 lb of material A at a standard cost of $1.50 per lb.	$ 90
30 lb of material B at a standard cost of $1.80 per lb.	54
10 lb. of material C at a standard cost of $1.60 per lb.	16
2. 100 lb. mixed having a standard cost of $1.60 per lb.	$160
3. With a standard yield of 80% should produce 80 lb. of product	
4. At a standard cost of $2 per lb. of finished product	

Assumed actual results for the period:

1. 200,000 lb. of raw material have been used consisting of:	
105,000 lb. of material A at an actual cost of $1.60 per lb.	$168,000
70,000 lb. of material B at an actual cost of $1.85 per lb.	129,500
25,000 lb. of material C at an actual cost of $1.70 per lb.	42,500
200,000 lb.	$340,000
2. Actual output: 165,000 lb.	

Computation of material price variance by type of material and in total:

	Quantity	Actual Cost	Standard Cost	Variance Analysis
Material A	105,000 lb. at $1.60 =	$168,000 at $1.50 =	$157,500	$10,500*
Material B	70,000 lb. at $1.85 =	129,500 at $1.80 =	126,000	3,500*
Material C	25,000 lb. at $1.70 =	42,500 at $1.60 =	40,000	2,500*
Total	200,000 lb.	$340,000	$323,500	$16,500*

*Loss

Computation of material mix variance:

	Actual Quantity Used, Pounds	Standard Formula for 200,000 lb. Input, Pounds	Difference Pounds	Standard Cost Per lb.	Material Mix Variance
Material A	105,000	120,000	15,000	$1.50	$22,500
Material B	70,000	60,000	10,000*	1.80	18,000*
Material C	25,000	20,000	5,000*	1.60	8,000*
Total	200,000	200,000	- 0 -		$ 3,500*

*Loss

Apparently it had been found necessary in the period under consideration to use a richer mixture than normal, i.e., one having a higher proportion of more expensive materials.

Combined material price and mix variance:

Material price variance (loss)	$16,500
Material mix variance (loss)	3,500
Combined variance (loss)	$20,000

The reader will note that the combined price and mix variance of $20,000 is the same figure shown as a price variance alone in the earlier example.

Direct Labor Time and Yield or Spoilage Variances

In an earlier illustration, a quantity variance in direct labor costs was shown as follows:

Standard labor cost of hours worked	
(64,500 hr. × $4.20)	$270,900
Standard labor cost of finished product output	
(165,000 lb. × $1.68)	277,200
Direct labor quantity, or efficiency, variance (gain)	$ 6,300

If the situation were such that direct labor normally had to be applied in proportion to the pounds of raw material handled, regardless of the yield of good product from that material, the quantity variance could be broken down to time and yield or spoilage variances, illustrated as follows. (The reader will recall that 200,000 lb. entered production; the normal processing time is 32 hr. of direct labor per 100 lb.; the standard yield is 80%; the actual hours spent were 64,500; and 165,000 lb. of product were produced):

Standard labor cost of hours worked	
(64,500 hr. × $4.20)	$270,900
Standard labor cost to process 200,000 lb.	268,800*
Time variance (loss)	$ 2,100

*200,000 lb. ÷ 100 × 32 hr. × $4.20 = $268,800

Another way to obtain this variance is to first compute the standard time to process 200,000 lb., which is 64,000 hr. Subtracting this from the actual time taken, 64,500 hrs., shows that 500 more hours than standard were expended. The 500 hr. × $4.20 per hour is the variance of $2,100.

After having eliminated the time variance, we can then find the yield or spoilage variance as follows:

Standard labor cost to process 200,000 lb.	$268,800
Standard labor cost of finished product output	277,200
Yield or spoilage variance (gain)	$ 8,400

As a check on this figure, the standard yield is 80% and, therefore, the expected output from 200,000 lb. is 160,000 lb. The actual output was 165,000 lb., thereby showing a gain in yield of 5,000 lb. The earlier figures showed the standard direct labor cost per pound to be $1.68. Thus 5,000 lb. × $1.68 = $8,400.

Summary:

Direct labor time variance (loss)	$2,100
Direct labor yield or spoilage variance (gain)	8,400
Direct labor quantity variance (gain)	$6,300

It would seem that breaking this total quantity variance down to its major components in this way would be worth the extra clerical work involved because it provides a much clearer picture of operating results.

Burden Time and Yield or Spoilage Variances

Earlier, the burden quantity variance was computed as being a $12,000 gain. This variance can be broken down to time and yield or spoilage variances, as in the case of the direct labor quantity variance.

Without repeating the details of analysis, we know from the labor cost analysis that 500 more hours than standard were required to process the incoming material. At a standard burden cost of $8 per hour, this represents a $4,000 unfavorable burden efficiency variance (with respect to utilization of time) for the period.

Similarly, we know from the earlier analysis that the yield was favorable for the period, showing a gain of 5,000 pounds, which at its standard burden cost of $3.20 per pound, amounted to a variance of $16,000 (gain).

Summary:

Burden time variance (loss)	$ 4,000
Burden yield or spoilage variance (gain)	16,000
Burden quantity variance (gain)	$12,000

Here, as in the case of direct labor, it would seem that the additional information just computed is worth the extra clerical work involved through its more complete explanation of operating results.

CHAPTER 24

Cost-Price-Volume Relationships

Knowledge of how costs are affected by changes in the volume of operations is important in planning and controlling business activities and in making decisions on a variety of problems. So too, for the same purposes, is knowledge of cost-price relationships for the given industry and company and of relationships between selling price and sales volume.

Many executives develop such understanding as a result of years of experience, rather than through formal studies involving technical aspects of accounting and statistics. There are, however, a few relatively simple techniques which are helpful in developing cost-volume relationships and which can easily be understood by anyone who might have occasion to use them.

In the present chapter, I shall deal largely with a. total costs and their fixed and variable components relative to changes in the volume of operations; and b. with profit analysis, break-even analysis, and marginal income analysis. In later chapters, I shall have more to say about cost-price-volume relationships with respect to individual products and with individual types of cost by department or cost center.

Quality Considerations

Cost, price, and volume are, of course, three of the major factors or variables determining the profitability of operations. Before considering these factors in some detail, it might be well to examine briefly a fourth major factor, that of quality. It is possible in studying the factors of cost, price, and volume to assume the factor of quality as fixed or given, and in fact we shall do this ourselves a little later.

Quality, however, is a factor affecting costs and is itself often determined by cost considerations; it influences and is influenced by the factors of volume and price and in the net has a decided effect on profits. In a practical business situation, therefore, quality should not be taken for granted.

The quality of a product is fixed by design and by specifications. Thus the selection of a particular quality can have a significant bearing on the price and sales volume which will be realized, as well as on costs and resulting profit.

In turn, maintenance of the selected quality through proper supervision, quality control, and inspection — and the control of costs through proper supervision, cost standards, and reports — are important in order to be able to satisfy the demand for this quality at available prices and to keep costs under control at satisfactory levels.

In situations where quality is a significant factor in relation to cost, price, and volume, it follows that if a company's profit situation is not satisfactory the quality factor, among others, merits investigation. For example, the volume of sales may be down because the quality of the product is not satisfactory.

On the one hand, this may be the result of poor design and specifications relative to competition or a failure to maintain quality. On the other hand, the quality of the product may be higher, with a correspondingly higher price, than the market is willing to support.

Allied with the pure quality factor there is also the matter of design in terms of style, taste, and utility which can have a bearing on cost, price, and volume. Redesign for product simplification, the use of alternative materials or manufacturing processes, and the standardization of parts used on more than one product can also affect cost, price, and volume.

While the foregoing matters are, for the most part, subjects of more immediate concern to designers, production supervisors, and salesmen, they are mentioned briefly here because changes in the design or quality of a product also represent a managerial alternative in attempting to correct a situation that is out of line with respect to costs or sales realization.

Historical Cost-Volume Relationships

The first step that many companies take in developing standards for their cost-volume relationships on a formal basis is to review their history of such relationships. To be sure, it is naive to assume that what has happened in the past is bound to happen again in the future, or that past cost-volume relationships necessarily represent the most desirable standards of such relationships.

Then again, it is equally naive to ignore experience. The least that can be said for experience is that it provides data against which standards proposed for the future may be checked, and departures from such experience should not be made without good reason.

The results of historical studies can always be tempered or adjusted by the introduction of a variety of assumptions to allow for current conditions or future expectations with respect to sales and production volumes, prices, and costs. Generally speaking, standards for these items should be changed when significant changes in conditions occur. But it is helpful if they can be developed and reviewed against a background of demonstrated performance as measured by historical records.

Practice varies as to the number of years of cost-volume history selected for study. Five years is a common figure, sometimes broken down by shorter periods within this span, although many companies have made studies over longer periods than this. The purpose has been to establish what could be regarded as representative relationships averaged out over time.

For such a purpose, it is often desirable to adjust historical figures by eliminating highly abnormal or nonrepetitive items of expense. This does not mean, of course, that abnormalities are not to be expected in the future. However, if a reliable base of normal experience can be established, the historical cost figures can be adjusted to allow for expected abnormalities in a particular future period or for abnormalities that have occurred during a period under review.

It must be granted that there are times when conditions have so changed that the cost-volume experience of previous years is markedly unsuitable as a guide in establishing cost-volume standards for current or future operations. Under such conditions, it is best to restrict the study of cost-volume relationships to a review by months for the most recent year or two or to deal only with projections of future expectations of these relationships.

Tabular Approach

Assuming that it is appropriate to study a company's cost-volume history, one procedure employed is to list all costs by type of expense for each year of the past five years. The amount of each cost is shown in one or the other of two columns. One column represents costs which

EXHIBIT 52

Examples of Development of Total Cost Standard: Five Years of Data

Year	Net Sales	Variable Costs	Fixed Costs	Total Costs
1	$ 9,000,000	$ 5,800,000	$ 2,000,000	$ 7,800,000
2	9,500,000	6,250,000	2,050,000	8,300,000
3	10,500,000	6,750,000	2,150,000	8,900,000
4	11,000,000	6,800,000	2,200,000	9,000,000
5	10,000,000	6,400,000	2,100,000	8,500,000
	$50,000,000	$32,000,000	$10,500,000	$42,500,000

Variable Cost %: $32,000,000 ÷ $50,000,000 = 64%
Fixed Cost: $10,500,000 ÷ 5 = $2,100,000
Total Cost Standard: $2,100,000 Fixed Cost + (64% X Net Sales) = Total Costs

Note: All numbers have been rounded.

vary significantly with changes in the volume of activity (variable costs). The other represents costs which tend to remain fixed regardless of changes in the volume of activity (fixed costs, or what some prefer to call "nonvariable costs"). Totals of these figures for each year are then brought together on a summary sheet, as illustrated in Exhibit 52.

It is recognized by those who make these arbitrary separations of fixed and variable costs that many of the costs listed as variable are actually semivariable. Some of the costs listed as fixed tend to vary somewhat with volume. Nonetheless, the designations of fixed and variable costs are considered to be close enough for the uses to be made of the data.

In establishing the relationship between total costs and changes in the volume of activity, a practical question arises as to what shall be taken as the measure of activity. Shall it be sales units? Sales dollars? Units produced? Labor hours or machine hours incurred? Or percentage of capacity operated?

Later, we shall note complications that arise in the analysis of results when a company's sales volume and production volume are quite different for a given period. For general purposes, however, we can assume that sales volume and production volume are the same at any given time. Or, in other words, that volume of activity can be expressed in terms either of sales or production, both of which would be measuring the same physical quantity of goods.

As a matter of fact, a more convenient measure of activity would be some physical common denominator such as pounds. However, since there are relatively few businesses in which such a common denominator exists, it is necessary for most companies to use a measure such as hours or dollars. For the present, let us assume that the measure of activity is to be net sales dollars, which at least have the virtue of being readily available.

The development of a total cost standard related to volume is illustrated in Exhibit 52. Here, the average percentage relationship of variable costs to net sales for the five-year period is computed by dividing total variable costs by total net sales; the result being 64% in this case. Again, the average fixed costs are found simply by dividing the total of fixed costs for the five years by 5; the result being $2,100,000 in this case.

Cost-Volume Formula

The company's period cost picture, or cost-volume relationship, can be stated as a formula, or cost standard, as follows:

Standard Fixed Cost Per Period + (Variable Cost % × Actual or Expected Net Sales for the Given Period) = Total Costs for the Given Period.

It should be expected that if, for example, the sales for a given year are $10,750,000 the total costs should be $8,980,000, computed as follows:

Fixed Costs of $2,100,000 + Variable Costs of (64% × $10,750,000) = Total Costs.

Therefore,

$2,100,000 Fixed Costs + $6,880,000 Variable Costs = $8,980,000 Total Costs.

Sales of $10,750,000 − $8,980,000 total costs shows the expected profit at this volume of sales to be $1,770,000. Incidentally, the costs illustrated in Exhibit 52 were intended to represent costs before income tax and, therefore, the expected profit just computed is before income tax.

Given a sales figure for a shorter period of time than one year the estimated fixed costs should, of course, be scaled down accordingly. But the same 64% for variable costs would be used in establishing the expected costs for such a period.

The cost-volume formula is most useful in forecasting or budgeting expected total costs and profit, given the expected sales for some period in the future. It is also useful for checking current results, or results of the past. However, this provides only a rough check on total figures, and it is no substitute for more detailed measures of performance.

Also, the formula is of use in connection with types of "what if" questions. For example, what would be the effect of a 5% increase in variable costs if fixed costs and selling prices were unchanged?

In this case, variable costs would become 67.2% of net sales. The contribution of each sales dollar toward the covering of fixed costs, and profit if any, would drop from $0.36 to $0.328. And sales volume would have to increase by almost 10% (actually 0.09753) for the company to be as well off as it was before the increase in variable costs took place.

I shall discuss the use of this formula in greater detail shortly in connection with marginal income analysis.

Regression Equation

What we have referred to as a cost-volume formula or total cost standard may be expressed in the form of a simple equation, $y = a + bx$, in which y represents total costs, a fixed costs, b a per cent or fraction, and x net sales. Having established values for a and b, it is possible at any time to compute what the total costs y should be at any given volume of net sales x, within the practical range of operations for the company concerned.

Graphical presentation. A company's cost-volume relationship can be expressed in the form of a graph, as illustrated in Exhibit 53, which is based on the figures we have just been dealing with. It is possible to read from this chart an approximation of what the total costs should be in this case at any given net sales volume from $0 to $12,000,000.

However, if more exact figures are sought than can be read from the chart, it is better to use the formula. Whether or not such a chart is used for reading values, it is a useful device for illustrating cost-volume relationships, and many people find it a useful visual aid in understanding such relationships.

The equation $y = a + bx$ is a general equation or formula for describing or defining a linear relationship between two variables. That is, a relationship which would be represented by a straight line when plotted on a graph having one variable measured on the vertical axis y and the other on the horizontal axis x.

As Exhibit 53 shows, the amount or value of a determines the starting point of the line, since in keeping with the formula, $y = a + bx - y = a$ when $x = o$. In our present use of the formula, it is clear, of course, that since variable costs are assumed to vary directly in proportion to changes in the volume of activity, there would be no variable

EXHIBIT 53

Costs Related to Sales Volume: Formula $2,100,000 Fixed Costs Plus 64% of Sales

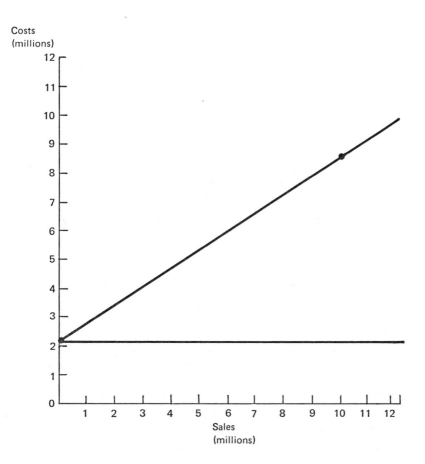

costs if there were no activity. At zero volume of activity, then, the total costs y would be simply a, the fixed costs.

The slope of the line is governed by the value of b. In the present case, b is a percentage or rate and, as x increases, the y value of the line increases at the rate of b. This might be visualized more easily if x measured units of product and b measured the variable costs per unit of product. Then, for each unit increase in x, the y value of the line would increase by b. Thus when $x = o$, $y = a$, when $x = 1$, $y = a + b$; when $x = 2$, $y = a + 2b$; when $x = 3$, $y = a + 3b$, and so forth.

To prepare a chart such as that shown as Exhibit 53, we can use the formula described earlier to establish the total cost at any single volume of sales, such as the $10,000,000 net sales illustrated, and then plot that point of total cost on the chart. On the y axis, we then plot point a representing fixed costs. Using these two points as guides, we can then draw the line of relationship $a + bx$, which in this case represents the relationship of total costs to sales volume.

It should be recognized that the cost-volume relationship pictured in the chart is based not only on arbitrary separations of fixed and variable costs, but also on an averaging of experience over a five-year period during which the volume of operations ranged from $9,000,000 to $11,000,000 of net sales.

The cost-volume relationship thus established is not necessarily a reliable standard for the future. Nor is it necessarily reliable for volumes of activity that are substantially above or below the range of volume on which the computed relationship was based. This does not mean that the results of such studies are not helpful to an understanding of cost-volume relationships, but only that they should be used with caution and common sense as rough guides.

Scatter diagram of cost-volume relationships.   Not only is a chart of the type just described useful in illustrating the line of relationship between costs and volume of activity, but one similar to it can also be used as a graphical approach in determining this relationship.

In this approach, the y axis and the x axis are drawn on graph paper with appropriate scales indicated for each. The known costs in relation to the known volumes of activity for the periods used for the study are then plotted on the graph, each such known relationship being indicated by a point or dot on the graph. The points so drawn then represent what is called a "scatter diagram" of cost-volume relationships.

Exhibit 54 illustrates such a diagram and represents a plotting of the data on total costs in relation to sales which were presented in tabular form in Exhibit 52.

The next step is to establish a straight line through the scattered points in such a way that the scatter above and below the line will be approximately equal. One method of doing this is by inspection. That is, by drawing a straight line through the points by eye, aided possibly by the use of a piece of thread or a transparent ruler.

At first glance, this appears to be a rather rough method, as indeed it is. It may serve adequately, however, to illustrate a principle or to establish approximations of correlation. Moreover, if there is any

EXHIBIT 54
Costs Related to Sales Volume: Five Years of Data

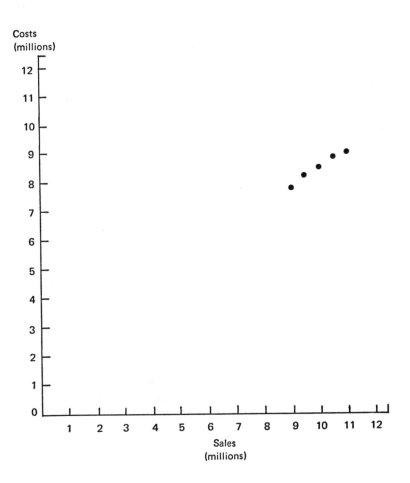

danger that the employment of a more accurate method will convince those using the results that the figures can be accepted without question, it is better to draw the line by inspection.

   In any event, the reader should remember that we are dealing here with approximations, tendencies, or probabilities, and not with the absolute. We are trying to establish some guides or bench marks that will be useful for a variety of purposes. For some purposes, a line drawn by inspection may be as useful as one which is more accurate mathematically.

Drawing a line by inspection, however, is not so simple as it may seem. Or, more specifically, it is frequently possible to draw in several lines, each of which taken by itself may appear to be a reasonable approximation of relationship. For example, people may draw quite different lines through the given points and each hold that his represents the most appropriate line of relationship.

As an experiment, the reader might try drawing a line by inspection through the points in Exhibit 54.

Mathematical Approach

The scatter diagram shown as Exhibit 54 does not contain many points and a line might be drawn more satisfactorily if there were more points. It is not necessary, however, to rely on inspection, since there are formulas available for regression analysis by means of which the relationship between cost and volume can be established readily, particularly on a computer.

Even without a computer, however, there is a procedure known as the method of least squares by means of which the line of relationship can be established without great difficulty. A line of relationship found by this method goes through the plotted points in such a way that the sum of the squares of the deviations from the line to the points is at a minimum. Deviations are always measured against the vertical scale, i.e., in terms of y.

We have already noted that the formula for a linear relationship is $y = a + bx$. The least squares method provides two equations, which when solved simultaneously determine the values of a and b in this equation. These two equations are as follows:

    1. $\Sigma y = Na + b\Sigma x$
    2. $\Sigma xy = a\Sigma x + b\Sigma x^2$

in which Σ = Sigma, sum of, summation; N = Number of items, classes, years, or plotted points of the data under consideration.

To illustrate the least squares method, we shall use data from Exhibit 52, with necessary computations added (Table 10).

The equations then become:

    1. $42{,}500 = 5\,a + 50{,}000\,b$
    2. $426{,}500{,}000 = 50{,}000\,a + 502{,}500{,}000\,b$.

TABLE 10

From Exhibit 52
(000's omitted)

Net Sales	Total Costs	Computations	
x	y	xy	x^2
1	$ 9,000	$ 7,800	$ 70,200,000	$ 81,000,000
2	9,500	8,300	78,850,000	90,250,000
3	10,500	8,900	93,450,000	110,250,000
4	11,000	9,000	99,000,000	121,000,000
5	10,000	8,500	85,000,000	100,000,000
Σx $50,000	Σy $42,500	Σxy $426,500,000	Σx^2 $502,500,000

It is now necessary to solve for a and b. The reader will recall that in solving two equations simultaneously we multiply either one or both the equations by such a figure or figures as will equalize the amount of one of the unknowns in both equations. Subtracting one equation from the other then eliminates this unknown and enables us to solve the value of the other.

In the present case to solve for b, we could multiply equation 1. by Σx, which is 50,000, and equation 2. by N, which is 5, in order to equalize the amounts of a in both equations. We can shorten our work, however, if we simply multiply the first equation by 10,000, which will increase the amount of a in that equation to 50,000 equal to the amount of a in the second equation. The first equation then becomes: $425,000,000 = 50,000\ a + 500,000,000\ b$.

Subtracting this equation from the second equation then enables us to solve the value of b as follows:

$$426,500,000 = 50,000\ a + 502,500,000\ b$$
$$425,000,000 = 50,000\ a + 500,000,000\ b$$
$$1,500,000 = \qquad\qquad 2,500,000\ b$$
$$b = 60\%$$

We can then substitute this percentage figure in either of the equations to solve the value of a. Taking the first equation as an example:

$$42,500 = 5\ a + 50,000\ b$$
$$42,500 = 5\ a + (50,000 \times 60\%)$$
$$42,500 = 5\ a + 30,000$$
$$5\ a = 12,500$$
$$a = 2,500$$

Converting the value of *a* to a full figure shows its value to be $2,500,000. The standard, or formula, for the cost-volume relationship in this case is then as follows:

Total Costs = $2,500,000 of Fixed Costs + Variable Costs of (60% × Net Sales)

Graphical application.   With this formula, we can, of course, find what the total costs should be at any given sales volume within the practical range of operations, based on the five years of experience, without bothering to prepare a graph of the line of relationship.

If we wish to prepare such a graph, however, we can easily do so. Taking the graph as it stands in Exhibit 54, for example, we can locate point *a* on the *y* axis at an approximation of $2,500,000. Applying the value of *b* (60%) to any selected sales volume within the given range of operations will give us a second point on the graph, which will enable us to draw in the appropriate line of relationship. Using $10,000,000 of net sales, as in Exhibit 53, the total costs at this volume of activity would be $2,500,000 of Fixed Costs + Variable Costs of (60% × $10,000,000) or $2,500,000 + $6,000,000 = $8,500,000.

An approximation of this point has been plotted on the graph shown as Exhibit 55 and the appropriate line of relationship has been drawn in. Exhibit 55 then represents Exhibit 54, plus a line of relationship established by the method of least squares.

The reader will note that the line of relationship established by the method of least squares (as would also the line drawn by inspection if it were done reasonably accurately) differs considerably from the cost-volume relationship established at the outset in Exhibit 52 and plotted in Exhibit 53.

This difference occurs because the cost formula developed in Exhibit 52 was based on an arbitrary division of costs into those that were considered fixed and those that were considered variable. In addition, the formula was based on the assumption that the variable costs varied directly in proportion to changes in the volume of activity.

The cost formula developed under the method of least squares, on the other hand, was based on the relationship of total costs to sales. It also took into account the fact that historically the variable costs were to some degree fixed and the fixed costs were to some degree variable.

As noted earlier, a graph of the type presented in Exhibit 55 is useful for illustrative purposes, but it is not necessary in developing cost-volume relationships when one has a formula developed by either the tabular approach or the method of least squares.

EXHIBIT 55
Costs Related to Sales Volume: Formula $2,500,000 Fixed Costs Plus 60% of Sales

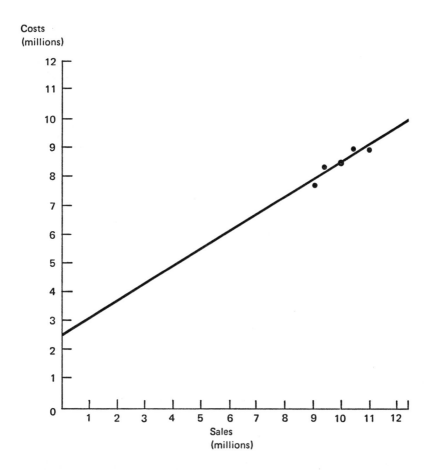

"Break-even Chart" or "Profitgraph"

Suppose we now prepare a graph showing the line of relationship of total cost to sales volume, as measured by dollars of net sales, and add to the graph a line representing sales revenue. Exhibit 56 shows such a graph using the same cost-volume line of relationship as presented in Exhibit 55.

This type of graph, with one line for total costs and the other for sales revenue, is known as a "break-even chart" or "crossover chart"

EXHIBIT 56
Costs Related to Sales Volume: Break-Even Chart

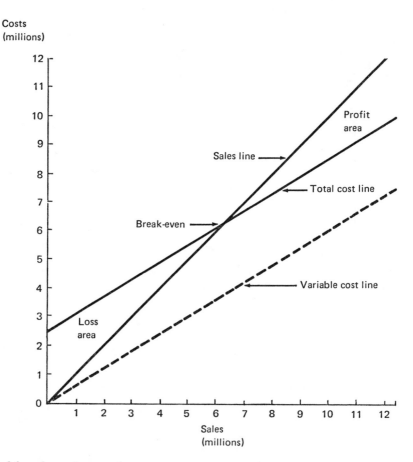

and has been in use for many years. It was pioneered by Dr. Walter Rautenstrauch and C. E. Knoeppel, the latter calling it a "profitgraph."

Under the assumptions on which the graph is based, the point at which the sales line crosses the total cost line represents the break-even point for this business. Above this point, the area between the sales line and the total cost line depicts the profits that should be expected when operating at volumes above the break-even volume.

In turn, the area between these lines below the break-even point represents the losses that should be expected when operating at volumes below the break-even volume.

Knowledge of a company's break-even point is useful in planning for the future and in stimulating action aimed at increasing volume, increasing or lowering prices, or reducing costs when volume threatens to be at or below this point. As long as volume can be kept above this point, one significant factor in profit is under control, to use the term "control" in a broad sense.

Management should not, however, be unduly preoccupied with the break-even point, if for no other reason than just breaking even does not constitute a healthy goal for the long run. The purpose of developing the break-even chart should be to further the understanding of the relationships of cost, price, and volume within a company's practical range of operations. It should not simply be to spot the point at which total revenue and total cost are equal.

A broken line representing total variable costs has also been inserted in the chart shown as Exhibit 56, and the space between this line and the total cost line represents fixed costs. In effect, fixed costs have been placed on top of variable costs in this chart whereas, in Exhibit 53, variable costs were placed on top of fixed costs.

In Exhibit 56, it is clear that at every point of volume the revenue from net sales is in excess of variable costs, and it would be a sorry state if this were not so.

The area between the variable cost line and the sales line represents the margin of revenue above the reimbursement of variable costs. Thus this "marginal income" can be viewed as the contribution toward fixed costs and profit, if any, for the range of operations pictured.[1]

Above the break-even point, this marginal income is of course adequate to cover fixed costs and to provide a profit. Below this point, it is not adequate to provide any profit and, as volume drops, it makes a decreasing contribution toward the coverage of fixed costs. Thus it shows in the net an increasing loss, until at zero volume the loss is exactly equal to the fixed costs.

Limitations of break-even chart. Although the data with which we have been working involve a top net sales volume of $11,000,000 and a low volume of $9,000,000, the break-even chart shows expected revenues and costs from $0 to $14,000,000 of sales volume.

One might reasonably question whether the pattern of relationships shown would hold at volumes substantially above or below the

---

[1] I am indebted to S. A. Peck for the use of the term "marginal income" here and elsewhere in the text. Peck introduced the term in his article, "The Managerial Aspects of Controls" (N.A.A. Bulletin, December 15, 1938), Section 1, p. 471.

limits experienced. For example, common sense would lead one to believe that, if the plant were to be shut down for any period of time, costs would be cut to the bone and might be less than those shown at zero volume in Exhibit 56.

Then again, if a shutdown were only temporary, it is possible that certain costs normally considered as directly variable might be continued. For example, certain highly skilled employees, whose wages along with those of other workers would ordinarily be considered as a directly variable cost, might still be kept on the payroll.

The break-even chart with which we have been dealing is based on the assumption that it is for a going concern operating essentially within the range of volume experienced in the most recent five years. If management contemplates a shutdown of any significant duration, it should prepare a separate estimate or budget of shutdown costs and not rely on a break-even chart for this purpose.

Also, if the expected volume of activity may be, or the realized volume is, substantially above or below that previously experienced, management should consider carefully item by item what the costs should be at such a level and not rely on a simple extension of cost curves. To state this in another way, if such a situation might or does occur, it is time to take another careful look at cost-volume relationships.

As indicated, however, historical experience is at least a useful starting point in the study of cost-price-volume relationships, and ordinarily historical data are readily available, so that such studies can be made with but little effort. Even if conditions have changed markedly, these studies provide a foundation of data that are useful in the development of perspective.

Moreover, as was noted earlier, it is often possible to establish relationships which, although based in large part on historical experience, are currently valid. For example, if the prices of materials bought or of goods sold have changed markedly, it is generally not too difficult to adjust historical data so that relationships can be stated in terms of current or expected prices.

It is possible, however, that changes in product mix, in the size of fixed assets subject to depreciation, or in the nature of operations may be so substantial as to make past cost-price-volume relationships invalid for current use or forecasts of the future. Under such circumstances, as we noted earlier, it is desirable to develop relationships restricted either to the most recent experience or to projections of expectations for the future.

The break-even chart is useful in developing an understanding of cost-price-volume relationships for operations as a whole and for visualizing and illustrating the probable effects of a proposed or expected change in cost, price, or volume. Since it represents a standard of a sort, it is also useful as a rough measure or check on performance.

A break-even chart is however developed on a relatively broad base of average conditions, either already experienced or assumed for the future. Thus it is no substitute for the fixed budget, variable budget, or standard costs for purposes of planning, controlling, and measuring performance.

A major weakness of the break-even chart, as either a planning or checkup device for a manufacturing business, is its assumption that sales volume and production volume are identical. In actual practice, this would never be the case.

In Exhibit 56, for example, what profit for the period should be expected if sales were $9,000,000 but production was at a rate sufficient to support sales of $10,000,000? Clearly, the full production costs would not be charged against the $9,000,000 of sales.

Thus the profit results computed for the current period would be dependent upon the extent to which production costs incurred had been assigned to the inventories of goods in process and finished goods to be carried forward into the next period.

Likewise, the results of the current period would be dependent in part on costs which had been carried forward in the inventories from one or more prior periods.

The computed results, in other words, would be highly dependent upon the company's methods of cost accounting and inventory valuation. The major factor involved would be how and to what extent the company charged fixed costs to inventories, rather than to the current period.

If inventories were charged with direct costs only, then, other things being equal, the actual profit for any sales volume experienced should be the same as that indicated for that volume on a break-even chart, regardless of production volume.

Except in a very few industries, however, manufacturers do include some charge for fixed costs in their inventories of work in process and finished goods. And in all manufacturing companies production volume and sales volume are not the same in any given period. Therefore, inventories fluctuate from period to period.

Hence in most manufacturing companies, even if all other factors were equal, the results computed in an income statement would not be

EXHIBIT 57

Example of Company Operating Costs: Eight Years of Data

Year	Net Sales (000's)	Actual Operating* Costs (000's)	Operating Costs per Formula (000's)
1969	$12,238	$10,519	$10,479
1968	11,608	10,051	10,064
1967	10,384	9,428	9,259
1966	9,826	8,780	8,891
1965	9,991	8,815	9,000
1964	8,821	8,265	8,230
1963	8,413	8,003	7,962
1962	7,838	7,604	7,583

*Actual operating costs shown here had been increased or decreased each year for changes in inventories of work in process and finished goods.

exactly the same as those which would appear on a break-even chart for the volume of sales actually experienced in a given period.

Break-even chart and expansion.   When prepared under conditions of expansion, a break-even chart may give a false impression of cost-price-volume relationships, which could be harmful under certain circumstances.

For example, if — in order to meet rising sales demands — a company purchases additional plant and equipment, there will be rising depreciation charges. When plotted along with other costs, these depreciation charges will seem to represent variable costs in relation to sales dollars. If sales volume should drop, however, the increased depreciation charges would not drop correspondingly, since they would in fact be fixed costs and not variable costs.

The cost-volume relationship computed by the method of least squares, based on experience under these conditions, could be useful as a rough indicator of what operating results might be expected under conditions of increasing sales. But the cost-volume relationship would give a false picture of what should be expected for net income should there be a marked drop in sales.

As a specific example, Exhibit 57 shows figures of an actual company for net sales and total operating costs, before other income and expense and income taxes, for eight years. It also shows the operating costs to be expected for each of these years, based on the cost-volume formula developed by the method of least squares from the net sales

EXHIBIT 58
Operating Costs: Actual and per Formula Related to Net Sales

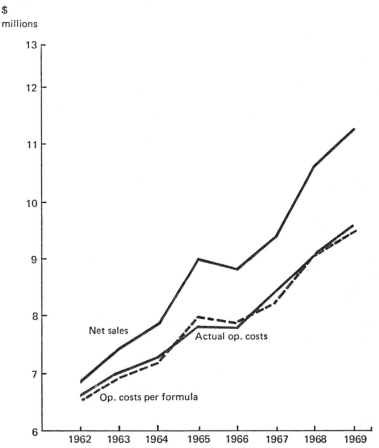

and operating cost data. This formula was as follows: Fixed costs of $2,425,000 + Variable costs of (65.81% × net sales).

The data from Exhibit 57 have been plotted in Exhibit 58. (Note that Exhibit 58 is not a break-even chart; the x axis represents time and not volume of activity.)

This company had found the use of a cost-volume formula, derived in the way we have just seen, to be of some aid in planning and in checking performance as long as sales continued upward. The company was aware, and had in fact found from the experience of fluctuating sales by months within the year, that the formula could not be relied upon when there was a marked drop in sales.

Through more detailed cost-volume studies of individual types of expense by departments and cost centers, the company had attempted to determine what the effects would be if a serious downturn should take place and continue with respect to sales volume.

The company also recognized that inflation was a factor to be considered when establishing a standard of performance for several years of data. But the company did not believe that inflation affected very much the figures used in Exhibit 57 and Exhibit 58.

An additional factor believed to be of some importance, however, was that in recent years the company had brought out new products having better product margins than some of its older products. The company had also trained its sales force to be more selective in the products on which it concentrated its efforts. Better profit margins should therefore result, and total costs should represent a lower percentage of total sales.

Profit-Volume Chart

Another type of break-even chart is one in which emphasis is on the profit-volume relationship, although it is really a reflection of cost-price-volume relationship, since profit is the residual of cost and price.

Exhibit 59 illustrates such a chart, based on the same figures as used in Exhibit 56. The profit line can be established by determining the profit at any two points within the given range of volume and by drawing a straight line through these points.

For example, in our case, one point might be established at $5,000,000 and the other at $10,000,000 of sales. Using the formula developed earlier, the total costs at a sales volume of $5,000,000 would be $2,500,000 of fixed costs plus variable costs of 60% × $5,000,000, or $5,500,000. For this sales volume, there would therefore be a loss of $500,000.

At a sales volume of $10,000,000, total costs would be $2,500,000 of fixed costs plus variable costs of 60% × $10,000,000, or $8,500,000. For this sales volume, there would therefore be a profit of $1,500,000.

The loss of $500,000 and the profit of $1,500,000 would then be plotted on a graph, and a straight line would be drawn through them, as in Exhibit 59.

The profit-volume graph is obviously a simpler presentation than the break-even chart shown in Exhibit 56. For this reason, it is often preferred. The break-even volume can easily be noted at the point where the profit line crosses the zero line, as measured by the vertical scale. With the amount of fixed costs known, it can also be seen that at zero volume of activity the loss is equal to the fixed costs.

EXHIBIT 59
Graph of Profit Volume

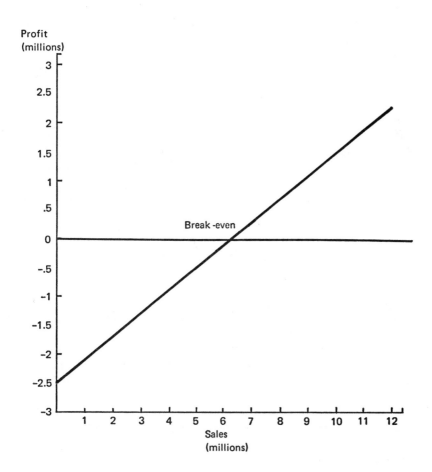

Marginal Income Ratio

The break-even point may also be computed very easily by the use of the marginal income percentage or ratio. Earlier in this discussion, marginal income was defined as a margin of revenue above the reimbursement of variable costs, which would be viewed as a contribution toward fixed costs and profit. The marginal income ratio is simply the percentage relationship of marginal income to sales.

In the figures we have been using in Exhibit 55, Exhibit 56, and

Exhibit 59, variable costs equal 60% of sales and the marginal income ratio is therefore 40% of sales. Consider:

Sales	100%
Variable costs	60
Marginal income ratio	40%

Marginal income may also be viewed in terms of the sales dollar. In the present case, $.60 out of every $1.00 sales is required to cover the variable costs of the goods involved, leaving $.40 to cover fixed costs and profit, if any.

If $.40 out of every $1.00 sales is available to cover fixed costs and profit, the number of sales dollars required to cover the fixed costs alone (or, in other words to break even) may be found by dividing the fixed costs by $.40, which gives a break-even sales requirement of $6,250,000. This is a simple way of arriving at the break-even volume without the use of a graph. Thus:

$$\frac{\text{Fixed Costs}}{\text{Marginal Income Ratio}} = \text{Break-even Sales Volume}$$

Percentage relationships of variable costs and marginal income to sales are also helpful in analyzing the effect of expected or proposed changes in costs and revenues. The effect of a change in selling price per unit can be seen with respect to its effect on the marginal income ratio and break-even point. The extent to which volume must be increased to offset a given drop in selling price may also be easily computed.

Similarly, the effect of a change in variable costs can be noted with respect to the marginal income ratio and break-even point. Thus the amount of increase in selling price required to offset an increase in variable costs can be readily computed.

In Summary

We have been developing a pattern of cost-price-volume relationships for an assumed company based on its experience over a five-year period. We have shown such relationships by means of formulas, graphs, break-even charts, and use of the marginal income concept. Using the company's historical experience, we have determined its average fixed costs based on this experience, and the percentage relationship of variable costs to net sales, as the measure of its volume of activity.

With this data we have prepared a break-even chart in which one may visualize what the fixed costs, variable costs, total costs, sales revenue, and profit or loss should be for this company at any given sales volume within the practical range of its operations, as well as its break-even point.

Assuming that we believe the relationships developed by the foregoing methods constitute reasonable standards of performance for the future, we are in a position a. to know in advance what volume of sales we must achieve in order to break even; b. to forecast what the variable costs, fixed costs, total costs, and profit or loss should be for a forecast volume of sales; and c. after the fact, to judge performance with respect to the actual variable costs, fixed costs, total costs, prices, and profit or loss for whatever sales volume was actually experienced.

Further, with these relationships developed from figures based on experience, we can project the probable effect of an estimated or proposed change in costs or selling prices. We can, for example, see how a proposed change in the selling price will affect the break-even point and the profit or loss at the various possible volumes of activity.

If a price cut is proposed in order to increase sales volume above that currently being obtained, we can see a. how much additional volume at the lower prices would be needed in order to maintain current profits; b. what additional profit, if any, might be realized in the net from the estimated increase in volume; and c. to what extent the break-even point would be raised. We can also see to what extent we shall be less well off if the hoped-for increase in volume should not be obtained.

In a similar manner, we can see to what extent the break-even point and profits will be affected by an expected or proposed increase or decrease in either fixed costs or variable costs. This includes situations where an increase in one type of cost is expected to result either in an increase in volume or a decrease in some other type of cost.

In addition to the cost-price-volume relationships already noted, a number of other significant characteristics of a business can be visualized quickly by the use of break-even charts and the marginal income concept.

For example, if fixed costs constitute a high proportion of total costs, the break-even point will be relatively high. It is of course well known that a business having high fixed costs, i.e., being capital intensive, must operate at a substantial percentage of capacity just to cover such costs. Above this point, profits increase rapidly as volume rises. Below it, recorded losses increase rapidly as volume falls.

For each situation, the break-even charts and use of the marginal income concept show such facts with a reasonable degree of exactness. Therefore, they help the people involved to visualize them more clearly.

Similarly, if variable costs constitute a high proportion of total costs, the break-even point is likely to be relatively low. Thus a company can well experience wide swings in volume and still show a profit.

On the financial side, however, increased volume brings with it a corresponding increase in variable costs for production and inventories. This causes a drain on cash, whereas, in a situation in which fixed costs predominate, a substantial increase in volume can take place without such a serious demand for cash.

From the foregoing, it can readily be seen that the suggested techniques should prove useful to any nonfinancial manager who must find answers to a variety of problems along the lines of those suggested. For, despite the fact that the results of such techniques may not provide complete answers, they can provide useful data on which judgments can be based in arriving at solutions.

CHAPTER 25

The Selection
of Relevant Costs

There are discussions now and then as to what aspects of accounting should be labeled financial accounting and what aspects managerial accounting. No harm comes from such discussions, although neither are they particularly fruitful. The fact of the matter is that all aspects of accounting in a business — except for pure mechanics — are, or should be, of concern to management. Thus, in this sense, all accounting comes within the term managerial accounting.

A major distinction commonly made between financial accounting and managerial accounting is that the latter uses data for some purposes that are not to be found in the accounts, particularly in connection with problems relative to the future.

This leads some writers to point out that the "accountant's figures" are not useful for such purposes. Such an observation is probably correct with respect to the accounts. But it is a bit unfair with respect to the accountant. In most companies, it is some accountant who is given the responsibility for deciding what data are to be gathered for these purposes, both apart from the accounts and from within them, and for assembling both types of data for management's use.

Whether one is or is not an accountant, however, the point is that figures to be used for any given situation should be relevant to the purpose for which they are to be used. And this is what is important, regardless as to whether they are from within or from without the accounts.

Different Costs for Different Purposes

The selection of figures relevant to a given purpose is particularly important in the use of cost data. As we have already noted, there are costs that are fixed, variable, period, historical, replacement, direct, indirect, controllable, noncontrollable, incremental, standard, and so on, which differ in character and serve various purposes.

To use such data wisely, one obviously needs to understand clearly the purpose for which their use is proposed. In addition, one needs to understand the nature, possible uses, and limitations of the specific data available or that which might be sought.

Cost for Inventory Valuation and Profit Determination

We have previously noted the distinction between those costs which might reasonably be identifed with goods or products purchased or manufactured and those which should reasonably be charged as period costs.

In this connection, there are differences in circumstances, as well as in viewpoint. These differences determine what costs shall be assigned to inventories and thus carried forward from one accounting period to another and what shall be charged as costs of the period against current revenues in computing net income.

Generally speaking, in a manufacturing business it is the full costs of material, and labor, and a fair share of factory burden, which are treated as product costs. Burden over- or underabsorbed and all selling and administrative expenses are accounted for as period costs.

All product costs, however, whether for goods manufactured or purchases for resale, eventually become charges against the revenue of a period when charged as the cost of goods sold. Thus, when the books of account are closed at the end of an accounting period, all product costs have either been charged to "Cost of Goods Sold" and in this way become period costs, or they have been applied to the inventories remaining on hand. The net distinction is therefore between inventory costs and period costs, rather than between product costs and period costs.

The problems in cost accounting for purposes of profit determination and inventory valuation are essentially problems in the proper allocation of historical costs to time periods. Solutions to some of these problems have developed over the years into accounting conventions.

Many others must, however, be faced as individual problems of individual situations, and their solutions call for the exercise of a high degree of judgment. In addition to the exercise of judgment and adherence to conventions, this area of accounting involves a large volume of clerical work.

Cost Relevant to Inventory Control

For inventory control purposes, items can be accounted for, issued, and re-ordered purely in terms of physical units based on an established minimum stock level and an order quantity for each inventory item. Tabulations of withdrawals provide records of experience which are useful in establishing such figures and in reviewing their appropriateness periodically.

Many companies establish somewhat arbitrary rules in this connection, although the rules do involve the intuition and judgment of experienced people. For example, the rule might be that the minimum stock level should be an amount equal to two months' estimated sales requirements and the order quantity an amount equal to six months' estimated sales requirements. Given these figures, inventory control is exercised by clerks either with the aid of visual perpetual inventory cards, which are hand or machine posted, or with a computer.

The records just mentioned can also be kept in monetary terms at additional clerical cost. The monetary figures used are product costs of the types we have examined in connection with inventory valuation and profit determination.

The use of monetary amounts in the inventory records can be helpful to the accounting process as a means of establishing the cost of materials used and the cost of goods sold. They add nothing to the control mechanism already provided in physical terms for assuring that items will be reordered in time to avoid stockouts. Nonetheless, for many people, data presented in financial terms is more meaningful and effective for control purposes than data on physical units alone.

Economic lot size. Cost computed outside of the inventory accounting records can be useful in determining the economic quantity of an item to be bought or manufactured. Such calculations can obviously be of importance not only to inventory control but to purchasing and production operations.

If purchase only is involved, as in the case of raw materials and of goods for resale, the differential savings in price from purchasing less frequently but in larger lots are measured against the differential costs of storing larger quantities. Similarly, where items are manufactured in lots, as distinguished from continuous production, savings per product unit in setup costs on larger orders are measured against the differential costs of storing. These savings include interest on the investment arising from the larger quantities that would have to be stored.

Formulas are available for determining economic lot size or economic order quantity, which involve the use of what are known variously as out-of-pocket, incremental, or differential costs. These formulas take into account incremental setup costs, other incremental product costs, and the expected sales or use requirements per year. Such formulas can be found in texts on mathematics or statistics.

Our immediate concern here, however, is to recognize the types of costs relevant to such problems, the difficulties involved in getting such data, and the possible shortcomings of using these formulas.

It should be clear that the costs under consideration in deciding the economic lot size of an item to be ordered or manufactured are not the same as the full product costs connected with inventory valuation.

For example, fixed costs such as rent and depreciation would be excluded. Assuming that in a given case it would be satisfactory to use cost experience instead of cost expectations as data for decisions here, much of the necessary data could be drawn piecemeal from the accounts, although it would not be found anywhere in the accounts completely assembled for use in determining economic lot size.

Judgment is called for, moreover, in determining what data should be sought, and what data available should be used, particularly where a type of cost might be fixed under some conditions and variable under others.

For example, if rent currently being paid on a warehouse which is not full cannot be reduced, there would be no incremental storage space cost for items purchased or manufactured in larger lots to fill it. If the additional space required would involve additional rent, however, the latter would be an incremental cost to be considered in deciding whether or not to purchase or produce in larger lots. Over the longer run, it might be necessary to determine which products should be produced in economical lots and which in smaller amounts.

Limitations of lot-size rules and formulas. The results of decision rules and formulas should be tempered by consideration of factors which they do not take into account.

For example, a company may have limited production facilities on which a number of items are produced. The economic lot size computed for any one of these items may be so large as to tie up the facilities for a long period of time. This may in turn cause shortages on other items, thereby forcing the production of uneconomical lots of these items in order to meet short-run sales requirements for them. Judgment or a more elaborate computer application is required in order to develop a longer run satisfactory production schedule under these circumstances.

So, too, seasonal fluctuations in demand may be such that automatic reordering when supply meets a minimum level causes a bunching of orders at some times, while at other times there are not enough orders to keep labor and production facilities employed to best advantage. Judgment is called for here in determining what shall be produced for inventory during slack periods.

Many companies place great emphasis on maintaining high rates of inventory turnover and on the avoidance of losses either from stock obsolescence or from carry-over of goods from one season to another. Data on these factors are very visible, and managers are held accountable for them. Unfortunately, there are no reliable records of business lost because potential customers could not be supplied with goods at the time they wished to buy them.

Along these same lines, unfortunately, there are no records of the amount of time and nervous energy expended by employees at all levels in an organization in maintaining inventories at low levels that might more profitably have been spent elsewhere. The stories one hears about plants being saved from forced shutdowns at the last moment, by flying in materials or parts, sound romantic. But, surely, these circumstances must exact their toll.

Cost Relevant to Budgetary Planning

Budgetary planning involves a blending of past experience and expectations for the future. With respect to costs, this does not mean a simple projection of historical costs, because such costs may well not represent the most desirable standards or goals for attainment.

It does mean, however, a review of historical costs by type of expense, by area of responsibility, and by type of product and product line. This review promotes cost consciousness by providing a means for a better understanding of cost relationships, particularly that of cost to volume of activity; and a better understanding of the company's cost situation, its areas of strength and weakness, as well as its trend.

The knowledge of past costs must be tempered by estimates of conditions to be expected during the budget period. On the revenue side, the expected volume of sales and the expected product mix are major factors to be taken into account for two reasons: because it is important to budget expected revenues; and because the expected sales volume and product mix obviously have a bearing on the nature and amount of costs to be budgeted.

Allowance must also be made for changes in the size of inventories; in plant capacity; and in methods of production, marketing, and distribution. Estimates must be made of the price level to be expected for materials, labor, and other expenditures.

All in all, of course, it is the expected costs of the budgeted period that are important for the purpose of budgetary planning. However, these costs cannot be developed in a vacuum.

Thus historical costs, used with common sense and tempered by expected changes in conditions, can serve as a good starting point in budgetary planning. The usefulness of historical costs in this connection is brought home most forcefully by their unavailability when one is attempting to prepare a budget for a new company or for an established company that has a new plant or is bringing out a new product.

Costs Relevant to Cost Control

Responsibility for cost control lies with supervisors, managers, and executives at all levels of an organization. They have the authority for incurring costs and the responsibility for the efficient utilization of men, materials, and facilities within their areas, whether the costs involved are incurred by them or by others.

Unfortunately, the truism that a supervisor, manager, or executive should be held accountable only for costs under his control has been accepted too literally. In fact, it has reached the point where the belief is widespread that no one short of top divisional and top corporate management should be made aware of what are termed the "fixed" or "standby" costs of operation.

In our age of increasing automation, when a higher and higher proportion of costs are becoming fixed, the efficient use of the facilities underlying these costs is of paramount importance in producing goods and services at low cost and in recovering the heavy investment in such facilities.

Therefore, it seems odd that control emphasis is restricted to spending connected with variable or direct costs. I shall have more to say on this point in later chapters on budgetary planning and control.

It can be agreed, however, that whatever costs are taken into account for control purposes must be identified with people. Therefore, they should be accounted for by type of expense within areas of responsibility, e.g., departments.

Where several different operations or functions are performed by a department, it is usually considered desirable to account for costs by smaller units, or cost centers, within the department. As we noted earlier, this is for the purpose of more accurate product costing as well as more accurate fixing of responsibility.

Where cost accounting for products is by process costing, the identification of costs is not only by product and type of expense, but also by process and, accordingly, by the individuals in charge of each process. Similarly, where products are costed by jobs or lots, their costs are identified not only by type of expense but also by the departments or cost centers that worked upon them and often by the individual workmen and machines involved.

Cost control requires cost comparisons. Any cost, standing by itself, is meaningless for control purposes. There must be a basis for comparison. Cost accounting provides standards by type of expense, by departments and cost centers, and by products to serve both as goals for attainment and measures of performance. This dual approach to cost control provides a working guide of cost allowances at the time expenditures are incurred. And it also provides successive tiers of management with the means of checking performance.

Actual costs. Various types of cost comparisons are provided by cost accounting. The simplest of these is a comparison of actual costs. Thus each item of the actual cost of a given product is compared wth previous actual costs for the same product. Actual departmental costs by type of expense are compared by periods, and by year-to-date with figures for the previous year.

Similarly, such cost comparisons are made by types of expense in successive profit and loss statements — per plant, per division, and for the company as a whole. In such analyses, percentages or ratios are often used in addition to absolute figures.

The technique of comparing actual costs may be criticized on the grounds that changes in industry, which take place continually, invalidate such comparisons because the actual costs are subject to random variations. Therefore, such cost comparisons may be criticized on the basis that they do not constitute desirable standards of performance.

Nonetheless, this technique is useful in noting trends and in flagging situations that should be investigated. In many cases, this is all that is needed in the way of cost reporting. After all, it is the action of investigation and improvement and not of refinement in the determination of the exact amount of a cost variance that is of the greatest importance.

Standard costs. Industry in general, however, has not been content to stop with simple comparisons of actual costs for control purposes. In the area of product costing, standard costs have been an effective tool in the control of labor and material costs and, to a lesser extent, in the efficient utilization of facilities.

The analysis of variances between actual and standard costs is an important part of the standard cost technique. The principle here is that of control by exception. That is, instead of attempting to follow a mass of cost data, the attention of those responsible for cost control is concentrated on significant variances away from standard.

If effective action is to be taken, the cause and responsibility for a variance, as well as its amount, must be established. Cost accounting can be particularly helpful, both through the proper classification and collection of cost data and through detailed variance analysis.

Costs Relevant to Control through Variable Budgets

The variable budget has proved to be a useful cost control technique for those costs which tend to vary in some degree with changes in the volume of activity. This technique has been particularly useful in the control of variable factory burden.

In developing the variable budget, costs by each type of expense are studied by areas of responsibility, such as departments or cost centers, in relation to changes in the volume of activity. These studies are somewhat along the lines of those described in Chapter 24 on cost-price-volume relationships, but in greater detail. Moreover, whereas in Chapter 24 total costs were broken down only to either fixed or variable classifications, the cost relationships developed for purposes of variable budgeting are more detailed and, in this sense, more exact.

Knowledge of the cost-volume relationship in a given department for a particular type of cost, e.g., supplies, provides a flexible standard with which, given a proposed or actual volume of activity for that department for a given period, it is possible to establish what the cost should be, or should have been. The variable budget thus provides a working guide in the form of predetermined cost standards or allowances for any volume of activity within the practical range of operations.

These same standards supply the means for checking spending performance on activity that has already taken place.

The variable budget is not ordinarily used in the control of material or labor costs. Nor, except possibly for the item of spoilage, does it set standards or measure performance with respect to the efficiency of operations.

It should be regarded as a useful guide and measure of performance relative to the input of expenses needed to operate a department or cost center. But it should not be regarded as a control or measure of performance relative to the output of goods or services of that department or cost center.

In other words, it is a technique which aids the control of spending efficiency but not the control of operating efficiency.

Costs Relevant to the Fixed Budget for Control Purposes

The fixed budget, also known variously as the "financial," "appropriation," "master," or "annual" budget, constitutes a goal or plan of action expressed in monetary terms.

The formulation of such a budget is in itself of assistance in controlling costs — that is, if, as should be the case, all those who have spending authority have had a part in it. The review of past costs and the making of estimates and commitments with respect to costs for the budgeted period stimulate cost consciousness, which is a basic requirement for effective cost control.

For many expenses, the fixed budget not only establishes a goal, but also sets a limit on expenditure. This places a control on the total cost of an expense item, although it provides no control over the wisdom or efficiency with which funds are expended. Control over the latter can be approached, however, if it is possible to define in detail the specific tasks to be accomplished by the funds to be expended.

Cost control is assisted to some extent by a comparison of actual results against the fixed budget. The knowledge that a "day of reckoning" is coming is salutary in itself. The check of actual results against the plan by time periods fixes responsibility for deviations and provides a knowledge of areas where corrective action is needed.

Costs Relevant to Efforts Aimed at Cost Reduction

Standard costs, variable budgets, and fixed budgets have assisted many companies to reduce and control costs, particularly when these standards are first established and studies underlying them have indicated that actual costs of one type or another are higher than they should be.

Moreover, for many individuals, standards represent not simply goals but challenges for the operations under their supervision to show favorable cost variances and thus to reduce costs. Not infrequently, the stated objectives for a period include the objective of beating a given standard.

The analysis of variances from standard costs and budgets can provide leads on where to apply efforts for cost improvement. If costs fluctuate markedly, it should be possible to find out what conditions lead to better than standard performance and to try to maintain these conditions so that average performance will be improved.

Despite these various possibilities, it must be admitted that if, over time, actual performance is brought into line with standard costs and budgets, which represent reasonably tight standards, enthusiasm is likely to wane for sustained efforts at cost reduction. Search may be continued for new materials, machines, and methods by which to reduce costs, but efforts for better performance under existing conditions are likely to drop.

In such circumstances, it is necessary to put on a special drive for cost reduction when a company wishes its operating costs to be further reduced. For such drives, many companies have found it effective to concentrate each time on a particular type of expense. In a manufacturing plant, for example, a cost reduction drive will be concentrated on one item such as spoilage, use of supplies, or downtime on machines.

The types of cost thought of commonly in connection with cost reduction are the direct costs of material and labor and the variable costs of factory overhead. These are costs which are potentially subject to reduction in the short run.

Not infrequently, such costs are also reduced in the long run by the substitution of fixed costs for them, as when a machine is purchased to supplant hand labor. From a company viewpoint, this approach is quite appropriate, provided that an adequate volume of business can be maintained over the long run so that the investment may be recovered, as well as a reasonable return on it.

Selling and administrative expenses as areas for cost reduction. There are also, of course, costs of selling and administration which should be taken into consideration when a company is attempting to reduce its costs of operation. Some of these costs vary with fluctuations in production or sales volume and some are fixed, in the same sense as fixed factory costs.

However, many of these costs, which mainly depend on management judgment, are known as "managed" or "discretionary" costs. Amounts spent for advertising, conventions, and training programs are examples of discretionary costs. While the incurrence of some amount of expenditure in such areas is influenced by what competitors are doing and by the desirability of maintaining employee goodwill, the total amount to be spent in any given period is discretionary with management.

Cost reduction here can mean doing less with less money, doing the same or more with less money, or doing more with the same money. Top management has the prerogative of reducing the allotment of money for such costs. But the wisdom and efficiency with which the money allotted is spent, of course, depends upon those doing the spending.

Some types of selling and administrative expenses are a combination of fixed, variable, and discretionary costs. In some companies, salaries and wages of the organization required for these functions at the lowest volume of operations likely to be experienced are considered as fixed costs. Here, admittedly, the structure of such an organization is determined in part by judgment, and the amount of salary or wage paid to individuals is discretionary within limits.

As the volume of activity increases, some additional help must be hired, and the costs connected with those hired are thus variable costs. Here again, the exact types and numbers of people to be hired and the amounts to be paid them are discretionary to a degree.

With respect to cost reduction, it is probably best to regard all types of selling and administrative expenses as discretionary in nature. The exception is depreciation on fixed assets, and even this is discretionary in the long run.

This view at least forces managers involved with these costs at various levels to accept responsibility for controlling and reducing them if necessary. Otherwise, such managers may not accept these responsibilities on the grounds that the costs involved are either fixed or completely dependent on the volume of activity being experienced, and that they are therefore beyond their control.

Costs Relevant to Joint Products and By-products

Some of the most interesting and perplexing cost accounting problems are met in situations in which two or more products are made from a single raw material. Somewhat similar problems are faced when two or more products, made jointly with the same labor and production facilities, are administered and sold jointly by the same sales and administrative organizations.

One approach to problems of this type is to adopt the viewpoint that no allocations of joint costs to joint products should be attempted. This view is based in part on the argument that all allocations of joint costs are arbitrary and, therefore, of questionable accuracy, since such costs cannot be allocated scientifically.

More important grounds, where they exist, are that such allocations do not aid the decision-making process or the efficient conduct of a business, and they may in fact lead to the wrong decisions.

From this viewpoint, a business should be regarded as a whole and not by its separate parts so far as products are concerned. Material and other joint costs taken together should be matched against the combined revenues from joint products in judging the profitability of operations, in the planning stage as well as after they have taken place.

Decisions with respect to shifting the direction of sales and production effort, and on such matters as adding or dropping individual products, can be made on the basis of studies of incremental effects on overall costs and revenues. Costs can be controlled through physical standards of performance and by such means as variable budgeting.

Finally, pressure can be applied to the sales department to get the best prices it can for all products, so as to realize the maximum possible contributions toward total cost and profit.

For example, in the case of a fishing trawler that has caught a mixture of cod, haddock, pollack, and miscellaneous other fish in its net, it can be argued that there is no point in allocating the costs of fishing to the quantity of each type of fish caught. A voyage would not be made unless it was believed that market conditions were such that enough would be realized on the mixture of fish that would probably be caught to make the trip worthwhile.

Thus the ship would be directed to the particular fishing grounds currently expected to yield the best total marginal contribution above total costs, the fishermen would be stimulated to fish at their best through share arrangements, and the running costs would be checked against budgeted amounts per day or for distance traveled.

Then, having caught its fish, the ship would head for home to arrive at the marketplace ahead of others, and whoever was responsible for selling the fish would get the very best prices available for the quantity of each type caught.

None of these particular factors of importance to end results would be aided by cost allocations to fish caught.

Why costs are allocated.   In the example just given, we assumed that all of the fish brought into port would be sold shortly after arrival. But suppose only some of the fish were sold immediately as fresh fish, while the remainder were sent in part to the fishing company's frozen food division to be processed into fish sticks and in part to its canning division where some parts would be canned for humans and some for cats. Clearly, the fish frozen or canned would not be sold immediately but would be sold gradually over several months (accounting periods) in the future.

There is, then, a dual problem here of determining the cost of goods sold for the fresh fish sold immediately and of determining inventory values for the fish in the hands of the frozen food and canning divisions.

Fixing Responsibility and Judging Performance

In addition to the financial accounting problems of determining cost of goods sold and inventory values, there are the matters of fixing responsibility and judging the performance of the various divisions of a business and of recording and judging the profitability of individual products and product lines.

Various Departments and Divisions

Some companies operate their departments and divisions as cost centers, which are essentially held accountable only for such costs as are incurred by them. In some of these companies, it is not considered necessary or desirable to charge a cost center for material furnished to it under joint product and joint cost conditions.

In some petroleum companies, for example, a refinery is not charged for crude oil furnished to it, nor are the marketing divisions charged for petroleum products furnished to them by the refinery. The refinery is held accountable for its operating costs, usually through budgetary control. It is also held accountable for the physical quantity of crude oil furnished to it and for the yields of the various products it is scheduled to produce.

Whatever inventories are on hand at the refinery at the close of each month are usually priced at a standard cost per unit established at the beginning of the year.

Similarly, the marketing departments are held accountable for their operating costs through budgetary control. They are also usually held accountable for showing an adequate marginal contribution of revenue above their own operating costs.

Inventories of petroleum products in the hands of the marketing divisions at the close of each month are commonly priced at a standard cost per unit. Nonpetroleum products, e.g., tires and batteries, are accounted for by the marketing divisions in the normal manner of accounting for goods purchased for resale.

In other companies, where divisions are operated as profit centers, i.e., held accountable for profits as well as for costs, and in many companies where divisions are accounted for as cost centers, charges are made for materials furnished by one division to another. Under joint product and joint cost conditions the transfers usually involve cost allocations.

Sometimes predetermined transfer prices are agreed upon by the individuals involved. In other cases, agreements are made with respect to the cost allocation formulas to be followed in computing transfer prices.

Where divisions cannot agree on transfer prices, or on transfer price formulas, it is necessary to have a means of arbitration or top corporate management decision with respect to one or the other when transfers are to be made.

Where divisions are regarded as cost centers, it is believed that divisions cannot be made to feel full responsibility for material furnished to them unless they are charged for it. Even though material yields and spoilage might be accounted for in physical terms, it is the belief that showing yield and spoilage in monetary terms is of importance in their control.

Likewise, where profit centers are in operation, it is believed that such centers cannot be regarded as standing on their own feet like separate companies unless charged for material and services furnished to them.

Moreover, there is the belief that profit centers are likely to overrate their contributions to total corporate financial results if all they see is the margin they have realized above their own operating costs. In particular, it is believed that they will not feel enough pressure to obtain the best possible prices for the goods they are selling or to maintain tight control over costs.

Individual Products and Product Lines

Whether or not separate divisions of a company are involved, it is believed by many that performance on individual products from the same raw material can best be judged if a full share of costs is charged to them. This includes the cost of the material used in making them, provided that these charges can of course be established on rational bases even though not scientifically exact.

We shall now briefly examine the common bases of allocating raw material costs under joint product and by-product costing and the basic reasoning underlying their use.

Raw material cost allocation in proportion to area or weight. A common basis of raw material cost allocation is the simple one of allocation in proportion to area or weight. Thus the cost of a given lot of raw material, and usually all processing costs up to the point where the material is separated into the parts for the joint products or for the main product and by-products, are allocated at an equal amount per unit, e.g., per pound, to the various products being manufactured from this material.

This is a reasonable basis in the vast number of cases where two or more products are made from the same lot of raw material and where the material used in each is identical in character with that used in the others, although different in size or weight.

For example, a variety of products of different shapes and market values may be poured from the same melt of brass. But, since identical material is used, each should be charged at the same rate per pound for material furnished. (This does not mean, however, that the cost per pound of good finished castings will be the same, since the products will differ on such factors as mold cost; proportions of sprues, gates, and risers; and percentage of spoilage.)

The area or weight basis is also acceptable in cases where the portions of material separated are not identical in character, but where the difference in cost allocation that would result from some other logical and more complicated basis are not considered to be worth the extra effort involved.

The conditions just stated would not be true in the classic example of joint products, cotton and cotton seed. The reasoning here is that cotton seeds weigh more than the cotton itself. To allocate raw material cost on a weight basis would mean charging more of the joint cost to seeds than to cotton, which would be unreasonable considering the fact that the market value of cotton is much higher than for seeds and the price of the raw material before separation of the two takes this into account.

There are any number of similar cases where the allocation of raw material cost on an area or weight basis is not acceptable because the various portions or segments of raw material differ markedly from one another in both character and known market value at the point of separation.

As a matter of fact, even though it is true that many products, like the items of brass mentioned earlier, are produced jointly from the same lot of material, they are not commonly regarded as being joint products when the material used in each is the same in character. For example, cotton and cotton seed are considered to be truly joint products, since they do differ in character and one cannot be produced without getting the other.

However, if two or more cotton products were produced from a given lot of cotton remaining after the seeds had been removed, they would not usually be regarded as joint products, even though produced from the same lot of material. The reason for this is that the material used in each would be identical in character and, from a production viewpoint at least, the material available could have been used to make any one of the products without having to make any other.

Market value as a basis of allocation. A second basis for the allocation of raw material costs is one which takes market value into consideration, as well as area or weight. The clearest cases for which this
approach is appropriate are those in which market values are available
for the various segments of raw material at the point of separation and
prior to further processing.

In meat packing, cattle parts, e.g., hides and hoofs, are bought and
sold in their green state — that is, in the state they are in immediately
after separation following slaughter — in sufficient quantities to provide the packer with acceptable market values as a basis for allocating
live cattle costs, whether he wishes to sell these parts as they are or to
subject them to further processing.

In these cases, the total of the market values of the different parts
at the point of separation is likely to be greater than the total cost of
the raw material they came from, unless market values have dropped
significantly since that material was purchased.

In any event, the total cost of the raw material will not be the same
as the sum of the market values of its parts, except by happenstance.
Since it is cost and not market value that is being allocated, the market
values of the parts are used simply to determine the proportions of cost
to be allocated to them.

For example, let us suppose that the costs of a given lot of material
up to the point of separation are $900, and that after separation its parts
have a market value of $1,000, broken down as follows:

Part A	$ 500
Part B	200
Part C	300
	$1,000

The $900 of costs would then be allocated:

50% to Part A =	$450
20% to Part B =	180
30% to Part C =	270
100%	$900

A more difficult problem in the allocation of raw material cost on
a market basis is faced when no market values exist for some or all of
the various parts at the point of separation, since they are not commonly sold in this condition. One approach here is to allocate costs on

an area or weight basis, even though it is believed that if parts were commonly sold in their condition at the point of separation they would probably show some differences in market value.

Another approach, where there are market values for some parts at the point of separation but not for others, is to assign market values to those parts for which they are available. The total of these values is then subtracted from the cost of the given raw material, and the balance of the cost is allocated to the remaining parts on an area or weight basis.

Use of market values of end products. A third method is to start with the market values, as of the date of separation, of the end products to be produced from each of the parts. Then, to subtract the estimated selling, administrative, and conversion costs to arrive at an approximation of the market values of the parts at the point of separation. These market values are then used to establish the proportions in which raw material cost is then allocated to the various parts.

This method should, however, be approached with caution. It not only involves additional clerical work, but also the differences in the market value of end products alone are not enough to justify its use.

The key to the matter lies in the question whether, if these parts were to be bought and sold commonly in their condition at the point of separation, these parts would in fact be exchanged at different unit values. And, if so, whether the relative values at which they would be exchanged would correspond with the relative values arrived at by subtracting estimated selling, administrative, and conversion costs from the market values of the end products to which they are converted.

An example of a situation in which it would not be appropriate to use end market values is that given earlier of the production of a variety of products from the same melt of brass. Here, the brass used for each product is identical at the point of separation at the melting pot. Thus the price differentials for the different products arise from factors other than differences in the cost or value of the raw materials used.

In contrast to this, with respect to cattle at the point where the parts are separated into dressed beef, hides, hoofs, and so on, the parts are different from one another in character and they are in fact exchanged at different unit values in the open market.

As we noted before, the brass example would not commonly be regarded as a joint product situation. Nonetheless, the point is that one product should not be charged any more than another per unit of raw material when the very same type of raw material, from the same lot of raw material, is used by both.

An argument sometimes used for charging a given cost to products on the basis of end market values is that this is a fair and reasonable basis because a product is then charged for the cost in proportion to its ability to bear it. Dignity has been lent to this approach on occasion by suggesting that it seems to follow a natural economic law. In other circles, the approach is known as "soaking the rich."

The fact that one product can absorb more cost than another and still show a respectable profit may be an excuse for charging more to one than to the other, but it is not a very good argument for doing so. Moreover, just because it may be logical to price different articles in terms of what the market for each can bear, it does not follow that it is equally logical to shift costs from one product to another on this basis.

Clearly, if the same type of labor at the same cost per hour is used for two different products, it would not be logical to shift any of the labor cost from one to the other just because the latter enjoyed a better selling price. Similarly, this is not a good argument for shifting raw material cost from one product to another when the raw material used by one is identical in character with that used by the other.

Raw material cost relative to expected uses. The main argument for the allocation of raw material costs on some sort of a market basis is that when a buyer purchases raw material from which joint products, or a main product and by-products are to emerge, he takes into account in the price he is willing to pay the probable yield and value of at least the major segments of that material.

In effect, he is buying a package containing a variety of different items. Thus he tries to determine their market value in arriving at a price that he should be prepared to pay for the lot.

After having bought the material on this basis, it is then logical for him, i.e., his company, to allocate its cost in proportion to the market values of the segments actually realized.

In a meat packing company, for example, the market values of dressed beef, hoofs, hides, and so forth are known each day, and the standard yields for types and weights of cattle have been established. These factors are combined, with the aid of a computer, to tell buyers what they should pay for the types and weights of cattle to be bought.

In other kinds of business, this type of analysis is not usually so detailed as in meat packing. Nonetheless, in a joint product situation the knowledgeable buyer has well in mind the uses of the material which he is to buy, and he knows approximately the cost limit within which he must operate for the joint products to be produced and sold profitably.

Main Product and By-product Costing

A large number of products produced jointly with others from the same raw material are labeled as by-products. That is, as products which are incidental to, and not so important as, the main products from the same material.

The distinction is largely a matter of size, and the point at which it is drawn is an arbitrary matter. Often rough rules are established, for example, that any product which contributes less than 10% of the company's total revenue shall be treated as a by-product.

If the only distinction between the main product and a by-product were a matter of size, it could be argued that as far as cost accounting is concerned by-products should be treated simply as joint products. Therefore, raw material costs should be allocated to them, as to other joint products, in proportion to area or weight, or in proportion to their relative market values at the point of separation, as described earlier in this chapter.

Main product and by-product costing, however, commonly differs from accounting for joint products. Under one theory of main product and by-product costing, all profits or losses for a company are accounted for only on its main products.

Moreover, the by-products are charged nothing for the raw material furnished by them. The cost of raw material and all processing costs up to the point where materials are separated are charged to the main products.

By-products are charged only for their own costs from the point of separation on through to completion. Then all revenues above these costs from the sale of by-products are treated as reductions in the cost of the main products.

Three arguments for this theory of main product and by-product costing are:

1. Raw material is bought for the main products and it would be bought for them even if there were no by-products; hence it would not be bought for the by-products alone.
2. The parts from which by-products are made would otherwise be sold as scrap and the proceeds used to reduce the cost of the main products; hence by-products simply represent improved scrap recovery.

3. It is necessary to treat the proceeds from by-products as reductions in the cost of main products in order to enable the latter to be competitive.

In similar fashion, there are three objections to this approach as follows:

1. The processing and sale of products from the same raw material take varying amounts of time. As of the close of each accounting period, not all of the units of product from some lots of raw material have been completed and sold. Moreover, parts of the output of many lots of raw material are still on hand, as either main products or by-products, while the other parts have been sold.

   Under these conditions, the failure to charge by-products for their material content causes distortions in inventory values, in the cost of goods sold, and in profit or loss for each period.

   It could be argued that the distortions of beginning inventories will offset distortions of ending inventories and leave the cost of goods sold and profit or loss as they should be. Even so, there are still likely to be shifts in the size and nature of inventories and in the goods sold from period to period to upset results.

2. Although the production and sale of each by-product may be small in relation to a company's total operations, in combination these are likely to represent a significant portion of the business that should be held accountable for showing a profit, and not for simply reducing the cost of main products.

   Moreover, from a control viewpoint, the divisions of a company responsible for processing and selling the by-products after the point of separation should be made to operate as independently as possible. In this connection, they should in effect be required to buy the material they process as though they were outside companies.

   Along these same lines, there is some belief that the philosophy of treating proceeds from by-products simply as reductions in the cost of main products encourages lack of aggressiveness on the part of by-product divisions in selling these products for the best possible prices.

3. Because of changes that are continually taking place, the by-product of today may become a main product tomorrow, e.g., as happened to gasoline. Therefore, by-products should not be accounted for in a manner so markedly different from the methods used for main products.

By-products charged for material at market value.   Another approach to main product and by-product costing, which meets the majority of the objections just stated, is to charge the by-product divisions for the material parts furnished to them. The charge can either be at the market values of these parts at the point of separation, or at predetermined transfer prices which are approximations of the market values of these parts.

Corresponding credits for these charges are used to reduce the raw material cost and operating costs up to the point of separation. The net of these costs is then allocated to the main products on an area or weight basis, or on a market value basis, whichever seems appropriate in the given case.

In this way, the by-product divisions are held accountable for showing a profit on their operations. Those handling the main products are held accountable for their skill in purchasing raw material and in processing it up to the point of separation, as well as for showing a profit on the further processing and sale of their products.

In smaller companies not having separate by-product divisions, the cost accounting just described would, of course, simply be product costing by separate products and not by divisions.

Allocation of Labor Costs to Joint Products

The great majority of labor costs can be identified directly with each product on which the labor has been applied. Thus no problem of allocation is involved. Frequently, a company's method of wage payment requires identification of specific products and thus incidentally provides the means for product costing.

Where workmen produce a variety of products each day and it would be too troublesome and expensive to account for the actual time spent on each, it is possible by observation or time studies to develop factors for use in making reasonable allocations of labor costs to goods produced.

In the production of joint products, the cost of labor and other operations applied to the processing of raw material up to the point of separation, along with the cost of the raw material, are prorated on an area or weight basis, or on a market value basis.

As suggested earlier, under main product and by-product costing, the labor and other costs applied to the processing of raw material up to the point of separation are commonly charged to the main products. Therefore, by-products bear none of these costs. Labor applied to any product after the point of separation is of course accounted for as a direct cost of that product.

Allocation of Factory Burden to Joint Products

Except where a single product only is being manufactured, it is necessary to allocate factory burden to products on some basis. The reason for this is that it is not possible to identify exactly how much of the total cost of items such as repairs and maintenance; heat, light, and power; and depreciation has been expended on any given product.

This assumes, of course, that it is considered necessary or desirable to allocate some, or all, factory burden to products from some purpose such as inventory valuation.

The reader will recall that costs within the category of factory burden are recorded by type of expense and charged directly, or allocated, to areas of responsibility such as departments or cost centers. Burden is charged to products on the basis of a burden rate, which may be at standard or represent the means of applying actual costs to products.

In the production of joint products, operating costs, including factory burden, involved in processing raw material up to the point of separation are allocated to products on an area or weight basis, or on a market value basis, as already discussed. Also, as noted in connection with labor costing, these costs are charged to the main product under main product and by-product costing and, therefore, by-products bear none of them.

After the point of separation, factory burden and any other costs involved in further processing are charged or allocated to the products processed. This is done in accordance with ordinary cost accounting practice, whether the items are considered to be joint products, main products, or by-products.

In Summary

The cost allocations we have been examining are for purposes of inventory valuation and measurement of performance of individual products and product lines. In particular, we have focused on those situations where it seems appropriate to establish the full cost of a product on some rational basis, even though it is impossible to establish its true actual cost in a scientific sense.

For other purposes, it is often desirable to compute only what are called the incremental or differential costs of a product instead of its full costs. This is particularly true of the costs of factory burden.

In deciding whether or not to convert some scrap material into a by-product, for example, the relevant costs to be considered — in the short run, at least — are simply the additional costs involved in converting the scrap that would not otherwise be incurred.

These additional (incremental or differential) costs include not only labor and material costs, if any, but also variable costs of factory burden. They also include whatever additional selling and administrative expenses might be involved in connection with these by-products that would not have been incurred in the disposal of the material as scrap.

Other examples of the use of incremental costs in deciding whether or not to make a product or provide a service are to be found in connection with pricing problems, which we shall examine in the next chapter.

CHAPTER 26

Relevant Costs
for Pricing Purposes

The relationship, or lack of relationship, between the cost and selling price of a product is a perennial subject of discussion and concern. It differs in importance between industries, between products within an industry, and varies in intensity under changing business conditions. Many pricing situations are exceedingly complex, and cost-price relationships represent only one of many matters to be considered.

Accordingly, our concentration here on the costs relevant to pricing should not be taken as implying that cost is necessarily the most significant aspect of pricing. Then again, we should not wish to minimize the importance of the influence of cost on price, as is sometimes done is discussions on pricing.

Obviously, cost affects selling price in cases where the price is established by adding what is considered to be a reasonable profit to the computed full cost of a given product. There is also a definite cost-price relationship in the many cases where products are so designed and constructed that their cost will come within the range of prices it is believed buyers will be willing to pay.

Similarly, even where it is said that price is set by the market, costs of one type or another are commonly taken into account in deciding whether or nor to produce and sell under the given conditions.

Differences Between Industries

It can readily be agreed that, in the short run, cost cannot have a significant bearing on selling price in industries where it is unknown or ignored by the great majority of companies. For example, among others, the shoe, textile, and job-printing industries have suffered over the years from a number of ills. Not the least of these has been the lack of knowledge of costs and the failure to pay adequate attention to costs where they have been known. Over a long period of time, after enough companies have been forced out of business through failure to recover their costs, those remaining in such industries do stiffen their prices so as to recover costs and, hopefully, some profit.

Thus over time, even in industries such as these, there is a relationship between cost and selling price. This is so both in determining who shall remain in business and in the fact that cost offers a resistance point to the lowering of price.

In contrast, the steel, automobile, and electrical equipment industries are led by large companies in which cost accounting as an aid both in managerial control and in determining price policy has been developed and used to a high degree.

Here, costs and prices are related in various ways at various times: in setting prices, in designing products to be made at a cost to meet available prices, and in restricting production when available prices do not bear a satisfactory relationship to costs. Great effort is expended to obtain information on both cost and market factors in order that marketing and production strategy may be planned and executed intelligently.

In the production of staple commodities such as flour and sugar, as well as in the processing of fresh meat, the relationships of cost and selling price are very close. Here, the miller, refiner, or packer aims to recover the price he pays for raw material, his processing costs, and a small profit per unit on a large volume of operations.

Raw material and finished goods prices tend to move up or down together, depending on conditions of both demand and supply. Thus many processors protect their profit position as best they can through contracts for raw material and other forms of hedging. On specialty items such as packaged cake mixes, the relationship between cost and selling price is not nearly as direct as it is on more staple lines.

Custom, in keeping with the denomination of coins, has established fixed prices for certain products such as candy bars, cigars, and ice cream cones. But these fixed prices bear no immediate relation to cost.

Over a period of time, the quality or quantity of the product per unit is likely to change, representing an adjustment of cost to the fixed selling price. Whatever penny candy is still available, for example, is now emaciated in appearance, while the few remaining ten-cent candy bars are disappointingly thin.

Over a longer period, the prices will themselves be changed in response to marked changes in cost. But the changes are likely to be large in percentage rather than gradual, e.g., by nickel intervals, rather than by pennies.

In more recent years, consumers and vending machines as well appear to be becoming more adaptable to changes in prices for items such as these. Thus the trend appears to be toward offering a somewhat larger quantity for an even greater increase in price, still within the denomination of coins — two neat but slender candy bars packaged together and sold for twenty-five cents.

There are some consumer goods such as shirts, neckties, and shoes for which the customer becomes accustomed to paying a certain price, or range of prices, depending upon their quality. Minor changes in quality can be made within a price range without unfavorable consumer reaction.

In general, the consumer's expectations with respect to both price and quality set up rigidities in the price structure and delay the adjustment of selling prices to changes in cost. Here, however, as in the case of prices based on the denomination of coins, the consumer's resistance to change is not as strong as in years past. Inflationary conditions have led him to become accustomed, if not reconciled, to rising prices; and, in some cases, to accept somewhat lower quality for the price he is able or willing to pay for a given item.

For a wide range of industrial goods, there are relatively close relationships between costs and selling prices. This is due partly to competition and also partly to the fact that the great majority of purchases of such items are made by professional buyers or purchasing agents. These people are not only shrewd buyers, but they are knowledgeable with respect to the probable costs to the seller of the items being purchased.

These buyers also are generally well aware of the uses to be made of the items they are purchasing. Thus, when they purchase raw materials and parts for production or goods for resale, they know within limits about what they can afford to pay if the costs of the items their companies are making or reselling are to be competitive.

Cost is the prime determinant of price in a wide range of products for use in war or defense. Here, cost means reimbursable cost, as defined by government regulations and cost manuals, and it is a vital aspect of pricing. The reason for this is that both the demand situation and competitive conditions are so abnormal as to prevent the establishing of satisfactory pricing through the ordinary means of competition.

This is unfortunate. It minimizes the value of contributions to the war or defense effort by such means as inventiveness, improved performance, and reduced costs. And it emphasizes simply the importance of being sure that all costs expended are reimbursable.

Thus far we have been considering cost in general terms and certain fundamental relationships of cost and selling prices, including examples of differences between industries in this relationship. Let us now examine the type of cost knowledge available to an individual manufacturer with respect to its possible relationship to prices and effect on pricing.

Historical Product Costs and Pricing

Except for work done on a cost reimbursement basis, and for all work in the sense of a resistance to the lowering of price, product costs gathered currently by the cost accounting department are not usually of immediate aid in pricing. Nor do current prices necessarily bear any relationship to them.

The actual material, labor, and overhead costs of products as gathered on cost sheets are subject to temporary fluctuations through: a. changes in price and variations in the yield of material; b. changes in labor rates and efficiency; c. price variances in certain types of overhead and differences of efficiency in the utilization of indirect labor, plant, and equipment; and d. variations in the volume of operations.

Moreover, the historical cost of any product involves cost allocations based on judgment, opinion, and custom. Therefore, the historical cost is arbitrary in nature. Over a period of time, however, a body of cost and physical data, e.g., material quantities, labor hours, and machine hours, can be built up.

Thus it is possible to develop average performance on products which can be of help in pricing, provided the basic figures gathered from experience can be tempered to allow for expected changes in material, labor, and overhead prices or costs, and in the volume of operations.

While current product costs may not have any direct bearing on current selling prices, this does not mean that they should be ignored. Instead, they should be compared with current selling prices as one measure of the profitability of current operations. Where profit margins are below normal, management should be stimulated to seek cost reductions, greater volume, or better prices.

Management may further be moved to drop lines or to make other changes to improve its profit situation. For example, management may concentrate the sales effort on products that currently offer the best profit possibilities because of their potential sales volume or because of their greater marginal income contribution per hour for the facilities involved in making them.

Clearly, management will not be stimulated to take any specific action along these lines when it is operating in the dark with respect to its product costs and profits or losses on individual products and product lines.

Standard Product Costs and Pricing

Although used primarily as a technique for the control of product costs, standard costs have provided many executives with a foundation of cost knowledge which, when used with caution and common sense, has been helpful as one aspect in pricing. In particular, the executives have been supplied with standards of performance with respect to material quantities, labor time, and machine time against which current or expected prices and costs could be applied for pricing purposes.

In some companies, standards underlying the standard product costs are so set as to constitute goals for attainment that are beyond normal expectations. While such standards are in these cases considered to be desirable spurs to improved performance, the standard product costs based upon them are too low to be used as costs for price considerations. Standards based on good average performance are more satisfactory for the latter purpose.

Standard costs are commonly adjusted at the outset of a new manufacturing season. In many companies, this means that they are revised twice each year. In other companies, the standard costs are adjusted at more frequent intervals in accordance with significant changes in raw material prices or labor rates, or with significant changes in overhead costs or volume of operations.

If standard costs are to be used in pricing considerations in industries in which finished goods prices tend to fluctuate with raw material prices, they should be adjusted with changes in raw material prices for them to be of practical value. The reason for this is that the replacement cost of the raw material at the time a price is quoted for a product is of greater significance to the price than some average cost would be. In fact, it is of greater significance to price than is the actual cost of the raw material which will be used to make it.

Relationship of Volume to Overhead Costs and Pricing

Practice varies among companies as to the basis on which the volume of operations will be assumed in determining standard burden rates and upon which, in turn, the standard product burden costs will be based. The major difference is that some companies base their rates on volumes expected in the coming season while others use the volume expected under normal conditions.

Beyond this, some additional companies, in hope or desperation, base their burden rates on an assumption of operation at full capacity, even though they know it is problematical whether such volume can be either achieved or maintained.

The use of burden rates based on volume expected in the coming season provides a forecast of expected actual product burden costs. But such costs may be harmful when used as the basis for pricing purposes, since they will be low when business volume is expected to be high, and high when business volume is expected to be low.

To the extent that they are allowed to influence the setting of prices, they will result in the company's charging too little when business is good and too much when business is poor. Carried to extremes, a company under such a policy would price itself out of the market during bad times and give its business away during periods of general prosperity.

The use of burden rates based on an assumption of operation at full capacity can have a harmful influence on pricing that is soon revealed when this assumption proves to have been false. The end result is not sweetened by the argument that such rates must be used because others in the industry are taking this approach; or that they must be used because otherwise costs will be so high as not to permit prices that are competitive.

Standard costs should be established objectively, based on costs and volume that are expected to be reasonably attainable. It appears to me that the use of normal volume in this connection is most appropriate where costs are to be brought into pricing considerations. The resulting standard burden product cost at least provides management with a workable concept of one element of cost that it should seek to recover in the average selling price over the long run.

In the meantime, if prices must be accepted which do not fully cover these costs, they will be accepted with the knowledge that they do not in fact cover these costs in full. It is better to know this at the time an order is accepted than to be made painfully aware of it only at the end of an accounting period.

The cynic may argue against the use of normal volume on the ground that it cannot be determined since it cannot exist in a world of constant change.

The practical businessman, however, has a pretty good idea of the volume of business he is likely to get on the average, having in mind seasonal and minor cyclic variations. As a realist, he knows that he cannot count on continual operation at capacity. Thus, with experience and study, he can establish goals that are reasonably attainable on the average.

Moreover, the businessman is accustomed to changing his sights on volume with major changes in his industry and in his company. Normal volume, to him, is therefore not a static concept. It changes with industry and company trends.

Cost-Volume Relationships and Pricing

Knowledge of cost-volume relationships relative to individual products and product lines can be of assistance in pricing considerations, whether figures from the past or projections of the future are used. In particular, studies along these lines make it possible to visualize the probable results of proposed or expected changes in cost, volume, or price.

Businessmen are often tempted to reduce prices on existing products in an effort to increase volume. The aim is, of course, to spread fixed costs over a larger volume of production and, thereby, more than make up for loss in price. The concept involves not only a careful estimate of the extent to which demand can be increased by a given decrease in price, but also a careful estimate of what the costs will be under the increased volume.

Such studies often reveal that it will take a considerable increase in volume to make up for the loss in price. And this statement is particularly true where variable costs constitute a large portion of the total cost of a product.

For example, assuming that the variable costs of a given product are $0.80 per dollar of sales, leaving $0.20 of marginal income, a reduction in selling price of 4% would require a 25% increase in volume for the company to be as well off as it now is. (A $0.04 drop in selling price would reduce the marginal income to $0.16 per "old" sales dollar. Thus it would require a 25% increase in volume to regain the $0.20 formerly received.)

However, the results from a given decrease in price have often been far more beneficial than was anticipated, even though forced by competitive conditions. This is particularly so where it has been possible to expand total demand and not simply to take sales away from someone else.

Both long-run and short-run considerations should, of course, be taken into account in deciding whether to reduce price, including the possibility of spoiling the market for the future and the probable reactions of competitors.

Budgeting as Related to Pricing

The preparation of financial budgets annually, and in connection with longer-range planning, involves the development of estimates and projections with respect to cost, volume, and price for the budgeted periods.

If initial budgets, although realistic, show expected unsatisfactory results for a given period, effort can be directed toward reducing cost, increasing volume, or making adjustments in price, so as to effect an improvement. Thus management will work toward developing a relationship between cost, volume, and price which will result in meeting a goal with respect to profit or return on investment.

Variable budgets, although designed primarily for control purposes, provide detailed knowledge of cost-volume relationships by type of expense, by departments, and by cost centers. This information can be helpful in pricing. Particularly so in dealing with tight competitive situations and in coping with problems of adding or dropping products, ·where knowledge of the variable, incremental, or differential costs involved is highly important.

Learning Curves and Pricing

Many companies find it useful to plot unit costs for individual products or models on graph paper with the y axis representing unit cost and the x axis the accumulated volume of units completed. Such graphs reveal the manner in which unit costs have been reduced as experience has been gained on successive units.

Over a period of time, typical learning curves or patterns emerge which can be used in establishing standards of cost performance on additional new products or models involving essentially the same production processes. These curves are most helpful in determining prices that must be received over time if profits are to be realized.

Learning curves are also helpful in determining the point in the accumulated volume of units completed at which a given unit selling price and the expected unit cost are equal. In other words, the point in accumulated volume at which the company will "break even" in terms of relationship of the expected cost per unit to the proposed selling price.

In the production of commercial aircraft, for example, the unit cost on initial units is very high. But it should be possible to reduce this cost with the production of successive units along the lines of a fairly well-defined pattern of experience.

The selling price per unit selected must, of course, take into account the demand and competitive situations, as well as cost. Thus it is not likely that a high enough price can be charged to allow a profit for some time in the production of a new model.

It is highly important, however, before accepting orders at a proposed selling price and starting production to know the probable costs of a new model, including expected reductions in unit costs in accordance with the expected learning curve, and to predetermine results by time periods based on the assumed selling price, assumed demand, and assumed productive capacity.

It is also highly important to know in advance the point in the accumulated output at which it should be possible to start realizing a profit on the new model and to use all the figures mentioned in establishing schedules, budgets, and profit goals for control purposes.

Cost-price relationships relative to product age or other factors. In most manufacturing companies, products differ in their cost-price relationships because of differences in age or other factors. We have just noted, for example, that it may not be possible to sell some new products at prices adequate to cover their full costs until costs are lowered through improved efficiency in manufacture and through increased volume.

Similarly, for competitive reasons and particularly to maintain customer goodwill, it is often necessary to continue to produce and sell some old products on which the price obtainable may not cover full costs. Likewise, it is often necessary to carry some items which are not profitable in order to be able to offer customers a full line of products.

In an outstanding article on pricing some years ago, the late E. Stewart Freeman of the Dennison Manufacturing Company likened an industrial company's products to the members of a human family. He stated, for example:

> Products, like humans, pass through a life curve from the early development of childhood, through the expanding period of youth, to the critical stages of middle age, and thence downward to the dotage of obsolescence. . . . It may be as unreasonable to expect all products to pay a like share of this year's cost as it is to expect the

baby, young sister, older brother, and grandparent to contribute alike toward the household expenses. Some are relics of the past worth preserving, some are the sustenance of the present, while others are the hope for the future.

The prosperous family is one which develops a lot of big strong brothers; yet, even in the prosperous family, all cannot be big brothers. We can save money today by not having any children, but when the present products approach obsolescence there may be none to replace them. On the other hand, balance is very important. No family or business can survive if at any given time it has too large a proportion of infant or infirm members to support. Likewise, it will be in a continuous state of unstable equilibrium so long as it depends too much on the contribution of a relatively few members. Such members might become sick or be attacked by competitors who have no weak sisters for their big brothers to support.[1]

I enjoy this analogy and appreciate the lesson it provides, even though I believe that it is the middle-aged parents and not the big brothers who actually provide the main support for a human family, as any middle-aged parent will agree.

Special Cost Studies on New Products

In pricing a new product, it is first desirable to estimate its costs under various volumes of production — basing this, insofar as practicable, on records of previous experience with respect to the operations through which the new product will pass. Then, to compare these costs with estimates of expected receipts from various volumes of sales at assumed selling prices. The object is, of course, to arrive at an attainable volume of production and sales that will bring in the largest total net receipts over time.

In the classroom, for example, it is a simple matter to assume a demand curve and a supply curve and to arrive at a theoretically desirable price. In practice, however, it is very difficult to develop for a new product either a demand curve or a supply curve that can be accepted with confidence.

The cost accountant knows well the difficulties of determining the cost of existing products at existing volumes, let alone the difficulties of predetermining the cost of a proposed product at proposed volumes of production. Even with the aid of a computer, it takes a combination of judgment based on experience; deduction based on field tests

---

[1] E. Stewart Freeman, *Pricing the Product* (Yearbook of the National Association of Accountants, 1939), p. 21.

or on the apparent experience of others now in the market with products of a similar type or class; intuition; and imagination to estimate what the demand for a new product is likely to be at various prices.

For that matter, it is not a simple problem to estimate the future demand for a product that is already on the market and on which a price has been established.

Full Cost and Pricing

The businessman has often been criticized for a tendency to favor a concept of pricing based on the estimated full cost of a product, plus what he considers to be a "reasonable" profit. Along with this, he has been criticized for not paying enough attention instead to such matters as total costs versus total receipts, incremental costs related to incremental revenues, and considerations of demand.

Granted that such criticism is valid, there is still something to be said for this homely viewpoint which seeks to get back what is considered to have been spent on a product, plus adequate compensation for effort expended and money invested. The difficulty lies in its inflexible emphasis on full product cost and failure to take into account many other factors of importance in pricing.

Although the full-cost approach has these limitations, it is understandable that many businessmen feel confident of their ability to establish the actual, standard, or projected costs of a product as a basis for pricing. They are much less confident of their ability to determine potential prices based on analyses of demand characteristics which are uncertain at best and for the most part beyond their control.

Moreover, as noted by Freeman, no company can be successful unless its products on the average are strong and healthy, which means being capable of realizing revenues in excess of their full costs. Thus a company should know its full costs; be aware of when it is selling at a price below full cost; and see to it that over time it receives full cost reimbursement, plus a reasonable profit on the majority of its products if it hopes to be successful.

Incremental Costs and Pricing

For a number of situations, the incremental or differential costs of a product are the most relevant costs to be considered for pricing purposes. These are, essentially, the additional costs that are incurred when an item is produced and sold, and that would be saved if the item were not produced and sold.

In producing a new product, for example, the incremental costs are a. the costs of the raw material and labor expended on it; b. the variable burden that would not have been incurred had the product not been taken on; c. the fixed charges on any new plant and equipment purchased to produce the new product; and d. the additional — if any — selling, delivery, and administrative expenses involved.

As a refinement, one might add interest on the capital required to finance the production and sale of the product. This would also include the additional investment in accounts receivable and inventories, provided that the same capital could otherwise be employed elsewhere.

If the possible incremental receipts from sales exceed these incremental costs, it is evident that as far as these factors are concerned the company would be better off to produce and sell the new product than it would be not to do so. This is not to say, however, that the company should proceed to do this without considering other factors.

Similarly, given the available selling price for a product, one can hold that incremental costs of the types just mentioned are the relevant costs to be considered in deciding whether or not to produce and sell it. Moreover, the margin available above these costs for any given product can be compared with the margins to be expected for any other products that might be made on the same facilities in deciding which are the preferable products to produce and sell.

Where prices are not given and the producer has some leeway in deciding what prices to ask for his products, preoccupation with incremental costs may move a management to set selling prices lower than is necessary under the actual conditions of demand. If the demand at various prices could be ascertained with accuracy, there would be little danger of this.

But, as we have observed, in most cases estimates of demand at various prices, i.e., demand curves, are not too reliable. Thus the temptation is to take the defensive and to quote prices that are lower than warranted. Moreover, such pricing may spoil the market for future sales and cause unfavorable reactions of other producers.

To be sure, incremental costing may be used only to determine the bottom limit of an acceptable price. Thus it does not necessarily prevent a company from charging a price that is both in keeping with the demand situation and that will yield a satisfactory profit. The danger is, however, that concentration on incremental costs may lead to contentment with prices that make only a modest contribution above such costs.

Importance of knowing both incremental and full costs. Surely, a company ought to know both the incremental costs and the full costs of its products. For Freeman's "infants," "weak sisters," and "problem children," it may well not be possible to charge prices that even cover full costs, let alone that provide any profit. Here, a knowledge of incremental costs can set a rock bottom to the selling price that can be accepted without incurring an out-of-pocket loss.

Knowledge of the full cost of these products will, however, be helpful in showing the extent to which whatever price is received is contributing to the covering of these costs. And it should spur some effort to get prices that will reimburse the company for these full costs to the extent possible. At least, accepting prices below full cost will then be done with eyes open and not in ignorance.

Similarly, it may be appropriate to charge less than the full cost of a product temporarily in order to get business to make use of idle capacity; to provide work for employees; or to meet a competitive market situation. Here, the incremental costs involved are the major cost considerations, although it should also be of some importance to know the full cost of the product for the reasons noted in the previous paragraphs.

If this product is one that is to become a major product, moreover, short-run cost and pricing considerations will not be enough. If the product is to become a major member of the family, it must in time take up its fair share of cost and profit responsibility.

As a practical matter, this must be taken into account in setting the price in the first instance. Obviously, it is very easy to lower prices but often difficult to raise them.

New products offering high margins. For many new products that are brought onto the market, the major consideration is the probable price people will be willing to pay for them. Even full cost is a minor factor in the picture, since whatever price is set for a product will be well above such cost.

With the passing of time, prices are lowered to widen the market or for competitive reasons. Thus full costs become of some importance in pricing considerations, at least in the sense that they offer a resistance to the lowering of price.

In the old age of a product, the selling price may have been worked down until it covers, with little or no margin, only the additional costs incurred in producing it. However, it is possible in some cases that, by this time, the demand may be restricted to a relatively few customers who are attached to the product for one reason or another and who are willing to pay a good price to obtain it.

In companies where products pass through the stages just

described, profitable operation depends upon the maintenance of a healthy average age of products by the periodic development of new products to take up the cost and profit responsibilities that can no longer be borne by products reaching old age.

Deciding whether or not to drop a product or product line. There are times when retrenchment is in order and the elimination of unprofitable products and less productive facilities can result in short-run improvement in profit, as well as in clearing the way for shifting capital, labor, and management effort into more profitable channels for the long run.

The relevant costs in deciding whether to drop a product or product line in the short run are costs of the type we have been calling incremental costs. These are the costs that would be saved if the product or product line in question were to be eliminated.

If the arithmetic shows that the available price for a product is adequate to cover these costs and to provide some margin above it, even though not adequate to cover the product's full cost, the expected decision is to continue to produce and sell the item. Otherwise, the company will be less well off in terms of total operations.

As we have noted a number of times, it may be desirable and even necessary to carry along some products that are incapable of bearing their full cost and profit responsibility. Over the long run, however, a company's products on the average must obviously provide more than this if it is to be successful.

Moreover, a point can be reached where a product or product line should be eliminated, even though available revenue on it exceeds its incremental costs and provides some contribution toward remaining costs. Thus the labor, facilities, and management time and energy now being expended on the product could be shifted to more profitable use for the long run.

In other words, the company should get going on a really worthwhile new product instead of limping along with an old product whose only contribution is to help the company lose money more slowly.

Relevant Costs Under Changing Economic Conditions

In slack periods of seasonal and cyclic fluctuations, available selling prices tend to drop. Therefore, it is not possible to realize as satisfactory prices as under more normal conditions. At such times, the usefulness of standard burden rates based on normal volume becomes apparent as far as pricing is concerned.

It is not to be expected that prices obtainable when business is slack are likely to be adequate to cover the full actual unit costs at such times and to provide a normal margin of profit as well. If a company is to be successful, it should, however, be possible, except under extremely poor business conditions, to sell the majority of its products at prices which show a reasonable gross margin per unit, with unit costs for burden being computed by the application of burden rates based on the normal volume of operations.

To state this in another way, if the company expects to be successful, the full standard cost of a product based on the normal volume of operations is the most relevant cost to be considered for pricing purposes under most conditions for a majority of that company's products.

This does not mean that a company is likely to make either the normal net profit per unit or the normal net profit in total during slack periods. After all, selling prices as well as the volume of operations would be below normal at such times. Hopefully, the higher prices and above-normal volume of operations obtainable during good times will balance off the unfavorable variances of slack periods.

Under extremely poor business conditions, it may well be that it is not possible to recover in selling price the full standard cost of even a company's strongest products. It is still, however, wise to compute the full standard cost of a product in such cases. The reasoning here is that when less than this must be accepted in selling price it will be done consciously, as was suggested earlier in pricing considerations for a company's weaker products.

Similarly, the incremental costs on such products should be established in order to know the minimum that prices might reach before the company would suffer an incremental out-of-pocket loss.

The cost elements of each product should also be known, particularly in terms of the major classifications of material, labor, variable burden, fixed burden, and selling and administrative expenses to the extent practicable. These cost elements are important not only for pricing purposes, but also for directing sales and production efforts under changing economic conditions.

Thus, if business conditions are poor, it may be important to identify products having a high labor and machine utilization content so as to concentrate sales effort on them in order to get as much business as possible to keep employees and facilities usefully employed. Similarly, when business is good and productive capacity is scarce, sales effort can be directed toward those products involving relatively larger amounts of material cost and relatively less labor and machine time.

It is the marginal contribution above incremental or variable costs that is of major importance in deciding which product to stress when demand is in excess of productive capacity. As a matter of fact, an analysis of the marginal contributions of products will indicate the relative preference for one over another, regardless of the state of demand. Obviously, such distinctions are academic during periods when demand is below productive capacity and when a company is glad to have whatever business it can get.

Care must be taken that the marginal contributions to be compared are those for time spent in the use of the same facilities. This is often spoken of as "marginal contribution per machine hour." A simple example may help to clarify this point:

Let us suppose the following:

	Product A		Product B	
Selling price per pound	$2.00	100%	$2.50	100%
Full Cost	1.80	90	2.40	96
Net income	$0.20	10%	$0.10	4%

It seems evident that when demand exceeds productive capacity the tendency here would be to push the sales of product A.

Let us suppose, however, that the variable cost analysis shows the following:

	Product A		Product B	
Selling price per pound	$2.00	100%	$2.50	100%
Variable costs	1.60	80	2.00	80
Marginal income	$0.40	20%	$0.50	20%

Now it appears that it would be better to push product B, since it shows a marginal contribution of $0.50 per pound, while product A shows a contribution of only $0.40 per pound. Curiously enough, however, the variable costs of each product are 80% of selling price, meaning that whichever product is sold the marginal contribution per sales dollar will be $0.20.

From this viewpoint, it is a matter of indifference as to which product is pushed. A million dollars of sales of product A will make just the same marginal income contribution as a million dollars of sales of product B. (Incidentally, the assumption here is that the costs with which we are dealing include selling and administrative expenses, as well as manufacturing costs, and that they have been identified rationally with each product.)

Let us now show the total costs and contributions as follows:

	Product A		Product B	
Selling price per pound	$2.00	100%	$2.50	100%
Variable costs	1.60	80	2.00	80
Marginal contribution	$0.40	20%	$0.50	20%
Fixed costs	.20	10	.40	16
	$0.20	10%	$0.10	4%

Looking at the fixed costs just shown, it is evident that product B uses the facilities, or whatever else is included in fixed costs, double the amount used by product A. If we can assume that the same facilities or other fixed costs are involved in making each of these two products, it is evident that two pounds of A can be made and sold for the same use of facilities or other fixed costs as one pound of B.

The contributions toward the same facilities or other fixed costs may then be illustrated for these two products as follows:

	Product A		Product B	
Sales	2 lbs. $4.00	100%	1 lb. $2.50	100%
Variable costs	3.20	80	2.00	80
	$0.80	20%	$0.50	20%

Assuming that the fixed costs illustrated are the limiting factor in this case, and that demand exceeds productive capacity, product A is the product that should be produced and sold in preference to product B.

As we noted earlier, however, short-run costs and contributions are not the only matters to be considered. In the present case, for example, it may be necessary to continue to produce substantial quantities of product B in order to hold the trade of customers whose orders will be needed in the future when times are not so good.

Costs Relevant to the Robinson-Patman Act

This act is designed to prevent price discriminations between customers that lessen competition and that cannot be justified on a cost basis.

It is the full cost of a product, and not simply the incremental costs involved in filling a particular order, that is required for justification.

In general, for example, if competition is thereby lessened, one cannot sell the same product to some customers at a price based on full costs and to others at a price based on incremental costs. The cost differentials, if any, between serving one customer and another must be based on the total costs involved in serving one versus the total costs involved in serving the other.

Cost-justification under the Robinson-Patman Act is an important and involved subject, not to be handled lightly or briefly. A point that can be stressed, however, is that before granting a more favorable price to one customer than to another, in a situation that might be subject to the Robinson-Patman Act, one should make a careful cost analysis in order to be satisfied that the price differential is appropriate. It can be an awkward defense if such an analysis is made only after it is discovered that the case is going to be brought into court.

Costs Relevant for Decisions to Make or Buy

This problem is the other side of the problem as to whether or not to make and sell a given item. As in the latter case, the costs most relevant to a decision are what are known variously as the incremental, differential, or variable costs.

In other words, these are the additional costs to make an item that would be saved if it were not made. If these costs are less than it would cost to purchase the item from someone else, the presumption is that it should be made and not bought.

Items on which the problem of make or buy arises most frequently are manufactured parts or components to be used in connection with the production of a larger item.

As an example, let us suppose that we have been making a part at a full cost of $5.00 per unit, and that we now find we can buy it from someone else for $4.50. Consider:

$5.00	full cost to make
4.50	purchase price
$0.50	possible saving

Analysis of variable costs:

$4.50	purchase price
3.50	variable costs to make
$1.00	out-of-pocket saving by making

Analysis of full costs:

	To Make	To Buy	Difference to Make
Variable costs	$3.50	$4.50	$1.00 saving
Our fixed costs	1.50	1.50	—
	$5.00	$6.00	$1.00 saving

In this example, the decision as far as the arithmetic is concerned is to continue to make the item. The fixed costs, by definition, will be with us whether or not we buy the part. Therefore, these can be left out of the calculation. If included in the calculation, however, they are included in the cost to buy as well as in the cost to make, as just illustrated.

To illustrate that the make or buy problem is the other side of the problem as to whether to make and sell a given item, let us suppose that the man who is trying to get an order from us for the part at a price of $4.50 has exactly the same costs as we. Let us also suppose that under normal conditions he would expect to price the item at $5.25. Thus:

Supplier's	Normal	Proposed	Difference
Price	$5.25	$4.50	($0.75) loss
Full cost to make and sell	5.00	5.00	—
Profit	$0.25	($0.50)	($0.75) loss

Proposed selling price	$4.50
Variable costs	$3.50
Contribution toward fixed costs	$1.00
Fixed costs	$1.50
Profit	($0.50) loss

In making the offer, the supplier hoped that his bid would be attractive enough to get an order. Thus he was attempting to get a dollar per unit contribution toward his fixed costs, even though the price of $4.50 showed a loss of $0.50 when related to full cost. Both sides in this example were therefore analyzing variable costs and the available marginal contribution above these costs in arriving at a decision.

Let us assume that the part under consideration has not been made previously and that it will require the purchase of machinery and equipment for production to be undertaken. In this case, the depreciation, maintenance, and other costs associated with such machinery and equipment should be included among the incremental costs to be considered, along with the material, labor, and variable overhead costs normally regarded as incremental costs.

Theoretically, if building space is available to house the new machinery and equipment at no extra cost, and if certain overhead expenses which will be charged to the part once its manufacture is undertaken will exist whether or not this part is manufactured, such costs should not be considered in cost comparisons between making or buying the part. However, if the omission of such costs is necessary in order to justify making the part rather than buying it, it is probably best to decide to buy it.

Given a choice, as certainly would be the case if we had not been making the part, a company should concentrate on those things that it can do best and avoid entering activities in which it can demonstrate only marginal performance. Here, the adage that "the shoemaker should stick to his last" is most appropriate.

Problems involved in deciding whether to make a part or buy it from outside sources are more complicated when a part is made, or might be made, by one division and sold to another within the same company.

We shall be considering this situation again later in discussing problems of transfer pricing for goods sold by one profit center to another within a company. The point here is that there can be a conflict of interests between divisions, as well as between a division and the best interests of the company as a whole.

In particular, a division may currently be able to buy a part at a lower price from an outside source than from another division within the company. This despite the fact that it is to the company's best interest to have the part made rather than bought outside, since a large part of its cost is fixed. To the buying division, the cost of the part is a variable cost, whether purchased internally or from an outside source.

For the selling division, however, and therefore for the company as a whole, part of the cost is fixed, whether or not the part is made. Unless the part can be purchased outside for less than its variable costs to the selling division, its purchase will involve an additional out-of-pocket cost for the company as a whole.

A ready answer to such a problem is that the selling division should always meet the competitive price. There is more to the problem than this, however, since the selling division is usually neither completely free to make what it pleases nor to increase or decrease its productive capacity at will.

While the view may be taken that one division which sells to another enjoys a captive market, the other side of this view is that it is a restrictive market, or at least one to which the seller has the first obligation. Surely, when demand is well in excess of capacity, the selling division is not completely free to sell outside and ignore the requirements of members of the corporate family.

In any event, a buyer-seller relationship between divisions a. should over time be mutually advantageous; b. should not normally be an on-again-off-again proposition depending on market conditions; and c. should be subject to review by top corporate management.

Most interdivisional transactions should be handled at the divisional level without serious conflict. Nonetheless, the way should be open to bring conflicts of interest to top management for settlement if necessary.

Factors of importance other than costs.   Other factors beyond costs are also important in decisions to make or buy a part. The importance of assured delivery or quality may lead to a decision to make a part, regardless of the savings that might be realized in its purchase. At times, it may be important to provide work to hold a trained force together, or to maintain skill in making a part, even though temporarily it might be purchased outside at lower cost, particularly during periods of business depression.

Occasionally, a potential supplier will offer a part at an attractive price, having in mind that he will raise the price on later orders once the buyer has become dependent upon him for supply. If such a case is suspected, it is wise for the buyer to maintain the capacity to produce the part, even though he actually buys it from the outside supplier.

Finally, if it is possible to buy a part for less than the incremental costs to make it, a number of questions should be raised.

Is it possible that either the company's cost accounting, or that of the potential supplier, is faulty? Is the company grossly inefficient in producing the part, or does the potential supplier have some type of machinery, equipment, or process which enables him to produce at much lower variable costs, if not total costs? Is it possible that the supplier produces this part for others as well and, therefore, that he has a marked cost advantage through high-volume production?

Answers to questions such as these are important in long-run decisions as to whether a given part should be made or bought.

Problems in Fixed Asset Selection

In the present chapter and in the one preceding it, I have highlighted areas where costs relevant for some purposes are not relevant for others. In particular, I have noted areas where decisions call for the analysis of costs in detail or in a form different than that used for purposes of inventory valuation and profit determination in the financial records.

One area of this type that we have not yet considered involves fixed asset selection and replacement, which is often discussed under the title "capital budgeting." This is an important enough area to be considered in a separate chapter and I shall therefore present it in the next chapter.

CHAPTER 27

Fixed Asset Selection and Replacement

Investments in plant and equipment are made for a variety of reasons not always directly connected with the improvement of profit or return on investment. Certain replacements, such as that of a general-purpose lathe which has worn out, are required simply to maintain existing operations and profits. Other expenditures are made to improve safety and working conditions or plant appearance with no measurable savings or profit improvement. Decisions on these items are made by managers at various levels without elaborate studies to justify them.

The investments with which we are concerned in the present chapter, however, are those which do improve profit and return on investment through cost reduction, improved quality of product or service, or expanded operations.

At any given time, in any progressive company having extensive facilities, there should be more ideas for investment in plant and equipment than money and time to make them. It is highly important, therefore, for such companies to maintain orderly procedures for proposing, reviewing, and approving capital expenditures. The end objective is that all proposals will be given adequate consideration and that within the yearly limits of time and funds available the most necessary and soundest expenditures will be made.

While lack of money is obviously an important limiting factor in making capital expenditures, another highly important factor is the limited amount of time and energy management is able to spend on new projects, while maintaining satisfactory performance on existing operations.

Moreover, new projects seem inevitably to involve more problems and to require longer time for installation and achievement of an acceptable level of performance than anticipated.

Deciding on the most appropriate mathematical formula to use in making selections among various alternative proposals for capital expenditures is a relatively unimportant problem in many companies. The real problem is that, again within the limits of money and management time available, there are more equally attractive proposals than can be undertaken.

Slight differences between these proposals in the computed return on investment or other criterion of selection are not conclusive. The reason for this is that there is the lack of certainty in the assumptions which must be made on the many variables underlying the computations. Nor does weighting these estimates by percentages of probability really do much to remove the uncertainty.

These comments are not meant to minimize the importance of using some formula that will help to eliminate proposals which are significantly less desirable than others. Moreover, just because there are many uncertainties in the typical capital expenditure is no excuse for compounding the uncertainty by using a crude formula, particularly when a more exact formula can be used with equal ease.

The point still is, however, that even a refined formula will not provide the final answer in a good many situations involving capital expenditures.

Data Required in Analyzing Proposals

The type of information that should be assembled in judging proposals for capital expenditures is indicated in some detail in Exhibit 60, Exhibit 61, and Exhibit 62. These exhibits illustrate the information requested by an actual company in connection with such proposals. The reader will note that the cost data are gathered in two parts: one covers the estimated investment costs involved; the other the expected operating costs once the investment has been made, together with present costs or the costs of an alternative proposal.

For all practical purposes, investment costs include all costs up to the point where the plant, machinery, or equipment is ready for regular operation. Adjustments are made for the estimated salvage value of any equipment replaced and for the estimated tax savings on the capital loss, if any, on the disposal of such equipment. These adjustments are made apart from the books of account in connection with the investment decision only. They would, of course, be treated differently for accounting purposes once the investment had been made.

More specifically, for accounting purposes the investment would be entered at its full cost and it would be depreciated accordingly

EXHIBIT 60
Request for Appropriation

Requested By_____   R/A No. _____
Department _____   Date _____
Delivery Date _____   Estimates
Source: 1. Total Cost   _____
                                                2. Savings or Profit after Taxes
                                                   but before Depreciation   _____
                                                3. Period for Cost Recovery   _____
                                                4. Efficient Productive Period   _____
                                                5. Return on Investment   _____

Reason for Request

To maintain existing operations and   To improve profit or return on invest-
profits, or to make improvements on which   ment through:
savings or profit results are not measurable:
_____ 1. Rebuilding and Replacement   _____ 1. Cost Reduction
_____ 2. General Plant Improvement   _____ 2. Improved Quality of Product or
_____ 3. Safety, Health—Working   Service
           Conditions   _____ 3. Expanded Capacity for Existing
                                                          Products
                                               _____ 4. New Products

Description and Discussion

Approval Date_____
Chairman of the Board
President   VP-General Manager
Treasurer   Director Res. & Eng.
                                               Plant Superintendent

_____

thereafter. The equipment it replaced along with its accumulated depreciation, would be removed from the accounts. And the capital gain or loss on disposal would be treated as a gain or loss for the period.

Operating costs per year are listed prior to depreciation, for reasons that will become apparent in later discussion, and depreciation is shown as a separate figure. Exhibit 62, although designed to compare costs per year under a present method with those under a proposal, may be used to compare costs between two alternative proposals. Or, in the case of expanded capacity for existing products or new products,

EXHIBIT 61
Investment Cost Check Sheet

For Use with Request for Appropriation

Request # _____
Date   _____
Cost by: _____   ESTIMATED   ACTUAL
1. Items purchased
   a. Total invoice cost
   b. Freight inward
2. Items manufactured
   a. Total labor
   b. Total material
   c. Burden at   % $DL
3. Installation
   a. Labor
   b. Material
4. Auxiliary items
   a. Added equipment
   b. Added tools
5. All other costs
   a. Service agreement
   b. Consulting engineers
   c. Break-in period
   d.
   e.
   f.
6. TOTAL COST
7. Related Equipment, etc.
   a.
   b.
   c.
   d.
   e.
8. Total Program Cost
9. Deduct
   a. Salvage value of replaced equipment
   b. Tax saving on capital loss, if any, on
       disposal of replaced equipment
10. Net Investment

it may also be used to compare expected incremental costs and revenues and to show the expected incremental profit per year. If operating costs and revenues are expected to differ among the years of the expected life of the investment, then separate schedules should, of course, be prepared to reflect these expectations.

EXHIBIT 62
Operating Cost Check Sheet

For Use with Request for Appropriation

Request # _____
Date   _____
Cost by: _____

Operating Costs and Estimated Savings per Year

Item	Present Cost	Cost under Proposal	Estimated Savings
Total before Depreciation			
Depreciation			
Total after Depreciation			

Estimated Savings per Year
  before Depreciation $ $ Return on Investment If
Less: Additional Depreciation   Held for Estimated Efficient
Net Taxable Savings   Productive Period of ....
Tax at _____ %   _____ Years = ... %.
Net Savings after Taxes and before   _____
  Depreciation $_____ $_____ ____ % if held for ____ years
                                                              ____ % if held for ____ years
Payback period _____ years (Net   ____ % if held for ____ years
  Investment ÷ Net Savings after
  Taxes and before Depreciation)

Use of the Payback Period

A common step in judging the relative merits of various proposals for capital expenditures is to compare them in terms of the speed with which the investment may be recovered. Indeed, in some companies this is the only arithmetical test applied to such proposals.

This payback period, expressed in years, is computed in each case simply by dividing the total amount of the investment by the expected annual savings or increase in income before depreciation. Thus, if a machine proposed for purchase requires an investment of $42,000 and it is expected to result in savings before depreciation of $10,000 per year, the payback period is 4.2 years. Consider:

$$\frac{\text{Investment} \qquad \$42,000}{\text{Savings per Year} \qquad \$10,000} = 4.2 \text{ Years Payback}$$

Increased income in terms of cash flow. The savings figure used is prior to an allowance for depreciation, since this figure represents the entire cash flow available for the recovery of the investment as well as for profit, if any, on that investment. To be more accurate, the figure used should be savings before depreciation and after income taxes. In other words, it should be cash flow, as we discussed in an earlier chapter.

For the moment, however, we shall defer income tax considerations in capital budgeting in order to simplify discussion. As a matter of fact, in many companies operating personnel are asked to make proposals without including the factor of income taxes. The proposals that pass initial hurdles are then turned over to tax specialists who report on the income tax aspects connected with them.

Criticisms of the payback method. As a basis for comparing proposals for capital expenditures, the payback method is strongly criticized on the grounds that it does not take the expected useful life of the investment into account. In the foregoing example, a machine having an actual useful life of exactly 4.2 years would be rated as highly as one showing the same payback but having a longer life. This would be so even though financial gain on the investment is to be realized only from income above the return of the investment itself.

Similarly, the payback period does not take into account adequately the rate of cash flow of one proposal versus another. In our example, the cash flow for one proposal might be received evenly over the 4.2 years. For another proposal showing the same payback, it might come in slowly at first and then accelerate as time went on. What is more important, in neither case is the time value of money taken into account.

Conversely, let us take a situation in which two proposals show an equal return on the investment, with the time value of money being taken into account, although differing in years of estimated useful life and in computed payback periods. In this case, there may be some point in selecting the proposal showing the shorter payback period, particularly if the future is uncertain and if there are ample opportunities to invest the funds recovered at a satisfactory rate of return.

Moreover, the payback period can be used as a quick and convenient test to eliminate the least desirable proposals, thereby reducing the number of proposals to be subjected to more refined analysis.

For example, the rule might be established that, except for some new product or project on which an early return was not to be expected, no proposal showing a payback period longer than five years after allowing for income taxes would be given further consideration. This rule would not apply, of course, to necessary or desirable capital expenditures to be made for reasons other than direct savings or profit.

Use of Return on Investment

There are a variety of ways in which return on investment is computed in analyzing proposals for capital expenditures. And refinements are still being introduced from time to time. Each company must therefore decide for itself the extent to which a given refinement will improve the quality of its decisions in capital expenditures.

Expected return on investment: first year.   One method of computing return on investment is simply to relate the expected annual savings after depreciation to the total investment. Using the same figures as those in the payback illustration of $42,000 investment and $10,000 annual savings, and adding the assumptions of ten years of useful life and depreciation on a straight-line basis, the return on investment is 13.8%. Thus:

$$\frac{\text{Savings after Depreciation}}{\text{Investment}} = \text{Return on Investment}$$

$$\frac{\$10,000 - (\$42,000/10)}{\$42,000} = \frac{\$\ 5,800}{\$42,000}$$

$$\frac{\$\ 5,800}{\$42,000} = 13.8\%$$

The cash flow here of $10,000 per year is considered to provide a recovery *of* the investment in the amount of $4,200 reimbursement for depreciation and $5,800 for return *on* the investment.

When this particular computation of return on investment is used, it is listed typically in request-for-appropriation forms under the title "Expected Return on Investment: First Year." This is in recognition of the fact that in later years, as the investment is gradually recovered, the percentage return will not be the same.

In fact, when the savings are estimated to be equal each year, this computed return on the investment based on the first year only is very conservative. Those companies using this method believe that if a proposal passes the test of a required percentage at this point it should be reasonably acceptable. Their reasoning is that if the savings continue to be the same as in the first year the percentage return will rise each year thereafter inasmuch as it will be related to a lower investment base. This point is illustrated in Table 11.

Although this approach has its shortcomings, it at least moves beyond the analysis of payback to include recognition of the estimated years of life for the investment proposal. For example, an alternative proposal to the one we have been considering, which also required an investment of $42,000 with the same expected annual savings of $10,000 but which had an expected life of 15 years, would show the same payback of 4.2 years but a return on investment of 17.1% for the first year. To illustrate:

$$\frac{\$10,000 - (\$42,000/15)}{\$42,000} = \frac{\$\ 7,200}{\$42,000}$$

$$\frac{\$\ 7,200}{\$42,000} = 17.1\%$$

The difference, of course, lies in the amount of cash flow considered to be a recovery of the investment via depreciation and its consequent effect on the amount considered to be the return on the investment. In the present case, the reduction of the estimated recovery of the investment from $4,200 per year to $2,800 raises the amount considered to be the return on the investment per year from $5,800 to $7,200.

Percentage return based on one half of the investment. A refinement in the computation of return on investment from that just discussed is one which recognizes that part of the investment will be recovered in

TABLE 11

Year	Investment	Savings	Recovery of Investment	Return on Investment	Percentage Return
1	$42,000	$10,000	$4,200	$5,800	13.8%
2	37,800	10,000	4,200	5,800	15.3
3	33,600	10,000	4,200	5,800	17.3
4	29,400	10,000	4,200	5,800	19.7
5	25,200	10,000	4,200	5,800	23.0
6	21,000	10,000	4,200	5,800	27.6
7	16,800	10,000	4,200	5,800	34.5
8	12,600	10,000	4,200	5,800	46.0
9	8,400	10,000	4,200	5,800	69.0
10	4,200	10,000	4,200	5,800	138.0

an even amount each year; therefore, on the average throughout its life, one half of the investment will be outstanding. On this basis, our first example would show a return of 27.6%. Consider:

$$\frac{\text{Savings after Depreciation}}{1/2 \text{ of Investment}} = \text{Return on Investment}$$

$$\frac{\$10,000 - (\$42,000/10)}{\$42,000/2} = \frac{\$5,800}{\$21,000}$$

$$\frac{\$5,800}{\$21,000} = 27.6\%$$

This method results in a more accurate picture of what the return on the average amount invested will be over the life of the investment, but it does not alter the relative attractiveness of alternative proposals. The results in each case are simply double those based on total investment and, in this sense, it does not further the process of selection.

If the possible returns on a great majority of proposals were relatively low, however, the use of return on investment based on total investment might discourage the acceptance of proposals which would look quite acceptable if computed on the basis of an average investment of one half the total investment. For this reason, as well as for the fact that it presents a more accurate picture of the return on the average investment involved, the use of one half investment as a base should be preferred.

Investments Not Involving Periodic Recovery

The investments we have been examining are those in facilities which are subject to depreciation, where the savings or incremental revenues to be adequate must provide for the recovery of the investment itself as well as a return on it. If the $42,000 in our example were to be deposited in a savings bank, the cash flow from interest received on it would represent a return on the investment. The full investment itself could presumably be recovered at any time desired, assuming that the bank had not failed.

Similarly, investments in inventories and accounts receivable connected with expansion of sales will not be reduced. This assumes that they are appropriate in amount relative to the amount of expansion which has taken place, unless there is a drop in sales volume.

Therefore, the cash flow resulting from the expansion as far as these investments are concerned is all gain, rather than partly gain and partly a recovery of the investment through reimbursement for depreciation. To be sure, there are likely to be inventory losses, and losses from bad debts, but these would be deducted as operating expenses before arriving at net income.

Discounted Cash Flow or Financial Method

The computations of return on investment just described are of assistance in making selections among alternative proposals for capital expenditures, and they go beyond the computation of simple payback in this connection to bring the useful life of the investment into consideration.

Nonetheless, these computations still lack the degree of preciseness in measuring return on investment now considered desirable in many companies. In particular, they fail to take into account the importance of timing in the valuation of the savings or other cash flows to be realized.

Therefore, the discounted cash flow method, also known as the financial method, has been widely adopted since it is one in which this financial viewpoint is inherent.

Reduction mortgage as an example. Most homeowners are familiar with the conceptual framework within which the discounted cash flow method operates in connection with the reduction mortgage on their homes. This is the method under which equal monthly payments over the life of the mortgage gradually reduce the loan and also cover interest at a fixed rate on the declining balance of the loan.

In negotiating the loan, the banker establishes the following information in consultation with the prospective borrower:

1. The amount of the loan requested.
2. The number of years over which payments of interest and principal are to be made.
3. The rate of interest to be charged.

Given these three factors, he then computes a fourth, namely, the amount of the monthly payment required for him both to recover his investment over the agreed upon years and to receive interest at the agreed upon rate on the balance of the loan outstanding between each payment. As a practical matter, the banker refers to published tables which enable him to establish quickly the monthly payment involved.

The reader who has a mortgage loan of this type knows well that initial monthly payments are largely payments of interest and provide only small retirements of debt. Fortunately, as both the mortgage and the mortgagor grow older, the required amount each month to cover interest diminishes and the retirement of debt increases correspondingly.

In granting the loan, it should be noted that the banker is really buying the right to receive a cash flow each month of a certain amount over a certain number of years. In financial terms, he is tacitly assuming that the amount of the loan is the present value to him of the payments he is to receive, discounted at the agreed upon rate of interest. This point has a bearing on the discussion of investments in fixed assets to follow.

Discounted cash flow applied to fixed asset investments. The same four elements just noted in the case of a mortgage loan are involved in applying the discounted cash flow method to an investment in fixed assets. Here, however, the information first established is as follows:

1. The expected cost of the investment.
2. The estimated useful life of the asset to be acquired.
3. The expected savings or other cash flows to be received each period (usually per year), by means of which the amount invested may be recovered and a return on the investment may be realized.

Given these three factors, the problem under the discounted cash flow method applied to investments in fixed assets is then to find the fourth factor, namely, the rate of return on the investment. When the rate is found, it can be checked as to whether or not it lies within an acceptable range established by the given company for this type of investment. Moreover, the indicated rate on this investment can be compared with rates estimated on other investment proposals in arriving at investment decisions.

In the example with which we have been working, figures for the first three factors just listed are as follows:

1. Investment required, $42,000.
2. Estimated useful life, 10 years.
3. Estimated savings before depreciation (cash flow), $10,000 per year.

These factors may be illustrated in diagrammatic form:

EXHIBIT 63
Fixed Asset Selection and Replacement

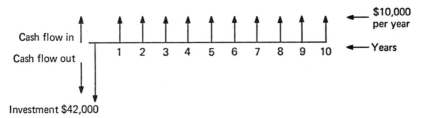

Exhibit 63 emphasizes the difference in timing between the investment and the cash flows expected to be realized from the investment over its useful life. It is also intended to help one to visualize that each succeeding cash flow per year is further and further away. Thus it is worth less in terms of its present value.

The major point the diagram is intended to suggest, however, is that a business investment is an amount paid for the cash flows expected over the life of an asset acquired. The investment is not simply the cost of a piece of property.

Admittedly, the individuals making an investment in a machine may well consider that they have simply bought a machine. Certainly, the accountant will duly record the purchase as an asset, with no footnote to the effect that what was really purchased was an expected cash flow.

Clearly, in our example the justification, if any, for making the investment is the expected savings before depreciation of $10,000 per year over the ten years of estimated useful life of the machine under consideration. It should therefore be evident that if the machine is purchased, the $42,000 paid not only represents the cost of the asset acquired but also what the investor considers the potential savings per year are worth to him at the time the investment is made. In other words, it represents the then-present value to him of the expected yearly cash flows.

We noted in the case of the banker and his mortgage loan that, in financial terms, the present value of cash flows is an amount equal to these cash flows discounted at a given rate of interest. In the banker's case, he knew the present value figure (the amount of the loan requested), the number of years over which payments of interest and principal were to be made, and the rate of interest to be charged. By deduction (actually, by the use of printed tables), he could then determine the monthly cash flow payments required.

In our example, we know the present value figure of $42,000 for the investment and that savings of $10,000 per year are to be expected for ten years. If we can find the rate of discount at which these expected cash flows will show a present value of $42,000, we shall then know the rate of return the investment offers.

To do this, we shall try discounting the expected cash flows at assumed rates until we find the rate we seek. To simplify our calculations, we shall assume that the $10,000 of expected savings each year will be received in a lump sum at the end of the year, even though they will actually be received over the year.

Present value formula. As a first trial, we shall discount the expected cash flows at a rate of 15%. The cash flow of $10,000 to be received at the end of the one year is equal to 115% of the present value of that cash flow as of the beginning of the year. This $10,000 divided by 115 and multiplied by 100 shows its present value for our purposes to be $8,700. As a check on this figure, $8,700 at 15% is $1,300 (rounded) and $8,700 plus $1,300 equals $10,000.

For the second year, the interest is compounded. Thus 115% multiplied by 115% equals 132% (rounded). The cash flow of $10,000 for the second year divided by 132 and multiplied by 100 shows its present value at the beginning of the first year to be $7,560 (rounded).

These two results, and present values for the eight remaining cash flows, can be found by the use of the following formula for establishing the present value of $1:

$$\frac{1}{(1 + i)^n}$$

Thus for the first year:

$$\frac{1}{(1 + i)^n} \quad \text{becomes} \quad \frac{1}{(1 + .15)}$$

$$\frac{1}{(1 + .15)} \quad = \quad 0.870$$

$$0.870 \times \$10,000 \quad = \quad \$8,700.$$

And for the second year:

$$\frac{1}{(1 + .15)^2} \quad = \quad 0.756$$

$$0.756 \times \$10,000 \quad = \quad \$7,560.$$

Fortunately, these factors have long been printed in tables such as those prepared by Jerome Bracken and Charles Christensen presented in Appendix 2. Thus the reader can turn to the column for 15% in Table A there for the remaining factors to complete the calculation of the present value of $1 as shown below in Table 12.

It is evident that the rate of return is greater than 15%. The reason for this is that discounting the estimated annual cash flow at 15% results in a present value of $50,190 for the total of this flow. whereas

TABLE 12

Year	Savings	From Appendix Table A Present Value of $1 Discounted at 15%	Present Value of Savings
1	$10,000	0.870	$ 8,700
2	10,000	0.756	7,560
3	10,000	0.658	6,580
4	10,000	0.572	5,720
5	10,000	0.497	4,970
6	10,000	0.432	4,320
7	10,000	0.376	3,760
8	10,000	0.327	3,270
9	10,000	0.284	2,840
10	10,000	0.247	2,470
		5.019	$50,190

the investment amounts to only $42,000. The problem then is to determine what rate higher than 15% should be used in discounting the estimated cash flow to arrive at a present value of $42,000.

Use of present value of $1 received annually for N years.   We could proceed to try factors from some column higher than 15% in Appendix 2, Table A. But, first, let us note that the sum of the factors for ten years in the 15% column just listed is 5.019. Furthermore, when this sum of the factors is applied to the annual cash flow of $10,000, the result is the total present value of the savings amounting to $50,190.

In Appendix 2, Table B, "Present Value of $1 per Period Received at End," we find the factor 5.019 already provided for us on line 10 in the 15% column. It is clear that the use of Appendix 2, Table B would have saved us 90% of our calculations. Had the savings been unequal each year, however, we would have had to use Appendix 2, Table A.

Now it is evident that for our present problem we can try using factors from line 10 in Appendix 2, Table B until we find the one that will come closest to $42,000 when applied to the annual cash flow of $10,000. This can be spotted easily in this case as being the factor 4. 192 in the 20% column. Thus the estimated return on this investment is approximately 20%.

The factor to be used can also be found quickly as follows:

$$\$10,000 \times X = \$42,000$$
$$X = \frac{\$42,000}{\$10,000}$$

$$X = \quad 4.2$$

It can be seen that the factor 4.192 in the 20% column of Appendix 2, Table B comes closest to 4.2. Note also that 4.2 is the payback figure for our investment. In an investment problem where the expected cash flow from the investment is an equal amount per year, the rate of return can thus be found quickly by first computing the payback and then by locating the factor which comes closest to the payback on the line representing the expected life of the investment. The column in which this factor is located indicates the approximate rate of return on the investment.

Comparison of ROI by different methods.   The reader will note that the discounted cash flow method shows a lower rate of return than we computed as a return on the average investment for our problem (20%

TABLE 13

Year	Investment	Interest Rate	Interest Amount	Savings	Recovery of Investment
1	$42,000.00	20%	$8,400.00	$10,000	$ 1,600.00
2	40,400.00	20	8,080.00	10,000	1,920.00
3	38,480.00	20	7,696.00	10,000	2,304.00
4	36,176.00	20	7,235.20	10,000	2,764.80
5	33,411.20	20	6,682.24	10,000	3,317.76
6	30,093.44	20	6,018.69	10,000	3,981.31
7	26,112.13	20	5,222.43	10,000	4,777.57
8	21,334.56	20	4,266.91	10,000	5,733.09
9	15,601.47	20	3,120.29	10,000	6,879.71
10	8,721.76	20	1,744.35	10,000	8,255.65
					$41,533.89

compared with 27.6%). This is because the discounting process gives a lower weight to savings the farther away they are from realization.

For example, if the useful life were fifteen years rather than ten, the discounted cash flow method would show a return of approximately 23%, whereas the return computed on the average investment would be approximately 34.3%.

Division of savings under discounted cash flow method. The manner in which the discounted cash flow method assumes the savings to be divided between interest and recovery of investment in our example is shown in Table 13 (the recovery of the investment does not quite balance out in these figures, because the rate of return is actually slightly less than 20%).

In a problem of this type, it should be made clear to those who are to decide whether or not to make the investment that the computed rate of return is the expected rate on the declining balance of the investment, as illustrated in the "interest amount" in the schedule just presented. Whether the amount of investment recovered each year can be reinvested at the same rate of return is another matter.

Moreover, whether the rate of return proves to be as estimated depends, of course, on the validity of the estimates of investment cost, savings to be realized, and useful life. For example, if the investment turns out to cost $42,000 and the savings are in fact $10,000 per year, but the useful life proves to be less than 4.2 years, the investment itself will not be recovered let alone any return on it.

In view of the uncertainty connected particularly with estimates of useful life, it is helpful to include in the proposal for a capital expenditure what the return on the investment will be if the useful life differs from a single expected figure. In the present case, for example, the following schedule could be drawn up easily by use of the payback factor and Appendix 2, Table B.

If the Number of Years of Expected Life Is	The Return on the Investment Will be Approximately
5	6%
6	11
7	15
8	17
9	19
10	20
12	21
15	23

Given such a table, those responsible for making the decision on the investment should be stirred to think about the probable useful life of the machine proposed. They should not simply accept without question a single number given to them, whether of expected life or of return on the investment.

Incidentally, in some companies the maximum life used in computing the expected return on investment under the discounted cash flow method for proposed investments in machinery and equipment is ten years. This is partly on the grounds that, owing to the many uncertainties with respect to the future, guessing what the useful life of a machine will be beyond ten years is an academic exercise. It is also partly based on the belief that this is carrying the arithmetical calculations far enough to sort out the projects which should then be given serious consideration on grounds other than their arithmetical justification.

In our example, we have used Appendix 2, Tables A and B covering savings, profits, or payments occurring in a lump sum at the end of each year. The reason for this is that tables of these two types are most commonly available and, therefore, they are most commonly referred to by those using the discounted cash flow method of determining the rate of return on an investment.

Appendix 2, Table C, which covers "Present Value of $1 per Period Received Continuously," is for the reader who wishes to compute somewhat more accurate arithmetical results.

Computation of ROI for unequal cash flows per period.   In the example we have been using, we have assumed that the same amount of savings will be realized each year. In many cases, however, the expected savings or profits will differ from period to period for a variety of reasons.

One approach in a case of this type is simply to use the average savings or profits expected per period. This may be close enough for practical purposes, particularly in view of the uncertainties in the many variables involved. If the expected results for different periods are markedly different, however, it is necessary to make a somewhat more involved analysis in order to compute expected return on investment with a reasonable degree of accuracy.

The approach is identical with that we have just been discussing, in the sense that it involves a discounting of the flow of payments, although the steps are a bit more complicated. An illustration will help to indicate the differences.

Suppose that the $42,000 we have been discussing as an investment to produce $10,000 of savings per year could, as an alternative, be invested in a different machine having the same useful life of ten years. Let us further suppose the alternative machine will offer savings of $4,000 per year for the first five years and $16,000 per year for each of the five years remaining thereafter. What would be the rate of return on the investment?

To determine this rate, under the discounted cash flow method we must proceed by trial and error, as we did in our previous example, to discount the expected savings until we reach the point where, at the indicated rate of discount, the total of the discounted savings equals the amount of investment. In other words, we search until we find the discount rate at which the total present value of the savings equals the investment.

We know from our previous example that an even flow in savings of $10,000 per year showed a return of 20% on the investment. If under the alternative proposal less than this amount per year is to be received in the early years and more than this in the later years, although the total savings will be the same, the rate of return will be less than 20%. The reason for this is that under the discounting process earlier payments are weighted more heavily than later payments in the average rate computed.

Suppose we first select 15% as a possibility, then test to see how closely this comes to fact. We could use Appendix 2, Table A in connection with our calculations and, as we noted earlier, we would have to use this table rather than Appendix 2, Table B if the expected savings differed each year. However, since the expected savings are the same per year for the first five years as well as the same per year for the last five years, we can use Table B more conveniently.

The cumulative present value of $1 per year for five years discounted at 15% is shown in Table B as 3.352. Applying this factor to $4,000 gives $13,408 as the discounted value (present value) of the savings to be realized for the first five years. The cumulative present value of $1 per year for ten years discounted at 15% is 5.019. Thus when we subtract the five-year cumulative factor of 3.352 from this, we get the factor 1.667 for the last five years. Applying this factor to $16,000 gives $26,672 as the discounted value of the savings to be realized for the last five years. In summary:

Years	Present Value Factor at 15%	Expected Savings per Year	Savings Discounted
1–5	3.352	$ 4,000	$13,408
6–10	1.667	16,000	26,672
			$40,080

Since the total discounted cash flow of $40,080 is quite a bit less than the investment figure of $42,000, we shall make another trial. For example, the figures with the savings discounted at 14% are as follows:

Years	Present Value Factor at 14%	Expected Savings per Year	Savings Discounted
1–5	3.433	$ 4,000	$13,732
6–10	1.783	16,000	28,528
			$42,260

Since the total discounted cash flow of $42,260 is quite close to the investment figure of $42,000, the indicated return on the investment is approximately 14%.

If with the same investment of $42,000 and estimated useful life of ten years the earnings were to be $16,000 per year for the first five years, and $4,000 per year for the last five years, the return on investment would be approximately 30%, computed as follows:

Years	Present Value Factor at 30%	Expected Savings per Year	Savings Discounted
1–5	2.436	$16,000	$38,976
6–10	0.656	4,000	2,624
			$41,600

The difference in results between the discounted cash flow method and return computed on the average investment may be noted by comparing our examples as follows:

	Return per Discounted Cash Flow	Average Return Based on Average Investment
Savings		
1. $10,000 per year	20%	27.6%
2. 1–5 years, $4,000 per year		
6–10 years, 16,000 per year	14	27.6
3. 1–15 years, $16,000 per year		
6–10 years, 4,000	30	27.6

Thus it is evident that the discounted cash flow method takes into account differences in the timing of the cash flows in measuring the rate of return on the investment. Obviously, the average return based on average investment does not. Under the latter, the three foregoing investments appear to be equally attractive, whereas under the discounted cash flow method the investment in which the cash flows are heaviest in the early years is by far the most attractive.

Present Value Method

Another technique for analyzing investment proposals is, for lack of a better title, known as the "present value method." Like the discounted cash flow method, it involves establishing the present value of the estimated cash flows expected from the investment over its useful life. Under this method, the flows are discounted at a predetermined rate. Here, the rate used is either the minimum acceptable rate for any capital investment made by the given company, or it is the required minimum rate for a given class of investment, having in mind the nature of the risks involved.

For example, let us assume that our company has set a required rate of return of 16% before income taxes for the type of proposed machine costing $42,000, having an expected useful life of ten years, and offering savings of $10,000 per year. From Appendix 2, Table B, we learn that the factor for ten years at 16% is 4.833. This factor applied to the expected savings of $10,000 per year shows $48,330 as being the present value of these expected cash flows.

Thus the present value is $6,330 above the $42,000 that had to be matched by the calculation just made to meet the required return of

16%. If this calculated evidence indicating that the proposal more than meets the required minimum rate of return is all the information the company needed, it would go ahead with the investment.

However, it might be possible to invest the $42,000 in our second example instead, in which the savings per year for the first five years are expected to be $4,000 and for the last five years, $16,000 per year. Here, the calculations would be as follows:

1. Factor for years 1–5, Appendix 2, Table B, 16% column, 3.274.
2. 3.274 × $4,000 savings per year = $13,096.
3. Factor for years 1–10, Appendix 2, Table B, 16% column, 4.833.
4. Factor 4.833 — factor 3.274 = factor for years 6–10, 1.559.
5. 1.559 × $16,000 savings per year = $24,944.
6. $13,096 + $24,944 = present value of $38,040.
7. Since this $38,040 is less than the investment amount of $42,000, the investment would not provide the required return of 16% and hence it should not be made.

It still could be possible, however, to invest the $42,000 in our third proposal in which the savings would be $16,000 per year for the first five years and for the last five years, $4,000 per year. Here, the calculations would be as follows:

1. Factor for years 1–5, Appendix 2, Table B, 16% column, 3.274.
2. 3.274 × $16,000 savings per year = $52,384.
3. Factor for years 1–10, Appendix 2, Table B, 16% column, 4.833.
4. Factor 4.833 — factor 3.274 = factor for years 6–10, 1.559.
5. 1.559 × $4,000 savings per year = $6,236.
6. $52,384 + $6,236 = $58,620.
7. Since this $58,620 is $16,620 above the investment amount of $42,000, the investment provides a return far in excess of the required 16%.

In fact, this $16,620, which is known as "present value profit," is well in excess of the $6,330 present value profit of the first proposal. Thus if only one of these proposals is to be accepted it would be the third one in preference to the first.

Advantages of present value method. The principal advantage of the present value method over discounted cash flow is in dealing with problems where alternative investment proposals differ in the length of their estimated useful lives. It also has some advantage where the best investments available showing a return above a minimum acceptable rate should be encouraged, even though they may not meet some higher return target set under the discounted cash flow method.

.In the case of dissimilar lives, for example, suppose as an alternative to the first investment proposal of $42,000 in a machine to effect savings of $10,000 over ten years of useful life, it is possible to invest $42,000 in a different machine, to achieve savings of $9,000 per year, over fifteen years of useful life. The new proposal has a payback of 4.667 years. When we trace this factor on line 15 of Appendix 2, Table B, we find the return on this proposal to be approximately 20% which, the reader will recall, is the same as the percentage return on the first proposal.

Thus neither proposal would be superior to the other in terms of percentage return on investment. However, since the first proposal has a somewhat quicker payback and a larger recovery of the investment in the early years, it might be preferred.

The application of the present value method to the new proposal presents a somewhat different picture. Assuming, as we did earlier, that the required rate is 16% before taxes. Thus when we apply the factor 5.575 from line 15, Appendix 2, Table B, to the expected savings of $9,000, we find that the present worth of the new proposal is $50,175. Then, when we subtract the investment cost of $42,000, we have a present value profit of $8,175. In comparison with the present value profit of $6,330 for the first proposal, the new proposal is to be preferred, as far as this arithmetic is concerned.

Incidentally, one could come to this conclusion with no more than mental arithmetic in this particular case. It can easily be visualized that an investment which showed a rate of return of 20% over a fifteen-year period would be preferred to investing the same amount for a rate of return of 20% over a ten-year period, if the only use that could be made of the capital as recovered would be to reinvest it at a return of 16%.

In some situations, there might at any given time be a dearth in the opportunities to invest at target rates established under the discounted cash flow method. Nonetheless, it could be better to invest in the best opportunities available that offered a return above a general minimum acceptable rate, rather than to have idle funds or simply to invest in government bonds or other low-interest bearing securities.

For example, if what is known as a company's "cost of capital" is 10% after taxes, it might in a given case be wise to invest in assets that would return something above this rate, even though under more normal conditions investments would be made only in assets that would return much more than this. One form of cost of capital where funds have been provided by bondholders (25%) and stockholders (75%) may be illustrated as follows:

1. Interest rate on bonds (after taxes)	4% × 25% = 1%
2. Average return on stockholders' equity (after taxes)	12% × 75% = 9
After tax cost of capital	10%

The present value method would also enable one to spot the proposals which offered the greatest present value profit above this minimum acceptable rate, although, of course, proposals could equally well be ranked by percentage of return under the discounted cash flow method compared against a minimum acceptable return.

As I suggested earlier, the problem is often one of having neither enough time nor money to invest in all of the many available assets or projects that offer highly acceptable returns, rather than a problem of settling on investments that barely cover the cost of capital.

Some people hold the belief that the discounted cash flow method assumes or implies that as the investment in a depreciable asset is recovered over its useful life the amounts so recovered are reinvested at the rate of return computed by the method. It may well be that one who does not understand the method can allow himself to believe that it makes this assumption.

But with careful study of the method, it should be clear that the rate of return computed is the rate to be expected on the declining balance of the investment over the life of the asset acquired and not on the original amount of the investment. A mortgagor knows that he will no longer have to pay interest on whatever amount of principal he repays, and the banker knows that as he recovers his loan he will reinvest each recovery in the light of opportunities then available and at a rate that does not necessarily have any relation to the rate received on the original investment.

Certainly, at the time a banker grants a mortgage loan he does not assume that as he recovers principal over the next twenty or more years it will necessarily be reinvested at the same rate of interest as that currently involved in the mortgage loan being granted.

The Profitability Index

When alternative investment proposals involve substantially the same amount of investment, their relative attractiveness in financial terms can be measured quite satisfactorily under the present value method by comparing what they show for present value profit. However, when alternative investment proposals show substantially the same present value profit under the present value method, but differ markedly in the amount of investment involved, their relative attractiveness is not so visible.

In the latter case, one can assume that the larger the amount of present value profit relative to the investment involved, the more attractive the investment. Many companies have found that the use of a "profitability index," in which the present value of the investment discounted at the target rate is divided by the amount of the investment, is helpful in establishing this relative attractiveness. The following example will illustrate the use of such an index:

	Proposal A	Proposal B
Expected cash flows per year over ten-year life	$10,000	$20,000
Discount factor for target rate of 16%	×4.833	×4.833
Present value of cash flows	$48,330	$96,660
Investment required	42,000	89,000
Present value profit	$ 6,330	$ 7,660

	Profitability Index
Proposal A: Present value $48,330 ÷ Investment $42,000 =	1.15
Proposal B: Present value $96,660 ÷ Investment $89,000 =	1.09

In terms of a simple financial rating, therefore, proposal A with its index at 1.15 is more attractive than proposal B with its index at 1.09.

General preference for discounted cash flow method. Although technicians prefer the use of the present value method, along with the profitability index for the reasons just suggested, many businessmen prefer the discounted cash flow method for appraising investment possibilities. Even where the present value method is used, these businessmen will often request that the percentage return on investment also be computed. This is because they are fairly well accustomed to thinking about profit or gain in terms of a percentage. They are not so familiar with the concept of a present value profit or the use of an index of profitability.

Income Tax Considerations

Up to now, in order to simplify our discussion, I have ignored income tax considerations connected with capital expenditures. Tax aspects are highly important in connection with such expenditures, however, since the amount of savings or additional profit from a capital expenditure taken by the government through taxation will not be available for payback or return on the investment to the company itself.

Also, depreciation affects the amount of income tax to be paid and consequent cash flow, while the tax gains or losses on items replaced can be important factors for consideration in proposals for capital expenditures to replace existing assets.

Although many problems arise in connection with capital expenditures that require the opinion of tax specialists, there are a number of tax aspects which can and should be generally understood by those involved in capital expenditures.

Savings After Taxes and Before Depreciation

The reader will recall that the savings figures used in computing return on investment under the discounted cash flow method, and that are discounted at a given rate under the present value method, are savings before depreciation. This is still true when savings after taxes are used, even though depreciation has been taken into account in arriving at the taxes involved.

Let us return to the example with which we have been working of an investment of $42,000, ten-year life, and $10,000 per year savings before depreciation and income taxes. Here, we shall add the facts that the company computes depreciation on a straight-line basis, and that its income tax rate for federal and state income tax combined is 52%.

Thus the manner in which the net savings after taxes and before depreciation are computed under these circumstances may be seen from the following figures:

	Per Accounting Records	Cash Flow
Savings before depreciation and taxes	$10,000	$10,000
Depreciation	4,200	
Taxable income	$ 5,800	
Income taxes at 52%	3,016	3,016
Net income per accounts	$ 2,784	
Savings after taxes and before depreciation		$ 6,984

The reader will note that the savings after taxes and before depreciation of $6,984 is the same as depreciation of $4,200 plus net income of $2,784, which is cash flow as described in an earlier chapter.

When using a savings figure after taxes and before depreciation under either the discounted cash flow method or the present value method, the target percentage set is, of course, much lower than when using savings before depreciation and taxes. There are no changes in the mechanics of the methods.

Accelerated Depreciation and Capital Expenditure Calculations

When accelerated depreciation is used for income tax purposes, the amount of the depreciation, and therefore the amount of taxable income and income tax arising from the use of a capital asset, is different for each year of its life. Normally, one would therefore expect to have to use the factors in Appendix 2, Table A in connection with either the discounted cash flow method or present value method in capital expenditure calculations when accelerated depreciation is to be used for income-tax purposes.

Fortunately, however, the tables in Appendix 2 provide present-value factors for calculating in a single computation the present-value effect of accelerated depreciation with respect to cash flow. Adaptations of these tables, presented as Appendix 2, Tables D and E, assume that the tax credit for depreciation will be taken in one lump sum at the end of the year.

Let us take up again our example of an investment of $42,000, ten-year life and $10,000 per year savings before depreciation and income taxes. Here, we now assume that the company computes depreciation by the sum-of-the-years' digits method, that its income tax rate is 52%, and that its target rate for return on investment is 10% after taxes.

Thus:

Calculation under present value method.

1. Present value of cash savings after taxes, as though there were no charges for depreciation:
   a. $10,000 (savings per year) × 48%
      (after-tax rate)   = $ 4,800
   b. $4,800 × 6.145 (Table B 10%
      factor for ten years)   = $29,496
2. Present value of depreciation tax shield:
   a. $42,000 (investment) × 0.701
      (Table D factor for ten years)   = $29,442
   b. $29,442 × 52% (tax rate)   = $15,310

3. Present value of expected cash flows
    discounted at 10% $44,806
4. Investment cost   42,000
5. Present value gain $ 2,806

Just a bit earlier, we noted that the savings after taxes and before depreciation, but assuming straight-line depreciation for tax purposes, was $6,984 per year. This amount discounted by the 10% factor from Appendix 2, Table B of 6.145 shows the present value of this cash flow discounted at 10% to be $42,917.

This figure, therefore, although more than meeting the requirement of matching the $42,000 investment, does not show as high a present value gain as when the sum-of-the-years' digits method is used in arriving at the present value of expected cash flows discounted at 10%. Thus this illustrates why this method of accelerated depreciation is used for tax purposes in preference to straight-line depreciation.

We can see from our previous calculation, using the present value method, that our investment is expected to yield a better than 10% return after taxes. Let us now see if perhaps it shows a return of 12%:

Calculation under the discounted cash flow method.

1. Present value of cash savings after taxes, as though there were no charges for depreciation:
    a. $10,000 (savings per year) × 48%
       (after tax rate)   = $ 4,800
    b. $4,800 × 5.650 (Table B 12%
       factor for 10 years)   = $27,120
2. Present value of depreciation tax shield:
    a. $42,000 (investment) × 0.659
       (Table D 12% factor for 10 years)   = $27,678
    b. $27,678 × 52% (tax rate)   = $14,393
3. Present value of expected cash flows discounted at 12% $41,513

Since the present value of the expected cash flows does not quite match the $42,000 investment cost, the return is somewhat less than 12% but well above the target rate of 10%.

Interest on Loans

In financing capital expenditures, interest on loans may be treated in the same manner as just noted for depreciation in arriving at a figure for estimated savings after taxes and before both depreciation and the payment of interest. Interest actually paid on the declining loans over the years could instead be taken into account as an expense in arriving at the amount of savings before taxes and depreciation under both the discounted cash flow and present value methods.

Because of the complications involved, however, and because it is in many cases difficult or unfair to identify specific loans with capital expenditures, as when some expenditures are financed by loans and others by retained earnings, interest is commonly omitted from the first calculations of return on investment.

Instead, the question of how an expenditure is to be financed is given separate consideration. Thus the net cost of interest after taxes is taken into account as an adjustment of the return on investment previously determined, if it is thought that the adjustment would be significant enough to have a bearing on the decision to be made.

Special Problems in Equipment Replacement

When the proposal for a capital expenditure is for the purchase of a new machine to replace an existing machine, the estimated disposal value of the old machine should be treated as a reduction in the investment required in the proposal. The reason for this is that it is the incremental investment against which the expected savings in costs between the two machines should be measured.

Loss on disposal of machinery or equipment replaced. If a capital loss is expected on the disposal of an existing machine, the estimated tax saving that would result should be deducted from the estimated cost of the replacement machine.

Except for the tax aspects just noted, a capital loss to be taken on an old machine should not have any effect on the decision to buy a replacement for it. However, this is in many cases a most difficult hurdle in arriving at a decision to buy a replacement machine.

Many businessmen simply dislike the idea of disposing of a machine before it has been fully depreciated in the books of account. And they dislike it even more if a capital loss has to be taken on the disposal, even though a substantial part of the loss may be recovered through its effect in reducing the amount of income tax to be paid.

One way of attempting to convince such individuals that depreciation on the old machine may be ignored except for its tax implications is to include it in the calculations for both the new machine and the old machine, as in the following example.

Let us assume that the new machine which costs $42,000 and offers a savings of $10,000 per year over its expected life of ten years would replace one which had cost us $30,000 and on which only $10,000 depreciation had been taken to date. To simplify our problem, we shall assume that the old machine could continue to be used for the next ten years. We shall also assume that the new machine is so superior no one would want to buy our old machine and, therefore, that it has no disposal value. Let us assume further that the volume of sales of the product made with the aid of these machines over the next ten years is expected to be the same, whether the old or the proposed new machine is used. Consider:

	If old machine is not replaced	If replaced by new machine	Difference
1. Expected income before taxes and depreciation for the next ten years on products to be made by the old machine that could be made on the proposed new machine.	$500,000	$500,000	$ —
2. Depreciation on old machine	20,000	20,000	—
	$480,000	$480,000	$ —
3. Estimated savings using new machine	—	100,000	100,000
	$480,000	$580,000	$100,000
4. Depreciation on new machine	—	42,000	42,000
5. Savings after depreciation and before taxes	$480,000	$538,000	$ 58,000

Thus we can see that the loss on the old machine has to be taken whether or not we buy the new one. It is really a matter of indifference whether we include this loss in the calculations for both machines or whether we omit it from consideration. This loss would, of course, be taken into consideration in connection with the tax aspects of the problem.

Unequal lives of proposed machine and the one it may replace. The estimated useful life of a proposed replacement machine is likely, of course, to be longer than the estimated remaining life of an existing machine. Despite this fact, in making cost comparisons of an existing machine with those of a proposed machine, many businessmen will assume that the old machine could be kept going, if necessary, for as long a period as the estimated life of the new machine. Therefore, they will simply spread the remaining undepreciated cost of the old machine over the same estimated years of life as the new one.

This may well be a satisfactory enough treatment where estimated lives used for capital expenditure decisions are the same as the conservative estimated lives used for accounting purposes. However, where the differences in probable useful lives are large, it is best to restrict the analysis to the years of estimated remaining life of the old machine, since the possible savings from the new machine versus the old will be valid for that period only.

The estimated value of the new machine at the end of this period may be treated as an additional cash flow as of that time under the discounted cash flow and present value methods. Or this value may be discounted at an amount considered appropriate and subtracted from the estimated investment under other methods of computing return on investment.

The point in the latter case is that the amount (cost) of the estimated investment is then considered to be the loss in the value of the new machine that would take place over a period of time equal to the remaining useful life of the existing machine.

While the true market value of the machine at the end of that time is difficult to forecast, it is probable that its estimated book value will serve adequately for computing purposes. If a very conservative valuation is considered desirable, it could at least be the estimated amount of tax saving involved if the book value of the machine at that time should have to be written off as a capital loss.

The same considerations as those discussed in the previous paragraph are also involved in cases other than those of equipment replacement where the salvage or trade-in value of the item proposed is expected to be substantial at the end of its use. Except for such cases, however, salvage value is generally omitted from calculations of return on investment, since it is not likely to be much in excess of the costs involved in disposal.

Depreciation on new versus old machine. In computing the present value of the depreciation tax shield on a replacement machine, only the difference between the depreciation of the two machines should be taken into account. The reason is that this is the only incremental depreciation applicable to the incremental savings.

Another way of allowing for this difference in depreciation is first to compute the present value of the depreciation tax shield on the new machine and then to subtract the computed present value of the depreciation tax shield on the old machine given up, as in the following illustration.

1. Estimated cost of new machine, $42,000.
2. Expected life of new machine, 10 years.
3. Expected savings on new machine, $10,000 before taxes and depreciation.
4. Undepreciated book value of old machine, $20,000. (Assume no disposal value for this machine and that, if retained, it would be depreciated over the next ten years by the sum-of-the-years' digits method.)
5. Depreciation on new machine to be based on the sum-of-the-years' digits method.
6. Tax rate, 52%, including capital gains or losses.
7. Target earnings rate, 10% after taxes.

Estimated cost of new machine	$42,000
Taxes reduced through capital loss on disposal of old machine $20,000 × 52% =	10,400
Net investment	$31,600

Calculation under present value method.

1. Present value of cash savings after taxes, as though there were no charges for depreciation:
   a. $10,000 (savings per year) × 48% (after-tax rate)   = $ 4,800
   b. $4,800 × 6.145 (Appendix Table B, 10% factor for ten years)   = $29,496
2. Present value of depreciation tax shield on new machine:
   a. $42,000 (cost) × 0.701 (Appendix Table D, 10% factor for ten years)   = $29,442
   b. $29,442 × 52% (tax rate)   = $15,310
3. Present value of depreciation tax shield on old machine given up:
   a. $20,000 × 0.701 (Appendix Table D, 10% factor for ten years) = $14,020
   b. $14,020 × 52% (tax rate)   =   7,290
4. Present value of net depreciation tax shield (2b—3b)   =   8,020

5. Present value of expected cash flows discounted at
   10%. (lb + 4) $37,516
6. Net investment   31,600
7. Present value gain $ 5,916

In Summary

I have suggested that it is highly important for companies to maintain orderly procedures for proposing, reviewing, and approving capital expenditures. The end result is that all proposals will be given adequate consideration and that within the yearly limits of time and funds available the most necessary and soundest expenditures will be made.

The use of more refined analysis in determining the gains to be expected from a given capital expenditure and in comparing various proposals would be a helpful step in many companies. The analysis should be as complete and scientific as possible within reason, even though judgment is involved in making the various estimates required.

While procedures such as the discounted cash flow and present value methods may at first appear to be quite complicated, they may be readily understood with a little study. The computations involved in a given proposal can be made with but little clerical effort. Where a computer is available on which these methods have been programmed, the clerical effort is, of course, even less.

CHAPTER 28

Budgeting: The Fixed or Appropriation Budget

In earlier chapters, we noted the simple technique of judging current performance by comparison with records of the past. We noted that such comparisons can be helpful in the control of costs by type of expense within areas of responsibility, e.g., departments, cost centers, and profit centers, as well as costs by the type of expense for the company as a whole. And we also noted that they can be useful in the control of product costs and the costs of services sold. Significant differences between current performance and that of the past reveal situations that should at least be investigated, if not corrected. The knowledge that such differences are likely to be investigated is in itself expected to have a salutary effect on cost performance.

We also discussed the use of standard costs for control purposes and particularly noted their usefulness in the control of material and labor costs of manufactured products. In the chapter on variance analysis, we noted the use of the variable budget formula in conjunction with standard costs in the analysis and control of manufacturing (burden) costs.

Budgeting provides another approach to financial control. It should be regarded as a desirable technique to be added to the others, not as a substitute for them. It provides the means for coordinating plans in financial terms, and the basis for comparing actual results against expectations for a given period, not simply against past performance.

All businessmen who have made financial plans of income and expense have in essence prepared budgets. If they have used these plans as guides, have tried to operate within them, and have measured actual performance against them, they have practiced budgetary control.

To be sure, the practice of budgeting can be very formal and elaborate and, to a certain extent, must be so in a large organization. But much is to be gained from even a simple approach, and no company should therefore avoid budgeting through fear of its complexities.

Although there are various types of budgets, those with which we shall be concerned in this chapter are known as fixed or appropriation budgets. In many companies they are known as annual budgets.

These budgets are fixed in a variety of senses. They are fixed with respect to the time periods involved, commonly a specified year ahead broken down by months. They are fixed in terms of set monetary amounts for the assets, liabilities, owners' equity, revenues, and expenses involved. And, of major importance, they are fixed with respect to the volumes of sales and production activity on which the great majority of the amounts budgeted are based.

Planning is, or should be, a more or less continuous process. This is true of budgeting, particularly in the development of background cost and revenue data. Based on such data and on estimates of economic conditions to be expected ahead, the first item commonly budgeted in a fixed budget is that of sales. The sales forecast, once accepted, establishes the fixed volume of sales activity on which much of the fixed budget for the year is based.

If the first sales forecast for a given year is not high enough to utilize properly the company's resources of people and facilities, decisions must be made as to what must be done to raise sales revenue to a satisfactory level, or to cut costs so as to have the best possible financial results under the sales revenue predicted, bearing in mind long-run as well as short-run considerations.

Similarly, if the sales demand first predicted is higher than can be met with the company's existing resources of people and facilities, decisions must be made as to how the organization and facilities will be expanded to meet the available sales predicted. Barring this, decisions must be made as to the particular products, services, and customers on which the limited resources shall be concentrated.

Once these decisions have been made, and the adjusted sales forecast accepted, plans are then made for purchasing or producing the goods necessary to meet inventory and sales requirements, including plans for adding or reducing personnel and facilities.

Schedules of expense allowances are developed by department, cost center, or other identified areas of management responsibility within the company. Cash requirements to meet these plans, and the cash receipts to be expected, are then estimated, as well as whatever loans, if any, might be necessary.

Thus the fixed budget sets sales and production goals for attainment, determines expense allowances within these goals, and provides a mechanism for coordinating and combining in financial terms the plans of the various departments of the business. As part of the annual fixed budgeting process, various budgets such as sales, production, cash, and capital equipment are developed.

The fixed budget in its final form consists of the detailed budgets just listed, schedules, such as sales quotas and the schedules of expense allowances mentioned above, and a series of budgeted income statements, balance sheets, and funds flow statements by months, year-to-date, and total for the year. Later, as one way of measuring performance, schedules and financial statements covering actual results for these same periods are measured against these budgeted statements.

The principal weakness of the fixed budget lies in the area of expense control and measurement of performance when the actual volume of operations for a period turns out to be different than that predicted and on which expense allowances were based. More specifically, under these circumstances the budgeted amounts are no longer appropriate for those expenses which should vary in some degree with changes in the volume of activity of the operations in which they are incurred. The control of expenses such as these is exercised more effectively by the use of a variable budget rather than by a fixed budget, as we shall note in the chapter to follow.

In many companies, it is the custom to adjust the fixed budget quarterly in light of significant changes that have taken place in operating conditions since the beginning of the year, when the budget was first placed in use. Where this is done, comparisons are not only made of actual results against the adjusted budget but also against the original budget, in the belief that there should still be some accountability for results as measured against original plans. Unless such comparisons are continued, it is feared that management may tend to allow the budget to follow actual results rather than strive to do the reverse.

Background for Budgeting

A formal budget is a presentation in financial terms of specified expectations with respect to the future. Nonetheless, it is based in large part on the experience of the past, which is then tempered by expectations of conditions to be met in the future.

In the development of either or both the fixed budget and the variable budget, it is particularly important for a company to have a concrete understanding of the way in which each cost or expense is affected by changes in the volume of activity for each area of operations being budgeted.

A desirable approach is through use of similar procedures as those described in Chapter 24 on cost-price-volume relationships. The reader will recall that the techniques described there were for developing formulas, tables, and graphs. The same techniques can also be used in developing the cost-volume relationships for each classification of cost or expense by cost center, department, or other area of responsibility in connection with budgeting.

Formulas and tables are most useful in establishing budgetary figures, while graphs can be helpful for educational purposes in explaining differences in the cost-volume relationship of different types of cost or expense. The types of graphs which might be prepared and the nature of the relationship of various types of cost to changes in the volume of activity may be visualized in the following diagrams:

1. A fixed cost, such as depreciation:

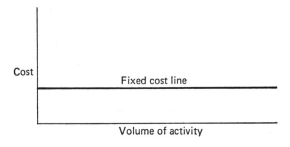

2. A directly variable cost, such as commissions on sales:

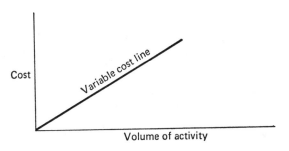

3. A semivariable cost, such as fringe benefits, where part of the cost varies with the amount of direct labor expended in the given cost center or department while part is related to supervision.

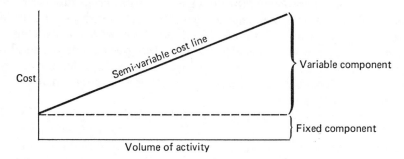

4. A semivariable expense, such as indirect labor or material handling, in which there is a fixed component plus a variable component, the latter rising in steps as volume increases because of the necessity of hiring another "whole" man rather than a "part-time" man for many jobs.

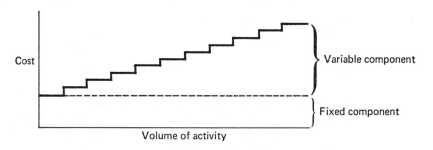

5. A semivariable expense, such as repairs and maintenance, some part of which may be deferred but undertaken later when financial conditions are more propitious.

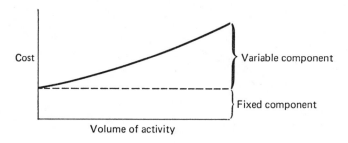

6. A semivariable expense, such as small tools or minor items of equipment charged off as expenses each year instead of being capitalized, where a certain portion has to be purchased regardless of volume, and more has to be purchased as the volume of activity increases, although the amount of cost per unit of activity declines as volume increases.

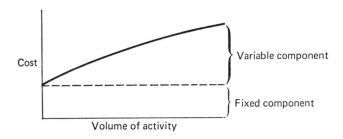

Elements of the Fixed Budget

A typical fixed budget shows expected revenues, at assumed volumes and selling prices, for the time period being budgeted, and it also lists expected expenses for the same period with due allowance for inventory changes. Projected income statements, balance sheets, and source and application of funds statements are included as summaries of such budgets.

As we noted earlier, the fixed-budget procedure also involves the preparation of separate budgets or schedules of sales, production, capital expenditures, and cash. In addition, many fixed budgets include percentage figures for various forms of return on investment and figures for miscellaneous items, such as average number of full-time employees, orders received and on hand, and sales and net income per thousand square feet of floor space.

To identify the budget with individuals responsible for performance, it is broken down to a separate schedule of revenue and expense items for each cost center, department, division, or other section of a business, to the extent considered appropriate by top management.

Budget Preparation

In small companies, the budget is often prepared by only one or a few members of top management. Ideally, however, each individual who is to be held accountable under a budget should have a separate schedule for the organizational unit under his supervision, and he should have a part in the preparation of that schedule.

Budgeting requires the support of top management, but the budget should be regarded as an operating goal and guide of assistance to all levels of management. Thus the preparation of the budget and the successful use of budgetary procedures should be accepted as the cooperative responsibility of all managers and not of top management alone, or of a budget director or staff reporting to top management.

The budget director and his staff should be responsible for educating managers in budget preparation and use. They should design appropriate forms, develop written instructions, and set timetables for budget preparation and review. In cooperation with the bookkeeping department, they should develop appropriate account classifications so that data to be used in connection with budgeting will be gathered through regular accounting routines, and thus duplication of clerical work will be avoided.

In the case of foreign branches, or subsidiaries, where accounts are kept in accordance with local governmental requirements, it may be necessary, or at least desirable, to supply the home office with summary data only for purposes of corporate budgeting and control, leaving detailed budgeting and control to the branches and subsidiaries.

Whatever discipline may be called for in comparisons of actual results against the budget should be administered by the heads of the organizational units involved and not by the budget director or anyone on his staff. The budget director should spark the budgeting program and provide aid for its success. He should not be expected to be, nor allowed to become a combined informer and disciplinarian.

Review of Past and Present Situations

In addition to studies of cost-volume relationships noted earlier, it is customary in preparing the annual fixed budget for companies to review near-term results with respect to revenues and expenses by major divisions and product lines and by type of expense for each cost center, department, or branch within each division.

It is also customary to analyze the present situation with respect to resources, strengths, and weaknesses so as to know how the company stands before planning what it should attempt to do in the year ahead.

Zero-Base Budgeting

The term *zero-base budgeting* has come into popular use, though it is a bit of a misnomer since, taken literally, at zero base there would be nothing to budget.

It is the practice in some companies to estimate what the expenses would be per month if operations, such as manufacturing, were temporarily halted. These expenses, sometimes known as shutdown or standby costs, are then identified as being the company's fixed costs per month. Although these are the costs that would be budgeted by these going concerns at zero volume of operations, this is not what is known as zero-base budgeting.

Zero-base budgeting is a procedure under which all expenses, indeed all activities, are reviewed in terms of their justification, as though the company or other organization being reviewed was starting from scratch. Missions and goals are redefined for all units of the organization. Simplifications, eliminations, and reductions of activities and expenses are sought, and usually expected, if not ordered. When carried out energetically this procedure can be a highly emotional and possibly shattering experience for the individuals involved.

A certain amount of soul-searching of this type should, of course, be undertaken each year in connection with the annual budget, and more in connection with long-range planning, but the review in depth called for in zero-base budgeting is best undertaken only at longer intervals, such as five years. To go through such basic and detailed review more frequently would not only be highly disruptive, but could kill any enthusiasm for undertaking it, and thereby destroy its effectiveness.

Assumptions With Respect to Economic Conditions

As part of the budgeting process, it is incumbent on top corporate and divisional executives, aided by whatever technical assistance they believe necessary or desirable, to define what they believe the economic conditions will be for the year ahead in general and for the given industry, or industries, in which the company and its divisions are located.

In addition to the advice of economists and others from within or outside the company, assumptions on the economic environment for the budget year are developed from the forecasts of statistical services and from reading government reports, financial publications, and trade reports of various types.

Major Corporate and Divisional Goals

It is also a responsibility of top corporate and division management to set broad or summary goals in terms such as rate of growth, percentage share of the market, and return on investment toward which each division, and the company as a whole, will be working.

Along the same lines, the annual goals of a corporation and its divisions should be fitted into goals established by long-range planning. Indeed, in many companies the annual budget is the same as the first-year plan of the long-range budget. Whether or not this is the case, planning in many companies has become a fairly continuous process, with discussions of ideas for the future flowing throughout the year among managers at the same levels and among managers at different levels.

Formal procedures call for specified steps to be taken in a circular fashion, with appropriate recycling within divisions and between divisions and corporate headquarters, and with goals periodically becoming solidified in the form of annual budgets and long-range plans. Procedures also involve appropriate periodic reviews of performance against such plans and budgets.

Budgeting for Sales

After having reviewed the past and present situations, and having been given broad and summary corporate and divisional goals for the future, it is then customary in developing the annual budget to forecast sales. This is a matter, of course, of estimating unit volume, product mix, and selling prices.

In companies where the assistance of individuals at all levels is sought in developing the annual budget, each salesman is asked to estimate what his sales will be by product line and by months for the coming year. Sales estimates are also made by branch managers, product-line managers, and other sales managers and executives at various levels in the organization. In many companies, additional sales estimates are made by customer classifications.

While one might suppose that salesmen's estimates would be cautious to avoid the possibility of later making a poor showing, the tendency appears to be for them to be somewhat more optimistic than forecasts of the economic climate would seem to warrant. Salesmen's estimates are usually, therefore, tempered a bit by the sales managers and executives above them, and even more so by the financial officers when it comes to putting the final budget together.

From an operational viewpoint, quotas for sales management pur-poses are often set higher than sales estimates in the financial budget. Thus the sales figures in projected income statements are the forecasts of sales executives tempered by the estimates of top general and finan-cial division and corporate managements. In the budget for sales man-agement purposes, sales are budgeted by branch, by product line, by customer or customer classifications, and by salesmen.

Example of the Budgetary Process

To assist in the discussion of the budgetary process, various schedules and budgets of a hypothetical company covering a period of six months will be presented. These exhibits are condensed versions of what would actually be prepared but should serve to illustrate the major elements involved.

The assumed company manufactures and sells a given type of product in a variety of styles and sizes. For budgetary purposes, how-ever, unit costs can be averaged and expressed in terms of four separate product grades. Similarly, sales expectations and production plans can be expressed in both units and dollars for each of the four product grades. The budgeted figures by grades can then be added to establish total budgeted sales and production figures.

The industry in which the assumed company is located has two main selling seasons, one in the spring and the other in the fall. Be-cause of this, and because there are marked seasonal differences in the products involved, it is the practice in this industry, and in our as-sumed company, to prepare six-month budgets instead of the twelve-month budgets common to many other industries.

Exhibit 64 shows the expected unit shipments by grades, and by months, for the budgeted six-month period. These figures would have been summarized from figures submitted by salesmen and others in the organization and passed upon by members of top management. Exhibit 65 shows the expected shipments in terms of sales dollars. These figures were computed by applying the following expected sell-ing prices per unit to the units developed in Exhibit 64:

Grade	Unit Selling Price
A	$28.00
B	23.75
C	19.40
D	16.00

EXHIBIT 64
Sales Budget
Expected Unit Shipments to Customers, January–June 19—

	Jan.	Feb.	Mar.	Apr.	May	June	Total
A	11,200	15,000	22,000	18,600	15,000	12,200	94,000
B	17,000	22,600	32,200	28,200	22,600	18,400	141,000
C	29,200	39,000	55,200	48,600	39,000	31,600	242,600
D	19,400	26,000	37,200	32,400	26,000	21,000	162,000
	76,800	102,600	146,600	127,800	102,600	83,200	639,600

EXHIBIT 65
Sales Budget
Expected Shipments in Terms of Sales Dollars January–June 19—

	Jan.	Feb.	Mar.	Apr.	May	June	Total
A	$ 313,600	$ 420,000	$ 616,000	$ 520,800	$ 420,000	$ 341,600	$ 2,632,000
B	403,800	536,800	764,800	669,800	536,800	437,000	3,349,000
C	566,500	756,600	1,070,900	942,900	756,600	613,000	4,706,500
D	310,400	416,000	595,200	518,400	416,000	336,000	2,592,000
	1,594,300	2,129,400	3,046,900	2,651,900	2,129,400	1,727,600	13,279,500

Budgeting for Production

Given the sales estimates, executives in manufacturing companies are then responsible for planning the necessary production to meet these shipping requirements. Thus they must keep in mind the desirability insofar as practicable of spreading production so as to maintain steady employment of men and machines and to produce economically.

Since sales typically are subject to fluctuations beyond the control of the producer, it is generally necessary alternatively to build up and draw down inventories in order to reconcile smooth production and fluctuating sales. The extent to which production can be leveled is, of course, dependent on whether goods must be produced on order or can be stocked; the risks of spoilage or deterioration of goods stored; and the cost involved in financing and storing inventory.

As we noted earlier, if initial sales estimates are far removed either way from production capability, decisions have to be made as to what is to be done about attempting to adjust sales to productive capacity or to adjust productive capacity and costs to anticipated sales.

Exhibit 66 shows the first work-sheet in establishing the production budget in our example. The company's products are stock items, produced in advance of customers' orders and stored in its warehouse.

EXHIBIT 66
Work Sheet for Production Budget (1)
January–June 19—

Grade	Month	Expected Shipments to Customers	Required Stock Level 1st of Month	Change in Stock during Month	Required Delivery to Warehouse
A	Jan.	11,200	16,800	+ 5,700	16,900
	Feb.	15,000	22,500	+10,500	25,500
	Mar.	22,000	33,000	− 5,100	16,900
	Apr.	18,600	27,900	− 5,400	13,200
	May	15,000	22,500	− 4,200	10,800
	June	12,200	18,300	0	12,200
B	Jan.	17,000	25,500	+ 8,400	25,400
	Feb.	22,600	33,900	+14,400	37,000
	Mar.	32,200	48,300	− 6,000	26,200
	Apr.	28,200	42,300	− 8,400	19,800
	May	22,600	33,900	− 6,300	16,300
	June	18,400	27,600	0	18,400
C	Jan.	29,200	43,800	+14,700	43,900
	Feb.	39,000	58,500	+24,300	63,300
	Mar.	55,200	82,800	− 9,900	45,300
	Apr.	48,600	72,900	−14,400	34,200
	May	39,000	58,500	−11,100	27,900
	June	31,600	47,400	0	31,600
D	Jan.	19,400	29,100	+ 9,900	29,300
	Feb.	26,000	39,000	+16,800	42,800
	Mar.	37,200	55,800	− 7,200	30,000
	Apr.	32,400	48,600	− 9,600	22,800
	May	26,000	39,000	− 7,500	18,500
	June	21,000	31,500	0	21,000

Experience has shown that in order to satisfy customer requirements with respect to style and unit size it is best to have on hand on the first of the month an assortment of units of each grade in an amount equal to one and one-half times the expected shipments to customers for that month. In addition to these arithmetical provisions, there must later be continual liaison between the factory and the warehouse to insure that production will be scheduled so as to provide the proper assortment of styles and sizes to meet customers' demand.

It can be noted in Exhibit 66 that 11,200 grade A units are expected to be shipped in January. This figure came from the Sales Budget, Exhibit 64. Column 2, in Exhibit 66, shows that the required stock as of January 1 is 16,800, which is one and one-half times the 11,200 expected shipments for the month. We do not know, at the moment, whether or not the amount of stock on hand will in fact be at least the required 16,800 units, but we shall check this matter shortly.

We can note that the expected shipments of grade A units in February is 15,000, and, that the required stock on hand February 1 to meet these shipments comfortably is 22,500. This means that the required stock level on grade A units rises from 16,800 on January 1 to 22,500 on February 1; an increase of 5,700 units.

In order to replace the 11,200 grade A units to be shipped from stock to customers during January, and also to build the stock level up to 22,500 units, it will be necessary to deliver 16,900 units from the factory to the warehouse during January (11,200 units + 5,700 units).

In contrast to this, when the required stock level of grade A units drops from 33,000 as of March 1 to 27,900 as of April 1, only 16,900 units need to be delivered from the factory to the warehouse during March since 5,100 units of the 22,000 units to be shipped to customers that month will come from drawing down the inventory.

In Exhibit 67, the required deliveries to the warehouse, which were developed monthly by grades in Exhibit 66, are listed and totaled by months.

The estimated productive capacity for each month was then entered in the form, e.g., 129,000 units for January. These estimates of capacity were developed by production personnel having in mind:

1. The required deliveries to the warehouse by months and by grades as presented in Exhibit 67.
2. The man-hours and/or machine-hours required per 100 units of each grade, for each phase of the manufacturing process.
3. The capacity in terms of man-hours and/or machine-hours of each cost center in which a phase of the manufacturing process would be carried out.

The production capacity of 129,000 units in January is 13,500 units more than the 115,500 units required for delivery to the warehouse that month. Knowing that delivery demands are to be heavy in February and March the decision is to produce at capacity. The production personnel have determined that the overproduction of 13,500 units will be spread among the four grades as listed in the first column of Exhibit 67.

The situation for February and March is not as happy with respect to production as that for January. The delivery demands for those two months are far in excess of their production capacity. Fortunately, the budget is being prepared in October, and it is known that there will be sufficient capacity, above the required deliveries in November and December, to build up a surplus of stock to be carried into the new year to meet the demands above the production capacities of February and

EXHIBIT 67
Work Sheet for Production Budget (2)
January–June 19—

	Jan.	Feb.	Mar.	Apr.	May	June	Total
A	16,900	25,500	16,900	13,200	10,800	12,200	95,500
B	25,400	37,000	26,200	19,800	16,300	18,400	143,100
C	43,900	63,300	45,300	34,200	27,900	31,600	246,200
D	29,300	42,800	30,000	22,800	18,500	21,000	164,400
	115,500	168,600	118,400	90,000	73,500	83,200	649,200
Prod. Cap.	129,000	112,900	97,000	128,000	132,000	97,000	
	Over	(Short)	(Short)	OK	OK	OK	
A	2,000	(8,700)	(2,600)				
B	3,000	(12,900)	(4,100)				
C	5,100	(20,600)	(8,800)				
D	3,400	(13,500)	(5,900)				
	13,500	(55,700)	(21,400)				

Surplus to be produced in November and December (on hand January 1)

Grade A	9,300
Grade B	14,000
Grade C	24,300
Grade D	16,000
	63,600

March. Accordingly, plans will include production of a surplus of 63,600 units in November and December, spread among the grades as shown in Exhibit 67. Thus, for example, a surplus of 9,300 grade A units will be produced in November and December, which together with overproduction of 2,000 such units in January, will offset the shortages of 8,700 units and 2,600 units expected in February and March.

The important point to note here is that budgeting for a single time period, such as a month, six months, or year, is not adequate just by itself. The probable situation in the time periods immediately preceding the time period being budgeted, as well as the situation in the time periods immediately following it, should be taken into account. This example also illustrates the wisdom of preparing a budget well in advance of the time period it is expected to cover.

EXHIBIT 68
Adjusted Production Budget
January–June 19—

	Jan.	Feb.	Mar.	Apr.	May	June	Total
A	18,900	16,800	14,300	13,200	10,800	12,200	86,200
B	28,400	24,100	22,100	19,800	16,300	18,400	129,100
C	49,000	42,700	36,500	34,200	27,900	31,600	221,900
D	32,700	29,300	24,100	22,800	18,500	21,000	148,400
	129,000	112,900	97,000	90,000	73,500	83,200	585,600

Figures for the months of April, May, and June in Exhibit 67 show that production capacity is expected to be well in excess of the delivery requirements for those months. The OKs in the columns are meant to indicate that these requirements, and those for the foreseeable future, can be met without difficulty.

In Exhibit 68, the figures developed in Exhibit 67 are brought together to form the final unit production budget.

Material and Labor Costs

Given unit production estimates by months for each product line, the next step is to estimate material and labor costs to be involved in producing these units. One approach here is to convert the unit production estimates into their values at estimated selling prices and then to apply to these estimated sales values percentages developed from experience of the relationship of material and labor costs to sales dollars.

A more accurate approach followed by many companies is to apply standard material and labor costs for assumed typical units within each product line to the total budgeted units to be produced in each line. Where standard costs are used in this way, it is necessary, of course, to prepare them in advance of their need for budgeting purposes.

Exhibit 69 shows the standard unit costs of material, labor, and manufacturing expense (burden) for each grade of product in the example we have been discussing. These are the expected unit costs for the budgeted period of six months, of what has been selected as the typical (i.e., average) style and size of product within each grade. The methods used in computing these standard unit costs for material and labor would be along the lines described in Chapter 22, Standard Costs. The

EXHIBIT 69
Standard Unit Costs

Grade	Material	Labor	Burden	Total
A	$9.05	$10.77	$2.20	$22.02
B	7.06	9.39	2.20	18.65
C	4.60	8.40	2.20	15.20
D	3.90	7.08	2.20	13.18

EXHIBIT 70

Material Costs

	Jan.	Feb.	Mar.	Apr.	May	June	Total
A	171,000	152,000	129,400	119,500	97,700	110,400	780,000
B	200,500	170,100	156,000	139,800	115,100	129,900	911,400
C	225,400	196,400	167,900	157,300	128,300	145,400	1,020,700
D	127,500	114,300	94,000	88,900	72,200	81,900	578,800
	724,400	632,800	547,300	505,500	413,300	467,600	3,290,900

Labor Costs

	Jan.	Feb.	Mar.	Apr.	May	June	Total
A	203,600	180,900	154,000	142,200	116,300	131,400	928,400
B	266,700	226,300	207,500	185,900	153,100	172,800	1,212,300
C	411,600	358,700	306,600	287,300	234,400	265,400	1,864,000
D	231,500	207,400	170,600	161,400	131,000	148,700	1,050,600
	1,113,400	973,300	838,700	776,800	634,800	718,300	5,055,300

method used in establishing the unit cost for manufacturing expense will be described in a moment.

Exhibit 70 shows the result of the application of the unit material and labor costs of Exhibit 69 to the expected number of units to be produced as indicated by Exhibit 58. It should be understood that the results shown in Exhibit 70 are the expected material and labor costs of units to be completed by the factory and delivered to the warehouse during the months budgeted. If the company keeps separate inventory records for material, work-in-process, and finished goods, the figures in Exhibit 70 represent amounts it would expect to transfer from work-in-process to finished goods inventories for the material and labor costs in the goods completed.

It can be appreciated that if the manufacturing time per unit is long, and if the volume of activity shifts markedly from month to month, there are likely to be significant differences between the cost incurred during a given month and the cost of the goods completed that month. Under these circumstances, it is necessary to budget the input costs of the factory by months as well as the costs of the goods expected to be completed in those months. Similarly, where major materials and manufactured parts must be purchased well in advance of their use, the budget must take into account the timing of their acquisition, as well as their entry to production and emergence as finished goods.

In our example, we shall assume that the manufacturing time per unit is short enough so that for purposes of financial planning, it is correct to consider the standard cost of material, labor, and manufacturing expense to be incurred during a given month to be the same as the standard cost of the goods expected to be completed in that month. This is not the same, however, as the budgeted costs leaving the finished goods inventory to become budgeted costs of goods sold, which we shall be discussing after some comments on budgeting factory burden.

As a final note on budgeting labor costs, the estimating of such costs by product line, by months, may be adequate for financial planning but not for production planning by plants, departments, and cost centers. For production planning, therefore, except on a broad basis, the labor estimates must be broken down to the operating units involved.

Factory burden. Here, as in the case of material and labor costs, a broad treatment can be adopted. Under this, the percentage relationship of factory burden to sales for periods in the past is applied to the estimated sales value of the budgeted production in arriving at the expected amount of factory burden to be absorbed by goods produced.

A better approach is through the use of standard product costs, as just suggested for material and labor costs. These standard product costs for factory burden, when applied to budgeted production, provide figures for the amount of burden expected to be absorbed by goods produced each month for the year budgeted. These amounts, which are in effect budgeted as being credited to production and charged into finished goods inventory, can be identified by product line if wanted.

In addition to budgeting the standard burden cost of the goods expected to be coming out of production, it is desirable to budget by type of expense the inputs of burden cost considered necessary to achieve this product output.

The variable budget (to be described in the next chapter) can be particularly helpful in this connection. Given the expected volumes of activity, such a budget can help to estimate the amount of burden to be expected each month of the budgeted year for each cost center or department, and by plant, division, and for the company as a whole.

The difference between the amount of budgeted factory input burden cost each month, and the budgeted amount of burden to be absorbed by goods produced each month, represents the expected amount of burden to be overabsorbed or underabsorbed.

The amount of this expected variance for any given month represents, essentially, the extent to which fixed or managed burden costs are expected to be overabsorbed or underabsorbed. This is because the budgeted production for that month is greater or less than the volume on which the standard product costs were based.

Depending on the company's policy, the budgeted variance either will appear as a loss or gain each month in the budgeted income statement, or its balance will be carried forward from month to month in the budgeted balance sheet, to be closed out at the end of the budget year.

Exhibit 69 shows the standard unit cost of manufacturing expense to be $2.20 per unit in the example we have been discussing. In an actual situation it would be likely that the manufacturing cost per unit would differ between grades because of difference in manufacturing time, as evidenced by the differences in unit labor-costs. In our example, however, the same rate per unit is used to simplify the presentation.

Also, as a simplification, the $2.20 manufacturing cost per unit is assumed to break down to $1.20 per unit of variable costs and $1.00 per unit of fixed costs for the 585,600 units to be produced in the six months budgeted. These burden rates are based on the volume of production for these six months, in contrast to the alternative practice of being based in the normal volume of operations over a number of years.

The upper section of Exhibit 71 represents the application of these burden rates to the total number of units expected to be produced each month from Exhibit 68. The results show the amount of manufacturing expense expected to be absorbed by the goods produced during the months budgeted. Normally, only the total rate of $2.20 would be used here. The rate has been applied in both its variable and fixed components in our example to illustrate the fact that the amount of fixed, as well as variable, cost absorbed varies from month to month with shifts in the volume of operations.

The lower section of Exhibit 71 shows the expected variable and fixed costs for the months budgeted. Here, the variable costs, being based on the expected volume of operations each month, are identical

EXHIBIT 71
Budgeted Manufacturing Expense
January–June 19—

	Jan.	Feb.	March	April	May	June	Total
Expected amounts of costs absorbed:							
Variable costs	154,800	135,500	116,400	108,000	88,200	99,800	702,700
Fixed costs	129,000	112,900	97,000	90,000	73,500	83,200	585,600
	283,800	248,400	213,400	198,000	161,700	183,000	1,288,300
Expected costs:							
Variable costs	154,800	135,500	116,400	108,000	88,200	99,800	702,700
Fixed costs	97,600	97,600	97,600	97,600	97,600	97,600	585,600
	252,400	233,100	214,000	205,600	185,800	197,400	1,288,300
Over or (under) absorbed	31,400	15,300	(600)	(7,600)	(24,100)	(14,400)	—

EXHIBIT 72
Budgeted Cost of Goods Sold
January–June 19—

Grade	Jan.	Feb.	March	April	May	June	Total
A	246,600	330,300	484,400	409,600	330,300	268,600	2,069,800
B	317,100	421,500	600,500	525,900	421,500	343,200	2,629,700
C	443,800	592,800	839,000	738,700	592,800	480,300	3,687,400
D	255,700	342,700	490,300	427,000	342,700	276,800	2,135,200
Total	1,263,200	1,687,300	2,414,200	2,101,200	1,687,300	1,368,900	10,522,100

to the variable costs shown in the upper section of Exhibit 71, also based on the expected volume of operations each month. However, the fixed costs in the lower section of Exhibit 71 are a fixed amount each month, being one-sixth of the total expected fixed costs of $585,600 or $97,600. This also represents an assumed average production of 97,600 units costing $1.00 per unit.

The figures in the bottom line of Exhibit 71 show the amounts by which fixed costs are expected to be under- or overabsorbed in each of the months budgeted. Thus in January and February, when the volume of operations is expected to be above the monthly average, fixed costs are expected to be overabsorbed. From March through June, when the volume of operations is expected to be below the monthly average, fixed costs are expected to be underabsorbed.

These expected under- and overabsorbed amounts affect the budgeted operating results of individual months, but are expected to offset one another, leaving no net under- or overabsorbed amount for the six months in total. Had the burden rates been based on the expected normal volume over a more extended period than the six months being budgeted it is likely that there would be an expected net under- or overabsorbed amount for the total of these six months.

Exhibit 72 shows the budgeted cost of goods sold for our example. These figures are the result of multiplying the budgeted unit sales in Exhibit 64 by the unit total product costs in Exhibit 69. The figures have been rounded to the nearest one hundred dollars.

Exhibit 73 shows the budgeted income statements for our example. The sales figures are from Exhibit 65. The allowances for returns and bad debts, computed at 0.0075 of sales, are subtracted from these figures to arrive at budgeted net sales. In turn, the budgeted costs of goods sold from Exhibit 72 are subtracted from the net sales to arrive at budgeted gross margin figures.

The manufacturing expense variances from the bottom line of Exhibit 71 are then subtracted to arrive at adjusted gross margin figures.

Cost of goods sold. The procedures just described for budgeting material, labor, and factory burden costs by months for the annual budget, as well as for budgeting the standard cost of goods completed each month by product line, have assumed both that a company has a standard cost system and that it wishes to plan its manufacturing costs in some detail by type of expense, by area of responsibility, and by the goods to be produced in each product line.

EXHIBIT 73
Budgeted Income Statement
January–June 19—

	Jan.	Feb.	March	April	May	June	Total
Sales	1,594,300	2,129,400	3,046,900	2,651,900	2,129,400	1,727,600	13,279,500
Less allowances	12,000	16,000	22,800	19,900	16,000	13,000	99,700
Net sales	1,582,300	2,113,400	3,024,100	2,632,000	2,113,400	1,714,600	13,179,800
Cost of goods sold	1,263,200	1,687,300	2,414,200	2,101,200	1,687,300	1,368,900	10,522,100
Gross margin	319,100	426,100	609,900	530,800	426,100	345,700	2,657,700
Mfg. exp. variance	31,400	15,300	(600)	(7,600)	(24,100)	(14,400)	—
Adj. gross margin	350,500	441,400	609,300	523,200	402,000	331,300	2,657,700
Sell. & adm. exp.:							
Variable	31,900	42,600	60,900	53,000	42,600	34,600	265,600
Fixed	51,000	51,000	51,000	51,000	51,000	51,000	306,000
	82,900	93,600	111,900	104,000	93,600	85,600	571,600
Advertising	70,800	70,800	70,800	70,800	70,800	70,800	424,800
Commissions	79,700	106,500	152,300	132,600	106,500	86,400	664,000
Total S & A exp.	233,400	270,900	335,000	307,400	270,900	242,800	1,660,400
Pretax income	117,100	170,500	274,300	215,800	131,100	88,500	997,300
Est. income tax	56,200	81,800	131,700	103,600	62,900	42,500	478,700
Net income	60,900	88,700	142,600	112,200	68,200	46,000	518,600

The same type of company can use its standard product costs per unit in budgeting the cost of goods sold for each month of the budget year. If not too many different types of product are involved, the standard cost per unit for each type can be applied to the quantity of that type expected to be sold to establish the cost of the goods sold.

If there are a great many different types of products, they can be grouped by major product lines and one type can be selected from each group as being representative of the average unit for that product line. The standard cost of the representative item for the group can then be applied to the expected number of units to be sold of that product line to arrive at the cost of the goods sold.

If the approaches just suggested seem too involved, the cost of goods sold can be budgeted in a far less elaborate way by the use of data on cost-price-volume relationships, discussed in Chapter 24.

Gross margin. After having budgeted both sales and the cost of goods sold by product line, it is only necessary to subtract one from the other to establish the budgeted gross margin by product line.

Earlier, we noted that in many companies the sales budget is broken down by sales district, by individual salesman, and by individual customer or class of customer, in addition to sales by product line. So too, in many companies, the expected gross margin is budgeted in these same categories to apply another dimension to expected sales revenues.

Selling expenses. In many companies, expenses coming under the general heading of selling expenses include those involved in packaging and warehousing finished stock, in handling incoming sales orders, and in shipping. These costs are often spoken of as "order filling costs." They should be responsive in some degree to changes in production and sales volumes, and they should be budgeted by month, accordingly.

Selling expenses such as salesmen's salaries, commissions, and travel; sales office salaries and overhead; and advertising are known as order getting expenses. They do not necessarily bear any short-run relationship to either production volume or sales volume.

Over the long run, there should be some relationship between selling expenses and sales achievement. This rests on the assumption, of course, that wise expenditures are made and sales efforts are applied efficiently.

Typically, the budgeting of order getting expenses starts with a review of the organization and expenses by organizational units for past periods, together with a review of past goals and tasks that had been budgeted and the manner in which these goals and tasks had or had not been met.

As we just noted, order getting expenses do not necessarily bear any short-run relationship to sales volume. Therefore, they would not be budgeted to fluctuate from month to month with budgeted sales. However, in budgeting such expenses, adjustments are made to allow for major changes in the volume of operations.

For example, if it were predicted that demand would be such that sales could be expected to rise markedly over the coming year, and for some time thereafter, the selling expense budget would include increases to cover the additional personnel and other expenses thought necessary to capture the predicted available increase in business.

In general, the budgeting of selling expenses, after a review of the expenses and accomplishments of the previous year, involves an analysis of the company's current strengths and weaknesses in the marketing area. It also involves a study of the environmental factors on which budgeted sales have been based and a discussion of established major corporate and divisional goals underlying the whole budgetary process.

Statements of marketing strategy are then developed, i.e., statements of specific marketing goals, of the means by which it is expected these goals will be met, and of the tasks involved. Budgets are then drawn up by month covering organizational changes as well as salaries, commissions, and wages to be met; facilities to be purchased; and estimated expenses to carry out the marketing plans.

Administrative expenses. As in the case of selling expenses, administrative expenses—other than those directly related to production or sales activities—bear no necessary short-run relationship to changes in the volume of either sales or production. Therefore, administrative expenses would not be budgeted to fluctuate from month to month with changes in the volume of operations.

If the costs of the payroll department are accounted for as administrative expenses, they could, of course, be expected to fluctuate somewhat with fluctuations in the number of persons employed. Similarly, the costs of the billing department could be expected to fluctuate somewhat with fluctuations in the volume of sales to be billed.

In general, however, administrative expenses tend to be relatively fixed from month to month. They are referred to as "programmed" or "managed" costs and are more subject to change by management decision than by exigencies arising from fluctuations in the volume of operations.

Procedures in the budgeting of administrative expenses are generally the same as those in the budgeting of selling expenses. Namely, the review of past expenses and accomplishments; the survey of current strengths and weaknesses; and the budgeting of organization, facilities, and expenses relative to plans tied into overall corporate and division goals.

In our example we shall assume, without illustration, that the company prepared detailed budgets by type of expense for each department of the sales organization, and each section of the administrative organization, along the lines just described above.

To simplify the presentation of the budgeted income statement, (Exhibit 73) selling and administrative expenses have been combined. It has been assumed in this exhibit that these expenses could be separated into those that for all practical purposes would be fixed each period, and those that would be expected to vary each period directly in proportion to changes in sales activity as measured by sales dollars. The total fixed expenses for the budgeted six months were expected to be $306,000 while the total variable expenses for this period were expected to be $265,600.

On the basis of these total figures the formula for establishing the expected amount of selling and administrative expenses for any given month was $51,000 fixed expenses (e.g., $306,000 ÷ 6) plus 2% of sales (e.g., $265,600 ÷ $13,279,500). Thus the budgeted selling and administrative expenses for January were $51,000 of fixed expenses plus (2% × $1,594,300) variable expenses, or $51,000 plus $31,900 = $82,900.

Although advertising expense and commissions are selling expenses, they are so significant in this case that they are treated as separate items in the budgeted income statement (Exhibit 73). The total advertising expense figure of $424,800 would have come from a separate advertising budget in which the types of advertising expected to be undertaken, and their expected costs, would be listed in detail. The total has been spread over the months in an equal amount each month on the assumption that despite the seasonal nature of sales, the advertising would be relatively steady from month to month to maintain publicity on the company's name and products.

Commissions were computed at 5% of the expected sales each month although actual payment to salesmen would be made in the following month.

Research and development expenses. Expenditures for R&D are important items to be budgeted in many companies. These are managed costs—that is, they are costs subject to management discretion. However, it is a fairly common practice to use as a guide a predetermined percentage of sales, in line with what competitors are spending on research and development relative to their sales.

As we noted in Chapter 12, companies used to be faced with the problem of deciding what R&D items, if any, should be capitalized, to appear in the balance sheet, and what items should be expensed, to appear in the income statement. The Financial Accounting Standards Board, however, in its statement of Financial Acounting Standards No. 2, October 1974, ruled in effect that all research and development costs shall be charged to expense when incurred. In the budgeting process, they would be budgeted to appear in budgeted income statements and not in budgeted balance sheets.

In addition to budgeting research and development expenses and expenditures by time periods, it is common practice to budget individual projects in considerable detail by jobs or phases, tying together time, money expenditure, and technical accomplishment. Formal techniques for project planning and control include CPM (Critical Path Method) and PERT (Program Evaluation Review Technique).

These techniques do not add anything to previous techniques so far as breaking projects down to jobs or phases, attaching time schedules to them, and budgeting manpower and costs for each one. Their particular contribution is the concept of identifying the critical jobs to be done—that is, the jobs that directly affect the total project time. Once these jobs are identified, control can be concentrated on them so that the project or program will be completed within or ahead of the time budgeted.

Knowledge of the critical jobs also enables studies to be made of the costs of shortening the time on any one or more of them relative to the benefits that might thereby result.

Both CPM and PERT typically involve the use of graphs which assist in identifying the critical path or paths, as well as the noncritical work to be done. However, such data can be developed, particularly on a computer, without reference to a graph. Nonetheless, the graph or "network" is useful in illustrating and communicating on the work to be done.

PERT, in connection with a project as it proceeds, typically involves the use of periodic graphs depicting the actual results to date compared with budgeted expenditures and technical accomplishment and forecasting the rate of expenditure and achievement of technical goals ahead to the current expected completion date of the project.

Comparison of Actual and Budgeted Income Statements

At the close of each month, the actual results with respect to sales and expenses as revealed by the income statement are compared against budgeted figures for the same items. Internal reports generally show both the budgeted figures and the actual results, along with the variances between the two for the month and year to date. Often, figures for the same month for the previous year are also shown, as are figures for the year to date for the previous year.

To the extent that budgeted figures have been established for revenues and types of expense for various divisions, branches, departments, or other organizational units of a company, so too reports of actual results compared with budgeted figures are prepared each month and sent to these units and to managerial levels above them.

In some companies, for some or all organizational units, adjusted budget figures are also included in monthly reports. These show what the expenses and results should have been at the levels of production volume and sales volume actually experienced. Thus managers are held accountable not only for performance relative to the fixed budget, but also relative to what their performance should have been, given the volumes of activity actually reached.

Exhibit 74 shows the comparison of actual and budgeted income statements for one of the divisions of an actual company. This company practiced a form of direct costing and calculated its gross profit as the difference between net sales and total variable costs. Fixed costs, including selling and administrative expenses, were then subtracted to arrive at the operating profit.

Exhibit 75 was the next step in this company's comparison of actual and budgeted figures. Here the variance in operating profit of $11,451 from the profit and loss statement was broken down to its major aspects of volume, product mix, revenue, cost, and inventory. Beyond this, but not shown here, the company developed analyses of variances by product line; comparisons of actual and standard material and labor costs; and comparisons of actual costs by type of expense against variable budget allowances, by departments and cost centers within the division.

Sales Analysis

From copies of customers' invoices, it is possible to analyze sales by class of customer; by type of product; and by division, district, and

EXHIBIT 74

Division H

Profit and Loss Statement — Month of May 1977

	Forecast	% of Sales	Actual	% of Sales	Variance
Total sales			5,562,633		
Less—returns			23,317		
Sales less returns	5,315,000	100.0	5,539,316	100.0	224,316
Less—cash discount	80,000	1.5	80,463	1.5	(463)
—allowances	80,000	1.5	133,947	2.4	(53,947)
Net sales	5,155,000	97.0	5,324,906	96.1	169,906
Less—cost of sales	1,975,000	37.2	2,154,696	38.9	(179,696)
Transfer premium	154,000	2.9	157,666	2.8	(3,666)
Variable factory departmental	604,000	11.4	619,276	11.2	(15,276)
Variable factory general	112,000	2.1	113,488	2.0	(1,488)
Commissions	35,000	.7	53,066	1.0	(18,066)
Transportation	144,000	2.7	132,635	2.4	11,365
Total variable costs	3,024,000	57.0	3,230,827	58.3	(206,827)
Gross profit	2,131,000	40.0	2,094,079	37.8	(36,921)
Less—fixed factory					
departmental	130,000	2.4	119,679	2.2	10,321
Fixed factory general	571,000	10.7	545,242	9.8	25,758
Laboratory and patent	64,000	1.2	71,518	1.3	(7,518)
Variances from standards	32,000	.6	41,024	.7	(9,024)
Selling and distribution	590,000	11.1	572,569	10.3	17,431
Administrative and general	271,000	5.1	259,596	4.7	11,404
Total fixed costs	1,658,000	31.1	1,609,628	29.1	48,372
Operating profit	473,000	8.9	484,451	8.7	11,451
Less—other expense	(10,000)	(.2)	(55,278)	(1.0)	45,278
Income before taxes	483,000	9.1	539,729	9.7	56,729
Less—income taxes	251,000	4.7	280,659	5.0	(29,659)
Investment credit	(7,000)	(.1)	—	—	(7,000)
Income after taxes	239,000	4.5	259,070	4.7	20,070

salesman. Sales data can also be developed by other factors such as type and size of package and by mode of transportation. To the extent that sales have been budgeted by these various classifications, actual results can be measured against budgeted figures. So too, results can be compared with the results of previous periods by the same classifications.

Sales analyses along the lines suggested are widely used by executives to keep them in close touch with the sales situation, to help them

EXHIBIT 75

Division H
Summary of Variances from Financial Plan — May 1977

	Volume Var.	Prod. Mix Var.	Revenue Var.	Cost Var.	Inventory Var.	Total per P. & L.
Sales	214,823	—	9,493	—	—	224,316
Cash discounts	(2,418)	794	(368)	1,529	—	(463)
Allowances	(20)	(613)	(794)	(52,520)	—	(53,947)
Cost of sales	(27,520)	(13,283)	—	(138,893)	—	(179,696)
Transfer premium	(15,593)	—	—	11,927	—	(3,666)
Var. factory departmental	(36,531)	(5,886)	—	27,141	—	(15,276)
Fixed factory departmental	—	—	—	867	9,454	10,321
Var. factory general	(8,919)	—	—	7,431	—	(1,488)
Fixed factory general	—	—	—	3,075	22,683	25,758
Laboratory	—	—	—	(7,518)	—	(7,518)
Var. from standards	—	—	—	(9,024)	—	(9,024)
Selling and distribution	—	—	—	17,431	—	17,431
Administration and general	—	—	—	11,404	—	11,404
Commissions	(1,736)	973	(2,093)	(15,210)	—	(18,066)
Transportation	(12,284)	(836)	—	24,485	—	11,365
Operating profit	109,802	(18,851)	6,238	(117,875)	32,137	11,451

spot areas requiring attention, and in general to serve as a useful aid in directing sales effort. Carried out in detail, management can not only spot where sales dollars differ from budgeted amounts, but it can also see these differences broken down to variances in price, volume, and product mix.

In smaller companies, sales analyses can be prepared manually by sorting copies of invoices in appropriate ways, e.g., class of customer, and by posting and combining figures from these invoices on columnar sheets with the aid of a calculator or adding machine. In larger companies, bookkeeping machines, tabulating equipment, or computers are used for faster and generally more economical results.

Gross Margin Analysis

By costing each invoice line of a copy of each customer's invoice, it is possible to establish the cost of goods sold in each of the categories covered by the sales analysis and to follow this by computing the gross margin contribution in each category. Standard product costs of the type discussed in Chapter 22 are particularly helpful for this purpose. Assuming that the cost of goods sold appearing in the company's income statement prepared for internal use is based on standard costs, the resulting gross margin is the same as would be a summary of the gross margin analysis of customers' invoices.

Standard product costs per unit are used in establishing figures for the cost of goods sold, both in budgets and in reports of actual performance. Thus the variances in gross margin between the two are variances in the sales volume, selling price, and product mix, and not differences in product cost.

This is appropriate, since the sales organization has some responsibility for sales volume, selling price, and product mix sold but usually no direct responsibility for the cost of manufacturing the goods that were sold. Manufacturing variances appear later in the income statement and, of course, the manufacturing organization is held accountable for them.

Gross margin analysis in detail, which ought to be more widely practiced, provides sales analysis with a qualitative dimension and assists to some extent in emphasizing the importance of the amount of marginal contribution from sales, and not sales dollars alone. Some caution must be used in the interpretation and use of gross margin analysis, since many expenses remain to be taken into account before arriving at net profit and return on investment.

However, shortcomings should not discourage gross margin analysis. It can be much more meaningful than sales analysis alone, and it is a necessary step in the direction of making an even more complete analysis of results. Moreover, the importance of the gross margin contribution should not be minimized; if a profit is not in the gross, it will never appear in the net.

Net Income Analysis

Ideally, it would be desirable to know the net income in each of the categories just mentioned for sales analysis and gross margin analysis and to relate the net income in each case where appropriate to the investment involved so as to determine return on investment by categories. Similarly, it would be desirable to be able to budget net income by these categories and to compare actual results against these budgeted figures.

To arrive at net income involves identifying selling and administrative expenses with these categories. However, if the analysis is performed with a reasonable degree of accuracy, it is time-consuming and expensive.

Moreover, as we have already noted, many of these expenses have only a very indirect relationship to specific goods either produced or sold, particularly in the short run. Therefore, the identification of these costs with specific goods involves arbitrary cost allocations. This does not mean that the allocations are made capriciously and without rational bases but only that the accuracy of results is subject to question.

A relatively simple net income analysis can be made by applying overall percentages to the figures for sales and cost of goods sold developed in the sales analysis and gross margin analysis. For example, the percentage relationship between selling expenses and sales for the company as a whole, or for a given division, can be applied to the sales in each category to arrive at an approximation of the selling expenses involved in each.

Similarly, the percentage relationship between administrative expenses and the cost of goods sold for the company as a whole can be used in establishing an approximation of the administrative expenses involved in each category. The net income figures resulting from subtracting the allocated selling and administrative expenses from gross margins by categories can be compared with budgeted net income figures, prepared in much the same way, in measuring the results of operations.

The allocation of selling and administrative expenses just described, however, may be far from accurate. They do not really advance the knowledge of the contributions by customers, products, divisions, districts, and salesmen beyond that known from the gross margin analysis, since they are developed from uniform percentages applied to all categories.

Sales, Gross Margin, and Expense Analysis by Salesmen

With respect to the performance of individual salesmen, the sales and gross margin analyses are useful in making qualitative appraisals of their contributions to income. It is common practice to maintain records of salaries, commissions, hotel, travel, and other expenses by individual salesmen.

Thus the total of these expenses for a period for a given salesman can be subtracted from the gross margin on the sales credited to him for that period in measuring his contribution to the business. There is little to be gained, compared with the work involved, in allocating other district, division, and home office selling and administrative expenses to individual salesmen so as to arrive at the net income on their sales.

Granted that while it is desirable to know how much above covering his own costs a salesman should be expected to contribute to the business in order to justify his existence, this is a matter that executives ought to be able to judge without making additional detailed cost allocations.

The sales and expense performance of a salesman can, of course, be compared with that of others within the company handling the same product lines and serving comparable areas. It is also useful to establish standard allowances and unit costs against which actual expenses can be measured. The latter include standards such as hotel and meal costs per day, automobile costs per mile, and average travel cost per call.

Sales, Gross Margin, and Expense Analysis by Customer Class

The extent to which it is practical to budget and measure results by customer classes depends considerably on circumstances within each company. The sales and gross margin analyses for these groups of customers would, of course, take into account any special prices, discounts, and allowances for each group.

By maintaining separate accounts receivable records for each group, it is also possible to identify collection experience and bad debt losses with each group. Where separate salesmen are assigned to separate customer classes, their salaries, commissions, and expenses can be similarly identified.

In cases where order-handling costs, freight, and express differ markedly between groups, it is possible to develop logical ways of prorating these costs to groups. And where separate products are sold to each group, it should be possible to make direct charges for expenses such as advertising.

Beyond the steps suggested, the more general selling and administrative expenses can be allocated to customer classes on bases such as percentage of sales or percentage of cost of goods sold, although the value of such allocations is open to question.

Sales District Analysis

Selling and administrative expenses directly incurred at the district level can easily be identified and deducted from the gross margin for each sales district, in budgets and in reports on actual results. These expenses include those of the types already discussed that are directly identifiable with individual salesmen and customer classes, as well as executive and staff salaries, rent, and other expenses of each district sales office.

The desirability of going beyond this point, however, in determining the contribution of each sales district is quite debatable. To go all the way to arrive at net operating income involves the allocation of both division office and home office selling and administrative expenses to each sales district.

To be sure, where specific services have been provided (e.g., time on a computer), equitable charges can be made to the districts. But where expenses are allocated simply on the basis of overall percentages of sales and cost of goods sold, the results will not really reveal any more information relative to the district contribution than was known prior to the subtraction of these expenses.

Then again, there may be a psychological benefit from deflating the contribution in this way in order to bring home to district management the fact that from a company viewpoint these divisional and home office expenses have to be taken into account before arriving at net income. In other words, it can help both to show that the district's contribution above the cost of goods sold and district expenses is not "all profit" and to indicate why a respectable marginal contribution at the district level is necessary.

Division Analysis

In establishing both the budget and measures of performance at the division level, data for sales, cost of goods sold, and gross margin are, of course, summaries of the same data developed at the district and salesmen levels. So too, the budgeted and actual expenses at these lower levels of the organization are brought into division budgets and income statements of actual results.

The selling and administrative expenses incurred at the division office level must then be allowed for in the budgeted figures, and brought into division income statements of actual results, in arriving at the expected and actual divisional income contributions before taking home office expenses into account.

The same questions arise about the appropriateness of charging home office costs to divisions, as we noted above in connection with charges to districts for home office and division office expenses. Where the home office provides services such as auditing, legal counsel, and engineering, it is possible to make charges to divisions for service rendered, although the rates charged are commonly considered to be too high by those in the units charged. The remaining home office costs are allocated to division offices typically as a percentage of sales or as a percentage of cost of goods sold.

Either basis leaves much to be desired, since the divisions that are most successful for a given period are made to bear more of the home office overhead, while the burden of bearing such overhead is lightened for the divisions that did not do so well. Moreover, under such methods of allocation, whatever the home office spends will have to be borne by the divisions, even though the home office may exceed its budget.

If it is considered desirable to allocate home office costs to divisions, over and above charges for specific services rendered, it is preferable to predetermine and budget a fixed amount to each division representing the expected cost of the home office support to be provided or, in any event, the amount of home office expense each division is expected to absorb. Also, the division should be charged, and the home office credited, each month for the same amount as was budgeted; no more and no less.

In this way, the division is made aware in advance of the amount that must come out of its income contribution before arriving at net corporate income. It is not charged more if it does a good job and less if it does poorly. And it is not charged more or less because of fluctuations in home office costs over which it has no control.

At the same time, the home office has pressure on it to live within its budget, since costs above budget will not be borne by the divisions.

Product Line Analysis

It is the practice of many companies to include data by product lines within the budgets and reports of actual performance prepared by operating units and for the company as a whole.

Sales, the cost of goods sold (using standard costs per unit), and gross margin figures can be developed by product lines without difficulty, except for the volume of clerical work involved. However, the identification of many selling and administrative expenses with product lines involves arbitrary allocations with results that are always subject to question.

Under these circumstances, whatever selling and administrative expenses can be directly identified with a given product line are charged directly to it. The remainder are allocated to product lines, commonly on a percentage of sales basis. The reason for this is on the grounds that the larger the amount of sales per unit and in total for a given product line the more time and money will be spent to administer and sell it, which may or may not in fact be the case.

Administrative expenses are sometimes allocated on a percentage of cost of goods sold basis, rather than as percentage of sales. The reasoning here is on the grounds that the cost of the goods in a product line is a reflection of company input actively calling for a proportionate amount of administrative attention.

Separation of fixed and variable costs by product lines. Fixed (or "standby") costs and variable costs are accounted for separately in some companies, for selling and administrative expenses as well as for product costs, even though the distinction between fixed and variable costs is of necessity somewhat arbitrary.

This separation is also carried out in product-line budgets and income statements. These first show sales, less itemized variable product costs, and itemized variable selling and administrative expenses, to arrive at marginal income. Then, from these, itemized fixed product costs, and itemized fixed selling and administrative expenses, are subtracted to arrive at net operating income.

The identification of variable product costs with individual product lines is, of course, not difficult. But the identification of variable selling and administrative expenses, and fixed costs of all types, with individual product lines is troublesome and arbitrary at best.

This type of presentation can be helpful to an understanding of the major characteristics of a company's costs. It stresses the amount of contribution from each product line above the covering of variable costs. And it may well bring home to some executives the size and importance of the fixed costs that must be covered before it can be said to have made a contribution to net operating income.

The disadvantages of this type of presentation are that costs are not summarized by the major functions of production, sales, and administration. Nor is a figure shown for gross margin, which is a key item in conventional income statements and which is considered to be an important measure of performance by many executives.

Of course, if a company wishes to do so, it can arrange its accounts so that both types of product-line budgets and income statements can be prepared as two different ways of looking at the same situation. However, if only the more conventional form of product-line budgets and income statements are prepared, studies should be made on the side to bring home to executives the nature of each of the company's major costs and cost-volume relationships.

Budgeting of Balance Sheet Items

As we have noted, the budgeting of sales, cost of goods sold, and operating expenses involve every operating section of a business and the managers as well as others connected with them. The budgeting of balance sheet items is not as involved. In fact, it often is developed by the financial and accounting executives and staffs with a minimum of participation by the line organization.

An exception to this is the balance sheet item of property, plant, and equipment, and its related account for accumulated depreciation. In all except small companies, requests for expenditures on property, plant, and equipment go through the hands of a number of people in an orderly process of study and presentation so that all proposals will be given a fair hearing. Thus the most desirable expenditures will be made within the funds available. This process is known as capital budgeting, which is one part of the total process of annual budgeting.

The computation of depreciation expense for a period, and its concomitant effect on the balance sheet item of accumulated depreciation, also involves a number of individuals outside of the financial and accounting departments.

Expenditures for property, plant, and equipment are financed, at least in part, by internally generated funds from operations, including customer reimbursement for depreciation that has taken place. If expenditures are budgeted for amounts in excess of expected internally generated funds, then the budget must also include plans for getting the necessary additional funds either through long-term debt or sale of capital stock.

The comparison of actual and budgeted balance sheets is carried out in the same way as when a balance sheet at the end of a period is compared with the balance sheet as of the end of the previous period. This type of analysis is described in Chapter 14, "Balance Sheet: Ratio Analysis," and illustrated at the outset of Chapter 15, "Construction of the Funds Flow Statement."

Cash Budgeting

Cash requirements to be budgeted as of the close of each month of the budget year are computed by deduction in some companies. That is, all of the other items in the balance sheet are estimated for each month of the budget year and the cash balance for any given month is then computed as the amount necessary to make the budgeted balance sheet for that month balance.

If the result shows a negative cash balance, or a balance that is inadequate relative to the size of other current assets and current liabilities, the amount necessary to increase cash to a desirable balance is then budgeted as the amount of necessary short-term debt outstanding as of the balance-sheet date.

The approach just suggested can be reasonably satisfactory in fore-casting what the balance sheet should look like at the close of each month of the budget year, particularly if operations do not fluctuate much from month to month. It is not likely to be adequate, however, in budgeting cash requirements for the treasurer who must face sizeable fluctuations in cash receipts and disbursements between balance sheet dates.

For the treasurer, a detailed cash budget is necessary which will budget expected cash receipts and disbursements on a weekly basis, if not by days. For this purpose, he must plan the timing and amounts of expected receipts from customers and the timing and amounts of payments of company debts. He must also plan the cash outflows for payrolls, rents, interest, and other expenses, as well as dividends.

A cash budget by months is commonly prepared as one part of the fixed budget. Exhibit 76 is an illustration of such a budget using figures from our earlier example of the sales, production, and income statement budgets.

It is assumed, for this cash budget, that amounts collected from customers each month will be equal to sales of the previous month, net of allowances. In Exhibit 76, sales for December have been assumed at $1,512,000, which, less sales allowances of $11,300, gives the expected collections from accounts receivable in January of $1,500,700.

Similarly, it is assumed in the example that payment for materials will lag one month behind the incurrence of material costs as budgeted in Exhibit 70. Further, it is assumed that the cost of materials in December is to be the same as budgeted in Exhibit 70 for January.

Labor costs, on the other hand, are assumed to be paid in the month incurred in this example. Thus the figures for labor in the cash budget (Exhibit 76) are the same as the total labor costs budgeted each month in Exhibit 70.

The payment of manufacturing expenses is assumed to lag one month behind their incurrence, as was the case with material costs. Also it is assumed that the cost of manufacturing expenses in December is to be the same as budgeted in Exhibit 71 for January. Although depreciation, a non-cash expenditure, would be the major item in the fixed costs budgeted, we shall assume that cash payments for plant machinery and equipment each month would be equal to the depreciation that has taken place and, therefore, that the fixed costs can be included here in the cash budget. In an actual case, the budgeted cash payments for such items would lag behind the acquisition dates scheduled for them in the capital budget.

EXHIBIT 76
Cash Budget
January–June 19—

	Jan.	Feb.	March	April	May	June	Total
Est. collections:							
Accounts receivable:	1,500,700	1,582,300	2,113,400	3,024,100	2,632,000	2,113,400	12,965,900
Est. disbursements:							
Material	724,400	724,400	632,800	547,300	505,500	413,300	3,547,700
Labor	1,113,400	973,300	838,700	776,800	634,800	718,300	5,055,300
Mfg. expense	252,400	252,400	233,100	214,000	205,600	185,800	1,343,300
Total factory	2,090,200	1,950,100	1,704,600	1,538,100	1,345,900	1,317,400	9,946,300
Sell. & Adm. exp.	81,200	82,900	93,600	111,900	104,000	93,600	567,200
Advertising	70,800	70,800	70,800	70,800	70,800	70,800	424,800
Commissions	75,600	79,700	106,500	152,300	132,600	106,500	653,200
Income tax	–	–	–	260,000	–	200,000	460,000
Total	2,317,800	2,183,500	1,975,500	2,133,100	1,653,300	1,788,300	12,051,500
Balance	(817,100)	(601,200)	137,900	891,000	978,700	325,100	914,400
Dividends	–	–	250,000	–	–	250,000	500,000
Month's balance	(817,100)	(601,200)	(112,100)	891,000	978,700	75,100	414,400
Cum. balance:							
Cash, 1st of month	760,000	692,900	691,700	579,600	720,600	1,099,300	
Balance	(57,100)	91,700	579,600	1,470,600	1,699,300	1,174,400	
Borrow	750,000	600,000	–	–	–	–	
Pay back	–	–	–	(750,000)	(600,000)	–	
Cash, end of month	692,900	691,700	579,600	720,600	1,099,300	1,174,400	

Payment for selling and administrative expenses, advertising, and commissions in Exhibit 76 is assumed to lag one month behind the budgeted amounts for these expenses in Exhibit 73.

The amount of income tax to be paid, and dividends to be distributed is an assumed amount so that something for these items might be included in the illustration.

One result of the budgeting of expected cash receipts and disbursements is to reveal the need and timing of bank loans, and the timing for repaying them. Thus in Exhibit 76, it is expected to be necessary to borrow money in January and February and to be able to pay back the loans in April and May.

Other Current Assets

The budgeting of expected accounts receivable balances for each month of the budget year is dependent on the sales budgeted by months and on the company's collection experience, i.e., the average number of days customers take to make payment. These data are the same as those on which the treasurer estimates his cash receipts from customers.

Inventories of raw materials, work-in-process, and finished goods are budgeted relative to the production budget, the sales budget, and budgeted income statements. The budgeting of prepaid expenses is based on these same sources of data plus the historical relationship of this balance sheet item to the total current assets.

Current Liabilities

The budgeting of accounts payable is dependent on budgeted purchasing, which is in turn dependent on the production budget and which ties into budgeted inventories.

Similarly, budgeting of wages and salaries accrued and other accruals is dependent on budgeted expenses which are summarized in the budgeted income statements.

The budgeting of short-term debt, e.g., bank loans, is dependent, as noted earlier, on the budgeting of cash requirements.

Long-term Debt

The budgeting of this item ties in with capital budgeting and with the company's long-range plans for expansion. It is also dependent on the company's policy with respect to its debt/equity ratio, on whatever long-term debt may be falling due and on expectations with respect to the money market.

Stockholders' Equity

The budgeting of this item involves the same considerations as long-term debt, together with the company's dividend policy. It also, of course, is highly dependent on the amount of net income estimated in the budgeted income statements.

CHAPTER 29

Variable Budgeting

For budgetary and control planning, we noted at the outset of the previous chapter that there are two types of budgets — fixed or appropriation, and variable or flexible. We noted further that the fixed budget in its final form is a series of budgeted income statements, balance sheets, and source and application of funds statements by months, year-to-date, and total for the year.

Later, as one way of measuring performance, the financial statements covering actual results for these same periods are measured against the budgeted statements.

The principal weakness of the fixed budget lies in the area of expense control and measurement of performance when the actual volume of operations for a period turns out to be different from that predicted, and on which expense allowances were based.

More specifically, under these circumstances, the budgeted amounts are no longer appropriate for those expenses which should vary in some degree with changes in the volume of activity of the operations in which they are incurred. Thus for the planning and control of variable and semivariable expenses, the variable or flexible budget is particularly helpful.

Under a variable budget, those managers in charge of a cost center, department, or other area of responsibility are provided with a schedule or table of allowances. With these, the managers can determine for each type of expense listed what the expense should be at any given level of operations within the normal or practical range of operations for their area of responsibility.

Thus, in theory at least, they know their spending allowances in advance when planning their operations. And they also know what they should be spending for the volume of operations at which they are currently working.

Beyond this, those in charge of an area of responsibility, and top levels of management also, can measure after the fact their actual expenses against what they should have spent for the volume of operations realized. Therefore, the variable budget is a planning tool, a spending guide as operations take place, and a rational means of checking spending performance.

The variable budget is particularly useful in the control of variable burden in manufacturing companies. It is inappropriate, or much less useful, in the control of selling and administrative expenses where costs are not readily responsive or cannot be quickly adjusted to changes in the volume of operations.

Thus while the variable budget can be more effective than a fixed budget in the control of certain expenses, it does not supplant the need of a fixed budget for other expenses. Moreover, even if the variable budget could be used in the control of every type of expense, it could still be highly desirable to use the fixed budget for purposes of planning and coordinating the efforts of a company's various organizational units. In fact, it may be said that all companies should have a fixed budget, even if only on an informal basis, whereas the usefulness of a variable budget is dependent on the circumstances in each given case.

Variable Budgeting

As we noted in the preceding paragraphs, the variable budget is particularly useful in planning and controlling variable and semivariable items of factory burden by cost centers, departments, or other operating units. It is commonly prepared in the form of a schedule or table of allowances. This shows the specific allowance for each type of expense at each volume of activity listed, with volume being measured by a factor such as direct labor hours.

For practical reasons, the schedule is restricted to the probable range of operations to be experienced by the organizational unit covered, rather than its possible range of volume, and its presentation is further restricted to intervals within the probable range of operations. For example, the expense allowances might be listed in columns at 5% intervals for the probable range of operations from 50% to 100% of capacity per week or other time interval for the operating unit budgeted.

Exhibit 77 illustrates this type of departmental variable budget showing the indirect expense allowances per week at intervals of 5%

EXHIBIT 77
Work Indirect Expense Budgets per Week

Direct Hours	1,000	1,100	1,200	1,300	1,400	1,500	1,600	1,700	1,800	1,900	2,000
Per cent capacity	50	55	60	65	70	75	80	85	90	95	100
Foremen	400	400	400	400	400	400	500	500	500	500	500
Clerical	240	240	240	240	240	240	240	300	300	300	300
Total	640	640	640	640	640	640	740	800	800	800	800
Oilers, cleaners	100	110	120	130	140	150	160	170	180	190	200
Internal transp.	70	70	70	70	70	70	90	90	90	90	90
Other indirect labor	350	380	410	440	470	500	530	560	590	620	650
Total indirect labor	520	560	600	640	680	720	780	820	860	900	940
Grinding wheels	40	40	50	50	60	60	70	70	80	80	90
Paints, lubricants	50	50	50	60	60	60	70	70	70	80	80
Stationery & office	10	10	10	10	10	10	20	20	20	20	20
Misc. supplies	50	50	50	50	50	50	50	60	60	60	60
Total supplies	150	150	160	170	180	180	210	220	230	240	250
Machinery	300	330	360	390	420	450	480	510	540	570	600
Motors	60	70	70	80	80	90	90	100	100	110	110
Small tools	900	900	1,080	1,170	1,260	1,350	1,440	1,530	1,620	1,710	1,800
Misc. equipment	40	40	40	40	40	40	40	40	40	40	40
Total maintenance	1,300	1,340	1,550	1,680	1,800	1,930	2,050	2,180	2,300	2,430	2,550
Total above charges	2,610	2,690	2,950	3,130	3,300	3,470	3,780	4,020	4,190	4,370	4,540
Depreciation											
Insurance											
Taxes											
Total fixed charges											
Total all charges											

for the capacity range from 50% to 100%. Given the number of direct labor hours the department plans to operate, is operating, or has operated, the foreman can determine what the expenses listed should be, or should have been, for the given week.

The feasibility of budgeting for a period as short as a week, and of holding supervisors accountable for these indirect expenses, is sometimes questioned. However, the reason for the weekly checkup is to enable the person immediately responsible for the area to know promptly when some expense is getting out of line so that he may take action to correct the situation. Those in authority above him should be content to wait for a longer period before judging his performance.

In many companies it is the practice to furnish year-to-date, or twelve-week moving average figures, in addition to the weekly comparisons of actual expenses against the budget. The emphasis in judging performance is then on the trend of expenses and not on the results of a single week or month.

It is a common experience to find that it is easier to hold expenses down as volume of production rises, than it is to cut expenses as volume falls. One reason for this is a supervisor's uncertainty as to whether production activity is to continue to fall or is about to start to rise again. Thus, for expense control, it is wise to inform a supervisor well in advance of an expected drop in production volume, and to give him some idea of the expected magnitude and length of the downturn.

Other Types of Variable Budgets

The variable budget may also be developed as a series of formulas, one for each type of expense involved in the operating unit being budgeted. A formula shows an amount expected to be the fixed component of the given type of expense plus a factor for the variable component to be applied to the base used to express volume. In Exhibit 51 of Chapter 24, for example, the formula for the total annual costs illustrated was $2,100,000 of fixed costs and variable costs equal to 64% of net sales.

Similarly, the formula for a given type of expense to be expected in a factory cost center would show a stated amount for the fixed cost for the length of time being budgeted, commonly a week. In addition, a factor for the variable cost component would be expressed as: a. a percentage of labor cost; or b. an amount per labor hour or machine hour; or c. per unit of product produced. Formulas of this type are developed by the techniques described in Chapter 24.

A third way in which the variable budget may be developed is in the form of graphs illustrated earlier in Chapter 28 and in Chapter 24.

Such graphs are likely to be more awkward for determining specific expense allowances for a given period than either a table of allowances or a formula. But they can be helpful for educational purposes in illustrating cost-volume relationships.

Comparison of Actual and Budgeted Expenses

Exhibit 78 shows the actual results of one of a company's cost centers compared to the variable budget allowances for the activity of that cost center for a given month. Figures were also provided by the company comparing actual results against variable budget allowances for the year-to-date, but these figures have not been included in our exhibit.

The company had established a list price for each of its products. Production activity was measured in terms of the list price value of goods produced. These list prices enabled use of the dollar as a common denominator by means of which dissimilar product units could be added together to provide what the company believed to be a rational measure of production activity. For the month illustrated, the product units which passed through this cost center had a list price value of $845,053.

In this particular variable budget, the cost of direct labor was included along with the usual items of factory burden. Variances were shown in percentages as well as in dollars to assist in flagging items that were significantly out of line, either favorably or unfavorably. The credits indicated variances that were in the red, i.e., unfavorable variances.

In this case, fixed expenses were included at the same amounts in both the budget and actual columns. The purpose was to make the head of the cost center aware of these expenses without holding him accountable for them in a spending sense.

As we have noted, the measure of activity in this example was the list price value of units produced. This meant essentially that the company used an output factor rather than an input factor in measuring the activity on which the variable budget allowances for the period were based. The significance of the difference between input and output measures of activity will be discussed in the paragraphs to follow.

Input vs. Output Measures of Activity

Since the "variable" referred to in a variable budget is volume of activity, the selection of an appropriate measure of that activity is an important matter. Direct labor hours expended, for example, are widely used as the measure of activity in establishing allowances for indirect labor.

EXHIBIT 78
Variable Budget Comparison

Department #
Cost Center #

	Budget	Actual	Variance	%
Production		845,053		
Direct labor				
Process A	1,589	1,497	92	5.7
Process B	1,940	1,876	64	3.2
Process C	420	329	91	21.6
Total	3,949	3,702	247	6.2
Indirect labor				
Equipment supervision	331	229	102	30.8
Trucking and handling wages	407	353	54	13.2
Cleaning and sweeping wages	46	16	30	65.2
Overtime premium	17	332	315 cr	852.9
Shift differential	151	174	23 cr	15.2
Training and breaking in	3	19	16 cr	533.3
Make-up allowance	35	4	31	88.5
Setting-up labor	77	58	19	24.6
Machine downtime	5	29	24 cr	480.0
Waiting for work	55	17	38	69.0
Wages for expediting	214	202	12	5.6
Miscellaneous indirect	19	—	19	100.0
Total	1,360	1,433	73 cr	5.3

A better measure of activity for establishing material-handling allowances, however, would probably be units, pounds, or tons of material handled.

Although a variety of different measures might be used in setting allowances for different types of expense, to simplify the procedure a single important measure of activity is usually selected for any one department or cost center. Different measures of activity are, however, often used for different departments or cost centers.

There is a marked difference in both philosophy and practice between the use of an input factor as the measure of activity for the variable budget and the use of an output factor for this purpose.

It is my opinion that the head of a department or cost center should be held separately accountable for his spending and operating performance. Generally speaking, variable factory burden should be expected to fluctuate with the time spent by a department or cost center or with the time of men and machines working within it.

EXHIBIT 78 (continued)

Department #
Cost Center #

	Budget	Actual	Variance	%
Variable expense				
Employee benefits	2,336	2,267	69	2.9
Process power	3	2	1	33.3
Mold expense	1,053	194	859	81.5
Misc. manufacturing supplies	12	74	62 cr	516.6
Printed forms and supplies	5	—	5	100.0
Repairs to machinery	968	161	807	83.3
Maintenance of molds	2,409	1,875	534	22.1
Part maintenance	—	11	11 cr	999.9
Repairs to templates	119	49	70	58.8
Repairs to tools	290	151	139	47.9
Maintenance to scales	63	90	27 cr	42.8
Lubrication and inspection	23	—	23	100.0
Total	7,281	4,874	2,407	33.0
Fixed expense				
Building depreciation	—	—	—	—
Rental expense	21	21	—	—
Depreciation mach. & equipment	637	637	—	—
Depreciation tools	11	11	—	—
Total	669	669		
Grand Total	13,259	10,678	2,581	19.4

Accordingly, expenses such as indirect labor, heat, light, power, and supplies take place while men and machines are working, and largely in an amount proportional to hours expended. What and how much is produced in these hours is another matter. The variable budget is, therefore, particularly useful for assisting in the control of spending relative to input measures of activity.

When variable burden allowances are based on an output measure of activity, the control responsibility is not clean-cut since spending efficiency and operating efficiency are merged. Standard costs rather than the variable budget should be used in costing the efficiency of operations. Thus the difference between the standard burden cost of input hours and the standard burden cost in goods produced is the measure of the operating efficiency with respect to burden realization.

Those who use an output measure of activity for determining variable budget spending allowances do so because they believe that spending control should be tightened when operating performance is below standard. It also, of course, sets a looser standard for spending when operating performance is above standard. But this is excused on the ground that there is no harm in allowing a department or cost center to spend a little more under these conditions.

Fixed Cost Considerations

In many companies, the variable budget is restricted to directly variable and semivariable expenses. Fixed costs such as depreciation, real estate taxes, and insurance, as well as the costs of many service departments, are omitted.

The primary arguments commonly given for not including these costs in the variable budget are that the department or cost center being budgeted has no control over them and that such costs are so large in comparison with variable burden that, if they are included in the budget, the manager of the budgeted area will be discouraged from attempting to control his variable costs, since they will appear to represent such a small part of total costs.

The fact is, however, that fixed costs are highly important from a total company viewpoint, and these are becoming increasingly more important with the heavy costs involved in increased automation. The only way to recoup these higher costs, short of liquidation, is to get orders for goods to be made by the facilities for which the costs were incurred and to make these goods efficiently.

Obviously, the supervisor of a department or cost center contributes to this process of recoupment when he sees to it that the jobs handled by his unit are done within standard time allowances and that scrap and spoilage are kept at a minimum.

Spending Control vs. Control of Operating Efficiency

It is probably a good idea in most companies to restrict the variable budget to items of variable and semivariable expense. These are items that the head of the cost center or department can do something about in a spending sense.

It is probably true, also, that the efficiency with which a department operates can be measured in physical terms and judged relative to physical standards. For example, in producing paper, the important matters from a cost viewpoint may well be to operate the paper machine at a standard speed for the grade of paper being produced, with a minimum of down time and a minimum of broke, i.e., spoilage.

Where heavy fixed costs are involved, however, these may well indeed be the most important costs from a company viewpoint. It may be far more important, for example, to keep reminding a foreman that he is the custodian of a $150 million machine and, therefore, that efficient use of the time of that machine is his major job, not the saving of a few pennies' worth of supplies.

The best approach here seems to be to use the variable budget for the control of variable and semivariable burden and to use standard costs in connection with the control of operating efficiency. Thus for the latter purpose, the foreman is charged at a standard rate per hour for the facilities under his supervision. He is then given credit for the standard burden cost of the goods produced. If he produces at standard efficiency, his credits will balance with what he has been charged for the use of the facilities.

There is nothing unusual about this. It is simply using standard costing for the money measurement of operating efficiency. In the meantime, the spending efficiency, in terms of spending properly for the time the department or cost center is operated, is controlled through the use of the variable budget.

Example of a Manufacturing Statement of Costs and Cost Variances

We shall now discuss the plant and departmental cost statements of a relatively large company having several divisions and plants within divisions. At both divisional and corporate levels, the company made appropriate use of typical planning, reporting, and control techniques including fixed budgets, a form of variable budgeting, and standard costs. Our discussion will be concerned largely with the control of manufacturing costs by type of expense, identified by plant and by departments within each plant.

The budgeted sales volume for the year ahead was the basis on which total production plans were made in this company, including the development of factory burden rates. This use of the expected volume of operations for the coming year as the basis on which burden rates were established is in contrast to the alternative practice of basing burden rates on the "normal" volume of activity.

Manufacturing cost statement. The statement shown as Exhibit 79 was a key report on manufacturing cost performance and was prepared for each plant, each month. The report for a given plant was reviewed not only by the plant manager but also by the divisional executive to

EXHIBIT 79
Manufacturing Cost Statement

	Month Ending 5-27			5 Months to Date		
	Actual	Variance	Ratio	Actual	Variance	Ratio
RAW MATERIAL:						
Mix Variance					76	100
Waste & Yield Var.	446,875	10,552	98	1,866,381	44,756	98
Direct Materials	24,935	—	100	112,366		100
Total Material:	471,810	10,552	98	1,978,747	44,832	98
DIRECT LABOR—	86,113	(1,019)	101	409,990	(6,587)	102
VARIABLE BURDEN:						
Indirect Labor—Mfg.	22,925	277		107,248	(2,290)	
Repair Labor	3,429	(353)		19,724	(6,131)	
Repair Supplies	4,714	3,214		29,327	6,147	
Operating Supplies	3,619	1,076		25,114	(2,773)	
Fringe Benefits	26,792	1,146		130,730	797	
Utilities	11,109	893		56,348	(1,724)	
Overtime Premium	13,674	(4,358)		54,984	(12,752)	
Total Variable:	86,262	1,895	98	423,475	(18,726)	105
FIXED BURDEN:						
Salaries	41,659	(3,967)		217,963	(20,079)	
Wages	5,521	699		30,236	2,424	
Fringe Benefits	7,657	(1,170)		40,712	(6,656)	
Utilities	4,956	(1,471)		22,716	(4,421)	
Repairs & Oper. Exp.	7,346	(1,038)		39,817	(6,701)	
Depr., Rent, Taxes & Ins.	21,885	—		114,896	—	
Office Exp., Tel & Travel	9,236	(3,467)		41,631	(11,343)	
Outside Storage	(1,114)	1,499		(5,500)	7,521	
Trials	324	1,984		8,081	4,035	
Reprocessing	2,642	(334)		7,936	4,180	
Miscellaneous	1,553	(511)		6,243	(773)	
Total Fixed:	101,665	(7,776)	108	524,731	(31,813)	106
Spending Variance		(6,900)	103		(57,126)	104
Efficiency Variance		10,993	94		50,150	
Book to Phys. Inventory Adj.		34,976			23,695	
Total Plant Controllable	745,850	49,621	94	3,336,943	61,551	98
Inventory Disposal		(9,120)			(30,396)	
Extraordinary Repairs						
Other—Detail						
Start-up		(12,185)			(30,046)	
GWI				19,169	(19,169)	
Material Price		1,077			13,307	
Volume Variance		28,536	130		98,484	120
Total Cost & Variance	745,850	57,929	93	3,356,112	93,731	97

whom he reported, as well as by other divisional and corporate executives.

The manufacturing cost statement served to highlight variances from predetermined standards and to indicate the major nature of these variances. The variances summarized the financial impact of these departures from standard or budgeted performance.

Although the reports supplied the plant manager with exact dollar amounts of variances, and summarized them appropriately by cost categories for the month and year-to-date, neither a favorable nor an unfavorable variance of any substance appearing in the report came as a surprise to him. That is, on the basis of daily or weekly reports of one kind or another, together with knowledge of the current rate of volume of activity in comparison with budgeted expectations, the plant manager could foresee whatever substantial variances were likely to appear in the manufacturing cost statement and could take corrective steps even before the report appeared, to the extent that such steps were necessary or possible.

One of the responsibilities of the plant manager was to send a memorandum to his executive supervisor detailing the reasons for variances appearing in the manufacturing cost statement and the action he had initiated to correct situations causing unfavorable variances or to promote the continuation of favorable variances. His comments were reviewed later by his supervisor to assure that action had been taken in deeds as well as in words.

The manufacturing cost statement combined in a simple manner use of the annual budget, variable budgeting, and standard costs. The steps involved will now be described in some detail.

Standard costs. Over the years, the company had established standard costs for each of its products based on engineered standards tempered by experience. New standard product costs were established annually. They were adjusted on individual items during the year when major changes in materials used, or in production methods, had taken place. They were also adjusted more broadly during the year with a major change in wage rates or raw material costs. These were exceptions, however, and in general it could be said that the company adjusted its standard costs once each year.

Raw material standard costs. The standard cost card for each type of product showed the standard quantity of each type of material required to produce the given unit of output, with allowance for normal waste and yield. Initially these standard quantities on a new product had to be established by estimate, based on experience with other products, and by trial runs. The initial standards were later adjusted in line with experience on the specific product.

Standard prices (costs) per input unit of raw material were applied to the quantities of each type of raw material called for in the formula to establish the standard cost per unit of product (output). These standard prices per input unit (per pound, for example) were the prices the company expected it would have to pay on the average during the coming year.

Material price variance.   Materials as purchased were accounted for in raw material accounts at their standard costs. Variances between these standard costs and the actual costs of the materials purchased were charged or credited to a material price variance account, the balance of which was closed at the end of the month to profit and loss as a gain or loss for the period.

The net amount of this variance for the month and year-to-date was shown at the bottom of the manufacturing cost statement. Whatever responsibility there might have been for such a variance was considered to be a purchasing department responsibility rather than one of manufacturing personnel. The variance was included in the manufacturing cost statement, however, because the plant manager had a strong interest in material costs and the extent to which they might vary from expectations, since such variances affected the profitability of operations which was one of the bases on which plant performance was judged.

The material price variance of $1,077 listed at the bottom of Exhibit 79 for the month of May was a favorable variance. It should be remembered that this variance applied entirely to materials purchased during the period, only some of which, and perhaps none, would have entered production during that period.

Mix variance.   In some of the company's plants it was possible, or possible and necessary, to alter the proportions of the different types of raw material mixed in batches to produce a given type of product. Where this was the case, a mix variance could result as the difference between the total of the standard cost of the actual quantity of each type of material used, and the standard formula cost of the total quantity of materials used. No such mix variance was involved however during the month of May in the plant from which the figures in Exhibit 79 were drawn.

Waste and yield variances. The figure of $446,875 in Exhibit 79 represented the standard cost of the actual quantity of raw materials entering production during the given month. Production was scheduled by batches. Materials in each batch were weighed at the time they entered the first department, and each time the batch moved from one department to another. In this way the actual yield and amount of waste was established by batch for each department.

Variances between standard waste and yield allowances, and the actual waste and yield per batch, were accumulated apart from the accounts. The work-in-process account was adjusted for the net variance (in dollars) at the close of each month, with a contra charge or credit to a waste and yield variance account. The net waste and yield variance for the month of May in our example was a favorable variance of $10,552. This was, essentially, the difference between the standard cost of the materials used and the standard material cost of the good units produced, for the month. Since the variance was favorable, it meant that more good units than would normally be expected were produced from the materials used.

Although not shown by the exhibit, in the plant from which the figures were drawn, by far the greatest amount of expected waste and shrinkage took place in the first department. For such waste as did take place in later departments, the cost accounted for included accumulated labor and variable burden costs as well as material costs.

Direct materials. This category covered materials other than raw materials which could nonetheless be identified with specific products. Packaging materials represented the major part of this cost. The company had not attempted to establish cost variances in the use of these materials.

Direct labor. The variance on direct labor of $1,019 for May measured the difference between the actual labor cost for the month and an amount computed by multiplying the actual machine-hours operated during the month in each department by predetermined machine-hour labor rates.

Essentially this represented an application of variable budgeting to the control of labor costs. The measure of activity was input machine-hours and the variance was what is commonly known as a "spending" variance. Direct labor was assumed to be a directly variable cost which would increase or decrease directly in proportion to machine-hours operated. The variance for May arose because during that month the average direct labor cost per machine-hour was greater than predetermined. Being related to input hours rather than output product, it was a matter of having spent more per hour than standard for time put in and not a matter of the efficiency with which time was utilized. Variances in connection with the latter will be discussed in a moment as "efficiency" variances.

Variable budget approach. Although the company did not use the term "variable budget" in connection with its manufacturing cost statement, it did practice variable budgeting in a simplified manner in connection with the control of factory burden as well as in the control of direct labor.

Items of burden were separated into those considered to be primarily variable in nature and those considered to be nonvariable or fixed As in the case of direct labor, the measure of activity was taken as machine-hours operated.

Variable burden items were assumed to vary directly in proportion to machine-hours operated, while fixed costs were assumed to remain unchanged with fluctuations in the number of machine-hours operated.

Variable burden. As part of the process in establishing the annual fixed budget, the production budget was broken down to the expected machine-hours to be operated by each productive department within each plant for the year. Variable burden was then estimated by department for each cost classification for the departmental volumes of machine-hours projected. The total estimated variable burden for the year for a given department was then divided by the estimated machine-hours to be operated in total for the year by that department to arrive at the standard variable burden rate per machine-hour for that department.

The percentage relationship between the amount budgeted for each classification of variable burden to the total amount of variable burden budgeted was also established for each department.

Variable burden spending variance. At the close of a month, the machine-hours operated in a given department were multiplied by the variable burden machine-hour rate for that department to determine what its variable costs should have been for the period. These results were then added together to determine what the variable costs should have been for the period for the plant as a whole. The difference between this amount and the total actual burden for the period was the plant spending variance for variable burden.

In the present case, the total sum of variable burden rates per hour applied to the actual machine-hours operated in May was $88,157. Comparison of this figure with the actual variable burden costs of $86,262 gave the favorable variable burden variance of $1,895 shown in Exhibit 79.

Having established the total variable costs absorbed by the application of the variable burden machine-hour rate to the machine-hours operated by a department, it is then possible to establish what should have been spent in each cost classification by applying the budgeted percentage relationship of each cost to the total variable costs absorbed. Thus if in the budget for a department, the item repair labor represented 4.6% of budgeted variable costs, then 4.6% applied to the total variable costs absorbed by machine-hours worked in that department for a given month would give the amount that should have been spent by that department on repair labor for the month.

The difference between this amount and the amount actually spent would be the variance on repair labor that month for that department. The total of the variances for all departments provided the figure for the variance on repair labor appearing in the plant manufacturing cost statement.

The results of the calculations just described can be seen first in Exhibit 80, departmental cost statement, where it will be noted that the total of the departmental variances comes to a net unfavorable variance of $353 for May. This same figure then appears in the variance column in Exhibit 79 on the line for repair labor under variable burden.

As with direct labor, it should be stressed that the variances for variable burden items shown in both Exhibits 79 and 80 are spending variances. They indicate that either more or less than expected amounts have been spent on items of variable burden to operate the departments for the actual machine-hours involved. They measure efficiency only in the sense of having spent more or less than standard on variable costs to keep the departments running for the hours operated. They do not indicate the efficiency of the department in turning out goods. Thus they are an input rather than an output measure of cost performance. The efficiency variance will be discussed after the discussion on spending variances has been concluded.

Fixed burden. The annual fixed budget included cost estimates on costs which were considered to be nonvariable or fixed within the range of production and sales volumes predicted by months for the year ahead. That is, they were costs which were budgeted as being fixed, even though changes could be expected in them over longer periods of time.

EXHIBIT 80
Departmental Cost Statement

Department	TOTAL DEPT. (Excl. Volume)			VARIANCE DETAIL									VOLUME
	*Actual	Variance	Ratio	Direct Material	Direct Labor	Indirect Labor	Repair Labor	Repair Supplies	Operating Supplies	Overtime Premium	Efficiency Amount	Efficiency Ratio	
1	8,088	1,828	82		(321)		(137)	214	317	(22)	1,777	87	1,641
2	19,692	2,804	88		(220)		283	761	(468)	628	1,820	95	6,332
3	6,995	(2,202)	146		(481)		(113)	367	122	(533)	(1,564)	116	(574)
4	5,353	(1,904)	155		171	(2)	(239)	113	69	(431)	(1,585)	123	510
5	1,524	199	89		(2)	(46)	(3)	78	15	(13)	170	94	(566)
6	93	(29)	145		(2)		2		3		(32)	127	(54)
7	11,443	994	92		87	497	(146)	1,051	1,548	(527)	(1,516)	109	4,775
8	1,455	3,222	31		110	(770)	(26)	24	75	(90)	3,899	21	379
9	24,676	800	97		(2,144)			65	33	(1,792)	4,638	84	16,135
10	3,651	337	91		(104)	57	(4)	(20)	37	(348)	719	81	1,263
11	5,053	(1,594)	146		887	116	(77)	20	30	(914)	(1,656)	121	1,726
12	78	593	12		126						467	30	
13	1,252	480	72		43		9		42	(51)	437	79	400
14	8,721	983	90		845	387	84	(106)	(582)	141	298	98	(643)
15	11,549	3,288	78		(14)	16		528	(314)	(133)	3,121	83	5,669
16	4,884	1,188	80			1,105	66	(224)	1	240			1,339
17	10,209	(1,024)	111			(999)	(52)	343	102	(418)			193
18	1,160	(49)	104						46				
19	8,598	(84)	101			(84)				(95)			(9,989)
Total	134,474	9,830			(1,019)	277	(353)	3,214	1,076	(4,358)	10,993	94	28,536

*Direct labor and variable burden less fringe benefits and utilities

Although the fixed costs were not expected to change from month to month with fluctuations in the volume of operations as measured by machine-hours, they were budgeted at higher amounts for periods assumed to be of five weeks duration than for periods which were assumed to cover four weeks. That is, although in this company operating periods were identified as months, the first two months of each quarter of the calendar year were accounted for as four-week periods while the third month in each quarter covered a five-week period. Estimated fixed costs were proportional to the number of weeks assumed for any given period.

Fixed burden spending variances.   The variances for items of fixed burden shown in the manufacturing cost statement were spending variances. That is, they represented the difference between the actual cost of these items for the number of weeks in the given period and the budgeted cost for the same period. They were not, at least to any significant degree, reflections of the current volume of activity or of operating efficiency.

Items of fixed burden were not included in the departmental cost statement, since it was believed that such costs were not within the control of department heads. They, and the variances on them, were, however, shown in the manufacturing cost statement partly because they did, after all, affect the profitability of plant operations and partly because some of them were discretionary in nature and in this sense were controllable by the plant manager, if not controllable by those under his supervision.

Total spending variance.   What was listed in the manufacturing cost statement as the spending variance was the sum of the direct labor, variable burden, and fixed burden spending variances. Thus, the $6,900 unfavorable spending variance listed in Exhibit 79 for May was computed as follows:

Direct labor spending variance	($1,019)
Fixed burden spending variance	(7,776)
	($8,795)
Variable burden spending variance	1,895
Total spending variance	($6,900) Loss

Efficiency variance.   It has been noted that a standard direct labor cost per machine hour, and a standard variable burden cost per machine hour, were established by the company for each producing department of each plant.

In establishing the standard cost of each product, a standard time per unit of product was established for each process (department) through which the product would pass. The departmental standard labor cost and standard variable burden cost per unit of a product could then be computed by applying the predetermined machine-hour rates to the standard time per product unit.

A record was maintained of the number of units of each type of product produced by each department each month. By reference to standard cost cards, the standard direct labor cost and standard variable burden cost per product unit could be located and then applied to the number of units produced. The difference between the resulting standard direct labor and standard variable burden cost of goods produced, and the standard direct labor cost and standard variable cost of machine-hours worked was an efficiency variance.

Thus, the difference between actual direct labor and actual variable burden costs and the standard direct labor and standard variable burden costs of machine-hours worked were accounted for as spending variances, while the difference between the total of these standard costs of machine-hours worked and the total of the standard direct labor and standard variable burden costs of goods produced was accounted for as an efficiency variance.

Input versus output measures of activity.   The company's practice just described is in contrast to the practice in some companies where variable budget allowances are based on output units of product as the measure of activity, rather than input machine-hours, and where only one variance, called a "spending" variance, is developed instead of both a spending and an efficiency variance. It seems evident that in the present actual case it was desirable to establish the two variances, particularly since one was a favorable efficiency variance of $10,993 for the month and the other an unfavorable spending variance of $6,900. To have merged the two would have resulted in a favorable so-called "spending" variance of $4,093. This would not have given the plant adequate recognition of its favorable production efficiency and would have concealed the fact that there was really an unfavorable spending variance for the month. Thus, to merge these two variances can seriously confound the problem of identifying variances from standard by cause.

Volume variance.   A volume variance was computed and shown at the bottom of the manufacturing cost statement. It measured the amount of fixed burden under- or overabsorbed by the current level of production relative to the budgeted level of production. The volume variance, whether favorable or unfavorable, was generally not considered to be the responsibility of the manufacturing unit, both because the budgeted level of production was based on sales department forecasts and because the sales department had primary responsibility for meeting these forecasts.

For product costing purposes, fixed costs were identified by departments, and a separate machine-hour rate for fixed costs was computed for each department based on the annual budget which established the expected fixed costs and number of machine-hours for the year by departments. Standard product costs included fixed costs computed by the application of the machine-hour rates just noted to the standard time required to process a product unit in each department. On the basis of production records, it was not too difficult to establish the amount of fixed burden absorbed each month by applying standard fixed burden product costs to the product output of each department. The volume variance could then be established by deduction as the difference between fixed burden absorbed and fixed burden budgeted.

Possible efficiency variance for fixed burden.   It will be recalled that in this company the efficiency variance accounted for the gain or loss with respect to labor and variable burden but omitted fixed burden. In an age when fixed burden is becoming in general a higher and higher proportion of total manufacturing costs, one might question whether such costs should be left out of consideration in judging the financial effects of gains or losses in production efficiency.

In the present case, for example, the fixed costs are larger in amount than either direct labor or variable burden costs. The efficiency gain of $10,933 for the month of May meant that the output per machine-hour was better than standard. This should have meant an equally more efficient utilization of facilities and the fixed costs associated with them. As it was, whatever efficiency variance there might have been was buried in the figure the company computed as the volume variance.

As an alternative, then, the company might have first computed the spending variance as the difference between the budgeted fixed costs and fixed costs absorbed by the application of fixed burden machine-hour rates to the hours actually worked. In turn, the difference between the fixed burden costs absorbed by the machine-hours worked and the fixed burden costs of goods produced would represent an efficiency variance on fixed costs to be added to the efficiency variance the company had computed.

Summary of spending, efficiency, and volume variances. These three variances shown in the manufacturing cost statement for May can be summarized as follows:

EXHIBIT 81

	A	B	A-B	C	B-C	B-C
	Actual	Actual Machine Hours x Std. Rates per hour	Spending Variance	Standard Cost of Output	Effiency Variance	Volume Variance
Direct labor	$ 86,113	$ 85,094	($1,019)	$ —	$ —	$ —
Variable burden	86,262	88,157	1,895	—	—	—
Total	172,375	173,251	876	184,244	10,993	—
			Period Budget			
Fixed Burden	101,665	93,889	(7,776)	122,425	—	28,536
	274,040	267,140	(6,900)	306,669	10,993	28,536

Adjusting accounts to physical inventory. Inevitably, raw materials entering production, waste removed from production, and goods moved from one department to another or to finished stock were not always weighed or counted with complete accuracy, and clerical errors also crept into the inventory records from time to time. Moreover, on some items, such as packaging materials, waste was not measured and standard usage was assumed in credits to Work-In-Process for goods completed. Thus when physical inventories were taken and priced at standard unit costs, the results were never the same as the inventory balances in the ledger accounts. Accordingly, adjustments had to be made to bring the ledger into line with the physical inventory. Fortunately in the present case, the adjustments for both the month and year-to-date were gains.

Inventory Disposal. This was a loss on disposal of slow-moving, obsolete, and off-grade products. While the figure for this loss appeared in the manufacturing cost statement below the plant controllable cost items, any excess over an established standard amount was considered to be a manufacturing responsibility.

Miscellaneous variances.   Such items as extraordinary repairs, start-up costs, and general wage increases (GWI) were isolated to relieve the manufacturing personnel of responsibility for charges which were not considered when the budget for the year was established.

Departmental cost statement.   This statement, shown as Exhibit 80, was referred to earlier. The actual costs shown by department on this statement were for direct labor and variable burden combined, less the variable costs of fringe benefits and utilities. The total variance shown for each department and in total for all departments was a combined spending and efficiency variance. Evidence of this can be seen in the following analysis:

Direct labor spending variance	$(1,019)
Variable burden spending variance	1,895
Total	$ 876
Less: Fringe benefits spending variance	1,146
Utilities spending variance	893
Net spending variance	$(1,163)
Add: Efficiency variance	10,993
Total variance	$ 9,830 (2nd. col. Ex. 80)

The spending variances by department for each type of expense listed and the efficiency variance in each department were matters of great interest and concern to the plant manager as well as to department heads. The departmental cost statement as shown in Exhibit 71 was sent to each department head who thereby knew the performance of other departments as well as that of his own department. Once each month the plant manager and all of the department heads met together to review this report. These meetings were believed to be helpful to all the people concerned.

The departmental cost statement included figures for the volume variance in each department. Department heads were not held accountable for these variances. They were included as information for the plant manager and department heads as to the level of output activity and its impact on operating results for the month. It was also useful in interpreting the spending variances for the month. Some judgment had to be applied in interpreting these variances when there were large variances in the volume of operations. Thus, showing the volume variances in this report gave an indication of the extent to which this judgment was called for in the current month.

CHAPTER 30

Formal Long-Range Planning

For a number of years now, it has been a common practice for companies to engage in formal long-range planning. What is considered to be long-range differs among companies, although five years seems to be a common number of years for which plans are made. It has, however, been the practice of public utilities to plan major needs for expansion over far longer periods than this.

Enthusiasm for long-range planning ranges from those who believe it is the most important line-management activity, particularly for top corporate and division management, to those who believe it is simply a "number-pushing" exercise which takes too much time and costs too much for the small benefit received.

Some companies have a strong centralized planning group actively engaged in the planning process. In others, planning is decentralized, although usually aided by a corporate planning officer. The functions of such an officer and his small staff are largely to spark the effort, in addition to developing the forms and routines and scheduling the program.

The formal planning system adopted by a company is highly dependent on the nature of the top corporate and division managements, as well as the nature of the situation with respect to the company and its industry. The following factors, among others, influence the nature of the formal planning system:

Organization structure.
Management background.
Management's aspirations for growth.
Operating style of the chief executive.

Growth rates of the company and industry.
Breadth of product line; single versus multiproduct.
Number of customer types and markets.
Capital intensity.
Degree of manufacturing integration.
Degree of technological complexity and change.

Strategic vs. Long-Range Planning

One major type of planning, often designated as strategic planning, typically involves only a few members of top management aided by a small but highly capable staff. This group determines basic objectives and goals for the company, decides the major strategies by which to attempt to reach these objectives and goals, and makes the necessary arrangements for the organizational and financial support required. In many companies, one of the major concerns of such a group is that of product diversification, including the starting of new divisions of the company and the acquisition of other companies.

Formal planning of the type with which we shall be most concerned, however, is engaged in by a large number of line managers at both corporate and division levels with staff assistance. It involves both the annual financial (fixed) budget and formal long-range planning. It is essentially an orderly process for establishing objectives, goals, and action programs in writing.

Although a revision of the long-range plan is made each year, it is usually developed separately from the preparation of the annual budget. In some cases, the long-range plan (typically, for the next five years) is made first, after which the annual budget is prepared. In other companies, the annual budget is first prepared in detail and represents also the first year of the five-year plan. After this budget is prepared, the plans are extended for four additional years, although in much less detail.

Thus, formal long-range plans include projected income statements, balance sheets, and funds flow statements for the number of years ahead for which plans are made. Except for the first year, these projected financial statements are much more condensed than the usual financial statements prepared at the close of accounting periods.

Long-range plans for the acquisition of plant, machinery, and equipment are commonly stated in terms of specific types and locations and thus are not simply projections of expected monetary expenditures. Similarly, projects such as the development of a new model of a product are described in writing, and tentative dates by phases and expected costs are estimated for them. Plans are also made of the ways in which these projects are to be financed.

The Use of Graphs

It is a common practice to prepare various graphs which start, for example, with the experience of the past five years for whatever item, such as sales revenue, is being depicted, and project the expectations or hopes for the next five or ten years.

Graphs of this type are particularly helpful in discussions of long-range plans. They help to dramatize, and focus on, critical areas where important decisions must be made. They can reveal with great clarity, for example, a gap between the projected sales expectations of the top corporate management of a company and a summation of the more modest sales projections of the divisional managers of that company.

Similarly, a single graph can depict results to be expected from the most optimistic, the most pessimistic, and the most likely estimates of sales or other types of activity. Graphs are also useful in picturing fund requirements for plant, machinery, and equipment; inventories; and accounts receivable, under conditions of expansion or contraction of sales and production activity.

Long-range planning is a circular process. Although it may seem most logical to start the long-range planning process with a statement of the major corporate objectives and goals, the process is more or less a continuing one. Since it moves from one aspect to another in a rotating manner, in a sense it does not make too much difference what one considers to be the starting point as long as the steps taken follow a reasonable sequence.

Thus, instead of starting with objectives and goals, one might start with a review of the past and appraisal of the present and eventually come around to setting goals after considering what the future might seem to offer.

In some companies, either at the outset of the program of formal long-range planning or at some later point, it is considered desirable to put into writing broad statements of the company's beliefs and objectives. This includes defining what kind of a business the company considers itself to be in, as well as its philosophies with respect to its relationships and responsibilities to shareholders, customers, employees, and the general public. The last point includes the company's role as a good citizen at international, national, state, and local levels.

Defining Qualitative Goals

Many companies include in their long-range planning what has become known as "management by objectives," which includes the setting of personal objectives by departments, plants, divisions, and the company as a whole.

Objectives are for example set in terms of:

Changes in organization.
Management development.
Employee opportunities for personal growth.
Employee welfare.
Employee work satisfaction.
Steady employment.

Similarly, in terms of citizenship, many companies include in their long-range planning moves to assist in problems of:

Minority interests.
Ecology and pollution.
Poverty.
Community welfare.

Budgeting considerations of quantitative factors. At some stage in the planning process, it is necessary to establish specific quantitative goals. These are likely to be tentative at first and made more firm at a later time. Typical quantitative goals are expressed as follows:

Rate of growth — sales.
Rate of growth — profit.
Return on investment.
Earnings per share.
Price of company's stock.
Price/earnings ratio.

Key Budgetary Questions

The following are typical questions that are raised and dealt with during the process of long-range budgeting:

What products or product lines should the company be in?
What markets should the company serve?

What will be the environment in which the company will operate?
  Nature of the industry.
  Nature of the competitive situation.
  Nature of the general economy.
  Political situation; local, state, federal, world.
What are the key variables?
  What does it take to be successful in this industry?
What are the company's strengths and weaknesses?
  In organization.
  In facilities.
  With respect to finance.
  What is the company good at doing?
  What is the company's justification for existence?
Where is the company now and where does it appear to be heading?
  What has the company accomplished?
  How does it stand financially, organizationally, and in its industry?
What can be expected from an extension of the company's present situation?
What assumptions should top corporate management make about the future with respect to sales, profit, growth, return on investment, and other factors?
How do the objectives and goals of the divisions of the company fit into the objectives and goals assumed by top corporate management?
What needs to be done to fill the gap between the two, assuming that a gap exists, or to change direction if change seems desirable? Specifically with respect to:
  New products.
  New markets.
  Development of existing products.
  Development of existing markets.
  Acquisitions.
  Capital equipment needs.
  Organizational needs.
  Financial needs.

Corporate Planning vs. Division Planning

Where a company has two or more divisions as well as a corporate organization, long-range planning should, of course, be done at both the corporate and division levels.

For overall planning purposes, it is necessary to have a common time schedule for the planning activities. But, beyond this, the degree of uniformity in the planning process throughout the company is highly dependent on the nature of the particular organization.

In some companies, for example, the forms to be filled in and the routines to be followed are set by the corporate planning office after having been cleared with top corporate management. In other companies, basic data must be furnished by the divisions to corporate headquarters according to a schedule set by the headquarters planning office, but the forms and routines are left up to the divisions.

Development of Budgetary Control

Historically, the development of fixed or appropriation budgeting preceded that of variable budgeting, while formal long-range planning is relatively a newcomer to the field. This sequence has also commonly been followed in the development of budgetary control within individual companies.

Sometimes, after having decided to adopt budgetary control, top management is impatient to have it installed at once throughout the company. However, the budgetary process should be a cooperative endeavor, involving managers at all levels as well as individuals more immediately responsible for the development and installation of a budget. In this connection, since a tremendous amount of educational work is involved, it has generally been found best to proceed with the development and installation in a more gradual manner.

In the development of variable budgeting in particular, it has been found wise in many cases to restrict the initial work to one or a few cost centers or departments believed to be most sympathetic to the program and most capable of benefiting from it. Once inevitable difficulties have been ironed out under these favorable conditions, and these cost centers or departments have benefited from the budgets installed, it is easier both to enlist the interest of other departments and to avoid difficulties in the installation of their budgets.

Another approach in variable budgeting is to start with one or two items of expense only, the items being those that everyone involved knows are out of line and ought to be reduced. If the budget proves to be effective in controlling these costs, it should not be too difficult to enlist cooperation in extending it to cover other items. However, if the process turned out to be ineffective in controlling the costs that those involved thought ought to be brought under control, the idea of variable budgeting should be quietly abandoned.

Benefits of Planning Process

In discussions of both annual budgeting and long-range planning, it has long been popular to praise the planning process as being more important than the plan itself. Many years ago, for example, the controller of a shoe company stated:

> None of the recent developments in business practice has done, or can do more to put a particular business concern on a sound and profitable basis than the preparation and carrying out of various budgets. The work that you and your associates do in the preparation of the sales budget will frequently open up unrealized sales possibilities. The work done in the preparation of a production budget often leads to the reduction of floor space required and the elimination of unnecessary machines. The work done in the preparation of an expense budget almost always throws a spotlight on glaring inefficiencies in operations. Even if the budgets on which you have spent so many hours are never used, the work in preparing them will bring to light so many things that your hours of labor are amply justified.[1]

Although specific benefits vary with circumstances, there are without doubt values to be gained from the planning process in addition to the usefulness of the budget itself. Worthwhile ideas cannot help but be generated from reviewing the past, taking stock of the present, and developing in cooperation with others plans for the future. These values are not to be realized if a budget is prepared by only one or a few members of a staff working primarily with statistical data.

At the same time, enthusiasm for the benefits of the planning process should not be allowed to minimize the values of the plan itself. If planning is to be undertaken, it should result in some sort of conclusions, otherwise no action will ever come from it. The plan, or budget, is simply a statement in writing of some of the current conclusions of the planning process. It should be regarded as an agreed upon program of constructive action, not as a straightjacket.

If a plan or budget really is not going to mean anything to anyone, there is no point in bothering to make it. There could still be some point in encouraging people to take time off from regular activities now and then to think about and develop improvements of one kind or another, but this activity should not be labeled as planning.

---

[1] See Harold S. Wonson, *National Association of Accountants Bulletin*, Vol. 16, No. 19.

The fact is, of course, that the plan itself is important, as well as the planning process. The least that can be said for a plan is that it gets some sort of a goal, program, or commitment down on paper and brings to a halt, temporarily at least, what otherwise might be an endless discussion getting nowhere.

CHAPTER 31

ROI and Other Goals and Measures

It has become generally recognized over the years that a business administrator has many responsibilities beyond that of showing a profit on the operations he supervises. These responsibilities include developing himself and his business as constructive units of society and concerning himself with the welfare and development of employees under his supervision. Thus, today, management objectives include qualitative aspects of living, as well as quantitative aspects of business.

To a degree, these qualitative and quantitative interests are inseparable. In particular, unless certain responsibilities not directly connected with profit are met, the business is not likely to be profitable. And unless the business is profitable, it will be difficult to meet certain responsibilities.

This is not to imply that a business must be successful before it can become responsible. Rather, that if a business is not profitable, its capital will wither away, and it will not be financially able to meet certain responsibilities it otherwise would be glad to accept.

In other words, neither an unhealthy individual nor an unhealthy business can be particularly constructive units of society. In our society at least, being a healthy business includes making a profit consistent with the risks involved; the creative capacity, skills, and goodwill developed; and the capital employed.

Need for Setting Profit Objectives

The primary purpose in setting profit objectives is the establishment of common goals to which all functions of a business will be directed.

The various activities of a business may be described in a variety of physical terms, but these generally cannot be added together to arrive at a meaningful whole, since they lack a common denominator. The dollar, however, provides such a denominator. Thus through proper accounting of revenues and expenses, it is possible to present meaningful summaries of these activities as well as to prepare budgets for them in advance.

The end result of revenue and expense — namely, profit (or loss) — is therefore not only a common goal for all functions of a business, but it also is an ultimate common denominator by means of which these activities may be combined in objective and judged as to result.

As we noted in the preceding chapter, setting profit objectives is part of the procedure connected with forward planning. Thus profit objectives are tied into plans for expansion or contraction of sales or production activity; contemplated shifts in productive capacity, product mix, and marketing strategy; and expected capital needs and the costs thereof.

Profit Relationship to Past Performance

Profits achieved in the past by the company as a whole — as well as by its divisions, product lines, and individual products — constitute a starting point for setting profit objectives for the future. Here, as in the area of cost control, there is a tendency to belittle references to past performance on the grounds that it is purely historical, is subject to random variations, and/or does not necessarily represent sound or proper standards for the future.

Nonetheless, in setting goals for the future, the practical businessman commonly starts with past performance in the belief that it constitutes a demonstrated base of achievement, rather than wishful thinking, and that as a minimum he should strive to do as well in the future as he has in the past. In other words, the past represents a known bridgehead from which to plan advancement. It has also been found useful to study past performance as a means of noting trends and spotting situations which merit investigation and possible corrective action.

Profit Planning for Expected Changes

In setting profit objectives, one should not, of course, stop with the past. Even if a company made no changes internally, there are bound to be external changes affecting profit. Thus, as a practical matter, no enterprising company is content to carry on its internal operations exactly as in the past.

It becomes necessary and desirable, therefore, to plan in terms of expected external and internal changes. Indeed, part of the planning is for making internal changes to meet expected external changes.

The setting of profit objectives in terms of dollars of profit is tied into these plans through budgeting by time periods for the future and through the development of projected profit and loss statements, source and application of funds statements, and balance sheets, as we noted in the previous chapter.

Profit Measurement Other Than Total Dollars

In addition to considering profit in terms of total dollars for specific periods of time, profit may also be viewed usefully in other ways. These include profit per direct labor man-hour or per machine-hour, as a percentage of sales, as earnings per share of common stock, and as a percentage return on investment.

Developing and measuring profit objectives in terms of profit per direct labor man-hour or per machine-hour can be particularly useful where a. the same men or machines produce a wide variety of products; b. the proportion of material cost to total cost varies markedly from product to product; and c. there are frequent short-run shifts in the product mix.

Here, the aim should be to achieve the desired profit objectives in terms of total dollars for the manpower and facilities used, regardless of the particular mix of products produced and sold for the period under consideration. Essentially, this is relating expected profit to "value added by manufacture."

The approach can be particularly helpful in forward planning under conditions where it is easy to plan for the manpower and facilities that will be in operation in the months ahead but extremely difficult to forecast with any degree of accuracy the specific product mix that will be involved.

Profit as a Percentage of Sales

Percentages of gross margin and net income to sales or net sales (by total sales, by product lines, and by individual products) are widely used as measuring units in setting profit objectives and comparing results. Actual performance expressed in these percentages can be compared with percentages of the past, with budgeted percentages, and with common percentages for the given trade. These will in turn provide rough measures of relative performance and will help to spot areas meriting investigation.

Preoccupation with gross margin as a percentage can however be disastrous if competitors have their eyes on total dollars of net profit, rather than on percentage of gross margin, and if they are willing to operate on smaller margins in order to increase volume. It is also clear that there is little comfort in having a high percentage of either gross margin or net income if the number of dollars involved is too small to represent an adequate return on effort expended or dollars invested.

EPS and Percentage ROI

Earnings per share of common stock represent a highly significant measure of profit to common stockholders and financial analysts for judging the performance of a company and its management. The ratio of earnings per share to the market price per share is also a matter of interest to these individuals.

Corporate managers are well aware of these interests in per-share earnings and in the price/earnings ratio, so much so in fact that sometimes they are thereby moved to make changes in their companies' accounting practices. For example, some companies that have used accelerated depreciation for their own accounting and for tax purposes have come to believe it necessary to change to straight-line depreciation as practiced by competitors in order to avoid being considered less favorably than their rivals in the stock market.

For many stockholders, earnings per share are most significant when related to the price they paid for their stock. Similarly, many companies view return on investment as of more significance both as a goal and as a measure of performance than such items as total company profit, gross margin, or net profit as a percentage of sales.

More specifically, many top managers favor return on investment as the best single or summary goal and measure of profit performance for the company as a whole and, where practicable, for its subdivisions.

Operations in many companies have been decentralized and managers of the resulting divisions or profit centers have been held accountable for showing a given expected return on the investment placed at their disposal. Insofar as practicable, managers have been encouraged to regard their operations as though they were in business for themselves. Manifestly, of course, there are limitations to the analogy, since decisions on a variety of matters are retained by top corporate management and since no man is truly in business for himself unless he receives full benefit or blame for whatever is realized in profits or losses.

Chart systems illustrating factors involved in ROI. The use of return on investment as a management control technique has grown tremendously in recent years following pioneer work by executives of E.I. Du pont de Nemours & Company and as the result of many articles and discussions on the subject. Various companies, following the lead of Du pont, have prepared chart systems to present figures in sequence covering sales, expenses, and investment leading up to and including ROI expressed as a percentage.

A chart prepared by the Radio Corporation of America for educational use to illustrate the relationships of factors affecting return on investment is presented in Exhibit 82.

It is common to speak of this use of ROI as a management tool. Nonetheless, Exhibit 82 shows that while return on investment can be both a useful goal and end result it is not an independent factor. Instead, ROI is dependent on all the factors leading up to it. It is something like the score of a game which is not in itself a controlling factor. Whatever control is exercised can only be spent on the factors beneath it. Thus ROI is a management tool only in a limited sense. It does not supplant other management tools, such as fixed and variable budgets, and standard costs.

Further reference to Exhibit 82 indicates that percentage ROI is computed in the chart by multiplying percentage earnings from sales by turnover of investment. Going back one step further in the diagram shows the computation to be as follows:

$$\frac{Sales}{Investment} \times \frac{Earnings}{Sales} = \text{Percentage ROI}$$

Return on investment could, of course, be computed with the sales figures omitted as follows:

$$\frac{Earnings}{Investment} = \text{Percentage ROI}$$

The reason for taking the longer approach is partly to define more clearly the factors affecting return on investment. And it is partly to indicate the two major lines of inquiry — investment turnover and profit on sales — should the ROI actually realized not meet expectations.

Return on investment as both a goal and measure of management performance may at first appear simple to establish and administer.

EXHIBIT 82
Relationship of Factors Affecting Return on Investment

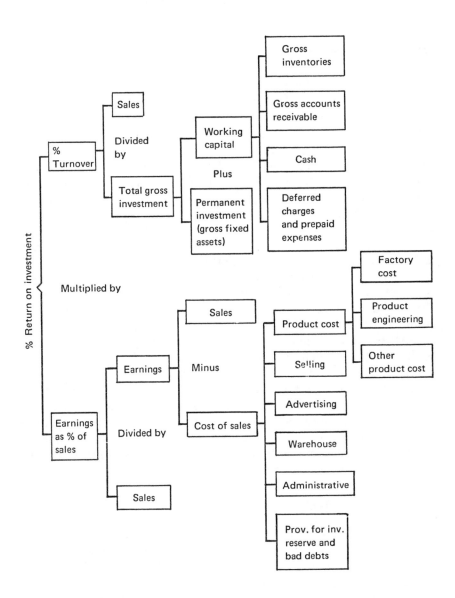

Nonetheless, it involves complexities. As with any other management control device, ROI has to be developed and used with a high degree of common sense if it is to be considered fair and acceptable by those held accountable under it.

What Is the Investment?

A basic problem at the very outset in adopting ROI as a management tool is the question of what constitutes investment.

Each stockholder has his own investment, i.e., the amount he paid for the stock he owns, against which he can measure return with respect to both company earnings per share and the yield from dividends received by him. Similarly, financial analysts and prospective investors can relate both earnings per share and dividends to the market value of a given stock as measures of current return and current yield, respectively. Here, market value per share is the current investment required to become an owner.

Another useful concept of investment is the combination of original capital and retained earnings, often called the "net worth" of the business, although it represents owners' investment and not "worth" in a market sense. In many company annual reports, the earnings for the year are related to this shareholders' equity, and the percentage result is shown as the company's return on investment.

All of the concepts of investment just noted, however, deal only with investment relative to the ownership of a business, whereas a company, and thus its management, is also provided with funds from other sources such as trade creditors, banks, and bondholders. In the use of ROI as a tool of control, management should be held accountable for showing an expected return on all of the resources placed at its disposal, regardless of source. Thus, for this purpose, the amount of investment is determined by examination of a company's assets and not by any measure of its ownership.

ROI as a Control Tool

It is most important to have it understood at the outset in developing ROI as a tool of control that this use is like a game. The rules have to be thrashed out by conferences with the participants and developed along lines that seem most appropriate in the given situation. Thus it is like a game in the sense that it involves players, goals, and scoring, and that it is subject to rules; but it is not a game to be taken lightly.

Unfortunately, in some companies using this technique, the rules are oversimplified. Here, the conditions under which various divisions of the business are operating are accepted as being comparable; and the same score as a percentage return on investment is expected from each division.

However, if ROI as a tool of control is to undertaken fairly and sensibly, the performance of a manager should be judged not only in terms of the general rules, but also in the light of the particular handicaps or advantages under which his section of the business is operating.

Thus the performance of the manager who is operating with old equipment in a high-cost labor area far removed from the source of raw material should be judged in the light of these handicaps. His performance should not be compared simply in terms of the same percentage return on investment with the performance of other managers who are operating under more favorable conditions.

Should the investment in fixed assets be taken at gross or net? Reference to Exhibit 82 will indicate that Radio Corporation of America uses gross assets rather than net assets as the base of investment against which return is measured, a practice which appears to be followed by many companies. More specifically, RCA and others include fixed assets in their investment base at gross value — that is, at original book value.

The use of gross fixed assets rather than fixed assets net of the allowance for depreciation tends to equalize the investment base with respect to old versus new fixed assets. To be sure, under conditions of rising costs, the gross cost of old assets will be below the cost on newer fixed assets, but the maintenance cost on them will probably be higher. In addition, the newer fixed assets should be more efficient, which is another equalizing factor.

Moreover, when net fixed assets are used in the investment base, some divisions of a company having older properties may be more hesitant than they should be about making replacements. The fear here is that there will be a heavy increase in the investment base without an adequately compensating return.

Granted, one may well argue that to the extent that depreciation has been taken, under conditions where the company has at least broken even, the investment has been recovered. Hence the capital recovered should not be included in the investment base except as reinvested.

The amount of depreciation accounted for, however, in many instances is subject to income tax considerations and to top management financial decisions that have no necessary direct relationship with the utilization of facilities. Such conditions render net fixed assets an unsatisfactory base in judging the performance of division management.

However, if gross assets are to be used in the investment base, the earnings to be related to this in computing the ROI should be before depreciation. That is, if, in the investment base, fixed assets are to be carried at original cost it hardly seems fair to deduct depreciation expense before arriving at the amount of income to be measured against the investment base in judging performance.

Some companies do in fact use net fixed assets rather than gross fixed assets in the investment base in the belief that this is the proper representation of funds currently invested in these assets for which management should be held accountable.

While I favor the use of gross assets and earnings before depreciation for the reasons stated in earlier paragraphs, the matter is admittedly debatable. As a matter of fact, provided that individual standards of performance are set for each division of a business, the selection of either gross or net assets as the investment base is not of paramount importance.

However, it is of great importance that the managers affected believe the base selected is appropriate. Beyond this, performance relative to budgeted expectations and the trend of performance are the most significant aspects to consider, regardless of the base selected. The provision here is that, once selected, the base is consistently followed.

Examples of ROI relative to the investment in fixed assets.   A simple example may be helpful in noting the various ways of computing ROI relative to the investment in fixed assets. Figures have been selected that can be identified with the present value tables in Appendix 2 at the end of the book.

Assume that at the close of a given year a company has the following assets.

Current assets		$167,300
Fixed assets (at cost)	$501,900	
Less: accumulated depreciation	200,760	301,140
Total assets		$468,440

Assume net income for the year to be $83,143.

ROI with fixed assets taken at net:

$$\frac{\text{Net income} \quad \$83,143}{\text{Total assets} \quad \$468,440} = 0.1775$$

As we have noted, some companies do use net fixed assets in the investment base because they believe that this is the current investment in such assets for which management should be held accountable.

ROI with fixed assets taken at gross:

Current assets	$167,300	
Gross fixed assets	501,900	
Total gross assets	$669,200	
Net income	$ 83,143	= 0.1242
Total gross assets	$669,200	

This computation of a 12.42% ROI is similar to the first return on investment computation shown in Chapter 27, Fixed Asset Selection and Replacement, and identified there as "Expected return on investment: first year." It is a very conservative computation of ROI since fixed assets are included in the investment base at their undepreciated cost of $501,900, while depreciation for the year, which, for our example, we shall assume was $50,190, had been subtracted in arriving at net income of $83,143.

As noted earlier, however, if fixed assets are to be in the investment base at original cost, it hardly seems fair to deduct depreciation expense in arriving at the amount of income to be measured against that base in judging performance. If we add back the $50,190 depreciation to the $83,143 of net income, we arrive at $133,333 as the amount of income after taxes and before depreciation. This figure, arrived at by adding depreciation for the year to the net income for the year, is what financial analysis term cash flow, as was discussed in Chapter 5, Cash Flow Analysis.

ROI measured by relating cash flow to total gross assets:

$$\frac{\text{Cash flow} \quad \$133,333}{\text{Total gross assets} \quad \$669,200} = 0.1992$$

This makes the return on investment appear to be much more favorable than either of the two previous figures for ROI we have computed.

But, have we not gone too far when we treat the entire amount of cash flow as a return on the investment? After all, the fixed assets involved are subject to depreciation, and by the end of their useful lives, their investment value will have entirely vanished. A significant part of the cash flow should therefore be regarded as simply a recovery of the investment, and not a return on it.

In fact, over the useful lives of the fixed assets, the amount invested in them must first be recovered before it can be certain that there will be any return on them at all. We shall not, however, be this conservative in our calculations of ROI. Instead, we shall now turn to the use of the discounted cash flow method in determining the ROI in fixed assets.

First we shall determine the percentage of total gross assets for current assets and gross fixed assets as follows:

	Investment	Percentage
Current assets	$167,300	25%
Gross fixed assets	501,900	75
Total gross assets	$669,200	100%

Next we shall determine the amount of cash flow applicable to each of these two classes of assets as follows:

Current assets	$133,333 × 25% =	$ 33,333
Gross fixed assets	133,333 × 75% =	100,000
		$133,333

The entire cash flow of $33,333 can be treated as the ROI relative to current assets since there is no depreciation on them. The percentage ROI is 19.92% computed as follows:

$$\frac{\text{Cash flow}}{\text{Current assets}} = \frac{\$33,333}{\$167,300} = 0.1992$$

The percentage relationship of the $100,000 cash flow to the investment in gross assets of $501,900 is also 19.92% but this is not the percentage return on these assets since they are subject to depreciation, and part of the $100,000 cash flow must be considered a recovery of investment and not a return on it.

If $100,000 cash flow was received each year the investment of $501,900 in fixed assets would be recovered in 5.019 years. This is a payback figure as described in Chapter 27, Fixed Asset Selection and Replacement.

Also, as described in that chapter, this is the factor to be used in connection with Table B, in Appendix 2 at the back of the book, in establishing the percentage return on investment under the discounted cash flow method.

We need one more figure, however, and that is for the average expected life of the fixed assets. The only way we can establish a figure for this in our problem is to divide the investment in gross fixed assets by the amount of depreciation taken for the year, as follows:

$$\frac{\text{Gross fixed assets}}{\text{Depreciation}} \qquad \frac{\$501,900}{\$\ 50,190} = 10 \text{ years}$$

Turning then to Table B, in Appendix 2, we search through the line of figures at the 10th period until we come to the figure closest to the factor 5.019 which we computed above. Since figures for our example were purposely selected to do this, we find our factor 5.019 in the 15% column. This tells us that the rate of return on our fixed assets is 15% as computed by the discounted cash flow method.

In our example, this means that a cash flow of $100,000 per year related to the investment in gross fixed assets of $501,900 will provide for the recovery of that investment over its useful life of ten years, and a return of 15% each year on the unrecovered amount of the investment as of the beginning of the year. In other words, the 15% return is the percentage return on the declining balance of the investment in fixed assets over their useful lives and not on their original cost except for the first year. This point may be clarified by studying Table 14 on the next page.

Under the discounted cash flow method of computing return on depreciable assets, the computed rate of return will be the same regardless of the specific year of estimated useful life in which the calculation is made. In our present case, for example, the computed rate of return on fixed assets will be 15% whether the assets are on the average two years old, eight years old, or any other age within the ten year average of useful life.

The computed rate of ROI on gross fixed assets will change, of course, with any change in one or more of the three factors on which it is based, namely: 1. the amount of gross investment in fixed assets; 2. the amount of cash flow; and 3. the estimated years of useful life.

The total computed rate of ROI on total gross assets is a composite

TABLE 14

Year	Investment in Fixed Assets at Cost	15% Return on Declining Balance of Investment	Cash Flow	Recovery of Investment
1	$501,900	$75,300	$100,000	$ 24,700
2	477,200	71,600	100,000	28,400
3	448,800	67,300	100,000	32,700
4	416,100	62,400	100,000	37,600
5	378,500	56,800	100,000	43,200
6	335,300	50,300	100,000	49,700
7	285,600	42,800	100,000	57,200
8	228,400	34,200	100,000	65,800
9	162,600	24,400	100,000	75,600
10	87,000	13,000	100,000	87,000
				$501,900

rate taking into account both the percentage ROI for current assets and for gross fixed assets. Earlier we noted that the rate of return on current assets was 0.1992 and that current assets were 25% of total gross assets.

The portion of the composite rate
for current assets is therefore 25% × 0.1992 = 0.0498
The portion of the composite rate
for gross fixed assets is 75% × 0.15 = 0.1125
The composite rate is 0.1623

This composite rate holds management accountable for the return on gross rather than on net fixed assets. At the same time it recognizes the importance of cash flow as the means of providing the recovery of investments in fixed assets as well as a return on them. It also recognizes a distinction, whether properly or not, between the relation of cash flow to the investment in current assets and its relation to the gross investment in fixed assets.

It will be noted that the composite rate of 16.23% in this example is more conservative than the rate of 17.75% computed with fixed assets taken at net. It is not as conservative as the rate of 12.42% computed when relating net income to total gross assets. It is, of course, much more conservative than the 19.92% rate of cash flow to total gross assets.

Historical cost or historical cost adjusted for price-level changes.
Under conditions of inflation, a case can be supported for establishing
the fixed assets in the investment base at historical cost adjusted for
price-level changes, rather than at historical cost taken from historical
records. By this means, the investment base is stated in the same
purchasing power of money as the current net income measured
against it in computing return on the investment.

The adjustment for price-level changes is made by the application
of a price index. Some companies are said to be using estimated replacement costs established for insurance purposes as the investment
base, although I have not seen an actual case in which this has been
done.

One could also argue for the use of reappraisals of property which
would bring market value into consideration, not simply price-level
adjustment. However, reappraisals are time-consuming and expensive.
And even though they are valuable in deciding whether to continue
using property for a given purpose or disposing of it, reappraisals are
not so necessary in setting goals and judging performance with respect
to its current use.

In theory, return related to the historical cost of the investment
adjusted for price-level changes, rather than unadjusted historical cost,
should be a more accurate measure of the rate of return. Moreover, it
should permit more equitable comparisons between companies, between divisions of the same company, and between different years both
for companies and divisions.

The division manager who is saddled with old equipment is not
likely to believe that restating his investment in this equipment, to
take account of the drop in the purchasing power of money, will put
him on a par with other divisions in making comparisons of ROI. He
knows that his maintenance costs are higher than in those divisions
having newer equipment, that his output per labor-hour and per
machine-hour is less, and that his rate of spoilage is probably higher.

The point is that differences in the timing of investment, coupled
with changes in the purchasing power of money, are only some of the
many variables causing differences in investment and ROI between
divisions and between companies. Clearly, it should not be assumed
that all can be made truly comparable simply by stating investment at
historical cost adjusted for price-level changes.

The decision whether to adjust the investment base to take account of changes in the purchasing power of money should be dependent on the degree of inflation experienced by the company and differences between divisions in the timing of investments and also on the

probable psychological effect of using the adjusted base versus historical cost on managers whose performance is to be judged.

In some companies, the majority of managers may believe that the
investment base should be adjusted for price-level changes. In others,
the majority may believe that this simply introduces another item of
contention and that historical cost which can be supported by documentary evidence is to be preferred.

Problems when government-owned facilities have been supplied. In
cases where government-owned facilities are a substantial part of the
resources that normally represent a company's investment base, ROI
as a tool of management is obviously not practical. In cases where such
facilities are less extensive, it should be possible to allow for them
either by including a statistical value for them in the investment base
or by requiring a higher rate of return on the unadjusted investment
base.

Problems when large sums have been expended on intangibles. In
publishing a newspaper, heavy expenditures are incurred in various
ways over the years to build up circulation. These outlays from current
earnings are really investments for the future, although their value is
so uncertain or possibly so ephemeral that they are wisely accounted
for as current expenses.

Similarly, manufacturing companies build reputations by means
of advertising, missionary sales work, and the development of new or
improved products involving costs which are not capitalized. A division of a company may spend years on research and experimentation in
a new field such as atomic power, charging all costs off as expenses
when incurred and thus having relatively little investment against
which to measure income by the time revenue materializes.

Other types of businesses develop intangible assets in different
forms. For example, a market research organization will spend years of
effort and much money in establishing a reliable panel of consumers
for use in market surveys. Many companies engaged in government
contacts incur heavy expenditures to assemble and train a group of
scientists, engineers, administrators, office and laboratory workers,
and skilled craftsmen. Members of law firms, public accounting firms,
and medical clinics have individually and collectively invested heavily
in education, training, and experience.

None of those expenditures by these organizations or individuals
are commonly listed among their assets, even though the assembled

and available skills, reputations, and knowledge are really their most significant assets.

There are sound management reasons, as well as tax advantages, for not capitalizing these intangibles, and I am not suggesting that they should be treated as investments in the accounting records. It could be helpful in some companies, however, to establish statistical values for them against which income could be measured. In fact, experimental work has been going on for some time to include people as assets in the balance sheet, although the work is still very much in an experimental stage.

For example, in a situation such as that of a market research organization having a consumer panel, it might be possible to make a reasonable estimate of what it would cost to replace the intangible item. If it would cost $1,500,000 to replace a consumer panel, this could be an interesting addition to the investment base against which income is measured.

Another approach where intangibles are significant factors in a business, although not included in its balance sheet, is simply to set a high standard for the expected return on the tangibles.

In cases where intangibles, including personal skills, are highly significant and where the investment is relatively low, ROI is not a useful management tool. The reason here is that the investment base is insignificant and other measurements are preferable.

While the owners of a successful magazine-subscription agency would, for example, enjoy receiving a high return on their relatively low investment, they would not find return on investment to be the most satisfactory device for use in establishing goals and measuring the performance of their sales organization.

What rate of return should be expected? The amount of return on investment sought is not only a matter of interest to investors, but it is also of interest, and indeed perhaps a matter of contention, among those whose performance is to be judged by this measure. In fact, it has been true that the difficulty in establishing an acceptable rate has been used as an argument against the use of ROI as a control tool.

If the various divisions of a company differ markedly in such matters as the amount of investment involved, the age of the facilities, and the percentages of material, labor, and overhead constituting their costs, it is not likely that any single rate that might be selected would be acceptable to all division managers.

A single rate that might be satisfactory on the average for the company as a whole could be unreasonably high for some divisions and unreasonably low for others. Furthermore, to set such an average rate as a goal and measure of performance for each division could be ruinous. The reason is that those who should be making more might be content to stop at the average expected, while the others could not hope to come up to this standard.

Thus while it is desirable to set a single rate of return both as a goal and measure of performance for the company as a whole, the probability is that such a rate will not be a satisfactory goal for each of the divisions of the company taken separatclv

Controlling and Investing Differences

In making investments, it is appropriate to have a minimum acceptable rate of return in mind, and even more appropriate to have different required minimum rates for different classes of investment depending upon the estimated risks involved.

Conditions do not, however, remain static. The return that should be expected in deciding on any new investment within a company is likely to be quite different from the individual rate of return that should reasonably be expected in any given division of that company from investments already made. In other words, the use of ROI in making investment decisions is different from its use in the measurement and control of operations.

With this in mind, the setting of a single company-wide average expected rate of return may be useful as a long-run investment guide. But such a rate is an oversimplified standard for controlling divisional performance.

Bases for Establishing Rates

In establishing either division rates or a total company rate or both, it is natural to start with a study of returns actually realized in the past. While such rates are historical and may or may not ever again be realized, they do represent rates actually achieved. As such, they provide a practical starting point for considering rates that should be reasonable and desirable in the future.

The next step should be to study the rates of return realized by others in the same industry, or in the separate industries in which divisions are located if they are not all in the same industry. For perspective, it is well also to study rates of return experienced by a wide range of industries.

At some stage, it would be well to establish a minimum acceptable rate and a maximum possible rate. These limits should evolve from discussions among the top corporate and division managers of the business and not be simply the recommendations of a staff. The purpose of the discussions should be to develop a feeling for the practical range of operating results.

For example, the minimum that might be set, say, at government bond interest, would represent a point at which drastic action should be taken for improvement, unless the relatively poor showing were considered to be only temporary. It could also be the point at which the company might begin to think about going out of business or of abandoning one or more product lines or divisions.

The maximum possible rate should be set high enough to require some reaching or stretching. But it should not be so high as to be beyond any reasonable hope of accomplishment and thus to represent an impossible goal.

Studies should also be made by divisions, and for the company as a whole, of the effect of changes in the volume of activity on the rate of ROI. This is essentially a refinement of break-even analysis, measuring the effect of changes in volume on investment return rather than on net profit.

These studies should assist in the development of a range of probable returns within the range of volume commonly experienced, as well as to emphasize the importance of maintaining volume in order to achieve desirable rates of return. In other words, it highlights the importance of both fixed costs and the volume of operations in establishing the rate of return realized.

Long-run vs. short-run rates of return. The various studies just suggested are particularly useful in setting return on investment goals and in measuring performance over the long run. They are thus helpful for long-range planning.

In the short run, the budget is the most useful planning tool, as well as the most useful general management tool for control purposes. The budget includes budgeted income statements and budgeted balance sheets by months, by divisions, and for the company as a whole.

Whether or not it is computed, these budgeted financial statements determine what the expected rate of return on investment will be. Thus if the budgeted net income for the year is $1 million and the budgeted total assets are $10 million, the expected return on investment is therefore 10%, regardless of whether it is computed and shown as a factor in the budget.

The point is simply this: No matter what the the long-range goal for return on investment might be, the expected return for any given year is, or at least should be, determined by the factors of revenue, expense, and investment budgeted for that year. Thus the expected rate of ROI should be different for each division of a company, since it is unlikely that the combination of budgeted revenue, expense, and investment would result in the same rate of return for any two divisions.

To state this matter in another way, it is not logical to establish a uniform rate of ROI as a short-run goal for all of the divisions of a business when budgeted figures for the same time period would not come to the same result. To be sure, one could force budgeted figures to end with a uniform return figure for each division, but this would be a witless exercise bound to destroy any faith in the budgetary process.

Problems in segregating investment by areas of responsibility. If an individual is to be held responsible for ROI, it is obviously important that the investment for which he is held accountable be clearly defined. This is difficult in many cases, as for example, where two or more divisions of a company are sharing buildings on the same plot of ground and utilizing joint facilities such as maintenance and engineering departments and storerooms.

Often a large piece of equipment, e.g., a press, will be shared by two or more divisions, which raises questions as to which should be held accountable for the investment and for how much of it, in each case. Similarly, there are questions as to whether operating divisions should be assigned any of the investment in a home office, or in an expensive piece of equipment, such as a computer, located at the home office and used for division purposes as well as for the needs of top corporate management.

One approach to many of the problems indicated in the previous paragraphs is to establish separate profit centers or service centers in situations where equipment, space, and services are shared. Thus no operating divisions are held accountable for investments in these jointly used facilities. Rather, each is charged at predetermined rates for services utilized.

In some instances where this is done, there is a set charge per month for the fixed costs involved plus an additional charge for variable costs in proportion to service rendered, usually on an hourly basis. If the jointly used facilities are truly to be established as profit centers and held accountable for showing a return on investment, their charges to the operating divisions must include a profit element.

To state this in another way, unless one is willing to assume that no return at all in jointly used facilities should be expected, either this investment should be prorated to the operating divisions and included in the investment base against which their returns are to be measured; or it should be identified as the property of the service centers, and a profit element should be allowed in their charges for service rendered.

In the case of home office facilities, there is likely to be considerable opposition from division managers either to the inclusion of a prorated share of home office investment in their investment base or to any charges which include a profit element for the home office. Controversy can be avoided if neither of these steps is taken.

Instead, the long-range goals set for each division should aim at a rate of return which top corporate management knows is adequate to provide the expected return on division and home office investment combined. This approach should be restricted to matters of general home office overhead. It should not include specific services for which charges to the divisions served are appropriate.

Transfer Price Problems

Managers of operating divisions under pressure to show a favorable rate of ROI will be highly critical of all service charges and of the prices they must pay for all items purchased from other divisions within the company. Up to a point this is good, since it stimulates the efficient production of goods and services. Beyond this point, however, valuable time and energy spent in bickering over and chafing about the prices at which people deal with one another within the company could better be spent in producing and selling goods and services to outsiders.

Transfer price problems are not adequately solved by broad policy statements such as "Goods sold by one division to another shall be at competitive prices," or "Each division shall be completely free to purchase goods or services at the lowest price either from within or outside the company provided it is satisfied that the supplier can meet quality and delivery requirements." Both these statements are sound long-run goals toward which to be working, but they are not adequate for short-run decisions on transfer prices.

For example, it is extremely difficult to establish a truly competitive price on items normally purchased from within a company and not commonly dealt with in the open market. Again, there are countless occasions when a division could buy an item normally purchased from within from outside at favorable out-of-pocket cost to it in the short run. Nonetheless, such a purchase could be detrimental to the company as a whole as well as to the division losing this business, because so much of the cost of the item would be fixed and would exist whether or not the item were produced.

The ready answer in such a situation is, of course, that the selling division ought to be objective enough to realize that any price received over and above out-of-pocket cost would be better than losing this piece of business. Therefore, the selling division should be willing to match the outside price.

However, the situation usually is not so simple. From a company viewpoint, while there would be a current benefit from keeping this business within the company, it does not follow that the selling division should always be expected to accept a drastic reduction in price in such a case.

The buying division which demands objectivity on the part of the seller, and a lower price when business is poor, is not likely to be objective enough itself to be willing to pay a high price when business is good and the item is in short supply. Under the latter conditions, the buying division is certain to consider that the inside supplier should meet the buying division's needs, even if outside customers are left wanting. The buying division may also consider that it should pay the selling division only for cost plus a "reasonable" profit, rather than a higher selling price.

Granted, there are some companies where division managers are free to decide whether they will engage in transactions with other divisions and on the prices at which the transactions, if any, will take place. Here, the belief is that even though the company may lose a little now and then because a division buys something outside that could have been made inside at a lower out-of-pocket company cost, the company will benefit in the long run because of the competitive pressure that the policy forces on the selling divisions.

In other companies, however, the profit center concept is not carried out to this extent. Even though divisions are allowed considerable freedom, there are restrictions on their captial expenditures. They are not free to produce whatever they wish, nor to sell to whomever they wish.

Moreover, a certain amount of productive capacity is often built to take care of needs within the company. Even in this type of situation, however, it is not likely that division managers who are being hard pushed to show a favorable return on investment will adopt a company viewpoint at the expense of their division showing.

This leads inevitably to differences of opinion on the prices at which interdivision transactions shall take place. If the best interests of the company are to be served in cases of this type, as well as essential fairness in judging division performance, there must be a means of having problems in the area of interdivision transactions passed upon by top corporate management if division managers cannot reach an agreement on them.

In some companies, such problems are submitted to a staff operating for top corporate management, with final decisions to be made by top management in the event that the division managers concerned are not in agreement with the staff recommendations. As a practical matter, division managers are likely to come to some sort of an agreement after a staff recommendation is received, rather than to carry the problem to higher levels.

Problems in Translating Profit Objectives

We have noted that return on investment is a matter of vital interest to stockholders, top corporate management, and top division management, since at these levels it is a meaningful unit of measurement in setting goals and judging performance. I have also suggested that it is desirable to acquaint managers at lower levels with the company's profit objectives in terms of ROI, in part to stimulate their company viewpoint and in part to sharpen their realization that what they do has a bearing on these end results.

An effective way to do this is to present figures in detail for the company as a whole and by divisions in chart form along the lines diagrammed in Exhibit 82. There should first be a presentation of budgeted expectations and later a review of actual results.

While the use of ROI is an important control concept, it should be recognized that it supplements and does not supplant other control mechanisms. It is simply an additional, although important, step taken in conjunction with the use of such controls as fixed budgets, variable budgets, and standard costs.

Analysis of Exhibit 82 will indicate that while return on investment is both an end goal and result, the factors affecting it are actually subject to control in various ways at various points throughout the company by lower levels of management having specialized interests and responsibilities.

Criticisms of ROI as a Control Tool

In recent years, some companies have lost their enthusiasm for ROI as a control tool, and some writers have taken to harpooning it with various criticisms. The root of the dissatisfaction in both cases lies in the unfortunate assumption that a single number could serve as the only necessary goal and measure of performance.

Companies that have become somewhat disenchanted with ROI as a control tool had expected too much from it. In particular, the use of one number had a tremendous appeal as a simple control mechanism. The fact is, of course, that the single number in this case — namely, the percentage return on investment — can control nothing in itself. It is simply the result of a myriad of activities each of which is, or is not, subject to control in various ways.

Thus although a given number for the percentage ROI may well be an appropriate figure as a top goal and measure of performance, the controls to reach it must be applied in various ways at various points and levels within the organization.

Similarly, the principal argument of the critics is that the use of the one number motivates division managers to attempt to reach it even if the methods used are harmful to the company. Thus it is suggested that division managers may sell equipment which is still usable in order to reduce their investment base against which their ROI will be computed.

Likewise, it is suggested that divisional managers will not buy certain facilities which could be beneficial to the company because they do not wish to risk lowering their percentage ROI. Moreover, they will be motivated to do all they can to improve their division showing in the short run, which often is not in the best long-run interests of the company.

However, unless top corporate management is callous, naïve, or imagines itself to be running a mutual fund instead of an industrial corporation, it will not use ROI as a single control tool. Even if corporate management uses return on investment as a summary goal and measure of performance, it is not a matter of indifference as to how a division manager achieves that ROI goal.

Generally speaking, top corporate managers have themselves moved up from division management and are well aware of the problems of and pressures on division managers. They can also spot exactly how a division manager is, or is not, meeting his ROI goal. In this connection, they place great reliance on the fixed budget, variable budget, and standard costs.

While it is true that ROI as a goal can motivate a division manager to take a short-run viewpoint, so too do other goals such as sales, dollars of profit, inventory turnover, and profit as a percentage of sales. The fact that there are these motivations for a division manager to take a short-run viewpoint has stimulated many top corporate managements to endorse and promote formal long-range planning. Thus everything does not depend on how well a man looks today, but also on his plans for tomorrow.

Anatomy of a Management Control System

I have tried to stress the usefulness of percentage return on investment as the top goal and measure of performance. At the same time, I have noted that this is an end goal and result which is dependent on all of the factors leading up to it. Moreover, these factors are controlled by various people at various levels using various techniques.

At the center of Exhibit 83, percentage ROI is shown as the top goal and measure of performance. At the left center, the revenue and cost factors leading up to earnings as a percentage of sales are illustrated, and this is data coming from the income statement. At the right center, the assets are illustrated, along with sales, leading up to a turnover figure for investment. The center section with its two columns is thus like Exhibit 82.

On the left side of Exhibit 83 are listed the major techniques for getting information and controlling items of revenue and expense, each of which I have discussed at some stage in this book.

On the right side of Exhibit 83 are listed the major techniques for getting information and controlling the assets that form the investment base against which ROI is computed. As with techniques connected with revenue and expense, so too each of these techniques has been discussed earlier at some stage in this book.

In Summary

My discussion of the problems involved in applying return on invest ment as both a goal and measure of performance has not been aimed at discouraging the use of this tool of control. Rather, I have focused on defining the major problems faced in its application and on stressing that ROI is not so simple a device as it may appear to be on the surface.

I have tried to stress that no one technique alone is adequate to control business operations and that a company should try to make

EXHIBIT 83
Anatomy of a Management Control System

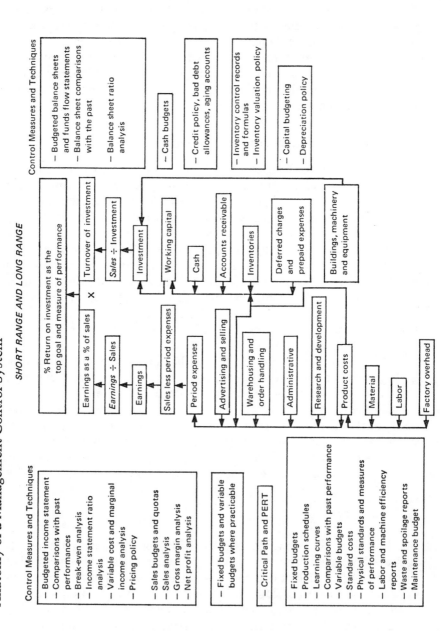

sensible use of all of the techniques available. Percentage return on investment is properly included among these techniques in setting goals and measuring performance in situations where the amount of investment is significant.

It has long been recognized that the value of a business property is dependent on what it can produce. As Samuel Johnson put it when asked what he really considered to be the value of a brewery he was assisting in selling: "We are not here to sell a parcel of boilers and vats but the potentiality of growing rich beyond the dreams of avarice."[1]

The other side of this coin is that in order to judge the value of the wealth created, we should take into account the property required to produce it. To stop short of return on investment and to judge performance only in terms such as net income fails to place full responsibility on management for efficiency in the utilization of capital employed.

There is a danger, as we have noted, that preoccupation with ROI may motivate division managers to adopt a short-run viewpoint which may be damaging to a company's long-run best interests. This must be guarded against by the use of additional types of goals and measures of performance.

Moreover, qualitative, as well as quantitative, goals and measures of performance should be used. In particular, top corporate management and division managers should use those goals and performance measurements which develop people as well as business for the future.

---

[1]James Boswell, *Life of Dr. Johnson* (Dutton, Everyman's Library Edition, Vol. 2), p. 376.

The Accounting Cycle

For the benefit of the reader who would like to know more about bookkeeping than that described in the text of Chapter 7, "The Analysis of Financial Transactions," I shall present a brief illustration of what is known as the accounting or bookkeeping cycle.

The complete cycle involves the "opening" of a "set of books," the journalizing (recording in chronological order) of financial transactions, the "posting" of the journal entries to the ledger (recording the transactions in ledger accounts under appropriate classifications), the "adjusting and closing" of the accounts, and the preparation of financial statements.

Under modern bookkeeping, particularly in connection with the use of a computer, the "books of account" are not the same as they used to be except in small companies. Nonetheless, the major steps in accounting for financial transactions remain essentially the same and are usually described in terms of the journals and ledgers common to earlier days.

Typical accounting transactions involved in starting a business were described in connection with the discussion of funds flow in Chapter 6, and the recording of these transactions was illustrated in Chapter 7. Now, in illustrating the accounting cycle, we shall deal with a business already started, and, in fact, will use data on the P. M. Stanton Company which will tie-in to the financial statements of this company presented in Chapters 2 through 15.

To simplify the presentation, I shall use a minimum number of account classifications, deal only with the major steps in the accounting cycle, and account for financial transactions as though they had occurred in summary form for the year.

EXHIBIT A
P. M. Stanton Company's Balance Sheet as of December 31, 1976

Assets		
Current assets:		
Cash		$ 930,250
Accounts receivable		765,162
Inventories:		
Raw material	$333,927	
Goods in process	194,748	
Finished goods	987,308	1,515,983
Prepaid assets		51,178
Total current assets		$3,262,573
Property, plant and equipment at cost less		
allowance for depreciation of $760,720		1,278,479
Investment in subsidiaries		34,401
Deferred development expenses		116,878
Total assets		$4,692,331
Liabilities and Capital		
Current liabilities:		
Bond sinking fund installment		$ 100,000
Accounts payable, (trade)		153,220
Provision for pensions		177,300
Provision for income taxes		226,675
Other accrued liabilities		224,974
Total current liabilities		$ 882,169
Provision for deferred income tax		103,418
First Mortgage 6% Bonds due 1984		800,000
Common stock		268,022
Paid-in surplus		2,152,198
Retained earnings		486,524
Total liabilities and capital		$4,692,331

The data with which we shall begin are presented in Exhibit A, representing the balance sheet for the P. M. Stanton Company at the close of the year 1976. These same balances also appear in the "T" accounts presented as Exhibit B, which illustrate the ledger accounts for this company in condensed form with beginning balances as of January 1, 1977.

For our purposes, the account balances, and transactions affecting them, will be recorded in rounded dollars, although the company actually carried out its accounting in dollars and cents.

EXHIBIT B
"T" Accounts for P. M. Stanton Company

	Assets					Liabilities and Capital	

Cash

Jan. 1	930,250	10	1,206,844
9	9,687,911	11	6,546,810
21	141,040	12	70,816
24	13,444	13	285,471
		14	8,731
		15	26,901
		16	100,000
		17	248,268
		18	367,901
		19	53,892
		20	826,075
		23	1,561
		Bal.	929,375
	10,772,645		10,772,645
Bal.	929,375		

Accounts Receivable

Jan. 1	765,162	8	68,243
7	10,058,729	9	9,687,911
		Bal.	1,067,737
	10,823,891		10,823,891
Bal.	1,067,737		

Raw Material

Jan. 1	333,927	2	1,421,661
1	1,385,824	Bal.	298,090
	1,719,751		1,719,751
Bal.	298,090		

Goods in Process

Jan. 1	194,748	Bal.	203,247
38	8,499		
	203,247		203,247
Bal.	203,247		

Bond Sinking Fund Installment

16	100,000	Jan. 1	100,000

Accounts Payable (trade)

10	1,206,844	Jan. 1	153,220
Bal.	332,200	1	1,385,824
	1,539,044		1,539,044
		Bal.	332,200

Provision For Pensions

17	248,268	Jan. 1	177,300
Bal.	163,500	31	234,468
	411,768		411,768
		Bal.	163,500

Provision For Income Taxes

18	367,901	Jan. 1	226,675
Bal.	417,300	33	553,409
		34	5,117
	785,201		785,201
		Bal.	417,300

Other Accrued Liabilities

11	6,546,810	Jan. 1	224,974
Bal.	246,800	3	1,568,346
		4	2,456,316
		5	511,188
		6	2,017,024
		30	15,762
	6,793,610		6,793,610
		Bal.	246,800

EXHIBIT B (continued)

Finished Goods					Dividend Payable			
Jan. 1	987,308	39	193,294	23	134,011	22	134,011
		Bal.	794,014				
	987,308		987,308				
Bal.	794,014						

Prepaid Assets					Provision For Deferred Income Tax			
Jan. 1	51,178	29	140,480	34	5,117	Jan. 1	103,418
12	170,816	Bal.	81,514	Bal.	98,301		
	221,994		221,994		103,418		103,418
Bal.	81,514					Bal.	98,301

Property, Plant and Equipment					First Mortgage 6% Bonds			
Jan. 1	2,039,199	25	16,131	20	800,000	Jan. 1	800,000
13	285,471	Bal.	2,308,539				
	2,324,670		2,324,670				
Bal.	2,308,539						

Allowance For Depreciation					Common Stock			
25	16,131	Jan. 1	760,720	Bal.	295,371	Jan. 1	268,022
Bal.	945,569	26	200,980			21	14,104
	961,700		961,700			23	13,245
		Bal.	945,569		295,371		295,371
						Bal.	295,371

Investment In Subsidiaries					Paid-in Surplus			
Jan. 1	34,401	Bal.	43,132	Bal.	2,398,339	Jan. 1	2,152,198
14	8,731					21	126,936
	43,132		43,132			23	119,205
					2,398,339		2,398,339
Bal.	43,132					Bal.	2,398,339

Deferred Development Expenses					Retained Earnings			
Jan. 1	116,878	27	50,275	22	134,011	Jan. 1	486,524
15	26,901	28	13,435	Bal.	908,337	44	555,824
		Bal.	80,069		1,042,348		1,042,348
	143,779		143,779			Bal.	908,337
Bal.	80,069						

EXHIBIT B (continued)

Expense and Income Accounts

	Raw Material Used					Sales		
2	1,421,661	37	1,421,661		35	10,058,729	7	10,058,729

	Direct Labor					Discounts and Allowances		
3	1,254,557	37	1,267,207		8	68,243	36	68,243
30	12,650							
	1,267,207		1,267,207					

	Service Labor					Cost of Goods Sold		
3	313,789	37	316,901		28	13,435	38	8,499
30	3,112				37	6,538,260	40	6,736,490
					39	193,294		
	316,901		316,901			6,744,989		6,744,989

	Fringe Benefits					Selling Expenses		
4	164,268	37	280,596		6	1,457,036	41	1,482,636
29	37,200				32	25,600		
32	79,128					1,482,636		1,482,636
	280,596		280,596					

	Tool Expense					Administrative Expenses		
4	606,044	37	606,044		6	559,988	41	595,604
					32	35,616		
						595,604		595,604

	Direct Burden					Other Expense		
4	672,528	37	699,348		19	53,892	42	79,967
29	26,820				20	26,075		
	699,348		699,348			79,967		79,967

	Other Direct Expense					Other Income		
4	1,013,476	37	1,013,476		42	13,444	24	13,444

	Indirect Burden (Except Depreciation)					Estimated Federal and State Income Taxes		
5	511,188	37	732,047		33	553,409	43	553,409
27	50,275							
29	76,460							
32	94,124							
	732,047		732,047					

EXHIBIT B (continued)

Depreciation				Profit and Loss		
26	200,980	37	200,980	36	68,243	35	10,058,729
				40	6,736,490		
Estimated Pension Expense				41	2,078,240		
				42	66,523		
31	234,468	32	234,468	43	553,409		
				44	555,824		
					10,058,729		10,058,729

Purchases of raw material on account for the year 1977 amounted in total to $1,385,824 as evidenced by purchase orders, receiving records, and invoices from suppliers. We shall account for these purchases by the following journal entry, as though they represented a single transaction:

1. Raw Material   1,385,824
        Accounts Payable (trade)   1,385,824

This entry, and also all entries to follow, will be posted by entry numbers to the accounts presented in Exhibit B. Normally, entries are identified in the accounts by date but the use of entry numbers here should help the reader to follow the flow of transactions.

Raw material withdrawn from the storeroom for use in production could have been charged to "Goods in Process," but the company preferred to charge these material costs to a "Raw Material Used" account. The raw material so used, as evidenced by material requisitions, amounted in total to $1,421,661 for the year. We shall account for it as a single transfer with a debit to "Raw Material Used" and a credit to "Raw Material" as follows:

2. Raw Material Used   1,421,661
        Raw Material   1,421,661

Labor costs for both production and service activities, supported by time cards and other documentary evidence, were summarized weekly and recorded as charges to the appropriate expense accounts, while the account for "Other Accrued Liabilities" was credited. On payday, the "Other Accrued Liabilities" account was debited and

"Cash" was credited for the amount of the payroll. In summary form, the labor costs for the year would be accounted for as follows:

3. Direct Labor	1,254,557	
Service Labor	313,789	
Other Accrued Liabilities		1,568,346

In addition to raw material and labor, there were various direct manufacturing costs the accounting for which in summary form may be illustrated as follows:

4. Fringe Benefits	164,268	
Tool Expense	606,044	
Direct Burden	672,528	
Other Direct Expense	1,013,476	
Other Accrued Liabilities		2,456,316

The company incurred indirect manufacturing costs such as supervision, production scheduling, and real estate taxes which in summary form would be recorded as follows:

5. Indirect Burden (Except Depreciation)	511,188	
Other Accrued Liabilities		511,188

The costs accounted for so far have been allied with the production of goods. In addition, the company incurred selling and administrative expenses which were actually recorded in detail in a number of accounts, identified by specific types of expense, but which we shall record in summary form as follows:

6. Selling Expense	1,457,036	
Administrative Expense	559,988	
Other Accrued Liabilities		2,017,024

Sales for the year, supported by documentary evidence in the form of customers' orders, shipping records, and copies of invoices sent to customers, amounted to $10,058,729, and we shall record them as follows:

7. Accounts Receivable	10,058,729	
Sales		10,058,729

Discounts and allowances on sales amounted to $68,243 in total, and we shall record them as follows:

8. Discounts and Allowances	68,243	
Accounts Receivable		68,243

There were thousands of transactions during the year involving the receipt or disbursement of cash and all were recorded by the company in detail as they occurred. Here, again, we shall treat the accounting for these transactions in summary form, beginning with the pleasant receipt of payments from customers which we shall record as follows:

9. Cash	9,687,911	
Accounts Receivable		9,687,911

We shall also recognize the payment of the company's debts to its suppliers of raw materials as follows:

10. Accounts Payable (trade)	1,206,844	
Cash		1,206,844

Also, payment of its debts to those who supplied labor, or debts involved in connection with various types of direct and indirect manufacturing costs, selling, and administrative expenses as follows:

11. Other Accrued Liabilities	6,546,810	
Cash		6,546,810

Insurance and some other items of expense were prepaid as follows:

12. Prepaid Assets	170,816	
Cash		170,816

We shall assume that purchases of property, plant, and equipment were cash expenditures. Also, for our purposes, the amount involved will be net of whatever cash had been received on the disposal of fixed assets:

13. Property, Plant, and Equipment	285,471	
Cash		285,471

A small addition to the investment in subsidiaries had been made as follows:

| 14. Investments in Subsidiaries | 8,731 | |
| Cash | | 8,731 |

Expenditures for product development were accounted for as deferred expenses as follows:

| 15. Deferred Development Expenses | 26,901 | |
| Cash | | 26,901 |

The liability for a bond sinking fund installment of $100,000 was paid during the year:

| 16. Bond Sinking Fund Installment | 100,000 | |
| Cash | | 100,000 |

Cash of $248,268 was sent to the trustees of the company's pension plan:

| 17. Provision for Pensions | 248,268 | |
| Cash | | 248,268 |

Federal and state income tax obligations were paid for $367,901 in total as follows:

| 18. Provision for Federal and State Income Taxes | 367,901 | |
| Cash | | 367,901 |

During the year, $53,892 for bond interest was paid:

| 19. Other Expense | 53,892 | |
| Cash | | 53,892 |

The bonds of $800,000 outstanding as of the first of the year were retired by payment of $800,000 principal and $26,075 premium:

20. Other Expense	26,075	
First Mortgage 6% Bonds	800,000	
Cash		826,075

Employees of the company exercised stock options during the year on 14,104 shares at $10.00 per share:

21.	Cash	141,040	
	Common Stock		14,104
	Paid-in Surplus		126,936

During the year, the directors of the company declared a stock dividend of 5% on the 268,022 shares then issued and outstanding. The market value of the stock to be given as a dividend was assumed to be $10.00 per share:

22.	Retained Earnings	134,011	
	Dividend Payable		134,011

When the dividend was actually paid, 13,245 shares were issued, while fractional shares to which some stockholders were entitled were paid for in cash:

23.	Dividend Payable	134,011	
	Common Stock		13,245
	Paid-in Surplus		119,205
	Cash		1,561

Minor items of other income amounted to $13,444:

24.	Cash	13,444	
	Other Income		13,444

Property, plant, and equipment disposed of during the year had been carried in the accounts at a historical cost total of $16,131. This amount had been removed from the "Property, Plant, and Equipment" account, as well as from the "Allowance for Depreciation" as follows:

25.	Allowance for Depreciation	16,131	
	Property, Plant, and Equipment		16,131

The transactions noted above, which I have numbered 1-25 and which represented visible financial activities or events, were for the most part routine in nature. These involved people who, among other things, developed the documentary evidence necessary to support entries to be made in the accounts.

A number of financial events, however, for various reasons, are not accounted for as part of the process of accounting for the daily activities of buying and selling, paying and receiving, making and managing. These events are accounted for at the close of an accounting period as "adjusting entries." Each of these entries affect one or more of the accounts to be reported in the balance sheet, as well as one or more of the accounts to be reported in the income statement.

One of the common adjusting entries to be made is that for estimated depreciation that has taken place during the period on property, plant, and equipment. It can be appreciated that the amount to be accounted for must be determined by someone in the organization as a special matter since it does not arise as the result of ordinary day-by-day business transactions.

Unless an entry is made for the estimated depreciation for the period, the costs of the period will be understated, and the net income for the period will be overstated, in the income statement. Similarly, the accumulated depreciation in the balance sheet will be understated, with a resulting overstatement of net property, plant, and equipment, and this will be matched by an overstatement of the "net worth" of the business.

In the present case, the adjustment for depreciation may be illustrated in summary form for the year as follows:

26. Estimated Depreciation   200,980
    Allowance for Depreciation   200,980

In a similar manner, someone has to determine how much of the accumulated deferred development expense should be charged off as an expense of the period. In the present case, $50,275 was written off in total and accounted for as follows:

27. Indirect Burden   50,275
    Deferred Development Expense   50,275

In addition to charging development expense to indirect burden where it, conceptually at least, became part of the cost of goods manufactured, the company in this case charged off some of the deferred development expense to "Cost of Goods Sold" as follows:

28. Cost of Goods Sold   13,435
    Deferred Development Expense   13,435

Another adjustment to be made was for the amount of prepaid assets such as insurance that should properly be charged as expenses for the period. In the present case, this adjustment in summary form is illustrated as follows:

29. Fringe Benefits   37,200
    Direct Burden   26,820
    Indirect Burden   76,460
        Prepaid Assets   140,480

The preparation of payrolls for direct and indirect labor is time-consuming, and therefore wage payments are commonly in arrears. At the close of an accounting period, it is desirable and a common practice to compute the wages earned but not yet paid as of the last day of the period, and to record the amount as an addition to the expenses of the period as well as an addition to the liabilities outstanding.

In the present case, this called for the following adjusting entry as of the close of the year:

30. Direct Labor   12,650
    Service Labor   3,112
        Other Accrued Liabilities   15,762

The estimated pension expense was computed each period and accounted for as both an expense and a liability. In summary form, the adjusting entry for pension expense for the year was as follows:

31. Estimated Pension Expense   234,468
        Provision for Pensions   234,468

The estimated pension expense was then prorated between manufacturing costs, selling expenses, and administrative expenses as follows:

32. Fringe Benefits   79,128
    Indirect Burden   94,124
    Selling Expenses   25,600
    Administrative Expenses   35,616
        Estimated Pension Expense   234,468

The estimated federal and state income taxes for the given accounting period call for an adjusting entry, which may be illustrated as follows:

33. Estimated Federal and
    State Income Taxes   553,409
        Provision for Income Taxes   553,409

In this particular case, the deferred income tax showed a net reduction for the year which we shall illustrate as follows:

34. Provision for Deferred
    Income Tax   5,117
        Provision for Income Taxes   5,117

Once the foregoing data shown in the form of journal entries 1-34 have been entered (posted) in the ledger (illustrated as Exhibit B), all of the transactions for the period will have been recorded in the accounts.

The next step, then, as far as the accounting cycle is concerned, is the closing out of the nominal accounts in arriving at the net income to be added to "Retained Earnings." Following this comes the preparation of financial statements.

The process of closing the accounts varies somewhat among companies. In the present case, sales and discounts and allowances were first closed to the "Profit and Loss" account. The "Cost of Goods Sold" account was then charged with the raw material used and labor and manufacturing costs for the period.

Adjustments were then made to the "Cost of Goods Sold" account for the changes that had taken place during the period in the inventories of goods in process and finished goods. For the current year, the inventory of goods in process had increased slightly, which called for removing this amount from the cost of goods sold. On the other hand, the inventory of finished goods had decreased substantially, which called for adding this amount to the cost of goods sold.

Once the cost of goods sold had been adjusted for the change in inventories, the adjusted figure and all remaining items of expense or income were closed to "Profit and Loss," after which the net income realized was transferred to "Retained Earnings." The closing entries to be made in the accounts may be illustrated as follows:

35. Sales   10,058,720
        Profit and Loss   10,058,720
36. Profit and Loss   68,243
        Discounts and Allowances   68,243

37.	Cost of Goods Sold	6,538,260	
	Raw Material Used		1,421,661
	Direct Labor		1,267,207
	Service Labor		316,901
	Fringe Benefits		280,596
	Tool Expense		606,044
	Direct Burden		699,348
	Other Direct Expense		1,013,476
	Indirect Burden		
	(Except Depreciation)		732,047
	Depreciation		200,980
38.	Goods in Process	8,499	
	Cost of Goods Sold		8,499
39.	Cost of Goods Sold	193,294	
	Finished Goods		193,294
40.	Profit and Loss	6,736,490	
	Cost of Goods Sold		6,736,490
41.	Profit and Loss	2,078,240	
	Selling Expenses		1,482,636
	Administrative Expenses		595,604
42.	Profit and Loss	66,523	
	Other Income	13,244	
	Other Expense		79,967
43.	Profit and Loss	553,409	
	Estimated Federal and		
	State Income Taxes		553,409
44.	Profit and Loss	555,824	
	Retained Earnings		555,824

Once these entries have been posted to the accounts in the ledger, the accounts can be balanced and ruled as illustrated in Exhibit B. The insertion of balancing figures in the balance sheet accounts in the ledger is done without bothering to have journal entries for them.

When the bookkeeping for the period has been completed, financial statements based on data gathered from the accounts can be prepared as illustrated in Exhibit C and Exhibit D.

The Work Sheet

It has been traditional for companies to draw up a list of the ledger accounts and their balances at the close of an accounting period prior

EXHIBIT C

P. M. Stanton Company's Income Statement for the Year Ending December 31, 1977

Sales		$10,058,729
Less: discounts and allowances		68,243
Net sales		$ 9,990,486
Less: Direct Manufacturing Costs		
Raw material used	$1,421,661	
Direct labor	1,267,207	
Service labor	316,901	
Fringe benefits	280,596	
Tool expense	606,044	
Direct burden	699,348	
Other direct expense	1,013,476	
Total	$5,605,233	
Inventory adjustments:		
Goods in process	-8,499	
Finished goods	+193,294	5,790,028
Margin above direct manufacturing costs		$ 4,200,458
Less: Indirect burden (except depreciation)	$ 732,047	
Depreciation	200,980	
Development expense	13,435	946,462
Gross margin		$ 3,253,996
Selling expenses	$1,482,636	
Administrative expenses	595,604	2,078,240
Operating income		$ 1,175,756
Other income	$ 13,444	
Other expense	79,967	66,523
Income before provision for income taxes		$ 1,109,233
Provision for Federal and state income taxes		553,409
Net income		$ 555,824
Retained earnings at beginning of period		486,524
		$ 1,042,348
Common stock dividend		134,011
Retained earnings at .nd of period		$ 908,337

to the preparation of adjusting entries. Such a listing is known as a "trial-balance before adjustments."

A minor purpose of this trial balance is to check whether or not the accounts are in balance, or in other words to check that the bookkeeping has in fact been double-entry. This check does not prove, however, that the correct accounts have necessarily been debited and

EXHIBIT D
P. M. Stanton Company's Balance Sheet as of December 31, 1977

	Assets		
Current assets:			
Cash			$ 929,375
Accounts receivable			1,067,737
Inventories:			
Raw material		$298,090	
Goods in process		203,247	
Finished goods		794,014	1,295,351
Prepaid assets			81,514
Total current assets			$3,373,977
Property, plant and equipment at cost less			
allowance for depreciation of $945,569			1,362,970
Investment in subsidiaries			43,132
Deferred development expenses			80,069
Total assets			$4,860,148

	Liabilities and Capital		
Current liabilities:			
Accounts payable (trade)			$ 332,200
Provision for pensions			163,500
Provision for income taxes			417,300
Other accrued liabilities			246,800
Total current liabilities			$1,159,800
Provision for deferred income tax			98,301
Common stock			295,371
Paid-in surplus			2,398,339
Retained earnings			908,337
Total liabilities and capital			$4,860,148

credited for each transaction. Protection on the latter point comes through establishing and carrying out routines of internal check and audit as part of the bookkeeping process.

A trial balance also provides a convenient means of seeing how the accounts stand at the moment. When drawn off prior to adjusting entries, it may assist in determining which accounts call for adjustment. A trial balance prepared after the adjustments are made but before the accounts are closed is often presented as a report to management on the current financial condition of the business.

A major use of the trial-balance before adjustments is its use as the first two columns of a work sheet, such as that illustrated in Exhibit E.

EXHIBIT E
P. M. Stanton Company Work Sheet

December 31, 1977	Trial Balance Before Adjustments	Adjustments Debit	Adjustments Credit	Income Statement	Balance Sheet
Cash	929375				929375
Accounts Receivable	1067737				1067737
Raw Material	298090				298090
Goods in Process	194748	38. 8499			203247
Finished Goods	987308		39. 193294		794014
Prepaid Assets	221994		29. 140480		81514
Property, Plant & Equipment	2308539				2308539
Allowance for Depreciation	744589		26. 200980		945569
Investment in Subsidiaries	43132				43132
Deferred Development Expenses	143779		28. 13435 27. 50275		80069
Accounts Payable (Trade)	332200				332200
Provision for Pensions	70968		31. 234468		163500
Provision for Income Taxes	141226		34. 5117 33. 553409		417300
Other Accrued Liabilities	231038		30. 15762		246800
Provision for Deferred Income Tax	103418	34. 5117			98301
Common Stock	295371				295371
Paid-in Surplus	2398339				2398339
Retained Earnings	352513				352513
Sales	10058729			10058729	
	10058729			10058729	

Discounts and Allowances	68243			68243				
Raw Material Used	1421661		37.1421661					
Direct Labor	1254557	30. 12650	37.1267207					
Service Labor	313789	30. 3112	37. 316901					
Fringe Benefits	164268	32. 79128	37. 280596					
		29. 37200						
Tool Expense	606044		37. 606044					
Direct Burden	672528	29. 26820	37. 699348					
Other Direct Expense	1013476	32. 94124	37.1013476					
Indirect Burden (Not Depreciation)	511188	29. 76460	27. 50275	37. 732047				
Depreciation		26. 200980	37. 200980					
Estimated Pension Expense		31. 234468	32. 234468					
		28. 13435	38. 8499					
Cost of Goods Sold		37.6538260		6736490				
		39. 193294						
Selling Expenses	1457036	32. 25600		1482636				
Administrative Expenses	559988	32. 35616		595604				
Other Expense	79967			79967				
Other Income	13444			13444	13444			
Estimated Income Taxes		33. 553409		553409				
Net Income				555824	5805717	555824	5805717	
	14529641	14529641	8188447	8188447	10072173	10072173	5805717	5805717

This type of work sheet is used by the accountant as a means of working out, apart from the books of account, the adjustments that appear to be necessary to bring the accounts up to date. It is also used to develop the elements of the income statement and balance sheet to be reported at the close of the period.

Among other things, the work sheet helps to avoid false steps when it comes to the actual adjusting and closing of the accounts and the preparation of the financial statements.

In the Exhibit E work sheet, the adjustments shown have been keyed to the adjusting entries illustrated earlier in this Appendix in order that the reader can in this way find their interpretation. It should be understood, of course, that the work sheet is actually prepared first and the formal journal entries are keyed to it.

Tables for the Analysis
of Capital Expenditures

These five tables, prepared by Jerome Bracken and Charles Christensen, published by the Harvard Business School, and copyright © 1961 by the President and Fellows of Harvard College, are adapted here by special permission for use in completing the calculations discussed in Chapter 27.

TABLE A
Present Value of $1

Period	6%	7%	8%	9%	10%	11%	12%	13%	14%	15%	16%	17%	18%	19%	20%	22%	24%	26%	28%	30%
1	0.943	0.935	0.926	0.917	0.909	0.901	0.893	0.885	0.877	0.870	0.862	0.855	0.847	0.840	0.833	0.820	0.806	0.794	0.781	0.769
2	0.890	0.873	0.857	0.842	0.826	0.812	0.797	0.783	0.769	0.756	0.743	0.731	0.718	0.706	0.694	0.672	0.650	0.630	0.610	0.592
3	0.840	0.816	0.794	0.772	0.751	0.731	0.712	0.693	0.675	0.658	0.641	0.624	0.609	0.593	0.579	0.551	0.524	0.500	0.477	0.455
4	0.792	0.763	0.735	0.708	0.683	0.659	0.636	0.613	0.592	0.572	0.552	0.534	0.516	0.499	0.482	0.451	0.423	0.397	0.373	0.350
5	0.747	0.713	0.681	0.650	0.621	0.593	0.567	0.543	0.519	0.497	0.476	0.456	0.437	0.419	0.402	0.370	0.341	0.315	0.291	0.269
6	0.705	0.666	0.630	0.596	0.564	0.535	0.507	0.480	0.456	0.432	0.410	0.390	0.370	0.352	0.335	0.303	0.275	0.250	0.227	0.207
7	0.665	0.623	0.583	0.547	0.513	0.482	0.452	0.425	0.400	0.376	0.354	0.333	0.314	0.296	0.279	0.249	0.222	0.198	0.178	0.159
8	0.627	0.582	0.540	0.502	0.467	0.434	0.404	0.376	0.351	0.327	0.305	0.285	0.266	0.249	0.233	0.204	0.179	0.157	0.139	0.123
9	0.592	0.544	0.500	0.460	0.424	0.391	0.361	0.333	0.308	0.284	0.263	0.243	0.225	0.209	0.194	0.167	0.144	0.125	0.108	0.094
10	0.558	0.508	0.463	0.422	0.386	0.352	0.322	0.295	0.270	0.247	0.227	0.208	0.191	0.176	0.162	0.137	0.116	0.099	0.085	0.073
11	0.527	0.475	0.429	0.388	0.350	0.317	0.287	0.261	0.237	0.215	0.195	0.178	0.162	0.148	0.135	0.112	0.094	0.079	0.066	0.056
12	0.497	0.444	0.397	0.356	0.319	0.286	0.257	0.231	0.208	0.187	0.168	0.152	0.137	0.124	0.112	0.092	0.076	0.062	0.052	0.043
13	0.469	0.415	0.368	0.326	0.290	0.258	0.229	0.204	0.182	0.163	0.145	0.130	0.116	0.104	0.093	0.075	0.061	0.050	0.040	0.033
14	0.442	0.388	0.340	0.299	0.263	0.232	0.205	0.181	0.160	0.141	0.125	0.111	0.099	0.088	0.078	0.062	0.049	0.039	0.032	0.025
15	0.417	0.362	0.315	0.275	0.239	0.209	0.183	0.160	0.140	0.123	0.108	0.095	0.084	0.074	0.065	0.051	0.040	0.031	0.025	0.020
16	0.394	0.339	0.292	0.252	0.218	0.188	0.163	0.142	0.123	0.107	0.093	0.081	0.071	0.062	0.054	0.042	0.032	0.025	0.019	0.015
17	0.371	0.317	0.270	0.231	0.198	0.170	0.146	0.125	0.108	0.093	0.080	0.069	0.060	0.052	0.045	0.034	0.026	0.020	0.015	0.012
18	0.350	0.296	0.250	0.212	0.180	0.153	0.130	0.111	0.095	0.081	0.069	0.059	0.051	0.044	0.038	0.028	0.021	0.016	0.012	0.009
19	0.331	0.277	0.232	0.194	0.164	0.138	0.116	0.098	0.083	0.070	0.060	0.051	0.043	0.037	0.031	0.023	0.017	0.012	0.009	0.007
20	0.312	0.258	0.215	0.178	0.149	0.124	0.104	0.087	0.073	0.061	0.051	0.043	0.037	0.031	0.026	0.019	0.014	0.010	0.007	0.005
21	0.294	0.242	0.199	0.164	0.135	0.112	0.093	0.077	0.064	0.053	0.044	0.037	0.031	0.026	0.022	0.015	0.011	0.008	0.006	0.004
22	0.278	0.226	0.184	0.150	0.123	0.101	0.083	0.068	0.056	0.046	0.038	0.032	0.026	0.022	0.018	0.013	0.009	0.006	0.004	0.003
23	0.262	0.211	0.170	0.138	0.112	0.091	0.074	0.060	0.049	0.040	0.033	0.027	0.022	0.018	0.015	0.010	0.007	0.005	0.003	0.002
24	0.247	0.197	0.158	0.126	0.102	0.082	0.066	0.053	0.043	0.035	0.028	0.023	0.019	0.015	0.013	0.008	0.006	0.004	0.003	0.002
25	0.233	0.184	0.146	0.116	0.092	0.074	0.059	0.047	0.038	0.030	0.024	0.020	0.016	0.013	0.010	0.007	0.005	0.003	0.002	0.001
26	0.220	0.172	0.135	0.106	0.084	0.066	0.053	0.042	0.033	0.026	0.021	0.017	0.014	0.011	0.009	0.006	0.004	0.002	0.002	0.001
27	0.207	0.161	0.125	0.098	0.076	0.060	0.047	0.037	0.029	0.023	0.018	0.014	0.011	0.009	0.007	0.005	0.003	0.002	0.001	0.001
28	0.196	0.150	0.116	0.090	0.069	0.054	0.042	0.033	0.026	0.020	0.016	0.012	0.010	0.008	0.006	0.004	0.002	0.002	0.001	0.001
29	0.185	0.141	0.107	0.082	0.063	0.048	0.037	0.029	0.022	0.017	0.014	0.011	0.008	0.006	0.005	0.003	0.002	0.001	0.001	0.000
30	0.174	0.131	0.099	0.075	0.057	0.044	0.033	0.026	0.020	0.015	0.012	0.009	0.007	0.005	0.004	0.003	0.002	0.001	0.001	0.000

Adapted by permission from *Tables for the Analysis of Capital Expenditures* by Jerome Bracken and Charles Christenson. Copyright © 1961 by the President and Fellows of Harvard College.

TABLE B
Present Value of $1 per Period Received at End

Period	6%	7%	8%	9%	10%	11%	12%	13%	14%	15%	16%	17%	18%	19%	20%	22%	24%	26%	28%	30%
1	0.943	0.935	0.926	0.917	0.909	0.901	0.893	0.885	0.877	0.870	0.862	0.855	0.847	0.840	0.833	0.820	0.806	0.794	0.781	0.769
2	1.833	1.808	1.783	1.759	1.736	1.713	1.690	1.668	1.647	1.626	1.605	1.585	1.566	1.547	1.528	1.492	1.457	1.424	1.392	1.361
3	2.673	2.624	2.577	2.531	2.487	2.444	2.402	2.361	2.322	2.283	2.246	2.210	2.174	2.140	2.107	2.042	1.981	1.923	1.868	1.816
4	3.465	3.387	3.312	3.240	3.170	3.102	3.037	2.975	2.914	2.855	2.798	2.743	2.690	2.639	2.589	2.494	2.404	2.320	2.241	2.166
5	4.212	4.100	3.993	3.890	3.791	3.696	3.605	3.517	3.433	3.352	3.274	3.199	3.127	3.058	2.991	2.864	2.745	2.635	2.532	2.436
6	4.917	4.767	4.623	4.486	4.355	4.231	4.111	3.998	3.889	3.785	3.685	3.589	3.498	3.410	3.326	3.167	3.021	2.885	2.759	2.643
7	5.582	5.389	5.206	5.033	4.868	4.712	4.564	4.423	4.288	4.160	4.039	3.922	3.812	3.706	3.605	3.416	3.242	3.083	2.937	2.802
8	6.210	5.971	5.747	5.535	5.335	5.146	4.968	4.799	4.639	4.487	4.344	4.207	4.078	3.954	3.837	3.619	3.421	3.241	3.076	2.925
9	6.802	6.515	6.247	5.995	5.759	5.537	5.328	5.132	4.946	4.772	4.607	4.451	4.303	4.163	4.031	3.786	3.566	3.366	3.184	3.019
10	7.360	7.024	6.710	6.418	6.145	5.889	5.650	5.426	5.216	5.019	4.833	4.659	4.494	4.339	4.193	3.923	3.682	3.465	3.269	3.092
11	7.887	7.499	7.139	6.805	6.495	6.207	5.938	5.687	5.453	5.234	5.029	4.836	4.656	4.487	4.327	4.035	3.776	3.544	3.335	3.147
12	8.384	7.943	7.536	7.161	6.814	6.492	6.194	5.918	5.660	5.421	5.197	4.988	4.793	4.611	4.439	4.127	3.851	3.606	3.387	3.190
13	8.353	8.358	7.904	7.487	7.103	6.750	6.424	6.122	5.842	5.583	5.342	5.118	4.910	4.715	4.533	4.203	3.912	3.656	3.427	3.223
14	9.295	8.746	8.244	7.786	7.367	6.982	6.628	6.303	6.002	5.725	5.468	5.229	5.008	4.802	4.611	4.265	3.962	3.695	3.459	3.249
15	9.712	9.108	8.560	8.061	7.606	7.191	6.811	6.462	6.142	5.847	5.576	5.324	5.092	4.876	4.676	4.315	4.001	3.726	3.483	3.268
16	10.106	9.447	8.851	8.313	7.824	7.379	6.974	6.604	6.265	5.954	5.669	5.405	5.162	4.938	4.730	4.357	4.033	3.751	3.503	3.283
17	10.477	9.763	9.122	8.544	8.022	7.549	7.120	6.729	6.373	6.047	5.749	5.475	5.222	4.990	4.775	4.391	4.059	3.771	3.518	3.295
18	10.828	10.059	9.372	8.756	8.201	7.702	7.250	6.840	6.467	6.128	5.818	5.534	5.273	5.033	4.812	4.419	4.080	3.786	3.529	3.304
19	11.158	10.336	9.604	8.950	8.365	7.839	7.366	6.938	6.550	6.198	5.878	5.585	5.316	5.070	4.844	4.442	4.097	3.799	3.539	3.311
20	11.470	10.594	9.818	9.129	8.514	7.963	7.469	7.025	6.623	6.259	5.929	5.628	5.353	5.101	4.870	4.460	4.110	3.808	3.546	3.316
21	11.764	10.836	10.017	9.292	8.649	8.075	7.562	7.102	6.687	6.313	5.973	5.665	5.384	5.127	4.891	4.476	4.121	3.816	3.551	3.320
22	12.042	11.061	10.201	9.442	8.772	8.176	7.645	7.170	6.743	6.359	6.011	5.696	5.410	5.149	4.909	4.488	4.130	3.822	3.556	3.323
23	12.303	11.272	10.371	9.580	8.883	8.266	7.718	7.230	6.792	6.399	6.044	5.723	5.432	5.167	4.925	4.499	4.137	3.827	3.559	3.325
24	12.550	11.469	10.529	9.707	8.985	8.348	7.784	7.283	6.835	6.434	6.073	5.747	5.451	5.182	4.937	4.507	4.143	3.831	3.562	3.327
25	12.783	11.654	10.675	9.823	9.077	8.422	7.843	7.330	6.873	6.464	6.097	5.766	5.467	5.195	4.948	4.514	4.147	3.834	3.564	3.329
26	13.003	11.826	10.810	9.929	9.161	8.488	7.896	7.372	6.906	6.491	6.118	5.783	5.480	5.206	4.956	4.520	4.151	3.837	3.566	3.330
27	13.211	11.987	10.935	10.027	9.237	8.548	7.943	7.409	6.935	6.514	6.136	5.798	5.492	5.215	4.964	4.524	4.154	3.839	3.567	3.331
28	13.406	12.137	11.051	10.116	9.307	8.602	7.984	7.441	6.961	6.534	6.152	5.810	5.502	5.223	4.970	4.528	4.157	3.840	3.568	3.331
29	13.591	12.278	11.158	10.198	9.370	8.650	8.022	7.470	6.983	6.551	6.166	5.820	5.510	5.229	4.975	4.531	4.159	3.841	3.569	3.332
30	13.765	12.409	11.258	10.274	9.427	8.694	8.055	7.496	7.003	6.566	6.177	5.829	5.517	5.235	4.979	4.534	4.160	3.842	3.569	3.332

Adapted by permission from *Tables for the Analysis of Capital Expenditures* by Jerome Bracken and Charles Christenson. Copyright © 1961 by the President and Fellows of Harvard College.

TABLE C
Present Value of $1 per Period Received Continuously

Period	6%	7%	8%	9%	10%	11%	12%	13%	14%	15%	16%	17%	18%	19%	20%	22%	24%	26%	28%	30%
1	0.971	0.967	0.962	0.958	0.954	0.950	0.945	0.941	0.937	0.933	0.929	0.925	0.922	0.918	0.914	0.907	0.900	0.893	0.886	0.882
2	1.888	1.871	1.854	1.837	1.821	1.805	1.790	1.774	1.759	1.745	1.731	1.716	1.703	1.689	1.676	1.650	1.625	1.602	1.578	1.556
3	2.752	2.715	2.679	2.644	2.609	2.576	2.543	2.512	2.481	2.451	2.421	2.393	2.365	2.337	2.311	2.259	2.211	2.164	2.119	2.077
4	3.568	3.504	3.443	3.383	3.326	3.270	3.216	3.164	3.113	3.064	3.017	2.970	2.926	2.882	2.840	2.759	2.683	2.610	2.542	2.477
5	4.338	4.242	4.150	4.062	3.977	3.896	3.817	3.741	3.668	3.598	3.530	3.464	3.401	3.340	3.281	3.168	3.063	2.964	2.872	2.785
6	5.063	4.932	4.805	4.685	4.570	4.459	4.353	4.252	4.155	4.062	3.972	3.886	3.804	3.724	3.648	3.504	3.370	3.246	3.130	3.022
7	5.748	5.576	5.412	5.256	5.108	4.967	4.832	4.704	4.582	4.465	4.354	4.247	4.145	4.048	3.954	3.779	3.618	3.469	3.331	3.204
8	6.394	6.178	5.974	5.780	5.597	5.424	5.260	5.104	4.957	4.816	4.683	4.555	4.434	4.319	4.209	4.004	3.817	3.646	3.489	3.344
9	7.004	6.741	6.494	6.261	6.042	5.836	5.642	5.458	5.285	5.121	4.966	4.819	4.680	4.547	4.422	4.189	3.978	3.786	3.612	3.452
10	7.579	7.267	6.975	6.702	6.447	6.208	5.983	5.772	5.573	5.386	5.210	5.044	4.887	4.739	4.599	4.340	4.108	3.898	3.708	3.535
11	8.121	7.758	7.421	7.107	6.815	6.542	6.287	6.049	5.826	5.617	5.421	5.237	5.064	4.900	4.747	4.465	4.213	3.986	3.783	3.599
12	8.633	8.218	7.834	7.478	7.149	6.843	6.559	6.295	6.048	5.818	5.603	5.401	5.213	5.036	4.870	4.566	4.297	4.057	3.842	3.648
13	9.116	8.647	8.216	7.819	7.453	7.115	6.802	6.512	6.242	5.992	5.759	5.542	5.339	5.150	4.972	4.650	4.365	4.112	3.887	3.686
14	9.571	9.048	8.570	8.132	7.729	7.359	7.018	6.704	6.413	6.144	5.894	5.662	5.446	5.245	5.058	4.718	4.420	4.157	3.923	3.715
15	10.001	9.423	8.898	8.418	7.980	7.580	7.212	6.874	6.563	6.276	6.011	5.765	5.537	5.326	5.129	4.774	4.464	4.192	3.951	3.737
16	10.406	9.774	9.201	8.681	8.209	7.778	7.385	7.024	6.694	6.390	6.111	5.853	5.614	5.393	5.188	4.820	4.500	4.220	3.973	3.754
17	10.789	10.101	9.482	8.923	8.416	7.957	7.539	7.158	6.809	6.490	6.197	5.928	5.679	5.450	5.238	4.858	4.529	4.242	3.990	3.767
18	11.149	10.407	9.742	9.144	8.605	8.118	7.676	7.275	6.910	6.577	6.272	5.992	5.735	5.498	5.279	4.889	4.552	4.259	4.003	3.778
19	11.490	10.693	9.983	9.347	8.777	8.263	7.799	7.380	6.999	6.652	6.336	6.047	5.782	5.538	5.313	4.914	4.571	4.273	4.014	3.785
20	11.811	10.961	10.206	9.533	8.933	8.394	7.909	7.472	7.077	6.718	6.391	6.094	5.821	5.571	5.342	4.935	4.586	4.284	4.022	3.791
21	12.114	11.210	10.412	9.704	9.074	8.512	8.007	7.554	7.145	6.775	6.439	6.134	5.855	5.600	5.366	4.952	4.598	4.293	4.028	3.796
22	12.399	11.444	10.604	9.861	9.203	8.618	8.095	7.626	7.205	6.825	6.480	6.168	5.883	5.624	5.386	4.966	4.608	4.300	4.033	3.800
23	12.669	11.662	10.781	10.005	9.320	8.713	8.173	7.690	7.257	6.868	6.516	6.197	5.908	5.644	5.402	4.977	4.616	4.306	4.037	3.802
24	12.923	11.866	10.945	10.137	9.427	8.799	8.243	7.747	7.303	6.905	6.546	6.222	5.928	5.660	5.416	4.986	4.622	4.310	4.040	3.805
25	13.163	12.057	11.096	10.258	9.524	8.877	8.305	7.797	7.344	6.938	6.573	6.244	5.945	5.674	5.427	4.994	4.627	4.314	4.042	3.806
26	13.389	12.235	11.237	10.369	9.612	8.947	8.360	7.841	7.379	6.966	6.596	6.262	5.960	5.686	5.437	5.000	4.631	4.316	4.044	3.807
27	13.603	12.402	11.367	10.471	9.692	9.010	8.410	7.880	7.410	6.991	6.615	6.277	5.973	5.696	5.445	5.006	4.635	4.319	4.046	3.808
28	13.804	12.557	11.487	10.565	9.765	9.067	8.454	7.915	7.437	7.012	6.632	6.291	5.983	5.705	5.452	5.010	4.638	4.320	4.047	3.809
29	13.994	12.703	11.599	10.651	9.831	9.118	8.494	7.946	7.461	7.031	6.647	6.302	5.992	5.712	5.457	5.013	4.640	4.322	4.048	3.810
30	14.174	12.838	11.702	10.729	9.891	9.164	8.529	7.973	7.482	7.047	6.659	6.312	6.000	5.718	5.462	5.016	4.641	4.323	4.048	3.810

Adapted by permission from *Tables for the Analysis of Capital Expenditures* by Jerome Bracken and Charles Christenson. Copyright © 1961 by the President and Fellows of Harvard College.

TABLE D
Present Value of Depreciation. Sum-of-Years' Digits Method

Period	6%	7%	8%	9%	10%	11%	12%	13%	14%	15%	16%	17%	18%	19%	20%	22%	24%	26%	28%	30%
1	—	—	—	—	—	—	—	—	—	—	—	—	—	—	—	—	—	—	—	—
2	—	—	—	—	—	—	—	—	—	—	—	—	—	—	—	—	—	—	—	—
3	0.908	0.894	0.881	0.868	0.855	0.843	0.831	0.819	0.808	0.796	0.786	0.775	0.765	0.754	0.745	0.726	0.707	0.690	0.674	0.658
4	0.891	0.875	0.860	0.845	0.830	0.816	0.802	0.789	0.776	0.763	0.751	0.739	0.728	0.717	0.706	0.685	0.665	0.646	0.628	0.611
5	0.875	0.857	0.839	0.822	0.806	0.790	0.775	0.760	0.746	0.732	0.719	0.706	0.694	0.682	0.670	0.647	0.626	0.606	0.588	0.570
6	0.859	0.839	0.820	0.801	0.783	0.766	0.749	0.734	0.718	0.703	0.689	0.675	0.662	0.649	0.637	0.613	0.591	0.571	0.551	0.533
7	0.844	0.822	0.801	0.781	0.761	0.743	0.725	0.708	0.692	0.676	0.661	0.647	0.633	0.619	0.606	0.582	0.559	0.538	0.518	0.500
8	0.829	0.805	0.782	0.761	0.740	0.721	0.702	0.684	0.667	0.651	0.635	0.620	0.605	0.591	0.578	0.553	0.530	0.508	0.489	0.470
9	0.814	0.789	0.765	0.742	0.720	0.700	0.680	0.661	0.643	0.626	0.610	0.595	0.580	0.566	0.552	0.527	0.503	0.482	0.462	0.443
10	0.800	0.773	0.748	0.724	0.701	0.679	0.659	0.640	0.621	0.604	0.587	0.571	0.556	0.542	0.528	0.502	0.479	0.457	0.437	0.419
11	0.786	0.758	0.731	0.706	0.683	0.660	0.639	0.619	0.600	0.582	0.565	0.549	0.534	0.519	0.506	0.480	0.456	0.435	0.415	0.397
12	0.773	0.743	0.715	0.689	0.665	0.642	0.620	0.600	0.581	0.562	0.545	0.529	0.513	0.499	0.485	0.459	0.435	0.414	0.394	0.376
13	0.760	0.729	0.700	0.673	0.648	0.624	0.602	0.581	0.562	0.543	0.526	0.509	0.494	0.479	0.465	0.439	0.416	0.395	0.376	0.358
14	0.747	0.715	0.685	0.658	0.632	0.608	0.585	0.564	0.544	0.525	0.508	0.491	0.476	0.461	0.447	0.421	0.398	0.377	0.359	0.341
15	0.734	0.701	0.671	0.643	0.616	0.592	0.569	0.547	0.527	0.508	0.491	0.474	0.459	0.444	0.430	0.405	0.382	0.361	0.343	0.326
16	0.722	0.688	0.657	0.628	0.601	0.576	0.553	0.531	0.511	0.492	0.475	0.458	0.443	0.428	0.414	0.389	0.367	0.346	0.328	0.312
17	0.711	0.676	0.644	0.614	0.587	0.562	0.538	0.516	0.496	0.477	0.460	0.443	0.428	0.413	0.400	0.375	0.352	0.333	0.315	0.299
18	0.699	0.663	0.631	0.601	0.573	0.548	0.524	0.502	0.482	0.463	0.445	0.429	0.413	0.399	0.386	0.361	0.339	0.320	0.302	0.286
19	0.688	0.651	0.618	0.588	0.560	0.534	0.510	0.488	0.468	0.449	0.432	0.415	0.400	0.386	0.373	0.348	0.327	0.308	0.291	0.275
20	0.677	0.640	0.606	0.575	0.547	0.521	0.497	0.475	0.455	0.436	0.419	0.403	0.387	0.373	0.360	0.336	0.315	0.297	0.280	0.265
21	0.666	0.629	0.594	0.563	0.535	0.509	0.485	0.463	0.443	0.424	0.407	0.391	0.376	0.362	0.349	0.325	0.304	0.286	0.270	0.255
22	0.656	0.618	0.583	0.552	0.523	0.497	0.473	0.451	0.431	0.412	0.395	0.379	0.364	0.351	0.338	0.315	0.294	0.276	0.260	0.246
23	0.646	0.607	0.572	0.540	0.511	0.485	0.461	0.440	0.419	0.401	0.384	0.368	0.354	0.340	0.327	0.305	0.285	0.267	0.252	0.238
24	0.636	0.597	0.561	0.529	0.501	0.474	0.450	0.429	0.409	0.390	0.373	0.358	0.344	0.330	0.318	0.295	0.276	0.259	0.243	0.230
25	0.626	0.587	0.551	0.519	0.490	0.464	0.440	0.418	0.398	0.380	0.364	0.348	0.334	0.321	0.309	0.287	0.267	0.250	0.236	0.222
26	0.617	0.577	0.541	0.509	0.480	0.454	0.430	0.408	0.389	0.371	0.354	0.339	0.325	0.312	0.300	0.278	0.259	0.243	0.228	0.215
27	0.608	0.567	0.531	0.499	0.470	0.444	0.420	0.399	0.379	0.361	0.345	0.330	0.316	0.303	0.291	0.270	0.252	0.236	0.221	0.209
28	0.599	0.558	0.522	0.489	0.460	0.434	0.411	0.390	0.370	0.352	0.336	0.322	0.308	0.295	0.284	0.263	0.245	0.229	0.215	0.203
29	0.590	0.549	0.513	0.480	0.451	0.425	0.402	0.381	0.362	0.344	0.328	0.313	0.300	0.288	0.276	0.256	0.238	0.222	0.209	0.197
30	0.582	0.540	0.504	0.471	0.442	0.417	0.393	0.372	0.353	0.336	0.320	0.306	0.293	0.280	0.269	0.249	0.232	0.216	0.203	0.191

Adapted by permission from *Tables for the Analysis of Capital Expenditures* by Jerome Bracken and Charles Christenson. Copyright © 1961 by the President and Fellows of Harvard College.

TABLE E
Present Value of Depreciation. Declining Balance Method

Period	6%	7%	8%	9%	10%	11%	12%	13%	14%	15%	16%	17%	18%	19%	20%	22%	24%	26%	28%	30%
1	—	—	—	—	—	—	—	—	—	—	—	—	—	—	—	—	—	—	—	—
2	—	—	—	—	—	—	—	—	—	—	—	—	—	—	—	—	—	—	—	—
3	0.920	0.908	0.896	0.884	0.873	0.862	0.851	0.841	0.831	0.821	0.811	0.802	0.792	0.783	0.774	0.757	0.740	0.725	0.709	0.695
4	0.898	0.883	0.868	0.854	0.840	0.827	0.814	0.802	0.789	0.777	0.766	0.755	0.744	0.733	0.723	0.703	0.684	0.666	0.649	0.633
5	0.878	0.860	0.843	0.827	0.811	0.796	0.781	0.767	0.753	0.739	0.727	0.714	0.702	0.690	0.679	0.657	0.637	0.617	0.599	0.582
6	0.858	0.838	0.819	0.800	0.783	0.765	0.749	0.733	0.718	0.704	0.690	0.676	0.663	0.650	0.638	0.615	0.594	0.574	0.555	0.537
7	0.840	0.817	0.796	0.776	0.756	0.738	0.720	0.703	0.687	0.671	0.657	0.642	0.628	0.615	0.603	0.579	0.556	0.536	0.516	0.499
8	0.821	0.797	0.774	0.752	0.731	0.711	0.693	0.675	0.657	0.641	0.625	0.611	0.596	0.583	0.570	0.545	0.522	0.501	0.482	0.464
9	0.804	0.778	0.753	0.730	0.708	0.687	0.667	0.648	0.630	0.614	0.597	0.582	0.567	0.553	0.540	0.515	0.492	0.472	0.452	0.434
10	0.787	0.759	0.733	0.708	0.685	0.663	0.643	0.623	0.605	0.588	0.571	0.555	0.541	0.526	0.513	0.488	0.465	0.444	0.425	0.408
11	0.771	0.742	0.714	0.688	0.664	0.642	0.620	0.600	0.582	0.564	0.547	0.531	0.516	0.502	0.488	0.463	0.441	0.420	0.401	0.384
12	0.755	0.724	0.696	0.669	0.644	0.621	0.599	0.579	0.559	0.541	0.524	0.509	0.493	0.479	0.466	0.441	0.418	0.398	0.380	0.363
13	0.740	0.708	0.678	0.651	0.625	0.601	0.579	0.558	0.539	0.521	0.504	0.488	0.473	0.459	0.445	0.421	0.398	0.378	0.360	0.344
14	0.725	0.692	0.661	0.633	0.607	0.583	0.560	0.539	0.520	0.501	0.484	0.468	0.453	0.439	0.426	0.402	0.380	0.360	0.343	0.327
15	0.711	0.677	0.645	0.617	0.590	0.565	0.542	0.521	0.502	0.483	0.466	0.451	0.436	0.422	0.409	0.385	0.363	0.344	0.327	0.311
16	0.697	0.662	0.630	0.600	0.573	0.549	0.526	0.504	0.485	0.466	0.450	0.434	0.419	0.405	0.392	0.369	0.348	0.329	0.312	0.297
17	0.684	0.648	0.615	0.585	0.558	0.533	0.510	0.489	0.469	0.451	0.434	0.418	0.404	0.390	0.377	0.354	0.334	0.315	0.299	0.284
18	0.671	0.634	0.601	0.571	0.543	0.518	0.495	0.473	0.454	0.436	0.419	0.404	0.389	0.376	0.363	0.341	0.320	0.303	0.287	0.272
19	0.659	0.621	0.587	0.557	0.529	0.504	0.481	0.459	0.440	0.422	0.405	0.390	0.376	0.363	0.350	0.328	0.308	0.291	0.275	0.262
20	0.647	0.608	0.574	0.543	0.515	0.490	0.467	0.446	0.427	0.409	0.392	0.377	0.363	0.350	0.338	0.316	0.297	0.280	0.265	0.252
21	0.635	0.596	0.562	0.531	0.503	0.477	0.454	0.433	0.414	0.396	0.380	0.365	0.352	0.339	0.327	0.305	0.287	0.270	0.255	0.242
22	0.624	0.584	0.550	0.518	0.490	0.465	0.442	0.421	0.402	0.385	0.369	0.354	0.341	0.328	0.316	0.295	0.277	0.261	0.246	0.234
23	0.613	0.573	0.538	0.507	0.479	0.453	0.430	0.410	0.391	0.374	0.358	0.344	0.330	0.318	0.306	0.286	0.268	0.252	0.238	0.226
24	0.602	0.562	0.527	0.495	0.467	0.442	0.419	0.399	0.380	0.363	0.348	0.334	0.320	0.308	0.297	0.277	0.259	0.244	0.230	0.218
25	0.592	0.551	0.516	0.485	0.457	0.432	0.409	0.389	0.370	0.354	0.338	0.324	0.311	0.299	0.288	0.269	0.251	0.236	0.223	0.211
26	0.582	0.541	0.506	0.474	0.446	0.421	0.399	0.379	0.361	0.344	0.329	0.315	0.303	0.291	0.280	0.261	0.244	0.229	0.216	0.205
27	0.572	0.531	0.496	0.464	0.436	0.412	0.390	0.370	0.352	0.335	0.320	0.307	0.294	0.283	0.272	0.253	0.237	0.223	0.210	0.198
28	0.562	0.521	0.486	0.455	0.427	0.402	0.380	0.361	0.343	0.327	0.312	0.299	0.287	0.275	0.265	0.246	0.230	0.216	0.204	0.193
29	0.553	0.512	0.477	0.445	0.418	0.393	0.372	0.352	0.335	0.319	0.305	0.291	0.279	0.268	0.258	0.240	0.224	0.210	0.198	0.187
30	0.544	0.503	0.468	0.436	0.409	0.385	0.363	0.344	0.327	0.311	0.297	0.284	0.272	0.261	0.251	0.234	0.218	0.205	0.193	0.182

Adapted by permission from *Tables for the Analysis of Capital Expenditures* by Jerome Bracken and Charles Christenson. Copyright © 1961 by the President and Fellows of Harvard College.

INDEX